# JAMES I

Also by OTTO J. SCOTT

*Robespierre: The Voice of Virtue*

# JAMES I

*Otto J. Scott*

MASON / CHARTER

NEW YORK 1976

**Library of Congress Cataloging in Publication Data**

Scott, Otto J
  James I.

  Bibliography: p.
  Includes index.
  1. James I, King of Great Britain, 1566–1625.
DA391.S35    941.06'1'0924    [B]    75–38591
ISBN 0–88405–123–4

*Dedicated to Orin E. Atkins*

# CONTENTS

PART FOUR: KING JAMES VI OF SCOTLAND

PART FIVE: THE MOST HIGH AND MIGHTIE PRINCE JAMES,
BY THE GRACE OF GOD KING OF GREAT BRITAINE,
FRANCE, AND IRELAND, DEFENDER OF THE FAITH, &c.

"If I were not a King, I would be a university man."
JAMES STUART, on a visit to Oxford

# PART ONE

*Conception,
Birth,
Infancy*

1

The figure of the Fool is widely misunderstood. He is neither a jester nor a clown nor an idiot. He is, instead, the dark side of genius. For if a genius has the ability to see and make connections beyond the normal range of vision, the fool is one who can see—and disconnect.

James Stuart was such a fool. He was an extraordinary one not only because he was learned and intelligent, but also because he was a king. The only son and heir of Mary Stuart, Queen of Scots, James later became the heir of Elizabeth I, the Queen of England. It was his high fortune to inherit the great prize over which these two queens contended: dominion over both Scotland and England.

James lived and reigned from the latter part of the sixteenth century to the middle of the third decade of the seventeenth. By then he had fulfilled the fears of his revolutionary-minded tutor, George Buchanan[1]—and unhinged all Britain.

His life began with his conception in 1565.

Lord Darnley[2] was thought to have the measles and took to his bed. The queen, who had earlier said he was "the best proportioned long man she had ever seen," decided to serve as his nurse. That tender duty kept her, on more than one occasion, in his bedchamber until after midnight. The young man—nineteen to her twenty-three—was surprised but delighted by her ardor and easily convinced that his own charm was responsible. The ladies in waiting giggled. News soon trickled from the palace that the Queen of Scots was in love at last and planned to marry.

When that rumor reached London, its romantic wrapping was quickly discarded by Elizabeth, who flew into one of her most frightful tantrums. She realized at once that Mary Stuart had tricked her, and the knowledge that William Cecil and other advisers had warned of this very possibility did little to assuage her anger.

The Virgin Queen—an ironic description at the time—had been so intent upon forcing Mary Stuart into a different sort of marriage that she had grown careless. It was common knowledge at the English court that the earl of Lennox and his lady, the obnoxious countess, had long harbored dreams of marrying their son, Lord Darnley, to the Queen of Scots. The countess was known to have discussed the possibility among the north English aristocracy. The earl asked permission to go to Scotland and carry Lord Darnley along—and had been abruptly refused by Cecil. It was Elizabeth herself who had overruled that decision and who had allowed the journey to be made. Her reasons, as well as the reasons for the marriage she preferred, were rooted somewhere deep in her nature, which has—then and now—baffled analysis.

Elizabeth had made it clear she was against any marriage between the Queen of Scots and any foreign prince. Such a union, she had said, would be considered an act of war. She insisted Mary Stuart must marry an Englishman. And the Englishman she finally produced as her proper—indeed, only—candidate was her own lover: Lord Robert Dudley.[3]

This prurient plan amazed even England, which had grown accustomed to the bizarre behavior of its queen, and created deep anger in many Scots. Elizabeth's intimacy with Dudley was notorious, though it took forms that baffled the naïve and was carefully shrouded from public view. Nevertheless, it was clear to all the world that Elizabeth loved Dudley, whose virtues were invisible and whose vices were glaring. When the Scots protested that Dudley's rank was beneath the dignity of their queen, Elizabeth elevated him to earl of Leicester.

Mary Stuart, confronted with a scandalous proposal, behaved with admirable patience. She demurred, but by graceful and subtle stages managed to convince Elizabeth that the grotesque marriage not only could, but probably would take place. Although Elizabeth regarded this conclusion with a strangely mixed combination of pain and pleasure, the Queen of Scots gave permission for the earl of Lennox and his heir, Lord Darnley, to come to Scotland. Cecil warned Elizabeth to be on guard and to forbid their trip. Elizabeth, lulled by her cousin's long docility and fascinated by the prospect of her favorite reigning as consort of the Queen of the North, overruled that advice.

News that Mary Stuart was enjoying herself in the bedchamber of Lord Darnley tore those dreams apart. A stream of messages, protests, and threats flowed northward from London. They were received by Mary Stuart with a small smile and an unanswerable argument. The Queen of England had insisted her cousin must marry an Englishman—and Darnley was the nearest prince of the blood of England. One of his grandmothers had been Margaret Tudor, the elder sister of King Henry VIII. He was an English subject, had been born in England, though of the Scots Stewart family—the same as Mary Stuart's own. What Englishman, asked Mary Stuart with arched eyebrows and wide eyes, could be more suitable—or even as suitable?

That was disingenuous, and everybody knew it. Lord Darnley was, after all, cousin to both queens and a member of the royal family in both realms. By marrying him, the Queen of Scots could combine their rights of inheritance beyond argument if Elizabeth died childless in the future. Even more menacing was the fact that together the two beautiful young people could present an attractive alternative to their strange and temperamental cousin on the throne of England.

Elizabeth's overweening self-confidence had allowed these two ambitious cousins to come together, and she raged at her Privy Council. A stream of letters and emissaries flowed north. Darnley was ordered back to England. His response was blunt. "I am very well where I am," he said, "and will remain."

In May 1565, the Queen of Scots made Darnley the earl of Ross. He knelt before her and pledged allegiance while the English cried treason. A couple of months later, on July 22, 1565, Mary Stuart raised her tall, blond cousin to duke of Albany. On July 28, six days later, heralds appeared in the hamlets, towns, and small cities of Scotland; trumpeted for attention; and then read aloud a proclamation naming Henry Stewart, earl of Ross and duke of Albany, the new King Henry of Scotland. The Queen moved with great speed; she had not even bothered to summon or obtain the consent of the Scots Parliament.

The day after the proclamation, King Henry married Mary Stuart, Queen of Scots, in a high Catholic ceremony at the Royal Chapel in the palace of Holyrood on the outskirts of Edinburgh. The archbishop of St. Andrews presided over an impressive gathering of high prelates attired in costly vestments, the air was heavy with incense and noisy with cheers, and coins were thrown to the crowds outside.

The marriage was like an abrupt display of a great, glittering heap of jewels long kept out of sight. In a single step, the Queen of Scots had outwitted the Queen of England and simultaneously thrown the gates of Scotland open for the return of papal forces the Reformers had once driven under. Suddenly, her intentions and the extent of her progress appeared, and Mary Stuart stood revealed as a figure of immense, though still largely potential, political importance.

By the time of their marriage, the newlyweds were no longer new to each other, but they were young and found embraces enjoyable. They vanished into their bedchamber to the noise of happy toasts. The small court of Scotland enjoyed four days and nights of revelry and was marked with unaccustomed gaiety.

Mary Stuart knew she had remaining obstacles. Elizabeth's anger was made plain in a variety of ways. John Knox, the leader of the Reform and a longtime critic, thundered from his pulpit at the church of St. Giles in Edinburgh. The queen's stepbrother, the earl of Moray, was deliberately absent from court.

Yet the queen, for the first time, was mistress of her situation. She had powerful Highland nobles around her and a strong young consort beside her. She had not only its approval, but a subsidy from the Vatican. From Madrid the most powerful monarch in the world—Philip II—sent his approval and hinted at impressive future support. The certainty of success gave her new radiance. Her chances of achieving the triumphs she planned were, indeed, excellent—had it not been for her husband's condition.

King Henry's easy disposition and gentle manners were well known in England and had smoothed his path when he first arrived in Scotland. Even David Rizzio, the deep-voiced singer whom the queen had raised to private secretary and who was bitterly resented by the Scots nobility, had found Darnley congenial and likable—at first.

But during his bout with the measles the young prince showed a new and uncertain temper. Visited by the elderly duke of Châtelherault, he took offense at some inoffensive remark and threatened to beat the old man as soon as he recovered. At another time he drew a dagger at a servant. Many jealously ascribed his mysterious and unpleasant change of personality to his abrupt rise in station, but the truth was even worse. Just before he left England, the heir of the House of Lennox had contracted, in some casual encounter, not measles but syphilis—at a time when that disease ran a short and frightful course.[4]

In the wake of the marriage, however, few people watched King Henry closely. More eyes were turned toward the man once closest to the queen, who was now the target of her anger; her stepbrother, the earl of Moray. Moray had objected to the union in blunt language. It would mean, he said, "mischief, sedition, and debate [argument]."[5] Mary Stuart's response was fierce and quick. She moved, in fact, to ruin Moray—and in that move showed herself to be remarkably free of any hindering sense of gratitude. After all it had been Moray—known then simply as Lord James Stewart —who, after the victory of the Reform and while Scotland was ruled by a council, had gone to France to bring Mary Stuart home to a throne.

In order to do that, he had, in effect, pledged to the other Lords of the Congregation and to the leader of the Congregation itself—John Knox—

that Mary Stuart would not overturn their accomplishment. Keeping that promise had not been easy. The queen brought her own priests to the palace and almost set off riots by having private Mass. Only Moray had calmed the reaction. It was Moray, also, who soothed the Kirk when Mary established a miniature Trianon in Scotland, a French court with Gobelin tapestries, gilt-framed pictures, and a library of French books. The queen "spoke French and lived French."[6]

He had, it was true, been rewarded. He was made an earl; his estates were increased. His enemy Patrick Hepburn, the earl of Bothwell, was sent abroad. For a time Moray appeared to be an uncrowned king; the queen seemed obedient to his every word.[7]

Mary Stuart, however, had arrived in Scotland a girl only in appearance: in reality she was a mature and worldly woman. She could rise with the sun and ride horseback across the landscape with abandon or join in a hunt and draw a bow in carefree manner. She alternated these bursts of energy with languid days in which she reclined in bed and received courtiers and even ambassadors in her peignoir. Six feet tall, regal, complicated, and cunning, she was beyond her stepbrother's experience.

John Knox was the only man who ever met Mary Stuart who was neither charmed nor deceived.[8] He spoke against her in the very flush of her return and was summoned to a special audience as a result. They clashed at once, and he said at that time that he saw "a proud mind, a crafty wit and an obdurate heart."[9]

Over a period of several years this beautiful, charming but amoral woman subtly undermined Moray's position—and not only Moray's. The Lords of the Congregation lost their revolutionary fervor and drifted apart from one another to compete for the favors of the sovereign. The Congregation itself, though lashed and warned by Knox, lost its influence in state matters. A pro-Vatican circle appeared and widened in the realm. David Rizzio, the queen's secretary, was widely considered an agent of Rome in this effort[10]—but the resentment he aroused was because of his foreignness, not his activities. The distinction was a sign of how far Mary Stuart had first softened and then deflected the course of the Reform.

Moray was one of the last to believe that his stepsister had maneuvered these changes deliberately. The realization came to him only after she announced her intention to marry Darnley. He had protested then, and she called him "a slave to England." The charge stung, because it was half-true. Moray, Knox, and the other Reformers had leaned upon England to achieve their victories, but they leaned, not because they loved England, but because they believed in the Reform.

Moray refused to sanction Mary Stuart's marriage to Darnley and heard rumors that the earl of Lennox and his followers would have him assassinated. In an effort to squelch that purpose, he made the rumors public. The queen, suddenly deadly and practical, demanded that he officially appear to prove such charges. Knowing the court was now stacked with his enemies, Moray did not answer the summons. Meanwhile, the queen sent for Moray's most dangerous enemy, the earl of Bothwell, to return from semiexile. She knew she would need a strong man for the test ahead.

Bothwell, with his deep-set eyes, chestnut hair, and simian features, was a fighting machine adored by women and detested by men.[11] "An ape in purple," said the poet George Buchanan in one of his unforgettable phrases.[12]

Meanwhile, the queen issued Moray a second summons, but the earl remained absent. He was trying to raise money from England, but though Cecil was willing, Elizabeth was not. The English queen waited to see if Mary Stuart would, indeed, marry in defiance of her opposition—and in the interim was content with sarcasms. The marriage was hailed and held. Moray, summoned for a third time, remained absent. The third summons left him open to further proceedings. If he did not appear in a set period, he could be declared in defiance to the Crown, his estates could be sequestered, and he could be outlawed.

Shortly after the wedding festivities at Holyrood, Moray appeared in the field with a small army. He raised the cry that the Reform was in danger, but only Knox agreed. The head of the House of Hamilton, the Duke of Châtelherault, who saw his family's chances for the Scots throne diminishing with the queen's marriage, provided some help—and so did a few other nobles. Many more sneered that Moray had lost his high place and his political power—and that not the Reform but his own estates were in danger. That charge, with its half-truth, did much to undermine the earl's position.

The people—or the Congregation, as Knox called them—were equally lukewarm toward the rebellion. The beautiful young queen had woven an effective and appealing legend. Her marriage to the tall blond King Henry was like the end of a fairy tale: two beautiful young people had come together despite the malice and hostility of the traditional English enemy and their strange, bejeweled queen. Mary Stuart gleamed in the sentimental regard of her people.

Nevertheless, Moray was determined upon rebellion. He was on the verge of losing more than his estates: the realm was being turned in new directions. Some money finally came from England—but not much. Elizabeth was always to believe that men should not obtain money from a female sovereign even when they fought on her behalf. Her support, though inadequate, was enough to enable Mary Stuart's supporters to raise the cry that Moray was funded by foreign sources and further undermined his effort.

Mary Stuart, on the other hand, enjoyed the support of many high Catholic nobles such as the earl of Huntly. They brought their troops to her cause, and she herself rode at their head. In a steel bonnet and corselet, with a dagger at her saddlebow, she made a fine show. She was flanked by King Henry in specially created gilt armor on one side and the hard figure of the earl of Bothwell on the other. The earl was a sinister figure in his black armor, with his long arms, restless eyes, and adventurously alert manner; but the queen had made him lord lieutenant of the realm. King Henry was not too happy about that; but the autumnal weather and their companionship, the newness of their wedding, and the sparkling humor of the queen combined to overcome the ignominy of his military role. The queen commanded and decided; the king watched and was petted. Later, diligent investigators determined that it was during this brief and easy campaign, with its pleasant stops at friendly towns and nights spent beneath the stars, that the queen conceived.


Moray had waited too long and been outmaneuvered. He could not rally a large enough force for a pitched battle and had to duck and dodge about the landscape. The Chase About Raids, his critics called this, and their ridicule was one of the weapons that defeated him. He could command no large castles or fortresses; no swarms of people joined the ranks of his followers; no large sums of money were available. The issues were stark and tragic to Moray, but most of his countrymen refused to see them and considered the rebellion a matter of personalities.

His effort soon ended. On October 6, 1565, Moray fled across the border to England, where a reluctant Elizabeth had allowed Cecil to persuade her into providing sanctuary. The man who, next to John Knox himself, was the living symbol of Reform in the land had been brought down and driven ignominiously away. He left behind a triumphant Mary Stuart, surrounded by hopeful pro-Vatican nobles and prelates and three especially close men. They were her new husband, King Henry; her Savoyard secretary and principal adviser, David Rizzio; and the chunky, sinister earl of Bothwell. They made a strange trio, but the woman who had ruined her benefactor now seemed their proper sovereign.


In London the advisers of another queen watched these events with dismay. By funding the Reform movement in Scotland in the first place, England had managed to turn Scotland into a puppet state, independent largely in name. Mary Stuart had ended that relationship in a series of lightning moves.

Cecil was under no illusions that the Queen of the Scots planned to stop with that remarkable accomplishment. His agents kept him informed of the now steady correspondence that flowed from Edinburgh toward Rome, Madrid, Savoy, and Paris. Mary Stuart, aware of her long-heralded claims to the English throne, had extended, with impressive speed, her new base into an effort to make a strong overseas alliance.

With a long eye to the future, Cecil received Moray in London and had a talk with him. Both were ardent Reformers—but their patron Elizabeth, indifferent to religious issues as such, was less sympathetic.

Moray had to be content with an audience in which he was kept on his knees and forced to listen to reproaches from the Queen of England for having rebelled against his lawful sovereign. To add salt to that experience, the sermon was delivered in front of the French ambassador, de Foix. Elizabeth's transparent purpose was to establish the myth that England had no hand in any Scots rebellion—and to remove, if possible, any French or Spanish intervention on behalf of Mary Stuart. Beyond that, however, the Virgin Queen had no plans. She had badly misjudged Mary Stuart; she would now wait and see what happened. Frowning at Moray, she told him he was lucky not to be clapped into an English prison and banished him from her court.

After this public humiliation, Moray withdrew north to Newcastle. There he sat, newly beggared, abandoned by his long-time patrons and most of his countrymen, with neither an estate nor an income, to reflect upon his sister's true character, the gratitude of princes, and his own ruined prospects.

Where Moray's future appeared closed, Mary Stuart's expanded. She had, during the Chase About Raids, established a Catholic provost in Edinburgh and cancelled the payment of revenues to the Kirk. That created great distress, and Knox sent eloquent communications around to alleviate the hardships that followed. They were many and were sharpened by one of the coldest of many cold Scots winters.

King Henry, however, felt a different sort of chill and did not suffer it in silence. Although their marriage had been launched in sensuality, it soon bored the queen, who found him irritatingly uxorious. He had desires, in fact, that radiated in all directions. His mother, the countess of Lennox, had been thrown into the Tower of London by an angry Elizabeth. King Henry urged her release. Elizabeth sent back word that the countess would be released only after Moray and his fellow rebels had been pardoned. That response outraged Mary Stuart and ended the matter as far as she was concerned. King Henry was aggrieved. Though not a notable drinker before coming to Scotland, he became a conspicuous toper and proved his head was weak by appearing drunk on numerous occasions. He also began to slip out of the castle and into various brothels. These expeditions, reported to the queen, did not help their marriage.

In addition to such urges, which seemed to master him with increasing frequency, King Henry was under pressure from his father, the earl of Lennox. The older man, whose ambitions were insatiable, wanted his son to now achieve the crown matrimonial. Technically, such a title would not add to King Henry's authority, but it made him the queen's heir if she died childless before him. To insist upon such a position at any time was tactless; to insist upon it at a time when the queen began to believe she was pregnant was horribly inopportune. Nevertheless, King Henry insisted. Queen Mary refused. He insisted again, and she refused again, and the ensuing arguments—ugly and passionate—extended from the privacy of their apartments into public view.

Yet the young king was crazily in love with his wife. She was his highest personal conquest; like many young men, he did not appreciate that sex can be as pleasurable, but also as light a matter, to a woman as to a man. He thought the queen was his physical slave because she had initially sought him out.

The queen was increasingly repelled. She began to avoid the young king's bed, pleading an infinite number of female indispositions. That worsened their relationship. King Henry, angry and sullen, drank more deeply and rushed more often toward the brothels. Even ladies of the court began to avoid him; he became a spectacular problem.

By November 1565, only a month after Moray's defeat and departure, the king was told that an iron stamp of his signature had been made. Educated for pleasures and responsibilities of state, he had spent his time hunting and gambling. He had resented the task of writing his name over and again to papers he had neither helped draft nor was encouraged to read. Rizzio, the king was told, would use the stamp. Even the news that the queen was pregnant could not slow King Henry's slide. An heir, as he knew even in his disordered condition, would only add to his redundancy.

At this point, some older and more experienced men, who did not have the excuse of illness, but who did have some shrewd realization of where Mary Stuart was carrying Scotland, began to draw near the young king.

The month of December 1565 passed in a whirl of snows and secret conversations. From England pressure began to be exerted on behalf of the earl of Moray, and the earl himself sent desperate letters. His money was running low, and his sources of income remained stopped. His estates were being given away; in a few months he would be destitute. William Maitland, the laird of Lethington, interceded with the queen. Mary Stuart, flanked by the formidable earl of Bothwell, listened with a marble face. It was known that Bothwell hated Moray; it now became clear that the queen shared that attitude. She also made it clear that, as far as she was concerned, English protests had ceased to be significant. Lethington, whom Buchanan later described as "the chameleon," lost no time in relaying that significant information back to Cecil in London.

In response, the English floated the rumor that Mary Stuart now hated her half brother, the earl of Moray, because he had discovered her in the arms of her secretary, David Rizzio. The story made the rounds with the speed of light and sent the unhappy King Henry into near frenzy.

By February 1566 two complicated plots were underway in Scotland. One was managed by the queen, working with Rizzio and a handful of others, and involved a cross correspondence with Philip II of Spain, the Vatican, and her Guise relatives in France to suppress the Reform and restore the papacy in Scotland. The other, of which the queen was unaware, involved the earls of Morton, Lords Ruthven and Lindsay, Lethington, and the king himself—to murder David Rizzio.

The king was now convinced the queen had been unfaithful. Rizzio's death and the crown matrimonial had become obsessive desires. His new associates, who had treated him with scant respect before, were now bluffly cordial and suitably respectful. They wanted the restoration of the Reform and the return of Moray. In true Scots fashion, the parties drew a bond to that effect. It did not, of course, mention Rizzio—but that was understood. Another understanding, insisted upon by the king, was that the deed be done in the queen's presence. That sick insistance carried; so did the agreement that the king would receive the crown matrimonial.

In early March 1566 the earl of Moray suddenly received a thousand pounds from Elizabeth, who had been informed of the plot by her ambassador Thomas Randolph. At the same time, he received a visit from a mysterious figure who showed him the bond. The earl came alive, but he did not lose his usual self-control. After reading the clauses, he inserted the word "lawful" in the pledge to support King Henry's future actions, as well as the phrase "according to the Word of God." Moray would not, ever, betray the Reform. Invited to share in the dread undertaking, he refused. He would return later; pressed, he agreed to return the day after Rizzio was removed.

On the evening of Saturday, March 9, 1566, Mary Stuart—now advanced in pregnancy—was having a quiet dinner at her private dining room in Holyrood Castle. She was not alone—queens were never alone—but the group was small. The countess of Argyll and the laird of Creich were with her, as well as the ever-present Rizzio. He was later described as having his head covered, in the French manner, and wearing an evening suit "of damask, furred, with a satin doublet and hose of russet velvet, with a jewel about his neck."

The party had finished eating and was enjoying wine; the silver candelabra lent a soft light to the scene when they were joined by King Henry,
who sat down next to the queen. He had not been with them long when Lord
Ruthven suddenly appeared, naked sword in hand, the gleam of his armor
visible beneath his fur-fringed mantle. Behind him crowded other armed
men, who had appeared without warning through the private entrance atop
the private stairs that led from the king's apartment below to the queen's.

The queen rose and demanded to know the reason for the intrusion;
she feared for her life. "I see a man here who takes a place that does not
become him," Ruthven replied, his eyes glittering with fever. He was, in
fact, ill.

Rizzio clutched at the queen's skirts, and she cried, "He is here by my
will," but matters were clearly out of hand. The men rushed forward; the
table rocked; Lady Argyll barely caught the candelabra before it fell; the
king pushed the queen against the wall. Later she believed the first dagger
blow against Rizzio had been delivered over her own shoulder; but that
fleeting impression, like so many that crowded into that turbulent moment,
might have been mistaken.

There was no mistaking, however, the fact that Rizzio was dragged
toward the door. He was terrified and shrieked, "Sauvez ma vie, Madame"
and finally, "Madonna, io sono morto, giustizia, giustizia!"[13]

In the large reception room on the landing, they stabbed and slashed
at him in a frenzy of hate; one ran and opened the casement window.
Finally, slipping in puddles of his blood, they picked him up and threw his
still-warm cadaver out into the courtyard below, where it landed with a
sickening smack. He had, in the grim phrase of the time, been *Scotched.*

In the shambles of her dining room, the queen shrieked at her husband.
A stream of invectives poured out of her and shocked him into letting her
go. "I shall be your wife no longer," she shouted into his face, "nor lie with
you no longer . . ." and more.

When she finally fell silent, they led her to her bedchamber. Attracted
by the uproar, the earl of Bothwell had appeared from his palace apartment,
sword in hand. The earl of Huntly had done the same, and the palace guard
had appeared, as well as a huge crowd of mixed citizens who emerged from
the night as though by magic.

King Henry went downstairs then and received a delegation in his
apartment. He said, "The Italian secretary is slain because he was detected
in an intrigue with the pope, the king of Spain and others—to introduce
popery into Scotland." The explanation had enough ring of truth in it to
satisfy the crowd, though in any event the five hundred armed men the
conspirators had placed around the palace in advance made them masters
of the situation.

The king retired. The queen was in her bedchamber, and her doors were guarded. In Berwick, a border town, the earl of Moray made preparations to return to Scotland and departed with the dawn. He was met en route by a large body of horsemen under the earl of Hume, who became his escort. All seemed successfully in hand, until the king was awakened with the news that the earl of Bothwell and the earl of Huntly had both slipped away sometime during the night—and that the queen was in labor.

A midwife was sent in, but reported the queen's time had not yet arrived. The king entered, as a natural matter of course. He found Mary Stuart pale and subdued on her bed, looking at him with woeful eyes. "Ah, my Mary," he said, and took her hand.

From that moment he was lost. She held him close, and their talk ranged into what he considered a reconciliation. In its course, he disclosed the nature of the conspiracy to her, and she assured him that in the future they would rule together and keep no more secrets from each other. At some interval when he was briefly absent, she sent the midwife away with messages for Bothwell, Huntly, and others. When the king returned, she resumed her task of charming him into docility—and complicity in her escape.

By the following day she had succeeded so well that she and the king were partners again. Moray arrived and found them smiling a welcome together. The three had a long private talk, and the queen assured her brother that he would be restored to favor. The Kirk would be retained. All the Lords of the Congregation would be forgiven; she understood that they had rebelled not against her, but against Romanism. Moray, wanting to believe, believed.

The lords appeared, strutting, to assure the queen of their allegiance. She listened warily. Their men at arms ringed the palace, her closest adviser had been butchered before her eyes, and King Henry had told her everything. Advanced in pregnancy, with her plans to control and lead her realm toward the papacy and the crown of England, she sat in the midst of the shambles of her plan. Moray and the rest were in league with Elizabeth— and her own physical safety, and that of her unborn child, hung by a thread. Nevertheless, she managed to smile and to assure them all that she was convinced, that all was well. They withdrew with broad grins, and the guard was withdrawn from her chamber. That was on Monday, the eleventh of March, 1566.

Later that night the king and queen, hand in hand, entered a secret staircase that led to an opening in the cellar of the palace and then up another staircase to the churchyard next door. The night was dark, and the king had to steer the queen around the high soft mound of a fresh grave. She guessed at once that it was Rizzio's and looked at it in silent anger. Then they reached Lord Erskine and some others, who were waiting with fresh horses.

King Henry, in a fever to get away, set their pace at a reckless gallop. He had—as he knew even in his sickness—betrayed men who had dared much with him. The queen, however, was pregnant and feared for her child. She called to him to go slower or to stop and rest and reminded him of her condition. At that his nerves snapped, and he said harshly, *"We can have more."*

That was a remark she would never forgive, and she placed it in her mind against him as they rode dangerously through the night.

The following day the queen was safe in the great castle of Dunbar and busy with her plans. She wrote a dramatic letter to Elizabeth in England, describing her narrow escape and the malignant activities of her subjects. Fighting men, led by the earls of Bothwell and Huntly, streamed toward her stronghold to her assistance. The reins of government were once again in her hands. The earl of Morton, Lord Ruthven, and their associates, who discovered in the morning that the king had deserted them, fled toward England. Only the earl of Moray remained, for he had taken no part in the murder of Rizzio or in the action against the queen.

He was still waiting when the queen, flanked by the earl of Bothwell, the only titular Reformer never to waver from her side, and the Catholic earls of Huntly and Atholl and with eight thousand troops behind her, entered the gates of Edinburgh on the eighteenth of March, 1566. The queen embraced Moray when they met and smiled upon her supporters. On the surface it was a great triumph for Mary Stuart, but underneath the surface it was a greater triumph for the earl of Moray. He had proven to his stepsister that she could not rule without him.

During the following weeks the earl of Moray worked to restore his position and to have the queen pardon and allow the return of Rizzio's murderers. The king, meanwhile, attempted to strengthen his own position with a public statement declaring he had not been involved in the conspiracy.

Unfortunately for Henry, however, the earl of Morton and his companions, smarting in English exile, sent copies of the bond to murder Rizzio, with all its incriminating details about the crown matrimonial for King Henry, back to Scotland for Mary Stuart to read. She studied the evidence carefully and with mounting bitterness. Her attempt to become the real sovereign of Scotland had failed through subversion shared by her own husband. Her plans to restore Catholicism to the land were in ruins. Though some of its leaders were scattered and John Knox had mysteriously vanished, the Reform was rising again. She knew that her respite was only temporary and that she would have to compromise, play for time, listen to Moray again—and await the birth of her child. Beyond that she had neither plans nor reliable associates.

A further difficulty was the rumor that David Rizzio had been her lover. Such evil suspicions cast a shadow on the paternity of her expected child, and it was necessary—even essential—that the king at such a time be kept by her side. That called for extraordinary powers of dissimulation, for she had grown to loathe him. Nevertheless, she smiled at the king and smiled, and smiled again.

Her time finally arrived in June 1566. Her labor was long but uneventful; the baby was a boy, born with a caul. Cannons boomed from the battlements of Edinburgh Castle, where Mary Stuart had retired for her ordeal. Bonfires were lit, and crowds gathered to cheer; the birth of a male heir was hailed.

Inside the castle the king was escorted to the queen's bedside, where a number of people had collected. Mary showed him the baby and said, "My Lord, this is your son and no other man's son. I am desirous that all here, both ladies and others, bear witness. He is so much your son that I fear it may be the worse for him hereafter."[14]

That bitter observation, uttered at such a moment, cast the entire room into an embarrassed silence. The queen, uncaring, turned toward Sir William Standen and said, indicating the infant, "This is the Prince who I hope shall first unite the two kingdoms of England and Scotland."

"Why, Madam, shall he succeed before Your Majesty and his father?" asked Sir William.

"Alas," said Mary, "his father has broken to me."[15]

The king, shamed before them all, said, "Sweet Madam, is this your promise that you made to forgive and forget all?"

"I have forgiven but can never forget," she said quickly. "What if Faudonside's pistol had shot? What would have become of him"—indicating the infant—"and me both? Of what estate would you have been in? God only knows, but we may suspect."

"Madam," said the king in a tone of distress, "these things are all past."

"Then let them go,"[16] she said and sank back, her triumph at the delivery of a healthy son forgotten in her contempt for its father. That was how, on June 19, 1566, the world and his parents greeted James Charles Stuart.

**2** While the infant James, who appeared healthy, slumbered peacefully, his mother flew from the small, dark, almost airless chamber she had selected for her delivery, like a creature released from a cocoon. By July 1566 she was spending much of her time at sea to escape the sweltering heat of the season. By the end of the month she was enjoying the cool river breeze of the Forth, at the castle of Alloa owned by the earl of Mar, attended by her court.

King Henry had not been invited, but he persuaded himself the oversight had been accidental. Accompanied by his few personal servants and his tiny guard, he rode to Alloa from Edinburgh—a trip only three miles to the south. Ignored when he arrived, he did not see the queen; her entourage snubbed him. He soon received a message, delivered through other parties, from his wife. His presence, the message said, was not desired; he was to leave. The young man rode away; it was painfully clear he could go wherever he chose: his activities were no longer of interest to the queen. She made no secret of her contempt. "It cannot, for modesty or the honor of the queen, be reported what she said of him," wrote the earl of Bedford back to William Cecil in London.[1]

That alarmed Sir James Melville, the Scots diplomat. He knew the arrival of James Stuart into the world created a crisis for Elizabeth. But he also knew the importance of gossip in politics. The contretemps between the Queen of Scots and her consort could, if it became common knowledge, injure the rising prospects of Mary Stuart.

Mary Stuart's marriage to the heir of the earl of Lennox had pulled the support of English Catholics in her direction. The Queen of England was only thirty-three years old, but she sat on the throne alone. Not long before the birth of James Stuart, the English queen had contracted smallpox. She had recovered, but for a time it seemed as if she would succumb —and the event sent apprehension through England.

Melville himself had brought the news of James Stuart's birth to London; it reached Elizabeth when she was dancing. She stopped abruptly and groped her way to a chair. "The Queen of Scots is lighter of a fair son," she said bitterly, "and I am but a barren stock."[2] That remark, poignant and self-revealing, was too rich not to be repeated. It went the rounds of Europe with the speed of light and became a part of the crisis created in England by the birth of James Stuart in Scotland.

Elizabeth was not an ideal sovereign. She was indecisive and stingy, reluctant to launch great enterprises. Her country was deeply divided and the queen's reputation was badly tarnished by her relationship with the earl of Leicester. With the men of the cities ardent for Reform and much of the countryside still Catholic, the death of a childless queen could leave future problems of succession that would be settled only by fire and sword.

Cecil and his associates considered it conceivable that Catholic England, if supported from the outside, could overthrow Elizabeth and place Mary Stuart on the throne. Such a coup would ensure that England would be headed by a sovereign whose legitimacy would be recognized by all the world, who had proved able to maintain the Reform in her own country while remaining Catholic herself. Mary Stuart was married to an English prince; she had an heir.

In Scotland the queen herself carried such speculations to their limits. She had already enlisted the support of the most powerful nation in Europe, Spain, for her marriage. If she could persuade Philip II to send an armada while she herself raised an army, England could be attacked from land, sea, and within; Elizabeth would be overthrown, and Mary Stuart would be queen.

It was not an impossible dream, but an impatient one. As matters stood during the summer and autumn of 1566, Mary Stuart had no need to plan any new large undertakings at all. Time was on her side. She had great and powerful friends in Spain and Rome; she had achieved independence from the Protestant Lords of the Congregation and the forces of John Knox; her rule was unquestioned. All she had to do was to steer a subtle and careful course and await events.

The earl of Moray, whose influence was now greatly diminished, pleaded that she pardon the remainder of those involved in the murder of Rizzio and allow them to return. Two of the exiles were especially important. One of these was William Maitland, laird of Lethington, long secretary of the realm, and a man so astute, worldly, and objective in his judgments that he had been nicknamed—after Machiavelli—*Michael Wily.* The other was James Douglas, earl of Morton, a man of cold, small eyes and burly body, formidable and feared. Both sent fervent assurances of good behavior in the future; both were influential men.

Mary Stuart, however, would not listen seriously to the earl of Moray. She was not anxious to see the return of the cool and calculating laird of Lethington or the dangerous earl of Morton. She turned, instead, toward the man whom Cecil had once described as "as mortal an enemy to our whole nation as any man alive; despiteful above measure, false and untrue as a devil"—the earl of Bothwell. He alone had never wavered from her side; he alone put his queen above religion and other alliances. What he whispered to her was their secret.

Toward the end of summer, 1566, the queen appeared to relax. To Moray's pleasure she issued orders that Lethington could return. The news that Lethington had returned sent young King Henry into despair. Men he had implicated in his confessions to the queen at the time of the Rizzio murder were seeping back to court. Their influence was on the rise again while his own continued to fall. The queen, in fact, now seemed to swing toward the theory that her husband alone was responsible for the bloody fright she had received. She used that assumption as an excuse to pardon everyone else. With Lethington back, the earl of Morton could not be far behind—and King Henry feared Morton. The Douglas leader was capable of cutting a man down on sight.

Had Mary Stuart cared enough, she could have calmed her young husband even in his disordered state. Instead, she attempted to manipulate his enemies against him. Learning that he was drinking heavily and making wild statements, she informed Moray that the king had insulted him. Her stepbrother received the information calmly and showed no inclination to pursue the matter. But the queen insisted the king should be made to apologize. Henry was dragged before them both and forced into a stammering statement of regret. Moray looked at the young king with some pity, bowed, and expressed himself satisfied. The queen bit her lip; it was clear she had hoped for more action and less understanding.

The air, in other words, was growing strange. Young King Henry traveled between the court and his father's seat at Glasgow like some uneasy and unwanted ghost. He began to write disjointed, semicoherent letters overseas. He wrote the pope that the Queen of Scots was a false Christian who had no intention of restoring papal power in the land and was merely bleeding the Vatican for money. He wrote Philip II in similar vein and offered himself to both these rulers as a more suitable candidate for their support.

By September 1566 du Croc, the French ambassador, who kept in touch with the king as part of his duties, learned the younger man planned to flee the country. "The queen would give him no authority; the lords had abandoned him," he told du Croc. There was an English ship in the Forth; he would take passage on it.

Du Croc asked where he would go, and King Henry thought the Scilly Isles might be a good place; he might become a pirate. Piracy was an avenue, however, for ordinary men and not for sick and despairing princes. Du Croc thought matters had gone too far and spoke to the queen.

The earl of Lennox, alarmed at his son's condition, wrote Mary Stuart at about the same time on the same subject. She sent word at last that her young husband should come to court. He appeared outside Holyrood Palace on the twenty-ninth of September, 1566, but refused to enter because the earl of Moray, Argyll, and Lethington were inside. The queen appeared in person and carried him in to her apartment. There he spent a night or two, and in that brief span she again turned him around.

The king's presence had long since been dropped from council meetings. State papers no longer carried even his stamped signature; the queen simply signed Mary R—*fiat*. But on September 30, 1567, King Henry was summoned to council. He entered hesitantly. The nobles, seated around a table headed by the queen, looked at him coldly. They represented all the factions of Scotland's nobility: the Catholic earls of Huntly, Caithness, and Atholl; the former Lord of the Congregation Moray, and others. The Frenchman du Croc had been summoned to be the world's witness. The queen read Lennox's letter to her aloud, and the king was then asked the cause of his dissatisfaction. His wife urged him to tell the lords whether he was dissatisfied with her.

"Say what you complain of," she urged him. "If the blame is with me —do not spare me."

One peer wondered how any man could leave "so beautiful a queen and so noble a realm." The king stared at him, wide-eyed, and the French du Croc quickly intervened to suggest that King Henry should not say anything to dishonor himself or his queen.

Finally, after a silence that affected even the men who held him in such deep contempt, the sick young king bowed. "Adieu, Madam," he said. "You will not see my face for a long space. Gentlemen, adieu."[3] He walked away destroyed—but somehow intact.


In England Elizabeth had been forced to call a Parliament and found herself embroiled in deep difficulties in consequence. The issue of succession was raised, and in the House of Commons speakers arose to name Mary Stuart. Elizabeth was outraged and threatened prison, the Star Chamber, treason trials, and all the instruments of suppression. But Cecil convinced her that sort of response could set off a conflagration. She had to promise —with a smile—that she would, indeed, marry and marry soon.

Negotiations were again launched with the Archduke Charles of Austria, and Cecil produced documents so detailed that they even discussed the archduke's living allowance after the wedding.

Parliament, however, was not dissuaded from its central purpose, which Cecil explained to Elizabeth time and again. The House of Commons wanted to make clear to the queen that the English people had the power to settle the election of sovereigns and intended to use that power. In addition, it meant to govern the high clergy; the Reform had no intention of allowing clerical despotism to emerge again in England.

Elizabeth's responses were varied and impressive, but Parliament held the power of the purse. The Crown would receive no money to use in quelling the eternal troubles in Ireland or in its disputes with France. The queen's economies notwithstanding, she could not maintain her throne without money.

Through autumn and to the edge of winter, the English queen struggled and finally managed to close that noisy Parliament down and send its members home—but the experience had been scary. She had barely managed to keep Commons from actually naming Mary Stuart heir to the throne of England and had to promise and promise again to marry. The issues were left with some open ends on all sides; her subsidy was granted on the basis of understandings and not formal agreements. She was past a great crisis for the moment, but it was understood that her heir—unless she had children of her own—would be Mary, Queen of Scots.[4]

In earlier years, that understanding would have contented Mary Stuart, but she had moved, in the months after the birth of her son, James, toward new needs. On the surface she was busy with innocent details of her son's baptism, but while Elizabeth grappled with an unruly Parliament, the Queen of Scots had a crisis of another, even more personal sort.

In early October Bothwell was busy putting down disorders along the border. His methods were quick, brutal, and decisive: he left loaded gallows and swinging bodies in his trail. In one of these affrays, however, he was wounded. The rumor swept the country that he was dead or nearly so— and not many appeared to sorrow. The queen, however, was concerned enough to make a trip to Hermitage Castle to see him. He was in pain, but would recover. She left for Jedburgh and fainted on arrival. Lifted from her horse unconscious, she went into delirium. That was followed by a fever and semicoma. On the twenty-fifth of October 1566 she grew still and cold, and it was feared she was dead. Her physician, Arnault, took heroic measures and she recovered. The cause of her distress was then unknown. Later it was diagnosed as a gastric ulcer "with a hysterical overlay."[5]

She had reason for hysteria that—as yet—few suspected. Sometime during that autumn, at a moment that only they knew and in a manner they held forever secret, the Queen of Scots and Bothwell had become lovers.

In early November, 1566, both recovered from their disabilities—he from his wounds and she from her ulcer attack—but neither recovered, nor would really ever recover, from their affair.

The queen made a slow progress to Edinburgh. En route she traveled close to the border, and as her entourage passed Berwick, the English guns of the town boomed an unprecedented salute. The understanding of Parliament, which reflected the sentiments of England, that she was the real heir to the Crown and in line to become the next English queen was echoed in that salute.

Mary Stuart returned to her capital, therefore, at the crest. She busied herself in plans for the baptism—by now somewhat overdue—of her son, James. Yet she did not seem happy. On a number of occasions her ladies found her weeping in bed, and du Croc wrote his masters that Mary Stuart's true illness appeared to be "deep grief and sorrow."

It was that, and more. The Queen was pregnant. She knew—as did everyone—that the father of her second child could not possibly be King Henry. In her new condition the king's existence altered from an annoyance to a positive menace; Bothwell undoubtedly came to that conclusion very quickly. Mary Stuart agreed, but the realization made her sick nevertheless.

She rested at the castle of Craigmillar on the outskirts of Edinburgh, and her melancholia brought Moray and others around in concern. "Again and again," du Croc wrote, "she says she wishes she were dead."[6]

It seemed the poorest possible moment for Moray and Lethington to press the queen for the pardon and return of the earl of Morton. Nevertheless, that was their desire. They conferred on how she could be persuaded, and Lethington—"Michael Wily"—brought up the subject of King Henry. It was not by any means a new subject: it was known the queen had written the pope regarding the possibility of a divorce—and had been advised to remain patient—and married.

Other means, Lethington hinted, might be found necessary. They stared at him, and he continued, "The best way to obtain Morton's pardon is to promise the queen to find a means to divorce her from her husband."[7]

Moray and Lethington then talked to the earl of Argyll, who did not see how such means could be found, failing papal approval. Nevertheless, he was interested and pulled the earl of Huntly into the discussion. That meant that both the Catholic and the Protestant lords were together, at least in principle. All of them next talked to Bothwell, who must have privately marveled at how skillfully the queen managed to move so many men in the direction she desired—and that he had suggested.

During the next few weeks the queen was busy with plans for the baptism of James Stuart, prince of Scotland. In darker corners an agreement

—a compact—was drawn and signed by the earls of Bothwell, Argylle, Huntly, Lethington, and a Bothwell cousin, Sir James Balfour, to "put forth" King Henry—"one way or other."[8]

The two preparations almost intersected when the queen went to Stirling Castle and was joined by the king at her invitation. That news, which seemed to indicate a reconciliation, was hailed in many quarters in both Scotland and England. When he arrived from England shortly afterward, the earl of Bedford was able to tell the Queen of the Scots that her claim to be Elizabeth's heir "should receive much favour." He also brought, as a sign of friendship and alliance, a magnificent gold baptismal font for the ceremony. It was ironic when Elizabeth, aware the gift and the baptism were both late and that the baby had by now outgrown the font, said it might do "for the next child."[9]

On the fifteenth of December 1566, a stream of torches lit the dark passageway to the chapel at Stirling and shed added light on the baptism of the young prince. The queen had spared no expense to make the occasion a grand one. The earls of Moray, Bothwell, and Argyll, among others, had been outfitted at crown expense in cloths of gold and silver and colors of red, green, and blue.

The baby prince was carried by the Count de Brienne, the French ambassador. One Scots noble carried the cierge, "another the salt, another the rood, another the basin and laver." At the door of the chapel they were met by the archbishop of St. Andrews and other Catholic prelates. The countess of Argyll held the prince at the font, and the baptism was conducted in the Catholic manner—"with the spittle excepted, which the Queen did inhibit."

James Stuart's titles were proclaimed: prince and stewart of Scotland, duke of Rothesay, earl of Carrick, lord of the Isles, and baron of Renfrew.

Later there was a series of feasts, masques, and fireworks; and it seemed as though all of Scotland gathered to do honor to its heir. Sir James Melville, who was present, never forgot it. At one banquet a scene came close to erupting between the visiting Englishmen and their hosts, "for a Frenchman called Bastian devised a number of men formed like satyrs, with long tails and whips in their hands, running down the meat. . . . The satyrs," Melville said, "not content only to make way or room, put their hands behind them to their tails which they wagged."[10] The English, well aware that rural people in Scotland still believed them to have tails, were outraged. Melville calmed them, and so did the queen herself and the earl of Bedford —but the incident was enough to show that the English and Scots alliance was still fragile.

Despite that near-crisis, the baptism and the festivities appeared a great success. Unfortunately, among the great nobles and guests one remained conspicuous by absence: the prince's father—King Henry.

The king of Scotland was at Stirling Castle, but did not stir from his apartment; he did not attend the baptism in the chapel, the banquets, the masques, or the dances. Some said he feared a public insult from the English, who officially persisted in refusing to recognize his status; others said he feared worse from the Scots.

Unwatched, disregarded, Henry crept from the palace early in the morning of December 24, 1566, and rode on horseback toward his father's seat in Glasgow. By the time he arrived, the true reason he had not appeared in public was horribly evident. He was lifted from his horse in a state of collapse. His whole body and face had erupted in "evil favored pistules"— the final and most fearful stage of syphilis.[11]


The queen spent Christmas in a state of somewhat spurious radiance. She attended Lethington's wedding to the beauteous Mary Fleming, one of her lifelong companions, in the Royal Chapel. Restless, the sovereign then moved from Drummond Castle to Tullibardine. Bothwell was, by now, in constant attendance. They heard the news of King Henry's real illness together. For a moment it must have seemed to Mary Stuart that her dilemma would be resolved by a happily opportune natural death.

In early January, however, news reached the court that the king was not only making a remarkable recovery, but had a ship waiting to carry him to Europe. That meant his tongue, with all its shameful secrets and wild babble, would sound through Flanders and Paris, Madrid and Rome, to slice Mary Stuart's reputation and undercut her position. It also meant that she would bear Bothwell's child in the king's absence and in that delivery, deliver herself to universal, inescapable disgrace.

Her reaction was, as always, swift. She signed a pardon for the earl of Morton and sent Bothwell himself to greet the exile when he crossed the border at Whittingham. Years later, in a dreadful moment of his own, Morton described how Bothwell greeted him with the news that King Henry had to be killed. Astonished, the Douglas leader said he was "newly come from one trouble, and in no haste to enter another." He wondered about the queen's standing in the matter, and Bothwell assured him "he knew what was in the Queen's mind."

Nevertheless, Morton was unwilling. The queen's effort to operate through others was not working—or at least not working fast enough. Bothwell returned to Edinburgh, and there were more whispered conversations. The king was in Glasgow at his father's house, where the Lennox family could not be frontally assaulted. He had to be brought, somehow, to Edinburgh. At that point the queen herself entered the game.

She arrived with her entourage at Glasgow on January 22, 1567. News of her coming had preceded her, and King Henry sent a man named Crawford to convey his regrets because of his indisposition. The queen was sharp with Crawford and wanted to know the real reason she was not being welcomed. Crawford, to his credit, said the king was afraid.

"There is no remedy for fear,"[12] she said shortly and swept on to the sick man's bedroom. He had prepared by putting on a taffeta mask. Once in his presence, she had no more problem than with a child. When she showed sympathy and some slight sign of affection, he dissolved in tears. She sat near his bed and played her part, though she later wrote to Bothwell that his breath "almost killed me." The treatment for syphilis then consisted of massive oral doses of mercury, which destroyed the gum margins and created a dreadful stench.

Not only did she endure that, but she convinced him that she wanted him in her bed. She proposed to take him from Glasgow to the castle of Craigmillar, where he could take the cold baths considered essential to the treatment of his illness. He demurred at that desolate location and—all sweet agreeableness—she then proposed Edinburgh itself, the capital; the proper site for a king. By then he was tired and, in the extremity of his illness, unable to maintain any further resistance.

She spent the night in Glasgow and sent French Paris—Bothwell's man—back to Edinburgh with some letters to the earl that described the king's condition and her own persuasions. "If I did not know his heart was wax, and mine a diamond, I could almost have pity on him," she said in part.[13] For the rest, she assured the waiting earl of her passionate love for him and stressed that she was taking all these pains and problems on his account. Her letters were enough, in time, to damn them both.

Her messages reached Bothwell on the twenty-fifth of January 1567, and he sent back word that lodgings would be prepared for the king in Edinburgh. They proved to be in a building owned by his cousin Sir James Balfour near the ruined church of St. Mary's, in a site known as Kirk o'Field. The building selected had once been occupied by Dominican monks and was not small. The king's apartment was cleaned and a handsome bed with black velvet hangings installed; the queen was to have an apartment immediately below.

Meanwhile, the queen's 36-mile journey from Glasgow with King Henry, conveyed on a litter, moved with snaillike pace. There was time enough for her to send messages, complaints, descriptions, and professions of love to Bothwell, and more than time enough for preparations to be made at Kirk o'Field.

The king was surprised at the location on his arrival, but the contagious nature of his illness made his isolation medically plausible. He was carried inside his apartment, and a stream of courtiers appeared to give the establishment the air of a miniature court. The queen herself had an apartment directly below his where she even spent a night. But on Friday she had her bed removed because the king had splashed it from his bath. To reassure her husband, however, she accompanied that decision with the news that she would sleep with him on Sunday night, after his last medicinal bath.

Sunday was February 9, 1566. The earl of Moray, who had been informed his pregnant wife had suffered a mishap, left the capital to go to his estate. Preparations were underway in the castle for a masque to be held in celebration of the wedding of two favorite servants. The queen spent most of the early evening in the king's apartment and then was reminded of the masque by French Paris, Bothwell's man.

She rose to leave, and the king was disappointed. In a charming apology she slipped a ring from her finger and gave it to him "as a sign of goodwill" and then leaned down and kissed him. She neared the door and her entourage prepared to depart with her. Just before she disappeared, she said aloud, as though suddenly recalling, "It was just this time last year Rizzio was slain." Then she was gone.

The king, startled by her parting words, was left with his page, Taylor, who generally slept in his room, and two servants. The servants, Nelson and Edward Seymour, could not answer when the king wondered why the queen had mentioned Rizzio. "What will she do?" Henry asked aloud.

A little later he drank a glass of wine. Then he asked for the English Prayer Book and—moved by an uncanny presentiment—opened it to the fifty-fifth Psalm. There he read:

> Hear my prayer, O Lord, and hide not thyself from my petition.
> My heart is disquieted within me, and the fear of death is fallen upon me.
> Fearfulness and trembling are come upon me, and a horrible dread hath overwhelmed me.
> It is not an open enemy that hath done me this dishonor, for then I could have borne it.
> It was even thou my companion, my guide and my familiar friend.[14]

He lay back in the bed and closed his eyes, and the page blew out the candles.

3 At two o'clock in the morning on February 10, 1567, a tremendous explosion tore the skies above Edinburgh and Kirk o'Field and brought down the entire side of the house where King Henry slept. People who rushed into that enclosure discovered Edward Seymour had been blown apart. Nelson, who had been in another wing of the building, had survived. In the garden, searchers came upon the bodies of King Henry and Taylor, his page. Both were in their nightshirts; near the page was the king's dressing gown and a chair. Both had been suffocated.[1]

The explosion awoke all Edinburgh. People in their nightcaps emerged to stand in clusters; large numbers poured toward Kirk o'Field. The guards at the castle gripped their weapons; messengers poured through the corridors, carrying the news of the murders. Oddly enough, Bothwell said he had slept through the noise and had to be aroused. He collected some guards and went to the scene, where he had some spectators arrested, to restore order. He returned to the castle inside a half hour and then waited, with unusual patience, for daylight.

The queen, usually so decisive and energetic, did not emerge from her apartment. Bothwell entered her bedchamber in the morning, with his man French Paris following. The windows of the room were closed, but it was draped in black and blazing with candles: the conventional signs of mourning. But the queen was still in bed and stirred only on their arrival. She sat up, and her breakfast—"a new laid egg"—was brought in; Bothwell went over to the bed and pulled its curtains around them. Paris could hear them murmur, but could not distinguish their words.

Later in the day a letter arrived for Mary Stuart from the Scots' ambassador to France, the archbishop of Glasgow. It contained a warning from Catherine de Médicis, saying the French court had heard rumors that an attempt would be made on the life of King Henry of Scotland.

That superbly ironic message impelled the Council of Scotland, now dominated by Bothwell, to compose a letter to the dowager queen of France, explaining that young King Henry had, indeed, been murdered. In effect, the reply amounted to a report. It stressed the violence of the explosion, which "left not one stone upon another" and the fact that the Queen of the Scots herself had left the scene only two hours before. The implication was that Mary Stuart had been the party endangered, as well as "a great many of the nobles and Lords in her suite." It was signed by the archbishop of Saint Andrews, a prelate of unsavory reputation who had lately grown prominent at Mary's court; the earls of Argyll, Huntly, Atholl, Cassillis, Caithness, Sutherland; the bishops of Galloway and Ross; Treasurer Robertson and officials Livingstone, Fleming, and Bellenden; Secretary Lethington; and, of course, Bothwell. The queen's signature was missing.

The news created a sensation in England. Sir Robert Melville, the brother of everybody's favorite Scot, Sir James Melville, carried the official message to Cecil and Queen Elizabeth. They had both received a stream of reports from their agents in Scotland, warning of plots and subplots against King Henry and connecting many figures with such plans. The names of the earl of Bothwell and his cousin Sir James Balfour had been prominent in these rumors.

Elizabeth sat down and wrote a tart, notably candid letter to her distant cousin, saying in part, "I cannot but tell you what all the world is thinking. Men say that, instead of seizing the murderers, you are looking through your fingers while they escape; that you will not punish those who have done you so great a service." Speaking, for once, in the tones of an honest sister, the Queen of England said in conclusion, "I exhort, I advise, I implore you . . . to lay your hands upon the man who has been guilty of the crime."[2]

It was a letter written in the shock of the moment by a woman who had herself been touched almost as closely by murder. The strange, broken-necked death of Amy Robsart Dudley, wife of Elizabeth's favorite, had thrown suspicion on Elizabeth. At that time the English Queen had drawn her skirts far from the man suspected of masterminding that too-opportune event: she now advised Mary Stuart to look, in similar fashion, to herself —and to her throne.


Events in Edinburgh, unknown to Elizabeth, made her words prescient. Bothwell, dressed in black armor and surrounded by guards, supervised the removal of the bodies of King Henry and his page. The council questioned a variety of servants. The examinations were awkward, for Sir James Balfour, the landlord of the property in which the king had died, was known to have purchased vast quantities of gunpowder—and Balfour was Bothwell's cousin and close companion.

A proclamation offering a reward of £2,000 was issued by the council, but it hardly had been posted before another appeared beside it—fastened in prominent places by parties unknown during the night. It charged Bothwell and Sir James Balfour with the crime and accused the queen of being "an assenting party." The poster was a new weapon, often used on the Continent, but previously rare in Scotland; a by-product of the printing presses that fueled the revolutionary doctrines of Luther, Calvin, and others, that had turned Europe into a jungle of dissension. Bothwell, furious, said he would "wash his hands in blood" and dared his anonymous accusers to come forward and claim their reward—and meet him in combat.

That was a rash response, for new placards appeared as if by magic, naming the queen's servants Bastian and Joseph Rizzio, the brother of the slain David, as well as the countess of Buccleigh, Bothwell's old light of love, and others. The new posters said that if these parties were arrested, accusers would appear. In the midst of this strange debate, conducted under cover of darkness on the part of Bothwell's secret opposition, one poster appeared that struck more deeply than any other, and copies of it were circulated, with devastating effect, throughout all Europe. It showed Mary Queen of Scots as a mermaid—the stereotype of a prostitute at that time —with naked breasts and a crown, lashing at pursuing hounds with a whip, while Bothwell, who was pictured as a hare—the crest of the Hepburns— crouched fearfully inside a circle of swords. The masses, who could not read, could grasp the significance of that illustration in a flash.

The king had been murdered in the early hours of February 10, 1567. His body was embalmed without an autopsy to determine the actual cause of death on the eleventh and placed on a bier in the Royal Chapel at Holyrood on the twelfth. The queen came then and stared down at her dead husband. She remained tearless and silent and soon departed. No special service—or at least no state funeral—was held. Henry Stewart, king of Scotland, was interred in the royal vault in the old Abbey Church at Holyrood on Saturday, the fifteenth, 1567. His horses and clothes were given to Bothwell. The suits had to be cut down; the young king had towered between six foot one and three; Bothwell was only five foot six. The tailor said the bequest was only proper, since the clothes of the dead were always the property of the hangman.

The following day the queen left the black curtains, closed windows, and lighted candles of the castle at Edinburgh for the more pleasant atmosphere of Lord Seton's estate a few miles from the city. The bishop of Ross, who was asked why the queen did not keep the usual forty days of mourning, had two ready explanations. The first was that "Darnley"—as the court now referred to the queen's husband, overlooking his later titles of earl, duke, and king—"was only a king by courtesy. He was a subject, and took his honour from his wife." In addition, physicians had decided that a darkened room in the French manner might be injurious to the queen's health.

The explanations, however, could not hide the fact that the queen's mourning was unusual. At Lord Seton's estate she played at golf and archery and seemed remarkably cheerful for a woman who had, only a short time before, openly wished she were dead. As various observers reported her behavior, opinion abroad began to harden. The French court decided, after brief discussion, to omit official condolences. Other quarters sent inquiries regarding the pace of the investigation; Elizabeth urged a trial. So did the countess of Lennox, finally released from the Tower of London by the death of her son; so did the earl of Lennox from his stronghold in Glasgow.

Meanwhile Bothwell, with the queen's consent, moved to expand his power. Granted control of the castles of Edinburgh, Blackness, and Inchkeith in addition to his border keeps, he removed the earl of Mar from Edinburgh and installed a lesser henchman first and finally the unsavory Sir James Balfour as governor.

In this atmosphere a note of new horror appeared when Lady Bothwell, the former Lady Jean Gordon and sister of the earl of Huntly, fell suddenly, mysteriously, and seriously ill. Rumors of poison began to float about; posters now charged the queen planned to marry Bothwell. The safety of the young Prince James entered into view: many were convinced that Bothwell would manage his murder, as he had managed the murder of his father, King Henry.

The Queen sought to persuade the earl of Moray to patch up his differences with Bothwell and come to her side. Moray, a deeply moral man who had grown horrified by the course of events, evaded that issue by saying he wanted to go abroad. He longed, he told her, to visit some of the famous places in Europe—and was retiring from political life.[3] She gave her consent with great reluctance and obvious disappointment.

The fact was the earl of Bothwell had become the *de facto* king of Scotland and was moving chess pieces around to prepare for future contingencies. Moray, writing Cecil for permission to travel through England— for it was a period when no man could travel without a passport—said he feared for his life if he remained in Scotland.

On March 23, 1567, a solemn high Mass was held for the murdered king at the end of the queen's official period of mourning. The fact that such an elaborate Catholic service was now held in a country that had mounted a spectacular rising against papacy was an indication of how far the queen had drifted from an understanding of the popular mood. Another was the fact that a few days after that ceremony, the queen gave Bothwell a number of costly church vestments so he could have suits made from them.

At the same time the pair now decided to hold the trial for which the earl of Lennox and others clamored. An official notice summoned the earl of Lennox to bring his charges and ordered the earl of Bothwell to defend himself against them. The effect of this proclamation, on the surface so hopeful, was weakened by the fact that it was signed by Bothwell himself, as head of the queen's council.

Crown policies then deteriorated even further. Lennox prepared to go to Edinburgh to press his case and, as days passed, alarmed the court by gathering almost 3,000 supporters in Glasgow. Bothwell, meanwhile, packed the streets and alleys of Edinburgh with 4,000 armed, fierce creatures from the battle-scarred border for his own defense. For a time it appeared a confrontation might occur, but the queen intervened. She sent Lennox word that by law he was restricted to six retainers when he appeared in court. She forbade him to bring more than that number to Edinburgh. With that word in hand, the earl of Lennox finally prepared to leave the realm and return to England. He had known all along that he would not receive justice, and the queen had furnished the proof he intended to show before a larger audience.

On the morning of April 12, 1567, the earl of Bothwell rode out of the yard of Holyrood Palace while the Queen of the Scots smiled at him from an upstairs window. To make their complicity unmistakable, their guards had held from the queen's presence a special messenger from England, bearing a letter from Queen Elizabeth, imploring Mary Stuart to act as a sovereign and not as the creature of murderers. Bothwell rode, in his black armor, down the streets of Edinburgh flanked by his troops and was, of course, in the absence of any accusers, acquitted by the court of the murder of King Henry.

Later that day his men rode about the city, nailing placards to various walls in which the proud earl offered to meet, in personal hand-to-hand combat, any additional accusers. By his standards and by the standards of an obsolete feudal period that the rest of the world had abandoned, he was in the clear and in the right by might. But when the queen rode from Holyrood a few days later to open Parliament, the women in the "Grass-market rose at their stalls as she passed and screamed after her, 'God save your Grace, if ye be sackless of the King's death—of the King's death.' "[4]

Knox had vanished; the earl of Moray was in London en route to Paris and other parts, and the earls of Mar and Glencairn had applied for passports. Most of the nobility was absent, and leaders of the Kirk were not invited to attend the opening of Mary Stuart's Parliament. Bothwell presided over a handful of seven nobles and five high Catholic prelates. The business of the gathering was as limited as those it represented, and the session was dissolved after five days.

Bothwell, using his own peculiar diplomacy, decided to host a lavish dinner at Ainslie's Tavern in Edinburgh. Later some of his guests, who included Huntly, Argyll, and Cassillis as well as a number of high Catholic prelates, pleaded the tavern had been ringed with Bothwell's hagbutters.[5] If so, that would not have been unusual. Bothwell had taken to moving about in the center of a strong armed force.

After seeing his guests fairly deep into their cups, Bothwell produced a document he asked the assembled company to sign. The first part of the statement cleared Bothwell of King Henry's murder and pledged the signers to resist any further such slanders on his behalf. The second part, which the rapidly sobering company heard with growing dismay, said, "The Queen is now destitute of a husband. Should her Majesty be moved, by respect of his faithful service, to take the Earl of Bothwell to her husband" the signers would agree to support such a union. At this the earl of Eglinton, who apparently had sipped rather than gulped at the hospitality, slipped away. The rest, numbering some twenty in all, signed their names in full view— they said later—of the hagbutters.

The end of the earl's game was now clear. The mock-merry gathering at Ainslie's Tavern came to its disorderly conclusion, and the earl of Bothwell clattered away, trailed by his men. There was no doubt regarding his destination: he was on his way to tell the Queen of the Scots that Scotland's nobles and prelates had agreed to their marriage, though he himself was still married.

He left behind some deeply disturbed men. One, Sir William Kirkcaldy of Grange, wrote an uneasy letter to the English earl of Bedford intended for the eyes of Cecil and Elizabeth. It was a curious letter: half report and half a muffled cry for help. He described the brief session of the Scots Parliament and how the Queen of the Scots had acted to protect Bothwell and Bothwell's plans to marry her. He described how men had pleaded with the Queen of the Scots not to pursue this course, and "She had said," he wrote, "that she cares not to lose France, England, and her own country for him, and shall go with him to the world's end in a white petticoat ere she shall leave him."[6]

The phrase, beyond the powers of masculine imagination to invent, had the ring of truth, of an angry woman rejecting advice against her lover. The Kirkcaldy letter concluded, however, on a note of great maturity. "Whatever is unhonest reigns presently in this Court," Kirkcaldy said. "God deliver us from their evil."[7]

Two days after the tavern gathering, the queen left Edinburgh to visit her son, James, at the castle of Stirling, 36 miles away. She was accompanied by Huntly, Secretary Lethington, Sir James Melville, and thirty horsemen. They arrived at Stirling on the twenty-second of April, 1567, and were met by a suspicious and unfriendly earl of Mar. He gave orders that only two of her ladies-in-waiting could accompany the queen inside the castle; the rest of her entourage would have to wait outside. His fear that the queen would kidnap the baby was as clear as if he announced it, but he need not have worried. Her purpose was not so motherly.

In the same way that Bothwell reasoned personal combat would resolve questions of guilt or innocence, he decided that his marriage to the Queen of Scots could be made both inevitable and acceptable if he raped her in public. While the queen was at Stirling, therefore, Bothwell raised a force of men at Edinburgh. News of his plans leaked widely—largely through Lethington, who hoped someone would stop Bothwell and Mary Stuart in their now mad enterprises. The earl of Lennox, already on the ship that was at dock in Glasgow and was to take him to England, wrote that Bothwell planned to kidnap the queen. If he knew, from his distance, then certainly others closer at hand knew equally well.

While the queen dandled the infant James on her lap at Stirling, Bothwell prepared his force in Edinburgh, and his minions prepared the castle of Dunbar, 29 miles from the capital. On the twenty-third of April, 1567, the queen left Stirling and the relieved earl of Mar, rejoined Huntly, Lethington, Sir James Melville, and their horsemen, and started back to the capital. She spent that night at Linlithgow, a halfway point. The following morning six miles from Edinburgh, on the Almond Bridge, an event was staged that was, by now, awaited by many. Bothwell appeared at the head of nearly a thousand armed men, rode forward, took the queen's bridle, told her she was in danger in the capital and that he was taking her away.

The queen received this information calmly, showing neither surprise nor alarm. Her bodyguard rode forward, but she spoke against bloodshed. Huntly announced himself a prisoner, and both Lethington and Sir James Melville allowed themselves to be taken. With Bothwell and the queen in the van, they rode toward the castle of Dunbar, 40 miles away. One of Bothwell's men, chatting with Sir James Melville as they traveled, told him it was all with the queen's consent.[8] That information, it was clear, had drifted far—and landed low.

The following morning Sir James Melville and Huntly were both released, and it was clear to Melville that the earl of Bothwell had carried out every step of his plan. "The Queen," he wrote later, "could not but

marry him, seeing he had ravished her and lain with her against her will."[9]
The information shamed the country.


Other obvious activities ringed the pair with odium. Two Bothwell
divorce cases entered the courts at almost the same moment that the queen
was carried off to her equivocal captivity. One, entered by Lady Jean
Gordon, charged the earl with adultery with her maid Bessie Crawford. Her
witnesses were numerous and explicit. If she won, the earl would be divorced, but, as the guilty party under canon law, could not remarry.

Bothwell, however, appointed the archbishop of St. Andrews, a prelate
so pliant as to be boneless, to head a special commission to determine if his
marriage had been legal in the first place. The archbishop, studying the
tangled geneologies of the families, made the happy discovery that the earl
of Bothwell and Lady Jean Gordon were fourth cousins. Since no papal
dispensation had been obtained, he ruled their marriage invalid.

On the sixth of May, 1567, the Queen of the Scots was escorted through
the streets of Edinburgh by the earl of Bothwell, trailed by his cutthroats
—a term then filled with dreadful meaning. The royal coffers were running
low; the queen had only 5,000 crowns. The gold font given to the Prince
James Stuart for his baptism was melted down and new coins minted from
it to pay Bothwell's forces. On the twelfth of May, 1567, the queen appeared
at the Court of Sessions to assure the judges she had no cause to complain
of the earl of Bothwell. That same day she raised Bothwell to lord of
Shetland and duke of Orkney and "placed the coronet on his head with her
own hands."

Their marriage banns were published, after Bothwell threatened to
hang the minister who demurred. Around them rose rumors of rebellion;
it was known that the fearsome earl of Morton together with Argyll, Atholl,
Mar, and others had gathered at Stirling and signed some sort of compact.

Nevertheless, on the fifteenth of May, 1567, at four o'clock in the
morning, the Queen of Scots married Bothwell. Until that moment her
policy had been directed toward the restoration of papal power and gaining
the support of Spain and Rome. But to the anger and disappointment of her
Catholic supporters everywhere, she bent to the will of her new master and
was married in a Reform ceremony conducted by the bishop of Orkney. The
bride, on her third appearance in that role, wore black and was presumed
to be mourning the death of King Henry, which had occurred a little over
three months before. The bridegroom had been divorced twelve days.


On the day she was married, the queen told du Croc, the French
ambassador, that she was miserable. Two days later Sir James Melville said,

"The Queen was so disdainfully handled and with such reproachful language that in the presence of Arthur Erskine, I heard her ask for a knife
to stab herself, 'or else,' said she, 'I shall drown myself.' "[10]

Bothwell was not, apparently, very happy either. Lethington, again at
court and still secretary, observed her new husband would "not let her look
at anyone, or let anyone look at her."[11] The fact was that they knew too
much about each other for any real trust to exist—a not uncommon criminal reaction after mutual crimes.

Yet they tried to make a brave show. A proclamation was issued saying
Scotland was still a Reform country and forbidding—once again—the holding of Catholic services. That was Bothwell's sop to rising sounds of discontent; he forced Mary Stuart—whose Catholicism had always been firm—
to agree. In public they were strangely formal; he would uncover his head,
and she would playfully put his hat back on for him. They made efforts to
become popular. On the twenty-fifth of May, 1567, a pageant was mounted
for the people of Edinburgh, with a sham water battle, at an expense the
Crown could not really afford. Tortured explanations of their union were
sent to France, Spain, and other important places—and were received with
contempt. In England, Elizabeth—as always—temporized. She was not too
distressed at the destruction of the Mary Stuart legend and on the other
hand could see no really good reason why she should assist rebels against
their lawful queen, especially—though she did not say it aloud—a queen
who had lost her important overseas support.

On June 6, 1567, Bothwell learned that Lethington, the secretary, had
vanished from court. That ominous signal was quickly followed by a message that a group of nobles, using Stirling as their headquarters and representing a broad union of both Protestant and Catholic leaders, were march-
ing toward Holyrood.

Bothwell's response was to head toward the border, where he had
forces of his own. He was accompanied by the queen, whom he left at the
castle of Borthwick, twelve miles south of Edinburgh, while he continued
onward. Intercepted by the forces of the dread earl of Morton, Bothwell fled
back to Borthwick and refuge. His pursuers followed, ringed the castle, and
shouted insults, which the queen answered in kind. During the night of June
tenth, showing his personal fearlessness, Bothwell slipped out of the keep
with only the young son of Lord Cranston as company. Young Cranston
was captured, but Bothwell rode away alone into the night.

After his escape, the besiegers proceeded to Edinburgh, where they
aroused the citizenry. As though on cue, huge banners appeared. Men
poured out of the crowded and steaming tenements of the city to fight
against the earl and a faithless queen. King Henry, despised in life, had been
inflated to tremendous stature as a martyr, and the queen's name was
blackened beyond redemption. Later observers were puzzled by this devel-

opment, but the eternally turbulent Scots had been altered by the deep and stirring chords of a religious awakening and were outraged by events that, in the past, would have been considered normal in high places.

Military dominance of Edinburgh was maintained by the great guns of the castle. These were in the hands of Sir James Balfour, a man identified with Bothwell. Both Bothwell and Mary relied upon him to hold the capital against the rebels. Yet the castle guns remained silent while huge preparations were made to organize a field force against Bothwell and the queen.

On the eleventh of June, 1567, with no besiegers left to keep her in Borthwick Castle, Queen Mary Stuart emerged disguised in male clothing. She was met by Bothwell in the road, and they rode together to Dunbar Castle, in East Lothian. They arrived at three in the morning, and the queen changed into some clothes hastily obtained from a servant. These were somewhat primitive and consisted of a short jacket with a red petticoat that reached barely below her knees. She did not mind. Her eyes blazed with excitement, and, in fact, the fierce activities, the danger, and the situation combined to restore her to her old self.

The following day, while Bothwell made still another attempt to reach his men at the border, the queen emerged from Dunbar at the head of a small force. She hoped to collect more as she proceeded—not realizing the depths of her unpopularity—and headed for Edinburgh, where Sir James Balfour held the castle. At Haddington she was joined by Bothwell with 1,600 men. On Sunday, June 15, 1567, they were intercepted on the road about eight miles east of Edinburgh by the rebels with 2,000 men, who were carrying an immense banner spread between two spears. It showed the figure of a dead man lying under a tree that represented Kirk o'Field. Beside this figure was a shirt, a broken branch, and a kneeling child. The legend underneath said, "Judge and revenge my Cause, Oh Lord." No better proof of how the powers of the new propaganda had overtaken the crests and banners of earlier times could possibly have been produced.

The two forces maneuvered for position as the sun came up that Sunday, and Carberry Hill appeared on the verge of receiving blood for its grasses. Du Croc, the French ambassador, who had accompanied the rebels as an observer, served as a mediator. He was empowered to ask Mary to abandon Bothwell and to resume her rightful place as queen alone.

The Frenchman found the queen sitting on a stone in her short red petticoat and begged her to reconsider her association. In reply, she demanded that the rebels sue for mercy. While they talked, Bothwell came up and said the nobles were jealous of him and that he would fight anyone they would select. Du Croc began the thankless task of running back and forth with these witless arguments, which at one point so enraged the earl of Morton that he proposed to fight Bothwell with two-handed swords, man to man. But as the parley extended, the forces of Bothwell and Mary Stuart began to desert.

It finally became clear the queen's forces would not and could not fight. She asked for final terms and was told to return to Edinburgh with her lords, where she would be well treated. Bothwell could go wherever he chose. They turned toward each other, and in full view of all the assembled men they held one another in a long embrace and a deep kiss. Then he climbed on his horse and galloped away, trailed by a handful of men.

The queen was conducted to the rebel lines by Kirkcaldy and met by the earls of Morton and Hume, who bowed before her. Shouts from the ranks broke that brief traditional moment. "Burn the whore," shouted the troops; "Burn the murderess!"[12] She burst into tears, and the parade started back to Edinburgh.

"I expected," said du Croc, "that the Queen would have been gentle with the Lords and have tried to pacify them. But on her way back from the field, she talked of nothing but hanging and crucifying them all."[13]

By the time she arrived at Edinburgh, she had killed their pity and quickened their anger. The crowds that emerged from hovels in the capital were dense, sweating, and angry. The great white banner with its legend of the murdered king bobbed behind her as she was led in single file through the masses; people hung out of the windows and women shrieked insults. It was the worse for her that the path led past Kirk o'Field, a place and event that inflamed the outcries. Rooms had been prepared at the provost's house and even supper—but she could not bear to look at food. She asked instead to be taken to her room. Once there, she was horrified to discover the crowd was storming the stairs to reach her; outside the windows the white banner and other banners— foul and bitter—bobbed before her gaze.

She had conversations that night with Lethington and others in which she accused them of treason and they tried to reason with her. It was all too late. The Queen of the Scots had closed her mind to reality and could cling only to being a queen. The world was wicked in not kneeling, and the people shouting outside the window should be chopped down. By morning she was hysterical. She threw the windows open and shouted—her clothes torn and her breasts hanging free—that she was being held a prisoner. Her captors waited till dark after what seemed an endless day and took her down the streets toward Holyrood with an escort of 300 through the thick crowds still shouting for her death. From Holyrood they hastened her to Leith and then across the water to Burnt Island. From there she and her escort rode twenty miles to huge Lochleven, whose vast waters contained an island that held a tower belonging to the Douglas family. There she was, at last, fastened and held down, silenced and out of sight—like some creature that men dared not release in day.

4 In the last week of June, 1567, the Reform movement in Scotland moved to revolution. Hundreds rushed to the Royal Chapel at Holyrood and stripped its "ornaments, melting down the chalices and grinding the crucifixes to powder." Groups ranged through cellars, alleys, attics, and corners of the city, searching for Bothwell's men. One—the laird of Blackadder—had already been captured, dragged through the streets, tried, convicted, hanged, and quartered—within the space of a single day. Torturers applied their dreadful pressures to Powrie and Patrick Wilson, who confessed to having carried bags of gunpowder to the house at Kirk o'Field.

These activities, however—on the part of both the nobles and the crowd and some authorities—were minor compared to the voice, power, and influence of John Knox.[1] Appearing suddenly like a genie in his podium at St. Giles, he rose to point his finger toward Mary Stuart and to remind immense throngs of his repeated warnings and prophecies that she would drag a trail of disaster through Scotland. Knox was echoed in this by other leaders of the Kirk—but he set the tone. His structured demands, for the first time, carried the Reform movement forward toward political rather than religious goals.

The queen, Knox said, should be put to death, not by crude assassination or through uncontrolled mob violence—though there was precedent enough for that in Scotland as well as other places—but through the cold machinery of state. An extraordinary meeting of the General Assembly should be called, at which the Council of Lords should be pressed to bring charges of murder and adultery against the queen. The demand was unprecedented at a time when most men believed a sovereign to be the law. Knox, arguing that the queen, no less than her subjects, was subject to trial and judgment by the people, was the first prominent figure to raise the opposite argument—and to convince a nation he was right.

The nobles, unprepared for a revolution to be raised around them, were —at that moment—confronted with an unexpected discovery. Before he fled the capital, Bothwell had entrusted a silver enameled box, or casket, as it was then called, to his cousin Sir James Balfour. Balfour, who had turned his coat and Edinburgh Castle over to the anti-Bothwell forces, was approached by Dalgleish, one of Bothwell's servants. The earl, who had temporarily taken refuge at Dunbar Castle, wanted the silver casket. Balfour gave it to Dalgleish and then sent word to the earl of Morton that one of Bothwell's men was on the verge of leaving the city. Dalgleish was arrested and the box given to Morton.

Morton assembled ten other nobles, and the casket was forced open. The men sat down to read a mass of documents that were mostly in French and represented a tangle of letters, agreements, official and unofficial correspondence. To their horror, some of the men found their names on some —and these were put aside. But the core of the mass was molten and fiery and consisted of letters Mary Stuart had written to Bothwell while she enticed King Henry to his death. The mixture of cruelty and unbridled sexuality they revealed was not unexpected—but proof that the queen had stooped to connive and assist in the murder of her own husband shocked even these hard men.


In London the Queen of England reacted in surprise and anger to developments in Scotland. Some sort of uprising against Bothwell was not unexpected: agents had kept her Privy Council well informed of that possibility. But the treatment of the Queen of the Scots—and in particular her confinement at Lochleven—touched Elizabeth in a sensitive place. She had herself been a prisoner in the Tower of London, placed there by her sister, Queen Mary Tudor. She had also been confined to her house, watched by spies, and cross-examined by enemies. Her quick imagination could share Mary Stuart's sensations—and the idea that a reigning queen could be so handled filled her with indignation.[2]

Better than her Privy Council, quicker even than the shrewd Cecil,[3] Elizabeth realized that the events in Scotland were far more than a simple uprising. They threatened the stature and position of royalty itself. She sent Sir Nicholas Throckmorton to the lords of the north with word their queen must be released and restored at once. She added that, of course, King Henry's murderers should be tried and punished—and that it would be best if Prince James were sent to England, where he could be reared in safety. Her tone was that of their ruler, and did Mary Stuart's cause more harm than good.


The reaction in France was far different. Catherine de Médicis, whose agents were closely watching the touring earl of Moray, had him called to her court. She had long since dismissed Mary Stuart—whom she deeply disliked—as of no consequence. Now she offered Moray all the help the French Crown could command, including an army and money and the regency of Scotland—if he would return to his country as an ally of France. She also thought Prince James should be sent to France, where he could be properly educated and trained for his future position. To her irritation, Moray remained inscrutably aloof. He said he knew nothing of events in Scotland and would have to decide such issues later. "He has," said Mary Stuart's former mother-in-law angrily, "an English heart."[4]

With French and English agents pouring in upon them, the people clamoring under the urgings of Knox and his associates in the Kirk, their own need for leadership and their own struggles with one another, the Scots nobility was divided. The Hamilton family, with some claim to the succession, intrigued for the Crown. The earl of Morton and his closest associates were political moderates; Lord Lindsay and others were ardent followers of Knox's extreme advice.

In this highly mixed situation, the lords sorely missed the cool counsel and strong presence of Moray, who had landed in London. They sent him copies of the casket letters, and by the time Moray talked to Queen Elizabeth he had come to realize that his stepsister was at the end of her reign. Elizabeth was deeply angered to be told that.

Mary Stuart, however, learned the news at first hand. On July 25, 1567, three men came to her at Lochleven. They were Lord Lindsay, who had thirsted to fight Bothwell; the young earl of Ruthven, whose father had led the murder of Rizzio; and Robert Melville, brother of Sir James Melville. Their purpose was to demand the queen's abdication, and they represented the Scots Council. Neither Lindsay nor Ruthven knew that Robert Melville carried a secret letter for Mary in the scabbard of his sword. It was a message from Elizabeth, assuring the Queen of the Scots of her undying support, telling her any agreement she signed under duress was illegal—and warning her that her very life was in danger.[5] Armed with this information, which Melville somehow made available to her, Mary Stuart signed the documents presented to her after only token resistance.

Two days later, on the 27 of July, 1567, Elizabeth sent word to the Scots that if they harmed their queen, she would send an army to invade their land and punish those responsible. The answer, composed with breathtaking speed, was that if a single English soldier crossed the border, Mary Stuart's throat would be cut at once. With their bridges burned, the nobles then turned toward a move they hoped would placate the Kirk, quiet Knox, resolve their own disputes, and settle all issues at once.

On the 29 of July, 1567, the earl of Mar and his entourage rode down the slopes of Stirling toward the old church of the village. Morton, Atholl, Hume, and a number of others had traveled 36 miles from Edinburgh to meet him. The interior of the French Gothic building showed the impact of the revolution. Niches that had once held statues of praying saints gaped vacantly; the altar and even its Cross had vanished and were replaced by a table. From the choir, where rows of boys had once chanted Latin orisons, a new preaching pulpit arched aloft like the prow of a strange new ship.

At its base, dressed in rich black, his deep blue eyes shining above his heavy black beard, stood the master of that particular vessel: John Knox. Around him crowded a small but fairly impressive group, including five earls, eight lords, a Catholic bishop, some gentlemen, and two superintendents of the Kirk.

The earl of Atholl carried the sword; the earl of Morton, the scepter; and the earl of Mar carried James, who was thirteen months and ten days old. All three were symbols of the Scots monarchy. One of the group read aloud Mary Stuart's abdication statement; another rushed through a proclamation naming Moray—still in England—regent. A third named the members of the new regent's council.

These legal forms concluded, the bishop of Orkney poured oil over James's head, poured more on his shoulder blades and the palms of his hands. The two Kirk superintendents then assisted the bishop to hold the crown over the infant's head while Morton and Hume took an oath, in James's name, to uphold the Reform and defend the realm. Then armored men came forward, one by one, to touch the tips of their swords to the crown as a sign of loyalty.

Then John Knox ascended the pulpit, and the lingering traces of Catholicism, as well as of the feudal era, vanished as in a clap of thunder. His text, chosen with stunning precision, was from the Book of Kings. It described how the boy Jehoash had been anointed and crowned by the captains and priests of Israel while the Queen Athaliah cried treason in her palace. He then read to them how the leaders had proceeded from that coronation to kill Athaliah, destroy the temples of Baal, and restore the faith of the prophets supreme in the land. No clearer call to kill Mary Stuart could have been conceived.

It was part of the genius of John Knox to be able to use the Bible as an instrument of revolution. His listeners had grown accustomed to his comparison of Mary Stuart with Jezebel, who as queen had allowed two forms of worship in her land as a matter of policy. Time and again they heard Knox argue against this practice; time and again heard him prophesy that the Queen of the Scots would be stricken in her pride and bring down all who associated with her. In the brief seven months before the coronation, all Scotland saw Knox's predictions uncannily fulfilled. No sovereign, apparently secure on the throne, had ever fallen so far or so quickly.

In the pulpit at Stirling, Knox pressed the point and relieved his listeners of any lingering sense of doubt or guilt over Mary Stuart's overthrow. The coronation of James VI was a forced event; a *coup d'état* reeking of illegality and uncertainty. But Knox managed to convince his listeners that the step was justified by a higher law. He wove Biblical events of the past together with the situation of the moment into a thrilling, convincing new doctrine. The *coup d'état* no longer seemed uncertain or illegal, but the very working of the will of God. No revolution was ever given a greater sense of historic inevitability.

The leaders returned to Edinburgh after the hasty ceremony at the old church at Stirling. There was much that remained to be done; they had to decide the future course of the country.

The earl of Mar and his entourage carried the infant James VI back up the slope of Stirling to the grim, walled complex at its peak. Inside the palace they handed the infant king back to the care of the countess of Mar and his wet nurse, Helena Little, whose milk would later be blamed for some of his defects. He was attended by four female "rockers," two musicians, and three Gentlemen of the Bedchamber. He slept, as he was to sleep for years to come, "in a gloomy bed of black damask, the ruff, headpieces and pillows being fringed with black."[6] On the wall was a portrait of his grandfather, James V. Life, whose conjunctions are always curiously mixed, had arranged that his first great gift would come to him as a result of his mother's humiliation.

5 While the infant James VI slept in his black bed at Stirling, noisy and impressive evidence of the popularity of the change resounded widely. The guns at Stirling and Edinburgh and other castles boomed salutes. Sir Nicholas Throckmorton, Elizabeth's personal ambassador, watching from an Edinburgh window, later wrote, "The people made great joy, dancing and acclamations, so it appeareth they rejoiced more at the inauguration of the new Prince than they did sorrow at the deprivation of their Queen."[1] He knew this would not please Elizabeth; he had been sent to Scotland to avert this very outcome.

Elizabeth did not realize—then or later—that it was not her intercession that saved Mary Stuart's life, but the actions of the man the Queen of Scots hated above all others: the earl of Moray.

Moray knew the contents of the casket Morton and others had seized, but did not tell Elizabeth about Mary Stuart's complicity in her husband's murder.[2] Instead he listened to arguments that no sovereign could be imprisoned, tried, or deposed by subjects and departed with as good a grace as possible. He arrived in Edinburgh thirteen days after James's coronation to find the capital still seething with revolutionary fervor.

His calmness did much to cool this heat. In an effort to make the new situation legally unassailable, he insisted on seeing the queen at Lochleven before he accepted the regency. This did not sit too well, but Moray, by remaining aloof from the violence and the plots of the revolution, had emerged as the only man whom every other man could trust. Nevertheless Morton, Atholl, and Lindsay were selected to go with him when he talked to Mary Stuart.

The four nobles reached the edge of the lake on August 15, 1567, and were rowed across to the island castle, where Moray's stepsister was "secluded." Moray was no stranger to the palace: it was his mother's property.

Moray found his stepsister changed enough to greet him with tears and an embrace—a considerable contrast to the cold, proud queen who had stood beside Bothwell. Later the earl described to Throckmorton the conversation at Lochleven—undoubtedly so that Elizabeth could be enlightened. He did not respond to his sister's warmth, nor answer her questions until she finally begged him to speak. Then, he told Throckmorton, he carried her step by step into a recapitulation of her behavior during the preceding two years, "like a ghostly [spiritual] father." The recital was dismal and depressing, and by the time he finished it was very clear that there was little space between Mary Stuart and an ignominious death at the hands of her subjects.

Yet the queen might have still resisted, had she not been relieved of her own secret and overwhelming burden by a miscarriage. That—and that alone—freed her from her obstinate reliance on Bothwell.

As it was, she was able to assure Moray that she would abandon the border earl at long last. For the rest she returned to her room to wonder through the night about her stepbrother's intentions. The following day she turned to that subject and was told she would, in effect, have to approve what had been wrested from her by Lindsay, Ruthven, and Melville in the name of the council.

Under the circumstances, their conversation could have only one outcome. Mary Stuart had learned that Elizabeth of England was at her side, and she knew consent obtained under duress could always be challenged later. It was an enduring proof of her self-possession and her ability as an actress that she was able to smile at Moray, to approve of him as regent, and to kiss him good-bye when he left.[3]


The earl of Bothwell, after galloping away from Carberry Hill, had taken refuge at Dunbar Castle. From there he made various sweeps about the countryside, attempting to put together a new force to rescue the queen and restore his own position. These efforts met with little success, and Moray, after he returned, moved energetically. By early September he had men in the field and received the submission of those nobles who had followed the border earl. Bothwell then fled north.

The queen had made Bothwell duke of Orkney, and he already held the hereditary title of lord admiral of Scotland. He fled toward these northern islands, where his family was respected and his name still held weight. There he collected a few hundred men and five small ships and embarked on a new career as a pirate.

Acting on Moray's instructions, four large ships with guns and carrying hagbutters were outfitted and sent in pursuit of the erstwhile duke. Kirkcaldy of Grange and Murray of Tullibardine were given orders to pursue Bothwell "with fire, sword and all other kinds of hostility." There was no particular intention of bringing him back alive.

A running battle was joined at Bressay Sound, and Bothwell barely escaped with two ships. A day or so later he landed at Karm Sound, Norway. He had hardly reached this port before a Norwegian warship appeared to demand his papers. Bothwell's explanations were confused, and he—and his men—were convoyed to Bergen. There, to Bothwell's horror, he learned he would have to tell his story to the governor of the Castle, Erik Otteson Rosenkrantz. The name was all too familiar to the earl: Rosenkrantz was the uncle of Anna Throndsen, a mistress he had abused and discarded. Fate had closed a ring about him.[4]

As regent, the earl of Moray made it his duty to lead a series of civilizing missions through the border. There, where disorder and theft were ways of life, he knew he could establish a cooperative effort with the English and create a *de facto* acceptance of his rule from English authorities.

To calm the fires of the revolution, Moray sat with the leaders of the Kirk and drew up a series of acts to establish the Reform in a final, permanent structure. It could not create the complete control Calvin had established in Geneva; and therefore Knox, though achieving a great victory, did not realize all his goals. The high nobles of Scotland retained papal titles to various profitable benefices, parishes, and estates. But the Kirk would receive at least enough money to support its ministers and superintendents—and many acts were prepared giving it authority over matters of education and morals in the land.

By December 1567, when the Scots Parliament convened, it consisted of "four bishops, fourteen abbots, twelve earls, fifteen lords, three eldest sons of earls and thirty boroughs."[5] This was the broadest and most representative gathering the unruly kingdom had ever managed to assemble— and it proved the most able of any till that time.[6] The acts of the Reformation Parliament of 1560, never ratified by Mary Stuart, were reaffirmed. Papal authority was abolished. The abdication of the queen, the coronation of James VI, and Moray's regency were approved. Then Parliament laid the cornerstone of a new structure by charging that Mary Stuart and Bothwell had conspired to murder the king. That charge, following the reasoning of Knox, gave the Scots the right to depose a ruling sovereign. It was not laid lightly, and the members of the Parliament examined both the depositions of men arrested for complicity in the crime and the documents discovered in Bothwell's silver enameled box—the "casket letters." Some believed they should be copied and circulated through Europe, but others decided the Scots people had already settled the issue and that further airing of dreadful details would only add to the odium already collected.

Shortly afterward the Scots Parliament ended its historic session. Sev-

eral Bothwell followers—Dalgleish, Powrie, Hay of Tallo, and Hepburn—
were hanged and quartered. Copies of the acts were sent to Elizabeth in
England and were received without official comment. Unofficially, the English queen was outraged that the subjects of any sovereign should so defy
long established and accepted theories regarding sovereigns and the state.
Bad monarchs were "scourges of God" visited upon people as punishment
for sins; good monarchs were blessings from the same source. Elizabeth's
sympathy was all for her cousin, who had been violently deposed and was
now imprisoned by those who had sworn allegiance to her. Her letters,
messages, and statements at court left no doubt about that; Mary Stuart
received a stream of assurances that Elizabeth would make every effort to
help her.

That gush of sympathy, however, did not prevent Elizabeth—whose
love of jewelry was notorious—from buying Mary Stuart's famous pearls
when Moray put these and other crown jewels up for sale.[7] Moray was
pressed for money. He was pressed in other ways as well. He distributed
as much patronage as he could, but—as in England—there were powerful
groups who were not pleased by the Reform and the wave of morality it
ushered into the land. The regent's strenuous and serious efforts to introduce law and order created indignation among men long accustomed to
behaving as they chose.

High moral positions are hard for ordinary people to maintain. Sentiment both in Scotland and overseas began to swing toward pity for the
beautiful Queen of Scots, immured and held prisoner by the dour forces of
piety. This reaction grew even at Lochleven itself, where the queen—her
spirits restored and no longer fearing death—enchanted young George
Douglas and led even Lady Margaret to smile. A Douglas might marry the
queen.

That rumor brought the Hamiltons alive; one of their family seemed
to them better suited for such a grand alliance. The French, whose ties to
the Hamiltons were close, sent a new envoy—de Beaumont—to Edinburgh
to see if this new thought might not lead toward a new alliance more
effectively than the abortive effort with the Regent Moray.

By March 1568 the laird of Lochleven had dashed one effort to rescue
the queen from outside and sent away his younger brother, George, whom
Sir James Melville described as "in a fantasy of love." Nevertheless, the
fascination of Mary Stuart, which enchanted millions throughout western
Europe, was too powerful to remain checked. A foundling page who had
been given the clan name and was known as Willie Douglas was persuaded
to help her. Sir William had given orders that the gates be locked each night
and the keys brought to him at dinner. Early in May 1568 the page casually
dropped a napkin over those keys and swept them off the sideboard. Then

he left and joined Mary Stuart, who was waiting in the courtyard. The queen was dressed as a servant and had a little girl by the hand. The innocent-looking trio passed the guards in fading twilight without attracting more than a casual glance, went through the gate and locked it behind them. Then they clambered into a skiff into which young Willie had foresightedly placed oars from the other boats and rowed swiftly to shore. There they were met by eager George Douglas and two other young men, who rushed them toward Lord Seton, who was waiting with an escort of fifty armed men.

Mary Stuart, surrounded by a small new group, rode all that night and into the following day until the party reached Lord Seton's home at Long-niddry. From there she sent a letter to her powerful uncle in France, the cardinal of Lorraine—and to Bothwell. A few hours later she was among the Hamiltons. Within a week a phenomenal force, conjured as though from the air, collected around her. The earls of Argyll, Huntly, Cassillis, Eglin-ton, Montrose, and others came rushing, followed by almost 6,000 troops. The Scotland of "feudalism, chivalry and sentiment,"[8] which resented the Reform and all its stern followers, had risen for the queen. Lines were drawn that week that were to divide the land for centuries to come and would fuel arguments whose elements were to pass from reason to legend.

Surrounded by ambitious Hamiltons, bishops anxious to regain their sees, adventurers, high-living, French-speaking young peers anxious to set-tle accounts with Moray—whose virtues made him hateful—Mary Stuart brimmed with plans and activities. She sent an emissary to Elizabeth and another to Paris immediately, carrying hastily drafted and dictated letters. Her story was essentially the same, but was shrewdly shaded toward each recipient. She sent the pope a letter brimming with religious zeal, claiming her difficulties were the consequence of her devotion to the Faith. To Madrid she wrote Philip II that she was not guilty of her husband's murder, but was instead the victim of trumped-up charges by the real murderers. The Prudent King received it without any noticeable softening: Mary Stuart's activities had created a disgust in him. Paris did not reply. Cather-ine de Médicis watched Spain and England—especially England.

In London Elizabeth was shocked back to earth. Cecil's repeated arguments that the victory of the pro-English Reformers of Scotland was a great blessing to her suddenly came home with great force—but at the same time she could not bring herself openly to oppose her cousin. Mary Stuart was, after all, a rightful queen; her fate at the hands of subjects could set a fearful precedent for England. The Virgin Queen took refuge in contra-dictions, in statements that baffled onlookers—and that left her room to maneuver, to wait, and to think.

Meanwhile, she sent "Mr. Leighton" to Edinburgh to warn Moray to submit to Mary Stuart "or she would compel him" and then to proceed to Mary Stuart to accept arbitration by Elizabeth "as her nearest kinswoman and neighbor"—and to warn her against calling upon the French for assistance—or she would change her mind about her. This message, which could not please any party, was accompanied by a letter expressing Elizabeth's pleasure at "the joyful news of your escape" and then proceeding to a scolding. "Had you cared as much for your honour as you cared for a miserable miscreant, all the world would have grieved for your calamities; whereas, to speak the plain truth, the number who have done so is small."[9] To that plain truth she added a final note of warning against turning toward any other quarter for help and succeeded in coining a memorable phrase in an otherwise notably disagreeable letter. "Do you, please," Elizabeth ended, "remember, that those who have two strings to one bow may shoot strongly, but they rarely hit the mark."[10]

Cecil, for one, obviously did not believe in that cliché: he sent a quiet message to Moray to crush Mary Stuart and her new army "without a moment's delay." The advice was hardly needed. Moray issued a call and all Glasgow—the heart of the Lennox family—rose as one man. The response from the other Lords of the Congregation and the now strong Reform movement among the people was equally swift. The earls of Morton, Mar, Lindsay, Ruthven, and others rallied their followers. It was a time when men "had but to buckle their swordbelts, put on their steel caps and breastplates, and strap a wallet with some cold meat and bread behind their saddles, to be equipped for a week's campaign."[11]

Men at such a time could move rapidly. The denouement between the two forces came suddenly near Glasgow. The Hamiltons, who lacked any leaders with military skill, rushed into the village of Langside, where Moray's men were waiting in ambush. The first fusillade broke the Hamilton ranks; the men reeled, were charged, and fled. The queen, who had watched from a hillside a half mile away, turned her horse in despair and galloped from the scene. Her army, summoned as quickly as summer rain, vanished with the same amazing speed.

Mary Stuart, flanked by only six followers, who included young Willie Douglas the page, ran without halting. Later she described how peasants rose with their scythes to menace her progress and claimed to have ridden ninety-two miles without stopping. It may have seemed that way; her flight was more complex, but it was, essentially, headlong and toward the south. On Sunday, May 16, 1568, she reached the Solway Firth and crossed in an open fishing boat. She landed at Workington, England, in the evening.

She rested there that night and in the morning wrote her "dear sister," Elizabeth. The news of her escape from Lochleven had started bonfires all over the Catholic north of England; her status as a heroine was unbelievably high. The word of her arrival in England was sensation piled upon drama and aroused soaring excitement; hundreds began to stream in her direction. A huge throng escorted her to Carlisle, where she rested and held court in the little castle. Even Thomas Percy, the earl of Northumberland, came to bow before her. She was—at once and forever—a counter sovereign for all Elizabeth's subjects.

6 The presence of Mary Stuart in England served to focus attention on John Knox's theory that subjects could depose—and even punish—erring sovereigns.

That thought was as unwelcome to Elizabeth as death itself. She sought to avoid it, to turn it aside, to suppress it in every way possible. Her first effort along these lines was to suggest that the Scots accept Mary Stuart as their queen, pay her due homage, but allow no real power to fall into her hands. That had always been Elizabeth's desire for her cousin.

Unfortunately for that argument, the Regent Moray was now fully aroused by Mary Stuart's escape and uprising. He finally accepted Knox's reasoning that not only a tyrant, but a tyrant's followers should be put to the sword. In that spirit, which contrasted with his former tendency to conciliate contending factions, Moray raged through not only the border, but also through the territories of Mary Stuart's supporters to burn and destroy their castles and country seats.[1] This had the effect of adding to his already outstanding list of enemies and to convince Elizabeth that the Reform movement was inherently rebellious and destructive. But Moray was mindful of London as well as his own country, and he was in close contact with Cecil.

Cecil took the occasion, as soon as Elizabeth paused for breath, to remind her that her cousin was not only a sovereign, but an adulteress and, very likely, a murderess. That had a cooling effect. Cecil then suggested that what the Scots could not accept in a queen the world might also reject— if it knew all the facts.[2] That thought riveted Elizabeth's attention. Anything that would reduce the dangerous popularity of her beautiful rival had obvious merit.

Finally, Cecil proposed that the Scots be asked to provide proof of their infamous charges against Mary Stuart—and that these proofs, if real, be sifted by a queen's commission. Elizabeth was entranced. She could become the arbiter of the situation, a position that would place her in clear superiority to Mary Stuart and that would allow her justice to shine clear before the world. She smiled at Cecil's thought. He smiled in return and bowed low. Elizabeth did not seem to realize that she had, in effect, been drawn into the vortex of Knox's reasoning. After all, there was little real difference between having a sovereign judged by her own subjects and having the case against her by her subjects judged in another land. Cecil knew that—but he was a true believer in the Reform.

Having once accepted the idea of a hearing, Elizabeth was drawn deeper by successive stages—and so was Mary Stuart. The Queen of the Scots resisted the plan strenuously, but her position was adroitly undermined by a series of vague promises, expressed in ambiguous terms, pressed with careful diplomacy.

The hearing was opened at York, England, in October 1568 and immediately drew itself into a series of knots that exasperated Elizabeth—and Mary Stuart as well— almost beyond endurance. But though it moved with the stately speed of a snail on the surface, its backstage discussions were heated, fervent, and complex. In its course, Moray refused to disclose all his evidence without some assurance that his stepsister would not be restored, if found innocent, to behead him and his associates. Elizabeth— breaking her promise to Mary Stuart that she was not being judged—sent that assurance.

During November and into December 1568, Mary Stuart's cause sank rapidly. The Queen of Scots knew that Moray and the Lords of the Congregation had claimed to hold some evidence against her—but she had not known what, specifically, they possessed. It was Bothwell, after all, who had kept the silver casket and the incriminating documents.

Moray and his associates produced these for the English in the Painted Chamber at Westminster. George Buchanan had made translations and written a somewhat hasty summary. The documents themselves were jumbled and incomplete. Some had been abstracted because they implicated such men as William Maitland, the laird of Lethington, in King Henry's murder. He had switched sides, and Moray wanted to protect him. At the same time, many of the queen's accusers were men who had known of various plots against the king. Evidence of that was withheld. Some of the letters might have been from Anne Throndsen, Bothwell's mistress; some, from other women from his numerous and shadowy conquests. But enough remained from Mary Stuart to convince and horrify Elizabeth and the commissioners.

Elizabeth's horror was mixed with pity for her cousin. That pity prevented her from allowing Moray's evidence to be presented to the world. Instead, in one of her more outstanding acts of sabotage against her own advisers, the English queen decided to issue her own verdict on the hearings.

Nothing had been proven, she said brazenly, against her dear cousin, the Queen of Scots. And at the same time she found no fault in Moray and his associates. This Delphic and confused statement convinced even Sir Francis Knollys, one of her principal advisers, that Elizabeth was incapable of being a ruler.[3]

Elizabeth's scrambled logic was received with bitter dismay by Moray and his Scots Reformers. It was true they had been left in place, but denying they had proved their case against Mary Stuart made their title to that place cloudy and uncertain.

Mary Stuart's supporters, on the other hand, greeted the official news of her innocence with relief and enthusiasm, followed quickly by indignation that their heroine was still—however loosely and luxuriously—held confined. The injustice of that situation created immense and widespread sympathy for the Queen of Scots and indignation against Elizabeth.

No possible verdict, by retaining at least the status quo, could have pleased Cecil more, while at the same giving him so much cause for concern. The Queen of England had exceeded, on this great occasion, even her own remarkable record for confusing important issues.

Elizabeth's verdict was greeted by John Knox with disgust. He called England "more foolish than foolish Scotland." God, he said, had delivered the "vile adulteress and cruel murderer of her own husband to their hands . . . and they sob for foolish pity."[4]

Knox was, as always, very close to political realities. He seemed to know all the patterns of conspiracy and plot—and by summer and autumn of 1569 these grew thick and dangerous. From her polite captivity under the pro-Vatican earl of Shrewsbury, the Queen of Scots spun a large and impressive web of connections across England and Scotland.

These efforts were helped by Elizabeth's complicity with pirates who sailed, quite successfully, against the treasure ships of Spain. The two nations drew close to war on that issue. In his anger Philip II relaxed his attitude toward Mary Stuart and encouraged her conspiracies through his ambassador in London, Don Guerau.

By autumn 1569 so many plots and strange movements were underway that few could follow events with complete understanding. All that was clear—though people held contradictory views on its significance—was that Mary Stuart was at the center of excitement, mystery, and much covert activity. Walsingham, in his reports to Cecil, found a phrase of his own for her: "the Bosom Serpent."[5]

By October 1569 the Queen of Scots had so lured the duke of Norfolk into an obsession to marry her that his importunities and arrangements alarmed Elizabeth, who cast England's first peer into the Tower of London.

On Sunday, November 14, 1569, Elizabeth was staggered to learn that the earls of Northumberland and Westmoreland had risen in rebellion in Northern England. They stormed into Durham with their followers. In the cathedral of that city, they "overthrew the Communion board, and tore the English bible and prayer book to pieces. The ancient altar was taken from a rubbish heap where it had been thrown and was solemnly replaced."[6]

From there the rebels proceeded south and gathered forces "variously estimated as from eight to fifteen thousand." Part of their purpose was to release Mary Stuart, and they came within fifty miles of Tutbury. An order from London transferring the Queen of the Scots to a new site at Coventry arrived before them. Discovering they had missed the glittering symbol essential to their gathering of more forces, the northern earls hesitated and turned back. Elizabeth's supporters gathered counter forces, issued proclamations, and marched North; the earls fled toward Scotland.

Moray, who had gathered a force and journeyed to the border himself, was able to lay his hands on the earl of Northumberland. It was traditional for each side of that frontier to grant asylum to the fugitives from the other. Moray broke that centuries-old tradition and had Northumberland imprisoned in Lochleven. That created a great outcry against him in Scotland, but it gave him at least one bargaining card vis-à-vis the English.

He needed that, as he needed all the cards he could collect, for in the period after the hearing at Westminster, his position had been undermined in Scotland much as Elizabeth's had been weakened in England—and for the same reasons. Where Elizabeth had Cecil, however, Moray had only John Knox—whose powers of analysis were unequaled, but who was not a politician and not a member of the government as such. He also had the handicap of dealing with William Maitland, the laird of Lethington— Michael Wily himself.

Unique among men of his time, Lethington laughed at religion. God, he said, "was a bogie for the nursery."[7] Assessing the course of the Reform, he came to the conclusion it was unpopular in Scotland and in England as well. The Vatican power combined with the might of Spain was irresistible. Therefore, he switched back to Mary Stuart and not only helped her lure the duke of Norfolk into her net, but in Scotland managed to divide Moray's supporters. He convinced Kirkcaldy of Grange, who followed him as blindly as a man under hypnosis. He swung Atholl and Hume and began to rebuild the Queen's Party in Scotland.

Elizabeth, badly frightened by the northern rebellion, reacted in anger. She gave severe orders and followed their execution personally. Hundreds were hanged; special courts were created. Most of those punished were of humble circumstances; England did not permit the queen to seize the property of rebellious earls without an act of Parliament. She was anxious, therefore, to lay her hands on Northumberland and Westmoreland. One was in Moray's custody; the other was enjoying the hospitality of the laird of Fernihurst. Her demands were phrased with her usual tact: that is to say, in insulting language.

Moray's response was bitter. He reviewed the difficulties of the recent past, the continued intrigues of the Hamiltons, and Elizabeth's own refusal to help the Reform in any substantial manner. He demanded money and support—and reminded the Virgin that her own fugitive rebels swelled the ranks of Mary Stuart's supporters in Scotland.

The justice of his remarks broke even Elizabeth's self-absorption, and she gave orders to help the regent. He did not have the pleasure of knowing this, however. Moray's life had turned into a nightmare of pursuit against enemies on all sides. He rushed to Dunbarton Castle to check a rumor that the queen's forces were ready to capitulate, learned it was ill-founded, returned to Stirling, then headed toward Edinburgh. En route he passed through Linlithgow—a town he had been warned against.

Moray spent the night in Linlithgow. The following morning he rode down the single street slowly and came abreast of a house owned by the archbishop of St. Andrews. There, hidden on the balcony by some washing strung for the purpose, a professional assassin named James Hamilton of Bothwellhaugh waited with a carbine. The bright sun and the closeness of his target made the shot easy. The ball, says Froude, passed through the regent and hit a horse nearby. Moray put his hand to his side while his murderer ran out the back of the house and galloped away on a waiting horse. Lord Semple helped Moray down. At first, the regent did not believe his wound was serious—but it was. Men gathered around; some blamed him for having been so lenient. He said he would never be sorry for that—and died while pursuers sought, in vain, for the murderer. He was thirty-five.[8]

On February 14, 1570, the earls of Morton, Mar, Glencairn, Cassillis, and Ruthven, and the Lords Lindsay, Ochiltree, and Glamis bore the coffin of Moray through the streets of Edinburgh and into St. Giles' Church. There, worn beyond his years but with his beard still black, John Knox waited. He remained silent while 3,000 people—an immense, tightly packed throng for the time and place—gradually settled into place. Then he spoke. His theme was: *Blessed are they that die in the Lord.*[9]

No orator of his time ever moved men as much or as often as Knox. He had the gift of eloquence,—in all times considered the most dangerous.

On the occasion of the murder of his old protégé, with whom he had so often quarreled on the issue of mercy, he brought his audience first to tears—and then anger, and then determination.

He coupled the murder of Moray with the murder of King Henry—and both murders with the ambitions and the crimes of Mary Stuart. He prayed for the life and health of the young Prince James—and called upon the people to make him king in fact as well as king in name. While he spoke, a new banner was being prepared and not long afterward was seen and described by Sir Thomas Randolph, Elizabeth's ambassador. It showed, as before, the figure of King Henry under a tree, with the infant James praying for heaven's help—and beside that, a new figure in a bed. That was Moray. His death had renewed the revolution, which now called itself the King's Party.

The king himself, still not yet four years old, was a pale child with reddish hair who resembled neither of his handsome parents. He was kept at the palace in Stirling: a structure improved along the odd tastes of his grandfather, James V. "Two antagonist systems seem at work," says an old guidebook, "in this remarkable building, the one producing an effect of eminent richness and grace when seen at a distance, the other rendering the very elements of these beauties grotesque when looked at close at hand. . . . The statuary, which produces a pleasing effect in the distant view, is found to embody all sorts of horrors. . . . Horrible commixtures of human and brute life—idiotic expressions . . . painful contortions, all clustered in reckless playfulness."[10] Such surroundings reflected the child king's situation with a grisly but uncannily accurate symbolism.

The death of Moray plunged Scotland into civil war. Elizabeth, in one of her rare exhibitions of militarism, sent an expeditionary force north. Unfortunately, the Virgin had troubles at home, and the situation was disheveled in both kingdoms.

By leaving the question of Mary Stuart dangling in limbo, Elizabeth allowed her rival to serve as a rallying symbol for English Catholics. These included most of the old nobility, who had long resented the Tudors and their "new men." These gathered, worked closely with the Spanish ambassador and agents of the Vatican, and began to plot a new rebellion.

"You have caused a rebellion in my realm," wrote Elizabeth to her cousin, "and you have aimed at my life."[11] In response, Mary Stuart protested she was misunderstood and pleaded for a personal audience.

That exchange took place while English armies marched briefly through Scotland and returned home. The English Catholics, outwardly subdued, were secretly conniving a new effort, which would become known to history as the Ridolfi Plot.

In Scotland, where his grandfather the earl of Lennox had been made regent in place of Moray, the young King James VI had passed his fourth birthday. To the alarm of his attendants, the child's legs were weak, and he walked uncertainly. He was pale and weak, but he seemed alert and quite intelligent.

His guardians had no time to concentrate upon that, however—they had larger problems with which to contend. The realm was divided by an uneasy stalemate, in which Lethington, leader of the Queen's Party, held possession of Edinburgh Castle and the capital. The Lords of the Congregation had the young king, Stirling Castle, Dunbarton, and Grange. Then a message arrived from Elizabeth, demanding that young James be sent to England for safekeeping. The Virgin wanted another important card in her own hands.

That brought the Lords of the Congregation together at Stirling to discuss some means of breaking the deadlock in their land. Morton, who was the strongest among them, suggested a concerted onslaught upon Lethington and his associates in Edinburgh. A spy reported this to the crafty laird, who thought a sudden raid might both throw the lords off balance and destroy their purpose. Buccleigh and Fernihurst, old border masters of the hit-and-run, undertook the assignment.

The Lords of the Congregation, with 2,000 men camped around the slopes of Stirling, were taken by surprise. On September 3, 1571, the border lairds, accompanied by Huntly, Lord Claud Hamilton, and a little over a hundred men, stole upon the scene late at night. Just before daybreak they moved in on various houses, whose locations they knew, and took Lennox, Argyll, Glencairn, Cassillis, Eglinton, and Sutherland prisoners—one by one. Only the earl of Morton awakened in time to barricade his door and fight them off. They then set fire to his house, and some of its inhabitants jumped to their deaths out of the upper stories. Morton emerged, blackened by smoke, and was taken prisoner by Buccleigh. If the raiders had then left, they might have succeeded—but they had tarried too long.

Reform troops appeared in force, and the undisciplined border fighters let their prisoners go and began to flee. Lord Claud Hamilton, in his flight, called an order to shoot the regent; a trooper did so, and Lennox fell to the ground. Then the raiders fled, taking 300 horses, leaving a dead Buccleigh behind. The earl of Lennox—mortally wounded—was carried up the slope and into Stirling Castle.

Years later King James VI said that his conscious life began the morning he saw his grandfather's bloody form being carried past him through the gates of the castle. It was a memory that not even a four-year-old could easily forget.[12]

While the Lords of the Congregation, now hot with fury, elected the earl of Mar to take the place of the dead Lennox, Cecil and Walsingham in England toiled with the mystery of the Ridolfi conspiracy. They suspected the bishop of Ross and behind him, his mistress—the Bosom Serpent herself: Mary Stuart.

Viewed overall, the situation was far from minor. Mary Stuart had fled to England at a time when many forces were heading toward a confrontation upon which the direction of Europe would depend. France was torn between the Calvinists and the pro-Vatican followers. Its queen, Catherine de Médicis, could not quite decide which path to take. Discussions were underway with Elizabeth to have her marry the French duke of Anjou. When it appeared this might occur, the French queen also made arrangements to have her daughter Margaret marry the Reform king of Navarre. If England's queen carried out her promise, then England and France would both take the Reform path against the Vatican. That could add their combined strength to the Reform provinces of the Netherlands, consolidate the great anti-Vatican effort of Calvinist Geneva, and create a counter power to Spain.

Mary Stuart, located inside England by accident, became a key to Spanish and Vatican efforts against the Reform movers. Spain and England had long been allies against France; the old English aristocracy wanted to continue this policy and restore the Vatican faith. In France, at the same time, the tentatively pro-Reform moves of Catherine de Médicis were opposed by the fanatically Catholic duke of Guise and his brother, the cardinal of Lorraine—both close relatives of Mary Stuart.

The captive Queen of Scots, therefore, was receiving funds from the Vatican, Madrid, and her own estates in France. She had the allegiance of traditionalists who, though sometimes against one another, could at least combine on her behalf. She was linked with a subversive movement in England and France and with the official government of the Vatican and Spain and had at least half of Scotland under her sway. In all, a remarkable performance by a captive woman.

Cecil resolved to prove Mary Stuart's intrigue and intentions to Elizabeth in a manner she could not ignore. The English queen might believe it was all personal; Cecil knew that far larger and more important issues were at stake.

The duke of Norfolk, released but still under surveillance, chose that delicate moment to accept some money, funneled from France to Mary

Stuart, and to forward it to her supporters in Scotland. One of the duke's secretaries sewed 600 pounds in gold in a bag, gave it to a merchant traveling north, and told him it was silver intended for a steward of the duke. The merchant looked inside the bag, discovered the gold and some coded letters, and turned both in to Cecil. The authorities retraced their source and took the duke's secretary into custody. Threatened with the rack, he said the key to the code was in the duke's bedroom. That chamber was searched, more coded documents and their key discovered, and the duke was again arrested. A series of disclosures led to the unraveling of the Ridolfi Plot. The names of all sorts of peers and commoners began to tumble into the net. The Queen of Scots was outraged to have her quarters searched and her servants reduced and the bishop of Ross—her ambassador at court —hauled off to prison.

The bishop was famous for his defense of his queen; he now became famous for his disclosures. He revealed the maneuvers that entrapped Norfolk during the time of Mary Stuart's hearing and other details of the many matters to which he was privy. In the process the bishop said the Queen of Scots was guilty of poisoning her first husband, King Francis II of France; had consented to the murder of her second, King Henry of Scotland; had brought Bothwell to Carberry Hill in the hope he would be killed; and would surely have murdered the duke of Norfolk had he managed to marry her. The bishop poured all this out to Dr. Wilson, an interrogator, who said, "Lord, what a people are these; what a Queen—and what an ambassador."[13]

Once Mary Stuart's activities were unraveled, Cecil had little difficulty in convincing Elizabeth she had been foolish in not publishing the reasons why Mary Stuart was considered dangerous and held in confinement. George Buchanan, the most famous man of letters that Scotland then or for many generations afterward produced, was encouraged to publish his famous book *The Detection of the Doings of Mary, Queen of Scots, touching the Murder of her Husband, and her Conspiracy, Adultery and Pretended Marriage with the Earl Bothwell.*[14]

Buchanan wrote in Latin, which was then the language that educated Europe spoke and wrote. His *Detectio* included an appendix of the casket letters in both French and Latin, was widely distributed, and created a sensation. Not since the days of Rome had a sovereign been so pitilessly, candidly, and mercilessly described—and even the Roman writers had waited until their subjects were safely dead. Written with a scholar's attention to detail and a poet's gift for vivid phrases, it created a sensation and was cumulatively horrifying.

The *Detectio,* however, issued from a Scots Reformer and not from the English authorities. Its validity was instantly assailed by a great army of

Vatican propagandists who termed Buchanan a forger and his proofs fraudulent. They contrasted the proofs he offered with the famous verdict of innocence pronounced by Elizabeth herself—who had seen the evidence. Buchanan's book was, therefore, swiftly caught in a vortex of argument that has swirled ever since.

Yet the great poet's effort had a deeper significance that many of its critics, and even its supporters, did not at the time clearly understand. John Knox was famous through his own writings and books—but Knox was a theologian and a religious leader. His fame did not approach, for a century or longer, that of George Buchanan—who was a great literary idol of Europe.

Until Buchanan became disillusioned with Mary Stuart, whose courtier he had been, he had always remained a man of high letters. His great fame rested on poems and plays whose political implications were shrouded in oblique references and masked personae, and appeared in hints and gleams—or in satire—and no more.

By fashioning the case against Mary Stuart in the beautifully balanced Latin cadences that had made him famous, Buchanan carried Knox's argument against the sacred prerogatives of sovereigns from the churches and castles of remote Scotland and England into the teeming centers of European thought. His *Detectio* did not so much state that case as rest upon it. That inner meaning sank more easily into the minds of his readers by being implicit. By arguing about the guilt or innocence of Mary Stuart, he led his readers—believers and critics alike—unconsciously to accept the idea that great sovereigns can be judged, like their subjects, on the rules of evidence and the law. His book, therefore, was a great weapon for Knox's revolution and its doctrines.

In January 1572 the duke of Norfolk was found guilty of treason and sentenced to death, and the Spanish ambassador was asked to leave England. In the wake of the revelations of the Ridolfi Plot, the English Parliament met from May to June, and many members called for the death of Mary Stuart. Her followers crouched as far beneath attention as they could manage, and Elizabeth finally sent a message to the Lords of the Congregation in Scotland that she would help them.

As usual, her promise was better than her performance. Despite proofs of the conspiracies against her, the English queen soon relaxed and took no decisive action. It was her custom to ignore, rather than confront, hard facts. Death was a forbidden subject—and so was the all-important matter of her succession. Rebels were misguided; she could not face the thought of her widespread unpopularity among the nobility and comforted herself with cheering crowds of commoners.

During the balance of 1572, Elizabeth allowed all Cecil's work to dangle unfinished. She delayed the execution of Norfolk, refused to allow Parliament to disinherit or punish Mary Stuart, and allowed her marriage negotiations with France to dither into futility. As usual, events changed her situation.

Reformers in the Netherlands erupted against Spanish rule. William of Orange led the resistance. Elizabeth refused to help. In France, Catherine de Médicis fulfilled John Knox's dark diagnosis of her character by setting in motion a plan to assassinate the Reformer Admiral Coligny. The attempt failed at first and then succeeded as part of a horrible holocaust known as the St. Bartholomew's Massacre, in which tens of thousands were butchered in Paris and other cities throughout France. The king of Navarre barely escaped with his life and his new bride; the realm was plunged into a civil war; the Guise relatives of Mary Stuart became the strongest force, virtually the masters, of the French crown.

Philip II sent Spain's greatest hero, Don John of Austria, half brother to the king and victor of Lepanto, to the Netherlands to reduce the rebellion. All this cheered Mary Stuart, but did not stir Elizabeth into any move in any direction. She was horrified by St. Bartholomew's, but soon recovered. Like many other nonreligious people, she considered religious arguments ridiculous and never quite understood that they seldom remain religious, but escape into every arena of national life: law, ideas of morality, the nature of lawful obedience, the rights of the individual, and the nature of authority.

The massacre on St. Bartholomew's Day shook the ancient respect in which Englishmen held the Vatican. Scenes of such cruelty could not be held consistent to the faith its name conjured. In England the recoil among Catholics was deep; the Anglican compromise really grew from that time forward. In Scotland the parallel repeatedly drawn by Knox, linking the Vatican to Anti-Christ, seemed awesomely fulfilled in the eyes of his followers—though Catherine de Médicis, and not the pope, had been responsible for the holocaust.

Only Lethington, who considered himself a realist, refused to believe that men are guided by matters of the spirit rather than material goods. Inside the castle of Edinburgh, surrounded by high peers, he was sure of victory. His associates, who held him in awe, relaxed in his assurance.

John Knox knew otherwise. He looked at the world from a high peak that he shared with only a few—if any—others. The man whom Calvin considered an equal was only in his late fifties, but was virtually worn out. He moved from Edinburgh to St. Andrews, where young James Melville, a boy at the time, later recalled seeing him walk slowly through the streets "well wrapped in furs." Knox had a staff upon which he leaned on one side, and a man to help him along on the other. He had to be assisted into and up the pulpit. Young Melville listened with pen and paper in hand, but Knox—who began softly—seemed to gather strength and force as he proceeded until he grew so immense that the boy dropped his pen in terror. He thought the man in the pulpit would smash it into splinters and fly out of it.[15]

Knox was, however, keen to the realities and politics of the moment. He deplored Lethington's hold over Kirkcaldy of Grange and sent David Lindsay—a minister of the Kirk—with a message for Kirkcaldy. "Tell him to leave that evil cause. If not, he shall be brought down over the walls with shame, and hung against the sun."[16]

Lindsay carried the message and returned to say that Kirkcaldy had seemed affected, until Lethington had ridiculed him. Knox listened without surprise. "I have been in earnest before my God about these two men," he said. "I am sorry about what will happen to one of them, but God tells me there is mercy for his soul. For the other—I doubt that he will ever be well."

Knox was, in fact, dying. He knew it. He also knew that the strains of the protracted civil war had brought Scotland to its lowest point. In Europe a revitalized Vatican, armed with the great wealth and power of Spain, seemed destined for inevitable triumph. The duke of Guise had become *de facto* ruler of France and was in the pay of Spain; the Queen of the Scots was still the hope of millions in England and her own peerage; from all material signs, he had, or would, lose the cause for which he worked. Instead he radiated calm. John Knox knew he had won.

He died over several days during which he entertained visitors, left instructions and advice, and ordered a new hogshead of wine opened for those who came to see him—for Knox was not a Puritan. When death arrived, on November 24, 1572, he found the leader waiting and smiling.[17]


Knox died the same day that James Douglas, earl of Morton, succeeded Mar as regent. Mar had died a natural death; few people expected the same of Morton. Reddish haired, fearless, and blunt, he was far from the austere sort of leader that Moray and others had been for the revolution. The number of Morton's mistresses and bastards exceeded probability, and he made no secret of his liking for money. Nevertheless, he had staked his property, as well as his life, in the Reform. Shrewd, practical, and fearless, he moved well.

By April 1573 he had managed, where so many others had failed, to persuade England to send siege guns and men north and led at last an attack on Edinburgh Castle. The siege was arduous and the defense firm, but by trenching and the poisoning of the castle water supply, the men inside were finally reduced. Kirkcaldy and Lethington were the last to come to terms and were lowered over the walls. Michael Wily was very ill, but his spirit was inextinguishable. At first there was some thought of sparing Kirkcaldy, but letters were found in the castle linking him to not only Mary Stuart—whom all the world knew and respected—but even to the duke of Alva, in which Spanish invasion plans were discussed. While his captors discussed his fate, Lethington died mysteriously. "The flower of the wits of Scotland," as Elizabeth called him, left a world whose surface he had adorned, but whose deeper meaning he never understood.[18]

Kirkcaldy, after several delays and reprieves, was conveyed in a cart from Holyrood to High Cross in Edinburgh. David Lindsay, who had brought him Knox's parting message, was at his side to comfort him. He was hanged looking up the street toward the castle, but as the cart beneath him was driven away, his body swung slowly around until it faced the setting sun.[19]

# PART TWO

*Childhood*

7 Stirling Castle gloomed atop an eminence near the river Forth and guarded the gateway of the Scots Highlands like some great blood-encrusted monolith to the god of war. It took George Buchanan—that strange mixture of worldly and unworldly elements—to inspire caravans into that great keep that carried not arms, or food, or guns, but books.

Buchanan's purpose was to educate James Stuart, known to himself and Scotland as James VI and as merely prince of Scotland to his mother and the vast Vatican world. The old tutor's collection was padded by almost two hundred volumes taken from the queen's library at Holyrood, which contained the French poetry of Ronsard, Marot, du Bellay; the Italian of Ariosto and Petrarch; Homer, Herodotus, Plato, and Euripides in Greek; Livy and Horace in Latin. Buchanan had helped Mary Stuart select these volumes and had often read them with her after dinner.

Buchanan launched his pupil on the saws and aphorisms of Aesop, Plato, and Plutarch and then prodded, pushed, cursed, and scared him into the history of the popes and the early Church, of kings, princes, emperors, countries, and conquests, as well as mathematics, logic, geography, grammar, rhetoric, and the dialectic of the Old Testament. James was carried from the study of early Christianity, with its wars against endless heresies and enemies, into the *Augsburg Confession* and the doctrines that alternately united and divided the Swiss, French, and German churches of the Reform movement. Intellectually, it was the education of a Calvinist, alleviated by an indoctrination into Greek and Latin, that opened a wide window to the civilization of an amoral past and that radiated toward the modern languages of French, Spanish, and Italian.

The overall sweep of Buchanan's course did not rush James over any greater territory than other boys of high station at the time, but they were usually allowed at least a carefree childhood until the ages of six or seven and then could experience grammar school with other boys until twelve or fourteen. Following that, they could suffer or saunter through university until they were in their early twenties. It was James Stuart's lot to be

plunged into education before he could think, and it was Buchanan's intention to have his pupil absorb—and absorb well—the learning of a doctor
before he reached and passed puberty. One result was that over six hundred
volumes, swelled by gifts and suggestions, poured toward the boy at Stirling.
Another result was the creation of a prodigy. Still another, less obvious in
its effects but poignant in its implications, was to place young James Stuart
under a head tutor who hated the boy's mother.

The Queen of Scots was well aware of that hatred. She read Buchanan's
*Detectio* with hoarse cries of rage. Pointing out that it carried neither a
printer's name or place, she demanded that Elizabeth have it suppressed.
The English queen, enjoying the confusion she had helped create, shrugged,
smiled, and turned away. Meanwhile, an edition appeared in French and
then in English and then in Scots. Geneva was energetic in distribution, and
scores of Vatican pens were diligent in producing anti-*Detectio* tomes,
charging Buchanan with forgery.

The issue of Mary Stuart's crimes became, in other words, entangled
in the landscape. England had crushed the pro-Stuart rebellion of its northern earls and assisted the Reform in Scotland to overcome the same Queen's
Party. Elizabeth could rest more easily for that and found it easy to forget
the source of her fright. With Scotland no longer an immediate threat, Spain
preoccupied in the Netherlands, France in a disorderly condition under the
strange Henry III, life in England began to assume the relaxed, smiling
aspect of peace.

The Queen of England believed she had triumphed. Secure again, she
several times alluded to Mary Stuart as her heir.[1] At the same time, rumors
began to float that Elizabeth was not in good health. These rumors, fanned
by the wishes of Mary, rapidly expanded into a giant whisper that the Queen
of England would soon die.[2]

The Queen of Scots, therefore, was treated by her guardian, the earl
of Shrewsbury, with great respect. She was allowed a miniature court of her
own and a cloth of state over her chair. She went riding and hunting,
accompanied by a well-dressed and respectful retinue, and would travel
"from Sheffield to Chatsworth and from Chatsworth to the baths at Buxton."[3] She received an income of 4,000 crowns from her estates in France,
and her correspondence was heavy and uncensored. She had many friends
at court in London and even drew, remarkably, the countess of Lennox,
Lord Darnley's mother, to her side. That alone did much to convince the
world she was innocent of the charge she had helped plot and pursue
Darnley's murder: the world did not know the countess of Lennox. She had
another son, Darnley's younger brother, whom she wanted to marry off.
The countess of Shrewsbury also drew near, and in short order the trio

began to weave a minor mare's nest.⁴ All this seemed small beer compared
to what had gone before and left little room for concern regarding the boy
at Stirling.

Sir Henry Killigrew, sent to Scotland to conduct some shadowy
negotiations in 1574, however, took the time and trouble to visit Stirling.
He found the eight-year-old prince had learned his lessons well. "The
King," wrote Sir Henry to Elizabeth, "seemed very glad to hear from your
Majesty, and could use pretty speeches, as how much he was bound unto
her Majesty, yea—more than to his own mother."

"He speaketh," Killigrew continued, "the French tongue marvelously
well; and that which seems strange to me, he was able *extempore* (which
he did before me) to read a chapter of the Bible out of Latin into French,
and out of French after into English . . . His schoolmasters Mr. George
Buchanan and Mr. Peter Young, rare men, caused me to appoint what
chapter I would. . . . They also made his Highness to dance before me, which
he likewise did with a very good grace."⁵

Tales of this prodigy traveled through the realm. James Melville, who
succeeded John Knox as head of the Kirk but lacked the great leader's
supernal perceptions, considered the young king "the sweetest sight in
Europe . . . for strange and extraordinary gifts of wit, judgement, memory
and language." He described how the boy, holding the hand of old Lady
Mar, would walk up and down and "discourse."⁶

The civil war had left Scotland ravaged and the Regent Morton received the same treatment from Elizabeth as his predecessors. She sent
orders and instructions that conflicted with both one another and common
sense and adamantly refused to part with any money. At one point she
wanted to trade young James for his mother—but Morton did not want
either the presence of Mary Stuart nor the onus of her fate on his hands.

Instead the head of a younger house of Douglas busied himself with
putting down disorder, and he did so with an efficiency that was remarkable.
In order to pay his troops and maintain the government at all, he introduced
taxes in every possible direction—a step that made him predictably unpopular. At the same time, he maintained his several mistresses and added new
ones whenever possible, which led to chilly relations with the Reform
ministers.

Time and seasons turned the world, and the great game of power
continued restlessly. In France the duke of Guise dominated the transvestite

Henry III while the Reform, headed by Henry Bourbon, king of Navarre, sought to ally itself with the Reformers of the Netherlands and Germany. Despite all the efforts of Cecil—now Lord Burghley—Elizabeth was reluctant to enter these efforts, but England was too clearly an obstacle to the peace of the Spanish empire to be ignored. London teemed with refugees from the Netherlands and the Inquisition. English pirates, carrying dubious credentials as "privateers" and in some instances financed by Elizabeth herself, created great anger in Madrid and a new, though lawless, industry in England.[7]

The two nations drifted toward war, and Burghley pushed Elizabeth, reluctant as always, into helping the rebels of the Netherlands against Philip II. It was his hope that the Queen of England would place herself at the head of a Reform league to counter the Vatican in all its reaches. That was a position Elizabeth refused to accept: she could not, nor would she ever, understand why men considered such issues important.

Meanwhile, James Stuart studied his lessons at Stirling. Two younger men from the Erskine family were assigned to teach him how to ride, to shoot, to hunt, and to play games. He had, as a companion, the youthful earl of Mar, who was eight years older and who had an aptitude for mathematics. From time to time, for varying periods, other lads joined the young king. The king loved horses; loved riding—at which he proved and would always remain reckless; loved hunting with a passion. The deaths of small animals and large—rabbits, squirrels, and deer—seemed to move him to an emotion close to passion. An odd reaction, and not his only oddity.

Buchanan, busy though he was with his duties in other areas—his writings, his history of Scotland—became aware that his royal pupil's docility concealed secret elements. The old man had, after all, taught hundreds, perhaps thousands, of boys; he was hard to fool. One afternoon, working in the library at the castle, the head tutor was disturbed by the noise of James and some companions in the garden outside. Rising, Buchanan stamped out to command silence and then returned to settle down again. The noise rose anew.

The old man rushed out and the boys fell silent—except for James. Putting his hands on his hips, he looked at the tutor boldly and said, "Who'll Bell the Cat?"—a saying famous in Scots history from the reign of James III.

Buchanan fell on him at once. James's howls produced the countess of Mar, as large in her farthingale as an overstuffed bed, bristling with indignation. She gathered the weeping James in her arms and turned to Buchanan.

"How dare you?" she asked, "How dare you lay your hands on the Lord's Anointed?"

Buchanan, breathing heavily, glared at her in contempt. "I have whipped his arse," he said. "You can kiss it if you like."[8]

Then he turned and went back into the library, leaving the bystanders doubled in laughter and a new legend to make the rounds. Yet the incident was clear enough: the king was growing up.

If the boy king was growing up, it meant that his elders were growing older—and their time shorter. England had become an active menace to Spain on the oceans; Philip II laid plans to send an army into Ireland to redress the balance. In France, where he had the powerful duke of Guise completely subsidized, another more complex plot was set into motion. Mary Stuart was encouraged; money began to flow into England, where a new Spanish ambassador was in residence—and into impoverished Scotland. The Hamiltons, led by the archbishop of Glasgow, the new earl of Argyll, and the earl of Atholl began to form a new Queen's Party. In the Netherlands, Don John planned another undertaking altogether: he would invade England, free Mary Stuart, defeat Elizabeth, marry the Queen of Scots, and rule that realm as king by her side.

Mr. Peter Young was no plotter: he was the king's day-by-day tutor. Newly graduated from the college at Geneva when he first found his post, he was always aware that his charge would someday rule the realm. He was careful, therefore, to sink on one knee and kiss the boy's hand when he came downstairs in the morning. Later he kept a notebook in which he wrote a record of James's witticisms and what seemed his more clever remarks. Predictably they reflected the dust of the books that surrounded them both. One day Young read about Absalom and stressed his handsomeness.

"He was felon fair above and fow fals in onder," James replied, and then—mingling Latin with his Scots—"the *unus ille naevus* made him a *knaevus.*" (The one fault made him a knave.)[9] James liked puns, and Master Young, extravagantly impressed with every feeble effort, dutifully scribbled in his notebook. He thought the king was very clever, almost wise.

He was not, but he was disconcerting. His humor took odd forms and unexpected twists. His memory was prodigious and he could pun and turn phrases inside out in a manner then fashionable among his elders and that Shakespeare, in the next generation, would establish for all the world. But James Stuart's eyes bulged from a pale face and he had a strangely soft body for a boy. He walked in a splayfooted, ungainly manner, almost as though crippled. The product of Darnley in the midst of syphilis showed a sort of inherited physical incompleteness. There was something wrong with his mouth, as if his tongue was too large. He dribbled when he drank, and his language, even for a boy (and boys like dirty language) was unusually foul out of Buchanan's earshot. Only his eyes, somewhat heavy-lidded, reflected Mary Stuart and were unexpectedly mature.

Buchanan now began to realize his pupil's nature. Alone, he unrolled the manuscript of a play he had written years earlier when he headed a college in Bordeaux and counted the youthful aristocrat Montaigne among his pupils. Cast in Latin verse, it was called *Baptistes*. The theme was tyranny—and its authorship had once almost cost him, in the hands of the Inquisition in Lisbon, his life.[10]

"This little book," he wrote carefully, "must seem to have a peculiar interest for yourself—inasmuch as it sets before you in the clearest manner what torments and miseries tyrants endure, even when they appear to be most prosperous. And this lesson I deem not merely beneficial, but absolutely necessary for you."[11]

He paused and looked, frowning into space and then continued. "Moreover, I wish my book to be a standing witness to posterity that not with your teachers, but yourself rested the fault."[12]

The dedication, blunt and direct, was an admission that the great educational effort with young James Stuart was—in the eyes of its architect —a failure. No clearer warning to the realm, or to the future, could have been composed, but Buchanan decided that this warning was not enough.

He knew, as keeper of the privy seal, that Mary Stuart's activities and position as heir to Elizabeth had once again drawn Spain and France toward her cause. The great issues raised by the Reform in Scotland were not only still unresolved, but their coherence had been unstrung by the twists and turns of Elizabeth, the arguments of the Vatican, and the shortsighted ambitions of people of the moment.

With Knox gone, the revolution had lost not only its leader, but its breadth of vision and its importance in the eyes of the world. Morton's regency was not recognized as legitimate even by the English court; it was a *de facto* situation. The Queen of Scots still sat under her cloth of state; the great issue of whether the rights of sovereigns were unlimited or whether subjects could frame laws not only for their own protection but to limit tyrants remained stifled and silenced.

Buchanan determined to carry Knox's argument to the world, and in that resolve the most famous writer of his day, sure of an audience throughout all western Europe, lifted the damaged banners of the revolution from the side of the road and began to set them where they would arouse the future.

One afternoon there was a scuffle in the garden over a bird. One of the boys caught it; James wanted it. The earl of Mar, taller, better looking, and stronger, refused to hand it over. In the sweaty but brief struggle, the bird was crushed to death. Someone told Buchanan, who was working—probably on his history of Scotland—in the library, and he summoned the two to come before him. James's answers were infuriating, and the old man in the black skullcap rose in anger and gave him a heavy blow that sent him staggering across the room.

*"You,"* shouted Buchanan in now open dislike, "you are a true bird of that bludie nest."[13]

Overheard, as was every whisper above the normal in that tiny court, the remark flew the rounds and added another touch to the endless speculation and discussion about Mary Stuart.

The Queen of Scots was, as usual, at the center of trouble. She and the countess of Lennox had persuaded Lord Charles Stuart, Lord Darnley's younger brother, to whom Elizabeth had given the Lennox estates in England, to marry the daughter of the countess of Shrewsbury.

That marriage, which involved a prince of the blood, was made without Elizabeth's permission and created a brief brouhaha. The countess of Lennox was returned to the Tower of London, to quarters by now familiar to her. The earl of Shrewsbury was called to court and humiliated, though he pleaded that his countess was uncontrollable. He begged to be relieved of Mary Stuart, who was costing him an extra £10,000 a year—an enormous sum at the time—and who did nothing but complain. His plea created harsh laughter in Elizabeth.

In the midst of this teapot excitement, Lord Charles Stuart and his bride both died, but not without leaving behind another waif for Elizabeth, Mary Stuart, and their respective factions to watch, quarrel about, and supervise. Her name was Lady Arabella Stuart. James, at Stirling, had another cousin.

By 1577, when James was eleven years old, his situation was still that of a child bound to his tutors—king only in name—and king only to a handful of people. Elizabeth refused to recognize his claim and would not send Morton any help whatever.

Her avarice, which was by now deeply imbedded, was belied by the glitter of her court and her own bejeweled presence. Few people excepting those in the inner circle could reconcile the hundreds of dresses, the dances and parties, the lavish granting of licenses and monopolies to her favorite

Leicester and his runners-up, with the tightfisted attitude of the English queen toward people for whom she had little regard.

At Stirling, however, a lack of funds kept those around the boy king in stringent circumstances beneath their station. The Regent Morton was widely suspected of receiving heavy English subsidies that he used for himself. He did not—but the rumor added to his troubles, which increased as time passed.

Morton not only had the animus and secret activities of the pro-Vatican, pro-Mary Stuart nobility with which to contend, but the Kirk as well. Andrew Melville, Knox's successor, thundered against the fact that high Catholic posts—and their attendant properties and incomes—remained attached to various peers of the realm. Knox had not liked that either, but had been enough of a realist to know that the retention of such privileges was the price the Reform had to pay for its alliance with the nobility. Melville—more of a doctrinaire and a purist of the type that later led to the minting of the term *Puritan*—was indifferent to such worldly nuances. He thundered—and the ministers of the Kirk echoed him like so many individual cannons—against the "Bishops."

The issue was not minor. Elizabeth ruled the Church of England through the power to appoint its bishops. In Spain, Philip II ruled the Catholic Church through much the same power. Through all Europe this combination of Church and State was centuries old and deeply imbedded and was considered essential to governmental control and stability. It was Knox's argument—as it had been Calvin's—that churches had to be free of such state controls. The Scots Reform, in arguing against bishops, was pursuing principles for which it had long struggled. The earl of Morton, however, was not a man to sit down and explain or to persuade Andrew Melville to be patient.

"There will never be quiet in this country till a dozen or so of you are hanged or banished . . ." he said when a Melville delegation approached him. His irritation was understandable, but did not help his situation. The Reformers were his great natural allies; the loss of their friendship was serious.

Anti-Morton rumors, many spread by pro-Vatican agents, began to flow. A young distant kinsman of the king, Captain James Stewart, returned from the wars in the Netherlands, arrived at Stirling, and fascinated young James with tales of derring-do and gossip against Morton. All sorts of people began to talk to James. When some mentioned, in a flattering way, his beautiful mother, Mary Stuart, it was soon seen that such comment was a quick way to his heart.

Copies of a Testament, written by Bothwell from his captivity in Denmark, found its way to Stirling—and was brought to James's attention by Lord Tullibardine.[14] Prepared while Bothwell's captivity was still fairly comfortable in Copenhagen, it was—as was to be expected—a long, extenuating, and self-serving chronology of events as seen from the viewpoint of Mary Stuart's third husband. It arrived at a time when Bothwell's death was rumored—though in reality he had simply been removed from sight and was immured in the fortress of Dragsholm. There he had been chained to a pillar in a cell half his natural height. Food was thrown into this dim pit; he was left untended. His hair and beard grew like an animal's; he wore marks around the base of the pillar in his tortured shuffling; in time his eyes glared madly into the gloom. Neither James nor his companions knew this; the Danes were not—then or later—anxious to acquaint the world with their cruelty—but the Testament traveled, in many copies, through wide reaches. It was reported that its explanation made James notably cheerful for several days.

The queen's friends gathered slowly at Stirling; some of the boy's attendants showed evidence of new and mysterious prosperity. Morton, alarmed at these changes, clattered importantly into the castle himself and was mildly alarmed to note a new, surly undertone to the boy's responses. The regent then—belatedly—took the precaution of placing some money himself among the attendants. One of these began to mention Morton in an admiring manner, and James looked at him with his strangely old eyes and said drily, "You have changed your coat."[15]

At this point the regent decided to crack down on the earl of Atholl. Like most of the Highland peers, Atholl ruled his distant domain like a petty sovereign; he was always subject to legal correction. Summoned to appear in court, the earl refused. His ally, Argyll, interfering, joined him in defiance. Several more summons were issued, and the two earls responded by calling their supporters to arms. A sudden threat of rebellion loomed.[16]

The news alarmed Burghley in London, and Elizabeth, reminded for the hundredth time that she had neglected the regent, sent him a sudden gift of some jewels. Unfortunately, she accompanied this token with instructions that he should settle his argument peacefully with the earls. More than that, she decided she should, herself, decide whatever issues were involved. Then she followed that suggestion with another message saying that if Morton did not accept the Queen of England as judge of the situation, she would send men to help the earls against him. These messages had the effect of leaving Morton with no immediate support in any quarter and forced Burghley into another campaign to calm his sovereign and lead her toward more rational grounds, if possible. Meanwhile Morton, having gone through the legal steps, declared both the earls outlaws. In response, they gathered their forces in large numbers and marched to Stirling Castle.

Their moment was shrewdly timed and had been planned with help from France. Money, funneled through the archbishop of Glasgow, Mary Stuart's ambassador to France, had been supplied by the powerful duke of Guise. But to young James the sudden appearance of his mother's old supporters, the sight of armed men camped in great numbers of the slopes of Stirling, and the appearance of two great armored, highly placed nobles who came to kneel before him was like seeing the pages of his history books spring to life. He was a king at last, and his eyes sparkled.

Word came from Morton that the two earls were outlaws. They should be denied a hearing and told to obey the law. If the king, Morton said through his messengers, would not uphold the laws of the realm—the regent would resign. That calm analysis of the issue, which reflected Morton's long tutelage under John Knox in the service of the Reform, made the leaders of the Kirk abruptly aware that significant movements were afoot and the Reform in sudden peril.

They had reason to be alarmed. The wheels of change were in motion and, as usual, were being moved by pro-Spanish, pro-Vatican, pro-Mary Stuart forces. From her easy captivity Mary Stuart watched absorbedly as the results of a torrent of letters, suggestions, orders, payments, and propositions began to emerge. In France her ambassador, the archbishop of Glasgow, conferred constantly with the duke of Guise. Their hopes were high; and their plan, eminently practical. If a pro-Vatican government could be placed in Scotland, then troops from Calais could reach Leith in three days. The Queen's Party, already renewed, could move into northern England, where it was sure of support, and the long dream to replace Elizabeth on the throne of England would once again emerge into life.

All these factors seemed remote and unreal to the twelve-year-old boy who sat on an elevated chair in one end of the King's Chamber at Stirling —a room where carved heads representing vanished royalty and figures from legend glared down from the great beams that crossed the ceiling.[17] The mighty earls of Atholl and Argyll entered to bow low before the boy king, while their men, camped on the slope outside, gave the region the look, sound, and smell of a military establishment. James's words on this occasion were not recorded; Mr. Peter Young's notebooks were absent. But there is no doubt about the immediate outcome. Regent Morton's resignation was accepted, and horsemen pounded away to carry the news, on March 12, 1578, that James VI had "accepted the Government."

The announcement was greeted with general dissatisfaction by the Reform. It was clear that a child could not rule, and the earls had other purposes in mind than they stated. The General Assembly of the Kirk met in Edinburgh and made speeches to itself—and to the Congregation—against bishops and Rome. Meanwhile, the earl of Morton, having seen his resignation accepted, retired to the island castle of Lochleven to await further developments. Word came from Elizabeth that he should move against the earls—but without any promise of help.

The palace at Stirling, so long a sanctuary against the turbulent world, rang to the harsh voices and arguments of the earls and their retainers. Drunken brawls took place, and the Chancellor Glamis was killed by the earl of Crawford.[18] James was soon awakened from his dream; he had merely changed guardians—and the new were not as interested in his education as the old. He and Peter Young bent over their books.

For a brief moment Mary Stuart's cause appeared high. In France the duke of Guise pressed his master, Philip II of Spain, for a decision. But the Prudent King, as he was called, decided to weigh the matter. That was an interminable process; like the movement of distant stars in their orbit, it could last for years. To the despair of the archbishop of Glasgow and Mary Stuart herself, the opportunity soon faded.

On April 25, 1578, the young, twenty-year-old earl of Mar, James's old schoolfellow, appeared at Stirling castle. He had sent word of his coming; he planned to hunt with his uncle, the master of Mar, who was serving as governor of the castle and guardian of the king. The young earl entered the gates followed by a number of armed men, presumably his huntsmen, more easily than Ulysses entered Troy—with much the same purpose.

The young earl had been approached, advised, and convinced by the earl of Morton that it was time for him to assume his full inheritance. The earls of Mar had traditionally been the guardians of the kings of Scotland in their minority; the governorship of the castle at Stirling was his due. Early in the morning of April 26 the men assembled in the Hall for the hunt. The guards of the castle were armed, but the earl and his followers appeared in armor. James, sleeping late in his black bed in the tower, was awakened by the clang and shouts of battle below. He rose and slipped down the stairs; near their base he stopped and watched in growing horror.

He saw a figure stagger and another slash viciously; still another received a heavy sword into his belly. The boy began to scramble back up the stairs in terror; men had to come to help him and their fierce figures made him hysterical. "He was in great fear," wrote Bowes, the English ambassador later, "and teared his hair."[19]

The Scots called it a "ruffle" but it was unforgettable to James. The master of Mar and the earl of Argyll were thrown bodily out of the castle; the young son of the master was mortally wounded. While preachers knelt by the young man's bed and prayed for him, the young earl of Mar—followed by several of his men—came pounding up the staircase where the boy king of Scotland cowered in his bedchamber. Soon women came with soothing draughts for the king, but Bowes wrote, "I have been informed his Grace by night has been by this means so discouraged as in his sleep he is greatly disquieted."[20] The boy, in other words, had nightmares afterward.

A few days later the earl of Morton appeared, radiating satisfaction. It was obvious he had planned the coup and equally obvious that the boy James, who trembled, was no obstacle. A call was issued to convene a Parliament at Stirling. Some highland nobles appeared, though Atholl and Argyll did not dare. Protests were raised with admirable lack of self-consciousness that Morton was holding the king a prisoner. If the king wanted help, the Highlanders said boldly, he could have it. They would restore his freedom and his rights on the spot.

At that, Morton turned toward the slight figure beside him and suggested His Majesty speak for himself.

James rose to his feet and said, in a shaky voice, "Least any man should judge this not a free Parliament, I declare it to be free. Those that love me will think as I think."[21]

His decision was good enough, since certainly Morton had interests at heart better than the Highlanders, but James did not speak from such a conviction. Even under the circumstances, it was difficult not to see that the boy, already famous for learning, was flawed by cowardice.

8 Morton's coup sent the pro-Vatican party in Scotland scuttling back to watchful waiting. From Paris the archbishop of Glasgow wrote bitter commentaries to Mary Stuart in England about the lethargy of Philip II and the opportunities lost. Mary Stuart, however, turned hopefully toward Don Juan, Spain's captain in the Netherlands, whose dreams of rescuing the Queen of Scots had become an open secret.

Unfortunately, Don Juan was a victim of plague that swept his forces and died suddenly in the autumn of 1578. He was succeeded by Alexander of Parma, another of the many excellent soldiers of Spain, who had neither romantic nor dynastic ambitions. At about the same time, the results of the death of the king of Portugal in an abortive adventure in Africa began to draw the attention of Philip II. Whether or not she knew it, Elizabeth was saved, once again, by changes beyond her control. The cause of Mary Stuart was set aside in Madrid, while Portugal was thoughtfully regarded.

During the next number of months, Morton, who did not bother to rename himself regent, toiled with the eternal problem of getting Elizabeth to recognize James as king of Scotland. The situation of the country would remain divided and uneasy so long as Mary Stuart sat under her cloth of state, had ambassadors, and claimed to be a sovereign. The countess of Lennox had died. Young James, as the son of the elder son, Lord Darnley, was clearly entitled to the Lennox estates and income. The Crown of Scotland had neither money nor a standing army. If Elizabeth would allow the Lennox properties to revert to James, he could live better, and such revenues would aid in establishing order. Morton sent the abbott of Dunfermline to Elizabeth to see if she could be persuaded. The abbott had to cool his heels because Elizabeth was loath to receive "the ambassador of rebels."[1]

Ordinarily, the English queen would have been more than happy to receive the ambassador of the Scots movement that was so markedly pro-

English; but, in fact, she was alarmed, incensed, and threatened by the fact
that this same group had suddenly reminded the world of its revolutionary
direction and goals in a sensational manner. It was not Mary Stuart's
sovereignty that Elizabeth had in mind, but her own—and that of every
other monarch in the world.

The man who rekindled this fire was George Buchanan. In January
1579, after several years of effort and having passed various handwritten
copies about, the great writer had combined the theories of John Knox with
the world about him and published a masterpiece. It was, of course, in
Latin, and the title was *De Jure Regni Apud Scotos*—"Laws for the Kings
of Scotland."[2]

It began with an ironic and prescient dedication addressed to the boy
James VI, which ended by saying, "I am forced to be somewhat jealous of
[concerned about] you, lest bad company, the fawning mother of all vices,
draw aside your soft and tender mind into the worst part; especially seeing
I am not ignorant how easily our other senses yield to seduction. . . ."[3]

This pointed dedication, however, was like the sound of cooing doves
compared to the text of the book. It was an astonishing work, a piece that
tolled like a great bell through time that was, in the end, to bring down all
the House of Stuart, the Bourbons and the Hapsburgs, the Hohenzollerns
and the Romanovs—the entire structure of kingly power. In 1579 it rang
as shocking as a scream in the night.

The fame of the author was assisted by the Calvinist diaspora, which
operated from Geneva and whose influence spread not only all across
northern Europe, but even into Constantinople. The dream of the leaders
of this movement was to smash the power of the Vatican and reunite all
Christendom into a new doctrine in which laymen would control the clergy,
but both would work together in a God-oriented new society. At least part
of this dream was attractive to the Jewish diaspora, and the Calvinists
received some cooperation from the Sephardic refugees from Spain who had
established themselves as commercially important in the Netherlands, Germany, and Portugal.[4]

Written in Socratic dialogue, *De Jure* argued that political power
ultimately belongs to the people and that all society consists of a series of
social contracts involving mutual obligations and restraints that bind both
rulers and people. The rights of the people, as expressed in a majority,
should prevail. If a tyrant abuses that understanding, the people have a right
to resist, to overthrow, and to punish.

It was Buchanan's great accomplishment to be able to state these
themes in the language of Europe's scholars as the leading voice of the
Humanist movement—a term then applied to classicists who had broken
the bonds of their predecessors to the works of Aristotle and who instead

ranged across the spectrum of learned antiquity. By being able to do that, Buchanan sounded a theme upon which the world of northern scholars, poets, literati, scientists, the politically restless and the ambitious, the Calvinists and the Jewish diaspora could all unite.

No more significant revolutionary contribution has ever been made; Knox's doctrines were renewed and revitalized. Buchanan created this masterstroke a hundred years before Hobbes and two hundred years before Rousseau took its themes, by then afloat in the air, to write his *Social Contract*. By that time Buchanan's name had faded like the Latin in which he wrote. In 1579, however, it might as well have been written in the sky over Europe. New editions of *De Jure* began to pour from the presses.

It was against this backdrop that the abbott of Dunfermline pleaded with Elizabeth to help the Scots Reformers. His specific case was, thought Burghley, more favorable to England than any agreement it had been able to reach through centuries of war—but Burghley was a Reformer. The abbott proposed that the Scots sign—or have King James VI sign—the Treaty of Leith. That would bind the two countries in firm alliance, keep the Scots king from pressing any claim to the English crown during the life of Elizabeth, and pledge Elizabeth to support Scotland's new government without casting doubt on the king's future rights of succession. That treaty had originally been drawn up when the Reform succeeded in 1561, but Mary Stuart had always refused to sign it. In captivity she still refused— though Elizabeth claimed that if she would sign, she would win her freedom. Her response was that she would sign when freed.

The abbott argued for a conclusion of the treaty with James and urged that the young king needed his revenues from the Lennox estates in England. The Virgin's answer was cold as death itself. She would not subvert her cousin Mary Stuart's sovereignty in such an underhanded step; she would keep the Lennox revenues in the clutch of the English Crown. The abbott departed after having been through a series that other Scots Reformers before him had experienced: warm words from Burghley; ice water and scorn from Elizabeth.

The English queen had similar answers for the Reformers—or rebels —of the Netherlands in their struggle against Philip II of Spain. In order to obtain help from her, these rebels were forced to accept a loan at interest and to turn over, as a pledge for repayment, the famous crown jewels of Burgundy. Then Elizabeth, gloating over the jewels, demanded her money. Not receiving it, she refused further support, and no arguments swayed her. "She stood at bay, fenced in by obstinacy, like a sullen dog."[5]

Meanwhile, she began a feverish distraction, which, despite their deep misgivings and distrust and the sardonic amusement of Philip II, drew the French court toward her once again. The latest diversion, like its predecessors, was based on her announced desire to marry. The chosen one was Monsieur, the duke of Anjou, "a small brown creature, deeply pock-marked, with a large head, a knobbed nose and a hoarse, croaking voice."[6] He was 25; the Queen of England was 46.

In April 1579 the earl of Morton attempted to establish some sort of general reconciliation by hosting a great banquet at Stirling. He invited all factions, including the earls of Atholl and Argyll. Unfortunately, the aftermath of his effort made his situation—already rendered difficult by Elizabeth's refusal of support—even worse. The earl of Atholl left the table saying he felt suddenly ill. About eight days later he died. Rumors connected his death with poison—and the poison to the earl of Morton.

At Stirling the king listened to this gossip with a frown. He was nearing his thirteenth birthday and had been greatly disappointed that Elizabeth would send him no money. The earl of Argyll, at his side again, whispered diligently; a younger brother of the Great Secretary Lethington, John Maitland, had appeared as did a number of others of Mary Stuart's party. John Maitland had been among the final defenders at Edinburgh Castle when his brother and Kirkcaldy had been taken; he was a minor hero. Like his brother, he was well-spoken and intelligent; the king liked him at once. All the Queen's Party, in fact, seemed to James to be men of singular congeniality, easy in their manner and filled with laughter and witticisms—in striking contrast to the dour and forbidding manners and austere outlook of the Reformers.

James's inclinations toward new friends was noted and relayed to his mother, Mary Stuart, and also by the English observers and the people around him in touch with the French court. There was no ambassador from France to Scotland, since James's title as king was not recognized. But Mary Stuart's ambassador at Paris, the archbishop of Glasgow, thought it was time someone was sent to the scene. The duke of Guise agreed, and so did Rome.

This move finally converged on Esmé Stuart, seigneur d'Aubigny. He was a cousin of James, a grandson of a brother of the earl of Lennox. He had already written that he would like to visit Stirling to unravel some inherited properties; someone suggested he be invited and James signed the letter. It is unlikely James attached much importance to it—he was more interested in a forthcoming visit to Edinburgh being arranged by Morton.

Morton worked hard to assuage the king's resentments and improve the king's real position. He had harried the Hamiltons into exile, and their estates had been seized by the Crown. Morton planned to hand this great present to the young king when Parliament convened in the capital. The time was also opportune to show the Scots people their learned young monarch—and Morton hoped the attendant festivities would reconcile the king to his situation.

Before James and the capital were ready for his visit, news came in September 1579 that his cousin, Esmé Stuart, seigneur d'Aubigny, had arrived at Leith. Richly attired, glittering with jewels, the newcomer was surrounded by an escort of twenty gentlemen and was carrying six fine-blooded horses as a present to the king from his even more distant, greater kinsman, the duke of Guise.

This glittering group traveled elegantly through Edinburgh on its way to Stirling. Scots gathered and clustered; nobles and lairds appeared as though from the earth to meet the king's cousin and to marvel at the number and size of the chests and trunks of the party. Their reactions were rewarded with munificence and fine words; Esmé Stuart had come to Scotland with forty thousand crowns in gold—more than Elizabeth had ever released to the northern realm in all her twisted and irritating dealings.

The seigneur d'Aubigny was obviously no ordinary visitor. Some said the duke of Guise himself had seen the nobleman off at Calais; Walsingham's agents reported in London that the archbishop of Glasgow, Mary Stuart's ambassador at Paris, had been closeted with d'Aubigny for weeks before he left France.

Great undertakings were planned. The Vatican, unable to endure Philip II's stately pace, had decided to enter the situation itself. Ardent young Jesuits led a revolt in Ireland; England's Catholics were to be reminded of their faith and their duty—and Scotland would be softened by Esmé Stuart with his charm, his gentlemen, and his gold.

The cousins met on the morning of September 15, 1579. James saw a tall, magnificently dressed, youthful man of 37, who bowed gracefully before him. He had a spade beard, auburn hair, pale skin, and flashing black eyes. The meeting seemed normal and casual to everyone but d'Aubigny, whose sharp eyes noted that the young king blushed.

# PART THREE

*Youth*

9 Esmé Stuart came to Stirling from the court of France, which, under Henry III, was one of the world's strangest. Henry Valois, prematurely white-haired and toothless though still only in his thirties, was a transvestite whose favorite costume was that of a lady-in-waiting. In low-cut gown and pearl choker, wearing the newly fashionable earrings, surrounded by a giggling circle of young men who frizzed their hair and bathed in perfume, the king of France alternated between bizarre entertainments and groveling repentance. Although notorious for faggotry and effeminacy, both King Henry and his *mignons* were difficult to classify, for their games were sometimes murderous. The king could assume normal clothes when he chose, and his whitened face could grow still and intimidating.

The king, however, did not rule. The duke of Guise, beloved of the people, virile and impressive, was the most powerful man at court. His influence was obeyed fearfully by Catherine de Médicis, the king's mother. Between these two, Henry III had little left but his strange games. Esmé Stuart, sixth of his line to be the seigneur d'Aubigny, married, with five children, a decade older than the king's favorites, was a figure who could go from the duke to the king and to the dowager queen and back again without leaving a ripple in his wake.

No mortal could entirely withstand the atmosphere of the French court, where Catherine de Médicis had a Flying Squad of beautiful young women who wormed their information in bedchambers, where the king giggled amid his dangerous but effeminate boys, and where the duke of Guise—in the pay of Philip II—strode about like a figure in search of a legend. In even ordinary times this overheated and hysterical atmosphere would have been difficult to withstand; it was made odder by the tides of fanaticism and religious revolution that swirled through the country to tear it between pro-Vatican forces headed by the duke and Reform forces headed by Henry Bourbon, ·king of Navarre. These yawning dangers kept the largest country in Europe too distracted and divided to maintain coherent policies.

In such a court, at such a time, the spectrum of experience open to an ambitious man stretched from the extremes of homosexuality through heterosexual orgies, secret political machinations, complex religious disputes, political events both staged and accidental, and interpersonal relationships that could change at a glance. No man could advance in such a great hothouse of ambition, greed, and religious fervor who did not develop special senses and perceptions and who could not use his natural attributes as instruments in his career.

Within a few weeks of Esmé's arrival at Stirling, the boy king was in love. All events seem inevitable in retrospect, and many reasons have been found and expressed for James Stuart's vulnerability to his cousin. All have surface plausibility in terms of d'Aubigny's social graces and witty conversation; his ability to convey a sense of the great metropolis of Paris—the largest in the world at that time; the luxury of the Tuileries; the lofty status of the anointed kings of France; the racy doings in the darker corners of the court. All these reasons, however, fade against the fact that the young king of Scotland disliked girls and made no effort to overcome that dislike. He was soon seen fondling d'Aubigny, indifferent to stares. The atmosphere at Stirling was suddenly equivocal. That was a turn of the wheel for which the earl of Morton, for all his shrewdness, had not prepared.

A month later, in October 1579, the cousins rode into the city of Edinburgh at the head of two thousand horsemen and a train of wealthy nobles, merchants, followers, and hopefuls. The atmosphere was pure delirium. Tapestries hung from windows; streets were blanketed with flowers; at every intersection figures costumed from legend and the Scriptures arose to declaim, bow, and retreat. Gates were wreathed with flowers and ribbons; floats and pageants appeared; casks of wine were opened and their contents poured for the crowds.

Morton, who had spent his own money, was going to great effort so the young king could see how well the realm had been put in order and how greatly his way had been prepared. Three days after his arrival at the capital, James VI—now officially in charge of his realm, though his real majority would not arrive until he was twenty-five—sat at the head of Parliament and received the estates confiscated from the Hamiltons. The holdings of that once-mighty family, now represented only by Lord John and Lord Claud—both in exile—included castles and villages, abbeys and farms, fields and woods, livestock and followers.

The king's reaction was to pluck the richest of the abbeys—Arboath

—with all its revenues and hand it over to his beloved. In addition, he let it be known that Esmé Stuart would soon become earl of Lennox.

The earl of Morton, who had risked so much so often for the Reform cause, was staggered. The leaders of the Kirk were alarmed. They did not regard the appearance and sudden ascendancy of a pro-Vatican French peer, loaded with gold and presents, as any addition to their cause. A rumor spread that James was being converted to Catholicism.

The young king had enough of Stirling and its memories of his childhood servitude. He liked Edinburgh and settled into the palace of Holyrood. Esmé Stuart was placed in an apartment next to the king's, and a court began to collect. It was enriched by the gold that Esmé had brought with him from France, which attracted the perennially impoverished Scots like bees to nectar. The earl of Argyll appeared and was joined by many of Atholl's supporters; Lords Seton and Livingstone came hurriedly, and Captain James Stewart, whom the King favored, exulted so loudly in the atmosphere that the Reform ministers assumed it was he who was leading the king down new pathways of pleasure.

Through the long gloomy Scots winter of 1579 and into the spring of 1580, the young king began to enjoy life in his own new fashion. He stamped about Holyrood in his ungainly and loud manner while Morton's enemies slowly gathered about him and the leaders of the Reform reflected a growing uneasiness. Events were underway in the great world that gave the Calvinists other reasons to worry as well.

The Vatican had gathered its strength and renewed the faithful throughout Europe. New reforms revitalized its structure; Loyola's soldiers of the pope—the Jesuits—sent out streams of ardent young men. Some landed in England; one was named Edmund Campion. In Ireland another —Nicholas Sanders—was setting a rebellion ablaze that was to plague England and Elizabeth for years to come. In Portugal the elderly King Henry died, and Philip II of Spain called grim Alva from the Netherlands to prepare an invasion.

In London Burghley watched these changes with concern. The great struggle in the Netherlands was unresolved, and Elizabeth would not help. Rebellion in Ireland made it essential that Elizabeth spend some money, send men and arms, and behave decisively—and that requirement was beyond her abilities.

Walsingham's agents left no doubt that d'Aubigny in Scotland was no innocent; that he had behind him the duke of Guise and Mary Stuart's ambassador, the archbishop of Glasgow. They did not have Philip II, who was intent upon Portugal—but they had the pope. That ruler, whose great possessions were both tangible and intangible, had enlisted the Knights of Malta and was proceeding to create a situation against England that he hoped Philip II would be forced to conclude.

In this atmosphere, with coded letters flowing from Scotland to Paris and from Paris to Madrid and from Madrid, Paris, and Scotland to Mary Stuart at Sheffield, the thirteen-year-old James VI undertook to convert his lover, Esmé Stuart, to the Reform. Far too clever to allow himself to be too easily persuaded, d'Aubigny held James in long, earnest conversations punctuated by wine and embraces behind closed doors. In the interim the Frenchman wrote Elizabeth a series of fawning letters, describing his situation as that of a man whose ties to France had vanished overnight and who had now found a new and true home.

Early in March 1580 the young king formally made Esmé Stuart the earl of Lennox. At the same time, assurances flowed from the little court toward the Kirk that the new earl had been greatly swayed by the unanswerable eloquence of the king and was inclining toward conversion. In alarm, Elizabeth sent Sir Robert Bowes, a man familiar with the strange and odd Scots, to assess the meaning of these events. Bowes wrote back that he found Edinburgh in "right strange humours."[1]

The new earl's ascendancy over the king had unhinged the situation. Ordinarily, it would have rallied the Reform in alarm, but the rumor that Lennox was leaning toward conversion touched the Kirk in a tender place. The faith of its leaders was based on the belief such conversions were real and could be accomplished; they could not rally against such an attractive possibility.

The subject of Esmé's religion was a key in both his relationship with James and to his rise in Scotland. The young king was immensely learned in a theological sense, although his ardor was less a matter of faith than of training. His effort to convert his beloved could not, obviously, fail without rupturing their relationship. On the other hand, d'Aubigny, already living one lie, was too astute to betray skepticism in an area so important. He and his masters in France had known he would have to assume whatever guise was necessary to achieve his goal—and that he would have to do so credibly.

The theological discussions between the worldly and skeptical courtier and the conceited young boy, therefore, were crucial to Esmé's progress. They proved so pleasant to James that he could hardly abandon them. The older man's retreat was so adroit, so gracefully conducted and gave so many convincing signs of being visibly impressed that it amounted to an enormous advance. Had Morton ever learned to mask superiority with the appearance of subservience so well, he could have remained regent.

Morton, meanwhile, was left with no tangible support from England and his own unpopularity. He withdrew to Dalkeith castle and even to Lochleven to await the time when Elizabeth and his countrymen would realize the nature of events and would be ready to act.

Sir Robert Bowes visited him and gave him a letter from Elizabeth in which she suggested he move first and thereby give her reason to come to his aid. Morton asked for more specific assurances, and Bowes added his endorsement. That convinced Burghley, but did not convince Elizabeth. That sovereign did not believe in futures; she hardly believed in events when they occurred.

When King James decided that he had sufficiently instructed his worldly cousin in the Calvinist faith, he sent him to the ministers of the Kirk so they could continue the effort. In Edinburgh, Lennox sat patiently while these men toiled with him and allowed himself to be gradually convinced. So the summer was spent, but it was not over before Philip II, whose armies had finally been organized, fell upon Portugal.

Within weeks the swords of Spain chopped down the richest prize in the world available at that time. Brazil and all its natural and real wealth, African outposts and splendors in India and the Orient—virtually half a world fell into the hands of Spain.

In one fell move Philip II had gained immense territories and riches, adding to the streams of silver and gold he received and poured across Europe and his empire. The influence of Spain, which already set the manners, fashions, and attitudes for most of Europe, rose to new, tremendous heights.


After signing Articles of Faith at St. Giles in Edinburgh, the earl of Lennox rejoined the young king—now fourteen years old—in a slow and impressive tour through at least the half-civilized part of the realm. A series of hunts and banquets were staged at Perth, Arboath, and Dunottar, ending at St. Andrews. The new convert, who shone in the reflected beam of royalty, was given the governorship of Dunbarton Castle while one of his followers was made governor of Edinburgh Castle. In addition, Lennox became a member of the Privy Council, lord chamberlain, and, of course, First Gentleman of the Bedchamber.[2]

These moves were far from honorary. The new earl created a sixty-man guard around the king to protect his sacred presence, and Captain James Stewart—one of Morton's worst enemies—was placed in charge of this force.

These moves sent Elizabeth into a flurry. Her scolding letters to James having been ignored, she sent instructions to Ambassador Bowes to have

Morton move against Lennox, with the assurance that English troops at
Berwick would come to his assistance. The former regent, whose power had
now melted, relieved to learn tangible help was finally available, sent messengers and messages around the realm to gather his forces. Two days later
a new message came from Elizabeth warning him against force, denying she
would help and recommending peaceful persuasions.

That left Morton exposed; Lennox's agents quickly seized evidence of
his efforts and brought them before the young king. The former regent was
plotting, in other words, rebellion. James was alarmed, but d'Aubigny was
calm and sure: he could handle all.

It was at this juncture that Sir Robert Bowes appeared at Holyrood and
asked for an audience with the king—in private. He wanted to present
proofs that Esmé was in the pay of the duke of Guise and was in reality
a double agent. James refused to listen and insisted his cousin should be
present to hear any charge brought against him. Bowes, whose instructions
were rigid, refused to show his proofs in the presence of the elegant, smiling
Frenchman. He left, therefore, baffled in his purpose—and was recalled
home. By that retreat, Elizabeth not only left d'Aubigny master of the
situation, but left Morton abandoned.

The net woven around Morton was subtle and sophisticated. The old
methods of physical assault were conspicuously avoided; by 1580 such
direct action was considered primitive. Instead the agents of the duke of
Guise, the Vatican, and the supporters of Mary Stuart decided to blend
Morton's downfall into a campaign to raise the Queen of Scots.

One level of this campaign was a great effort to revive the Catholic
cause in England. A number of youthful English Jesuits were sent secretly
into the country during the year. The most gifted of these were Edmund
Campion and Robert Parsons. Both had been converted while at Oxford by
Dr. William Allen during the reign of Queen Mary Tudor and had studied
at the seminary Allen created at Douay, France. While the earl of Lennox
moved to strengthen pro-Vatican forces in Scotland, therefore, these ardent
agents held secret meetings and told Englishmen that they owed no true
allegiance to the excommunicated Elizabeth.

It had always been Mary Stuart's contention that she was not only
innocent of her husband's murder but that the true murderers had been her
rebellious accusers. As part of her defense, she portrayed the earl of Moray
as a self-server. The earl of Morton and others, she claimed, had killed the
king and placed the blame upon her. This argument carried weight in many
quarters because Elizabeth had never allowed proof to the contrary officially to appear. Buchanan, said the Vatican propagandists, was simply a

forger and a tool of the revolution, a scholar false to his learning.

Toward the end of 1580, therefore, Sir James Balfour—who had played a key role in the conspiracy that ended in Lord Darnley's murder—was secretly brought over from France, where he had prudently remained for many years. He was prepared, James was assured, to testify to the truth.

At that point, James VI spent a curious day in the company of his old regent. The original plan had centered around inviting Morton to court and to the Council, of which he was no longer a member. When he arrived, however, the king took him hunting. He was not only friendly but solicitous and toward the end of the afternoon said, "Father, only you have reared me and I will therefore defend you from your enemies."[3] That was somewhat histrionic, but James was a florid speaker.

Morton was puzzled, and Lord Robert Stuart whispered to him that he was in danger and should fly. The earl looked at the king's smiling and friendly face and could not believe it.

On the evening of December 31, 1580, the earl of Morton was placed under arrest at his apartment in Holyrood Palace. That was a Saturday. On Monday morning he was conveyed to Edinburgh Castle under guard headed by Captain James Stewart, while—as Sir James Melville later wrote —"all looked through their fingers to see his fall."[4]

It was not the news of Morton's fall that disturbed Elizabeth so much as the news of the charge that was to be placed against him. He was to be tried for the crime the Reform imputed to Mary Stuart—and even the Queen of England, rapt in her own pleasures, could grasp the meaning of that.

Finally alarmed, the English queen gave Burghley permission to move at last. Walsingham's secret agents, who had been carefully tracking the youthful Jesuit invaders, swooped down and arrested several. The young priests, in the country illegally, were conveyed and imprisoned in "underground cells lighted by tunnels sloping toward and closely grated to prevent communication. The prison diet was bread, beer, salt fish and water not the freshest."[5] They were questioned and as the year 1581 slowly extended, were brought, one by one, to an intimate acquaintance with the rack—which stood "in a long vaulted chamber beneath the Armory."[6]

The use of torture had long been forbidden in England, and Elizabeth was fond of reminding the world that her kingdom—unlike Spain and its Inquisition—did not persecute people for their inner beliefs so long as they respected the outer forms of the official religion. But the disputes that arose in the wake of Luther, Calvin, Knox, and others had opened the gates of rebellion and unrest in every country of Europe—and ushered ideological war, with all its subterranean moves, propaganda, enforced conformities, and conspiratorial trappings, into life. Torture—for the first time since the days of the Caesars—was once again a part of the dark underside of all Europe's governments.

The plight of the young priests in the Tower of London fed the agitation created by the efforts of Campion and Parsons. The Catholic cause in aristocratic England and in the traditional-minded countryside began to flare into renewed life. For the first time considerable numbers openly refused to attend Anglican services; incipient rebelliousness began to emerge into open defiance. In response, the government passed severe laws against secret Catholic services or meetings—or failure to attend the official Anglican Church. The Treason Act had several side effects: one was to bind the bishops of the Church of England and the Crown together—another was to put Elizabeth into better standing with a Reform-dominated Parliament.

In May 1581, however, Mary Stuart's cause received impetus from the trial of the earl of Morton in Edinburgh. He had, for almost six months, been held in the fortress of Dunbarton—in irons. Then he was brought to trial in Edinburgh, where, said Sir James Melville, "he had few friends to appear or to act for him. His gold and silver was transported long before by his natural son James Douglas, and one of his servants called John Macmorran. It was first carried in barrels and afterward hid in secret parts; part was given to be kept by some who were looked upon as his friends who made ill account of it, so that for the most landed in bad hands."[7]

The result was that the proud earl arrived under custody in Edinburgh destitute and "when he went through the streets to the Tollbooth toward his assize [trial] was compelled to borrow twenty shillings to distribute to the poor, who asked him for alms, for God's sake."[8]

His judges consisted of men he had balked: Argyll, Seton, Maxwell, Eglinton, and others. Officially, the charge was high treason; its substance consisted of the fact that Morton knew in advance of the plot to kill Darnley —and had not spoken against it. Sir James Balfour testified that Bothwell had brought Morton back from exile for the purpose of committing the murder and no defense was allowed. The deliberations of his judges were as predictable as the seasons, and mercifully brief. The verdict announced that Morton had been guilty of being "art and part of the murder of King Henry."

"Art and part!" Morton cried, striking the floor with his staff. "Art and part! God knows the contrary."[9]

His sentence was to be hanged, drawn, and quartered. After Morton had been hustled from the courtroom, the time was set at the following day. His judges did not want any time to elapse, lest Morton be somehow rescued. The procedure then in vogue was grisly and protracted. It called for the condemned to have his genitals cut off and burned before his eyes, to be strangled to the edge of death and then resuscitated, and finally to have his head chopped off and his body divided into four quarters—and for these parts to be displayed in prominent public places.

In his last night—though he was not informed of this—Morton wrote an appeal to the young king. James, ensconced in Holyrood, shrank from examining what his former guardian wrote. "He would not look . . . but ranged up and down upon the floor of his chamber, clanking with his finger and thumb."[10]

The king did, however, cheat the ever-present crowds of at least part of its grisly and morbid pleasure by indicating that Morton's head alone would satisfy his sense of royal justice. That decision, hailed as a sign of mercy by some parties then and later, shortened the earl's ordeal.

Morton ascended the scaffold in the melting heat of June 2, 1581. His gaze flickered upward at The Maiden—a weighted blade enclosed in a frame that he had himself installed.[11]

He spoke bravely to the crowd, ignoring grinning faces, and said the king was losing a good, a dutiful servant. Then he walked over and put his head under The Maiden. The ministers began to pray aloud, and Morton's voice could be heard joining theirs; he made a signal with his hand. The blade flashed down, his head tumbled, and an immense fountain of blood gushed forth like a red sewer. Later his head was "sett upon a prick, on the highest stone of the gavell of the Tolbuith, toward the public street."[12]

Elizabeth, when she heard the news, said, "That false Scotch urchin!"[13]

10 The Vatican, which had not forgotten that its faith emerged from martyrdom, watched while the age-old formula worked once again in England. The authorities pursued, arrested, and mistreated the Jesuits, and, as a result, a wave of sympathy for these ardent young men washed across the land. Their leader, Edmund Campion, operating underground, famous for his eloquence and constantly on the move, nevertheless found time enough to compose and find a printer to publish a pamphlet entitled *Ten Reasons for Being a Catholic.* Its appearance created a sensation, and Campion left the safety of the sprawling tangle of London for a daring speaking round of secret speeches in the pro-Vatican countryside.

This effort brought him near his old school, Oxford. He could not resist a visit. Old colleagues and youths attracted by his fame rallied around, and their enthusiasm was so great that he agreed to give a speech at the manor home of the Yates family a few days later. The news reached Eliot, an agent of Leicester, and on the appointed day the authorities surrounded the house. Campion spoke after a Mass was served, and the authorities rushed the residence. Campion and two other priests took refuge in a secret room reached through a narrow between-wall stairway, whose entrance was hidden behind Mrs. Yates's bed. The search took a long time and was almost unsuccessful until Eliot thumped a section of wall that returned a hollow sound. It was broken down, and Campion, together with the other priests, was discovered and hauled away.

Within a few weeks Campion, who confronted his interrogators bravely, was stretched on the Tower rack. His arrest caused great excitement; his confinement and ordeal sent the Vatican world into frenzies. Don Bernardino de Mendoza, the Spanish ambassador to England, was besieged by appeals to have his great master, Philip II, intervene.

Don Bernardino would have been delighted. The behavior of the Queen of England had made his duty a nightmare to the point where he openly prayed to be relieved. She had received the notorious Francis Drake upon his return from an extended trip that left looted and sunken treasure ships of Spain, huge Spanish losses of life and property behind him. Not only had Elizabeth received Drake, but she accepted a large share of his loot and made him a knight.

When the pretender to the Portuguese throne, Don Antonio, appeared in London, Elizabeth received him and even lent him money. Don Antonio, in return, had to pledge the Braganza diamonds. Don Antonio then bought some ships and was having them outfitted to plague Philip II over the crown of Portugal.

At the same time, the English queen let it be known she was madly in love with the duke of Anjou and wanted to marry him as soon as possible. Since the duke had meanwhile involved himself with the Netherlands, this led the Spanish to believe that England and France would unite against them.

In all, the post of Spanish ambassador to London was no pleasure while Elizabeth ruled. Don Bernadino would certainly have snatched at any reasonable plan for Spanish intervention. His master was, indeed, slowly turning his cool and calculating gaze in that direction. But the key to the conquest of England at that point, Don Bernadino said, was in Scotland. Mary Stuart agreed.


The Queen of Scots, whose mail was uncensored and whose captivity in the Shrewsbury mansion was easy, had watched events in Scotland with painful eagerness. The death of Moray had been such a pleasure to her that she pensioned his murderer. The death of Morton was equally wonderful in her eyes, and her constant thought was on how she could reenter her realm.

The years had taken their toll of Mary Stuart. Beneath her wigs—and she never appeared without one—her hair had turned gray and was kept closely cropped. Her once graceful figure had thickened, and she had acquired a double chin. Her lips were tight, and her face had the sharp, wary look of an unfree person. She had grown noticeably pious and spent a great deal of time at her devotions. Attended by a priest, who was allowed to remain though his disguise was transparent, she had come to believe that her troubles were due to her religious affiliation and not to any fault of her own.

Falling into an argument with the countess of Shrewsbury, she found that virago had filled the air of England with scandalous inventions about her, including the charge that she had conceived and then murdered several bastards while in captivity. She wrote Elizabeth a long letter of complaint on this matter—and repeated in it, with open relish, charges the countess had made against her own queen as well. These had included the whisper

—widespread in the realm—that Elizabeth had some physical abnormality that made normal intercourse impossible and that she satisfied "her lusts in different ways." She threw in, for good measure, the charge that Elizabeth's ulcerated leg, which resembled her father's, was in fact a sign of syphilis. Her hatred, in other words, could no longer be contained.

That remarkable letter, whose contents are still occasionally used to chop at the legend of Elizabeth, resulted in the earl of Shrewsbury's having to appear before the queen to explain his wife's attitude. The earl was not surprised to hear about the countess's tongue and its activity. She had, he told the queen, called him a "knave, fool and a beast and mocked and mowed at him."[1] Elizabeth laughed and let him go. But Mary Stuart was transferred from the comfortable Shrewsbury establishment—however uncomfortable psychologically—to the cooler and more rigorous charge of Sir Ralph Sadler and the moated and uncomfortable Tutbury Castle.

As usual, there was more to the move than appeared on the surface. The letter and the revelations about the countess of Shrewsbury were nothing new; it was the revelations of the captured Jesuits that concerned the Privy Council and the queen. The strength of the Vatican Party in England was rising—and Mary Stuart remained its pole star.


The fall of Morton left Esmé Stuart the most powerful man in Scotland. He not only held the king in thrall, but was raised to the title of duke of Lennox and acknowledged as the first prince of the blood. It seemed, in fact, that he could do no wrong in the eyes of his cousin—and the secret of his power had begun to seep out of the confines of the court. "His Majesty having conceived an inward affection to the Lord d'Aubigny, entered in great familiarity and *quiet purposes* with him."[2]

Other signs often seen in homosexual circles began to increase. Worthy men became subjects of ridicule, conversations were loaded with filthy innuendoes, and the young king—formerly noted for precocious learning— soon displayed a truly unusual, even staggering talent for scatology.

This was not the best of atmospheres for Esmé to press toward lofty goals, but he was caught between the pressures from France and rising dissatisfactions from the Reform movement of the Scots. That movement had not watched the ruin of Morton and the subversion of its case against Mary Stuart without understanding the event, or Esmé Stuart. Andrew Melville, Knox's successor, was in just as close contact with the Calvinists in Europe as his predecessor—and had the advantage of the writings of George Buchanan—which served as an intellectual bridge between theology and politics.

Melville and the Reform leaders moved rapidly. In early 1581 a second

*Book of Discipline* was issued that carried Knox's theories straight into the political arena. Where Knox had talked of the Kingdom of God, of a realm where the principles of early Christianity would dominate, Melville and his followers talked of two kingdoms: one of the world, and one of the Lord's. The state, which represented the world, could have control over all worldly matters—but the Reform would rule the rest. Divided powers, in other words; separation of Church and State.

No greater contrast to Vatican reasoning could be found. The Scots Reformers had, by now, established through Knox and Buchanan an intellectual presence in the international Calvinist diaspora that affected the theories and approaches of the greater body. Buchanan's *De Jure Regni,* which argued the limits of sovereigns and was distributed widely through northern Europe, joined *Vindiciae Contra Tyrannos,* written by Hubert Lanquet—a book along the same lines—and hundreds of pamphlets broke their bulky contents into more easily digestible splinters for the average man.

The response of the Vatican, however, was impressive. No new movement could approach its deep, subtle, and experienced techniques, refined through a thousand years of experiment and observation. It not only had treasures of the past with which to lure and convince, but new works—such as *The Dark Night of the Soul* by Juan de Yepes—appeared, accompanied by hundreds of pamphlets. In a political sense, the Vatican not only controlled and ruled vast areas and millions of people, but was master of a system that blended Church and State in a manner that Philip II conspicuously followed to create a monolith.

Internationally, Spain and the Vatican cooperated to create a Catholic League, headed in France by the duke of Guise, which coined a slogan appealing in its simplicity and easily argued: *One Faith, One Law, One King.*[3]

No group could have seemed less able to affect such great movements, tides, and ideas than the grotesque coterie that had gathered around the reedy, youthful, and boorish young putative king of Scotland or his dwarfish court. Yet France and the Vatican were involved and served Esmé Stuart as he softly persuaded James to write—and to listen—to his exiled mother, Mary Stuart.

The king listened and wrote some dutiful letters that were joyfully received by the exile. Meanwhile, the court at Holyrood gradually filled with figures from Mary Stuart's past. The once-young George Douglas, who had helped her escape from Lochleven, appeared and became a favorite. The laird of Fernihurst, who had taken part in the raid at Stirling that resulted in the death of the king's grandfather, appeared and received a full pardon. The earls of Huntly, Eglinton, and Caithness; the Lord Seton; and others grew tall on the landscape once again.

Meanwhile, the boy king found life more enjoyable, in every sense, than any he had ever known. Buchanan and his books were gone; the old scholar was back to his own writing. Morton was gone; the Reform leaders and their complaints seemed no longer fearsome or important. The young king had fallen into the habit of obscenities in which the name of the Deity appeared more often than not—and some ministers remonstrated. "I thank you," he said and laughed aloud.

The young king was, in his opinion, liberated—and enthroned. Esmé was at one side to handle the serious matters of the realm, and the former Captain James Stewart, a major instrument in the ruin of Morton, was at the other. The young king loved Esmé and liked James Stewart, to whom he had given not only a large part of the Hamilton estates, but the Hamilton title of earl of Arran as well.

His favorites gave James's court a curious aspect; it seemed half French and half traditionally Scot. The new earl of Arran was an adventurer about the same age as Esmé, interested in nothing but himself, with a reputation as a fighter and swashbuckler. Under his encouragement, James developed and extended his flair for filthy jokes, for scatology in general; indulged his passion for hunting prodigiously; and relaxed in dissipation. To the suspicious and watchful eyes of the Reform, the earl was leading the young king toward loose women, "provoking him to the pleasures of the flesh and fostering him in foolish talk."[4] He was, in other words, a foil who helped the young king to maintain a facade of normality—and his presence showed an intuitive craftiness in the young boy with the old eyes that was both remarkable and unpleasant to contemplate.

That slyness showed in another area to disconcert even Esmé Stuart. Young James was a rapt listener to tales of how the authority of Catholic kings was supported by their bishops. That pleased him; he was in favor of that. But he resisted any efforts to incline him toward the Vatican faith as such, and his interest in his mother was tepid.

That was made plain when Mary Stuart, acting in concert with the duke of Guise, proposed that she and James form an "association" and share the crown of Scotland. The offer would enable James to achieve at least quasi-recognition and exchange ambassadors with other nations, could push him into becoming his mother's champion, and lead toward a renewal of the Scots alliance with France.

That proposition brought Elizabeth running, politically speaking. She sent an agent north with instructions to bribe the earl of Arran and to foster the creation of a new pro-English party and was dashed to discover the border was closed. That was alarming, and the English queen stood before the window in front of her ladies-in-waiting and exclaimed angrily, "That false villain of Scotland! That villain for whom I have done so much! The night before Morton was taken he could call him father. He could say he had no friend like Morton who brought him up and that he would protect him. And the next day he had him seized and cut off his head. What must I look for from such a double-tongued scoundrel as this?"[5]

The double-tongued scoundrel, however, had no intention of becoming his mother's champion. He was living in an adolescent paradise, where every wish was gratified, and he was daily introduced to pleasures he had not before known. His relationship with Esmé provided the euphoria of an early love affair. He began not only to write poetry, but to surround himself with poets and scholars whose hothouse personalities balanced the rough huntsmen and the earl of Arran. When Arran, jealous of Esmé's great powers and closeness to the king, provoked an argument, James showed an unexpected firmness and had the argumentative earl banished from court. Nobody could come between him and his fascinating cousin.

That relationship, however, had now been assessed by the leaders of the Reform. They had watched the gathering Vatican nobles around the king, and the *Second Book of Discipline* had marked the areas they chose for contention. Esmé had not realized that and proposed to appoint the chaplain of Stirling, one Robert Montgomerie, to the post of bishop of Glasgow.

That decision provided the Reform with an issue, and its leaders proceeded to make the most of it. Morton had retained bishops, and the majority of these were sees left over from Vatican days, in which high nobles retained title and the revenues of important properties. Gradually, the former regent had introduced his own men into these posts in an arrangement where they kept only part of the incomes and funneled the rest back to the government. The Reform labeled that practice "simony" in its official documents—and "Tulchan Bishops" in its explanations to the people. A *tulchan* was a calfskin stuffed with straw that fooled a cow into letting down its milk. The analogy made the issue clear to an agricultural nation.

In an era without newspapers, the ministers of the Kirk, privy to the bulletins that circulated through the Calvinist diaspora, served the people as combinations of political leaders, moral judges, and journalists. Their orations on Sundays and at the endless Bible and prayer meetings conducted through the week provided information as well as exhortation and direction. Their campaign against Esmé's decision to plant Montgomerie into the see of Glasgow and siphon its funds for court pleasures and political purposes was an ideal issue on which to rally the people against a foreign favorite. It personalized the aura of corruption that surrounded Esmé and James and even Arran. Beyond that, as Melville and his associates knew well, loomed the great issue of separating Church and State—of whether the clergy could select its own leaders, or whether the king could act as a petty pope.

A delegation of ministers called upon James and insisted that the appointment be withdrawn—or Montgomerie would be excommunicated.

"We will not suffer [let] you," James said bravely.

"We obey God rather than men," John Durie answered. "We pray God remove evil company from about you. The welfare of the Kirk is your welfare, and the more sharply vice is rebuked the better for you."[6] That dissolved the young king's self-confidence and sent Esmé into a rage. He was placed in a position from which he could not retreat without being weakened and could not go forward without increasing his troubles.


While Esmé and James struggled with the Reform in Scotland, the English government tried to smother the influence of Edmund Campion and his ardent young Jesuits. At one point, the queen had Campion brought to the palace for a private conversation—for she remembered him as one of the stars from Oxford years earlier. Despite the confrontation, he remained firm.

Campion found the attentions of his interrogators savage. They pulled his fingernails and racked him several times. He appeared in court in late November with a broken arm. Despite that, he defied his judges eloquently; his speeches were widely reprinted and distributed. He and a number of younger priests were sentenced to be hanged, drawn, and quartered. The execution took place a few days before Christmas 1581; all the men went to their deaths nobly. The slaughter evoked waves of sympathy and aroused fervent pro-Vatican reaction among many. Tidal waves of propaganda from Rome and its supporters, and from Geneva and the Reform, washed across both realms.

Toward the end of 1581 and into 1582 the positions of the English and Scots governments and their mirror-image problems intersected when Crichton, a young Jesuit trained by Dr. Allen in Rome and acquainted with the pope—followed shortly by another named Holt—scurried in disguise across the border to talk to Esmé and James.

The young priests were encouraged, to some extent, by the Spanish ambassador to England—Don Bernadino de Mendoza. He assured them that if James converted, he could expect help from Philip II of Spain. That assurance seemed a statement of the obvious, since such help would be almost inevitable if the young king of Scotland made so great a turn. In the hands of the Jesuits, however, it was converted into a proposition.

Mary Stuart, kept informed of these moves, added a stream of secret messages, exhortations, suggestions, and plans that gave her the illusion of participation and, in fact, encouraged much running about by parties who shared her confidence.

Over several months the Jesuits crept in and out of Scotland, back and forth from France to London, and their conversations expanded into a complex and wildly unrealistic plot. The Scots, who were attracted, did not quite understand that the young priests were not the pope, any more than others could realize that the pope was not Philip II.

Propaganda had carried the issues beyond reality and encouraged expectations that exceeded all possibilities. Mary Stuart came to believe that Philip II would evoke an army from the air that would descend upon England to free and enthrone her. The pro-Vatican party in Scotland, infused with the same belief, haggled with the young Jesuits over terms. In due course, Mendoza and his master, Philip II, were both staggered to learn the Jesuits had promised that Spain would send 15,000 troops to Scotland at once.[7]

While this great chimera floated aloft, the Reform movement in Scotland mounted its campaign against Esmé and his new bishop of Glasgow. Montgomerie appeared in the city, attempted to enter the pulpit, and was physically thrown out of the church. Crowds gathered; agitation was constant—and the Reform was in direct opposition to the Crown of Scotland for the first time since the days of Mary Stuart.

An indication of its methods was provided when a foreigner, a Frenchman—carrying messages from the duke of Guise to Esmé—was tracked by the Calvinists from Paris to Edinburgh. Once in Edinburgh, he was pointed out to crowds as a man known to have taken part in the St. Bartholomew Massacre. He barely escaped death in the outcry that ensued. By this time ministers were thundering from their pulpits, and John Durie rose in Glasgow to denounce Esmé as "the corrupter" of the young king.

Summoned to Dalkeith Castle before Esmé to answer for these charges, Durie later said the duke's French cooks had emerged from their smoky kitchen caverns to menace him with their skewers and great knives. Esmé called him *un petit diable* and he was ordered—with his followers—out of the capital. Durie obeyed the banishment, but the leaders of the Kirk excommunicated Montgomerie.

In the midst of this seething scene, Crichton appeared before Esmé again to assure him he could obtain 15,000 seasoned Spanish troops from Philip II if he could convert James. The Frenchman's response came close to hysteria. If he could not convert the boy, he said, he would force him to act in unison or he would seize him physically and send him to Spain to be converted, or he would depose him and place Mary Stuart on the throne, or—and he paused—he would wait to hear what Mary Stuart recommended. In other words, he was lost in depths too deep for him to fathom.

The king, meanwhile, hunted and wrote poems. A portrait was painted, at about this time, by an unknown artist of considerable skill. It shows a youth with a long, pale, closed face, whose deeply socketed eyes look warily at the world.[8] He had found companions who included Alexander Montgomerie, a poet of some talent, and Robert Hudson, who had been one of his musicians at Stirling. His old nurse, Helena Little, came to court and made him a present of some poems by Du Bartas, the French Huguenot—for news of his inclinations had traveled far. Yet it was significant that none could actually trace any specific decisions—and many were made—to the suggestions or opinions of the boy who had passed his sixteenth birthday and was heading into early manhood. He seemed content, though uneasy from time to time, to watch his favorite's progress almost like a spectator at his own life.

Esmé's problems were more complex. He was a foreigner, and his mastery of the language of Scotland had been slow. That was a handicap. A greater handicap was an inability to attract first-class men. He turned, after their reconciliation, toward Arran—but that greedy individual quarreled with virtually everyone, including the earl of Mar and the earl of Glencairn and Lord Lindsay.

Esmé was being isolated, while the Reform agitation over the appointment of the bishop of Glasgow, Montgomerie, soared into a huge dispute. When the General Assembly of the Kirk met in June 1582, Melville made it clear that not only was Montgomerie excommunicated, but that the Kirk was meditating the expulsion of Esmé as well. Melville declared that bishops were a papal disguise and that as soon as Esmé had planted enough, he would drop the disguise for the reality. The argument left the favorite no room to retreat because it demanded he not only drop Montgomerie, but the entire institution of bishops.

In response, Esmé wanted to know whether the Reform or the king ruled the realm. The Reformers replied that James was being false to his trust, his contract with the people. Knox's doctrines, as expanded by Buchanan, had become imbedded in their attitude. They drew the argument into a statement and, headed by Melville, carried it to the palace to place it before the boy king.

"Who dares subscribe to these treasonable articles?" asked Arran, who was beside James at that moment.[9]

"We dare," said Melville. "We dare, and will render our lives in the Cause." He snatched a pen from a clerk and wrote his name in large angry letters before the earl and the king. His supporters crowded around him to add their names as well and Esmé stalked out of the chamber in purple anger.

In an attempt to prove that the Reform leaders did not really have the support they claimed, Esmé sent Montgomerie back into Edinburgh with yet another armed guard. A crowd collected, and the guard decided to take the unhappy new bishop to the tollbooth, where he could be safe behind thick stone walls, but some unknown parties vanished with the keys. They reached the gate, and the crowd at their heels formed a great jeering cluster. In short order, missiles were brought up from the Grassmarket, and the air began to fill with eggs, vegetables, stones, horse droppings, and whatever came handy. The miserable Montgomerie had to be taken down side alleys and hustled out of sight.[10]

The description of it sent James into gales of laughter, but it was clear the court was in trouble. When James and Esmé attended a service in Perth together, the minister leaned over the pulpit to berate the duke to his face. Esmé's temper cracked, and he jumped up to shout his answers in heavily accented Scots; James pulled him down and put his hand over his mouth.

Matters were obviously headed for a climax of sorts, and Esmé made preparations, together with pro-Vatican diehards Lords Maxwell, Ker of Fernihurst, and others, to obtain soldiers from the duke of Guise and put down an incipient rebellion. The target date for this effort was set for August 27, 1582. James, hunting as usual, was assured all would go well. On the twenty-second of the month, only five days before Esmé's elaborate plans were to be realized, the young king on his way from Perth was met near the castle of Gowrie by the earl. It was suggested that he favor the Ruthven family by staying overnight. Smiling, the boy king rode into the castle surrounded by a group who seemed more grim than the occasion warranted.

The following morning James rose and dressed and was about to leave when the master of Glamis barred the way. The king pretended to be surprised and blustered profanely, but the men grinned. Suddenly, he broke into tears, and their faces registered contempt. Glamis, his lips turned down, said, "Tis no matter of his tears. Better that bairns should weep than bearded men."[11]

# 11

The coup had been well planned, and its purposes extended beyond the old Scots practice of holding the king hostage for mere personal gain. James, the very child and symbol of the Reform, which named him king against all the world, was to learn its power was unbroken.

Removed to Stirling, the castle where he first learned discipline and the Calvinist theology, James found himself forced to listen to John Durie, the fiery little minister whom Esmé had banished from the capital. At the same time the Lords of the Enterprise, as they termed themselves, placed a bitter proclamation in front of him. Despite his tears and a refusal to eat, he was forced to sign a statement in which Esmé and Lennox were "charged with having conspired to destroy religion, to corrupt his own morals, to break the alliance with England and betray the country to the Pope."[1]

He did not—then or later—comprehend that such a proclamation in his own name restored him to the most powerful group in the country and placed him, at least on paper, at their head. Instead, wrote Sir James Melville, the young king "took the matter further to his heart than any man would have believed, lamenting his hard estate and mishandling by his own subjects, and how he was thought but a beast by other princes for suffering such indignities."[2]

Arran had been seized at Fife and sent to Edinburgh under guard, where the provost, a supporter, kept him in easy confinement—but kept him. Esmé, uneasy at Dalkeith, also traveled to the capital and at first attempted to brave the situation. On the first Sunday after the king's capture Esmé attempted to retain his standing by attending services in the capital. He heard himself denounced from the pulpit at the same time that his young conquest, James, was listening to harsh words from John Durie in the pulpit at Stirling.

On the fourth of September 1582, Esmé received an object lesson difficult to ignore. John Durie, the fiery little minister he had banished from the capital indefinitely, returned in triumph. The Kirk had spread news of his coming and prepared a demonstration. The response of the city was overwhelming. Thousands of people poured out to surround the little man at Gallows Green and packed about him, chanting Psalms, as he passed through the streets and reentered his church. For the first time Esmé saw the crowds that had sent Mary Stuart into hysterics years before and realized the depths of the revolution that coursed beneath the surface of the realm.[3]

"The Duke," it was said, "was more afraid of that sight than anything he had ever before seen in Scotland."[4]

It was enough, in fact, to send him out of the capital under cover of night, and he did not stop riding until he had reached the castle of Dunbarton. There he was in pro-Vatican territory, where Fernihurst and others crowded about with suggestions. They had border men who were waiting to be called, but the duke of Lennox had strangely altered. The flashing courtier who had so charmed the boy king and had seemed so sure in all situations sat, drumming his fingers on the side of his chair, or paced back and forth without giving any instructions or drawing any plans.

James was also undergoing an ordeal he was to never forget. It was as though a nightmare had come alive: he had been plucked from early manhood and plunged back to the status and the conditions of childhood. He wanted to go riding, and the earl of Gowrie carelessly refused permission. He rushed at the door and the earl casually put his booted leg across the sill and barred his passage. The young king shouted he would not bear such treatment and would appeal to his subjects; and Gowrie, grinning, shouted for someone to bring a rocking horse.

One day a messenger arrived from Esmé and was allowed to enter. James shouted that he was prisoner and that he wanted to be rescued. That was, in fact, his dream—and it died hard.

Meanwhile, a new proclamation was placed before him. It declared the king had no intention of ruling the Reform and that the Kirk was free. That great step, separating Church and State, evoked more wild outcries from James. "The ministers were a pack of knaves, and he would rather lose his kingdom than not be avenged upon them."[5] But he signed.

He signed because beneath the bluster he knew there was a limit to his resistance and to the patience of his captors. He had been taught the history of the realm, and he knew that for more than a century every king of Scotland had died by violence.

One night, filled with self-pity he wrote on a wall:

A prisoner I am
And liberty would have.

The following morning he was chilled to read some unknown hand had
added two more lines beneath his. They read:

A Papist thou art and friend to a slave;
A rope though deservest and that thou shalt have.[6]


In September 1582 the young king heard, with no regret, that his old
tutor George Buchanan had died. Buchanan's last year or two found him
living in a modest house in Kennedy's Close in Edinburgh. Andrew Melville, Knox's successor as leader of the Kirk, called upon him in these last
months. He found the old poet teaching the alphabet to his only remaining
young servant.

"I see you are not idle," Melville said, and Buchanan grinned.

"Better this," he said, "than tending sheep."

Not long afterward the old man could not get up. He asked the young
servant how much money was in the house and commented that it would
not be enough to pay for his funeral. "Give it to the poor," he ordered.

"But who is to pay for your funeral?" asked the servant.

"It doesn't matter," Buchanan replied. "They can either let my body
stay here, or do whatever they choose with it."[7]

The town chose to give him a quite proper funeral and placed him in
a new cemetery called Greyfriars. He was (and would remain for centuries)
its greatest resident.


The bleak winter of 1582 slowly shifted into 1583, and the world
turned with little notice of the boy king of Scotland and his erstwhile
favorite, Esmé Stuart, duke of Lennox. Some suggestions drifted from
London to Scotland that there would be no grief in England if both Esmé
and Arran were to die—but the Scots Reform leaders were not inclined to
behave in that manner.

The Kirk in Scotland, unlike the Church of England, whose bishops
bowed before their queen, was genuinely religious. Melville and other Scots
divines never instituted any blood purges.

The Reform nobles in Scotland, however, continued to hope for English money. The sums they had in mind were not large: £10,000 in an
immediate lump and £5,000 a year from the Lennox estates in England
would be enough. Such an income would so establish James in reasonable

comfort that he would forgive their rough handling. While sending agents south to plea for that support, they pressed the young king to banish Esmé from Scotland.

Unfortunately, Elizabeth would not help with money. After many delays, she offered £2,500 a year. The Scots, regretfully, considered that too close to an open insult to accept. Their position was frozen by the unshakable hostility of the English queen to their Reform revolution and all its principles. The Kirk proclamations on the separation of Church and State had been regarded by her with loathing and anger. No matter how irritating her behavior, Elizabeth could not shake the conviction that Mary Stuart was the true queen of Scotland and her son merely a tool in the hands of rebels who threatened all royalty. Esmé's downfall, now clear to all observers since he lacked the will to organize an opposition, seemed to her proof of her own great sagacity. She turned toward an old idea that Mary Stuart herself had conceived: the Queen of Scots should hold the throne with her son, but use no authority.

In Paris, where King Henry III, his mother Catherine de Médicis and the duke of Guise were all disappointed at Esmé's difficulties, some other plans emerged. Perhaps a stronger Frenchman could hold Esmé's pro-Vatican party together. Perhaps James could marry into the French royal family—or close to it. The duke of Guise had nieces, princesses of Lorraine, whom he could produce.

In Madrid, Philip II, informed as always by his spies, began to reassess the entire situation. The king of France was killing himself with weird and obscene practices. His gaunt white face with its feverish dark eyes resembled death itself. The heir was the duke of Anjou, who was fighting Spain in the Netherlands. Behind them stood the king of Navarre, a Reform sovereign. Elizabeth's sea war, though undeclared, was costing Spain millions in real treasure and almost as much in terms of influence. If the pope could be brought to spend some of his vast fortune, perhaps Spain would move.

The French sent an ambassador toward Scotland. He was La Mothe Fénelon, who had once served as ambassador to England, and was well known to Elizabeth. That sent all sorts of alarm through Burghley and the Privy Council, and they delayed the diplomat while they sought to discover the nature of his orders.

The long wait had been hard on James and even harder on Esmé. Walled in the castle of Dunbarton, his provisions ran low, and he was increasingly isolated. At one point, he took ship for France, but for various reasons returned and took refuge at Blackness Castle. The Lords of the Enterprise, meanwhile, forced James to send several orders for Esmé to leave the country, but their wording was so unlike the boy that Esmé realized they had been obtained by force or threat of force.

Finally, however, a scrawled note arrived. It was real, and Esmé knew that at once. It repeated James's love, but said his life was in danger as long as Esmé remained in Scotland. He was asked to leave, and the young king assured him that when he had regained his authority, he would have him return, and all would be as before.

The note arrived on the heels of a safe passage guarantee from England, whose queen wanted to see him. That miraculous coincidence was more than enough: Esmé saddled and rode south. Ironically, he met La Mothe Fénelon and an English observer, Davison, at the border. The two Frenchmen whispered together in the rain while the Englishman Davison tried, in vain, to eavesdrop. The downpour, he said afterward, kept him from catching even a single word.[8]

In London a little later, Elizabeth regarded the fallen favorite with intense curiosity. She knew the nature of his relationship with young James, but the court of England, as indeed all of Europe at the time, was familiar with homosexuals and she did not dwell on that subject. Her interest was in assessing Esmé as a political force.

The Virgin was in one of her gracious humors. She allowed Esmé, as a duke, to keep his hat on in her presence; she had, after all, triumphed over his efforts in Scotland. She taxed him with having been sent to Scotland by the duke of Guise, of consorting with Jesuits against her, and seeking to ruin the English alliance with the Scots—but she did it without the icy menace she knew so well how to convey.

Esmé protested these accusations were all false, all based on lies told by enemies. He had been converted by the king of Scotland, and his conversion had been sincere. He had struggled with the Scots on behalf of England; he had never dealt with the duke of Guise. Elizabeth estimated the graceful figure, very much at his ease in a court, and looked thoughtfully into Esmé's sparkling black eyes. The Virgin was not always wise and had many faults, but her ability to judge the quality of men was unequaled. She smiled and turned from Esmé Stuart as though from a piece of furniture. He was never again to enter her thoughts or her conversation.

The duke then sent a hurried, coded letter to Don Bernadino de Mendoza, the Spanish ambassador, protesting that he remained a true pro-Vatican supporter beneath his disguise as a Reformer—which was essential to his return to Scotland as soon as its king was restored. He then fled to Paris.

**12** With Scotland almost in their hands again, Burghley, the Virgin's principal adviser on the Privy Council, and Walsingham, the spymaster *extraordinaire* for England, were dismayed to learn that the queen had decided to handle matters herself. They groaned but could not protest.

Months of maneuvering had brought the pro-English reform faction in Scotland to the fore and placed the young King James in its power. The remaining problem was to swing James toward England. It was believed that could be done, provided that the young king were given the income from his grandfather's English estates.

Elizabeth disagreed. She hated to part with money unless the recipient was near her personally. Turning toward the lawyers, she received a ruling that no foreigner could benefit from the income of English lands—and clung to that point with fanatic obstinacy. Meanwhile, her devious and unfathomable mind conceived an elaborate new scheme.

She had an elaborate agreement drawn up, in which she offered Mary Stuart her liberty providing her cousin would agree to abandon her claim to the English throne, promise never to meddle in political matters again, live in England and remain within a ten-mile radius of an estate, "associate" her sovereignty with her son, James—and pay her own expenses. That offer was read to Mary Stuart, who listened in a darkened room—the atmosphere in which she usually heard Elizabeth's messages—and was eagerly accepted. The Queen of Scots, at that point, would have signed in blood to gain her freedom.

Then Elizabeth, having obtained Mary Stuart's signature, had Sir Robert Bowes, her emissary in Edinburgh, carry a copy to James. The young king recoiled. It suddenly appeared as though his captivity had been aimed toward such a conclusion and his "kingship," as he called it, was in most fearful jeopardy. Pressed for an immediate answer by the experienced Bowes, the boy stammered that he wished his mother "would give over her plots. He must look toward his present as well as his future interests. He refused to be a party to any agreement in which he himself was to be compromised until he saw more deeply into his mother's meaning."[1]

Elizabeth was delighted. She was now able to tell Mary Stuart she could not release her because her son did not agree to her generous offer. At the same time, she had a new insight and a marvelous new weapon over James. By threatening him with his mother, she could control his future behavior.

While Elizabeth was enjoying, amid other distractions, her latest cat-and-mouse game with Mary Stuart and James, the Frenchman La Mothe Fénelon and another—the Marquis de Mainville—were spreading gold coins among the nobility of Scotland with a heavy hand. The earls of Argyll, Huntly, and Montrose benefited, as befitted old allies; the earl of Arran, who had been released from captivity and was eagerly awaiting James's restoration, was also enlisted.

The earl of Gowrie, the master of Glamis, and his other captors, meanwhile, found their reasons for holding the young king had diminished with the disappearance of Esmé Stuart. The king himself had stopped weeping and made an adjustment; conversations were now civil. Since they had acted in the king's name, it was necessary to allow him to appear on state business, to receive foreign visitors, and to resume his normal role.

To release the king, however, would have placed the earl of Gowrie and his associates in peril of their lives. To keep him meant to pay 300 armed men serving around the clock, indefinitely. They could not afford to have the king taken by the pro-Vatican faction, and his continued detention would bankrupt them. Their need for money grew increasingly acute. Finally, they sent two men—Colonel Stewart and Sir John Colville—south to plead again with Elizabeth.

To help their allies in Scotland, Walsingham and Burghley attempted to pave the way for the Scots commissioners by proposing a budget of £10,000 a year. Elizabeth turned icy and said she "would sooner marry James than give him that much money."[2]

The Scots commissioners arrived and presented James's own solution. The young king asked for only £5,000 a year or his grandparent's estate. If either request were granted, he would forswear any foreign entanglement and would be a firm English ally. Otherwise, he would have to look for help where it could be found.

Since James's commissioners had not mentioned his mother, Elizabeth immediately said no treaty could be signed unless Mary Stuart was a party to it. Then she offered to lend some money, providing "the large towns and chosen persons of the nobility of both factions would be sureties for the repayment."

Walsingham attempted to intervene, and Elizabeth's temper, always savage to her most trusted men, flared in response. "Her servants and favorites," she raged, "professed to love her for her high qualities. Anjou for her beauty and the Scots for her crown—but they all meant the same in the end. They wanted nothing but her money, and they should not have it."[3]

Esmé found Paris greatly changed and the court almost unfamiliar. King Henry III turned a cold white face toward him and, in the oddly formidable manner he could assume, forced the duke of Lennox from his presence. Catherine de Médicis was similarly antagonistic. Esmé felt it necessary to maintain his facade of being converted and attended Reform services, and the pro-Vatican court snubbed him for his effort. The duke of Guise was deeply involved in new and mysterious ventures; the onetime key to the Scots situation found himself on a low level.

The taste of power and the experience of intrigue are difficult to overcome and are addictive to its devotees. Esmé, smarting in his new and lower status, sent a Scots servant to the English embassy with a message for the ambassador, Sir Henry Cobham. Intended for Elizabeth, it warned of a plot to send James to France and revealed the names of various of Esmé's collaborators in England during his days of power in Scotland. The duke was now trying to become a double agent, or perhaps a triple.

His information went disregarded in England, where the authorities— as usual during revolutionary times—were swamped with thousands of denunciations and purported revelations. But Esmé was in a new Paris, swarming with spies and seething with the cross-purposes of the king, the duke of Guise, and the tides of a civil war against the Crown being fought by the king of Navarre. In such a city no men could contact and send a servant in and out of the English—or any other—embassy unseen or unfollowed.

D'Aubigny soon returned to his ancestral estates. It was an uncomfortable return; his wife had been forbidden to join him in Scotland, and the base nature of his domination of the king of that country was no secret to her. He was sick, and his thoughts turned toward his children. In the end it was their inheritance that occupied his mind. He established their future in the only way left open, by restoring his credit with James.

In June 1583 the young king of Scotland passed his seventeenth birthday, was in his eighteenth year, and nearing manhood. His situation had grown considerably easier; his captors were seeking some honorable and mutually easy way to withdraw from their role and had grown respectful. A letter arrived from Esmé, and James read it with pleasure. The favorite apologized for his long silence, renewed his pledges and support, said he had been ill, but longed for the day he would be called back to Scotland.

On its heels the news came that Esmé was dead. At first James refused to believe it—but it was true. A final letter arrived, dictated on the day Esmé died, saying he had died true to his conversion—and his king. The diagnosis was dysentery and gonorrhea. The rumor was poison.[4]

James wept and wrote a number of poems, but his eyes were soon roving.

On the seventh of July, 1583, James rode out of Falkland in the company of Sir James Melville and Colonel Stewart. The English observer, Sir Robert Bowes, watched them depart with no stirrings of suspicion; the king had his falcon with him and was in obvious good spirits. Once out of sight, the men and their hunters rode hard until they reached St. Andrews, "swarming with Gordons," where the earl of March was waiting. Other pro-Vatican lords had been informed and were heading toward the scene. The king was delighted. He lingered in the village inn and reveled in the sensation of freedom.

Within a few days pro-Vatican nobles converged at St. Andrews, and James sent for the earl of Arran. The earl of Mar, the master of Glamis, and other Reform leaders of the coup fled to Ireland. The earl of Gowrie had to make a crawling approach and a humble plea for forgiveness. The young king was gracious toward Gowrie, but his eyes showed little friendliness.

A delegation of ministers, seeing the wind change so sharply, called on James at St. Andrews and requested no "new course" in the government's policy. James's response was savage. No king, he said, would have borne what he had borne from the Kirk. The response of the delegation was icy.

"You have been well brought up," said David Fergusson, "not to behave as other kings."[5]

The behavior of other kings, however, was what James wanted to emulate. They were engaged, in France and Spain and other parts as well, in building strong central governments. The greatest of all kings, Philip II of Spain, had crushed local parliaments in the various provinces of his country and operated as a supreme master, to whom even the Vatican, at least in his territories, was largely subservient. Until 1583 Philip had many other problem areas with which to contend and had hoped that by forbearance and patience he could restore his once-firm alliance with England. By the time James broke away from the restraints of his Reform nobles and their supporters in the Kirk, Philip began to change his mind.

That stately alteration in course was conducted, as was his habit, with subtle changes that resembled nothing so much as the changing of the seasons. His men, distributed throughout the vast Spanish empire, would chafe and rage against the slowness of the Prudent King—but there was no denying that when his changes reached their peak, they were as formidable and far-reaching as the gulf between July and December.

Philip's new direction began with a series of meetings and coded correspondence that involved the duke of Guise, the papal nuncio in France, and Dr. William Allen, the pope's leader of rebellious English Catholics, the duke of Parma—Philip's general in the Netherlands—and various highly placed English and Scots nobles.

By the time James gained his freedom at St. Andrews and sent for the earl of Arran as his strong right arm, these maneuvers had resulted in a complex and serious military plan. Guise no longer believed Scotland was essential: he had been persuaded by Dr. Allen and the Jesuits that all England was seething with rebellion and needed only outside assistance to rise and overthrow Elizabeth.

A plan was evolved—not without many interarguments and disagreements—in which 4,000 men from Parma's Spanish forces in the Netherlands would cross the Channel in Spanish ships supplied by Philip II. Dr. Allen—or Father Allen, as he preferred to be called—would go with the expedition and speak to the Vatican Englishmen in the name of the pope. Both Allen and Don Bernadino de Mendoza, the Spanish ambassador to England, who was party to the plot, were of the opinion the French considered religion only "an accessory of politics." Spaniards were more sincere and, as ideologically convinced fighters, more effective.

Mary Stuart, who had dreamed for years of obtaining the help of the mighty Philip II, was in secret transports of delight over these developments. After years of frustration, circumstances were, at last, converging toward her triumph. She received word that James had previously acted under duress and was leaning toward her.

The Lords of the Congregation, after all their previous successes, were split, in flight, or dead. Scotland was again dominated by the earls of Argyll, Huntly, and other men who had crowded about Mary Stuart in her brief return from Lochleven—or their successors. They were being financed by the French duke of Guise, who—as a secret agent of Philip II of Spain— did not bother to let them know of the new, larger Spanish plan.

That plan was, however, carried into the English Catholic world. It enlisted the support and hopes of leading families of the old aristocracy, as well as many ardent young university students whose tutors had labored long in their indoctrination.

Elizabeth, meanwhile, was blissfully unaware that her realm was being penetrated in hundreds of secret places by persons dedicated to her over-throw and to changes that would affect every sector, class, and activity of her nation.


For that reason, the Virgin was astonished when Mary Stuart abruptly announced she would not accept release on the latest terms. The scent of coming victory impelled the imprisoned queen to raise her price. She now said she would accept release only if it was understood she would continue in the Vatican faith, renounce none of her rights, be made an English duchess—and acknowledged as heir to the English throne.

Incensed, Elizabeth dashed off a caustic letter to James and told Wal-singham to deliver it in person. The treasurer was taken aback. Carrying messages for Elizabeth had ruined many a man's honor, because they changed with the weather. Mendoza wrote Philip that Walsingham swore "by the soul, body and blood of God that he would not go to Scotland if she ordered him to be hanged for it—he would rather be hanged." Never-theless, he went.[6]

Walsingham took his time getting to Scotland, where the young king enjoyed his new, or renewed, station. James had the earl of Arran beside him to see that his commands were obeyed, he had sweeping plans for the Reform, and he had received a significant letter from the duke of Guise. His answer was based on the belief—which Guise did nothing to upset—that the old plan to send French troops to Scotland was still being plotted.

"Your proposal to send troops here is most agreeable to me," James wrote. "I will accept it or not accept it as circumstances shall require. I hold myself happy in having so brilliant and distinguished a kinsman . . . ready to take arms in my behalf. M. de Mainville, you tell me, has been pleased to speak *of the virtue's and rare qualities which God has bestowed upon me.*" The underlining was added later by none other than Philip II himself, to whom the letter was forwarded. The Prudent King, to whom irony was second nature, wrote on the margin "a modest young gentleman."[7]

Walsingham came upon James at Perth in September 1583. To the young king he must have seemed like a specter from his Reform childhood; the famous Englishman was tall, thin, heavy-browed, with a swarthy com-plexion and a severe, tightly controlled face. The treasurer was the most successful spymaster in England's history and had no high opinion of amateur politicians. Apparently, the two men detested one another on sight.

James heard Walsingham's message with a flushed face. It was to the effect that Elizabeth would increase her offer to pension him, though his claim to English estates would have to be settled in court with his cousin Lady Arabella Stuart. But he would have to dismiss the earl of Arran and all his recent appointments and restore the earl of Gowrie and other pro-English Reform leaders.

What did the Queen of England have to do with his councillors? he wondered aloud. He did not advise her about her own. Let her select the men she preferred, and he would do the same. Walsingham drew himself up; the comparison between this ungainly young man and the fearful regality of Elizabeth Tudor was not to be borne.

England, the older man told James, had no need of his friendship; he had not been sent to seek it. His mission was to charge James with "unkind dealing, and to demand satisfaction, excuse or reparation."[8] At that the earl of Arran and Colonel Stewart, who flanked James like two guard dogs, expressed great open-eyed wonder and attempted to interrupt, but Walsingham refused to listen to them. In response, Arran took a peculiar revenge that vastly amused James. He hired a notorious scold and nuisance called Kate the Witch to "sit in the entry of the king's palace and revile her majesty's ambassador."[9]

Such behavior toward one of England's most powerful men was proof —if any was needed—that Arran was not overbright and that James's education had not penetrated very far. Walsingham, even in poor health, was a dangerous man to provoke. He endured the filthy ravings of Kate the Witch as he entered and departed from the court for a full week—but became busy on other levels as well.

He held series of secret conversations with the earls of Gowrie and Mar, Lord Lindsay, and other Reform leaders. They were in agonies at the successes of the Vatican Party and their own fall and anxious to have English help for a new coup. Walsingham could not promise anything, but he could—and did—promise to try to get them help. He said he would write Elizabeth and put their case as strongly as possible and wait at Durham for an answer.

Some hint of these proceedings may have reached James because his tone softened before Walsingham announced his departure. He was ready, he said, to forget the Raid of Ruthven, to forgive the nobles involved, and to restore them to their positions as councillors. Walsingham remained impassive and asked for these promises in writing. "A dark and ambiguous answer"[10] was returned.

Walsingham's conclusion was pessimistic. "I have no hopes of the recovery of this young Prince," he wrote Burghley. He warned James could, or rather would if he had the power, be a dangerous enemy. He believed the young king of Scotland was "depending on Spain and the Pope" and that his mother was "layer of the plot."

The information failed to interest Elizabeth. In the autumn of 1583, as in the years before, she felt a vast impatience with Reformers in general and the Scots in particular. Her opinion was that they were common rebels and deserved harsh treatment.

The English queen was supported in that view by the man she appointed as the new archbishop of Canterbury: John Whitgift. Whitgift had watched how Burghley and Walsingham had thwarted the pro-Vatican underground with approval and their protection of the English Reformers with disapproval. Beyond that, Whitgift believed—as did Elizabeth—that a sovereign was the final authority of the national Church. It was his intention to use a special High Commission, created years before but left dormant, as an instrument by which he and his bishops, with the queen's blessing and support, would cleanse the Church of England of its numerous dissenting ministers and congregations.

Before Whitgift had his machinery in place, however, the pro-Vatican underground erupted. First, a young man named John Somerville appeared in London, talking, somewhat wildly, about assassinating the queen. Carried off to the Tower, he was introduced to the rack and named his father-in-law, Arden, as an accomplice, together with a priest harbored in their household. All three were tried, convicted, and sentenced to death. Before the sentence could be carried out, Somerville strangled himself to death in his cell, but his head was severed, impaled, and placed on exhibition anyway. His father-in-law's head soon appeared as well. The priest, who turned his coat, was released.

It was a grim season and soon grew worse. Sir Nicholas Throckmorton, who had been Elizabeth's ambassador to Scotland and who had witnessed the wild celebrations attendant upon James Stuart's premature coronation, was a staunch defender of the English queen—but he had a brother, Sir John, who was equally staunch for Mary Stuart. One of Sir John Throckmorton's sons, Francis, was also ardently pro-Vatican and was under surveillance by Walsingham's men in Europe and London. In London his house became a center of activity. It was rushed by the authorities and young Throckmorton was caught with a list of English pro-Vatican leaders, plans of English harbors, piles of pamphlets, and other interesting arcana.

The authorities knew they had snared a conspirator, but at first had no idea of the extent and seriousness of Throckmorton's activity. He was shown the rack in the Tower, and it was suggested that he cooperate—while a choice was still available. He refused, and official permission was obtained from Elizabeth to proceed with "the pains." Racked, the young man remained adamant, but his interrogators were heartless. As soon as he had recovered, they brought him into the slanted chamber in the Tower again.

A second sight of the rack was too much. "When he was laid again upon the frame, before he was strained to any purpose, he yielded to confess everything that he knew."[11]

Before he finished, his questioners were horrified. The place where the invasion was to land; the names of great English noblemen involved; the communications system between the pope, the king of Spain, the duke of Guise, the Spanish ambassador in London, and Mary, Queen of Scots; the locations of hidden priests and their protectors—all sorts of details came tumbling forth.

It was as though a thousand bombs went off at once under England. Elizabeth was shaken to learn the extent of her danger. Philip II of Spain was a ruler over greater territories and larger resources than any the world had ever before seen, even in the greatest days of the Roman Empire.[12] When that dread figure began to draw plans to invade her realm, depose her, turn her nation in new directions, and place Mary Stuart on her throne, the English queen had at last some glimmering of her peril. Acquiescent to her advisers for once, she signed every paper they placed before her. Troops, horsemen, special agents, and hastily created commissions poured across the landscape.

The long Elizabethan toleration came to a sudden end. Pro-Vatican officers in the navy, tacitly tolerated for years, were abruptly removed. Persons long hidden in the recesses of society, or harbored by sympathizers in high places, made a rush to get out of the country before they were arrested. A vast manhunt occupied the authorities during the Christmas season of 1583. Before it slackened, it was estimated that 11,000 people were under some form of arrest.[13]

For the first time since the days of Mary Tudor "conformity in religion was made a condition of admission to the bar." The pro-Vatican Inns of Court, training schools for the nation's lawyers, were raided and the students made to swear their allegiance. Even magistrates were not exempt; special tribunals met and questioned—and since the search was for traiters, there were no bounds to the powers of the questioners.

In January 1584, while the manhunt, searches, and trials were being organized, the Spanish ambassador, Don Bernardino de Mendoza, was expelled from the country.[14] Mendoza was the fourth representative of Spain to be so expelled, and the two countries grew visibly closer to war.


Both Burghley and Walsingham had foreseen some such development and were agreed—as were most of the Reformers of England—that the Vatican and Spain presented dangers that had to be confronted. But Elizabeth regarded the situation somewhat differently—and so did the new archbishop of Canterbury, John Whitgift.

The queen and the archbishop saw the issue as one of "conformity." They considered the growing tendency of the people to adopt individual attitudes toward the national Church of England as a danger from within that transcended factions. Elizabeth did not believe—and would never believe—that religion itself was a serious issue. She regarded religious dissent as simply a mask for rebellion, as a pretext to avoid her authority and to diminish her right as queen to rule the Church of England.

The queen had been impatient with Burghley and Walsingham for years because they had protected Reformers. Whitgift, therefore, had her full support in moving, with his High Commission, against the Reform-minded dissenters in the Church of England and against those who shared the views of John Knox, George Buchanan, and the Kirk of Scotland.

Whitgift announced his intention to examine all printers and books, ministers and "disordered persons." His commission consisted of a "dozen bishops and a score of deans, archdeacons and civil lawyers." He had the power to examine, to punish, to fine or imprison.

The sweep of the High Commission extended not only to canon law and ecclesiastical rules, but included "heretical opinions, seditous writings, contempts, conspiracies, false rumours, and slanderous words." This enormous net over the realm was cunningly crafted, and those who refused a summons to appear could be fined or jailed. Those who did appear were ordered to take an oath to answer truthfully any question put to them. Refusal to take the oath was tantamount to conviction. Answers that did not please the commission provided the basis for official charges and the evidence for conviction. The commission could summon, question, charge, convict, and punish and allowed no lawyers for the defense. Before Whitgift's commission even began, the Privy Council was deluged by complaints from the Church of England ministers who could not subscribe to Whitgift's doctrines as laid down and who were already thrown out of their posts. Burghley and Walsingham, as well as the entire Reform element of the cities and countryside, were appalled.[15]

In effect, Whitgift—with Elizabeth's approval—had created an English inquisition. Like its counterparts in Europe, it sought to protect a doctrine created from on high and to force—by examinations into inner beliefs—complete and abject conformity. Between the new High Commission and the activities of the Privy Council with its Star Chamber proceedings against suspected Catholic traitors, all England was placed on a rack. By early 1584 the whole country began to be stretched slowly out of recognition.

# 13

In Scotland, Mary Stuart's son, James, watched these events avidly. He learned of the plot to invade England and place his mother on that throne with some surprise. Somewhat hastily he sent a secret letter to the duke of Guise, approving such an effort and claiming a filial loyalty he had not before revealed. Just to be on the safe side, he sent a parallel letter to the pope, in which he stressed the helplessness of his situation and asked for help from the Vatican.

At home, however, he exulted in Elizabeth's decision to move against the Reformers. His hatred of the Reform was too bitter to be concealed. His escape from Ruthven and the other Lords of the Congregation left him burning for revenge. The earl of Arran, anxious to enrich himself, was willing to move in the name of the young king; the archbishop of St. Andrews, Patrick Adamson, whispered that only bishops obedient to the Crown could maintain proper authority.

When Andrew Melville and John Durie thundered from their pulpits that the young king had surrounded himself with "Papists and atheists," they were summoned before the newly formed Council to answer for their charges. Both were defiant and claimed the right of the Congregation to preach the Word; both were threatened with imprisonment; both fled to England. That left the Congregation without its strongest voices.

The Lords of the Congregation, divided and handicapped, sought to organize and recapture the young king. The earl of Gowrie was at Perth, but the earls of Angus and Mar were in exile. They returned secretly, but Arran learned of their plans and arrested Gowrie. The earls of Mar and Angus gathered a small force and captured Stirling Castle—from which they issued a call for the countryside to rally and sent a messenger pounding toward England to ask Elizabeth for help. Her reaction was to refuse. That word had barely reached Scotland when the English queen changed her mind and sent a token £1,000—a pitiful sum. Her change was too late. Word had already traveled that England would not intervene. Secure in that knowledge, Arran and James marched toward Stirling; made insecure by the same knowledge, the earls of Mar and Angus fled. Those who remained in the castle were immediately hanged.

The result was that the earls of Mar and Angus were declared outlaws and their estates were seized by the Crown. The earl of Gowrie, who had not taken any physical part in the latest rebellion, was hastily tried, found guilty, and hanged. His estates were confiscated and taken by the earl of Arran.

Elizabeth's confusion, the diminished position of the Reform in England and its inability to support its comrades in Scotland, the whole series of unlikely events that had gushed forth following the arrest of young Francis Throckmorton had, improbably, elevated the young, seventeen-year-old king of Scotland into a strong position.

Had Arran been James's only adviser, that strength might have been temporary, but John Maitland had become a member of the king's Council. Maitland, as indifferent to religious issues as his famous elder brother, the great Lethington, aimed at becoming secretary of the realm and the king's first minister. He came forward with a subtle plan to end the domination of the Reform in Scotland over the Crown.

In May 1584, following this plan, James called a Parliament. No word leaked of its purpose, and it met for only four days in complete secrecy. Its proceedings produced what were later called the Black Acts. The king was declared head of the Church, he and his Council assumed complete authority over all ecclesiastical matters—and anyone who denied this authority was declared a traitor. The church was forbidden to hold a General Assembly or any other meeting without permission; ministers in the pulpit were forbidden to "utter any false, untrue, or slanderous speeches . . . or to meddle in the affairs of his highness and his estate."[1]

As if this were not enough, the Reform church was to pay for a king's bodyguard; all vacant benefices were to go to the Crown; all those holding benefices were to pay a portion to the Crown. In one fell swoop, the heir of the revolution claimed all its gains for himself.

In former years, the Reform in Scotland would have been able to organize instant demonstrations against the Black Acts—but Knox was gone and Andrew Melville a fugitive. The archbishop of St. Andrews was in close contact with Whitgift's bishops in England and was planning some sort of joint enterprise, in which the Church of England and Scotland would unite. This was a twisting of Burghley's tactics with a vengeance, but that statesman was still busy untangling the information gathered in the torture chambers of the Privy Council and engrossed in tracing out and arresting all those involved in the invasion plot.

The Calvinists from Scotland, operating partly from hiding places in England, had to be content with issuing pamphlets calling James a bastard of Mary Stuart and the Italian singer, David Rizzio. Meanwhile, the Queen of Scots exulted. Some of her oldest enemies were being destroyed by her son, whose protestations of support on her behalf had been relayed to her from France and Rome. As usual, the Scots queen moved to take advantage of the developing situation and sent a Frenchman—M. de Fontenay—to Scotland to see her son.

Fontenay had several instructions. One, intensely personal, was to report what James was like. Another was to urge that Lord Lindsay, an old enemy, be executed. Another, by far the most important, was to persuade James to associate himself with his mother and to work for her release and restoration.

Her agent arrived in the summer of 1584 and found the young king just after he had passed his eighteenth birthday. Portraits showed a sad-eyed young man with a long, thin, Celtic face and a wary expression. Fontenay, however, found a boastful and conceited youth.

It was a time when royalty walked surrounded by a nimbus of descent, and Fontenay's description—which he sent to his brother, the queen's secretary at Sheffield—began with the usual flattery. "For his age," Fontenay wrote, "one of the most remarkable princes that ever lived." He then added all sorts of superlatives, in full awareness that Mary Stuart herself might read his words. "He apprehends readily, he judges maturely, he concludes with reason. His memory is full and retentive. His questions are quick and piercing and his answers solid. . . . In religious argument I have known him to establish a point against adversaries who in the main agree with him, and I venture to say that in languages, sciences and affairs of State, he has more learning than any man in Scotland. In short, he is wonderfully clever. . . ."[2]

Having said all that, Fontenay then proceeded to withdraw all these conclusions in a series of observations that sharpened as they extended. "For the rest," he said, "he is full of honorable ambition and has an excellent opinion of himself. Owing to the terrorism under which he has been brought up, he is timid with the great lords, and seldom ventures to contradict them.

"He dislikes dances and music, and amorous talk, and curiosity of dress, and courtly trivialities. He has an especial detestation for earrings. For want of instruction his manners are rough and uncouth. He speaks, eats and dresses like a boor, and he is no better in the company of women. He is never still for a moment, but walks perpetually up and down the room, and his gait is sprawling and awkward. His voice is loud, and his words sententious. He prefers hunting to all other amusements, and will be for six hours together on horseback, galloping over hill and dale. . . . His body is feeble but he is not delicate; in a word, he is a young old man."

That was bad enough, but Fontenay was not through. "Three unfavorable points only I observe in him," he continued, as though his portrait thus far had been benign. "He does not understand his own insignificance. He is prodigiously conceited, and he underrates other princes." Then, carefully, Fontenay hinted at the homosexual element. "He irritates," he said, "his subjects by indiscreet and violent attachments." And, returning to business, he added, "He is idle and careless, too easy and much given to pleasure— particularly to the chase, leaving his affairs to be managed by Arran, Montrose and his secretary. Excuses, I know, must be made for so young a man, but it is to be feared that the habit may grow upon him. I once hinted something of this kind to him. He told me that whatever he seemed, he was aware of everything of consequence that was going on. He could afford to spend time in hunting, for that when he attended to business he could do more in an hour than others in a day. He could listen to one man, talk to another and observe a third. Sometimes he could do five things at once."

Fontenay attempted to cut through this bluster with some blunt questions. There was a rumor floating about that James would forsake his mother and make some arrangement with Elizabeth. Was it true? The young king, faced with this question, suddenly turned sharp. He would take good care of his mother, and Fontenay should be less curious in matters that did not concern him. Fontenay added that to the fact that James had not asked any questions about his mother, showed no curiosity about her health, or how she spent her time, or how she looked. Added together, the indifference—even irritation—was ominous for Mary Stuart's expectations from her son. Even more ominous were the graceful presence and rising fortunes of Patrick, master of Gray, in the rude little circle that James considered his court.

The master of Gray was as beautiful, in the eyes of his contemporaries, "as Lucifer." Like that great prototype of pride and sin, Gray's ambitions were not restricted by conscience. After graduating from St. Andrews University, he had gone to France and there was employed by Mary Stuart's ambassador to that country, James Beaton. That led him, by natural and easy stages, to the attention and into the pay of the duke of Guise. Mary Stuart came to consider him one of her agents. In the autumn of 1583 he was entrusted with the task of carrying Esmé Stuart's young heir from France to Scotland. James was instantly attracted, and Gray was careful not to show any soaring ambition before the suspicious eyes of the earl of Arran. As a result, he fell into the posts of master of wardrobe—and Gentleman of the Bedchamber.

In that position he shared James's bed and his secrets. They were few and not difficult to learn; one was that the young king of Scotland was not anxious for his mother's release from her English captivity. That was enough to switch Gray from the people for whom he had worked so many years into an opposite direction. In that switch he joined most of the other nobles at the Scots court, whom Fontenay had described in withering terms. "Money and preferment," he said, "are the only Sirens which charm the lords of Scotland . . . They care nothing for the future, and less for the past."[3]

Arran headed the pack. When James had been taken prisoner by Ruthven and the Lords of the Congregation, Arran had been also taken and there was some talk, at that time, of putting him to death. His life was saved by the intervention of the countess of Gowrie. In the fall of 1584, however, the earl of Gowrie was dead, and his countess and children were homeless and destitute. According to Davison, the English ambassador, Lady Gowrie waited before the Tollbooth in Edinburgh and threw herself at James's feet when he passed, to beg for mercy for her children. Arran thrust her away with his foot and strode across her body as she fainted.[4]

Scotland, in other words, was in the hands of unscrupulous men. Between them, they created unrest—but Arran, being the most clearly villainous, attracted more odium than the young king. Arran, in fact, was detested on all sides. He had obtained much of the Hamilton estates and the possessions of the Douglases and the Gowries. The king's court was poor and barren, but his strongest courtier became conspicuously wealthy. But Arran's course was curious because the Reform had assumed his intention was to restore the Vatican and Mary Stuart. Time, however, proved that Arran had no interest in religion and less in the Queen of Scots: his own destiny was the only one that interested him.

That realization trickled into England slowly, and Elizabeth sent Lord Hunsdon to visit Scotland and appraise its latest strong man. Hunsdon met Arran in Fouldren Church a few miles from Berwick, near the border. Arran appeared with Lord Rothes and several others of James's Council, and Hundson was impressed by the fact that these leaders walked "five hours in the churchyard, seeming all as servants" while Arran talked inside the church.

The Englishman, who had expected some rude figure, was dazzled by the tall, handsome, and elegant Arran. His conversation included interjections in Latin and even Greek, and he carried himself with almost regal grace. Hunsdon did not know, or perhaps did not fully realize, that any man who gained James Stuart's complete confidence had to have a dazzling presence.

He listened to Arran, who assured him the young king of Scotland was in his hand. The issues, said the earl, were not religious, since religion was "a superstitious terror to the consciences of the people to hold them in awe and obedience."[5] If Elizabeth would forget the Lords of the Congregation and abandon the English plea that the earls of Angus and Mar be restored, would disown the Reform ministers, and recognize James—Scotland would be firm in its alliance.

Hunsdon was almost convinced. He asked if James himself had not, for a time, dealt with the Jesuits on behalf of his mother. "A slander," Arran said. "The King has never seen a Jesuit." That lie was one too many. Hunsdon knew better.[6] His report gave Elizabeth pause; she believed in her own right as a queen to lie, but was scornful when other people stooped so low.

The Virgin had, however, larger problems than Arran presented. The duke of Anjou, her frog prince, died that summer at Château-Thierry. A month later, in July 1584 a fanatic named Balthazar Gerard, anxious to claim the immense reward offered by Philip II, inserted himself into the household of William of Orange, waited for the right moment, and fired "three poisoned balls" into the prince's body.

The assassination of the man who had led the struggle of the Reform Dutch against Spain for fifteen years created despair, horror, and anxiety in the rebels of the Netherlands. Combined with the death of the duke of Anjou, it also created a new international situation. Henry of Bourbon, leader of the French Huguenots, was the next heir to the throne of France. Elizabeth, whose assistance to the Reformers of the Netherlands had been grudging and half-hearted, was confronted with the need either to enter that arena or to allow Spain to regain its control. For their part, with their leader gone, the Netherlands rebels turned toward England and offered a complete union.

Such a result would give England territory on the continent of Europe, unite two emerging maritime powers, and create, in effect, a Reform empire, or the strong beginnings of one, that could stem the tide of Spanish advance. King Henry III of France and his mother Catherine de Médicis, would do almost anything to stop such a union from coming into existence: the Netherlands could unite with France as well as England—but Elizabeth would not allow that. The Queen of England, in fact, would neither plan nor allow any plans. She blew, as always, hot and cold and swayed while her Privy Council begged and argued. It was not a time when the people were kept aware of these tides by newspapers; most Englishmen were prospering too much to want full-scale war. The troubles in Europe had resulted in a swing from Bruges and Ghent to London and Bristol; new industries were rising and English maritime trade was extending even into the Mediterranean with the Turk. Although the Channel was heavy with pirates and English "privateers" prowled the oceans, trade with Spain was also lucrative.[7] Both nations struggled against one another in the Netherlands, but in an undeclared fashion; English volunteers fought alongside the Spanish against other English volunteers fighting with the Dutch.

With so much to consider and so many factors to weigh, Elizabeth and her councillors could hardly be blamed for indecision. In the interim, almost absently, like a naughty child pulling apart an insect, the English queen toyed with her cousin Mary Stuart.

These efforts had, as always, provocations to bring them forward. The Shrewsbury family had been torn apart by the long responsibility and the endless coilings around the Queen of Scots. The countess of Shrewsbury now had a granddaughter who was a princess of the blood—Arabella Stuart. With such a prize growing up, the countess intrigued with Leicester to marry Arabella to the favorite's son. In the course of these subterranean plottings, the countess turned against Mary Stuart and spread an incredible number of horrible stories—including the charge that the earl of Shrewsbury was sleeping with the Queen of Scots—who was pregnant.

That accusation created great problems inside the Shrewsbury family. The children believed their mother; the earl was outraged. When Mary Stuart learned the difficulty and its cause, she erupted. Elizabeth, informed, had the countess hauled before the Privy Council. Burghley, Walsingham, and the others forced the notorious scold to her knees before them and squeezed an admission from her that she was a liar and that her charges were false.

Elizabeth then allowed the long-suffering earl of Shrewsbury to appear before her and listened to his expostulations and troubles. When that pleasure palled, she informed him he was transferred to a new command in Lancashire. The poor man kissed her hands and thanked her for removing him from "two devils."

Meanwhile, Mary Stuart was told again that if she capitulated and abandoned all her hopes, she would be released. It looked, in fact, as though Mary Stuart's course was almost over. Her son was maturing; her supporters in Scotland had taken her money and then gone their own way; Philip II was no closer to an invasion than before; France was torn between three contending factions; and the duke of Guise could not persuade the Spanish to assist his own plans on her behalf. Elizabeth seemed, at last, tiring of the game.

At that point—probably the last real moment of hope that Mary Stuart had in reality—Father Crichton and another Jesuit, who had been close to the bishop of Ross, were captured in the Channel on their way to Scotland. Carried to the Tower, the priests revealed, under the agonies of the rack, the long, wearisome, and tangled history of the Vatican efforts against Elizabeth—beginning with the mission of Esmé Stuart. There was nothing they had to reveal that was new to Walsingham or Burghley, but these powerful members of the Elizabeth's Privy Council took advantage of the arrest of Crichton and his fellow Jesuit to disclose the situation to the country.

Their timing was astute. The mass arrests of pro-Vatican supporters, the executions of priests, the groaning prisons had all created a sympathy for Catholics that had maintained sympathy for Mary Stuart. When Elizabeth teetered on the brink of releasing her cousin, the revelations of Crichton were used to swing sympathy the other way.

The effort was so successful that a great wave of concern for Elizabeth's safety swept the realm. Mass meetings were held and hysterical speeches mounted. The Privy Council sent, in this wave of excitement, a statement around the country called the Bond of Association. This bond, patterned on the productions of John Knox and drawing upon his numerous bonds, covenants, and associations, called upon all Englishmen to rally to protect the queen—and also to deny the succession to any who involved themselves in the queen's death.

No stroke was more surely aimed against Mary Stuart, was so remarkably masked in concern for Elizabeth—or brought the matter of succession more naturally to the foreground. Elizabeth was placed in the position where she could neither charge treason nor pretend that the succession was of no concern to her subjects. The theory that the people had a voice in the election of monarchs could hardly have been more flatteringly presented—but it was presented.

This development had the effect of holding the liberty of Mary Stuart in abeyance, and created a great wave of anti-Vatican sentiment. While England flocked to sign the bond on behalf of Elizabeth, the Queen of Scots was moved to Wingfield—another comfortable house owned by the earl of Shrewsbury, to be greeted by a new guardian—Sir Ralph Sadler. She still had her attendants, her priest, her cloth of state, and her comforts; and she learned that Patrick, the master of Gray, was being sent to England by her son, James, to arrange a suitable treaty. The news cheered her; Gray was her agent since his youth. She did not realize that the same revolutionary tide that had swept her out of Scotland was now moving under the surface of England.

# 14

In Scotland young King James had a better realization of the depth and meaning of those tides, for they had surrounded him from birth. Buchanan was dead but his book—*De Jure Regni apud Scotos*—spelling out the limits of monarchs, the rights of subjects, and the intellectual basis for tyrannicide, had become required reading at the University of St. Andrews and fueled the arguments of ministers against the Crown.

Editions had poured out of the presses of London and Edinburgh, Geneva and other places where the Reform was strong; one of James's first acts after Arran had helped him establish himself had been to ban and order the burning of that inflammatory political handbook. Adamson, the archbishop of St. Andrews, placed in charge by James, did not find these orders uncongenial: quite the contrary. But they were difficult to enforce, short of searching every home in Scotland—and the students at St. Andrews were not easily converted by a king's order. They formed the habit of appearing in crowds at the archbishop's windows at night, under the cover of darkness, to shout curses and threats and to cast stones.

The young king, however, was living on another level, in a different dimension. Esmé Stuart and the first court he had created around James at Holyrood had extravagantly admired the boy's learning and facility in languages; by 1584 James recreated that atmosphere for himself. He was surrounded at night with poets—all hard drinkers like himself—and while bonfires were being made of Buchanan's works, issued a book of his own verse to edify and impress his realm. The *Essayes of a Prentice in the Divine Art of Poesie* revealed the young king to have a tendency, like many who have been overinstructed, to confuse injunctions with composition. To prove it, he produced a preface on the art of poetry in which the rules, long known, were gravely repeated. The slender little volume also carried a series of rhymed tributes to His Majesty from his admiring circle of subjects and, finally, a series of tortured efforts of his own that revealed more learning than talent.

Despite these deficiencies, however, the fact that the young king of

Scotland supported poets as well as politicans and soldiers created a great stir. His little volume was sent everywhere and was received with enormous praise—especially from the vast sector represented by impoverished poets, *littérateurs,* and teachers whose dreams of paradise were crowded with the figures of wealthy and benevolent patrons.

Few of these lovers of the arts, then or later, drew any conclusions from the paradox presented by a young monarch who loved culture, doted on debate, and was generous with his companions—but who burned opinions that differed from his own or imprisoned men for holding them.

Gray's handsome, self-assured presence charmed Elizabeth—but she was even more pleased with the significance of his conversations. The Queen of Scots had funded Arran and arranged the release of her son, James, in the expectation, nurtured for years, that this would lead to her own release, her return to Scotland, and joint rule.

The success of her efforts was clear, so far as James and his position were concerned. In advance of Gray's arrival in London, Mary Stuart had paved the way by sending lavish presents to the English Privy Council; sent her secretary, M. Nau, to London; and issued instructions that she would sign any agreement whatever—even if it cost her the support of the Catholic world. At that point, Elizabeth could see no other alternative. The Reform earls of Mar and Angus were exiles in her realm and the Reform cause was being reduced by Whitgift and the High Commission in England and by the archbishop of St. Andrews and his supporters in Scotland. The release of Mary Stuart would remove an irritant in her relations with Spain and restore her own reputation as a merciful and just sovereign.

Patrick Gray, however, offered new alternatives. He first revealed the coded correspondence he had received from the Queen of Scots, proving her promises hollow. Then he assured Elizabeth that James was not interested in a joint association with his mother. To her horror, Mary Stuart learned he recommended that she be imprisoned for life.

While Mary raged and her agent, M. Nau, sought frantically to salvage the situation, a book appeared in Europe charging that far from being a martyr to the Vatican cause, she had weakened under her tests. The pope believed she should sacrifice her life to a greater cause. When Elizabeth questioned Gray regarding Mary Stuart's party in Scotland, he blandly assured the Virgin that—after sixteen years—the Queen of Scots was a vague and unhappy memory; her influence was lost in the mist.

He did not stop there; Master Gray had caught the illness to which courtiers and politicians are so peculiarly subject: he wanted to rise forever. Arran, he told Elizabeth, was untrustworthy. That agreed with her own idea, and she smiled at him. The tall, debonair Scot then pressed his point. If he could have the support of England, he would both unseat Arran and arrange a suitable treaty between the two countries. It took weeks for the conversation to reach this final and most sensitive level, while around them reverberated great echoes of Burghley's anti-Vatican, pro-Reform campaign.

Parliament was assembled, amid the uproar, to specifically deny the crown and the right of succession to Mary Stuart. Its members were the result of new elections—the first in twelve years. Burghley had drawn its plans very closely. They called for an interim government in the event of Elizabeth's death and elections "by secret balloting, as in Venice"—for her successor. Elizabeth was not pleased. She wanted the protection represented by the association—but the matter of succession was, in her eyes, no business of Parliament. Her sure instinct warned her against making an open issue of that.

The queen was also anxious to dampen the outcries rising against Whitgift, the archbishop of Canterbury, and his High Commission. In operation through the year, one of the first victims was a clergyman named Edward Brayle. He appealed to the Privy Council, whose Reform members shared his views. Sir Francis Knollys remonstrated on Brayle's behalf with Whitgift, and asked that "only Jesuits be fenced." Parliament, the archbishop was told, had not intended Reformers to be so treated. Burghley added his voice. An examination of the High Commission, he said, convinced him that "even the Inquisitors of Spain use not so many questions to comprehend and trap their prey."[1]

The Reformers, however, were on treacherous ground. The argument that only their opponents should be persecuted for their beliefs was inherently unfair—and Whitgift lost no time in making that clear. The archbishop, in fact, warned the Privy Council he acted under the queen's personal authority—and the threat of that silenced, though it did not please, Burghley, Walsingham, and Knollys. It did not silence the clerk of the Privy Council, Robert Beale. He wrote a book against the system of forcing men to testify against themselves and claimed the Magna Carta itself forbade the practice. It did not, but the claim was instantly accepted, picked up, recirculated, and widely used. Like Buchanan's claim that the early kings of Scotland were elected, the historical claim fitted magnificently into the propagation of a new element in an evolving revolutionary doctrine.

Beale's book joined Buchanan's works in circulation; both were additions to Knox's legacies, and each was surrounded by a sea of pamphlets that was now swollen by arguments against the High Commission. New authors added to their detail, and genuine precedents against tyranny were unearthed from previous centuries and writers. Under the pressures launched by Whitgift, the Reformers of England began to organize along the same Calvinist lines as Knox had organized Scotland. Each congregation was to split into cells; the cells would elect other cells to meet with other congregations and in turn would create a national synod.

The same Commons that passed, amid tumultuous approval, a measure to banish all Jesuits and other Catholic priests from England within forty days also drew a bill to create a Genevan-style church, along the lines of Knox's establishment in Scotland. Although many members were in favor, almost all knew that Elizabeth would never allow such a measure to be realized. After raising the threat, therefore, the bill was removed and a petition drawn up against the High Commission and its forced oath. The petition urged the restoration of clergymen ousted by Whitgift and an end to the High Commission's reach for authority into matters of belief.

Elizabeth was far too slippery to be so easily snared. She did not debate sensitive issues; she diverted them. Her gratitude for the concern of her subjects regarding her safety was superbly expressed. The question of how her bishops behaved was something she would investigate. Meanwhile, she wondered if subsidies to the Crown might not be better topics for discussion. Overseas events might make measures in the national defense necessary. Having deflected the question of her successor and the matter of the High Commission, she then wondered if an adjournment might not be timely, since time was required to examine the issues brought before her. Commons bowed and dutifully withdrew. Burghley had planned well, but had not carried the day beyond anti-Vaticanism.

By that time the master of Gray had convinced the Virgin. In January 1585 he turned back toward Scotland after coming to a secret understanding that he would be supported by England in his efforts to unseat Arran. No man, on a single diplomatic mission on behalf of his country, had ever managed so many conflicting interests so smoothly or more to his own advantage.

That same January 1585 Mary Stuart found herself unexpectedly moved from the comforts of Wingfield to the cold confines of Tutbury Castle once again. The site was familiar to her, but even her adamant spirit could not keep from sinking when she arrived. More like a fort than a residence, it was located on a dreary and treeless plain and consisted of little more than a great, thick, high wall surrounding a rude, rustic, poorly kept structure, drafty and cold.

The sympathetic earl of Shrewsbury was gone, but Sir Ralph Sadler assured the Queen of Scots her stay would be short. She was allowed to hunt and to ride, but her new guardian had her surrounded by fifty heavily armed men on each occasion. Regarding this poor liberty, Sadler responded grimly that any interference would result in those weapons being directed first at the Queen of Scots. The master of Gray and her son James had demolished her position.

Elizabeth used the adjournment of Parliament to regain her control. She called Burghley and other members of the Privy Council into a special session she headed and at which Whitgift appeared. Since all the men held their office at her pleasure, she did not spare any. Versed in Italian as well as Latin, Greek, and French, she quoted a proverb from the land of Machiavelli with telling effect. "From mine enemy let me defend myself, but from a pretensed friend, Good Lord deliver me."[2] She would favor neither faction, for she feared the Reform as much as the Vatican.

When Commons assembled again, she sent her orders directly and said there was something in the Reform "that was dangerous to kingly rule."[3] Then she placed Whitgift on the Privy Council, where he could contend with Burghley, Walsingham, Knollys, and Beale on an equal level—and gave his High Commission authority to use torture.

The times were extraordinary and beyond control. France split apart. One faction, centered in the great cities, was fanatically pro-Vatican and led by the duke of Guise. Another represented the Huguenots led by Henry of Bourbon, king of Navarre. Persons caught in the middle were placed in the unenviable position of hoping the transvestite King Henry III would live forever. The Catholic League, headed by Henry of Guise, declared the Reform king of Navarre would never succeed and instead named his younger, pro-Catholic brother, the cardinal of Bourbon. The "war of the three Henrys" began.

That narrowed Elizabeth's choices. In the Netherlands, the duke of Parma was advancing against the rebels, and the internal troubles of France —funded by Spain—removed that country as a threat. England was confronted with an unsettled situation in Scotland and a diminishing situation in the Lowlands. Since both areas were gateways to England, the Virgin had to agree to send help—in the form of men, arms, and money—to the Dutch. Typically, she demanded payment for what was unavoidable: she wanted three coastal cities.

As news of her resolution trickled out, Philip decided to show that he was far from supine. In May 1585 with no warning, every English ship in every Spanish harbor was suddenly seized and all their captains and crews cast into gloomy Spanish prisons. The cargoes were confiscated—and the people of England suddenly realized that war was close.

That same May 1585 Elizabeth sent Sir Edward Wotton to Scotland to conclude an alliance with James. He arrived to find that the master of Gray had worked well—and that Gray had made a partner, for the moment, out of John Maitland, the secretary.

The results of their efforts were evident. Arran had grown wealthy, arrogant, but fearful. His negotiations with the English had alienated the pro-Vatican nobles who had first assisted him—and his greed had alienated the rest. Aware that plots were forming against him, Arran went about heavily armed; always guarded.

The young king, on the other hand, was pleased with life. Patrick Gray had promised him money from England, as well as a gift of hounds. The dogs had not arrived, and James was very upset. Sir Edward Wotton, however, arrived with some fine horses, sent for the delayed hounds—and proved an amiable companion during the hunt.

The young king had, however, taken a revealing step. He had received reproaches from his mother in England, and he wrote her that he had never promised to any "association" with her—and never would. It was his last communication.

The Queen of Scots received that dismissal with boundless fury. Sir Ralph Sadler had been removed, at his own request, and was replaced by a new Reform guardian, Sir Amyas Paulet. Paulet, governor of Jersey, had once been ambassador from England to France and was Calvinist to the core. The famous beauty had turned pudgy and sharp-nosed and tried to charm her new jailer without success.

With grim efficiency, Paulet set about the creation of a new security system. The laundress, the coachmen, all her attendants, her letters, and belongings were all subjected to a thorough and unremitting search. For the first time the real position of Mary Stuart turned into that of a prisoner of state. Her rooms were located to confront a courtyard; she was deprived of a sight of fields lest she use the windows from which to signal. Neither anger nor reproach nor prayer nor argument nor silence nor screams could swerve this experienced spymaster. As firmly as a man closing a window, Paulet drew the blinds between the Queen of Scots and the world.

15 Through the summer and autumn of 1585 events began
to assume a sort of symmetry. Elizabeth, forced by
circumstances toward action, wavered over her assistance to the Dutch, and vacillated regarding Scotland.
But every passing week brought her nearer inescapable
decisions; and her Privy Council nudged, cajoled,
pleaded, and plotted her toward resolution.

James had been promised £5,000 and a treaty. He was avid to get the
money and would sign anything. John Maitland, his secretary, bargained
with the English to gain some advantage for Scotland. His propositions
were farsighted. He wanted the subjects of both realms to have mutual
commercial privileges. He wanted Scotland guaranteed against invasion. He
wanted more money for King James. Each of these desires, accompanied
by various skillful internal programs to levy taxes, to reach a compromise
with the Reform Church, and to establish some system of justice, raised him
in the eyes of his young king, made him less popular with the nobility—
but steadied the realm.

A border incident, in which the heir of the English earl of Bedford was
murdered, temporarily delayed the signing of the treaty. Elizabeth, with her
usual miserly second thought, reduced James's stipend to £4,000. He saw
it receding and wept before the English ambassador. Arran, blamed for the
border incident, was placed under arrest. Patrick Gray, double-dealing as
ever, thought the earl unjustly imprisoned, and James immediately released
the monster. That set everyone back, and the English Privy Council, finally
out of patience, allowed the earls of Mar and Angus to return to Scotland.

The Reform leaders were met at the border by the Lords Hamilton,
and people flocked to them as if they were saviors. A plague had spread in
Scotland, and the ministers had declared it a punishment of God, visited
upon a realm that allowed the godless to rule. The combination of genuine
grievances against Arran, revolution, and superstition created an irresistible
movement against Arran and his few remaining supporters. James fled to
Stirling, flanked by Maitland and Gray, who were determined to keep him
aloof from Arran. The fallen favorite appeared, made a futile plea, and then

fled through the water gate.[1] James was so alarmed that he tried to flee himself. He was overwhelmed when the earls of Mar and Angus appeared, knelt before him, and pledged their loyalty. Within days he convinced himself he had won a great victory.

Elizabeth, who had sanctioned this latest coup, had the audacity to send the young king of Scots—held once again by the Lords of the Congregation—a letter offering her assistance in case he needed it. It ended with a postscript remarkable even for the Virgin, reminiscent of the terms in which she once wrote his mother.

"Fear not," she said, "for their life must be yours, or else they shall smart, every mother's son of them."[2]

In the same autumnal season of 1585 the English queen received the Dutch towns of Flushing, Brill, and Rammekins as security for a generosity she was forced to display and reluctantly allowed her favorite, Leicester, to leave at the head of a small army for the Netherlands. At the same time, she allowed Sir Francis Drake to undertake one of his extraordinary forays against Spanish shipping. In the course of this adventure, Drake stormed and took Santo Domingo, then proceeded to take Cartagena. He extracted immense ransoms in gold from both cities and was planning to move against Panama when disease hit his crews, and he had to turn homeward.

News of these exploits, which seemed to pit Drake alone against all the immense power of Imperial Spain, sent his name—and the name of England—soaring before the eyes of Europe. The action of Philip II in seizing helpless English merchantmen in port without warning seemed savagely—and unforgettably—revenged.

For the balance of 1585 and into early 1586 both Spain and England gathered their strength for a conflict—but Elizabeth still believed it could be avoided. Her thought was that she would trade Philip II the three Dutch ports she had obtained for a treaty of peace. The Prudent Monarch, however, was a far different man from any other with whom Elizabeth ever had to contend. He knew England; some of his most arduous days had been spent there as the husband of Mary Tudor—and as king. The only real debauch of his life had taken place, in fact, on the occasion he last left those rainy shores. In the years since, he had struggled with a series of popes, privately ordered the execution of his own son, stemmed the Turkish advance into the Mediterranean, subverted the government and the stability of France, conquered Portugal, and extended his immense empire to the Western Hemisphere and the Orient and organized the first ideological state since Rome. Later historians would call it the Elizabethan Era, but it was really the Age of Philip II. No Caesar had ever sent his troops so far so successfully; no monarch before or since ever personally managed as many details of his possessions. Forced by destiny to deal with female sovereigns in England, France, and Scotland; harassed by zealous clerics, opposed by the Calvinist and Jewish diasporas; envied, feared, loved but never absent from anyone's thoughts for long, Philip, in his conclusions and the steps by which he reached them, seemed as remote from ordinary men as the brooding sky itself.

He had long ago, by 1586, lost interest in Mary Stuart, her claims, and her position. Elizabeth was saved only by the watery moat around England. If the borders of her country had been in Europe, her court and courtiers, her proud subjects, and her green lands would have been put to the Spanish torch and either reduced or, as in the Netherlands, been turned into a battleground for a generation. As the direct descendant of John of Gaunt, Philip II now turned toward England as its proper master—and asked the pope how much money he would provide for the task ahead.

The Virgin Queen of England did not believe in war and did not believe any reasons existed for wars. The pope might be in an agony over the division of Christendom and the loss of immense Vatican revenues from England and other vanished branches of the church; Philip II might be intent upon keeping sea routes safe for his empire and equally intent upon suppressing rebellions; the Calvinists of Geneva, France, England, and Scotland might be genuinely convinced that religion had to be wrested out of the control of men interested only in power and money—but Elizabeth considered all these reasons and attitudes childish. Living in a world torn asunder by ideas, she did not believe ideas were real.

Forced into siding, at least on the surface, with the Dutch against the Spanish, she sent her favorite, Leicester, to lead her 8,000 troops in the Netherlands. Her first and major instruction was to garrison the three towns she had obtained as payment for her help: Brill, Flushing, and Rammekins. She warned Leicester not to take a step without permission. Before Leicester even arrived, she had threatened Sir John Norris, who was in charge of the English already landed, not to offend again by fighting. The English, said the Virgin, were "to defend and not to offend."[3]

Meanwhile, she was contacted by the pro-Vatican leaders of the southern provinces of the Netherlands, who were loyal to Philip II and the Vatican and anxious to mediate between Spain and England. The English queen was delighted. Her perceptions were verified; her statesmanship would prevail. She plunged into subterranean negotiations and delayed sending ammunition, provisions, or money to her army.

As usual, however, Elizabeth overlooked facts as represented by other people, who persisted in behaving independently of her wishes. Robert Dudley, the earl of Leicester, arrived at Delft and was greeted with tumultuous, cheering crowds. Hailed as a savior on every hand, feted and provided with a homage he never before knew, the favorite began to glow in a new and exciting independence. His progress raised enormous hope; England's entry into the arena against Philip II sent the entire Calvinist world into transports of joy.

The States, as they called themselves, had many reasons to cling to Leicester. Their long struggle had reduced them; their rebel government was on the thin edge of collapse; they needed a new leader to lift their banner. They pressed Leicester to become their king; and he colored, quivered, and was visibly affected. Such a soaring honor was impossible, but—perhaps—governor. Governor and captain-general, the rebels replied; and the earl, who owed his belt to qualities far removed from the battlefield or government, undertook to obtain permission. Letters of persuasion were drawn for Elizabeth, and others went to Burghley, Walsingham, and the men on the Privy Council who might help Robert Dudley, the earl of Leicester, toward a new and different sort of consummation.

Leicester's letters arrived as the year 1585 ended and 1586 began and were received with considerable interest. Burghley and Walsingham, who watched the landscape assiduously through dozens of paid eyes, knew about the queen's secret negotiations with the Spanish. Burghley was even officially informed and kept such a calm presence to the news that Philip II was told the councillor was favorably inclined.

There was no record made, and certainly none left, of how Burghley and Walsingham discussed these developments or how they planned their next move. But they were Reformers, steeped in the doctrines of Calvin, Knox, and their supporters. They knew that the best-laid plans of princes could be balked by appeals to the people; but they also knew that such appeals, in order to be effective, had to rise as though from the air—spontaneously. The design—and especially the designers—could not be visible.

They turned, therefore, in a direction that had served them well before in the anti-Vatican cause.

# 16

The Queen of Scots suffered at Tutbury Castle under the grim and unsleeping regime of Sir Amyas Paulet. Her local charities had been stopped; the stream of secret correspondence sewed into the lining of books or concealed in the heels of shoes and the invisible writings on linen returned from the laundress had all been halted. The queen's correspondence was limited to open letters, subject to examination and review, to the French ambassador.

This regime was made intolerable by news that her son in Scotland had made himself head of the Kirk and was loud against the Vatican. Great events were circling, and Mary Stuart was immured, as in the bottom of a well. She complained, she was sick, and she was declining. Rumors of her ill health had considerable basis in fact; she had never been robust or without some medical problem. Elizabeth was told that her captive should be moved lest she be accused of having created circumstances that led to her death. That alone would not have moved her, but Walsingham explained that the realm had lost a valuable observation post when it sealed Mary Stuart into isolation. He thought the Queen of Scots could be useful as a means of discovering the real attitudes of her son, James, and the situation—always uncertain—in Scotland.

Having obtained permission by telling part of his reasons, Walsingham then suggested that the Queen of Scots be moved to the home of the Gifford family in Staffordshire. Sir Amyas Paulet was astonished. The father of the family had been imprisoned for being a Catholic recusant—that is to say, a subject who refused to attend Church of England services. One son, it was true, was a Queen's Guard. But one was a Jesuit, who served at Dr. Allen's seminary at Rheims. The third, Gilbert Gifford, who had been out of England since he was eleven, was a dean of the Vatican faith living in Paris. Bristling with suspicion and filled with wonder that the home of such a family should be suggested to harbor his charge, Paulet surveyed the Gifford manor. He discovered features that displeased him. The neighborhood was "ill-affected"—in other words, pro-Vatican. The house had neither moat nor wall, and the windows opened onto a garden into which all sorts of persons could creep under the cover of night. He made his report, and his feelings were soothed when Walsingham gravely agreed the choice was unsuitable.

Paulet was then sent to one or another of several large dwellings in the same region, and he turned each down for lacking the warlike security he preferred. Eventually, the choice narrowed to the home of the earl of Essex —a manor called Chartley—that sat inside a watery moat and was large, comfortable, and well-furnished. The young earl objected, but the Privy Council made short shrift of that. Paulet was under the impression he had made the choice, but the site was next to the Gifford estate.

Elizabeth sent Mary Stuart a nasty letter emphasizing her own kindness and generosity and her cousin's ingratitude, treachery, and general worthlessness. The move itself covered only twelve miles and drove Paulet into a terrible temper. Many carts were needed to transport the queen's books, dresses, and mementos, and she was not settled with her secretaries, her priest, ladies-in-waiting, and servants until Christmas 1585. Then a coded letter—the first in a long time—miraculously found its way to her hand.

It was from Morgan, her trusted—and trustworthy—agent in Paris. By that time, Paulet had been informed by Phillips—Walsingham's secretary. Phillips' post, as the right hand man of the chief of England's secret police, required many talents. He had bribed a brewer in the vicinity of Chartley. The brewer had caused a special cask to be constructed with a false bottom. Mary Stuart's secretary, M. Nau, had then been made aware the brewer was secretly sympathetic and would take a bribe. The letter from Morgan, after all these twists and turns, was then carried in to M. Nau and his mistress in a false bottom at the base of the beer keg.

The letter from Morgan was genuine, but had been decoded and placed in the beer keg by Phillips. It contained an introduction to Gilbert Gifford, the graduate of Rheims, the dean in the Vatican faith and resident of Paris, who had made Morgan's acquaintance and gained his confidence—and who was in the pay of Walsingham.

The queen was told that Gifford would be her central correspondent in England. She could code her letters, put them in the beer keg bottom, and resume her contacts with the world. The brewer, an ordinary citizen of the realm, seemed born for his part. He demanded that Mary Stuart pay him high sums of money for his cooperation. This scandalized Paulet, who knew the brewer was already being paid by Walsingham; he was even more scandalized when the brewer raised the price of the beer itself. Mary Stuart and M. Nau, however, were rendered trusting by this sign of greed. They would never have credited an idealist; corruption seemed reassuringly normal.

They began to reestablish their pro-Vatican contacts, and Morgan helpfully sent along a new code—and its key. Walsingham's secretary, Phillips, moved into Chartley, ostensibly to assist Paulet—and busied himself decoding, copying, and replacing the letters that coursed in and out of Mary Stuart's new residence. In London, Walsingham settled down to wait.

Once the overthrow of Arran had been accomplished and the Hamiltons, the earls of Mar and Angus, and other leaders restored to their estates, the coalition in Scotland began to separate. Mar was once again governor of Stirling Castle; Hamilton, in charge of Dunbarton; Bellenden, of Blackness. Sir James Hume became governor of Edinburgh Castle. These mighty keeps once represented the keys to the power of Scotland—but times were changing—and the nobles were behind the times. Some, however, merely burned for spoils. The young earl of Bothwell, for instance—nephew of Mary Stuart's third husband—was disgruntled and dissatisfied. He considered he had been slighted, and was loud in his resentment.

The great peers, however, reflected a ruling group whose influence was being eroded by a rising class of lesser landowners, known in Scotland as lairds, as well as by clergymen and merchants. These new men, as they were known in England a generation earlier, were represented in the king's court and on his council by Sir John Maitland. Maitland, like his famous elder brother, Lethington, was not religious-minded, but unlike his brother had a keen understanding of the great significance of the Reform. In other respects, he was much like Burghley in England: cool, patient, and farsighted; a true servant of the State—whose interests he placed above all other measures.[1]

Knowing that James hated the Reform ministers above all other men, Maitland encouraged the King to be stern with them. Their return, in the wake of Arran's downfall, was only reluctantly allowed. Discovering no intention to repeal the Black Acts, their sermons immediately resumed at the point they had been interrupted. One—James Gibson—compared James to Jeroboam, who "did evil in the sight of the Lord" in ancient Israel, in the classic Knoxian manner. James, who attended numerous sermons and heard echoes of others, had Gibson summoned to him and to his council. The exchange was bitter, and Gibson charged the king with being a persecutor. James grew loud and sharp, and Gibson expressed some surprise, saying he had often before preached before the king without reproof.

That reminder of his past subservience sent James into a fury. "I give not a turd for thy preaching," he shouted.[2]

Gibson was dragged from the council chamber and thrown into a cell in Edinburgh Castle. Shortly afterwards a statement was issued saying his crime had not been religious; that he was guilty of treason. James, meanwhile stormed against the ministers. He called them "loons, contemptible fellows and seditious knaves." There was no doubt that he hated them and, left to his own devices, would have created such a storm, so many martyrs, and so much material that the revolution itself might have been reawakened.

Fortunately for James, he was neither alone, untended, or free. The Reform earl of Angus, one of the "great lords" to whom Fontenay had referred, whom the king regarded with awe, moved in with soothing words. Patrick Gray, intent upon concluding the treaty with England that he hoped would ensure his own position, was also anxious to see matters go smoothly. But it was Sir John Maitland, the most farsighted and coolest man at court, who saved both James and the day.

It was clear James would not remove the Black Acts, but Maitland went about assuring the ministers that these laws would be "interpreted" easily. Bishops would be no more than ministers with administrative duties. The General Assembly would—at some distant date—be allowed to meet again. James flared at that, but Maitland smoothly promised the assembly would be limited to unimportant ecclesiastical matters.

Having so stilled and calmed the waters, even while Andrew Melville and the archbishop of St. Andrews cursed, anathematized, and eventually excommunicated one another, Maitland moved, surefooted as a cat, to organize and structure the government of lawless Scotland. He launched a quiet census of properties and holdings, examinations into benefices, reforms of the courts, collection of taxes, and numbers of appointments of lairds and commoners to official posts. Without a sound, the instruments of administration began to swing from the control of the high nobles to the new men he himself so well represented.

From Chartley, the Queen of Scots sent out inquiries regarding events, which were decoded and read by Phillips and then replaced in the bottom of the beer keg. The reports she received were conflicting, but contained little that was new. Some thought her cause "decayed," and others were still ardent. In an effort to untangle the discrepancy, a young Jesuit named John Ballard traveled into England "under the name of Captain Fortesque, disguised as an officer with blue velvet jerkin and cap and feather." He toured about the splendid homes of the old aristocracy and found Lord Henry Howard, Lord Arundel, and others—Sir William Catesby, Lord Montagu, Lord Vaux—a new earl of Northumberland—eager in the pro-Vatican cause. He even learned that Lord Claud Hamilton and Lord Maxwell, the latter especially pro-Vatican, would help from Scotland.[3]

Once again the pieces began to form a pattern and—once again—centered on the person of Elizabeth. If the Virgin were to be killed, with the succession still open to Mary Stuart, an uprising on her behalf might still win the day. Relayed to Don Bernardino de Mendoza, now located in Paris, burning with hatred for Elizabeth and her Reform Council members, and busy as the paymaster of the Holy League, the plan grew more detailed. Not only Elizabeth, but Burghley, Walsingham, and Knollys would be killed—and the English world would suddenly upend.

Morgan could not restrain himself from sending a hint to Mary Stuart. "There be many means in hand," he wrote, "to remove the beast that troubles all the world."[4]

Summer in Scotland is fair, and in July 1586 the young king found the world very much to his liking. Elizabeth had sent old Sir Thomas Randolph north to conclude her arrangements and to offer no more than a yearly pension of £4,000. Maitland wanted more, but Elizabeth could barely part with anything; James's desires were limited. He wanted some more horses and some deer. The horses were refused; the deer were sent. Randolph wrote a brief thumbnail in one of his reports. "The King still follows his hunting, riding and writing in metre."[5]

On the surface, the master of Gray, who had inserted himself into the negotiations as James's principal adviser, had won a great victory and had led the English to the treaty they sought. Maitland, who had delayed the signing by insisting on better terms, withdrew to the background. James, however, had won more than Gray, the Reform nobles, or anyone—except Maitland—seemed to realize. England had spent many thousands of pounds, men, arms, armies, efforts, and agonies over more than a generation to secure Scotland. Now the Lords of the Congregation, the Congregation itself, Patrick Gray, and every other figure had been superseded by the young king of Scotland himself. By virtue of descent, which Elizabeth prized above all other accomplishments, James Stuart had become England's man in the North.

Among the many men to whom the release of Mary Stuart was a sacred cause was one who had been a page at her court in Sheffield, grown into reedy manhood, named Sir Anthony Babington. It was Babington's lot to inherit a considerable fortune that removed him from learning the realities of a harsh world. Ballard had contacted Babington, in his secret visits, and encouraged the young man—who, with his fortune, had little difficulty in maintaining a circle—into a plan to rescue the Queen of Scots physically and carry her off to freedom and triumph. With Ballard's assurances that vast overseas help would ensue and anxious to play a great role in a heroic undertaking, Babington wrote a detailed letter to Mary Stuart—in code— describing how eager he and his friends were to assist her. Their plans were laid, but some loose ends remained for her consideration. A harbor had to be selected where her foreign allies could land safely, she had to be taken from the custody of Paulet, and Elizabeth had to die.

By the time that letter reached Mary Stuart, George Gifford had returned to England from Paris to alert Walsingham. Phillips, Walsingham's secretary, was at Chartley and watched the beer keg with its contents carried in to the queen's chambers. Mary Stuart had grown accustomed to Phillip's presence: "a spare, pockmarked, impassive, redhaired man, something over thirty."[6] He later reported to Walsingham that he knew when she read that letter.

It took Mary Stuart five days to answer. Her mail was heavy, and she had many other letters to dictate. Her practice was to sit at a table with M. Nau or her other secretary, Curle, waiting across from her. She spoke French, as always; they wrote; she read and corrected; and they would rewrite. Then it was coded; the queen would examine it again and seal it herself.

The outgoing mail on this occasion included a letter to Lord Paget in Madrid, mentioning a movement underway on her behalf, saying she had given instructions, and recommending that he alert the pope and Philip II that the time had come for action. She took the precaution of sending some harmless letters to persons she did not fully trust. Then she answered Babington, giving specific orders regarding men, horses, and places where she took her air, and suggesting various approaches and diversions. These included setting fire to the stables at night to draw men away, a large mounted body to overcome Paulet and his force on her rides, or a rush into the manor itself in the guise of deliveries. She ended with the words "burn this immediately."

Phillips, with the insatiable hunger of a born policeman, added a postscript in handwriting very nearly—but not quite the same—as the body of the letter. It said, "I would be glad to know the names and qualities of the six gentlemen who are to accomplish the design. . . ."[7]

It took the response ten days to reach Babington, who had been living dreamily. Together with almost a dozen young gentlemen like himself, he had sat happily at taverns, eating and drinking hugely, deep in excited discussions of how they would shift the axis of the world. They were so fond of themselves in this future role that Babington commissioned a group portrait—so history could know how they looked on the verge of their great design. Later it was shown to Elizabeth, who recognized some of the faces.

Toward the end of July, about three weeks after James had signed a treaty with Elizabeth, Babington went to London and applied for a passport. It was his intention to go to Paris to talk to Don Bernardino de Mendoza and arrange for Mary Stuart's "foreign friends" to come to an English harbor.

One would imagine a man on such an errand would have dispensed with proper papers or arranged to carry false credentials or would have sent an agent. Babington, however, thirsted for glory and high place. He talked, at some length, to Mr. Pooley, who was serving as secretary to the man who issued passports: Sir Francis Walsingham. Deciding he had found a sympathetic ear in Pooley, Babington then wanted to meet the great Sir Francis himself. He was ushered in and explained that he had to go to Europe on business and would be happy to serve as a spy upon the refugees who clustered in Paris.

Walsingham appeared impressed, but the matter of a passport was slightly delayed. Two weeks later, on the evening of August 13, 1586, Babington was in a tavern with his friends when they learned that a servant of the disguised priest, Ballard, was a spy for the authorities. Babington, in a panic, sent a sudden secret letter to Walsingham via Pooley, saying he had unearthed a conspiracy.

While he waited for a reply, the authorities themselves arrived, looking for Ballard—the disguised priest. The warrant, which was shown, was signed by the lord admiral—and not Walsingham, and the charge was being a disguised priest. Ballard, looking pale, was led away, and the rest were left to stare at one another.

The boldest of them was named, appropriately enough, Savage. Babington had hired him to kill Elizabeth and in sudden haste scurried around to his lodgings and told him to act at once. Savage protested that his clothes were so shabby he would not be allowed inside the court—and Babington threw a purse at him. Then, wild-eyed, the pseudoleader ran to Pooley and asked to see Walsingham. He wanted to inform him of a plot. To his astonishment he was told to come back in a day or so. Instead, he fled the city of London, which had grown suddenly dark and strange around him, taking four of his circle with him for comfort's sake.

Their attempt at evading capture was on a level with their abilities as conspirators. Having plunged into St. John's Woods, they stained their faces with walnut juice—a white, pale face then being a mark of the upper class and a sun-darkened face being the sign of a laborer. Then they hid in a barn.

At Chartley, Sir Amyas Paulet, in an unusually cheerful humor, suggested to Mary Stuart that they go hunting in Sir Walter Axten's park for deer. The park was nine miles away and contained a lodge known as Tixall. Almost all her entourage, including her two secretaries, were invited to attend; as they rode along, her spirits rose. For a while it seemed almost as if she were free.

As they neared the gates of the park, which opened toward the lodge, the Queen of Scots saw a party of horsemen waiting along the road. Her breath came short; for a moment she was sure her rescuers had arrived. Then one rode forward and stopped before her, touching his cap. He was Sir Thomas Gorges, a familiar at Elizabeth's court. He handed the Queen of the Scots an order and then turned and shouted "Take them away! Do not allow them to speak to her!" Mary Stuart saw her secretaries, Nau and Curle, led off while other hands took the bridle of her horse and led her toward the lodge, Tixall.

While the Queen of Scots was held in the tiny and uncomfortable lodge with no change of clothing and virtually no conveniences, Babington and his associates were hunted, with tremendous hue and cry, through the countryside. The news of a vast Vatican conspiracy to murder the queen and members of the Privy Council, invade the country, burn, pillage, and massacre swept through England. Search parties ranged the landscape in every direction; agents plucked the erstwhile heroes from their barns, haystacks, lodgings, and other impromptu hiding places; only two managed to escape to Europe. News of the captures and arrests were hailed by the tolling of church bells and bonfires; every home and tavern echoed to excited conversation.

At Chartley, investigators invaded Mary Stuart's apartment and forced open drawers, boxes and cabinets; prized apart books; probed every conceivable nook and cranny. Every scrap of written material was seized: notebooks, letters, memorabilia, mementos of eighteen years of confinement were carried away. More than sixty different codes were discovered, as well as a mountain of letters from various English subjects who had, in many cases, written with an eye toward the possible future Queen of England. The mixture—far greater than even the most careful watchers had suspected— was packed and sealed and sent to the Privy Council.[8]

The members of that council, who had been kept in the same darkness as the rest of the country, sat tight-lipped with shock as Walsingham spread his proofs before them. One intercepted letter had claimed Parma had a special army in Normandy on the verge of invasion. Calls were sent out to muster arms; Portsmouth and Plymouth were placed under special guard; messengers were dispatched to warn King James and his Scots to be on their guard against landings.

The news hit Elizabeth, even though she had given Walsingham permission for each of his steps, almost as hard as it did the rest of the country. Although she had given Walsingham permission to proceed, she had not anticipated the huge dimensions of the excitement that would ensue: the crowds that gathered to cheer before the palace, the tolling of the bells, the massing of troops, and the reaction of the people. Presented with a list of names to comprise a special commission, she could find no good reason not to sign; but, as usual, she sought to delay. She refused to name a time for the commission to meet—or a place. Meanwhile, she sent a hasty letter to Mary Stuart, urging her to reveal whatever she knew, in strict confidence.

The letter arrived shortly after Mary Stuart was conveyed back to Chartley. Kept at the Tixall lodge for a fortnight, she had returned "in a wild condition; disheveled for want of attendance and change of clothes." A crowd of beggars were squatting at the gates of the manor as she was convoyed through, and she shouted, "I have nothing for you. I am a beggar as well as you; all is taken from me."[9]

Inside her apartment she stood still in shock. "Some of you will be sorry for this," she said to Paulet. He looked at her with apprehension; Mary Stuart in anger was chilling. Hastily the guardian sent word to London that a stronger and more secure place was needed; he feared a general rising, he said. Actually, for the first time, he had come to fear his prisoner.


The Babington trial was public and held at Westminister, where an enormous crowd could be accommodated. Seven prisoners were brought before a tribunal consisting of peers, judges, and Privy Councillors. The throng listened intently as the deposition of Savage, the intended assassin, was read. He had not been tortured; his confession was clear, concise, and complete. Babington and his associates, however, pleaded conscience and lofty motives; they credited the seminary at Rheims with having taught them that a higher cause excused lower methods. Such a defense stained the Faith they claimed and linked the Vatican cause into treasonable behavior at precisely the moment Elizabeth had considered herself close to a settlement with Philip II. The queen's private feelings about this coincidence and its impact broke out when she crossed Burghley's name off an appointment as lord lieutenant of Hertfordshire.

On September 20, 1586, Babington, Savage, Ballard, Barnwell, Tichborne, and Tilney were "drawn on hurdles" to St. Giles in the Fields. As usual, each was allowed to speak to the crowd, and their explanations were interrupted with shouts, jeers, curses, and demands for their punishment. Their execution was protracted and conducted according to the letter of the terrible sentences that had been passed upon them. They were strangled and then brought down, their bodies cut open slowly, castrated, and carved apart over a period of hours during which their groans could be heard. The crowd, savage as it was, was slowly horrified, and its anger turned upon the executioners. Elizabeth, informed, was sickened by the recital. She gave orders that the remainder of the group, executed the following day, be speedily dispatched. She knew, as did her Privy Council, that Babington and his associates were merely curtain raisers for the first act of a larger drama that was now unfolding, in which she and her cousin Mary Stuart were being forced to play roles not of their own choosing.

At first, James and his advisers in Scotland considered the Babington case another of the seemingly eternal scandals associated with his mother. The young king, still contented with the recognition of his position implicit in Elizabeth's treaty, his pension, his efficient secretary, and his "bedmates" expressed the thought regarding his mother that he did not mind "how strictly she be kept, and all her old knavish servants hanged."

Walsingham, a stage manager whose talents approached genius, then sent him significant excerpts from Mary Stuart's intercepted correspondence—and especially the portions that cursed him as an unnatural son and named Philip II as the queen's heir, and that mentioned his being carried off to Spain to be "educated."

This was not pleasant reading; few men can withstand a mother's dislike. Yet James could not believe his mother was in any danger; his sense of sovereign rights was too strong for that. His advisers, however, were split. Maitland, always an ardent Scot, came to the point very quickly. The king of Scotland could keep his mother safe if he threatened to break off the alliance with England in the event any harm was done her. He knew that James shrank from boldness, but pressed the point nevertheless. If "England stand strict," he said, "they are no more to be trusted, and foreigners to be sought."[10] In other words, Scotland was not so helpless it could not protect the mother of its king.

The master of Gray, however, was in close touch with James Douglas, a lawyer who had recently been appointed James's ambassador to England. Douglas was well known and widely held in low esteem, mainly because he was remarkably unscrupulous even in those corrupt times—but he was quick and intelligent. Douglas's advice from London was to forget about Mary Stuart and remember, instead, the great question of succession to the English crown. If the Queen of Scots were to die, James Stuart would be the heir.

The same thought had come to Elizabeth, and she did not like its appearance. She had the best of both worlds while Mary Stuart was her captive and had all along made sure her cousin was treated with the respect and comfort due an heir. Few monarchs had enjoyed such a truly secure position of total control over their heir, who served as a hostage as well. That was not a situation Elizabeth was anxious to change. James was in Scotland, king of a realm, and beyond her reach. She wondered aloud if he would "play his mother's part." Davison, secretary of the Privy Council, sought to assure her, but she remained uneasy. Meanwhile, the furor over the Babington conspiracy continued, inexorably, into the next stage.

On October 8, 1586, the twelve-man special commission that had examined Mary Stuart's mountainous correspondence held another meeting at Westminister. This time the throng represented the nobility of the realm, who heard the confessions of M. Nau and Curle, listened to Babington's letter and Mary Stuart's response, and were asked to vote upon the question of whether the Queen of Scots should be tried for conspiring against the Crown of England or not. The response was predictable: only a lunatic would have protested at such a moment. The commission ruled that every peer of England who was in the country, of age and not "elsewhere engaged on public duty," was to go to the castle of Fotheringhay to constitute a court.

That huge court, whose judges were the assembled peers of England and which included its Privy Council and officers of state, assembled in the Great Chamber of Presence in Fotheringhay Castle, in Northamptonshire on October 11, 1586. The Hall was sixty feet long, and a chair of state, with a canopy over it, was placed at one end. That chair represented Elizabeth —and was empty.

Burghley, nine earls, and Viscount Montagu sat on benches on the right side of the immense room, and thirteen barons sat on benches on the left. Behind both these high nobles were the Privy Councillors Hatton, Walsingham, Crofts, Sadler, Mildmay, and Sir Amyas Paulet. In front, before the earls, sat Chief Justices Wray and Anderson together with the Chief Baron Manwood and four more judges. The attorney general and solicitor general sat at a small table in front of these figures, and in the center of the room a chair was placed for Mary Stuart.

The queen protested that she was a sovereign and could not be tried by the subjects of another country. She was not in England by her own will; she was not bound by its laws. These were strong arguments and had sustained her for years—they had persuaded Elizabeth to place her cousin beyond judgment on the occasion of her first trial years earlier. But that issue had centered around Mary Stuart's complicity in the murder of her second husband, Darnley. In October 1586 the security of the Crown of England was at stake. And where Elizabeth had kept the first proceeding secret and muffled its conclusions by issuing her own confused and confusing verdict, Walsingham and Burghley made the second trial as public and as official as possible. The entire House of Lords was present; the little village near Fotheringhay Castle was crowded with two thousand of its armed retainers; observers from all quarters representing powers overseas were at the scene.

Protesting, the Queen of Scots nevertheless appeared. She wore a simple dark dress with a white headdress and veil.[11] A maid carried her train; two men supported her at each side; her physician, apothecary, and three ladies-in-waiting trailed her; as she moved, one leg dragged. The effect was of an aging, helpless woman, infirm and unable to threaten anyone. Nevertheless, her spirit was irrepressible; she moved at once toward the large red armchair under the canopy and when directed toward the chair in the center instead, said, "I am a Queen by right of birth and my place should be there under the dais."[12]

Having made that point—which she regarded, always, as her special right to be above the laws of ordinary people—she sat down in the defendant's place and looked about. "So many Councilors," she said sarcastically, "and none for me."[13]

The trial was one-sided and pitted one woman against the assembled brains of the ruling group of England. She conducted herself brilliantly and with no sign of fear. When the court produced copies of her letters to Babington, she demanded the originals. Told they were in code, she wondered how anyone could prove she wrote them—since it was neither her handwriting nor beyond possibility that anyone could transcribe her codes and then produce a forged letter. Walsingham, she said pointedly, was well equipped to manufacture such proofs. That drew blood, and the head of the secret police had to overlook covert smiles.

Forced to listen to the depositions of her arrested secretaries, Nau and Curle, the Queen of Scots made the same point again. Men in prison, foreigners without defenses could be made to say anything for money—or for fear of their lives.

Within hours she reduced the court to angry shouts and accusations, which she interrupted with eloquent discussions of her sincere Vatican faith, her sovereign rights, her mistreatments—and the lack of law involved in her situation. With centuries of canon law behind her, which argued the duty of subjects to obey their leaders, she dwelled on points to which her judges were especially sensitive. Their questioning grew scattered and repetitive. At the end of the second day she rose to leave, pausing at the last moment to pardon them all. Her defense had been made; she had closed with a request to be heard either by the full English Parliament or Elizabeth herself. She left behind an impression not uncommonly achieved by great criminals. Her abnormal self-possession, her smiling indifference, her very ability to shrug away so calmly the most damning evidence had left little room for ordinary compassion. Instead, it evoked the subliminal recognition that she lived and thought in a different dimension from that of ordinary mortals.

They were considering that phenomenon when a note arrived from Elizabeth in London with "a few hasty lines scribbled at midnight." The Virgin ordered the trial suspended and summoned its organizers back to London to make a report. The leaders announced proceedings would resume in the Star Chamber—the room used by the Privy Council for its trials—in ten days.

The Queen of England was distraught. It seemed to her she was surrounded by enemies, by unseen antagonists. Walsingham's evidence, culled from the mountainous correspondence of Mary Stuart, had been devastating. She read letters to her cousin from her favorite Leicester. She burned these, but they seared her mind. In the Netherlands the same Leicester was flouting her orders and was behaving—as best he could—as a commander of forces against Spain, while she had hoped to bring peace between her country and that mighty power.

The Babington conspirators had come very close to Elizabeth in an emotional sense. One was a pensioner of hers, another was the son of her master of wardrobe, and still another the son of her undersecretary. Several of the others had relatives or friends at court. She read letters to the Queen of Scots through the years from her highest peers and well-placed gentlemen, many of whom had knelt before her and received her patronage. She was inundated with Walsingham's proofs and hated them; she was never quite to recover from their deadly effect. Nevertheless, she stopped the trial at Fotheringhay; but when her councillors returned, it was clear matters could not be so stifled.

The country was raging for a conclusion to a situation that had coursed out through the Ridolfi Plot, the Throckmorton revelations, and dozens of lesser scares in between. Foreign observers, for the first time, began to send dispatches home saying that Mary Stuart's case was turning dark.

The Star Chamber met on October 25, 1586, and disposed of those objections that Mary Stuart had raised in her two days of trial. Her secretaries were produced and repeated their testimony—but Elizabeth remained frozen. She would neither judge nor move, and the council advised her that Parliament was gathering to hear the conclusions of its House of Lords. The matter, in other words, had moved beyond Elizabeth's powers. Commons, crowded with Reformers, heard exhortations and was given the evidence; the House of Lords hashed the matter again and again. The members were reminded of the association they had signed to protect their queen and that Mary Stuart had plotted in violation of that pledge. A delegation went to the palace, and Elizabeth sought to soften their resolution, but on the twenty-ninth of November, Parliament passed a sentence of death. All that remained to Elizabeth was to sign the warrant and name the day.

The news was received in Scotland with anger among the people and much of the nobility, with secret pleasure by the Kirk, and consternation by James. Maitland, who had pointed out a course straight and true as an arrow, insisted that he threaten England with an end to the alliance. At first, James agreed and sent Elizabeth a letter to that effect. Harassed and pushed into avenues she resented, feared and resisted, the Virgin exploded. She cursed James, and every repeated word gave him the shakes.

Around him the Vatican nobles stirred. The earls of Huntly, Crawford, Montrose, and others emerged from their relative silence; even the former earl of Arran, Captain James Stewart, reappeared on the scene. A convention of the Estates was called, and the peers of Scotland declared they would fight if their former queen was done to death. James, however, would not hear of this; and after watching his reaction, Maitland decided to drop the matter and step aside. He pushed forward Patrick, the master of Gray— the man who had risen so far with English influence and who had played so large a role in the negotiations that ended in the alliance and James's pension.

Gray was appalled. He was ordered to go to London, and he could see no way from which he could emerge from such a commission with any personal profit. "Refuse I," he wrote to James Douglas, the Scots ambassador, "and the King will think I know already what will come—and if she die, will quarrel with me. Live she, I shall have double harm."[14] He added more to the same effect, but as the established man of England at the court, he was caught.

The year 1586 ended with bells tolling and bonfires lit for the end of Mary. In the palace the queen's Christmas was darkened by deputations.

The French ambassador had warned of the terrible reaction on the part of the pro-Vatican world; agents from Philip II had crept softly in and out. The situation in the Netherlands was chaotic; Elizabeth was besieged by conflicting viewpoints.

It was clear that the attitude of Scotland was very important—even crucial—to Elizabeth's final decision. Gray left for London with a letter authorizing him to negotiate this delicate and complex matter and with another—somewhat ambiguous—letter for the earl of Leicester from James. The earl, back in the English capital, had somehow managed to turn Elizabeth's wrath away and had resumed his position as the most powerful peer at court. In this capacity he treated James Douglas, the ambassador from Scotland, to a ride in his carriage.

Leicester knew Douglas, as indeed the world knew him, as a man to whom principle was a word without meaning. The favorite skillfully extracted what Douglas knew and what Elizabeth yearned to know: that James Stuart would not fight for his mother and was anxious only about his own right of succession. Gray arrived to discover his position, already weak, had been hopelessly undercut.

Gray spoke to Elizabeth, flanked by Robert Melville and Sir William Keith, on behalf of Mary Stuart. Leicester, who was present, as well as a number of others, listened in silence. The Scots requested that the Queen of Scots be reprieved and sent home. Elizabeth asked what assurance she would have against any further efforts on Mary Stuart's part, and they replied that their king and the Scots nobility would guarantee her safekeeping.

"That would be to arm my enemy with double power," Elizabeth said sharply, "and to make him the stronger to do me hurt."[15]

The Scots were astounded, and their faces reflected it. The Virgin, seeing their consternation, softened briefly. "I swear," she said, ". . . I would give one of my arms to be cut off, so that any means be found for us both to live in assurance."

Keith thought he saw an opening and spoke somewhat confusedly. He was out of his depth; Elizabeth wondered if, since James was so concerned for his mother, he would renounce his rights to the succession in the event she misbehaved in his charge.

At that, the master of Gray intervened. Mary Stuart's support, he reminded the Virgin, was based on her faith—but James was of the Reform. If he were named the heir, Mary Stuart would, by that easy act, lose her support.

Elizabeth then let out one of her short curses. "Is it so?" she said furiously. "Get rid of one and have a worse in her place? By God's Passion, that were to cut my own throat, and for a duchy or some Earldom to yourself, you—or such as you—would cause some of your desperate knaves to kill me. No. By God, he shall never be in that place. Tell your King what good I have done for him in holding the Crown on his head since he was born, and that I mind to keep the League that now stands between us—and that if he break it, it shall be a double fault."[16]

They begged her to delay; not to let matters end on that note, to wait a bit. "Not an hour," she said and dismissed them. They had not only failed, but they had made matters worse. They were back in Scotland by February 7, 1587, and were ironically thanked by the king's council for their effort. Then, like the rest of the world, they settled down to wait.

Sir Francis Walsingham had signed some notes as security for Sir Philip Sidney—one of the flowers of the English court—who had died in the Netherlands. Sidney, whose death was mourned throughout his country, had been careless in his affairs. When it came to be settled, it was discovered his will was poorly drawn, his estate was tied up—and Walsingham was liable for a fortune. The creditors descended, and Walsingham appealed to Elizabeth for help. She had received, as a result of his efforts, the estates of the Babington conspirators; as a result of his various discoveries, heavy fines and other properties had fallen to the Crown. Nevertheless, she turned away. Babington's estate was given to Sir Walter Raleigh, and Walsingham was reduced to near-penury. He retired to his house; he feared Elizabeth would never forgive him for the disclosures he had forced her to confront.

Burghley, meanwhile, was ill. He was at Theobalds, his palatial estate, suffering from a variety of disorders. The other members of the Privy Council, whom the queen regarded darkly, were left without instructions and forbidden her presence. The sense of silent pressure was almost visible, and Elizabeth paced the floor of her apartment alone, while her ladies in waiting could hear her muttering to herself.

Finally, Lord William Howard of Effingham—her uncle—came to her and told her she would have to act. She told him to have William Davison, Walsingham's assistant, who was acting as secretary in his absence, come to her.

Davison, who had been waiting in the park, came in upon Lord Howard's instruction, carrying a number of documents. Elizabeth asked him what he had, and he said, "Divers things to be signed. . . ." The queen sat down and began to sign them all, moving rapidly from one to the next, dropping each on the floor when she finished—Mary Stuart's death warrant among them. Humbly, Davison bent down and retrieved them, and when he straightened was surprised to have the queen ask him if he were sorry.

He answered stoutly that it was a matter of justice. She smiled faintly and said he should go and tell the lord chancellor—and tell him the Hall of the castle was a more suitable place than "the green, or the courtyard." Then, she added, he ought to tell Walsingham. "The grief of it might kill him," she added sarcastically.

Davison, feeling uncomfortable, started to leave when she called to him to wait and mentioned the association—that famous signing of a national agreement to protect her. If a "loyal subject" relieved her of the embarrassment of killing her kinswoman, she said, it might "disarm the resentment of Scotland and France—and give their Kings an excuse not to quarrel with her." Davison should speak to Walsingham about that and remind Paulet and Sir Drue Drury, his coguardian, that they were members of the association. Davison realized then that she still wanted to evade the responsibility, though her signature was still fresh on the warrant. He was bold enough to say such a message would be "lost labor," but the Virgin insisted—and like a mother talking to a boy, told him what words to use. He bowed and fled.

Davison, whose actions were later retraced in infinite detail, then carried the warrant to the Court of Chancery, where it was sealed without being read and continued to Walsingham. That eternal servant of the state heard the queen's message and wrote a letter to Paulet and Drury, making it clear they could save everyone a great deal of embarrassment. Then Davison went to his office, where the warrant was witnessed and signed, and sent it off. That was on Thursday, February 12, 1587.

On Friday the queen sent Davison a note telling him to delay. He ran to the palace, filled with foreboding, and told her it had already been sent. She seemed displeased, and he reminded her he was following orders and wondered if they had changed. They had not, but everyone was placing the responsibility on her; she did not like that. He murmured it was all honorable and just, but she walked out of the room.

At Fotheringhay, Paulet read the queen's hope and was horrified. In her service he had dealt with spies, traitors, greedy and unscrupulous men, but he had held her above these. He showed Drury the hint that they should relieve Elizabeth by turning to murder. He then sat down to write an indignant reply. "God forbid I should make such a shipwreck of my conscience," he said in part.

Meanwhile, Davison went to Burghley, who assured him he had acted irreproachably. The members of the commission were summoned. Lord Kent and Lord Shrewsbury were named as official witnesses. They had to be informed and brought to Fotheringhay. Robert Beale, the secretary of the Privy Council and the opponent of Whitgift, hurried off on that task. Not long afterward, Davison, again with Elizabeth on some official matters, was told she had dreamed the Queen of Scots was executed and was so angry that if she had a sword, she would have run it through him. Davison, now deeply concerned, looked at her anxiously, but she was smiling. He smiled too and asked her if she would go through with it. "Yes," she answered shortly.

A few days later Paulet's letter arrived, and she cursed against "precise fellows who in words would do great deeds, but in deed perform nothing." The next day she brought the matter up again and said it was time it was dispatched. Davison started to tell her the date had been settled when some ladies entered the room, and he never got around to telling the queen the day.


The Queen of Scots had been kept waiting six weeks when she was told that Robert Beale, the secretary of the Privy Council, had arrived. The news was like the tolling of a bell.

The others arrived after Beale, but nobody brought the news to Mary until Tuesday, February 7, 1587. The heavy meal of the day, dinner, was then held around noontime. Soon afterward, a servant appeared at the queen's apartment to announce visitors. They appeared shortly afterward: the earl of Shrewsbury, who had been her sympathetic guardian for so many years and whose appointment to this task contained a touch of malice; Lord Kent, a stern Reformer; Beale; and Sir Drue Drury. They told her that her sentence would be carried out, and for a brief few minutes her nerve broke. Turning toward her physician, she began to speak about some debts of hers in France, and then she stopped and asked—When?

Eight o'clock the following morning. She was stunned, and said, "The time is very short."[17]


The following morning the provost marshal knocked on the door of the queen's apartment. He received no answer and went for the sheriff, but when he returned, the door opened, and Mary Stuart, dressed as for a court appearance, emerged. She was in black satin with a long white veil that trailed behind her shoulders and down her back. She carried a crucifix and a prayer book and entered the great castle Hall to find three hundred spectators waiting. A fire was blazing in the chimney; the furniture had been removed. At the upper end of the Hall was a small platform a little over two feet high and twelve feet square covered with black cloth, surrounded by a small black-covered railing. On the platform was a black block; on its top was a black cushion. Behind that was a black chair; each side of the platform also held a black chair for the official witnesses Shrewsbury and Kent. Two men, dressed in black, with black hoods from which their white eyeholes gleamed, waited silently. The axe leaned against the inside of the railing.

The warrant was read aloud. Dr. Fletcher, dean of Peterborough, with the strange insensitivity that clergymen occasionally betray, came forward and exhorted her to change her faith. She answered sharply, and a sort of argument took place that ended when the queen sank to her knees to pray. When she began, Fletcher raised his powerful preacher's voice to drown hers, but she did not falter, and he stopped while her Latin continued.

Finally, she rose and put her crucifix on one of the chairs; an executioner stepped forward to claim his right, but was ordered off. The rules, on this occasion, were to be different. Her ladies came forward then, and the veil was lifted off carefully to show her shining coifed wig. Then the black robe was lowered, showing a red velvet petticoat; the black jacket was removed and revealed another red undergarment. One of her ladies handed her a pair of red sleeves which she used to cover her arms and was, at last, bloodred altogether. Barbara Mowbray tied a handkerchief around the queen's eyes, and she knelt before the block. She murmured, *"In manus, Domine, tuas, commendo animam meam."* The axe swung and missed; the second blow severed her head entirely except for a shred. The executioner cut that off, reached down for the head and lifted it up by the hair, but it came apart in his hand. He held up the wig while the grizzled, wrinkled face of an old lady rolled horridly across the platform. Mary Stuart, the White Devil, was dead—and in that moment the destiny of her son, James, suddenly rose aloft like a star.

# PART FOUR

# King James VI
## of Scotland

# 17

In Scotland, James listened to the first reports of his mother's execution "and moved never his countenance."[1] Some observers were puzzled at this, but the young king—now past twenty—was quick with the explanation that he did not believe the report.

In England the Virgin chose melodrama. She left on a hunt on February 10, 1587, just as young Lord Talbot, the heir to the earl of Shrewsbury, arrived from Fotheringhay on a mud-splattered horse. Talbot rushed in to tell Burghley, and the aging councillor nodded wearily. He advised the young man to wait; the queen would know soon enough. By midday the news was echoing through the palace of Greenwich; the queen heard the bells of the city tolling and was informed when she returned. She flew into her chambers and gave way to a storm of weeping, while her mind turned the event around for retrospective analysis.

By Friday, the following morning, she decided she had been tricked; the revolution that had sent Mary Stuart into exile had used the Queen of England as an instrument to try publicly, convict, and execute a sovereign for the first time in the history of the world. She had not only been tricked, but used; her policy of peace had been undermined and her Privy Council had maneuvered events and wrested their control and direction from her hand. The more she wept, the more convinced she became that cunning men had undermined her.

On Friday, February 11, 1587, she sent for Christopher Hatton, the new lord chancellor, and told him that Davison—that sly and deceptively humble man—had deliberately deceived her. The warrant she had signed had been but a mere instrument—a threat to be held against contingencies; she had never been told it would be executed without her express permission.

On Saturday she summoned the Privy Council, whose members bowed and even wept before her anger. The storm broke mainly against Burghley, whom the Virgin considered the archplotter who had misled her into a tremendous offense against all princes, and she ordered Davison to the

Tower. The entire group fell to its knees, and the unhappy undersecretary was dragged away on a charge of high treason. No official so charged had ever emerged "in one piece" through the Traitor's Gate. Burghley protested and was ordered out of the chamber.

As the news of the queen's displeasure spread, the Reform celebrations at the downfall of the great Vatican symbol began to falter. Sir Robert Carey, sent to Scotland with a letter from Elizabeth describing Mary Stuart's death as "an unfortunate accident" and offering to increase James's pension and even to acknowledge him as an heir, was stopped at the border.

When James himself finally received official notice toward the end of February, 1587, he announced his "deep displeasure" and went to bed without supper. He had decided upon a proper expression of grief and announced he wanted to be alone, journeying to Dalkeith in "a dull weed of purple"—the color of mourning. The earl of Bothwell, discontented and anxious for action, said "a suit of mail" would be more appropriate. The air rang with threats from various of the dead queen's pro-Vatican supporters.

The reaction from Europe was delayed because Elizabeth, in her fury at having been outwitted—and there was little doubt her resentment was well-founded—had closed all the English harbors and stopped the overseas mails. These steps had not been anticipated; the Reform movement had planned to take advantage of Mary Stuart's removal as a great and disturbing symbol of the Vatican cause by mounting a massive demonstration in the House of Commons.

Elections had been held, and the Commons was packed with Reform members. Their position was that God was above all queens, kings, and princes—and they assembled in the cheering conviction that the death of the Queen of Scots for violating God's laws had proven the point beyond argument. They had spent previous months in an amazing effort, in which a survey of the nearly ten thousand churches of England had been undertaken. Many had been discovered without resident pastors, performing no useful purpose—while Crown-appointed prelates enjoyed a variety of privileges. The purpose of the survey was to prove that Whitgift's High Commission, "which had cruelly treated many ministers, depriving them, imprisoning them and holding them in irons," was proceeding in the wrong direction.

All these grievances, surveys, and observations culminated in a "General Supplication Made to the Parliament" against the forced oaths and proceedings of the High Commission against the Reform as part of a great plan to establish a Church along Genevan lines. Elizabeth, aroused to the full meaning of this movement, used her high anger over her cousin's death as reason to turn savagely on these efforts and to quash them.

The Virgin was determined to restore the program the Reform had so seriously undermined. She listened impatiently to James Douglas, the ambassador from Scotland, who told her that James was not convinced of her innocence in his mother's death. She heard, with mounting fury, words that sounded sarcastically familiar. The young king demanded proofs of Elizabeth's innocence and punishment of those guilty. Her response was that her position as a sovereign placed her beyond such a need; it was the same defense Mary Stuart had herself mounted. Elizabeth was enraged at the irony; she had no sense of humor where her own dignity was involved.

The Queen of England, however, was able to convince herself of anything she wanted to believe and was capable of carrying out dramatics to prove any point. She hated the Reform with all her heart, and with Whitgift acting as archbishop of Canterbury she intervened in Commons to prevent the Reformers from gaining any advantage from Mary Stuart's execution. At the same time, she pressed the courts to bring a charge—any charge—against Davison in order that he be punished and her own innocence emphasized.

A commission consisting of a number of notoriously pro-Vatican peers, Whitgift and one of his bishops, was appointed. Even this heavily stacked tribunal, however, found it impossible to find Davison guilty of anything except zeal; he was convicted of "precipitancy"—a charge created for the purpose, after the event, and unknown to any book of law. He was fined 10,000 marks—a heavy sum that equaled his resources—and was sent back to the Tower to remain imprisoned at "the Queen's pleasure."

By March 1587 the Virgin had so stamped upon the lesson of Mary Stuart that Peter Wentworth rose in the Commons to deliver a paper on freedom of speech, with telling effect. He questioned the queen's right to dictate men's beliefs, cited the Magna Carta and the arguments of the Reform, and demanded that the reform be extended to the Church of England. He was clapped into the Tower of London immediately. A day later Wentworth was joined by four more members of Parliament.

The Reform leaders in Scotland, however, moved to support a king they had themselves created. The loss of Mary Stuart was a gain in their eyes; they worked among the people to make that view popular. The pro-Vatican lords did not share that attitude; they were contacted by the duke of Guise, Don Bernardino de Mendoza, and the duke of Parma. These moves took some time to mount, however, and Maitland was busy on James's behalf.[2] Learning that Lord Maxwell was threatening to burn Newcastle in retaliation, he had James order the firebrand out of the country. Somewhat surprisingly, Maxwell obeyed.

At the same time, Maitland was happy to catch the master of Gray in contact with incipient Vatican rebels. He laid the proofs before James and raised the charge that Gray had deceived the king and had encouraged the English to murder Mary Stuart against the king's wishes. That had the effect of creating a scapegoat.[3] The switch in emphasis helped James immeasurably.

The young king of Scotland showed, in fact, unexpected dexterity—though not on an order or a level to impress Elizabeth. She was told his wounds could be healed with money; the news relieved her. The Virgin had a fine scorn for anyone who liked money even nearly as much as she did herself. She sent back a scathing reply. James, she said, had raised a point of profit rather than honor.

That would have abashed an ordinary man, but James Stuart was born without a sense of shame. He simply named the profits he wanted: an English dukedom, which would enable him to obtain the Lennox estates and incomes in that realm, and an acknowledgment that he was now the heir to the throne of England. Elizabeth, seeing he was back in his proper state of subservience, turned toward other problem areas of far greater import and the reactions of mightier men.

The mightiest of these was Philip II of Spain, and the next in importance was Pope Sixtus V. They provided a study in contrasts. Philip had spent immense sums creating the combination monastery, tomb, chapel, and headquarters called the Escorial. Hidden from sight in a small group of rooms that opened above the altar onto the church within, he served as the chief administrator, clerk, magistrate, commander, and unseen presence of his vast empire. As the years passed, he was increasingly indifferent to social events and disliked appearances. His world was one of the mind, in which he ruled—as no king before or since—through reports, memorandums, notes, and thoughts whose patterns were his alone.

Sixtus, on the other hand, chattered incessantly. His thoughts were as hidden as Philip's, but by a cloud of words rather than silence. In anger he would "fling his dinner plates about." Italian to the core, he discussed his plans, in variations, with anyone who lingered nearby. This habit did not mean, however, that anyone knew what Sixtus would do or planned to do.

Between the two men were two more who served as brokers for a crusade against England. Like brokers, they would gild the offer of one to the other or diminish it by cautious shading to elicit a counteroffer. They were both English, both zealous, and both priests. One was Fr. William Allen, a former master at Oxford and longtime refugee, who had grown white in the service of his faith and Mary Stuart. The other was younger, shorter, and darker and was named Robert Parsons. Parsons was a Jesuit who had accompanied Edmund Campion to England and, unlike Campion, had survived the experience. Both men switched, on the news of the execution of Mary Stuart, their allegiance to Philip II.

Their efforts had, among other inventive strokes, resulted in the publication of a genealogy for Philip II, demonstrating, or trying to demonstrate, that he was the rightful heir to the throne of England after the Queen of Scots. On the eve of her execution, they were immersed in conversations between the king of Spain and Pope Sixtus V regarding the financing of an invasion. In its wake, the pace of these talks became brisk and businesslike.

The Virgin, in fact, was slow to realize the extent to which she had been entangled. Sir Francis Drake had persuaded her to invest in one of his expeditions again and even talked her into contributing six of her naval vessels. By April 1587 she had Leicester back in the Netherlands and was receiving a stream of requests for money from that chaotic arena, and Drake was on the verge of sailing against the Spaniards. The queen did not want these warlike events to continue; she could not believe that there were issues worth a war.

Intent upon the course interrupted by Mary Stuart's execution, Elizabeth sent Leicester back to the Netherlands with instructions that amounted to orders to be ineffectual. In the earl's case they were hardly needed; he was personally brave and clambered about busily, but a large campaign was beyond his capacity. At the same time the queen sent agents to Parma and his master, Philip II, to offer them the towns she held as security from the Dutch rebels—Brill, Flushing, and Rammekins—as an inducement for peace. This offer to betray the Reform in the Low Countries came as easily to her as taking a breath; she was no friend to rebels whatever their faith.

Unfortunately, the English queen also had to deal with a group later times would call the public. It consisted, in her day, of merchants and "new men," sea rovers and adventurers, as indifferent to religion as possible—but also as adamant against Spain as possible. She had been seduced again and again into investments by such as Hawkins and Drake, in their expeditions against the treasure ships and ports of Philip. Sir Walter Raleigh had landed a colony on a vast territory in the Western Hemisphere that he called—to her delight—Virginia. Sir Francis Drake had not only persuaded her to invest in a new expedition, but also to include six of her naval vessels. She recalled this in time to send word that they should delay, but Drake sailed ahead of schedule in April 1587 to avoid receiving just such a message.

To the delight of England and the amazement of western Europe, Drake did not head for the Indies or treasure, but for the coast of Portugal, where Philip II was assembling a great fleet. This destination, a clear violation of the queen's expectations, was in line with secret instructions from Walsingham and other members of the Privy Council, who were alarmed at the extent of Spanish preparations. By the end of the month, he was off Cadiz, which was crowded with Spanish transports. Against the protests of Admiral Burroughs, the sea warrior carried his fleet into the harbor, sinking a galleon en route; halted beyond the range of shore guns; and proceeded to sink, according to his own estimate, thirty-seven galleys and cargo vessels. A day after this carnage, he sailed toward Cape St. Vincent, sinking, on the way, more galleys and cargo vessels and leaving behind a trail "of smoking ships." In need of water, he stopped at Faro, sent boats ashore, stormed, and took its forts. Admiral Burroughs's protests continuing, Drake had the admiral confined to quarters. From there he headed toward Lisbon, where he planned to attack and sink the entire Spanish navy. En route he delayed at Lagos, where his soldiers were unable to take the fort; proceeded to Cape Sagres, where he did take the castle—which he burned. Five days later he was off Lisbon and sent in some insulting challenges to Santa Cruz, Philip's admiral. Then he sailed back to Cape St. Vincent to the port of Sagres for outfitting and some rest for his men.

Drake's idea of resting was strenuous. He had some ships out at all times, sweeping up and down the coast for distances each way. In the course of the efforts, he sank more than a hundred vessels—mostly small—which included many fishermen, but also many that carried hoops and "pipe staves." These were essential to Philip's fleet for the creation of casks that carried supplies.[4]

In early June, Drake suddenly left Cape St. Vincent and sent a part of his squadron back to London; it arrived safely. Then, sailing with six ships, he overtook and captured a carrack–a huge vessel named the *San Felipe,* loaded with spices and Oriental goods, gold, silver, jewels, silks, and ivories worth well over £100,000.

He returned to find his name had soared high into the firmament; Elizabeth's share of his prize was £40,000—and he had delayed the great Armada of Spain. Elizabeth bit her lip. She was pleased and irritated at the same time; her negotiations for peace had been dealt a severe blow—and yet she loved the fame, the excitement, the money, and the great victory Drake had achieved.

18 The king of Scotland would be twenty-one years old on
June 19, 1587. His government maintained its official
anger over his mother's death in England, but unofficial
communications were seeping back and forth. In the
meantime, with great powers moving about on the
landscape in mysterious maneuvers, James sought to
show a friendly face to every quarter.

As long as Maitland was in charge of his efforts, they were shrewd,
subtle, and cool; his own took peculiar forms. One, on May 15, 1587,
undertaken while Drake was creating havoc off the coast of Portugal, was
to summon his peers to a great banquet in Edinburgh. "The King came
from the palace of Holyroodhouse to the castle of Edinburgh; from that to
the Tollbooth and . . . to the Market Cross, where a long table was set,
furnished with bread, wine and sweetmeats. The Cross was covered with
tapestry, and upon it the trumpeters blowing, and the musicians singing."[1]

There James drank to everyone, and every lord drank, virtually, on
command, to every other. "The gibbets at the Cross were broken down with
fire-balls and fire-spears; the glasses, with wine, sweetmeats, were cast
abroad in the streets." Afterward the fierce feudal lords, who left an enduring definition in the very word *feud,* walked up High Street with each man
holding hands with his worst enemy, while the cannons of the castle thundered. This love feast was silly on the surface, but serious enough in intent.
James had an adviser in John Maitland, who was, for the first time, not only
congenial to the young king, but intent upon improving the king's position
as well as his own.

Unlike every previous favorite there was no sexual implication in
Maitland's relationship with James. They came together in a mutual dislike
of the Reform and of the high nobility as well. Fontenay had noted, years
before, that James held the great nobles of his realm "in awe." Maitland
held them to be disturbers of the realm, representatives of a group that kept
the country in turmoil and the Crown deliberately weakened. If Scotland
was to be properly managed, the nobles had to be reduced.

His approach to this task was so stealthy, complicated, and shrewd that even historians in later years were not sure of what they reviewed. James held his banquet, and shortly afterward a new Parliament was assembled. Maitland rose before it and spoke so spiritedly regarding Scotland's disgrace over the execution of Mary Stuart that the nobles were bathed in sentiment and knelt in unison to vow revenge. The English were alarmed and thought a new Scots assault was being meditated.

The pro-Vatican faction was immensely heartened. Its leaders had been in touch with the duke of Guise; with Don Bernardino de Mendoza, Philip's man in Paris; and with the duke of Parma. This trio offered help and muttered—not for the first time—about barges loaded with troops that would land in Scotland. The earl of Huntly, one of the leaders in this subversive program, was encouraged when James gave him most of the rich estate of Dunfermline, which he took away from the fallen favorite Patrick, master of Gray. Colonel Sempill, an agent of Philip who appeared from the Netherlands, was allowed to lope across the landscape unchecked, and Robert Bruce, a Vatican agent in charge of coordinating some efforts, corresponded secretly with the court.

Yet Maitland and James, at almost the same moment and in the same breath, received Robert Carey from England and discussed the size and nature of Elizabeth's contribution to the king. At the same time, they sent letters to the duke of Guise and to Henry III and even to other parts, asking for assistance, and opened a correspondence with Henry Bourbon, the king of Navarre—enemy of Guise and leader of the Reform in France. Bourbon was pleased; he needed all the allies he could get, and he had a sister he thought a suitable wife for the rising young monarch of Scotland. To help that union, he sent du Bartas, a famous Huguenot poet, to Edinburgh as his personal ambassador. James was delighted; du Bartas's writing was familiar to him, and famous writers had not yet grown common. He toured with the Frenchman and encouraged Andrew Melville to orate before them on church government, though Melville's views kept James "in anger all the night."

Nevertheless, the marks of favor toward the Congregation that James and Maitland had to make were immensely important in retaining the support of the people. Another set of moves, far-reaching in significance, showed more of the adviser's cool and calculating mind than of James— though the king was an aware participant. These were plans to reorganize the courts and the method by which their rulings were enforced, the creation of commissions to regulate the coinage, and, most important, the Crown annexation of all Church benefices. This measure was carefully guarded by mounds of fine print to keep the Reform and its ministers from mounting a new rebellion. It left the Kirk, therefore, much as it was, but cut the power of the nobility in this area and transferred it to the king. James suddenly had, in other words, the immense and important power of patronage.

The ministers were delighted, for the step seemed to undercut bishops as well as nobles, though such offices remained on the books. At the same time, Parliament itself was expanded to include lairds—who had to pay, however, for the privilege. New election rules were drawn, and the Crown eventually obtained some £40,000 as a result.

These sweeping changes did not, at the time, mean too much to the great nobles. Other Scots Parliaments had drawn great plans that had vanished as soon as their ink had dried; there were those who expected no more from these. But Maitland, who was given estates and a variety of new titles—as well as the office of chancellor "for life"—was to prove that the changes of 1587 could be made permanent. Meanwhile, the pro-Vatican faction did not argue: all the world knew the mighty Philip II was getting ready for war, and they believed his inevitable victory would bring the real changes they desired.

In midsummer 1587, while James and Maitland attempted to bring some coherence into disorderly Scotland, the duke of Parma moved toward the coast of the Netherlands. The Spanish plan was beginning to form. Father Allen and Father Parsons had convinced the Prudent King that an assault against England would be greeted with joy by the Vatican followers of that realm. Sixtus V had agreed to pay a million crowns toward this effort —but refused to hand any of the money over until Philip's troops were actually on English soil.

Philip hoped to keep his intentions as secret as possible as long as possible, but that was impossible in any negotiation involving Sixtus V. The pope discussed the plans with everyone who came into sight and sent rivers of suggestions toward Spain, which annoyed Philip II almost beyond endurance. The king of Spain was notoriously devout, but he did not worship the clergy.

Fathers Allen and Parsons, however, were in their great moments. Philip II had received them, had listened to them, and recommended that Allen be made a cardinal and the legate for England. That would mean, in the event of success, that Allen would be the new archbishop of Canterbury in a restored Catholic country.

The duke of Parma was involved in the great plan from another point. Like many others, he may have wondered where Spain was getting the money for the most sweeping plans the world had ever seen—especially since paying his own troops in the bottomless war in the Netherlands had not always been easy for him. Nevertheless, he was told that his part would consist of obtaining coastal ports, assembling a vast number of barges, organizing his troops, and joining them to the Armada being created. Parma would lead the soldiers, in other words, in the subjugation of England. He did not anticipate any pleasure in this task. His opinion of English fighting qualities, formed from experience, was high. Nevertheless he prepared by driving first toward Ostend and then at Sluys. That port, relatively sparsely defended in terms of numbers but considered virtually impregnable from land, soon found itself besieged by the best engineer and soldier of the day.

Elizabeth was taken by surprise. She had persuaded herself that her negotiations for peace were calming the situation. While she adjusted to reality enough to allow Burghley back to her presence, Parma settled down to a siege grim even by the standards of one of the most vicious and protracted of Europe's wars. By early August 1587, Sluys capitulated, though an English fleet carrying troops under Leicester appeared on the horizon and could not puzzle its way to the defenders. That gave Parma Dunkirk, Sluys, and Nieuport. He began to collect hundreds of flat-bottomed barges and a mixed but veteran force of Spaniards, Germans, and Italians.

Another polyglot collection was being formed in Lisbon under the veteran naval hero—as famous at sea as Parma on land—the Marquis de Santa Cruz. Santa Cruz had more ships than the world had ever before seen assembled; he had at least 20,000 soldiers, an equal number of seamen, and an almost equal number of slaves.

Had the Armada sailed at that time, the English had no collected naval force with which to greet them and would have had to defend their country on land for the first time since William the Conqueror. Elizabeth, however, was scornful of the danger and intent upon negotiating a peace. Domestic matters, in fact, obsessed her—as they had ever since Mary Stuart's death.

She listened to Whitgift, the archbishop of Canterbury, who agreed with her that the Crown's greatest danger came from dissident church groups. Whitgift even unearthed a small group of fanatics who were immediately termed Separatists, who had decided the Church of England was as corrupt as that of Rome and who wanted to establish a completely new sect apart from the state in every sense.[2] These subversives, whose views created a shudder through the country, were thrown into the Clink and their leader, Barrow, sought everywhere.

Meanwhile, the queen heatedly defended Leicester, whose efforts to rescue the defenders of Sluys had cost a fortune and resulted in a display of impotence, evoking charges of incompetence. The earl was incompetent along the lines that Elizabeth preferred. He was a soldier who did not create any damage in the field. The queen, in fact, now began to voice a new theory, to the effect that professional soldiers and maritime adventurers were deliberately attempting to pull her country into war in order to achieve glory and profit for themselves.[3] She made it clear that the Crown would not listen to such counsels; that military men could not be trusted to discuss matters of high state.

As always, Elizabeth had some intuitive shrewdness in her opinions. In Spain, Philip the Prudent read dispatches from Santa Cruz that called his attention to a multitude of deficiencies in the preparations underway, to the need for more ships, more men, more guns, more powder, more stores —and more time. The month of September came and passed, and then October arrived with its winds. The seas of the north Atlantic grew stormy and cold.

In France, Henry Bourbon fought, to universal surprise including his own, a battle against the Catholic armies—and won. While eyes turned toward that event to assess its significance, the duke of Guise took a small army against a much larger German force near Chartres and also won. These twin surprises left King Henry III in his old position between contending forces, but he found his grip on his crown slipping. If it failed altogether, Guise would be the new sovereign of France—and Guise was in the pay of Philip II.

By that time, however, it was November, and too late for the Armada to sail. Fortune, whose gifts are unpredictable, had given the Virgin a reprieve.


Elizabeth and Whitgift used that time to set a great hunt into motion against the Separatists, who denied the doctrine that the head of the government, or the government itself, had any right to interfere in religion. The leader of the sect, Henry Barrow, was arrested when he visited one of his flock in the Clink.[4] In short order he was brought before Whitgift, who salivated at such a prize. The prisoner began the struggle by asking why he had been arrested. He was told that information would be given as soon as he took an oath to tell the truth. Barrow agreed to swear, but only if he was not forced to swear. Then he said he would not swear until he knew why he had been arrested. Whitgift, breaking his own system, said he was arrested for not attending church and therefore for defying the queen.

Barrow said these were charges. When evidence was produced, he would swear. Whitgift, beginning to sweat, assured him his responses would be credited more than any other evidence and asked him to swear to tell the truth. Barrow said, "I would know to what I swear—before I swear."

Whitgift, amazingly, held his temper long enough to run around that circle again. If anything "unlawful" was asked, he said, Barrow need not answer. "I have not learned to so swear," Barrow replied. "I will first know, and consider the matter before I take an oath."

The exchange ended, as everyone knew it would, with Barrow being hauled back to prison, but Whitgift's difficulties resumed at the next session. Barrow's stand was so difficult to penetrate that the archbishop humored him to the unprecedented extent of producing the charges against him, based on a manuscript that had denounced the Church of England. The reading was considered a "rare favor." Barrow disagreed and refused to take an oath. "Where is his keeper?" Whitgift shouted, ". . . Away with him; clap him up close, close, let no man come at him."[5]

Though the High Commission had similar difficulties with other Reformers, their principles did not extend as far as Barrow's, and his case created a sensation. A special commission was created to deal with him at the special order of Elizabeth herself, who followed the matter with great interest. Barrow, who had some legal background, would simply not cooperate in providing the government with testimony with which it could punish him. His stand was shared by virtually all Reform ministers who had no objections to an established church, but many to the one that Elizabeth had established.

Yet the High Commission was generally effective. Searches, secret agents, tortures, savage confinement in barbarous conditions, mass arrests, fines, and loss of livelihoods were gradually reducing resistance.

It was remarkable, in view of these activities, that James and Maitland in Scotland were taking a somewhat different course. King James had settled down, or so it appeared, and was busying himself in the long Scots winter evenings by composing comments on the Apocalypse and writing sermons against "the Papists and the Spaniards."

For the first and practically the last time in his life, James Stuart drew close to the Congregation of his country. He and Maitland had learned that Scotland was included in the vast plans of Philip II. While the Armada was being organized in Lisbon and Parma was collecting men and barges in what would become Belgium, the pro-Vatican nobles of Scotland had been told that ships would be leased in Scotland to carry grain to Parma at Dunkirk—and would be sent back with Parma's troops.

The delays of the entire great expedition had delayed that Scots part of it as well, but James was not the only one that winter to believe that immense forces of immeasurable significance were forming.


For generations the awful imagery and prophecies of the Book of Revelation had intrigued, impressed, and drawn the imaginations of men in all walks. Magicians and astronomers, scholars and their schools had created systems of analysis that ranged from the Cabala to numerology—and for many years had prophecied that the final battle between the forces of Good and Evil would arise in the year 1588. James Stuart, king though he was, was part of his times. His writings on the subject during that winter were prepared as though original, but echoed a widespread feeling that swept across the international borders of all western Europe. A sense of imminent doom, of huge invisible forces coming into conflict, of the end of the world itself suffused the atmosphere. Melanchthon had written of a cyclical pattern to events based on multiples of ten and seven and had prophesied that only seventy years remained after Luther's defiance of the Vatican, before Armageddon. That grim forecast repeated an even earlier one by Regiomontanus, the mathematician who created the tables that guided Columbus and others. As the dread year 1588 came into being, a rush of prodigies, omens, and grotesqueries was reported to give credence to the sense of impending change. Almanacs appeared describing dreadful calamities to come.[6]

To the duke of Parma these calamities did not need to be contained in almanacs. The long, cold, wet winter swept across his fine army of 30,000 men—kept in the open in expectation of an Armada that did not appear. Disease appeared and plucked his troops in clusters that ran, as the weeks passed, into hundreds and finally thousands.

Word came from Philip II to delay with Elizabeth's peace ambassadors as long as possible. That kept Parma from falling upon Ostend, which was barely defended and sinking into ruins. Elizabeth, however, was sure there would be no war, providing the talks were continued. She was willing to force the Dutch rebels into a settlement and thought Philip II could establish a "toleration" along her own lines, in which formal observances of the official faith would be sufficient. The Virgin could never grasp that religion was real.

The English Privy Council, however, had different views. A system of warning beacons along the coast was established and a network of inland preparations undertaken. Companies, regiments, and militia were organized to respond to emergency or to invasion. Sir John Hawkins had created a modern fleet of eighteen large and seven smaller galleons and a number of pinnaces capable of outsailing and outgunning any other on the water.

To his disgust, however, and the irritation of the lord admiral, Charles Howard, Elizabeth would not allow these fine instruments to be used against Spain. There would be no repetition of Sir Francis Drake's expedition; she kept her fleet at home and her seamen on half-rations or less. In January 1588 when Philip II and his Admiral Santa Cruz were exchanging letters on the progress of the Armada, England was still relatively bound down by the stern orders of its peace-minded sovereign.

The King of Spain grew impatient, a condition in which he was rarely seen. His reasons were mainly financial. Parma's efforts and armies cost a half million crowns a month; the preparations for the Armada cost at least as much. Sixtus, who believed his own million crowns were the objects of Philip's efforts, refused to listen to these statistics and also refused to share any of the costs of the crusade. The pope, fiercely Italian, could hardly himself have said whether he really wanted Spain to win or not. It would mean Spanish control of the waters around England, the subjugation of the Dutch, the control of France—and with these accomplishments the mastery of western Europe and half the world beside. On the other hand, it could mean the restoration of Christendom, as the new Cardinal Allen claimed. That vision, in Allen's mind, soared beyond all others.

None of these arguments, however, were sufficient to spur Admiral Santa Cruz. He had thirteen elderly galleons, four galleasses, and a weird collection of nearly seventy other ships of highly mixed design, crews, and capacities. He wanted fifty new galleons and another hundred well-armed, well-provisioned ships, and he struggled in vain to convince his master that the Armada was not, in reality, the huge and awesome instrument the zealots believed. Santa Cruz was a real admiral, not a showpiece. He had fought against the Turks at Lepanto and pirates in between, had supervised invasions and sea engagements beyond number, and was a holdover from the days of Charles V, the king's father.

His explanations, however, were largely disregarded. A condition of mysticism had swept Spain; the will of God—as enunciated by the priests —seemed sufficient. Legends and myths surrounded a theory that right always wins; it infected even Philip II, the man whose private office window looked down from under the vast ceiling of a church upon kneeling worshipers below.

In January 1588 he gave Santa Cruz final, irrevocable, and ultimate orders to sail at once. The old admiral instead took to his bed with an indisposition and died in early February.

# 19

There are patterns in events that appear governed by rules as yet unknown. A run of cards will suddenly begin to flow toward certain players in a game, or a series of numbers begin to recur in roulette. The Vatican cause had been organized and directed from Madrid and Rome and—despite the jealousies and difficulties in that uneven relationship—had prospered beyond plausibility. In France the duke of Guise had made himself more powerful than the king. In the Netherlands the duke of Parma had pushed the Dutch rebels very near the brink of exhaustion and defeat. In Scotland the pro-Vatican nobles headed in the north by the earl of Huntly, head of Clan Gordon, by Lord Claud Hamilton and Lord Maxwell in the south, had gathered in great strength. England was internally divided; many of its people were still pro-Vatican, and the Crown was disputing the Reform contention that its greatest defense was in permitting their minority to govern.

Then, following the death of Santa Cruz, the run began to change. In Scotland, Huntly, Hamilton, Glencairn, and Montrose gathered at Linlithgow with their men, while forces under Lord Herries and Lord Johnston advanced on Edinburgh. To their surprise, the ministers of the Reform rallied the people at the capital, who appeared, armed, in opposition. Maitland and James issued announcements against Herries, denounced him as a Papist and a rebel, and organized a force to put him and his associates down.

Their move was supported by Andrew Melville and the Congregation, which was delighted that the young king was finally siding with the forces of virtue. Maitland and Melville held a secret meeting and came to an understanding. The king would not wound the Reform; the Reform would support the king. The General Assembly was allowed to meet amid awesome prophecies about Armageddon, the immense preparations of Spain, and "the enemies of the truth against Christ's Kirk."[1]

A petition was sent to James to pursue Papists and Jesuits and to send and protect Reform ministers to the pro-Vatican north, where Huntly ruled like a petty king. James agreed to enter this situation on behalf of the

Reform through his Chancellor Maitland. His reputation began to rise, and
the propagandists of the great Calvinist diaspora, as diligent as ever, began
to mount encomiums about the young king's immense learning, his deep
piety, his theological astuteness, and other qualities that entered into the
lists of legend with remarkable speed and ease.

With this switch in emphasis, James's reputation began to improve in
the English Privy Council. Lord Herries, seeing the wind change, capitulated, appeared before the Kirk, and promised to behave better. Maitland
and James decided to move to settle the turbulent border and led a very
successful expedition. They were beginning to rule, and to rule skillfully.

In Spain the duke of Medina Sidonia was appalled to find himself
appointed to lead the Armada in Santa Cruz's place. Philip II had appointed him because of his lofty station in Castile and his lack of enemies.
The duke protested against the honor. "My health," he wrote, "is not equal
to such a voyage. I know by experience of the little I have been at sea that
I am always seasick and always catch cold. . . . I have no experience either
of the sea, or of war . . . I know nothing of what the marquis of Santa Cruz
has been doing . . . I feel I should give a bad account of myself."[2] There
was more to the protest, all along the same lines, and all equally candid and
useless.

Medina Sidonia went to Lisbon and found confusion verging on
anarchy. Santa Cruz had pressed men from hospitals and prisons; had
presided over a chaos of orders; had thrown men, supplies, and arms hastily
aboard his odd fleet in order to meet the king's last orders to sail. As a result
some ships had more men, more guns, and more provisions than they could
place or use, and others were inadequately crewed, unarmed, and almost
starving. The duke of Medina Sidonia had to meet the veteran sailors under
his command, untangle the confusion, delay the king's plans, get acquainted, organize, and reschedule the entire enormous effort.

He ordered new guns to be cast, and the king, reading his description,
agreed to detach eight fine galleons from the Indian fleet of Portugal for
him. By various means the duke also obtained some very large fine merchant ships, powder and ball. The duke was, in fact, an excellent administrator, and had he been appointed to assist Santa Cruz, there is little doubt the
Armada might have sailed when England was still unprepared. As it was,
the duke did his best during the months of February, March, and April. At
the end of that time he had forty large galleons and eight other well-armed
ships for his first line and forty large, heavily armed merchantmen for his
second. All had been repaired and strengthened. Then the neat, gray, civilized duke turned unhappily toward the purpose of all these efforts.

During the same period in early 1588, events in Spain, England, and France moved toward a vortex of interlocking effort. King Henry III, desperately trying to retain control, called Swiss troops into Paris. The duke of Guise, whom the king had ordered away from the city, chose to return in defiance. The Paris mobs, organized by Spanish and Vatican agents into districts, rose to hail their hero. Barricades were mounted, and the leaders of the Holy League, commanded by the Committee of Sixteen and the Spanish ambassador, Don Bernardino de Mendoza, prepared for a revolution that would make Guise—the puppet of Spain—the ruler of France.

Events in Scotland appeared, in contrast, remote and unimportant. But the northern realm was considered an important bastion of the Reform faith. While the duke of Guise was pressing King Henry III to break with England and side with Spain, Lord Maxwell returned against orders to Scotland. James, alerted, appointed the Reform earl of Angus lord lieutenant of the Marches—and another order went out declaring Maxwell an outlaw.

A force was gathered and marched against Maxwell's strongholds before he could rally his followers, and Philip's Scots representative was captured and clapped into prison. News of this prompt behavior was received with great satisfaction in London. Elizabeth—who was now convinced the Armada existed and was being prepared against her—sent James £2,000 sterling. True to form, the young king immediately raised his price. He had heard, as all the world had heard, that the Armada was nearly ready to move. He stated his terms to Sir William Ashby, the new ambassador from England.

They were not new. A dukedom; a pension of £5,000 a year; money enough to support a royal bodyguard of fifty men and a border guard of one hundred and fifty.[3] Whether James Stuart actually expected Elizabeth to turn generous is problematical; the fact was that Cardinal Allen's denunciations of England had propounded the theory that Philip II—not the young king of Scotland—was the proper heir to the English throne. That had hit James hard. When an envoy suggested he might be spared in the event of a Spanish victory, James said such an outcome would gain him the promise Ulysses received from Polyphemus—"to devour him after all his fellows were devoured."

On April 25, 1588, the archbishop of Lisbon presided at a great Mass in the cathedral to bless the Armada. Captains knelt to receive benedictions; standards and banners were brought forward. The papal nuncio, sent to the scene to report every movement to Sixtus V, told the Cardinal Montalto that he later talked with one of the leaders of the expedition after the ceremony and asked him if he expected to win. The captain said he did, but for reasons that, for all their piety, did not imbue the pope with great expectations.

"The English," said the veteran, "have faster and handier ships than ours. They know their advantage as well as we do. They will never close with us at all, but stand aloof and knock us to pieces with their culverins. We are sailing," he concluded, "against England in the hope of a miracle."[4]

The delays had, finally, aroused the last person in England who believed in a Spanish threat: Elizabeth. She dropped her sarcasms against Burghley and Walsingham and began to work in earnest with the Privy Council. Every town and hamlet responded to the call of Crown and country with amazing ardor. The air, however, was so thick with rumors and alarms, excited predictions and inventions that for the first time the queen allowed the publication of a "news-paper." Called the *English Mercury,* it was printed daily to overcome gossip and misinformation, and its appearance day after day served to weld the country in rare unity against the invasion.[5]

That threat became real when the duke of Medina Sidonia finally left Lisbon in early May. His departure, like everything else about the effort, had been cumbersome and difficult; the Armada represented an amalgam of three nations—Spain, Italy, and Portugal—and each was subdivided by groups from provinces who could barely understand one another. In all, six different major languages were spoken in the duke's assembly, whose peripheral posts included galley slaves from Constantinople and Algiers, as well as exiled English and Irish priests, Scots renegades, and men gathered into the imperial net from all parts of the globe.

The flotilla included galleons, galleys, armed merchantmen, frigates, freighters, and supply ships. It carried huge and unprecedented supplies, and its inventory was published, for the edification of the faithful, in the name of The Fortunate Fleet. Its ships carried the flower of Spain, as well as some of its dregs. Each had several squadron commanders who carried pilots familiar with the Channel and the North Sea; every Captain had charts of adjacent waters. The leaders of 30,000 men and 130 ships headed toward the coast of the Netherlands, where they would pick up the duke of Parma and his barges and troops.

The Duke of Parma had assembled 30,000 men himself, but the cold and disease-racked winter had reduced that number to a little over 17,000

—slightly more than half. The great commander had assembled a fleet of canal boats that had neither masts nor guns nor sails. They were barges, flat-bottomed and used to transport cattle. He had written Philip II that he could not move his men in these without the protection of the Armada. That was a major point; an even more important one was that they rested in shallow water the huge vessels of the Armada could not penetrate. Parma had asked permission to assault and occupy Walcheren, the port to Flushing. There the Armada could enter and escort the barges out to cross the Channel. That request was ignored. The rendezvous between the Armada and the commander of the forces that it carried and that it expected to invade and conquer England remained set at Dunkirk. Yet the waters around Dunkirk were shallow, and Spanish galleons could not come close to its shore. English ships, drawing less water, could interpose themselves at that point—and neither Parma nor Medina Sidonia would be able to stop them. That inability to close the links of the immense chain that had been wrought made the entire plan impossible—even if nothing else occurred. Yet it remained gaping and disregarded.

As the great moment drew nearer, Queen Elizabeth became excited. She had appointed her favorite, Robert Dudley, the earl of Leicester, commander of her armies. Windsor Castle itself was ringed with 23,000 troops. Leicester was supposed to block the Thames at Gravesend. The English fleet, now assembled and manned, had almost as many problems as the Spaniards with the matter of supplies, food, and expense. Its command was under Lord Howard, with Sir Francis Drake as vice admiral. Drake had some fifty ships and formidable companions, including Sir John Hawkins. All told, the English had over 200 ships to go against Spain's 130; they were smaller but faster, and their guns had a longer range.

It was the end of July before "the English descried the Invincible Armada ships with lofty turrets, like castles, in front like a half-moon, with wings thereof spreading out about the length of seven miles, sailing very slowly though with full sails, the winds being, as it were, tired with carrying them and the ocean groaning with the weight of them."[6]

The English fleet was divided into several places, for its leaders did not know where the Spaniards would appear. It collected; Medina Sidonia conferred and on July 31, 1588, approached Eddystone near Plymouth harbor. The English attacked the half-moon's nearest tip. The longer range of their guns enabled them to stand off and fire; the Spaniards, waiting with grappling hooks to board their enemies, waited in vain.

The first day resulted in little damage; the Spaniards withdrew with their formation unbroken. The English were admiring; so were the invaders. The leader of the Armada, however, was frantic. He could not discover where he could rendezvous with Parma. He sailed, while waiting for a return message, with the English fleet following like shadows. On August 5, 1588, he entered the Strait of Dover and the following day dropped anchor in Calais Roads. The English crowded behind him; across the Channel were Dutch flyboats—small swift craft—and the English army under Sir Henry Seymour. The Spaniard could not afford to wait long.

Parma sent word he could not emerge to join him yet and had no flyboats to send to help him. His men were working as hard as possible, but he could not come out in flat-bottomed barges. The news filled Medina Sidonia with alarm; he had already spent half his ammunition in the first engagements; the English were in much the same condition.

On Sunday, August 7, 1588, the English held a council of war aboard Lord Admiral Howard's flagship, the *Ark Royal*. It was decided to use "fire-ships." Eight of the volunteer vessels that had attached themselves to the fleet were obtained, "their rigging smeared with pitch and their hulls filled with combustible materials. The sky was cloudy. The moon was late in its last quarter and did not rise till morning and the tide, toward midnight, set directly down from the English position."[7] The ships of the Armada were huddled.

The duke of Medina Sidonia had been warned the English were preparing "strange fireworks and diabolical inventions." The duke had "hellburners" in mind, inventions of the Italian Giambelli, which were bombs capable of killing many men on detonation. These weapons were myths that were widely believed to exist; Giambelli had actually been hired by the English and was working for them.[8]

What the Spaniards actually saw, however, were eight blazing ships that seemed like something from a nightmare, with flames licking all about them and lighting up their masts and sails, coming straight toward them in a lurid light of their own creation.

The Spaniards sent pinnaces after these apparitions to seize them with grappling hooks and drag them away from their fleet—which, wooden and heavy with tar, hemp, and cloth, could catch fire and blaze beyond control in a flash.

Two of the flaming threats were maneuvered out of the way, but their guns, loaded, exploded, and a great shower of blazing pieces fell in a spray around the pinnaces and scattered them. Six of the fire ships continued straight into the Armada, whose formation shattered as captains cut their cables and attempted to move out into the sea; several collided and began to drift; others blundered onto the beach, and the English began to move in for the kill.

The rest of the engagement has often been told. Once their formation was broken and the chain of command that held it together severed, the great galleons and merchant vessels of the Armada were individually pursued and hounded. Many strays went aground or were simply lost. Medina Sidonia and his flagship *San Martin* dueled with Drake himself on the *Revenge*. While the action continued, other Spanish vessels—galleons and smaller ships alike—came to their leader's side and reformed their half-moon. "A remarkable feat," said the English in wonder, "of Spanish discipline and seamanship."[9]

The engagement lasted all day, and the Spaniards fought like tigers chained to rafts, their priests among them blessing and saying prayers over the dying and dying themselves. Nevertheless, their ranks were depleted, and the English advantage in gunfire made their cause hopeless; toward the end of the day the seventy remaining ships of the Armada appeared doomed until a squall appeared. The wind, which had been carrying the Spanish ships toward shore, shifted abruptly. The English were blinded by the torrent, and the Spaniards moved north and, in incredible defiance, re-formed their half-moon. The English could not respond; they were virtually out of ammunition and the day was nearly over. Their commanders watched the Armada move, orderly as the spears of their king, into the mists of the North Sea.

Later that night the duke discovered he had lost 4,000 men and virtually all his ships were damaged and carried many wounded men. Dawn arrived to find the English fleet shadowing them; the Armada headed for the Sea of Norway in the hope it could escape toward home around the western coast of England.

The English followed them past the Firth of Forth, in Scotland, and then turned back. The duke of Medina Sidonia, who had hardly paused since the nightmare began two weeks before, wearing only a doublet and a short cape, leaned on the taffrail watching long after their sails vanished.

Six days later the queen left Windsor and proceeded on the royal barge, surrounded by many others, crowded with yeomen of her guard, to inspect the army at Tilbury. The encampment was waiting for the duke of Parma, whose coming was predicted as confidently as had been the Armada's. The Virgin arrived to find her favorite, Leicester, now white-haired, red-faced, and stout, coming to meet her with a broad smile. She proceeded to an inspection, riding a white gelding, dressed all in white velvet, carrying a silver truncheon, with jewels in her hair.

Her reception was so thunderous and enthusiastic that she repeated the whole performance the following day. The day after that someone insisted Parma was on his way, and she went back to Windsor for safety's sake and at the insistence of her captains, but in reality her danger was over. Elizabeth, who had tried to avoid that moment with all her heart, was lifted by it into legend.

# 20

It is not only events that change human relationships but what is thought about events. The Armada returned to Spain with two-thirds of its fighting ships and men.[1] Yet the myth of Spanish invincibility, based upon genuine prodigies of achievement, generations in the creation, was shattered. Men began to stir and look about western Europe with new eyes, as though recovering from an illness.

In Scotland, James threw the Spanish agent, Colonel Semple, into prison. In Rome the pope told Count Olivares, the Spanish ambassador, that he had expected the defeat all along. When Cardinal Allen, heartbroken, asked permission to join Parma in the Netherlands, Sixtus V sneered and openly wondered if he could be of any value anywhere.

In England, the Virgin sent word to Scotland that the promises made in her name by Sir William Ashby, in the peak of England's peril, had exceeded his authority. James would not become an English duke, would not receive money for a bodyguard, or a border force, nor the open acknowledgment as an heir that he had been promised. The Virgin was at the crest: her country credited her with its remarkable victory, the largest in its history. Cheering crowds massed at her every appearance; the "Protestant Wind of God" was credited with giving England recognition. In that benign humor, the queen softened her tart message to James with a cash gift of £3,000 sterling. It was a small sum to a nation that had remained at her side during a dangerous period, but James received it with gratitude. He knew it was immense to Elizabeth.

In common with that of everyone else, including even the Spaniards, his view of England underwent a fundamental and enduring change. The realm—small beside the huge bulk and teeming millions of France, the might of Madrid and its empire, the variegated riches and strengths of the German states, or the palaces and wealth of the Italian—was a new world of power, impregnable and formidable. To become the heir of such a throne was a lure that was irresistible. James looked aloft at that image and felt the greatest hunger of his life.

In the first flush of victory, Elizabeth turned, as she always turned, toward Leicester and told him she would make him the lord lieutenant of the realm. The Privy Council protested and the Virgin had to retreat; Leicester grew angry and they had words. This meant nothing; Leicester was unwell, having caught "a fever" at the Tilbury camp, and the Queen shared his disappointment. She suggested he go to Buxton and try its waters as a cure. En route he stopped at Cornbury and unexpectedly died.

He was fifty-five years old, the same age as Elizabeth. She gave way to boundless grief, but it was a time when death was a frequent visitor. She recovered and emerged, after days in her chamber; and her court life, dances, flirtations, and activities resumed.

The remainder of the year 1588 was one of slow change. In his office the king of Spain worked as diligently as ever, reading the mass of reports that flowed in from his empire, assessing the damage, and estimating ways to resume the effort. Stories were told of his reaction; and though their specifics varied, they agreed only that it was calm, philosophical, and restrained. His blond hair, however, which had been slowly turning gray, lost its remaining sheen. His face, according to paintings before and after that year, showed that Philip II grew old sometime in 1588.

In France many changes took place. The duke of Guise had entered Paris on the eve of the Armada against orders, and his Holy League conspirators had raised the city against King Henry III. The king had escaped, and after the battle off Calais, Dover, and in the Channel, was at Blois. Under duress from Guise and his mother, Catherine de Médicis, Henry had signed all sorts of documents. After the defeat of the Armada, he slowly began to form a new resolution, though Guise's men crowded the castle.

The duke of Guise was awakened at seven in the morning on December 23, 1588, by a message that the council would meet in an hour. He arrived to find his brother, the cardinal of Lorraine, and their ally, the archbishop of Lyon, had preceded him. Some routine business was discussed when word came that the king wanted to see the duke. Guise rose and walked toward Henry's apartment. At the threshold he realized he was being followed, whirled around, and was struck by a dagger. He tried to draw his sword, but his arms were seized and held from behind; he struggled and was struck again, shook himself loose, staggered, took a step, and fell headlong.

Henry III emerged then to look down at him, and said, "How tall he is. I had not realized he was so tall."[2]

On the body the searchers found a note prepared for Spain, which said in part, "To continue the civil war in France will cost 700,000 livres a month."[3]

In the long run the death of Guise was almost as heavy a loss to Philip II as the defeat of the Armada—and might not have occurred if his fleet had succeeded.

In Scotland, a land on the periphery of the great world, changes came more slowly. The young king, whose experience was still limited, enjoyed his hunting, his poetry, and his favorites. These included Alexander Lindsay. Hume was tart about the handsome young man, whom James called Sandie. "The King's only minion and conceit . . . his nightly bed-fellow," said Lord Hume.[4]

Thomas Fowler, an English agent who watched James and his uncle, agreed. "It is thought," he wrote, "that this King is too much carried by young men that lie in his chamber and are his minions."[5] His words were precisely chosen: minion at that time was a word used to describe a mistress.

Lindsay, however, was not, being a minion, anyone to fear. That cautionary emotion was aroused by another handsome young man who had the looks, presence, and intelligence to charm James—and the power to ensure his respect: the young earl of Huntly.

The earl was leader of the pro-Vatican faction of Scotland, a faction that was slow to realize the significance of the Armada's defeat and remained intent upon realizing old, long-standing goals. Huntly, a complex man, proceeded subtly. In 1588 he married Henrietta Stuart, the sister of Ludovic, duke of Lennox—Esmé's heir.

In order to make the marriage, Huntly had to convert to the Reform faith. Typically, he combined this necessity with the task of charming the king. James played the schoolteacher with delight. His mock-pupil was, however, no ordinary sycophant: in the north he ruled his own territories with a cruelty remarkable even in Scotland. At one point he "captured two cooks from an enemy clan and roasted them alive, and adorned the turrets of his castle of Strathbogie with the severed limbs of his foes."[6]

This fearsome individual, whose smooth manners hid his nature, allowed James to convert him and accomplished the marriage he desired—and even became captain of the king's guard. The minion Lindsay was one of his creatures and was made vice-chancellor, while Huntly made it his business to lull the suspicions of Maitland, the real chancellor.

Maitland, more intelligent than the nobles of Scotland, took it for granted that the defeat of the Armada ended the dreams of the pro-Vatican faction. He did not realize that Huntly was combining with the young earls of Angus and Crawford—nor did he ever quite realize that his own rise was deeply resented. Like most competent men, Maitland would never understand that his talents made him hateful to the untalented.

His efforts included levying new taxes, organizing the government of Scotland virtually from scratch, and negotiations for a possible marriage for the king. The candidates had narrowed to Catherine de Bourbon, sister of Henry, the king of Navarre, and Princess Anne, the younger daughter of the king of Denmark.

The French alliance had been discussed, on and off, for several years, but contained difficulties. James was not anxious to ally with a faction still at war in France. He was not told, but another difficulty resided in the lady herself, who was seventeen years older than James and deeply in love with the count of Soissons.

The Danes, on the other hand, offered a beautiful, blond fifteen-year-old, whose portrait was tempting and who appeared in combination with a handsome dowry. Predictably the dowry attracted James the most. The prospects of increased trade in the Baltic drew the support of Scots merchants; the Reform leaders greatly favored such a Protestant alliance.

With such interesting prospects before him, James, therefore, was annoyed in 1589, when, on February 27, he received a packet of letters from Sir William Ashby, the English ambassador. These were written by Huntly and his pro-Vatican associates to the duke of Parma in the Netherlands. They expressed regrets over the Armada, repeated the long-standing idea that England could be invaded from Scotland, and asked for men and money so they could undertake that task. James read how Huntly had pretended to become converted and how deeply he deplored the necessity. This revelation of how he had been duped was only part of the sting: the rest was supplied by a covering letter from Elizabeth. "Good Lord," she wrote with her usual tact, "Methink I do but dream. No King a week would bear this. Pluck up treason by the roots," she continued, like a scolding mother, "take speedy order lest you linger too long."[7]

The Virgin, as Burghley told her to her irritation, did not understand the situation. "The King," Burghley wrote, "hath not so absolute authority there as she hath here, and the nobility . . . are themselves in a sort absolute."[8]

James, with little money to pay troops and caught between contending forces, sent the laird of Easter Wemyss to London to ask Elizabeth, once again, to honor the promises made to him on the eve of the Armada for a dukedom, money, and a pension. Meanwhile, he went through the forms of punishing Huntly, whose easy remorse deflected anger.

The earl was removed as captain of the guard and told to remain inside Edinburgh Castle. He was, said the king, a prisoner—but he followed that remark by visiting him and sharing a table with him the next day. Fowler, the English spy, wrote—in mingled disgust and wonder—that James not only treated Huntly favorably, "kissing him at times to the amazement of many," but allowed free access to the earl's wife, servants, and friends.

A few days later Huntly was free, and James restored him to his captaincy. Maitland, at that point, threatened to resign. The king gave way reluctantly. Huntly was told to leave the court. Fowler, an absorbed witness to the argument between James and his chancellor, was fortunate enough to learn the king's reasoning later.

"When it comes to justice," Fowler wrote Burghley, "he fears to deal . . . [for] his forbears that were the best and severest justices were always cut off untimely."⁹ He was not so much forgiving, in other words, as fearful.

The consequences of his timidity were predictable. Huntly went north; collected his men, the earls of Errol and Crawford and their followers; told his region that James was a virtual prisoner in the hands of Maitland, who planned to send him a captive to England; and marched south.

From the south the earl of Bothwell, nephew of Mary Stuart's beloved and just as wild, wicked, and witty as his relative, organized his unruly border followers and marched north. Their purpose was to converge and overthrow Maitland, the chancellor whose policies threatened their noble privileges.

James learned of these moves on the afternoon of April 6, 1589, and rode to the capital in a great hurry. There he rushed into Maitland's home at three in the morning and aroused the chancellor. The speed, efficiency and courage of the Crown's actions were hailed, at home and abroad, as proof of James Stuart's abilities in a crisis. Since they had never before and never later emerged, they seem better proof of Maitland's. Messages poured forth to Reform leaders, who responded immediately. The news that the king was on the move melted Bothwell's supporters in the south. By April 10, 1589, James sallied forth from Edinburgh, with Maitland at his side, to meet Huntly and his men. "The Chancellor keeps his watch nightly," wrote Fowler. "He is daily in his armor and marches in the vanguard."¹⁰

James himself attracted praise by talking to everyone, traveling around the camps at night, and giving the appearance of leadership. The contending forces converged at the Bridge of Dee outside Aberdeen on April 17, 1589. It was a period when armies maneuvered, and the side with the worst position was apt to retreat; the news that the king himself was in the field demolished Huntly's propaganda that he was a prisoner, and the northern leader's supporters vanished. The earl himself followed them into the night.

A few days later word came through the master of Glamis that the erring nobles would come to James and beg forgiveness, providing that forgiveness was guaranteed in advance. That was a soft offer that pleased James, since it left him honor and did not force a hard decision. He returned to Edinburgh in triumph to enjoy the universal belief that he had displayed conspicuous courage. His chancellor, whose role in the victory was ignored, was dismayed to discover that his enemies were busily creating the legend that he was against the king's Danish marriage.

In May 1589 the rumors gave rise to demonstrations against the chancellor in Edinburgh. Fowler, watching, was astonished to see that James had to make a public announcement of his intentions to conclude that arrangement in order to restore order. The Englishman, who shared his countrymen's lofty disdain for the Scots, expressed himself proudly. "I should say," he wrote, "a most vile people."


Fowler's verdict was prejudiced: there were worse places in Europe than Scotland; France was one. The murder of the duke of Guise had been followed by the death of Catherine de Médicis at the age of 70. In Paris, the headquarters of the Holy League, fanatics rose to tear down the royal arms from public places, to smear excrement on the statues of the Valois kings, and proclaimed their hatred of Henry III.

The duchess of Guise, residing in the city, became the idol of the masses; the streets filled with people caught in excess who danced naked in mindless demonstrations. Presses rolled and propaganda poured forth against the king; the *History of Henry III* by Boucher appeared. It charged the king with sodomy, atheism, black magic, and murder.[11]

The death of his mother, Catherine de Médicis, and his release from the duke of Guise left Henry III independent for the first time in his life; the rebellion of Paris left him without the center of his support. He turned toward Henry Bourbon, king of Navarre, and announced that Navarre was his heir. That step cheered the Huguenots of France, the Reformers of Holland, and Protestants across all northern Europe. Their leaders, in the aftermath of the defeat of the Armada, saw great opportunities for their cause loom suddenly into view. Their eyes turned toward Elizabeth and England.

Their great hope was that the Protestant queen would send men, money, and arms to help the Dutch shake off the Spanish yoke. Beyond that, some dreamed—and Henry of Navarre was one—of forming a great new coalition of Protestant powers that would launch a final assault against Madrid, the center of the Vatican's military support.

These dreamers did not realize that the Virgin was only a half-Protestant at best.[12] She was not interested in empire or in striking any blows for any religion. She considered "innovations in religion to be the work of the devil"[13] and considered the Reformers to be inherently dangerous to all monarchs. She was determined to remain aloof from the quarrels of Europe and to create her own church system in England, along lines of her own choice, that would make that island a very Eden.

**21** Under Elizabeth, the Church of England was gradually transformed into a hybrid "incredibly Catholic and impossibly Protestant."[1] The queen, whose private chapel contained "a crucifix with wax-lights burning round it,"[2] inclined toward the ancient liturgy, the costly vestments, the celibate clergy, and the outer trappings of Catholicism. She restored these and also restored the Episcopal system and anointed bishops. Since she appointed these anointed, from Whitgift down, they bowed low before her.

To ensure that her subjects understood and obeyed a church that she made both Catholic and Protestant, the queen's High Commission increased its search and sanctions against open dissenters. The majority of her subjects seemed willing enough to obey, but true believers among both Catholics and an increasing number of Protestant sects, were, understandably, of different minds.

The defeat of the Armada had depressed and disorganized Catholics in the realm, and Reform leaders who had expected that victory to enhance their positions were also disappointed. Burghley, Walsingham, Beale, and others remained important, but their protests against the High Commission and the turn being made by the Church of England were dismissed by the queen. At this juncture a series of pamphlets written by someone signing himself Martin Marprelate appeared to puncture the facade of enforced conformity with shafts of sarcasm, wit, and irony.

Their author was never discovered, and history, therefore, has never been able to credit one of the most remarkable and talented writers England ever produced. Filthy and funny, Martin Marprelate lampooned the bishops of Elizabeth and Whitgift and presented Reform principles so well, so wittily, and so sharply that the Virgin herself issued angry answers.

The High Commission was strengthened not only by a royal command to root out such rebellious libels, but also by the addition of Dr. Richard Bancroft, a cleric with the instincts of a policeman and the brain of a lawyer. In Bancroft, the Reform movement found a pursuer as capable as any the Inquisition had ever produced—and as unbending.

Dr. Bancroft created a network of spies, informers, double agents, and investigators that spread through all England, sat in on Presbyterian meetings and councils, tracked the followers of Barrow, and amassed dossiers on many leaders and quick intelligences of the Reform. Mrs. Crane was arrested because her home harbored Martin Marprelate's press; the bookbinder who sewed the pamphlets together was captured and turned his coat; the printer and his assistants were tortured on the rack. Their eventual—and inevitable—revelations sent the authorities running in search of more persons.

Against these grim and cheerless happenings the discussions and preparations for the marriage of James Stuart and Anne of Denmark appeared innocent and inviting. Maitland, ever anxious to drive a hard bargain for his sovereign and fated to be eternally disappointed, sent the earl marischal, a wealthy Scotsman, to Denmark with instructions to ask for an enormous sum of money—£1 million (Scots); clear title to the Orkney Islands, an old area of dispute; reciprocal rights for the merchants of both countries; and whatever else he could devise. The Danes listened to all this with astonishment and rejected everything. Fortunately, their queen paid little attention to such matters; she was engrossed in marrying off her daughter and had hired a small army of tailors and various workmen to make ready. Anne was to be provided with a wardrobe beyond complaint, a coach with silver hinges, and other marvels. The earl marischal sent word back that matters had proceeded beyond recall; James sent another envoy. On August 28, 1589, the marriage was held by proxy in Copenhagen. James received a slender blond girl a little over fifteen years old and 75,000 Danish thalers. Maitland's other conditions had been waived, though the chancellor was among the last to learn that.

After this abrupt conclusion, the king began to look, somewhat frantically, for money with which to prepare to receive his new queen. Maitland, pressed into service on this end of the matter, persuaded the burghers of the towns of the realm to produce £20,000 (Scots). James contributed by sending out letters asking his well-heeled peers to contribute horses and provisions. From London, Elizabeth sent a gift of plate worth £2,000 and £1,000 in cash. As usual, she considered this gesture handsome beyond bounds, and James thought it niggardly. He was dissatisfied, therefore, with her gifts, and she did not consider his acknowledgments sufficiently grateful.

The new Queen of Scotland set sail from Denmark to join her husband, but her ship was driven back by storm. After several tries the Danes turned back to Copenhagen, but at the insistence of the Scots finally carried their princess to Oslo, rather than return her home. In Scotland, where James waited in a somewhat uncertain state, days passed with neither news nor bride.

It is curious that the king now whipped himself into a condition of an ardent and thwarted lover. In his entire life he had never shown the slightest flicker of interest in any woman, and no trace of sexuality along normal avenues. Now he began writing poems about his aching heart and told everyone within earshot that he was passionately in love.

When he learned in October, 1589, that Anne had been delayed by the weather and that she would not make the trip for some time, his reaction was tinged with some hysteria. Bothwell, hereditary lord admiral, he decided, should take a fleet and get the king's bride. Bothwell, always able to infuriate his sovereign, drew up an enormous budget of the expenses involved, and James angrily shouted that he would go himself, in a single ship, if necessary.

It was up to Maitland to solve the latest problem. The chancellor put up enough money for a ship and a half; his "friends"—a kind word for his appointees—put up some more. James occupied himself with composing an explanation for his trip. It was, in both wording and attitude, pure James. Unlike his efforts in scholarship, it was surprisingly original, though it revealed him in a curious light.

He explained his long delay in getting married as due to his orphaned condition and said he had kept his intention to travel toward his bride a secret "from the chancellor . . . for two reasons. "First . . . because he would be blamed for putting it in my head" and then, "remembering what envious and unjust burden he daily bears, for leading me by the nose, as it were, to all his appetites, as if I were an unreasonable creature, or a bairn that could do nothing of himself, I thought it unfair to be the occasion of heaping further unjust slander upon him."[3]

After this graceless indication of how deeply he resented his most valuable man, the young king went on to write that he was leaving his realm not only to meet his bride, but to prove that he was "no irresolute ass who could do nothing of himself." For the rest, he sermonized, told everyone to live in peace until his return, and announced the composition of the government in his absence. It consisted of putting the contending factions in a position to rule jointly. Whether Maitland had a hand in that or not is unknown; the odds are that he did not. Yet it showed a shrewdness in terms of the interrelationships that was remarkable. James had, beneath his many personality problems and defects of character, a lucid understanding of his associates. Two councils were created. One held Bothwell, the young duke of Lennox, and other nobles who would not combine for any reason. The other was staffed by the leaders of the Reform. Each council could keep the other under watch and strain.

When Elizabeth learned that James was actually planning to leave Scotland, she was appalled. Horsemen streamed toward Scotland with messages against such a project, but the king was gone. He took Maitland and 300 escorts with him—including a large number of troublesome peers. In five days his ship saw the shores of Norway, but it traveled slowly along the coast, and he did not land until November 11, 1589.

He entered Oslo in some state, wearing a red coat and a black cape, and met his bride at last. They were allowed only a half hour, being surrounded by officials and the sort of persons who prefer ceremony over significance. The following day he was welcomed with official speeches in Latin, and the Norwegians marveled at his patience during long orations. They did not realize the extent to which the Kirk had accustomed him to such exercises.

On November 23, 1589, the marriage was celebrated in the bishop's palace in Oslo and a genuine ceremony performed in French by the minister of Leith. The bishop of Oslo added another long oration on the significance of marriage to the occasion, and a month of festivities followed.

The festivities were marked by heavy drinking on all sides and a considerable number of disputes and arguments among the Scots. Maitland and the earl marischal argued over money; the ambassador wanted to be reimbursed for his expenses from the bride's dowry and the chancellor would not agree. In the midst of these mingled activities and disputes, the relations of the bridegroom and bride seemed somewhat peripheral, but James was loud in protestations that Anne was all he had dreamed. It was clear that though he had never before had a woman, he had no difficulties in that respect. Yet the lack of comment about the newlyweds speaks, by omission, rather significantly. They were, by this tacit sign, not conspicuously ardent, but that was not unusual in a state marriage.

Just before Christmas James agreed to accept an invitation from the Danes to visit Copenhagen and to stay there until Anne's elder sister married the duke of Brunswick. The entire, huge, drunken party with its secret dissonances, luggage, and servants was carried across the northern snows on sleds. The experience was not difficult for Scots; their own realm was one of long winter nights, deep cold, and blazing skies; their route was circuitous and traversed Sweden. It was well into January 1590 before they were escorted by a glittering assembly into Kronborg Castle in Copenhagen.

The Danes drank even more than the Norwegians. James, whose capacity for strong liquor was beginning to rise toward the remarkable levels that distinguish a true alcoholic from a merely social drinker, was delighted. He wrote his old minion, Alexander Lindsay, whom he had, significantly, not forgotten, saying "we are drinking and driving . . . in the old manner."[4]

The Danes showed him their outstanding sights, including a visit to the island observatory of astronomer Tycho Brahe and lectures at the Royal Academy. The king was complimented on the Latin in which he was truly accomplished. Most of the time, however, was spent carelessly. Week after week passed without a mark. It was not until April that his hosts managed to dislodge James and his entourage. He had not obtained a huge dowry, but there was no doubt he had put them to huge expense.

On May 1, 1590, he finally landed at Leith with Anne and was greeted by a welcoming party swollen by curiosity. Their progress to Holyrood, in Anne's coach, which was covered with a cloth of gold, was more elaborate than any seen in Scotland since the now-forgotten days of his mother. On May 17, 1590, Queen Anne was crowned in a seven-hour ceremony at Abbey Kirk.

The event was preceded by a bitter argument between the king and the Reform, in which James's special approach to theology emerged. James had somehow formed the idea—probably from his Bible reading—that "anointing" was the integral part of a coronation. He referred to himself as an anointed king; in time, the phrase would become one of his clichés. He did not, obviously, realize that his own coronation had been a rude, hasty, *pro forma* exercise in the midst of a *coup d'état.* Nor would he ever admit, either to himself or anyone else, that he was called a king at the age of thirteen months because it suited the tactics of the Reform revolution. He seemed to believe he was a king because he was anointed; he would later erect a towering theory on that slender point.

Meanwhile, his queen had to be anointed. The ministers protested, saying such a rite was pagan, Jewish, and "Papastical"—but James was adamant. When the Kirk threatened not to officiate at all, James retorted he would produce a bishop. That threat prevailed, though at the cost of great irritation.

Having aroused the Kirk, James then proceeded to sprinkle salt into the wounds of the nobility by raising Maitland, already greatly unpopular for his many reforms and innovations, from a knight to baron of Thirlestane.[5]

The recognition was ill-timed. The nobles had finally seen the danger to their powers and privileges in Maitland's programs. A whispering campaign against the chancellor had risen during the marriage negotiations and caused a riot in Edinburgh. All factions were beginning to unite against the advisor. The new queen had her ears filled very quickly. She learned, with indignation, that the chancellor had been against her marriage from the start and had preferred a union with a French princess.

That alone was enough to prejudice Anne, but she was provided with more material reasons after the coronation. Established at Holyrood Palace, the queen had her expenses paid by the income from the abbey of Dunfermline. That arrangement, however, did not include money from the lordship of Musselburgh, which Maitland had been given in 1587 and which he was allowed to retain.

The young queen loved dancing, games, hunting, and parties and soon proved to be extravagant. She was very young and had no idea of economizing in any direction—and Maitland was quick to tell the entire court that its revenues were limited and that it could not afford great displays. The queen, smarting because Maitland enjoyed some revenues to which she believed herself entitled, formed a great dislike for the chancellor. She was soon drawn into the backbiting intrigues of the realm. Instead of a confidant to whom he could turn, James soon discovered, to his discomfort, that his young bride was capable of shrill argument and embarrassing behavior.

## 22

In France an assassin hired by the Holy League finally ended the unhappy life of Henry III, the last of the Valois. Henry of Navarre claimed the crown and termed himself Henry IV. The Holy League, however, unearthed a candidate of its own, and the civil war in France, already virulent, went into a paroxysm known as the War of the Three Henrys.

As if to prove the defeat of the Armada had not sapped its vigor, Spain increased the severity of its campaign to reduce the rebels of the Netherlands. The duke of Parma, tireless and diligent, marched his troops into France in the hope of tipping the scales against the Reform Henry IV.

Spain's intention to control France as well as Holland posed a great threat to England. If Madrid could make its control of Dutch coastal ports firm, it could mount a new invasion attempt against the English. Elizabeth was urged to help the Dutch Reformers in their struggle, but the Queen of England remained reluctant.

Like James Stuart, the Queen of England was a product of the Reform, but resisted its arguments. Her dislike soared in 1590, when the argument that only the Reform kept the Vatican forces of England from overthrowing her no longer held its former force. Her Privy Council was weakened, from a Reform viewpoint, by the death of Sir Francis Walsingham. The brilliant intelligencer had spent his fortune on her behalf, and paying the debts of Sir Philip Sidney had completed his private ruin. His last two years were unhappy; he died so poor his family could not afford a suitable ceremony; he was buried late at night in virtual secrecy, as though he had been a criminal.[1]

His departure was a serious loss for both the realm and the Privy Council. Burghley remained, but he had grown old and sick. Burghley's younger son, Robert Cecil, who was now serving as an assistant to his father, was a hunchback who seemed quiet and clever, but was still young and untested. The queen's favorite on the council was Sir Christopher Hatton, once her dancing partner at court, and a man whose pliancy so gratified the queen she made him lord chancellor.

The queen also appointed two new men to the Privy Council to support her new chancellor. They were Lords Cobham and Buckhurst. Both were anti-Reform, and both had been recommended by Whitgift, the archbishop of Canterbury. The balance of forces, in other words, had shifted in England. The Reform leaders, so ardent in their opposition to Spain and the Vatican, were alarmed to discover that in the wake of the Armada defeat it was they—and not the pro-Vatican followers—who became the objects of determined Crown prosecutions.

These had been spurred by the discovery of Barrow and his Separatists and by an avalanche of unlicensed books and pamphlets. The most effective were those of Martin Marprelate, and the effort to apprehend that mysterious genius resulted in many arrests. One of the more prominent was John Udall, a minister who had already experienced the rigors of an investigation before the High Commission and who had been forced into official silence. Udall was the author, or one of the authors, of the *Book of Discipline,* which had held aloft the vision of a Geneva-styled church, had attracted the House of Commons, and alarmed Elizabeth.

Brought before the High Commission, Udall used the same defense as Barrow before him. Asked to swear to tell the truth, he declared he would swear allegiance but not swear "to accuse myself or others." As a loyal subject, Udall said, his duty was to be obedient, but there was no law that could press him into helping the prosecution.

The High Commission, after much thundering, ordered him to prison. Udall said he was happy to go to prison with a good conscience; happier than he would be if freed with a bad conscience.[2]

That sort of reply lends itself to public attention. The examination of Udall did not reveal the High Commission in a very flattering light—a circumstance of which it was aware. The High Commission wanted him to apologize, and, therefore, to lose the immense sympathy and respect he was gaining in many quarters. Such quarters, however, were far from court. The leaders and supporters of the Reform were to be found among merchants, bankers, lawyers, landowners, and solid citizens more quiet and austere than the average.

All this, however, seemed far from court, which served as a great stage that both inspired and entertained the realm. The queen glittered in her bejeweled costumes, surrounded by her nobles, courtiers, and hangers-on. Robert Dudley, the earl of Leicester, was gone, but younger men had taken his place. Sir Walter Raleigh was one of these, but the real successor to Leicester in the queen's affections was his stepson Robert Devereux, the earl of Essex.

Essex was, like all Elizabeth's favorites, tall, athletic, and good-looking. He wore a fortune in clothes, but so did the queen. Her costumes, in fact, grew ornate almost beyond belief. Her dresses, in the voluminous folds and trains of the times, were tapestries with embroidered animals, flowers, motifs from myths, and curiosities worked in gold and silver threads on fabrics of velvet, satin, and other rich materials. Her capes were equally ornate and expensive; hosts of mantles, veils, kirtles, and other garments blossomed in profusion; even her handkerchiefs were works of art. She appeared with jewels in her hair, on her fingers, pinned to her clothes, like a creature from a living legend.

With crowds running behind every time she went on a progress, with her courtiers kneeling when she entered or left a room and able to stand only with her permission, the Virgin's pride soared far beyond a sense of reality except when money was involved. Her taste for flattery, already gluttonous, coarsened to the extent where no compliment was too outrageous to elicit an accepting smile. A young woman might be forgiven such vanity, but Elizabeth was 57 in 1590, and such an age was then considered advanced. Her figure had sharpened from slenderness to skinniness; her teeth were bad; her makeup, heavy and thick; and her temper, uncertain. The queen grew dangerous to cross as her popularity and her reputation soared; the success over the Armada contributed toward her sense of authority and made it increasingly difficult to tell her unwelcome truths.

Lord Burghley, however, was still a towering figure, and many of his plans seemed to meet with the sort of easy success that competent men so often accomplish. No area was of greater satisfaction to him than the alliance now established between England and Scotland. Maitland was a man after his own heart, whose cool intelligence was reassuring, especially when contrasted with the wild and unpredictable behavior of the Scots nobility.

Letters flowed from London to Edinburgh replete with mutual satisfaction. Maitland, secure in the knowledge of this great friendship, was also well equipped to deal with James. The chancellor was, like his more famous brother, a man of wit, who could mix jokes into discussions of state in a manner that enlightened his topics. Learned in Latin, skilled in writing poetry in several languages, he could amuse, entertain, and inform the king without leaving any bitter aftertaste.

Nevertheless, by 1590 Maitland's enemies began to reach formidable numbers. There was little he could do about Huntly or Lennox; both were born steeped in intrigue, and both were leaders of the pro-Vatican faction. But the chancellor also knew that faction could not cause any serious trouble unless it received heavy assistance from abroad. The only possible source was Spain, and Philip was still smarting from the defeat of the Armada.[3] That left the earl of Bothwell.

The fifth earl, hereditary lord admiral of the realm, a great border leader, was a man of many talents and abilities, greatly underrated by the historians later—a strong and even frightening force for James VI. He had inherited his title from his mother's side; she had been a sister of the Bothwell who had become entangled with Mary Stuart. On his father's side he was descended, though on the wrong side of the blanket, from James V. He was, therefore, the king's cousin and shared the strange elements that distinguished all the Stewarts, or the Stuarts.

At first, James liked Bothwell, who was described as "young, well-favored and dissolute." Bothwell was also a favorite of the Reform, because he was firm, or at least protested that he was firm, in its faith. For the rest, the young earl had great presence and was utterly fearless—a quality that carries men far. He had another, special gift—greatly admired then and now—that his contemporaries felt more than historians: eloquence.

"This nobleman hath a wonderful wit," wrote the dean of Durham, "and as wonderful a volubility of tongue as of agility of body on horse and foot. Competently learned in the Latin, well languaged in the French and Italian, much delighted in poetry, and of a very resolute disposition both to do and to suffer." Thomas Fowler, whose task it was to assess the leaders of Scotland, was almost lavish, and his involuntary admiration could not be concealed. "There is more wickedness, more valour, and more good parts in him than in any three of the other noblemen," he wrote.[4]

Fowler's opinion was curious, because the agent died in Edinburgh in April 1590 shortly before the king returned from Denmark. James and Anne arrived to discover that Bothwell was claiming, as his right, some Lennox jewels from Fowler's estate. James believed he should have them himself; an immediate dispute arose to exacerbate their relationship.

It was not too good in any event. Bothwell had been appointed to some interim authority in James's absence and had used the time to woo the Kirk, pose as an ardent Reformer, and poison the air against Maitland. By midsummer 1590 the chancellor called a convention of the Estates—which he preferred to a Parliament—and renewed his efforts to establish order and some control over the nobles and, in particular, Bothwell.

The border had been the scene of intermittent violence for a century or more, but the good relations established with England had accomplished much, except in Bothwell's territory. The earl refused to act, and Liddesdale was a serious trouble spot. Still, matters were not too difficult; Maitland thought the earl could be bought off and struggled toward that end.

Scotland was, with its newly married king and the prospect of a royal family for the first time in a generation, in relatively good condition. The leaders of the Reform were concerned, however, by developments in England. They had learned of the denunciation of their system of "Presbyteries" by Richard Bancroft and had watched the activities of the High Commission with deepening anger.

They were alarmed when Elizabeth wrote James a letter on the subject, saying in part, "There is risen, in both your realm and mine, a sect of perilous consequence, such as would have no kings but a presbytery and take our place while they enjoy our privilege. Yea, look we well unto them. I pray you stop the mouths or make shorter the tongues of such ministers. . . ."[5]

Maitland would have no part of such an effort. Like Burghley in England but for different reasons, he considered the Virgin's campaign against the Reform to be impolitic for Scotland. Elizabeth, however, ruled over a complex kingdom that crossed many barriers. The activities of Huntly, Lennox, and Bothwell in concert with the Spanish had been uncovered by her agents, and she wanted them punished. James's indolence in that respect annoyed her.

She sent the earl of Worcester to Edinburgh to give the now fully established king of Scotland the emblem of the Garter—an honor held highly in England. The earl was instructed to press for the punishment of Huntly et al, and James agreed. It was his habit to agree easily, but not his habit to do much more. As the summer passed into autumn. Elizabeth sent caustic reminders, but her concern was evident. Finally, James said he could not move against such powerful nobles because he lacked funds. In a rare moment of belief, Elizabeth sent him £3,000.

The young king could hardly be blamed for enjoying the situation. The earls of Huntly, Lennox, and Bothwell, by their overtures toward the Spaniards, had provided James with a chance to show a veiled independence of the English. Sheer indolence had done the rest, and he had received high honors and money as a result. This reversal of their usual cat-and-mouse game was far too delicious to bring to an end—no matter what the long-range consequences.

It took Chancellor Maitland to change the play and swing the king's mind into new directions. His timing and the method he chose seemed merely coincidental. But it was a suspiciously helpful coincidence when the master politician whispered into the king's ear of dark and sinister plots against the royal person. He mentioned witches, warlocks, Satanic schemes —and the earl of Bothwell. James started from his chair in alarm.

**23** Great religious periods evoke great antireligious reactions. The splintering of Christianity gave birth to witches, warlocks, demons, ghouls, and perverts. The Devil presided over orgies, over banquets held in fields and meadows at night and sometimes in churches when their custodians were absent. Black Masses, in which the symbols of Christianity were reversed and desecrated, sabbats in woods, covens in homes were held all across Europe. Hundreds of thousands of witches appeared to follow new, secret leaders and met in great enclaves in France, Germany, Italy, Sweden, and other lands; certain localities became infamous and eerie.[1]

The antireligious phenomenon created another: witches aroused witch-hunters. Courts and clergy were drawn into pursuit, and new forms of police work, new types of police came into being. The Inquisition, in fact, had begun against Satanism and extended against other forms of heresy. Devil worship, however, remained the central sin; the great blasphemy.

Witches came late to Scotland, but as in other lands, torture came in their wake. King James's library contained huge tomes on the subject. He would not have considered himself—nor have been considered—learned, had he not delved into the subject. It was, in some respects, the psychiatry of the time. It explained the dark and irrational elements in human beings, their tendency to develop baseless hostilities, and their delight in pointless vice. Black magic provided rationalizations for misfortune and gave adversity a human face. It transferred guilt to evil elements and gave both its practitioners and its opponents a sense of power, knowledge, and authority.

Scotland was swept by the fashion and by the time James's attention was personally drawn in the winter of 1590, proved it held persons as inventive as any in Italy, Germany, France, or England in the art of extracting confessions from the accused. England had discovered "pricking," which consisted of sticking needles into a suspect until a dead spot was discovered. The superstition was that Satan had licked that spot as a mark of his dominion; the needle would discover it and the witch was proven.

The Scots accepted that theory, as did everyone else, and built some frightful instruments of their own. The witch-bridle was one. It consisted of "a band of iron fastened around the face, with four diverging points thrust into the mouth. With this the accused was secured immoveably to a wall. . . ."[2]

Other instruments were copied from other countries. The pennyzinkus was a vise that crushed fingertips and toes. But the most often used was the Spanish boot, which fitted around the lower leg and could be tightened with screws until the shin was shattered: an excruciating sensation.

Following interrogations, witches and warlocks were tried in court and their confessions were read aloud and entered as evidence. Witnesses appeared to testify to misfortunes suffered at their hand. The accused would often only not claim credit, but would describe other triumphs, as well as their experiences with the Devil. Punishment was by burning. Mercy meant being strangled to death before the pyre was lit.

In the autumn of 1590 the king of Scotland was told that confessions were being obtained that mentioned his name. Irresistibly lured, he rode to the prison and descended, well wrapped in his furred cloak, accompanied by his closest servants, into the depths of the stone dungeons. There he watched, fascinated, as the examiners approached the accused, stretched naked on stones if a woman and shackled upright if a man, with their instruments. He heard the screams and the stories and was caught into the drama. Bending over the culprits, he put questions himself and suggested ways to break their resistance.


The prisoner who attracted James's attention was named Dr. Fian by some, and John Cunningham by others. Fian was a schoolteacher and a learned man and had been named by a maidservant—Geillis Duncan—who worked for David Seaton. Taken into custody after numerous accusations by persons in her neighborhood, the old servant had been subjected to the pennyzinkus and to having a rope tightened about her head. These pressures resulted in the names of three women and three men.

They were, unlike most persons caught in such a dragnet, of better than average quality. One, Agnes Simpson, was a midwife known as the Wise Woman of Keith. She was matronly, dignified, and intelligent. Sir James Melville and the king listened to that impressive woman with horror as she related her part in two conventicals.[3]

At the first, Agnes Simpson described how she was "delivered to the Devil" while wrapped in a linen cloth. After he had finished with her, he gave her a wax image, which she passed to her companion and which was then passed around. The Devil said, "This is James VI, who is ordered to be consumed at the instance of a noble man, Francis, earl Bothwell."[4]

The next meeting was in a church at North Berwick. The Devil was there, "clad in a black gown with a black hat upon his head." His worshipers kissed his buttocks. Then the Devil spoke from the pulpit amid a circle of lighted candles. He wanted to know the effect of their activities and in particular whether the destruction of the wax image of the king had been successful upon its original. "An old plowman named Grey Meuill," said Agnes, "said nothing ailed the King yet, thanks be"—and the Devil gave him a "great blow." The coven marveled that all their efforts had been fruitless and the Devil answered, "He is a man of God," in French.[5]

That sent James into a state of high excitement. When Dr. Fian, or John Cunningham, was in the position for interrogation—that is, shackled —the king was present and anxious.

Fian confessed; there was seldom an interrogation without a confession —failures being due largely to death's intervention. His story tallied with that of Agnes Simpson, but was replete with more details. It carried the Satanic plot backward in time to when Anne of Denmark was unable to reach Scotland though on a stout ship captained by a Danish admiral. The storms she encountered were the result of spells and the activities of demons. The same sinister elements had sent mists to blind the crew of James's own ship when he fearlessly sailed to meet his bride. The plan of the forces of evil was to cast the king on the shores of England—which inspired thoughts of another Scots sovereign once held captive by the Virgin of that country. Fian also admitted being "the clerk" of the black figure that appeared in a black cape and a black hat in the pulpit at Berwick.

It was the identity of that figure that James wanted, and the king suggested new tortures to the examiners, who were surprised that was possible. They were tried to no avail. Dr. Fian would say no more, though the men all believed he could, if he but would.

Tried in Edinburgh on December 26, 1590, Fian was found guilty and burned to death. The records of the trial do not mention the earl of Bothwell. Behind the scenes the interrogations continued.


On January 7, 1591, the king was in Edinburgh and emerged from the tollbooth. A retinue followed that included the duke of Lennox and Lord Hume. They fell into an argument with the laird of Logie and pulled their swords. James looked behind, saw the steel flashing, and fled into the nearest refuge—which turned out to be a skinner's booth. There, to his shame, he "fouled his breeches in fear."[6]

The king's affliction—cowardice—was rare both then and now. It was a time when violent dispute could erupt as quickly as in a schoolyard and be as quickly forgotten by the survivors. It was James's agony to be cursed with disabling fear.

Bothwell knew the king was a coward and therefore paid no attention to his dignity; he was never to be able to take a coward seriously. In the same month that James disgraced himself in a skinner's booth, Bothwell decided to intervene in a divorce case.

The laird of Craigmillar was suing his wife, whom he accused of misconduct with the laird of Niddrie. A witness to the adultery was lodged, for safekeeping, in the tollbooth. Although James was sitting in session with his council in a nearby room, Bothwell appeared, carried the struggling witness away to Crichton Castle, and there debated whether or not to hang him.

The earl, in other words, was behaving as though Scotland had no king. James bit his lip and waited.


On April 15, 1591, the Crown case against the earl of Bothwell, based on the confessions of captured witches and warlocks, was at last complete and released to an astonished realm. The earl was hauled before the Lords of the Secret Council on a charge of conspiring with Satanists toward the king's death. That was, of course, treason.

Bothwell protested, but was committed "to ward" in Edinburgh Castle, and his friends and allies were forbidden to come within ten miles of the king. To lend support and add credence to the charges, the witches—male and female—who remained were publicly tried. A dreary round of burnings and stranglings set into motion.

One witch—Barbara Napier—was acquitted. That event so angered James that he wrote personally to the court on May 10, 1591, ordering a sentence of death and had the jury called into custody. To make sure they understood their particular offense, the king himself presided at a new hearing—which could hardly be called a trial—and was gracious enough to release them without punishment when they reversed their verdict.


With Bothwell in custody and these subordinate figures convicted, James was upset to learn that his case did not arouse as much horror and indignation as he had expected. The leaders of the Kirk were of the opinion that pro-Vatican elements such as Huntly, Lennox, and others, were far more dangerous than Bothwell. His behavior was too impulsive and his temperament too familiar in a rough country to be taken as sinister or steeped in diabolism. As an opponent of the Chancellor Maitland, the ease with which such a case could be manufactured was too clear, even for men who believed in witches. And in the final analysis, great nobles were not to be handled like maidservants, midwives, schoolteachers, and the like.

Bothwell was in custody; the king had to be satisfied with that for a time.

In England the High Commission moved against the heart of the Reform by arresting Thomas Cartwright and nine of his associate ministers. The event combined personal, political, religious, and civil issues rolled into one great undertaking; Whitgift and Cartwright had been opponents on theological matters for years. The charges were complex. Cartwright had been a leader in the creation of the *Book of Discipline* for England, had been exiled and in exile had—like Knox before him—engaged in exile politics, and headed a church based on the Calvinist principles. If the archbishop of Canterbury, armed with weapons equal to those used by the Vatican in England generations before, was ever to extirpate dissent to the established church, the demolition of Cartwright had to succeed.

The argument took a now familiar form: Cartwright objected to the mandatory oath in advance unless he heard the charges. The High Commission did him the favor of reading them, and its members were enraged when he then asked for a lawyer and said he would answer on a selective basis. Given permission to frame his answers in prison, Cartwright and his companions composed a statement or a series of statements that lacked legal acuity but carried immense moral force.

Dozens of secret printing presses in England and their companions in Geneva rolled day and night, and the controversy spread across the land. In Scotland Andrew Melville and his companions in the Kirk, deeply alarmed at these attacks against principles they espoused, appealed to James VI to speak up on behalf of Cartwright.

Their interest entailed more than sympathy. Whitgift and the High Commission had drawn a connection between Presbyterian principles and treason and called upon the Privy Council of England to try Cartwright and his associates in the Star Chamber. If Presbyterianism, the name that was now attached to Calvinist approaches in Scotland, was to be synonymous with treason in England, the leaders of the Congregation in the North feared the effect on their own sovereign and their own ultimate standing.

Whitgift, whose anger against Cartwright was deep and implacable, meanwhile betrayed the traditional tenderness of a thwarted theologian. The Star Chamber, where the Privy Council held its trials, could impose a variety of punishments. These ranged from lopping off noses to clipping ears and public whippings, banishment, and service in the galleys as slaves. The archbishop thought banishment for life would be sufficient.

The High Commission had authority to question men regarding their inner beliefs; the Star Chamber on their behavior. The chamber proceedings, therefore, were conducted with at least some recognition of the common law. Though defendants could be tortured in cases of suspected treason, they were also entitled to be charged with specific acts and confronted with evidence corroborating their own confessions, if obtained. The Privy Council had no intention of torturing a man like Cartwright, and the clergyman refused to provide any testimony against himself. The case entered a labyrinth in which lawyers, judges, clerics became embroiled.

In Scotland, James issued a statement, pleading with Elizabeth on behalf of the Reform defendants, and his own Kirk leaders warmed toward him. For a high moment the heir of the revolution seemed on the verge of appreciating his duty—but James was actually more intent upon reducing the earl of Bothwell.

On June 21, 1591, Chancellor Maitland visited Bothwell in his locked apartment at Edinburgh and told him to prepare himself for exile. The earl, who believed Maitland was at the bottom of all his problems with the king, was told to think it over. Instead, he escaped that very night.

James was frightened and furious and invoked an old sentence for treason passed once against Bothwell and rescinded. The earl was "put to the horn" and declared an outlaw. The statement giving the reasons for this step declared Bothwell had "given himself over altogether in the hands of Satain, continuing in all kinds of filthiness, heaping treason upon treason against God and His Majesty." These latter figures were drawing closer together in James's mind.

Bothwell, however, was at large and had many friends. His argument on his own behalf was shrewd. He claimed Maitland was using him as an instrument with which to destroy the powers of all the nobility—and that the king was after his property to reward pro-Vatican courtiers. His call was issued to the nobility and to the Congregation—and the fact that he was able to travel about, be feted and received, and rally some defenders was evidence that his campaign had appeal.

The chancellor, however, had created a governmental network that kept Bothwell on the periphery, instead of allowing him into the center of resistance. Maitland gathered a force and, with James bobbing alongside, traveled through the border. Many lairds, thankful to the chancellor for their improved status, signed bonds against the rebel earl. Lord Hume and the laird of Buccleigh, who had at first sided with Bothwell, repented, recanted, and agreed to accept temporary exile as a punishment. Bothwell was unable to raise any considerable force.

Elizabeth watched all this through the summer somewhat abstractedly. Her attention was devoted to various efforts on land and sea against Spain. They were not impressive but they were expensive, and that distressed the queen. She was having some difficulties with her latest favorite, the young earl of Essex, who did not take well to orders.

It was not until mid-October, 1591, when Bothwell's estates were given by James to the pro-Vatican duke of Lennox, that the Virgin grew angry. She had warned James again and again to move against the pro-Spanish and pro-Catholic elements in his realm; he had not only ignored such injunctions, but elevated these nobles.

The king of Scotland, however, was harassed. His queen had turned toward the pro-Vatican courtiers with considerable enthusiasm. She argued against Maitland, spent more money than the Crown could afford, listened to Huntly and Lennox, and even had words of praise for the young earl of Moray, who sided with Bothwell. The king had no army and little money with which to raise one. His seat, in other words, was shaky.

On December 27, 1591, Bothwell made that shakiness terribly evident. Accompanied by Douglas of Spott, the laird of Niddrie, Archibald Douglas, John Colville, and forty or fifty others, the earl appeared through a secret staircase opened from within by someone in the court at Holyrood. The same sort of entrance had been made a generation before by the earl of Gowrie and others against David Rizzio and Queen Mary Stuart.

The king was dining apart from the queen, a circumstance that had become habitual, when he heard the tumult and fled upward into a tower. Meanwhile, Bothwell's men, armed with huge hammers, began to break down the doors of Maitland's apartment. While the intruders hammered, the chancellor and his entourage shot muskets out their windows to arouse help. Bothwell himself, believing the king to be with the queen, hammered on her door. Before he could complete his purpose, soldiers and guards arrived from the city and the earl had to flee so hastily he left nine of his men behind.[7]

The following day a gallows was constructed and Bothwell's nine men were hanged. James himself went to St. Giles Church—Knox's old pulpit —to tell the Congregation his troubles. He found them, in the main, unsympathetic. The minister declared the realm was poorly handled, and there was no doubt the king was floundering.

His suspicions, by this time, ranged wildly. He wondered if his queen was his friend; his chancellor was the subject of innumerable satires and jeering poems and pamphlets. Bothwell—though an impure champion— gained popularity by boldness and the effect of his eloquent propaganda.

Early in January 1592 the king was told the rebel was lurking in the environs of Edinburgh and rode in that direction with some followers. Unluckily, he fell off his horse into the waters of the Tyne, "and had almost been drowned in a pool, had he not been rescued and pulled forth by the neck of yeomen, where the courtiers durst not venture."

The contrast between the proud nobles, the bold Bothwell, and the pitiful James VI, who so repeatedly disgraced himself before his subjects, was devastating.


Matters were far more solid in England, where the queen's rule was iron and the country prospering. That prosperity, however, did not extend to Elizabeth's ventures. She sent the youthful earl of Essex, who seemed to her like a beautiful but willful son, to France to help Henry IV. Essex spent huge sums, made a great display of his personal qualities, and proved to have little or no common sense. Summoned home, he knighted twenty-four of his men on his own authority as a field commander. The Virgin bit her lip. Great sums were being wasted in military adventures conducted as though by boys; it would be necessary to call another Parliament to raise money.

The Star Chamber, meanwhile, had no better luck with Cartwright and his fellows than had the High Commission. They refused to testify against themselves, and their arguments were secretly assisted by Robert Beale and even Lord Burghley himself and by a spate of Reform pamphlets.

All of this irritated the queen. Her "dancing Chancellor" Sir Christopher Hatton died; her subjects were thinking and behaving along patterns new and unexpected; the world was moving in odd directions. Elizabeth ended 1591 in a mood of exasperation. The news from Scotland in early 1592 of the ludicrous and ineffectual activities of James VI did little to lighten her humor.


In the new year 1592 the young earl of Moray, a great favorite of the Congregation, returned south. He had recently lost his wife, and he carried his five young children and sister to the castle of Donibristle on the north shore of the Firth of Forth to place them with his mother, Lady Doune.

The king had mixed feelings about Moray's presence. The earl was a friend and ally of Bothwell's. James feared that Moray would give Bothwell refuge at his strong estate, Darnaway, in the north—and perhaps join him in his efforts.

The earl of Huntly, whose handsome presence the king found so congenial, had very clear ideas about Moray. They were embroiled in a blood feud of great depth. On the morning of February 7, 1592, Huntly announced he was going to Leith to see the races. He departed with a considerable number of armed men, but instead of going to Leith, went to Queensbury. There he crossed the river and had the ferry stopped so none could follow or leave. By nightfall, he was at Donibristle, which he had his men surround, and issued a command that Moray should emerge. The women and children obeyed, but Moray refused. Huntly then set fire to the castle.

Moray finally emerged, but the plume on his helmet caught fire. Immediately beset, he rushed to the water's edge and was wounded, fled into a cavern, was followed, and killed. Huntly, it was said, delivered the last, most savage blow: a slash across the face.[8]

The circumstances of the murder were so dramatic that poets and minstrels began to strum as soon as they heard the details. Moray's mother, Lady Doune, had her son's corpse carried into Edinburgh and vainly pleaded with James to come and view it.

The king, with an insensitivity that resembled his mother's reaction to the murder of Darnley, chose instead to go hunting within sight of the smoking castle of Donibristle. He discussed chasing Huntly, who had discreetly vanished, but made no move in that direction. Lady Doune had an artist draw a picture of the dead Moray, brought it to the king, and handed him one of the bullets recovered from the body.

As days passed and it became clear that James would take no action, show no grief and submit no proper explanation, a deep and serious resentment began to rise. The murder of one of the Reform's leading supporters by a pro-Vatican peer already distrusted, already associated with Spanish plots, and already too influential at court was too much to endure in silence. Ministers began to raise their voices; Elizabeth stirred in England.

She had sent many remonstrances north to the effect that James should reduce the pro-Vatican and pro-Spanish peers of his realm. Now, for the first time, she issued orders to assist Bothwell.[9] The Reform in Scotland, which had held the rebel earl in somewhat light esteem, began to consider his value as their champion.

At that critical moment, Bothwell issued a masterly statement—one of many—denouncing Maitland as the mastermind; the fox behind all the evils of the moment. His contacts with the Spaniards, the earl explained, had stemmed from a natural resentment of the English execution of Mary Stuart —but he had learned Huntly was actually Spain's man—and therefore had withdrawn. Maitland, he charged, had maneuvered the death of the Regent Morton and then the earl of Gowrie. He had inspired the activities of the now-disgraced archbishop of St. Andrews. He had contrived the witch's plot against Bothwell—and his long-range purpose was to destroy the nobility of Scotland, to place his own men everywhere, and to rule the puppet king. "A puddock-stool [toadstool] knight," Bothwell termed the Chancellor, usurping the place of "two ancient cedars"—himself and Lord Hume.[10]

The uproar surrounding this paper and its argument, the apprehensions of the Kirk and its leaders, the deep anger against Huntly and the pro-Vatican faction combined to create tremendous pressure. James, however, was obsessed. He hated Bothwell as he was to hate few men, and regarded the dead Moray as a man who had supported the man he hated. Far from showing grief, he made no effort against Huntly and did not bother to deplore the murder.

Instead of calming the storm, James insisted on riding, at the head of hastily assembled forces—against Bothwell. Maitland himself vanished into his house at Edinburgh; his public appearance created disorder. For weeks stretching into months the king of Scotland presented the spectacle of a bumbler beset by forces beyond his control and could hardly be said to be ruling. In London the queen listened to Sir Robert Bowes, her ambassador to Scotland, report on the disheveled condition of the northern realm with impatience. She sent Bowes back with a peremptory message to James to the effect that if he did not take his responsibilities in hand, pursue, and punish Huntly and his associates, his pension would be reduced. Then she reduced the pension anyway.

The queen had reason to wonder. England was far from free of unruly men; even her Star Chamber—loaded with faithful creatures of the Crown —had been unable to convict Cartwright and his followers of treason. But the ordeal of the accused had been so onerous that following their release in May 1592, they were quieted for all time. That was, after all, the result the queen and Whitgift had sought. Why could not James do the same?

Yet James Stuart's weakness was, in a way, his best defense. Any strong man could dominate the king of Scotland, and all the realm knew it. No crimes committed in the king's name, therefore, were considered his own. They were, instead, laid at the door of the man nearest the king, the dominator. Since Chancellor Maitland was widely considered the king's intellectual master, it was Maitland—and not James—who was held responsible for allowing Huntly to murder Moray with impunity.

Seeing that the king's justice would not be invoked against Huntly, the Kirk discussed Huntly's excommunication. That was a very real penalty since it forbade all church members from dealing with an outcast. James wondered why the Kirk had not, long before, excommunicated Bothwell. That inquiry set off an angry shouting match in which the ever-fortunate Huntly found his case set aside.

Queen Anne, who knew her husband probably better than she liked to admit, was only one of the many persons who now pressed her ideas upon him. The queen liked Huntly and hated Maitland. Unfortunately, she liked Bothwell also—and she had liked Moray. Anne, in fact, liked anyone that James disliked and was always swayed against her husband's opinions. Now she added her voice to the pack against Maitland, whose wife she also disliked. The queen's household, headed by the duke of Lennox, took on a definite pro-Vatican aroma. Toward the end of March 1592, James gave way to these pressures and sent orders to the man who introduced coherence and created a network of civil servants who were quietly establishing the basis for order—instructions to leave the court till further notice.[11]

Maitland obeyed and retired to Lethington. His banishment from the scene was not total; James continued to ride and visit him intermittently and secretly sought his advice. But it was enough to create great exultation among the nobles, since Maitland had been considered the real ruler of the realm.

In May 1592, after many delays, James called a Parliament. Following Maitland's advice, he proposed a softening of the Black Acts against the Kirk. The Golden Acts, as the propagandists of the Reform labelled these, legalized the presbyteries, their benefices, and their authority in ecclesiastical matters. In reality, little was changed, but the ministers did not at first realize that. They mounted orations recalling the days and triumphs, ideas and principles of Knox and Buchanan. Some of the more intelligent among them—notably James Melville—made handsome acknowledgment of their debt to John Maitland.

These moves, which strengthened James and allowed Maitland to remain a power behind the throne whose appointees remained in charge of the administration of the Crown, were more sophisticated than Bothwell's tactics. That rebel was enraged because the same Parliament, suddenly suffused with amiability toward the king, ratified the seizure of the Bothwell estates and his status as an outlaw.

On June 27, 1592, the earl collected about 300 men from the border and, accompanied by the now desperate master of Gray, who clutched at any movement that would accept him, assaulted James at the palace of Falkland. The earl had a very simple purpose: he wanted to take physical custody of James. He was convinced that the king was so personally feeble that he could be bullied into anything.

For a number of hours that night the earl and his men thrust themselves against the back door of the palace with a battering ram, while James quaked inside a locked room in a tower. By daybreak rescuers were on the way, and Bothwell abandoned his effort. His ruffians stole some horses from the palace stable, and the party fled in disorderly fashion. Later a number were caught in the surrounding countryside; the earl himself rode to the western borders and finally to England.

The Queen of England was almost sixty and growing strange. Her ladies-in-waiting found her quick to scold, to slap, and to take scissors to their dresses, if they threatened to compete in elegance with her own. The earl of Essex, bold and impudent, was like her crown prince at court, who could do no wrong.

Sir Walter Raleigh, a man of startling impact who had long enjoyed the Virgin's favor, busy outfitting a small fleet to assault Spanish treasure, was clapped into the Tower for having made Elizabeth Throckmorton pregnant before he married her. No greater sin existed in the Virgin's eyes; she had developed an older person's unpleasant habit of becoming prudish about the sexual behavior of the young.

The Queen of England was, however, still the darling of Fortune. Raleigh's fleet sailed without him and, under the command of Sir John Burrows, captured a great carrack loaded with gold, silver, diamonds, emeralds, musk, ambergris, pepper, perfumes, and other gleaming, costly cargoes from the Orient. It was the greatest prize ever captured at sea in England's history. Hauled into Dartmouth, it attracted crowds, hordes, masses. Raleigh offered the lion's share—£80,000—to Elizabeth, and she unbent enough to accept it. The great bribe gained him his freedom from the Tower for the crime of marrying, but he remained in disfavor at court.

That court was growing odd. It was as though the queen were determined to stop time, to freeze further change around her. Her method was to dance strenuously and to pretend that all was as it had been, that nothing was new. If newness appeared, the Virgin put it aside.

She had a great accomplice in that effort in her "black husband," the archbishop of Canterbury. He and his High Commission had uncovered a small number of Separatists: men who believed in the unholy theory that the government should have no control whatever over a church. The first leaders discovered, including Greenwood and Barrow, had been locked up after sensational trials. By the end of 1592 the movement had grown remarkably and developed new leaders against whom the High Commission now moved. Francis Johnson and Cuthbert Bainbrigg, both Fellows at Cambridge, became converts and invigorated the movement. Another was John Penry, a notorious dissident. Arrests of these men included their following, which led the High Commission downward into the very centers of the people—haberdashers, glovers, apothecaries, housewives. These men and women, some aged, were thrown into chill dungeons and placed in chains and kept in starving condition.

Their leaders had written books against the established church and had compared Whitgift's High Commission to the Inquisition. The comparison was apt; there was little intellectual difference—and the printing presses extended the parallel and pressed it into the mind of the realm. The sequence was one that would become familiar in later ages: dissent, persecution, martyrs, sympathy, more dissent.

It boiled to the surface of the new Parliament, called in early 1593.

James Morice, a lawyer who had written an immense tome against the High Commission's authority, arose in February in the House of Commons against the expressed injunction of the queen. She had warned against "licentious" speech. Her position was that no subject had a right to discuss religion or a scheme of government. Morice tore that argument to shreds, citing the Magna Carta, the common law, and precedent. His peroration was stirring and ended with the statement that if he and his generation allowed their patrimony to be destroyed, posterity would blame them for passing on slavery. He also introduced two bills ensuring that the church authorities would be bound by the rules of common law, citing ancient English liberties.[12]

Morice was far from alone. The Privy Council had members who agreed with him and who—in all probability—had selected him to spearhead their latest effort to curb the Virgin and her tame clerics. Sir Francis Knollys was one; Robert Beale was another. Sir Robert Cecil, Burghley's son and assistant, a growing power in the administration, did not appear openly, but his support was clear—and behind him, that of his father. Sir Edward Coke, a lawyer of impressive abilities whom the queen liked, was serving as Speaker of the House. When Morice was finished for the moment, Elizabeth called Coke into a private conversation. Morice, meanwhile, was taken into custody. Beale was placed under house arrest. The High Commission thundered. The protests were stifled. New rigid laws were passed against Catholics and against Separatists as well. It was all the Reform could do to soften the measures clearly aimed against any idea excepting those held by the queen.

Elizabeth had been maneuvered against her will into the execution of her cousin Mary Stuart and into a war with Spain. She had learned her lesson; she was never to have to learn it twice. The Queen of England was as determined as her father, Henry VIII, to rule as she chose, to brook no arguments—and like her father, so cleverly mixed her favors that she managed to make her every act popular. Yet the movement she sought to stifle continued to grow beneath the surface. Like time itself, its pace was subtle but irresistible, invisible in motion but visible in its effects.

In Scotland, a land that now seemed racked with perpetual disputes and scandals, the winter had passed, and James brooded in his palace—cursing Bothwell, drinking, hunting, working on a book to be called *Dæmonologie,* and letting matters drift.

He was caught in a strange paralysis of the will. The earl of Huntly remained unpunished for his murder of Moray; the earl of Lennox was large at James's version of a court, and numerous pro-Vatican factions plotted before the king's very eyes while he stared as though blind.

Maitland was in isolation; and though James continued to seek his counsel intermittently, it was his constant presence, his mixture of jokes and suggestions, that had kept the king's policy coherent. In the chancellor's absence—he was still officially chancellor—the English ambassador, Sir Robert Bowes, and his agents kept a sharp and constant vigil upon the scene. The leaders of the Reform, having now learned their king was neither trustworthy nor alert, constituted another network of watchers. For the first time in years English money helped in this activity. It was soon proven worthwhile.

On December 27, 1592, Andrew Knox, the minister at Paisley, halted George Ker as he was about to sail for Europe. Ker was searched and found to be carrying letters from Jesuits and pro-Vatican persons in Scotland to their associates overseas. That was a good haul, but what was truly alarming was that Ker was also carrying a number of blank sheets signed by the earls of Huntly, Angus, and Errol, with their seals, as well as the seal of Sir Patrick Gordon.[13]

Torture extracted a garbled story from Ker, as well as the names of some of his confederates. Unraveling truth from their falsehoods was not, then or later, easy. All that emerged was that the Jesuits were again working on an international effort to draw Philip II of Spain into another action against Elizabeth in England, using Scotland as a base. William Crichton and Father Tyrie, who had crept in and out of their Scots homeland for years pursuing this dream through all vicissitudes, had persuaded Huntly, Angus, and Errol to sign some blanks and hand over their seals by saying that Philip needed proofs of their sincerity. Apparently, other Jesuits in Spain planned to fill in the blanks with the sort of promises, protestations, or propositions Philip would find persuasive.

On the Scots end, the Jesuit James Gordon had convinced Huntly and his followers that Philip II would send 30,000 men—provided he could obtain their support. The plan, according to the dreams of unworldly clerics who considered themselves as truly adroit, formidable, and sophisticated as their enemies claimed, would not upset James Stuart on his throne. Only four or five thousand men would remain in Scotland; the rest would enter England, rally the faithful and accomplish the overthrow. In effect, the Jesuits were again attempting to broker a project into life.

Elizabeth sent one of her tart masterpieces to James and had Lord Burgh carry it north to emphasize its seriousness. She herself, she said untruthfully, had never—in thirty-four years—suffered any disobedience from her subjects. Once again she warned of Spanish dangers and urged the punishment of Huntly et al. And she said she knew nothing of Bothwell and his whereabouts, though everyone knew he was in England raising money.

James answered at great length, and they exchanged their usual disjointed messages regarding money. The Virgin increased her pressure by reducing her payments; James begged and complained.

In reality, he lost a great deal of ground by the discovery of the Spanish Blanks—and Bothwell's propaganda seemed more convincing than ever. The Reform began to wonder aloud if the plague that had struck in London were not a punishment against the Virgin for her High Commission—and if Bothwell were not a whip of God to urge James against the forces of Anti-Christ in his own realm.

With the Kirk thundering, Elizabeth's ambassador urging action, and the Crown revenues dwindling fast, James led a small force northward in the direction of the earl of Huntly. He also arrested Angus, but that noble escaped with suspicious ease from Edinburgh Castle almost at once. The king made no move against the estates, the supporters, or the families of the pro-Spanish nobles. Only David Graham, an underling, was hanged for complicity in the blanks. The king contented himself with obtaining some "sureties" from the people of Aberdeen and returned south without having penetrated the savage Highlands.

Upon his return from this pseudopursuit, the king again announced he needed money. If money and support were forthcoming, he would move against the pro-Vatican conspirators involved in the Spanish Blanks. But in the meantime he was determined that Bothwell should be captured and punished. The Kirk might thunder, but the king's determination in this respect was clear. First Bothwell, and then other matters. To ensure that all understood, he said a Parliament would be summoned—but not until summer. Then he settled back to wait; the only policy in which he was always firm.

---

In England the queen, having suffocated the objections of Parliament, turned Whitgift loose upon the Separatists. In March 1593, Barrow was convicted of having slandered Her Majesty and executed in April. In that same month John Penry was sent to death for having denied the Virgin's supremacy over religion.

Matters were going well in other areas for the queen. The formidable duke of Parma had died the previous December, and the war with Spain was not overly burdensome; Philip II was more intent upon the situation in France.

The queen, however, would hear nothing of any successor; she had Peter Wentworth cast into prison for bringing the subject up in Parliament. Time, it was clear, would bow to the imperious will that now seemed to her invincible.

Between April and May, 1593, the uproar over the Spanish Blanks having somewhat subsided, the king of Scotland made some efforts—strenuous in his terms—to restore his Chancellor Maitland to court. In this undertaking he had the assistance of the English ambassador, Sir Robert Bowes, and behind Bowes the shrewd and longsighted Burghley in England. The Virgin had briefly chosen Bothwell, but Burghley knew that Maitland was the more intelligent and therefore the best man to support.

Since Elizabeth and Whitgift had savagely reduced the power of the Reform movement in England, the queen may well have warmed toward Burghley; at any rate, she accepted his advice and wrote Scotland's Queen Anne a friendly letter—recommending Maitland.

Queen Anne's intelligence had not improved, but her influence was undeniable and she was in the forefront of Maitland's enemies. James talked to her; his councillors talked to her; Maitland sent an abject letter from his exile in Lethington. Her sense of importance at last being recognized, she began to soften.

One result was somewhat surprising. James grew amiable, curbed his sarcasms, and the royal couple began to draw together. They were seen entering the bedchamber together. An air of unaccustomed normality began to lift the atmosphere of James's court. Sometime in May he succeeded, although it would be some while before he knew, in making his queen pregnant. The fact that he could do so was proof that his ardent pursuit of his own sex was not based upon any physical abnormality or inability, but simply a preference for that vice.

By June Maitland ceded revenues of the lordship of Musselburgh to Queen Anne—proof that her surrender had some financial basis. James had driven a bargain that did not quite debase Maitland, however—the estate was to revert to his family in the event of the queen's death.

These developments greatly angered the duke of Lennox. He had no intention of allowing Maitland to resume his dominance, and he decided to take steps. Lennox waited while James's Parliament—always a somewhat feeble gathering—came together. It met in July, 1593, and convened after George Ker, the carrier of the Spanish Blanks, had managed to escape from custody in Edinburgh.

James, however, was not interested in Spain nor Huntly nor Lennox nor any of their associates—but only in the earl of Bothwell. At his insistence, the Scots Parliament, hoping the king would later become more cooperative, tried Bothwell *in absentia* for his invasions of Holyrood and Falkland. The earl was declared a traitor and his outlaw status ratified. The Bothwell coat of arms was torn by heralds in front of the great Cross in Edinburgh, and his disgrace sounded throughout the realm.

Having attained his objective, James then declared that since Ker had escaped from custody, no witnesses remained in the case of the Spanish Blanks and that no proceedings against Huntly and the pro-Vatican earls were possible. That amazing stance, otherwise inexplicable, may have been part of Queen Anne's hard bargain with the king before agreeing to Maitland's return: Anne had secretly converted to Catholicism.

James then dissolved his Parliament, and howls immediately rose from the Reform faction. Elizabeth sent another angry message from London and a new ambassador—Lord Burgh—appeared before the king to remonstrate —and to suggest that Bothwell be pardoned.

To the surprise of the English, James exploded. "Touching that vile man," he said to Burgh, "his affronts to me are unpardonable."[14] He went so far as to write Elizabeth in her own sort of language when aroused, saying he "would rather be a slave in the Turk's galleys" than forgive the rebel earl. His animus against Bothwell was so fierce, in fact, that it gives rise to the suspicion that something had happened between them the world did not know.

In view of this adamant attitude, which set the face of the Reform in his realm against him, irritated the foreign ally that kept him on his throne, and aroused widespread discontent in many quarters, the events of July 27, 1593, were all the more humiliating for James.

They began, as far as the king was concerned, while he was sitting in his closet at Holyrood at 8 A.M. Hearing noises, he emerged with his pants in his hands, still in his nightgown, to see the earl of Bothwell coming toward him with a naked sword.

Behind Bothwell were the figures of the laird of Spott, William Leslie, and John Colville. The trio were carrying large pistols. The earl, looming before the astonished king, took a tone somewhere between contempt and a horrid jolliness.

"Loe, my good bairn," he said. "Ye have given out that I sought your life. Now, it is in my hands. What a wrong you have done me!"

James, white as his gown, ran toward Queen Anne's door and hammered on it, but it remained closed and still. Bothwell, moving easily, caught him by his nightgown and turned him around. James, flattened against the door, stammered.

"What do you mean?" he asked. "Are you after my life? You can get it, but you will not get my soul!"

Bothwell, however, sank gracefully to his knees and offered the sword. He was loyal; the king could strike him if he did not believe it. Matters had gone far enough; it was not necessary to frighten the king to death.

From then on, Bothwell later told the dean of Durham, who sent it all to Burghley in England, matters turned in more familiar directions, "the two alone withdrawing themselves to a window, capitulated a while . . . how importunately the King embraced him about the necke, kissed his cheek and as it were wooed him diversely, *to disclose what her Majesties part was in the Earl's attempt to take the King.*" The dean, in his description to Burghley, expressed some disgust.[15]

James was now in the hands of Bothwell. A crowd had appeared outside the palace, and the king, leaning out the window in his usual unregal way, told them all was well. All was well—for the Stewart clan. The duke of Lennox was high; Bothwell was again at court and smiling hugely at his friends; the earl of Atholl and Lord Ochiltree—more Stewarts—walked about in high good humor.

The leaders of the Kirk, who were aware of the earl's intention, approved of the change in the air. Lady Gowrie, "who had the family flair for making King James' flesh creep" and who had opened the palace door to Bothwell, was pleased; Lady Atholl, who had overseen Bothwell's arrival the night before, was pleased—and James announced himself to be delighted.

On July 26, 1593, only days after his coat of arms had been publicly destroyed and his name banished from the annals of the realm, Bothwell's reputation was announced, by Royal Proclamation, to be above reproach, and all subjects forbidden to "slander, murmer, or reproach" his "partakings."

The ministers appeared to arrange a more orderly shift in the situation, and it was agreed that the earl would appear in a formal court to clear his name of the odious charge of witchcraft. James was sullen when the trial, packed with Stewart followers, acquitted Bothwell—though the verdict was an obvious conclusion. He swallowed the subsequent steps as well; and on August 14, 1593, he agreed to pardon Bothwell, restore the earl's estates, and, in general, to make his abject condition plain to the world. For the moment there was little else he could do; Maitland was told to keep away from court. At one point, James thought of fleeing to the north and placing himself under the protection of Huntly and the great pro-Vatican nobles in the Highland fastnesses, but Bothwell accused him of "breach of promise," and the king subsided.

Nevertheless, the rebel earl had to do more than keep the king of Scotland in a state of personal fear. The times when even James could be held a captive were over; the world had moved toward more civilized practices; Scotland had moved since James was a child. The duke of Lennox was at court and had no intention of allowing moves against his ally,

Huntly, if he could help stop them. The earl of Atholl, who had helped Bothwell, was angry because Bothwell—for all his personal force—could not move James against the Highlanders.

Furthermore, as soon as Bothwell felt secure, he began to swagger. That drove the earls of Mar and Morton, Lord Hume, the master of Glamis, and other Reform nobles away; they had no intention of setting up another strong man. Bothwell needed support, and he was bold enough to ride away from Edinburgh and rash enough to travel into England. He stopped in Berwick and talked to Lord Hundson, but the English were apprised, through their network of spies, that a Reform coalition was already forming against the earl.

Elizabeth, underhanded and curious as always, wanted to know all particulars. Henry Lock, her agent in charge of negotiations with Bothwell, was told to reprove him for handling his king so arrogantly and to hold him in discussions about money until the air was cleared.

Meanwhile, James rode to Stirling. Joined by Maitland, he conferred with Lord John Hamilton—a very powerful figure—the master of Glamis, Lords Hume and Maxwell, and the other Reform leaders for whom Bothwell had now served his purpose. His courage restored, James declared he had been "a captive and thrall" and that his pardon of the rebel earl had been obtained "by force and fear." A larger man would have been ashamed of such an admission, but it was James's peculiar strength to be below pride and to be held so generally beneath the ordinary expectations of men that his weakness was both known and, strangely, forgiven.

At Stirling it was agreed that Bothwell would be pardoned at the next Parliament and would afterward be sent into exile. In the interim the king issued an order that the rebel was not to come within ten miles of the court. The news did not greatly please the Kirk, which had just learned that Henry IV, the great Reform leader of France, had abruptly announced his conversion to Catholicism, in order to obtain the surrender and support of Paris.

With Elizabeth having repressed the Reform tide in England and with pro-Vatican nobles retaining the support of their own king, the Reformers of the Kirk decided to move on their own. In late September, 1593, the earls of Huntly, Errol, and Angus, as well as Lord Hume, were excommunicated.

James, however, was a hard king to help. He had a satiric bent, since his weakness allowed him few other means of expressing his real sentiments, and he devised a playlet based on Bothwell's more spectacular dramas. On October 12, 1593, as he was proceeding toward a visit with Maitland, he pretended to be surprised by the appearance of the excommunicated earls near Fala. They knelt, asked his pardon, and claimed they wanted a fair trial

—and the king "warded" them on their promise to appear a little later in Perth.

That action, which reduced the hopes of the Reform, confounded Elizabeth, made no sense as far as the king's position was concerned, and threatened to start a civil war.

The Reform decided to rally in force at Perth to make its powers to excommunicate valid. The earls, in response, planned to bring hundreds, or even thousands, of their armed followers. The king, caught almost as off-guard as by Bothwell, had no idea of what to do. It remained for Maitland, probably the best servant of the worst master in the history of Scotland, to devise not only a way out of the impasse, but to open the gates of resolution for the entire situation.

The chancellor explained to James that the issues at stake were too serious to trust to a trial. He suggested that the earls be given terms and a compromise be reached. The king, who had no other voice available, listened—as usual—to the closest. The duke of Lennox, the earl of Mar and Maitland, after unknown private struggles, drew up a plan that was presented to the Estates in the name of the king and made public November 26, 1593. Its terms were so civil, and its long-range implications so far-sighted, that only Maitland can be credited with its invention.

The chancellor's intent was to resolve disputes, reduce the rebellious pro-Vatican nobles, and placate the Kirk. But beyond these details, he was intent upon establishing the king of Scotland over both the nobility and the clergy. Therefore, he called a meeting of the Estates—from which both the nobles and clergy were barred. The Estates then passed an Act of Abolition, in which only one faith—the Reform—was to be allowed in the land.

After that act, the earls and all other Scots were instructed to accept that faith by January 1, 1594, or go into exile. That exile, however, would not affect their estates or their incomes. They had one month—until February 1, 1594—to make their choice.

Only a man inherently indifferent to the huge arguments based on religious rights at the time would have presented such a proposition. The great argument in Elizabeth's England was against the government's resolving by fiat, force, argument or any other means, the beliefs of the people. The larger issue involved was whether men would be subject, in the medieval sense, to their rulers—or free to choose their faith, as citizens. The Maitland plan, by taking the resolution of the Vatican earls away from punitive powers of the Kirk, placed the king above them all.

James thought it was masterly. The forgiveness of the earls extended only to the matter of the Spanish Blanks and did not include any "murders or other criminal matters." Maitland, whose interest—like that of Burghley in England—was for Crown and country, was also pleased. If the earls refused, they would be rebels. If they accepted, they would be gone. Furthermore, the solution was reached without English intervention, either intellectually or in any other way; and as a Scot, the chancellor was pleased.

It did not please Elizabeth, but then nothing that anyone did without her instructions pleased the Virgin. She sent word to Sir Robert Bowes to seek the king's ear and carry her usual torrent of ambiguous suggestions. He sent back word that it was difficult for him to reach James. The king could not see him because he had a toothache, or was off on a hunt, or was busy.

Elizabeth decided she needed a new ambassador and sent Lord Zouche. He carried the usual insulting letter, which said in part, "For your own sake play the King, and let your subjects see you respect yourself."[16]

On January 19, 1594, the queen of Scotland gave birth to a son. This event, so normal in any other nation and so unlikely in the case of James Stuart and his queen, created the most popular demonstrations on behalf of the Crown in years. One observer described how it was "a great comfort and matter of joy to the whole people . . . bonfires were set out, and dancing and playing used in all parts, as if the people had been daft for mirth."[17]

The king's position was improved in a dynastic sense, but the matter of the Catholic earls and the Kirk was slowly unraveling. Maitland, a man born out of his proper time, was aghast at the denunciations that came from the pulpits against his plan. The leaders of the Reform believed that exiles with vast incomes was no answer, but a means of putting powerful pro-Catholics overseas in a position and funded to take part in new conspiracies.

From London the Virgin, who was by now convinced beyond recall of her own shrewd and capable brilliance, meddled with her usual results. Her ideas were similar to those of the Kirk: the pro-Vatican nobles of Scotland had to be punished. She turned her mind toward Bothwell again and told Lord Zouche to deal with him secretly while dealing with James openly. Her thought was to pressure the king. Zouche misunderstood and thought she meant what she said.

The Virgin's representative moved according to his instructions. Reflecting the general English disdain for the unruly and poverty-stricken Scots, he talked to James in terms the king deeply resented. The king was sharp and reminded the Englishman he could not be treated "as if he were not a sole Prince, who must render account."[18]

Then Zouche met with Bothwell, or Bothwell's agents, and gave him £400. That might have caused a great deal of trouble, for the earls of Huntly, Errol, and Angus had surveyed the situation and decided not to accept the Maitland plan. They would not give the "surety" demanded against their future conduct; they would not accept exile—and they prepared to remain in their northern keeps.

All this puzzled Zouche, as it would puzzle any foreigner unused to the kaleidoscopic maneuvers and lightning shifts of the Scots. He was so bewildered he thought Maitland was taking bribes from the pro-Vatican earls and wrote Robert Cecil to that effect. Cecil was inclined to agree; he thought Maitland was "slippery."

The king's position was growing oddly similar to the one Mary Stuart had occupied a generation earlier. By failing to take action after the murder of a popular noble—in his case, Moray, and in hers, Darnley—they had both aroused the leaders of the Reform and a few determined peers. In both instances, they had sought support from the powerful pro-Vatican, dissolute, but charming nobles of the north in order to remain on the throne. In both instances, they refused to follow the English alliance, in which subservience was held to be a test of trustworthiness.

In James's case, however, matters did not proceed as far as in his mother's. He was saved, not by any shrewdness of his own, for his intelligence was never his guide, but by the mistakes of his enemy—the earl of Bothwell.

The earl had the lukewarm support of the Reform and equally lukewarm and tentative support from Elizabeth. Instead of building upon that support, he decided to move. On April 3, 1594, he abruptly rode into Leith, the seaport of Edinburgh, with "four cornets"—four hundred men.

The news galvanized the capital and aroused James into a state of high excitement. Bothwell had an effect on him no other person could arouse. The king appeared at the High Kirk at eight in the morning and addressed the congregation and the assembled ministers in probably the most effective speech of his entire life.

"If you will assist me at this time," he said, "I promise to persecute the excommunicated Lords, so that they shall not be suffered to remain in anie part of Scotland . . . if the Lord give me victorie over Bothwell, I salle never rest till I passe upon Huntlie and the rest. . . ."[19]

The reaction was instantaneous. These were the words the people and their leaders wanted to hear. "The toun putteth on their armour; the Chancellor putteth on his jacke" and men ran to get their swords, pikes, and muskets. They rushed out, and Bothwell, seeing their numbers, retreated until he reached Niddrie.

There he collected his men on a hill and waited. Lord Hume led the king's force, accompanied by the master of Glamis. Bothwell divided his defense with Lord Ochiltree, whom Hume charged and scattered. Bothwell, however, led a charge of his own, and some mixed fighting took place. Finally "trumpets sounded the retreat," and Bothwell retired; he had fallen off his horse and dislocated his shoulder blade.

Unfortunately, James did not remain on the field that long. When the tide flowed toward him, the king fled. "He came riding into Edinburgh at the full gallop, with little honor."[20]

It was, nevertheless, a great victory—for it swung the Kirk around to James. The king sent letters to Elizabeth, charging her with having assisted rebels, and asking—as ever—for money. For her part, she sent secret word to Bothwell to rest for a time and waited to see if the king of Scotland would move, as he had promised, against the pro-Vatican earls.

Robert Cecil, who had moved far into his father's place, though Burghley was still on the scene and available, persuaded the Virgin that she had to provide more tangible assistance. She sent £4,000.

The tide, in other words, was finally shifting. Sir Robert Bowes wrote Cecil that James would do the right thing and rid his realm of Huntly and his associates. Cecil, who had his father's habit of scribbling comments on edges of the reports he received, wrote *"Credo in Deum"* ("I believe in God"). But James was, for once, moving.

In May 1594 the Scots Parliament met, and the earls were found guilty of treason. Maitland took advantage of a series of agreements with the Kirk to have another measure passed, which required a prior submission of all proposed legislation to a committee of the Estates, in other words, the king —first. A series of money-raising bills were passed, for the benefit of the Crown and for immense, ponderous, elaborate preparations for the baptism of the infant Prince Henry—James's heir and pride.

Through the summer the chancellor restored the administrative machinery of the Crown while James busied himself with the details of his son's baptism. In some instances, he addressed invitations personally and even composed some of the entertainments to be presented.

These innocent activities lulled Huntly and his associates. The Highland nobles were inclined to mock the rumors that seeped from the Crown regarding more serious preparations underway behind the scenes. Ships had arrived from Europe, and some had carried more Jesuits and even money from the Vatican. The pro-Vatican faction, aware it needed help in the south, held the lure of this money out for Bothwell, and he tumbled into oblivion by reaching for it.

Elizabeth received a letter from the rebel earl, in which he said he had been offered £40,000 to switch sides: to abandon the Kirk and also to abandon the English and to help Huntly, Erroll, and Angus. Unless she matched the offer, he would have no choice. Bothwell also contacted the Kirk and though he was not so blunt with the ministers, hinted that he might have to shift his stand. The Virgin refused to match the pro-Vatican offer, and Bothwell announced his change. In doing so, he stood revealed as a complete adventurer, available to the highest bidder. The response of the Kirk was indignant, and the people were contemptuous. In a single step,

Bothwell had destroyed his own credibility and remarkably cleared the path for James and Maitland.

On August 30, 1594, young Prince Henry was baptized in the Royal Chapel at Holyrood, and a series of festivities, masques, and entertainments followed. James appeared in one as a Knight of Malta, other nobles played various parts, and some were even persuaded into women's clothes. An elaborate ship, eighteen feet long with silken lines and cloth of gold sails, awed the court; mock windmills, Moors, chariots, and lesser marvels followed.

After all this, James began to move, like a fierce snail, toward the north and the mighty earls of the Highlands. He accumulated men as he progressed and levied money from the various towns and hamlets, as he proceeded, to pay his expenses. These sums were increased by payments from those who wanted to be excused from fighting, loans from peers and lairds and burghers, and special levies on districts.

On October 3, 1594, the earl of Argyll, commanding Crown forces, met and fought against Huntly and his men. The pro-Vatican leader was credited with a victory, but it was an expensive one, and he had to withdraw. James and his men arrived at the Huntly castle of Strathbogie to find it undefended and set it afire. They did the same to the seat of the earl of Errol at Slaine. The two earls and their supporters, meanwhile, vanished into the infinite recesses of the mountains, whose trails they knew by heart.

By year's end James returned to Edinburgh in triumph. Early in the new year 1595 the Kirk capped events by excommunicating the earl of Bothwell. In London the Virgin learned that the king of Scotland, whose fortunes a year earlier had dwindled to the vanishing point, had made a remarkable recovery. Without the help or the money of England, the Scots Crown was once again secure. She was astonished, with good reason. James Stuart had floundered, been frightened, fled, wept and ran, and somehow emerged in the strongest position of any king of Scotland since Robert the Bruce.

From afar, this was inexplicable. At home, jealousy and meanness kept the Scots from admitting that these triumphs were achieved not by the King or the Kirk, but by the adroit moves and policies of the chancellor, John Maitland.

# 24

James, following tradition, ordered the infant Prince Henry placed at Stirling Castle under the protection of the earl of Mar—the hereditary guardian. The king had known the earl since childhood, and, though their relationship had its uneven moments in the past, had grown fond of him. Queen Anne, however, rose in protest. She wanted to take care of her son herself. James explained the situation as well as he could, but the queen's demands rose with each session. She wanted to be given Edinburgh Castle and the prince; she would handle all.

Their argument grew rancorous, for Anne had developed a talent for nagging, weeping, scolding, and amateurish plotting. She soon became the center of a confusing coalition, and even Maitland was drawn into the vortex. The chancellor was trying to regain his position at court and hoped for the queen's assistance. Unfortunately, he and the earl of Mar became involved in a separate dispute, and for a time James had several different quarreling groups on his hands.

Maitland, however, never put his personal interests ahead of the Crown. He approved of Mar as the guardian of James's heir; and he also revealed a plot to James, in which Anne was involved as a cat's-paw, to seize the royal infant. James did not need to be told what that meant. The history of Scotland was replete with interludes where nobles reigned in the name of a captive child-king; he himself had been one.

Alerting James to that danger and ensuring the safety of the prince at Stirling in the hands of the reliable Mar was Maitland's last great service to James.[1] It also convinced the king, permanently, that Queen Anne could not be allowed into matters of state.

Coincidentally, the queen fell ill at this point, and James visited her at Falklands. She was sorrowful, tearful, and apparently repentant; James was magnanimous, and a reconciliation took place. Maitland, ill himself, retired to his estate. His condition was serious.

Robert Bruce, one of the leaders of the Kirk, found the chancellor wondering about his ultimate fate and wondering also whether his efforts had been worthwhile. "He broke out in plain speeches," Bruce said, "confessing he had negligently heard the word and omitted to that good . . . which he might and ought to have done."[2] He bargained, publicly, for time. If he could live a little longer, he would live differently. His castle at Lauder, whose creation had so filled him with pride, he now deplored—and wondered aloud why he had not built a hospital.

The chancellor's remorse impelled the ministers, who usually swarmed to urge repentance, into reassurances. That was difficult, for Maitland was too intelligent a man not to feel a deep shame at having worked so long as a servant for such a master as James Stuart. Yet the Kirk's leaders were right; Maitland had carried his countrymen far toward a stable and coherent society.

Nevertheless, James's problems pursued him to the end. Asked on the evening of his death what advice he would leave the king "for the managing of his estate," Maitland turned his head away. The question, he said, came too late. His thoughts were on another realm, which he entered on October 3, 1595.

The king heard the news of Maitland's death with proper seriousness, but it was not unexpected. He had composed a sonnet in advance that ended, typically, on a note of self-pity:

So for himself most happy doth he lie,
Though for his Prince it most unhappy be.[3]

Maitland had barely vanished when James set about slandering his memory. He made a great fuss about what he claimed to be inefficiencies he discovered that had been previously hidden and announced he would leave the chancellor's office vacant in the future. His reasons varied with the person and the group with whom he talked. Ambitious peers seeking the office were told such an appointment would make "a great man better attended than the King himself." Commoners were told, with a cruel undertone, that he had his fill of the "start-ups" (upstarts).

The king, having explained away his ingratitude, then busied himself in sudden flurries intended to establish his sovereignty and spread "order" in the realm. He began with a soaring proclamation of authority over everything that moved in Scotland. He next used some of the £3,000 that Elizabeth had sent north in August 1595 to hire soldiers and undertake a series of sallies toward the border to scare that criminal region into temporary civility. Between these exercises he held hearings in Edinburgh in which persons at feud or accused of breaking laws were hauled and hectored before the king and his council.

James was also very displeased to discover the extent of his poverty. This condition, in which he had lived all his life, seemed worse when he examined the accounts for himself. When Maitland had been managing his affairs, the king simply demanded that something be done. Managing his own was a different matter. He muttered darkly that untrustworthy men had enriched themselves at his expense.

His humor was not improved when, at New Year's Day, 1596, Queen Anne triumphantly produced a purse of £1,000 that her council had managed to save through the year from her expenses. She shared half with her husband and convinced him he was badly served. He had some harsh words for the master of Glamis and other officials of his Exchequer and on January 9, 1596, announced the creation of a new committee to handle the finances of the realm. Since it consisted of eight men, it was immediately dubbed the Octavians.

James composed—he was fond of compositions—a sort of charter for the Octavians, in which they were to control the royal revenues, and he promised not to overrule their decisions on what was financially sound. He was very jovial about this and said he enjoyed having a council that was "hangeable"—a clear reference to the greater lords he had ousted from the Exchequer and to their predecessors.

The step did not meet with any great burst of applause. For one thing, at least half the Octavians were known to be secret Papists. For another, the king was impugning the nobility in a rather careless fashion. The courtiers did not like this intrusion of a sudden new element, and a group called the Cubiculars formed in reaction.

The spectacle of higher civil servants setting policy and jealous courtiers competing for the favor of the sovereign resembled, at least in outline, forms long familiar in England. There the earl of Essex, the Virgin's great and reckless favorite, struggled against the influence of Lord Burghley and his son, Robert Cecil, to achieve dominance.

There was an odd, almost unnatural relationship between the queen and Essex; it was as though he was her real son, though they maintained a flirtation that was the queen's fond contact with the emotions of youth.

Elizabeth's struggle against time had caused her to banish mirrors from her palace and to persist in a round of progresses from one stately home to another, one dance to another, one series of flattering subjects to another—endlessly. But the years were coursing, and death plucked, one by one, her old associates. Sir Francis Drake and Sir John Hawkins were gone, lost in an expedition the year before. Hatton was gone; Sir Thomas Randolph was gone; the earl of Shrewsbury was gone; Leicester's brother was gone; and Lord Burghley was old and sick.

New men rose on all sides, and Essex was their leader. He developed a habit of pushing the queen toward directions and appointments against her will. At times he baited. The high post of secretary of the Privy Council had long been vacant, and Essex urged the queen to appoint William Davison, who had been the object of her wrath in the wake of the execution of Mary Stuart and who had been so heavily fined and placed in the Tower.

In the intervening years, Davison had been quietly released and the fines forgiven, but he was a living reminder of one of the queen's most scalding experiences. To propose a new eminence for him was, to say the least, insensitive. But Essex liked to test his limits.

Essex found those limits when he tried to force Francis Bacon into high office. Bacon and his brother, Anthony, were cousins of Robert Cecil and sons of Sir Nicholas Bacon, the former lord keeper. Their father died unexpectedly, leaving Francis in reduced straits. He served Essex as an adviser and writer, and the earl wanted to have him advanced. Robert Cecil and his father, Lord Burghley, advised against it.

The queen sided with the Cecils. She did not like Francis Bacon;[4] he was a homosexual fond of his own brilliance. Neither quality was attractive to her. Bacon was passed over. Essex, angered that his own favorite was not elevated, gave Bacon a small but tidy estate with an income attached, out of his own soaring wealth, as proof that the queen's displeasure did not mean any man would suffer, so long as the favorite liked him. It was a display of pique, which the young earl confused with power.


Elizabeth's belief that time stood still seemed almost true. In 1596 the situation regarding Spain was as it had been for many years. Once again rumors of an invasion swept through England; reports arrived that Philip II was building an immense Armada, that pro-Vatican aristocrats and supporters in England were continuing their secret conspiracies, and that the Crown of Scotland was sending warm private letters to Catholic powers in Europe.

There was a new pope—Clement VIII—but the policy of the Vatican regarding the Virgin was as virulent as ever. From Spain the tireless Father Parsons authored and issued a new book, called *A Conference Regarding the Succession of England*—which argued, amazingly, the right of subjects to overthrow an unlawful sovereign. The propaganda of Knox, Buchanan, and others had affected the propaganda of Rome.

As before, however, there was a split between the Vatican and Madrid; the Church was in favor of a restoration of its faith in England and Philip

II now regarded that realm as a suitable gift for his daughter, the Infanta.

As before, England was divided between a war party and a peace party, and its sea dogs barked to be released. In France, Henry IV begged for aid that came in reluctant trickles from Elizabeth; her delays cost England the possession of Calais. That defeat, which provided the Spaniards with a new springboard port for invasion, created great excitement. Preparations were renewed, and bitter, internecine arguments rose about military command. Essex, of course, wanted all.

In May 1596 the English sent an Armada of their own against Spain. Command was divided among four men: Sir Thomas Howard, Lord Admiral Charles Howard, the earl of Essex, and Sir Walter Raleigh. The force was formidable and consisted of more than 100 ships and over 10,000 men; its commanders bickered all the way to Cadiz.

Overall, the expedition succeeded in destroying the major part of Philip's invasion fleet at port. It seized Cadiz and created considerable damage. Essex argued with Raleigh and the others and took part in some disastrous undertakings of his own insistence. The English left just before an immense Spanish treasure train arrived.

Essex returned a hero to the people and with more enemies than ever before at court, to learn that the queen had made Robert Cecil a knight —and secretary of the Privy Council. Sir Walter Raleigh, a man whom Essex deeply resented, was made captain of the Queen's Bodyguard and was tall at court again.


These great events had stirred the Kirk of Scotland, but were largely disregarded by its king. James was enjoying a season in the sun. At the age of 30 he was, at last, sovereign of his realm. His tiny court grew flattering, obsequious, and deferential. Lady Huntly and Lady Errol knelt before him and begged forgiveness for their husbands. James easily agreed that the exiled Catholic earls could return. That forgiveness set off a violent response from the leaders of the Kirk.

Andrew Melville and a group of his ministers appeared at the palace at Falklands to remonstrate with James, but the king was in full flush and "used his authority in a most crabbed and choleric manner." Melville lost his patience and his temper and called James "God's silly vassal."

"Sir," he said, "You are brought in extreme danger both of your life and your Crown. And with you the country and Kirk of Christ is like to wreck. And, therefore, Sir, I must tell you, there are two Kings and two Kingdoms in Scotland. There is Christ Jesus the King, and his Kingdom the Kirk, whose subject James VI is, and of whose Kingdom not a King, nor a lord, nor a head, but a member!"[5]

That was drawing the issue very plainly, and James—whose distinction it was to never argue with angry men—immediately backed down.


The Queen of England had problems of a different nature. She had grown dependent upon Essex for a connection with emotion and with a sense of being alive, wanted, important, and likeable as a woman. The earl, however, was in a great temper because she had distributed honors to other men in the wake of the expedition to Cadiz.

The court missed the handsome earl, who sulked at his estate and refused to appear, even on command. The queen had developed a habit of constant "progresses"—visits from one great noble house to another. These processions, despite the bone-wrenching discomforts of her coach, carried her past cheering crowds, staring faces, and gave her a reassuring lift.

But as the autumn of 1596 extended, the shadows grew longer. Lord Hunsdon, an old favorite, sick and ailing, described a vision. He "saw come to him, one after another, six companions already dead. The first was Dudley, the Earl of Leicester, all on fire. The second, Secretary Walsingham, also in fire and flames. Puckering, the Lord Keeper, so cold and frozen that touching Hunsdon's hand, he thought he should die of cold. Then came Sir Christopher Hatton, Lord Chancellor, Heneage and Sir Francis Knollys, all flaming, and standing round Hunsdon's bed told him to prepare to join them, with Cecil [Burghley] who was, as yet, alive."[6]

Elizabeth could not stand it. She announced that Essex was her new earl marshal of the realm, and he condescended at last to join her, smiling and handsome, making her laugh—helping to melt the chill of time.


Despite his promise to the Reform, James Stuart welcomed the earls of Huntly and Errol back from exile. His excuse was almost domestic. Queen Anne had a new baby—a daughter—in August, 1596, and the king wanted his nobility united around him. The realm erupted. Ministers rose in their pulpits to thunder; the heir to the revolution was against turning toward the Vatican and all its creatures.

David Black, minister at St. Andrews, drew a public comparison between the course that James was choosing and the path taken by his mother, Mary Stuart, upon whom "God's judgment" had fallen. The king called Black before him and attempted to argue him down and did not succeed. That was a great crime in James's eyes, greater than the substance of any argument.

Black then created an international incident in the pulpit of St. Andrews when, in the presence of English observers, he declared that Elizabeth was an atheist, that religion in England was "an empty show," that English bishops were persuading James toward a similar course, and that the king had connived at the return of Huntly and Errol. Satan ruled the court, said Black, and went on to the call the king's judges "cormorants" and said Queen Anne was a woman for whom the Kirk prayed, but from whom no good could be expected. He ending by wondering aloud whether or not all kings were not children of the Devil.

The fires that Knox and Buchanan had kindled were, it was clear, still burning bright. James protested, but the Reform was in a mood to draw lines and test wills. The king wrote a lengthy document, as was his habit, and the ministers under Melville responded. James wanted Black tried before his council, and the Kirk declared the Crown had no right to censure sermons or to pass upon their content; the spirit of prophecy could not be contained by a government.

This carried the issue beyond Whitgift's High Commission in England and onto higher ground. In years to come it would lure the entire island, but in December 1596 it was premature. For all his searching intelligence, Andrew Melville lacked the supernal powers of the great Knox, but for a moment the balance seemed very close.

On December 17, 1596, the congregation at St. Giles was excited by an oration against the king's council—the Octavians. A courtier, whose appearance was timed to take advantage of the oration, appeared at the door to shout, "Save yourselves! Armour, armour! Bills and axes!"[7] People rushed toward the tollbooth and hammered at the doors, alarming James and the council. The flurry did not last long. A short time later James rode toward Holyrood Palace on the outskirts of town, and the streets were already quiet.

James was, however, armed with a council of intelligent men, intent —as Maitland had been intent—upon centralizing the government and ending the turbulent patterns of the realm. The day after the short-lived Edinburgh alarm, the king rode easily to Linlithgow accompanied by his entire court. There the council officially declared that Edinburgh had committed treason and would lose its status as the capital of the realm.

While the burghers and merchants of the city recoiled in shock, the king's canny new councillors sent more messages. A fine of twenty thousand marks was levied, free election of city magistrates was cancelled, and the court would not return. These economic and social sanctions, which resembled the punishments of England's High Commission against individuals, completely altered the situation. A howl went up from the Edinburghers; merchants rose against the ministers and four of them had to flee the city.

These were masterful moves on the part of the king and were followed in February 1597 at a General Assembly. There, royal agents went to work with their powers of patronage, and many ministers of the more extreme sort were replaced by their more compliant brethren. There were protests, but the Kirk had been penetrated, and the Reform movement was, at last, split. "Where Christ had guided before," said Melville in despair, "the Court began to govern all."[8]

An anonymous letter of the time was quick to point toward the source of James's inspiration: Elizabeth. "There is not a Popish prince in Europe that dares claim [to be head and judge of all causes] . . . and none but her Majesty of our neighbor country. And ye know . . . how King Henry VIII got that title, and how she had borne it since. . . ."[9]

Some of the outcasts wrote to Essex for help, but his response was chilly. The earl was not interested in religious issues or persons. Meanwhile, James and his councillors managed to turn their victory into stones that rained upon the Reform. Ministers were to restrict their oratory to ecclesiastical matters and to cease thundering about the state. The king of Scotland, having succeeded over his nobles with the help of Maitland, was now winning against the Reform with the help of Maitland-trained men.


The Virgin had lost many of her teeth, and those that remained had turned black. Her wigs were as red as ever; she dressed with her customary splendor; her manner was as regal; her hold, apparently as secure. "She was dressed," said one observer, "in white silk bordered with pearls the size of beans and over it a mantle of black silk, shot with gold thread. Her train was very long . . . borne by a marchionesse. As she went along in all this state and magnificence, she spoke very graciously first to one and then to another."[10] But her reign in 1597 was thirty-nine years old, a longer span than the average life of her contemporaries—long enough for people to learn, and to grow sick, of her every habit and mannerism, every nuance and turn. Her young ladies had grown afraid of her; not all her bowing courtiers bore her much love.

Later even the captain of her guard, one of her most celebrated and favored men, Raleigh, was to say, ". . . she seemed a great and good mistress in the eyes of the world, but she was unjust and tyrannous . . . to him."

That simmering discontent infected Essex as well, though he was the envy of all because of the immense gifts the demanding old queen showered upon him. The earl corresponded with James in Scotland through his sister, Penelope. The exchange had little solidity, but it seemed to keep all of them in some sort of harmony, which James—always seeking English allies—treasured. One note from Essex to his sister described his emotions at court as "melancholy, merry, sometimes happy and often discontented. . . . The time wherein we live is more inconstant than women's thoughts, more miserable than old age itself."[11]

From Madrid the aging Philip II, his hair white and his face pale as a ghost, watched the collapse of his hopes in France. Henry IV, by changing to the Vatican faith, had gradually drawn all the reins of his country into his hand. The great empire Philip II had sought to extend forever had reached its limits and was settling.

In 1598 Henry moved toward peace negotiations without regard to his English allies to the relief of everyone except Essex, who saw his chances for glory and advancement diminishing in times of peace. The earl's passionate arguments in favor of continued English action against Spain on the French land mass, despite the intentions of Henry IV, were heard in the Privy Council in silence. A mood of weary disgust with Essex's ambitions seeped into the chamber. Lord Burghley alone had the temerity to pull out his Prayer Book and opened it at the fifty-fifth Psalm, from which he read aloud words many would later recall, "Bloodthirsty and deceitful men shall not live out half their days."[12]


From Scotland another young, ambitious man watched the course of events with an impatience that approached agony: James Stuart. A border incident in which Buccleigh had rescued a Scot from the clutches of the English in a daring raid created an argument in the spring and cost the king of Scotland his yearly pension from Elizabeth. To James, whose need for money was always critical, the calamity was the fault of the Cecils, whose collaborations with the Kirk through the years had been one of his great problems. The lord treasurer, James believed, would seize upon any excuse to cut off his money.

He exchanged bitter letters with Elizabeth, in which they again wrote past one another. He asked, for the hundredth time, for the Lennox estates in England, to which he considered himself the rightful heir. For the hundredth time he was told in response that no foreigner could inherit English land. That raised an old bugaboo: if a foreigner could not inherit a private estate, how could a foreigner inherit the entire crown of England?

The issue was enough to perplex any man. Force had undermined religious principles that once buttressed the laws of Europe. In Scotland during James's own childhood force had intruded into the law, and nobles had taken physical steps to bend legal decisions toward their own desires. The international European states, creatures of rising sovereignty against the Vatican system of supranational sanctions, had taken the same course. From Spain the mightiest monarch of all time had overridden the claims of the Braganzas to make himself king of Portugal and produced a tortured genealogical claim to the throne of England. An alliance with Spain, therefore, would not help James Stuart become king of England.

Spain, however, was merely the greatest Catholic power: it was not the only one. The Vatican still ruled over vast areas; its faith was held by millions. Rising troubles in Ireland made it clear its ability to sway people and shake thrones was still strong. If James were to become king of England, he would be wise not to offend the great international movement whose tentacles continued to extend into that realm and into his own as well. King James, therefore, decided to send ambassadors to Italy and to other parts of the Vatican-dominated world to ensure that his claims to England would be understood—and his own peaceful inclinations made evident.

At the same time, there was the Protestant world to consider. James was considered the prize example of great teachers; the product of Knox and Buchanan, the hope of the Reform. To ensure Protestant support, he spent money he could not afford to send ambassadors to Denmark and Germany and to other parts as well.

These were efforts based on persuasion: his only weapon. It was part of James's remarkable good fortune—and perhaps his greatest unearned gift from fate—that he mounted his argument at a time when the printing presses had introduced mass propaganda into the world and when its effect was electric.

The king of Scotland was educated by a great name in European literature: George Buchanan. James, who resented the lessons he learned, argued against most of them and hated his teacher, but never forgot that Buchanan's power came from his writings. He emulated his mentor at an early age when he published his first slim book of poems, and the praise that rained upon him as a result was like strong drink.

When the earl of Bothwell made his days and nights hideous, James turned again to that defense, and composed—with considerable assistance from his coterie—the tome *Dæmonologie.* Issued from the presses in 1597, it emerged during the height of the great witchcraft movement and antimovement and contained a mountain of incredible detail about Satanism, which fit the learning, prejudices, and attitudes of the time so precisely that its popularity was inevitable and long-lived. The king of Scotland became an internationally known author.

In his struggles with the ministers of his own country and his program to become heir to Elizabeth, it was natural for James to turn toward more writing. His methods, familiar in later times, were novel in his own and widely misunderstood. The king did not sit down to create; he put his assistants to work and then altered, edited, amended, and extended their productions—and issued them in his own name. In this he was ahead of his time—but in no other way.

In 1598, using the talents of William Semple, the writings of other authors in his extensive library, and his own memory (which sometimes played him false), James produced *Basilikon Doron.* It was an effort to argue down the Kirk and its ministers regarding the role and stature of monarchs, a series of pious injunctions about how kings should rule their realm and homilies on the human condition, all rolled into one.

Drawing heavily upon the Old Testament and his own anti-Buchanan ideas, James argued that kings—anointed kings, that is—were chosen by God. This was a common part of the Vatican faith since time immemorial; James fused the thought into the argument that kings, divinely chosen, had, therefore, divine rights. Building upon that premise, which gave his claim to England's throne the greatest of all sanctions and which resembled the Vatican argument that kings had to have theological approval, James went on to buttress his claim by all sorts of examples of his wisdom.

James Melville, the leader of the Reform, saw one of the first drafts of this opus and was alarmed to see James's idea of a proper church. Melville took notes and declared the king of Scotland's theories were "anglo-pisco-Papistical." There was no doubt he was right. James wanted a national Catholic church, complete with mitred bishops, incense, and obedience to a national king-pope, along the lines that Elizabeth had established.

*Basilikon Doron,* however, was not put into print right away. Books then were heavy and expensive projects, and their printing was not quick. James used the effort more to put his ideas down in organized fashion; the results were what later officials might term a working paper, upon which his policies, in both the short and long range, were made clear to his growing group of able assistants.

In the meantime, in Ireland, The O'Neill, earl of Tyrone, urged into action by diligent Jesuits and Spanish gold, mounted a rebellion. The ties between northern Ireland and Scotland were close in terms of both geography and blood; James exchanged warm letters with The O'Neill. He was anxious to leave no possible bridge unbuilt, no contacts left forgotten.

O'Neill was powerful and dangerous, treacherous beyond belief; and the Irish tides behind him made his rising a serious matter. Discussions were held in London regarding the troubled island, whose position was as potentially dangerous to England as Scotland, and where no common bonds had been established. The Irish combined their Vatican faith with their national desire to be free; the seeds of eternal rebellion were thickly sown.

As usual, the issue quickly entangled the rivalry that had developed between the Cecils—Lord Burghley and his son Robert—and the earl of Essex. Essex had great power with the queen and enjoyed a monopoly that enabled him to live in high state. He was not so successful in placing his men in positions in the government. Elizabeth had always preferred to keep her court and her council in a state of mutual tension, so she could steer between. Nevertheless, Essex, who, unlike his predecessor Leicester, had grown popular in the realm, was persistent in his efforts.

Late in July, 1598, the queen discussed the post of lord deputy of Ireland with the favorite and with Sir Robert Cecil, while the earl of Nottingham listened. The contenders presented a study in contrasts. Essex was tall and powerful, with golden tints in his brown hair, spectacularly handsome, able to blend an easy familiarity with a lack of menace that the opposite sex—and the queen—found almost irresistible. Cecil, on the queen's other side, was only three inches over five feet, with a pale, long face and tapering hands, dressed in dark clothes, his back hunch faintly visible beneath his carefully tailored jacket. The queen called him, with the demeaning familiarity she knew so well how to assume, her Pigmy.

Cecil had, with his usual foresight, prepared several names for the queen's consideration as lord deputy of Ireland. Sir William Knollys, Sir Charles Blount, and Sir George Carew were sent into the air; Essex interjected that Carew should be the man. The queen looked at him in contempt, gave one of her sharp, sarcastic yelping laughs, and made a dismissing motion with her hand. It was clear he was not to enter into serious discussions. The earl turned his back to hide his contorted expression, and Elizabeth gave him a hard crack along the head. "Go," she shouted, in her high voice, "and be hanged!"[13]

Essex wheeled around instantly, hand on sword, and said thickly that he would not take that and that he would not have taken that even from the king, her father—when Cecil's gasp brought him to his senses. He backed away then, then fled—leaving behind a memorable shambles.


The Virgin did not have time to worry about Essex, though his conduct had scandalized her court: Burghley was dying. The queen went to see the old man, who was past 77. She sat beside his bed and fed him soup with her own hand; it was an act that sprang from her deep and true femininity, for which men loved her.

Burghley's death was slow but welcome to him; he was annoyed at efforts to keep him alive. "For God's sake, let me die quietly," he said to the hovering physicians. Nevertheless, it hit the queen hard. She went into seclusion, and the very name of her old councillor could bring her close to tears for months afterward; it was like losing an older and beloved brother.

Three weeks later, the news that Philip II of Spain, the Prudent King, had also died, did little to lift the Virgin's spirits. She remembered Philip from girlhood, when he had appeared to marry her sister, Mary. His passing, despite the troubles that racked their countries and held them finally in war, recalled him as the very image of male competence and mystery.

The entire Catholic world, and especially the Spaniards, mourned Philip II; his death had been slow, agonizing, and terrible. He had met it with a fortitude almost incomprehensible. "Look, my son," he said to the future Philip III at one point, "at how Kings die."

The world was changing; and the signs of its change, slow and subtle as the shift of seasons, few and scattered at first and then thick and heavy, had altered Elizabeth's landscape beyond recognition. On every hand new trees towered and new figures appeared.

The earl of Essex protested in a letter to Elizabeth that "I was never proud, till you sought to make me too base."[14] The queen did not answer, and none dared to bring the matter up before her. Her favorite remained from court for two months. During that period he had the good fortune to fall ill, and the news—coming on the heels of the death of Burghley and Philip II—touched the queen where no other news would have sufficed. She sent her personal physician to him and in that action tacitly forgave his temper. By October he was back at court, back at the meetings of the Privy Council, and his position seemed unchanged. The queen, however, had the quiet expression of someone who has just begun to realize that a favored son might have grave defects.

Essex proceeded to prove that suspicion by attempting to become lord treasurer—the post held by Burghley. The queen demurred, softly, and the post remained—for the nonce—unfilled. The subject of Ireland emerged again. In August 1598 The O'Neill had encountered a force of 3,500 men under Sir Henry Bagnal at the Yellow Ford on Blackwater River—and killed them all, including Sir Henry. Then the earl had proceeded, at the head of a wildly enthusiastic country, to raise more forces and extend his territories in Ulster. The discussion that had caused Essex to erupt once was again brought up again at the Privy Council.

The name of Sir Charles Blount recurred, and Essex again protested. The queen looked at him with an enigmatic expression and observed that he seemed to know better than all the council, or than she did herself, the qualities of a new lord deputy and what the situation required. In that event, she concluded, he should perhaps go himself, as the new lord deputy.

The council was stunned, and Essex was taken aback, but he was caught in a position from which he could not retreat; his ambitions would be put to the test.

The Virgin hoped her favorite's abilities would match his words and gave him more generous support than his predecessors. That alone was a mark of her affection, but Essex decided, before he was ready to embark in

March 1599, that he was being ill-treated. "Banishment and proscription to the cursedest of all islands," he called it in a farewell note to his sovereign.[15]

The queen had promised 16,000 men and 1,300 horses—and forbade Essex to make any more battlefield knights, as he had in Spain. His instructions were to go after The O'Neill and defeat him in battle and end the rebellion. The Irish leader was in the north, in Ulster. Essex arrived in Dublin and sat in long conferences and left the city to march south. He was staggered to discover the land was "soft, watery, woody" as well as rainy and swampy. The Irish had developed guerrilla warfare tactics for which the earl's court tourneys, with their bugles and rules, had not prepared him. Like guerrillas everywhere, the Irish considered retreat a basic tactic and secret attacks heroic and existed with no visible means of support.

The earl lost men first singly, then in handfuls, and finally in clusters as he traveled. Eventually, he was able to send news to London that, in the midst of his calamities and complaints, he had captured a castle. The queen said aloud she was paying Essex £1,000 a day "to go in progress." She sent stern orders that the earl should turn north, search, find, and destroy O'Neill.

Instead, Essex asked for more men, more money—and returned to Dublin. He complained the Privy Council was not providing enough support and hinted he was being deliberately placed in a hopeless position. His humor was not improved when, in his absence, the post of lord treasurer went to Buckhurst and the lucrative honorific of master of wards was given to Sir Robert Cecil.


Essex marched out of Dublin in August 1599 with a diminished army whose leaders included 59 new knights he had named, in direct violation of the queen's injunction. His rationale was that such promotions would add to their enthusiasm—a quality he confused with competence.

He found Tyrone and his army in early September. That was not too difficult; the Irish earl had a larger force and was in a mood to be found. Essex, seeing himself outnumbered, marched away from a confrontation and sought better ground; Tyrone asked for a parley. Essex, miserably aware his position was weak, weakly agreed.

The earl of Tyrone had abandoned that title because it was granted by Elizabeth and had reverted to calling himself The O'Neill. Raised partly in England, he was better aware of Essex and his personality, his position and weaknesses, than the Englishman dreamed. Irish eyes had watched developments closely in England, and O'Neill had spent the summer preparing for this moment.

Once face to face with Essex, O'Neill—"a compelling and majestic figure with strong features, long luxuriant black hair and a heavy beard . . . a flowing black cloak about his shoulders"—held the younger man spellbound.[16] All he wanted, murmured the Irish noble seductively, was to have the complaints of his country heard by the real leaders of England.

O'Neill proposed a truce for six weeks, presumably so Essex could acquaint the English government with the fact that they did not confront a rebellion, but merely armed and murderous demonstrations. He wrapped this absurdity in terms that Essex accepted as reasonable: an armistice at once, renewable for periods of six weeks indefinitely, to be broken only after two weeks' warning. Persons afraid of war always place great emphasis on conversation; Essex wanted to believe and did. To the next question, which involved some proof of this agreement, The O'Neill drew himself up in regal fashion. Surely the word of Ireland's leader was enough, as was the word of the earl of Essex himself. This loftiness impressed Essex and convinced him he had achieved a diplomatic triumph.

He reached Dublin to find a letter waiting from Elizabeth. The Virgin did not stint her sarcasm. "You had your asking," she reminded him and said he had wasted it in aimless marches in directions he had not been ordered and had listened to an Irish council in Dublin rather than the commands of his queen. Filled with his agreement, he decided to return to England to convince Elizabeth of how brilliantly he had resolved the great Irish rebellion. He departed on September 24, 1599, accompanied by the reckless earl of Southampton and Sir George Carew and some of the men he had made knights, leaving his army behind and his sword of state with the Archbishop Loftus.

Friday morning, September 28, 1599, the earl of Essex and his escort arrived in London, learned the queen was at Nonsuch Palace just outside town, commandeered some horses, and rode hard. They had learned Lord Grey was ahead of them, and they wanted to reach Elizabeth with their news before Grey. They reached Nonsuch and were told Grey was inside, talking with Robert Cecil.

Essex raced up the steps of the palace and rushed inside, still wearing his dirty, mud-splattered clothes, raced past Elizabeth's guards and into her bedchamber. The Virgin had just risen and was sitting in a wrapper thrown over her nightgown, without her wig or makeup, with her thin gray hair "hanging about her ears." No more hideous moment could have been conceived.

Somehow the queen got rid of him and was able to dress. Robert Cecil, meanwhile, questioned the earl's men and learned of the circumstances in which they had left Ireland. The Privy Council met, and Essex had the experience of being called before it—not as a member—but as a man left standing, forced to answer questions posed by men clearly under the domination of the Pigmy.

Essex was placed in house arrest at York House in the care of Lord Keeper Egerton. His luxurious home, Essex House, was closed and its 160 servants dismissed. The queen, whose patience had grown into a weapon, waited, and the year slowly ground around toward its end.

She was unhappily aware that her favorite was the most popular man in the realm—at least with the people. London teemed with veterans of the Irish wars, and they sympathized with the earl, whose disgrace—based, according to rumor, on an effort to bring peace—seemed to them admirable.

In Ireland the rebels continued to flourish; Dublin itself was threatened. Elizabeth, who brooded through Christmas, finally appointed the man she had originally in mind: Sir Charles Blount, who had succeeded to the title of Lord Mountjoy. As the new year lengthened, it was clear he had been the right man all along; he began to redress the situation.

Essex, however, suffered agonies. He first became sick and virtually wasted away; that caused Elizabeth to send physicians to him. They returned to report that he was ill, but not in any mortal danger. The queen said she did not mean to ruin him, but only to correct him—and sent broth.

Essex, however, had not acted without some provision against disaster. In Ireland he had plotted with his associates that, in the event he was clapped into the Tower or otherwise punished by the queen, they would rescue him. At the same time he sent secret letters to James Stuart in Scotland, urging that James announce his rights to the throne of England. Then Essex himself would call a Parliament and James's status as the heir would be made official. In that manner the earl hoped to become a kingmaker and the favorite of the new king.

It was a scheme filled with holes, packed with "ifs," born of ambition, jealousy, and greed. James answered cautiously from Scotland. He himself was almost as driven as the earl; he walked, ate, slept, and dreamed in a state of longing for the English throne. If the earl of Essex would bring him nearer, he was carefully pleased.

Essex was moved to his own Essex House in March 1600 and barraged the queen with abject and beseeching letters. He was convinced that if he could confront her, he could charm her into elevating him again. That conviction was part of his delusion, but had some basis in reality—for the queen was old and lonely. Meanwhile, the earl's enemies were in high places and watched him with unwinking eyes. In June 1600 a hearing was convened to deal with his offenses.

Aware the queen still held Essex in great affection, the judges were careful to treat him gently. Eighteen men were appointed for this task; and when the earl appeared and sank to his knees in submission, the archbishop of Canterbury, Whitgift, who was harsh toward the dissenters to his churchly rule, suggested the earl be given a cushion.

His old protégé, Francis Bacon, had drawn the charges against Essex. He had been careful not to make them too sharp. The queen, to whom he brought them, reminded him that Essex was marked "for chastisement, not destruction." She was well used to the ways of her Privy Council and wanted no repetition of Mary Stuart—unless she herself so decided. Bacon made his understanding clear, and the queen signed.

After considerable oratory, in which the earl was reminded of his disobediences, he was fined—but the fine was forgiven. He was removed from offices, and that was left standing. Then he was released from imprisonment. The queen ratified all this, and the earl was told he was free, but banished from court—and from power.

Essex withdrew to the country to take stock of his position. It was almost ruinous. His debts were enormous, and his enemies were in high office. The queen would not receive him, nor answer his letters. His monopoly on sweet wines, which provided the bulk of his income, was due to expire—unless it was renewed. He wrote Elizabeth, this time without a shadow of pride, and implored her to rescue him from the depths that yawned in his path. That was unfortunate, for the Virgin had always recoiled when her affections were mentioned in the same breath as money. She told Francis Bacon, who was still creeping about on the periphery of Essex's affairs, that the earl had written "some dutiful letters, but what she took to be an abundance of the heart, she found to be but a preparative for the renewing of his farm of sweet wines."[17]

Curious about the value of that monopoly, the queen had the matter examined and discovered it was worth £50,000 a year. She was astonished and ordered that it revert to the Crown. Essex went nearly wild. He faced bankruptcy. He returned to London and to Essex House. The authorities were at first surprised and then made curious and finally alarmed by the numbers and types of persons who crept, heavily cloaked and muffled, in and out of that establishment at all hours.

In Scotland the King had written, after his fashion, another book. It was called *The Trew Law of Free Monarchies.* In it he elaborated the theory he had obliquely approached in *Basilikon Doron*. It was, in its way, a sequel. Where *Doron* had sought to instruct his son and heir, Prince Henry, the *Trew Law* was designed for his subjects. Buchanan had taught him when

he was a young prince, king largely in name; he would now—being a king
—instruct all Scotland.

The *Trew Law,* designed for general distribution, was written in simple
language, without the wealth of elaborate scholarship that James was adding to *Doron.* It cited, in bald terms, the James Stuart theory that "Kings
are called gods" and were to be considered "loving fathers" to their nations.
Heavy with Old Testament documentation, James argued that subjects
owned total, complete, and abject obedience to their sovereigns and could
resist only with their tears, if they proved unjust. Kings were made by God.
James believed that a king, to his subjects, should be like God.

This theory, which distorted the theology of the ancient Hebrews and
Christians alike, though qualified by careful phrasing, was a denial of every
principle Buchanan had sought to inculcate into his pupil years before. It
was an argument against the Reform and all its political consequences, a
twisting of history, and a throwback to pagan ideas about emperor-gods,
which James had apparently absorbed in his classical Latin and Greek
studies.

The *Trew Law* was finished, but not yet printed on August 5, 1600,
when James emerged early in the morning from Falkland Palace to go
hunting. His entourage included the duke of Lennox, the earl of Mar, James
and Thomas Erskine, Sir Hugh Herries, a page—John Ramsay—and a
hawker. Before the hunt began, James was approached by the nineteen-
year-old master of Ruthven, who was attached to Queen Anne's court and
whom the king liked. The master begged a private word, and the two men
walked apart from the rest and talked briefly. Then the hunt began, with
the young master riding among the rest.

The kill was made at about 11 o'clock in the morning, and the king
told the duke of Lennox he was proceeding to Gowrie House with the
master, "to pick up a treasure." The courtiers, apparently under instruction, were to wait for fresh horses and follow later. They also sent for swords
—a preparation that throws a strange light on what occurred afterward.

The earl of Gowrie, the twenty-four-year-old older brother of the
master, seemed surprised to see them, but escorted the king into the house.
A little later, James was ushered into a small room on the ground floor,
where he was served dinner alone, as a mark of respect. The courtiers, who
arrived shortly afterward, ate in the great hall.

After finishing his meal, the king and the young master of Ruthven
went upstairs together. The courtiers by then were scattered about, with the
larger number in the garden. Time passed and the men grew impatient.
Someone said the king had left, and the men ran for their horses, the earl
of Gowrie among them. At the gate, however, the porter said no one had
departed. They returned and were milling about the courtyard when they

heard a shout. Looking up, they saw James's face at a turret window. "Help, my Lord Mar! Treason! I am being murdered!"

The king's hat was gone, his face was red, and a hand appeared over his mouth. The men pounded up the stairs, swords in hand. John Ramsay, the page, was first on the scene. The young master of Ruthven was on his knees, James had his arm around the master's head, and the master's hand was raised, searching for the king's face, as though to stop his shouting.

Other men piled in behind Ramsay, and the king cried, "Strike him high; he has a chain doublet on him." Ramsay flew at the master with his dagger and slashed him on the neck and face. The young man rose, staggered back, and fell down the stairs. He had time only to say, "Alas, I was not to blame," when Herries ran his sword through him and killed him.

At that point, the earl of Gowrie came panting up the stairs and, looking about, asked for the king. The men turned and cut him down.

The melee, the shouts, the stamping feet had sent the servants of Gowrie House running for help; the great bell of the town was tolled and townspeople came running. The local officials gathered their forces and arrived on the scene; people milled outside in a state of high excitement. As the news ran through their ranks that the young earl of Gowrie and his brother, the master of Ruthven, had been killed by the king and his courtiers, their mood shifted instantly. Shouts rose against James. "Come down, thou son of Seigneur Davie," they cried.

The skies overhead darkened and it began to rain; it was evening and the crowd was dispersed by the bailie and his men before the king emerged, surrounded by his men, to return to Falkland.[18]

Later the king gave his explanation of events. It was a tale from the lower levels of fiction, incredible and fantastic. The master of Ruthven, according to James, had approached him with a story that he had discovered and taken into custody a mysterious stranger who was carrying a pot of gold coins. Taken to Gowrie House, he and his brother, the earl, had decided the king should be informed.

During the hunt, said James, the master had continued to urge the king to come to Gowrie House and view the treasure. After the kill, the king decided to make the trip and told Lennox of it. Lennox then sent for fresh horses and swords, being suspicious.

After dining, the master took the king to the turret room, pausing en route to lock the door of every room they passed through. Once in the turret room, James was confronted by a man in armor with a dagger in his belt. The master of Ruthven took the dagger, confronted the king, and told him he must die. James then turned the force of his marvelous eloquence upon the two, and the man in armor, overcome by these compelling arguments, opened a window. The king then called for help, while Ruthven struggled with him, but James overcame the young man. Everyone knew the rest.

What happened to the locked rooms, through which the courtiers raced without impediment? Where did the man in armor go? Nobody knew.

The king, however, not only produced that explanation, but made it clear it had to be accepted. The ministers were summoned and heard the tale and were told to repeat it to their congregations. Their reactions reflected incredulity. "I see, Mr. Roberts," said the king to one, "that ye would make me a murderer. It is known very well that I was never bloodthirsty . . ."[19]

His story, however, could not be accepted. The ministers refused to endorse it, even after being called before the council. They were stripped of their posts and other, more compliant clergymen appointed. After this punishment, all decided to suspend their doubts except Bruce—one of the most effective leaders of the Kirk.

The full powers of the Crown, which had grown large, were brought into play. The reluctant ministers had to travel about and repeat their acceptance; the Kirk itself issued a Proclamation of Thanksgiving at the king's escape and the fifth of August was set aside as a special day.

The House of Gowrie, meanwhile, was destroyed; and the name Ruthven, abolished. The bodies of the young earl and the master were stripped and divided into quarters, like beeves, and displayed as a warning to traitors. The Ruthven properties reverted to the Crown, though Sir John Erskine received a small part. The page, John Ramsay, hugely credited by the king, was made a knight.

The skill with which the king turned the events of August 5, 1600, into personal profit was remarkable. His version of events met with ridicule in London and was rejected out of hand in Paris—but was forced, in defiance of logic, upon the Kirk and the people of Scotland. In one swoop James suddenly assumed the sinister aura of real power, eliminated a family he loathed, increased his holdings—and was able to forget, at last, the £80,000 he had owed the last earl of Gowrie.


By the end of the year 1600 the skies of England were dark and ominous. The queen raged in her palace and "stamps her foot at ill news." The Privy Council, meanwhile, examined the information presented by Robert Cecil and decided to place men at strategic spots inside Whitehall, the Tower, and the Mint. Spies had penetrated the gathering at Essex House and learned, without too much difficulty, of the earl's plans. They followed the mad outlines created earlier: he would emerge at the head of his immediate followers and rally the city. The earl would rush the palace and confront Elizabeth. Once his victory was secure, messengers would acquaint the country of a new Parliament. The king of Scotland had sent a personal, handwritten letter to Essex, whose contents were unknown, but which the earl carried in a leather pouch on a chain around his neck under his shirt. The implication was that England would have a young new king and that Essex and his discontented young men would assume the high posts of the realm.

Their preparations were curious. One effort consisted of hiring the actors of the Globe Theatre to stage *Richard II*—in which a king is deposed. The players performed, but only after receiving a special cash advance. The play, they protested, was old and not too popular anymore. The earl's young men, however, had found the theater a great inspiration; they had some difficulty in separating it from life—and apparently thought the people were in the same condition.

On Saturday, February 7, 1601, a messenger appeared suddenly at Essex House commanding him to come before the Privy Council. The earl said he was ill and closed the door. His supporters crowded about him excitedly; their plot was discovered—he had to flee. They spent the night ranting at one another, and early Sunday morning Sir Charles Danvers arrived, in a panic, to say the guards at Whitehall had been strengthened. He was heard with fear; it was obvious the conspirators had lost the advantage of surprise upon which they had so heavily relied. Nevertheless, the courtyard at Essex House began to fill with several hundred of the earl's followers, who were anxious to get started. Their leader, however, continued to hesitate.

At 10 o'clock that Sunday morning high Crown officials, the earl of Worcester, Lord Keeper Egerton, the lord chief justice, and Sir William Knollys, arrived, pushed their way through the mob, and hammered on the door. They wanted to know the meaning and purpose of the gathering. Essex took them into the library while the hotheads outside shouted for their death. The earl locked the officials in the library, saying he would return.

He emerged from Essex House, was immediately swept up by the crowd out the courtyard and down the street toward the palace. The young men waved weapons and shouted their cause. Sir Christopher Blount marched at their head, calling for volunteers, but people watched from windows and doorways and did not move. The ministers had told them not to move against the queen; Essex—who loved the theater and despised the church—never understood how the people were really led.

At the Strand, instead of turning toward the palace, Essex turned toward the City. He wanted to increase his force and to secure the great rallying mobs he expected. He had been told the sheriff's force contained 1,000 of his followers, and he headed for the sheriff's house on Fenchurch Street. He entered it, but the sheriff had fled. The earl, like a man dreaming, sat down to wait. Sitting there, he decided to return to Essex House, take his prisoners out of the library, and, using them as hostages, obtain entry into the palace and the confrontation with Elizabeth that he believed would alter the situation. If he could only get to the queen, he would be great again.

It was too late for that. The elder Cecil, Thomas, who was now Lord Burghley, and others had arrived in the city with heralds and the proclamation that the earl of Essex was a traitor. Essex emerged from the sheriff's house and, still at the head of the same band that nobody had joined but from which some had vanished, walked down the street toward his home. At Landgate near St. Paul's the authorities had set up a chain and some soldiers with pikes and muskets. Essex demanded they give way, and Sir Christopher Blount struggled with them, was wounded, and taken prisoner; a page was killed and a melee erupted. The earl ran down a side street, threw some money at a boatman, and was rowed to the water steps of his house. He dashed inside, tore open a case containing his files, tore the leather bag from the chain around his neck, and threw papers, letters, notes, bag, and all into the fire.

While he was busy in this task, during which he shouted he would leave "no tales to hurt his friends," his men straggled in, and on the third floor of the mansion his wife and sister and their servants set up shrieking laments.[20] The authorities arrived and surrounded the house, demanding his surrender. Inside the theatrics continued but the end was inevitable; cannons were threatened. Essex emerged in the cold air of evening to be taken first to Lambeth Palace and later, when the tide was low, to the Tower.

The trial was held on February 19, 1601, with Sir Edward Coke as attorney general, twenty-six peers of the realm as judges—with Essex's protégé, Francis Bacon, in charge of the case against him.

For Bacon, who had already achieved a reputation with his writing and was renowned for learning as well, the case against Essex was a great chance to prove he was not connected with rebellion, was loyal to the Crown even against his own benefactor—and had soaring abilities. His charge was clearly stated, direct, documented, and deadly.

The earl of Southampton, a fellow defendant, argued no specific act against the queen had taken place, but Bacon cut that down in withering terms. He cross-examined the man to whom he owed his small estate and permanent income and exposed him without mercy. Essex reminded Bacon that he had helped compose his letters to Elizabeth, and Bacon replied he had been a friend to the earl only when the earl had been loyal. The outcome was never in doubt: Essex left the chamber following a man who held an ax with its edge turned toward him; a sign of the verdict to the waiting crowd.

In the Tower the earl dissolved and confessed in great detail. He named all who had worked with him and added the name of his sister—Beatrix, Lady Rich, terming her an adultress as well as a traitor. He was abject enough to spill his tale before his old rival—Robert Cecil, the Pigmy. By the time he was led to the block on February 25, 1601, nothing remained of the tall, husky, proud earl of Essex but a pale figure in a satin suit, felt hat, and cloak of "wrought black velvet." It took the executioner three heavy blows with the ax to sever his head.

Essex came closer to affecting the course of history than either he or the spectators realized. James Stuart's agony was that Elizabeth had not, and would not, name him heir. He had no means of knowing whether the English would accept a foreign king—particularly one from Scotland, which they regarded as a realm barely human, occupied by inferiors.

The earl of Essex, in establishing an understanding with The O'Neill in Ireland and then seeking to establish another understanding with James in Scotland, had not proceeded without some shrewdness. James longed to be made certain of the English inheritance, and Essex promised to provide that security. Knowing the earl was immensely popular in England, James was very much tempted. Only a saving fear—one of the many weaknesses that kept him from common male mistakes—kept James from falling into the pit with Essex. But he came to its very edge.

The letter that Essex carried in a leather bag in a chain around his neck was one sign of how close James had drawn; another was his dispatch of the earl of Mar and the titular abbot of Kinross, Edward Bruce, to London to deal with the earl.

Typically—and luckily—James wavered as he moved. Essex had asked the Scots king to send his agents to London on February 1, 1601. James did not let them leave until the eighteenth of the month, after news of the actual uprising reached Edinburgh. Then Mar and Kinross, acting under orders, lingered on their journey, traveling at a snail's pace, until James learned the outcome of the Essex effort. He learned it with a sort of quiet horror, for it gave rise to the next question: how much did Elizabeth know?[20]

His phenomenal luck, however, held. When Elizabeth did write, it was to say that a plot "divers years in the making" had been broken in only twelve hours. The queen, it was clear, had not been told about Scotland—and neither James's name nor the name of Scotland was aired in the course of the Essex trial.

James Stuart had many weaknesses, but a lack of intelligence was not among them. He immediately sent Mar and Kinross new instructions. They were to see Elizabeth and rehash the usual grounds about money, the Lennox estates, and his right to inherit the crown. But more important, they were to lobby on their king's behalf among the English courtiers—and in particular to talk in secret with Robert Cecil.

Essex had dragged ninety proud young men down with him. Though only four went to their deaths, the rest were heavily fined. In effect, the old queen had reduced a youthful wave. A sense of loss suffused the taverns, theaters, and soul of England. Songs appeared, extolling Essex's memory; he was called "England's Sweet Pride."

Recollections of the great days of the Armada had vanished into the misty past; most people were too young to recall that event. It was a new century, whose coming was predicted in some quarters as the end of the world. The Church of England, under the iron hand of Whitgift and the High Commission, had stamped out dissent. An underground had appeared, heavily populated with strange new cults. The Rosicrucians, based on the Jewish Cabalists of earlier times; the Freemasons; magicians; and astrologers flourished. Love potions, amulets, aphrodisiacs, brothels, gambling dens, and houses with rooms for rent for transient amours flourished.

A sense of decay hung over the City of London and seeped through the queen's palace. The Virgin was old and tired. One day she asked for a hand mirror; for years she had refused to look into one and had relied upon her ladies-in-waiting to make her up. She stared, while the women held their breaths, at the ravages of time, and her eyes filled with tears. "I have been abused by flatterers," she said—and several fled from her presence.[21]

In a short time, however, her iron will returned and she resumed her state. The progresses continued, though now the spectators had thinned in number, and the old queen heard no more cheers. She made a trip to Dover and hoped for a visit from Henry IV, who had made himself a strong king of a reunited France. She was disappointed; Henry IV was too practical to make a sentimental trip.

Yet the queen was still mistress of England and was determined to hold that authority, if not forever, for at least as long as she was alive. She listened to Robert Cecil more closely than anyone else; he had become the leading member of her council. He persuaded her to increase James Stuart's allowance—from £3,000 to £5,000.

In October 1601 a new Parliament was called. The queen, who had never liked Parliaments, appeared at its opening in heavy court dress and had to lean on an arm in order to walk. She noted the surprising youth, or what now appeared to be youth, of the gathering. Its reception was not enthusiastic, and she insisted that Cecil tell her the reasons.

Crown monopolies. These rights, granted by the queen in lieu of Crown salaries, had become abusive, obsolete—and restrained the growth of trade. Meanwhile, the Crown's expenses had been affected by the tide of inflation that had swept all Europe; prices were rising on all sides; unemployment, increasing; discontent, growing. The queen announced she would abandon monopolies, and the Commons exploded with enthusiasm for her. At the close of Parliament a great crowd of members came to see the queen, and she spoke of her love for them all so well that the memory of her words lingered in the air like perfume, for generations.[22]

Sir Robert Cecil was 10, Lord Henry Howard was 3, Sir Walter Raleigh was 2, the Queen of England was 24, and James VI was 30. There were forty numbers all told, and each represented a key person in the correspondence that passed between the king of Scotland and Queen Elizabeth's most important councillor, Robert Cecil.

The letters were sent through the French duke of Rohan to the Scots earl of Mar and back. Rohan had visited Scotland and liked James VI; the exchange was facilitated, as a courtesy to a high noble, by the couriers of the English and Scots governments.

The regular English agent in Scotland, Nicholson, noticed that the king, Mar, and Kinross always drew together when de Rohan's letters arrived and suspected something undefined was underway. He reported his suspicions to Cecil, who was not amused and who went to some efforts of deeper concealment.

The actual intermediary between the two was Lord Henry Howard, a younger brother of the ill-fated duke of Norfolk, who had become entangled in the earliest and first web woven in England by Mary Stuart. Lord Henry was an old agent of Walsingham who had somehow wormed himself into James's confidence. He was also employed by Cecil on matters too dark for ordinary men. He had long been in the habit of writing letters to the king of Scotland that James complained were "ample, Asiatic and endless."

Cast by unexpected good fortune into a role between the most influential man in England and the king of Scotland, Howard routed letters, interlarded with his own, between the two men. Howard's letters were dark and devious.

Cecil, in contrast, wrote clearly and cleverly. He was careful to address James as though that king were was a mighty emperor and to lard his expressions with Biblical references and Latin tags. He gave advice so softly that it seemed merely comment, and James was an apt pupil.

The secret was well kept and had its effect. For the first time it was clear the way to his inheritance in England could be prepared by a power able to make such preparations. James's letters to Elizabeth noticeably improved. Whining stopped and a sudden flattery appeared; every line exuded patience and tolerance. The queen was surprised and complimented him.

These maneuvers were unsuspected by everyone except Queen Anne. She tried to get in touch with Cecil herself, and he sent his alarm through Lord Henry Howard, who advised against letting the queen know anything at serpentine length.

The queen also tried hard to have James restore the remaining members of the Ruthven family to their position. The earl's sister was secretly brought back to her court and thrust before the man who had ruined her brothers and her estate. Two more Ruthven brothers had fled to England, and Anne tried to obtain their pardon.

The queen had converted to Catholicism and made a great matter of secretly seeing priests—which created intense irritation in the Kirk. To some extent this fitted James's desires. He himself secretly encouraged Catholics in England and elsewhere to look upon him as their great hope —much as the Reform already regarded him.

Relations between James and his wife, uneasy at best, grew even more strained. Anne was a meddler and could not resist annoying her husband deliberately; as their great inheritance grew closer, they grew individually further apart.

The year 1602 passed, and Cecil, James VI, and Lord Henry Howard drew—at least on paper and intellectually—closer together. James was warned against Sir Walter Raleigh and his friends, the Earl Northumberland and Lord Cobham.

The year 1602 seemed, to James Stuart, to crawl. In Spain, Philip III, son of a great monarch, proved stupid. "I shall never fear a Prince who was twelve years learning his alphabet," said Elizabeth with scornful hyperbole.[23]

The queen had reason to feel sure. The long, costly war with Spain had inflicted great blows upon both parties and achieved nothing. That in itself was an achievement: who wins in war is not always as important as who does not lose. Spanish forces had landed on Ireland to assist The O'Neill, but had been defeated by Mountjoy. Once one of Essex's discontented young men, he had found himself on the field of battle.

Toward the end of 1602, on December 27, the queen received a visitor: Sir John Harington. Harington was a young man whose wit made him welcome everywhere. "I found her," he later wrote his wife, "in a most pitiable state." He spent the day and noticed the queen's memory had grown uncertain. She called for persons she had, in moments of anger, dismissed and forgotten their dismissal. "Who, dearest Moll," wrote Harington, "shall say, 'Your Highness has forgotten'?"[24]

He read some of his light verse in an effort to lift her spirits, but her smile was thin. "When thou dost feel creeping Time at thy gate, these fooleries," she said, "will please thee less. I am past my relish for such matters."[25]

Yet on February 6, 1603, she received Scamarelli, the Venetian ambassador, in great state. Wearing a crown and an elaborate costume dappled with "pearls the size of pears," she noted the Venetian's awe with satisfaction. She spoke to him in Italian, a language she said she had hardly ever used since her childhood lessons. The ambassador later wrote his masters "I can believe the fame of her past beauty."

Three weeks later, however, her cousin Robert Carey came to see her and found her in a small "withdrawing" chamber. Carey kissed her hand and complimented her on looking so well. Elizabeth clutched his hand hard, and said earnestly, "No, Robin, I am not well."[26]

She was mourning the death of a friend since childhood: Kate Carey Nottingham. Robert Carey sat beside the queen and said he had not heard so many sighs or seen so many tears from her since the death of Mary Stuart. That unlocked the gates; the queen wept passionately and said Mary Stuart's death had been against her will; she had never consented to it.

The next day was a Sunday, and the queen was expected at services, but did not appear. She had told several of her attendants that she could not rest and that her dreams showed her "exceeding lean and fearful, in a light of fire." Never religious, she was suddenly afraid of hell.

She refused to go to bed, therefore, and had cushions put on the floor, where she sat without eating. News of her circumstances flew about the city and the Privy Council met; the queen was "moping and sighing and weeping." The council issued an order forbidding conversations regarding the queen's health, which had the effect of loosening tongues everywhere.

The siege wore on everybody's nerves. The earl of Nottingham arrived and created another storm of tears by his mourning attire. Sir Robert Cecil came and listened. The queen refused to go to bed, because, she told the earl, "If you saw the things in bed that I see, you would not ask me to go there." Cecil wondered aloud if she saw spirits, and the queen flared at him.

"To content the people, you must go to bed," the adviser responded and she said, "Little man . . . the word *must* is not to be used to Princes." A little later, she added, "You know I must die, and that makes you presumptuous."

She was put to bed by force and stayed there fifteen days, but got out of it and "sat on a stool for three days." Forced off the stool, she "obstinately stood on her feet for fifteen hours," wrote Lady Southwell.

Finally, on March 23, 1603, after three days of silence in her bed, she said, "I do not wish to live any longer, but desire to die."[27] She seemed to believe she could summon death, as she had summoned so many during her reign.

Instead, the Privy Council appeared. The men stood around. One suggested she hold up a finger, or put her hand to her head when her heir was named. When they mentioned James Stuart, she raised her hand.

The council left and Whitgift arrived. He prayed for a long time, but when he started to rise from his knees, a gesture from the bed forced him down again. He prayed for another long stretch, and one thin hand reached for his. He held it, as Thomas Cranmer, an earlier archbishop, had held the hand of the dying Henry VIII. The queen slipped into a coma from which she did not awake. It was March 24, 1603. In Scotland, where he was at ease, James Stuart was silently lifted by a second woman's death into a second kingdom.

# PART FIVE

*The Most High and
Mightie Prince James
by the Grace of God
King of Great
Britaine, France
and Ireland
Defender of the Faith; &c.*

## 25

In Whitehall the English Privy Council, in session since before dawn on the morning of March 24, 1603, summoned Roger Aston, a messenger in the service of James VI. While the man waited for his package, one of the councillors leaned back for a moment of relaxation and asked, idly, how he thought his master felt about the great change underway.

"Even, my lords," said Aston, "like a poor man that hath been wandering in the wilderness for forty years and hath at last come within sight of the Land of Promise."[1]

A great roar of laughter erupted.

A little later the earl of Northumberland arrived with some other peers, trailed by a hundred of his armed men, to announce loudly that if James VI were not acknowledged as the new king of England, he was prepared to fight. Cecil sighed. Proclamations had been composed, printed, and distributed in advance. Warships sat in the straits of Dover and outside key harbors; the armed forces were on alert; dissidents had been quietly arrested and sequestered; streams of secret understandings had been exchanged between Edinburgh and London; everything had been foreseen and arranged. The earl was making a great and foolish display while Cecil had placed, oiled, and set the machinery of the English government into smooth motion to receive the new sovereign.

Within days all England was ready, and a great mixed crowd began to pour toward the north, where an unlikely new sun was rising. Composed of the ambitious, the needy, the curious as well as the official, the mob sprang from all quarters; the sound of running feet was almost audible. Even James was astonished.

"Shall it ever be blotted out of my mind," he said later, "how, at my first entry into this kingdom, the people of all sorts rid and ran, nay, rather flew to meet me—their eyes flaming nothing but sparkles of affection—their mouths and tongues uttering nothing but sounds of joy—their hands, feet and all the rest of their members discovering in their gestures a passionate longing and earnestness to meet and embrace their new sovereign."[2]


In his own fashion, James had prepared for this moment for years. He had scattered letters and secret agents over virtually all western Europe, stressing his right of inheritance and begging for support. Boasts, whines, and hints about his possible course had been sent to every power—whether Reform, Catholic, or in between, without consistency. His efforts had created astonishment.

"He practices in Rome, in Spain and everywhere else as he does with me," said Henry IV, "without attaching himself to anyone, and is easily carried away by the hopes of those about him without regard for truth or merit. Hence I foresee he will allow himself to be surprised on all occasions."[3]

The analysis was shrewd and worldly, but too rational. The king of France had survived a dynastic struggle and changed his religion in order to gain his crown and had then issued his Edict of Toleration in an effort to overcome deep-seated religious divisions in his realm. He had, all his life, been forced to contend with great powers and subtle men. It was natural for him to consider intelligence and character the keys to success. He overlooked luck.

James had benefited from the efforts of a series of regents and advisers and inherited a realm burgeoning with wealth, undisturbed by invasion for five hundred years. He came into his new kingdom at the very moment the Irish rebels faltered and fell and when the mighty power of Spain was held in the nerveless hands of Philip III and the corrupt duke of Lerma and was on the verge of bankruptcy. The king of France had great gifts—wit, intelligence and courage—but they were chilly compared to the warm embraces of fortune that enveloped James Stuart.

Promising all things to all men, James himself never realized that his most inviting attribute was his own weakness. Any man who could get near him could talk or force him into anything. That simple and notorious fact encouraged all factions to plot avenues toward him. Every faction had good reason to consider James its hope, in a manner they could never have regarded a stronger man.


The swarm descended before James could even leave Edinburgh. Cecil sent his private secretary, Sir Thomas Lake, with one hand and with the other issued an order forbidding Sir Walter Raleigh and his associates from traveling north toward the new king. Whitgift, the archbishop of Canterbury, sent the dean of Canterbury to prepare James for the attitudes of the Church of England; the Scots themselves quivered eagerly.

On April 3, 1603, James attended services in St. Giles, Knox's old church, in Edinburgh. The congregation had mixed emotions. The pride of Scotland in sending its monarch to rule over England as well—an event that stood centuries of English struggle on its head—was darkened by the realization that Edinburgh would lose its court patronage and would sink to the status of a provincial, instead of a national, seat.

James interpreted the long faces as sorrow over his personal departure. Rising in the church to make an oration—an old custom of his—he assured them he would remember them all. That brought tears to many who saw their livelihoods vanishing beneath oceans of words.

Two days later, surrounded by Lennox; the earls of Mar and Argyll; Lord Hume; Sir George Hume of Dunbar; his secretary, Sir James Elphinstone; Sir Robert Ker of Cessford; his Gentlemen of the Bedchamber; and others, he said good-bye to Queen Anne in the street before a marveling crowd. James's ideas of ceremony were his own. The queen was tearful; she could not accompany him because she was pregnant again—a tribute to an unlikely marriage in its fourteenth year. Then the king clattered away, his entourage trailed by dozens of hopefuls, on his journey to the Promised Land. It was to last weeks, to cost enormous sums, to confound observers, and to set a tone all England would find familiar in years to come.

On April 6, 1603, the caravan reached Berwick, where the city fathers gathered on the outskirts to present among other gifts a purse of gold. The cannons of the city roared a simultaneous volley that astounded even its artillery; great clouds of smoke rose. James received the keys of the city and knighted the man who handed them over. The sequence was to be repeated, over and again, as he proceeded. The king of Scotland was dazzled by his reception, astonished at the wealth and luxury he discovered, and amazed at the immense throngs of people who appeared.

He tarried in Berwick a day, inspecting the cannons and even firing one; but as he left that city and entered Northumberland to discover more waiting officials, more crowds, and more ceremonies, he grew impatient. Sir Robert Carew, a wealthy man, was waiting at Widdrington Castle, almost forty miles away. James galloped in that direction with his followers falling behind and covered the distance in only four hours. As he entered the park of the castle, he saw some deer grazing. The sight was too much for him; he dismounted and ran into the park to kill two of them. He spent the night in the castle, but was on the road again the next day and rode into Newcastle, where he pardoned all prisoners except those guilty of treason, murder, or papistry. After three days of enormous eating, drinking, and knighting men, James and his coterie proceeded to Durham, where he was entertained in the Episcopal palace by the bishop, who bowed low. The new king was delighted; this was the sort of prelate he enjoyed; their conversation grew dense with theological details. From there the places and the banquets, the parks and manor houses grew closer and more luxuriant; the feasts, more elaborate; the discussions, chaotic.

England had five times the population of Scotland, had been civilized longer, was dotted with palaces and crowded with wealthy men, and teemed with new learning and new sights. Great full-length portraits, unknown in Scotland, graced the halls of England's homes; libraries, statuary, rich clothes, elaborate carriages, blooded horses, game-stocked parks, graveled walks, geometric gardens, gleaming jewels, beautiful women, and handsome men shimmered before James's eyes.

The green hills and the fat towns with their richly dressed officials had the effect of sharpening James's desires. He had originally agreed to meet the Privy Council, whose members he had verified in their posts, at Burghley; but he now decided that these gentlemen should have traveled farther toward him. He wanted Cecil at once; he wanted more money, jewels, and clothes for himself and more for his queen in Edinburgh. Cecil traveled to York and knelt humbly before him, was jostled when he rose by the king's courtiers and local officials anxious to be noticed—and to be knighted. James distributed these honors almost like a man paying bills as he picked up presents and purses, bows and compliments, feasts and entertainments. At the end of a week, Cecil returned to London and the cares of the kingdom to find himself burdened with new details: the king wanted new coins with his own head, crowned, to be minted at once. He was also interested in the timing of his coronation and other weighty matters. Cecil departed, however, with the royal consent to dismiss Raleigh as captain of the guard.

Nobody will ever know what Cecil thought as he rode away from that first meeting and these first hasty conferences, but there was little doubt that most Englishmen found their new king of absorbing interest. James in 1603 was between 37 and 38 years old, a mature age then, dressed in heavily padded clothes that gave his body a bulk belied by thin legs that emerged in somewhat comical fashion. His brown hair was beginning to gray; his beard was thin and scattered; his tongue was in great evidence when he spoke and he spoke—it seemed—endlessly.

His conversation created astonishment. A waterfall of words tumbled out of him that inundated the kingdom. "His mind passed easily from topic to topic, and he applied the vocabulary of one set of ideas to things entirely different, throwing discordant images into grotesque juxtaposition. His wit was the rollicking foolery of the court jester, enriched by his extensive knowledge."[4] He was apt to mix the religious and the scatalogical, the trivial and the important, the personal and the official, and personalities with the impersonal.

The English were, at first, delighted. Their new king had a shambling walk and was apt to appear leaning upon his courtiers, but he was a married monarch with a family; his masculinity was in itself pleasing to many who had tired of living under a female. It was noticed that he was very quick and settled business matters curtly, that he attended churches everywhere, and seemed easy to approach.

At Newark on Trent, however, the genial mask slipped briefly. Told that a pickpocket had been caught amid the welcoming crowds, James ordered him to be hanged at once. As if to balance this harshness, he also issued the usual pardon to all the prisoners in the castle—with the usual exceptions. At the moment, persons were inclined to treat the hanging as a natural error on the part of a sovereign accustomed to a ruder realm, but Sir John Harington was ironic.

"I hear," wrote Sir John, "that our new King hath hanged one man before he was tried. 'Tis strangely done. Now, if the wind bloweth thus, why not a man be tried before he hath offended?"

The larger point, that James considered himself Lord of Life and Death, was lost in the euphoria of the moment. But it was to recur later.

En route south, the king was presented with the Millenary Petition, which its authors said represented the opinions of a thousand Reform clergymen. It called for some relaxation of the stern restrictions, mandatory doctrines, and practices by Whitgift, his High Commission, and Bancroft, the archbishop's strong right arm. Tremendous hopes had been attached to this petition; the king received it and said he would study the situation.

By the time he reached Theobalds, the home of Sir Robert Cecil, James had heard enough arguments and seen enough wonders and marvels to become sated. Yet the "fairy tale palace, with its courts and fountains and elaborate gardens and turrets of rosy brick, surmounted by gilded weather vanes and a loggia on whose walls was depicted in brilliant colour the history of England, and a great green hall lined with artificial trees, complete with bark and bird's nests, and a ceiling adorned with a sun moved by machinery and stars which, after dark, shone and twinkled,"[5] reduced him to open greed. He was never to rest till he held this magnificence in his own hands. Meanwhile, he lolled in his chair, sipping the innumerable cups of white wine he preferred, but did not insist upon. The king liked all spirits, so long as they were sweet.

Cecil and the Privy Council had a number of matters to settle, and James was, in the main, agreeable to their advice. One subject of great importance was his policy toward the Catholics. He had aroused great hopes in this quarter before he received his inheritance; but on the way to Theobalds, now assured of his new property and reminded of his implied promises, he had demurred. "Na, na," he was heard to say, "we'll not need the Papists now."[6]

That meant that the fines exacted from Catholics for refusing to attend the services of the Church of England would not be forgiven, as rumor had it, but would be collected as usual. The Crown, Cecil explained, needed the money. He needed no stronger argument.

Other steps were taken that were popular with the influential Reform minority. Monopolies were to be examined; the Privy Council was retained but the fourteen men who had served Elizabeth were increased by twelve more whom James I advanced. One of these was Lord Henry Howard, the third party to the undercover correspondence in Elizabeth's last years, a man so creepy that Walsingham used him without open acknowledgment —and who was soon slated to become earl of Northampton. Five of the new Privy Councillors were Scots who had accompanied James to England.

On May 13, 1603, the new king made Cecil baron of Essendon and created three other new barons at the same time. He had already named crowds of men knights; he would create more new peers shortly.

These innovations, though somewhat rushed, were inserted between discussions on foreign affairs—always among the first topics of a new national administration. Spain did not appear to be much of a menace, for Philip III was indolent, and his adviser, Lerma, was anxious to end the war with England. But the Reform in the Netherlands was continuing its gener-ation-long struggle, which Elizabeth—however reluctantly—had assisted, as did Henry IV of France. His Privy Council learned that James detested the Reform; he considered the Dutch common rebels against a lawful sovereign. The new king was, in fact, against war at any time, by any power, for any reason. England and Spain were still, officially, at war—but to make his opinions known at once, James issued orders that no more Spanish ships should be taken at sea.

Meanwhile, James rushed to London to make a hasty inspection of the crown jewels at Whitehall. He did not linger; plague had struck the City and was spreading. The sovereign had a number of outlying country man-sions to enjoy and spent the next few months traveling from one to another. He had discovered that these properties and their environs contained game and immediately plunged back into the activity that had occupied him almost entirely in Scotland and was to occupy him all over again in England: hunting.

Almost at once complex matters of state began to pile up for his attention. In Edinburgh, Queen Anne, who heard about her husband's triumphs with increasing exasperation, launched a furious quarrel with the earl of Mar, via correspondence, tantrums, and tears, regarding the custody of Prince Henry. The Scots queen wanted that custody, as always, and wanted the nine-year-old prince to accompany her to England. She did not succeed; the countess of Mar fought back bitterly, and Anne suffered a miscarriage. Unworthy suspicions floated that the accident was a means of punishing the king, but he appeared unmoved; it was not her first.

The queen left Edinburgh after her ordeal, accompanied by the seven-year-old Princess Elizabeth, to go through the same series of fetes and banquets, welcoming city fathers and gracious hosts, in a progress of her own. The English began to realize how fortunate they had been in their solitary and spinster queen in the past; it was a reflection that would grow deeper in years to come.

The new royal family was reunited, at least in public, at Windsor, and James played the doting family man to enormous cheers. The event, however, was misleading, for the king of England was never again to live with his queen. Three courts were established, in effect: one for the king, one for the queen, and a third for little Prince Henry. None of them would, apparently, see any more of each other than circumstances made unavoidable.

The queen, whose behavior in Edinburgh after James departed was embarrassing, proved even more embarrassing in England—where she made no effort to conceal her Catholic leanings. That subject, which hounded James forever, surfaced almost as soon as he arrived in the south and was exacerbated by his own past promises, which bobbed in his wake.

One of these had been made to William Watson, a priest but not a Jesuit, whom James had received and to whom he had been rashly gracious. Watson took that as a promise of toleration. News that James would continue the fines against Catholics who refused to attend Church of England services enraged Watson; rumors of the king's peace feelers toward Spain convinced him the monarch had fallen into the clutch of Jesuits. His solution was a plan to kidnap James and hold him until he came to better conclusions.

As usual, the fanatic had fanatical friends as unworldly as himself. These included several other priests, Sir Griffin Markham and George Brooke, a brother of Lord Cobham. Brooke was a Reformer who was disappointed regarding an appointment; he drew in Lord Grey of Wilton, a malcontent similarly motivated. This oddly assorted group planned to seize the king at Greenwhich, hold him in the Tower, and bend him to their will. The design reflected some insight into the nature of the king, but none into the intelligence network maintained by Cecil.

As so often happens, the conspirators were conspicuously talkative, and news of their plans soon reached Blackwell, the head of the Catholic priests in England, and Father Henry Garnet, the head of the Jesuits in the realm. It dismayed them both. Pope Clement VIII had received a letter from James as king of Scotland that had convinced the Vatican a conversion was possible. With the pope excited over such a possibility, orders had been issued to cooperate with the monarch in all matters. The rumor, in fact, was coursing through all Europe and merged with other rumors regarding a peace with Spain.

The Watson conspirators, in other words, had succumbed to impatience. James himself was making overtures toward the Catholic world. He was surrounded with pro-Vatican Scots nobles; and Lord Henry Howard of England, high in his favor, was a secret Catholic. In fact, the pro-Vatican and pro-Spanish leanings of the new king of England were so clear that they alarmed Reform leaders everywhere.

King Henry IV of France, who was assisting the Reformers of Holland against Spain and had long-range anti-Spanish plans, sent the Marquis of Rosny, his closest adviser, to England at once. Rosny—later better known as the duke of Sully—had instructions to offer James an alliance sealed by a dynastic partnership. Henry offered his eldest daughter to Prince Henry and his heir—the dauphin—to Princess Elizabeth. He also asked James to help support the Reformers of Holland against Madrid.

Meanwhile, Fathers Blackwell and Garnet informed the English authorities of the Watson plot. The plotters, learning they had been discovered, fled in different directions. Because his brother was involved, Lord Cobham was called in for questioning. Lord Cobham then told several stories, and Cecil moved. The secretary's move, like the secretary himself, was oblique but shrewd. It managed to tilt the king without bringing Cecil's own plans into view. Yet it achieved results that Cecil found congenial.

The secretary's instrument was Lord Cobham, who proved capable of telling a different story on each interrogation. One of these stories implicated, though vaguely, Sir Walter Raleigh. Raleigh, hauled before the council, declared he knew nothing of Cobham's brother or the Watson group. Later, however, Raleigh wrote a letter to Cecil, charging that Cobham himself had been secretly dealing with the Archduke Matthias of Germany through an Antwerp merchant named Renzi. The letter was a fatal error on Raleigh's part, because Cecil had him arrested and thrown into the Tower.

The news created a sensation. Raleigh had been an intermittent favorite of Elizabeth and when she died had been captain of the guard. His personal attributes, his pride and fearlessness, his inability to flatter inferiors into any sense of equality, and his arrogant personality, however, had made him widely unpopular. It was notorious that he had vied against Essex, the darling of poets, players, and younger persons in general, and was widely believed to have indecently exulted at the favorite's fall. Tavern singers had mounted many dirges to Essex, and Raleigh, who had been nicknamed The Fox, was held to be completely contemptible. He seemed to have a remarkable facility for creating a jealous envy in every man who ever knew him.

The details of Raleigh's offense were, at first, a secret, though tantalizing hints floated through the air. The Privy Council was, of course, told the entire matter. The covert Catholics among them listened glumly as Cecil unveiled a complex and far-reaching plot—far overshadowing Watson and his feckless fellows—that linked Lord Cobham, Lord Grey, Sir Walter Raleigh, the count of Aremberg, ambassador from the Spanish Netherlands, and various agents in a plan to overthrow James I, install Arabella Stuart, install the Vatican faith, restore ties with Spain, and, in general, reverse the government, its policies, and its leadership.

King James I of England and Queen Anne were crowned on July 25, 1603, at Westminster Abbey. The event was less elaborate than it might have been because hundreds of people were dying of the plague in London every week. The peers held fine handkerchiefs over their mouths as they passed through the streets, and the ceremony was shortened in view of the risk to their health. The archbishop of Canterbury, Whitgift, grown older and more feeble but still sternly alert, presided. Queen Anne, who seldom overlooked an opportunity to embarrass, refused to accept a Reform communion. She sat stiffly in her seat, leaving James, wearing the robes of Edward the Confessor, to make that gesture conspicuously alone.

After the coronation, the king fled to the country. With parks and palaces at his disposal, he plunged into obsessive hunts. The Privy Council, its clerks and servants, the Gentlemen of the Bedchamber, and the hopeful were all forced to gallop in his wake. The pattern James had established in Scotland, of indifference to details and reliance on his advisers, was established in England.

The realm gradually learned its new king did not care for crowds; they frightened him. His padded clothes were protection against a sudden, treacherous knife thrust. The assassin lurked, for him, behind every appearance of the people. When some interfered or rose in his path during a hunt, he was outraged. "What do they want?" he asked, and someone said they wanted to see the face of their king.

"God's Wounds!" shouted James in a frenzy, "I will pull down my breeches and they will also see my arse."[7]

At first it was assumed the spreading plague in the south of England kept the king from Whitehall and forced him to spend so much time in the country. But as weeks and months passed, the English were to learn their monarch detested the City and all the details of government. He rose early and plunged on horseback in chase of stags marked the night before for death.

He would ride, at breakneck speed, following the baying of the hounds, accompanied by his gentlemen. The dogs would bring the deer down—if they were lucky—and the king would dismount to slit the animal's throat and to open its belly and play with its blood. To be smeared on the face by the king with the results was a mark of high favor; James was convinced that plunging his arms into the entrails of a dying stag, and sometimes standing in its opened cadaver, held great, though mystical, medical values.

A successful kill led to a happy supper later and a jovial monarch. He would then listen to letters from his Privy Council and dictate replies and go to bed leaning on one or another arm in great good humor. Lack of success led to curses, dark threats, and complaints about the fickleness of heaven. Rainy weather led to long cardplaying sessions; good weather led to the chase. Business was left to be wedged between. It was unavoidable that this routine be interrupted, however; the king had to appear to receive ambassadors and attend other great occasions.

Then he would fasten expensive jewels to his clothes and indulge in another great pastime: discussions with the clergy. James found no men more congenial—outside the bedroom—than the high prelates of England. Their sonorities, their eloquent bows, their admiration of his learning warmed him from the start. He knew the structure of their faith very well; this had been part of Buchanan's teaching and part of Knox's efforts. He also knew the doctrinal differences that had arisen through the years, against which Whitgift and his High Commission struggled. The Millenary Petition had sought to bring him into this arena, and James was resolved to prove his great wisdom by judging these issues. The prelates were surprised; Elizabeth had not entered into such details—but they were delighted, as the king continued his discussions, to help him make up his mind.

Whitgift's faction in the Church of England was not the only one that sought to help the king. The universities of Cambridge and Oxford also entered the lists to argue against freedom of thought—for any who dared to criticize the archbishop's Articles of Faith. This position was whipped into being by the archbishop, who also undertook a survey of the number of his ministers in the realm, the number of Catholics who did not appear at services, and a poll of those suspected of mental reservations.

The king, however, spun out his discussions and allowed all sorts of hopes to arise both from the Reform faction and from the archbishop's followers. His position was not easy to define. For instance, in September 1603 he was asked to continue the ancient Vatican practice of appearing before persons with scrofula in order to heal with the royal touch. James laughed at this and said he didn't believe in it; it was a Romish rite. It was argued Elizabeth had followed it, and James finally, reluctantly, did the same. He would not touch the sick, but he waved his hands over their disfigurements. It was difficult, in the end, to tell whether the king shrank from the sores or the sense of the occasion.

He expressed so many opinions, however, that the framers of the Millenary Petition had almost as much reason for hope as did Whitgift and Bancroft. The Reform requests, after all, were not without reason. They asked for relatively minor relaxations in the rites of the Church of England. Infants were not to be questioned before baptism or the sign of the Cross used; caps and surplices not made mandatory for the clergy; sermons to be given before Communion; and the ring not to be exchanged in marriage; and the congregation not to bow at the name of Jesus. Other requests had more significance: the Reformers wanted an end to absentee pastorates, which would have restricted the huge benefices enjoyed by some prelates, and asked that the clergy—allowed to sermonize—be better educated. Obviously, the suggestions were negotiable.

Whitgift and Bancroft, however, were caught at the end of the chain that intolerance fastens upon all authorities. They regarded any changes arising from any men except themselves as inherently dangerous. They did not believe that all benefices should be distributed or that the clergy should express its differing opinions. They pressed James to establish his authority as head of the Church. Learning that James had many jests to make about this, the Reform ministers, who were beginning to be called, mockingly, Puritans because they wanted to purify everything, hoped for the best.

Sir Walter Raleigh was carried from the Tower to Winchester on November 12, 1603, through a howling mob that raged so violently against him it seemed, for a time, that he would not survive the journey. Raleigh himself, aware that few defendents ever emerged alive from a treason trial, had tried to commit suicide in the Tower.[8] Conveyed by carriage through the streets of London and to the outskirts, where the plague was less in evidence, however, he decided to go down fighting.

He had already, with the accession of the new king, lost much. Before his arrest he had been removed as captain of the guard, had been forced to resign the lucrative post of warden of the stannaries, had lost the sweet wines monopoly, and been abruptly ejected from possession of Durham House, where he had resided for twenty years. He was, therefore, regarded as a ruined man capable of any action to restore his fortunes. Beyond that, he was a symbol of a past that many persons, tired of war and talk of war, wanted to bury and forget. There is a dark side to heroism and fame, beneath which jealousy and envy lurk, that emerges when fashions change. Raleigh had circumstantial evidence against him, had glittered in the sun too long, and was a little over fifty years old.

The government staged Raleigh's ordeal with great craft. It prepared the way by trying the priests Watson and Clarke, together with their erratic group members Markham, Brooke, Copley, and Brookside, for their plot to kidnap the king.

They were found guilty amid foaming oratory; the priests and Brooke were sentenced to death. They had been barely hauled off when Brooke's elder brother, Lord Cobham, who held the high hereditary post of warden of the Cinque Ports, and Lord Grey of Wilton were hauled before the thirty-one peers who sat as commissioners. Grey conducted himself with considerable dignity and spirit, but Lord Cobham groveled before the court. He charged that Raleigh had been the leader in a scheme to restore Spanish power over England and Arabella Stuart on its throne. After all this, which resulted in a conviction and death sentence for Grey as well as Cobham, Walter Raleigh appeared alone before the bar.

Since treason trials were conducted outside the common law, the discredited hero had no attorney, was not allowed to confront his accuser—Cobham—and was confronted with evidence elaborately prepared in advance while he languished in solitary confinement. His guilt was assumed. It was his task to outargue spontaneously whatever case was presented.

Raleigh had the disadvantage of being confronted by Sir Edward Coke, the great rival of Francis Bacon; a man whose eloquence, force, and fierce abilities were virtually irresistible.[9] Coke was a walking compendium of precedent and statutes, a living encyclopedia of the law, who was armed with proof that Raleigh knew, at least in part, about actions by Cobham that were treasonous in intent. Raleigh's own letter to Cecil made the proof irrefutable.

The great advocate made the most of his moment. He called Raleigh a viper and a traitor, the rankest traitor in all England. Raleigh protested he was innocent and Coke shouted, "Nay, I will prove all. Thou art a monster; thou hast an English face, but a Spanish heart."[10] His denunciations ranged from that beginning into peaks of invective while statements of Cobham and various other depositions were produced. Raleigh was, inevitably, caught in contradictions. By the time the case reached its summation, the outcome was visible. Raleigh asked, as a special privilege, for the last word. Cecil quietly overruled Coke, who sat down in a great display of injured dignity, while the famous defendant pleaded, somewhat brokenly, for his life.

On the twenty-ninth of November, 1603, the priests Watson and Clarke went to their deaths. A week later, Brooke, Cobham's brother, appeared before the crowd, withdrew some of his confession but not all, and was also executed. That gave James a thought.

Lord Cobham, Lord Grey, and Markham had been sentenced to death, as had Raleigh. On December 10, 1603, Lord Cobham and Grey were each brought before the executioner. While they surveyed the crowd for their last words, they were asked about Raleigh's guilt. As each insisted on it, a king's messenger arrived to halt the proceedings and to carry them back to prison, to the loud astonishment of the crowd.

James, who had hoped for last-minute revelations, was disappointed. Nevertheless, he commuted the sentences for Copley, Brooksby and Markham and had them exiled from the realm. Cobham and Grey were sent to the Tower. Raleigh's sentence was reprieved; his forfeited property was restored. He was shifted to a set of rooms on the top floor of the Tower, where his wife and young son, Wat, were allowed to join him. He could have servants, writing materials, and other comforts. He settled down for a memorable stay—and the king relaxed in the belief that he had shown a great mercy. He had, but it seemed mysterious and a little odd—like the king himself.

The king not only delighted in the hunt and blood, but also in feasts, banquets, masques, parties, drinking, scandals, and excess. At Hampton Court in the Christmas season of 1603—James's first in England—the realm witnessed a great explosion of extravagance that paled any previous demonstration in opulence and license. The entire tone of the court went reeling in directions Elizabeth would never have countenanced, to resemble a tavern party by persons who had mysteriously found the cornucopia of plenty.

Banquets of staggering opulence were mounted. Masques, balls, and plays appeared. Players discovered the king liked low comedy and high satires; they produced what pleased him. Queen Anne, whose love of costumes, parties, dances, and plays was almost childlike, dressed as a goddess and, trailed by her ladies-in-waiting, headed a train of worshipers before His Majesty. The king supervised and beamed during the marriage of his favorite, the earl of Montgomery, to Lady Susan Vere; the following morning he rushed to their bedchamber to learn the details of their first night, lolling familiarly between them.

The procession of floats; the nights of gambling, dancing, seduction, and revelry, which included a special show by the queen and her ladies in blackface; the display of jewels and costumes that cost thousands of pounds each; the drinking, the food, the caresses, the hugs, the laughter, the great monstrous scale of these proceedings marked a court that knew no bounds.

It was all the more amazing, therefore, that the same Hampton Court, barely cleared of the stained linens and the debris of roistering, should have been the site of a great conference at which the king would judge the issues raised by the Millenary Petition and the resistance to those issues mounted by the archbishop of Canterbury on January 14, 1604.

James was engrossed in the abstractions of religion; he seemed to consider the entire subject, which wracked the world of Europe and had led to millions of deaths, to be one that could be settled by conversation. In particular, he was caught by the structured reasoning of Richard Hooker, who argued the Church of England was really old Catholic, since it was based on the early ideas of Christianity, as formed before the Vatican created the pope and moved into worldly channels.

The king was so impressed with this theory, with which the English prelates largely and eagerly agreed, that he wrote to Rome asking the pope to give him the power to excommunicate "turbulent" Catholics in his realm. He was surprised not to receive that permission: he had been so reinforced by the easy compliance of the archbishop of Canterbury and the bishop of London, Bancroft, that the question of his religious supremacy now seemed to him beyond discussion.

In a withdrawing room inside the Privy Chamber, a number of councillors, including Cecil, and the hierarchy of the Church, including Whitgift, the archbishop; Edward Bancroft, bishop of London; six other bishops; seven deans; and two conforming clergymen, listened to King James. He made a long speech about the relations between men individually and vis-à-vis the State, and although it was difficult to follow, it was clear he believed his wisdom alone could resolve all issues. He also thanked God "who brought me into this Promised Land . . . where I sit before grave, learned and reverent men, not as before, elsewhere, a king without state, without honor, without order, where beardless boys would brave us to our face."[11]

Then, while his Privy Councillors, at his request, departed, he spent the day discussing mutual ideas with his high prelates. The scene was visually impressive. The bishops wore their mitres and rich vestments and carried their crosiers; the king "sat in his furs in the cold weather as the fire roared . . ."[12]

It was the king's belief that he was confronted with the sort of Reform that he knew in Scotland and associated with the theories of Calvin, the deeds of Knox, and the teachings of Buchanan. That would have surprised and even astonished the four men selected to represent the mild objections of the Millenary Petition, who waited patiently outside the chamber all during the first day of the conference. All four, after all, were ministers of the Church of England and were never associated with extremism of any sort. Dr. Reynolds was president of Corpus Christi College at Oxford; Laurence Chaderton, master of Emmanuel College at Cambridge, Dr. Thomas Sparke, an archdeacon, and Rector John Knewstubs were all highly respected figures. Not being among those allowed to stand behind the king's chair, they did not realize how different James was personally from his towering reputation as the product of the great Reform of Scotland, the hope of the Protestants of Europe.

While they waited to be called before the heads of their own church and their king, they speculated regarding the discussion that was proceeding on the other side of the closed doors. Their common view was that James was resisting his bishops and their heavily Catholic doctrines. Instead, James was telling the bishops the fine points of their position.

The king called at times for the Bible and at other times for the Book of Common Prayer and instructed his Bishops from these. His homilies were digressive, in which he told anecdotes from his life in Scotland and repeated instances of how he had outreasoned the rebellious Kirk of that land. The bishops marveled at his wisdom and penetration. At the close of the first day it was later said they "departed filled with wonder . . . so admirably, both for understanding, speech and judgment, did his Majesty handle all parts . . . as the greatest scholars and most industrious students there present might not outstrip him. . . ."[13]

The atmosphere changed after the doors opened and the minority spokesmen appeared.

The second day of the conference opened with young Prince Henry seated on a stool beside his father's great chair. Some Privy Councillors, including Cecil, were present, as well as some spectators. One of these was Sir John Harington, who later wrote his impressions. As before, the bishops were in their vestments.

The king listened while Dr. Reynolds began to discuss some changes in the Articles of the Church and in the rite of confirmation. Bancroft interrupted. Years of sitting on the High Commission and bearing heavily down upon all dissenters was too much for him. Throwing himself on his knees before the king, he called for recollection of the laws, which forbade dissent and "any man speaking against his Bishop." He wanted Reynolds stopped on the spot.[14]

Even James could not accept that; there would be no conference at all, if Bancroft had his way. Nevertheless, Bancroft had made his point. The little group for whom Reynolds spoke were dissenters—rebels against authority, breaking laws with which they were familiar. James looked at them with a lowering expression.

Reynolds avoided trouble for a time. He dwelled on doctrinal matters, to which the bishops replied, but which the king could follow and comment upon shrewdly. He did so, and a hum of applause rose in the chamber to bring a smile to his face.

Reynolds discussed the lack of learning of many clerics. The bishops replied that some ministers showed disrespect for the liturgy by walking up and down the aisles, or even outside, until they could rise to preach. James brushed that aside. He thought those that could preach should, and those who could not should be let alone.

When Reynolds then suggested that a new English translation of the Bible be prepared, James agreed. He did more: he discussed how it should be prepared and expressed opinions about marginal notes. Finished with that point, he leaned back, greatly relaxed and said, "Surely, if these be the greatest matters you be grieved with, I need not have troubled . . . and, looking toward the Lords, shook his head smiling."[15]

The minority then raised the matter of a more learned ministry, ignoring the whispers and laughter among the bishops and the spectators. They endured a considerable discussion on that point; and when they passed on to the Apocrypha, whose reading they did not approve in church, James called for the book and discussed it in detail. This was his forte, and he made jokes. Turning toward the audience, he wondered aloud why the Reformers objected to Ecclesiasticus. "By my soul, I think he was a Bishop," he said, arousing appreciative laughter.

He was, however, growing bored as the day neared its end. The minority, intent upon making all its points, pushed forward. Dr. Reynolds wanted a restoration of "prophecying"—a practice once allowed by Whitgift's predecessor and halted by Elizabeth on the grounds it led to "disturbances."

If any new disturbances were so created, said Reynolds, unaware he had wandered onto sensitive ground, "the Bishop and his Presbyters" could handle it. At that, James suddenly flew into a rage. "If you aim at a Scottish Presbytery," he shouted abruptly, "it agreeth as well with monarchy as God and the Devil. Then Jack and Tom and Will and Dick shall meet at their pleasure to censure me and my Council and all our proceedings. Then Will shall stand up and say, It must be thus; then Dick shall reply and say, Nay, marry, but we will have it thus. Stay, I pray you, for one seven years, before you demand that from me, and then if you find me pursy and fat, and my windpipes stuffed, I will perhaps hearken to you, for to let that government be once up, I am sure I shall be kept out of breath. Then shall we all have work enough, both our hands full. But, Doctor Reynolds, until you find that I grow lazy, let that alone. How they used that poor lady my mother is not unknown, and how they dealt with me in my minority you all know."[16]

He turned toward the bishops. "My lords the Bishops," he said, putting his hand to his hat, "I may thank you that these men plead thus for my supremacy. They think they cannot make their party good but by appealing unto it, but if once you were out and they were in, I know what would become of my supremacy, for *no bishop, no king.* I have learned of what cut they have been . . . passing over in silence my being supreme governor in causes ecclesiastical."

"Well, doctor," the king ended, while his son stared at him from his stool with round eyes, "have you anything more to say?"

"Nothing, Sire," said Reynolds miserably. James rose to leave the room.

"If this is all they have to say," he announced loudly, "I will make them conform themselves, or else harry them out of the land." He passed through the door, leaving the balance of his words to float back on the air, "or else do worse."[17]

The last day of the conference was marked by the presence of many lawyers representing both Church canons and the courts of the realm. The discussion was highly important and revolved around the mandatory oath employed by the High Commission in its inquiries into beliefs. No record was kept of who said what; but apparently Lord Burghley's letter, written years earlier, comparing the approach of the High Commission to the Spanish Inquisition, was read aloud. Archbishop Whitgift denied the parallel and said defendants could refuse to reply if the issue involved "life, liberty, or scandal." That reply ignored many dead and imprisoned men and amounted to a flat lie.

The argument against the mandatory oath was further undercut by Ellesmere, the lord chancellor, who explained the same oath was used in the Star Chamber and "in divers Courts." The king then launched into one of his schoolteacher's expositions where he orated at some length without fear of interruption or contradiction and explained why the High Commission's oath was necessary, wise, and lawful.

It was this oration that imbued Archbishop Whitgift to exclaim, delightedly, "Undoubtedly your Majesty speaks with the special assistance of God's spirit."[18] Bancroft, the archbishop's great assistant, added his voice and said, "I protest my heart melteth with joy . . . such a King as, since Christ's time, the like hath not been given."

The delight of these prelates was echoed—at least outwardly—by most of the audience of advisers, courtiers, and spectators. Those who disagreed did so privately or in the freedom of their personal notes. Sir John Harington, a confirmed skeptic so far as James was concerned, was caustic about Whitgift's Holy Spirit. "The Spirit," he wrote, "was rather foul mouthed."[19]

That coarseness was in loud evidence when Drs. Reynolds, Kewstubs, Chaderton, and Sparke were called in to hear the king's conclusions. They were treated to a display of the monarch's invective and told they would have to "conform themselves, or they would hear more of it."[20] They bowed submissively, and James swept out, followed by a loudly admiring entourage.

The conference, however, was deceptive. The numbers of admiring bishops and the sharply reduced voices of dissent did not represent the actual condition of England. In the last years of Elizabeth's reign, when her life was clearly drawing toward its close, the High Commission had fallen into relative inactivity; the laws against Catholics had been relaxed by bribery and indifference, and the absolutism of the Tudors had lost its lustre.

James had been expected to bring an expanded view to old and narrow arguments, to usher change, lighten an atmosphere grown stale and sour. Instead, he turned toward the past. In the weeks following the conference, even Archbishop Whitgift was heard to worry and to say he hoped not to see the new Parliament. That hope was granted. Toward the end of February, 1604, Whitgift was on his deathbed.

The king came to see him, but the old man was beyond knowing. He could only whisper over and again, *"Pro ecclesiâ Dei; pro ecclesiâ Dei."*[21] He left behind, however, a church of God headed by James Stuart.

# 26

Great success brings greater dreams. The new king of England had endured years of unregal scrabbling, fear, and poverty. He had crawled, wept, and pleaded to survive. In early 1604 he was rich and powerful, surrounded by sycophants, victorious over all his enemies.

He appeared before the new Parliament—the first of his reign—on March 19, 1604—to tell them of his dreams for the future. One was a union between Scotland and England, a blessing "which God hath in my person bestowed upon you." As he orated, a vision rose of "One King, one faith, one language; one law, one parliament, one people alike in manners and allegiance."[1] The old divisive names would vanish. England and Scotland would combine in a new blended realm called Great Britain.

Speaking thickly in his broad Scots accents, the king waxed about this as though seated at one of his hunting lodges with his intimates. "Hath he not made us all one island . . . of itself by nature indivisible? And in the end and fullness of Time he hath united the right and title of both kingdoms in my person, alike descended of both the Crowns?"[2] There was a sort of logic about this, as there is about all simplifications, but James could not keep himself out of any subject that interested him; he had a unique facility for homely metaphors and coarse parallels. "What God had conjoined let no man separate. I am the husband and all the whole isle is my lawful wife. I am the head and it is my body. I am the shepherd and it is my flock." That eerie echo of the great words of the Bible, and the hint that the king thought he was God sent a shudder through the Puritan minority of Commons and struck even the indifferent as grotesque and unpleasant.

"I hope, therefore," the king continued, unaware of the reactions he aroused, "that no man will think that I, a Christian King under the Gospel, should be a polygamist and husband to two wives; that I being the head should have a divided or monstrous body or that being the shepherd to so fair a flock should have my flock parted in two. And as God hath made Scotland the one half of this isle to enjoy my birth and the first and most unperfect half . . . and you here to enjoy the perfect and last half . . . so can I not think that any would cut the one half of me from the other."[3]

That was only the beginning. The king wanted Commons to know his mind in all matters. The man who considered himself God's representative told Commons how his far-ranging intellect regarded the petty ideas of men and how the Reform dissenters being "ever discontented . . . maketh their sect unable to be suffered in any well governed commonwealth." He read the text of his proclamation to the bishops, ordering them into a great convocation, being held at the same time that Parliament was in session, that would order beliefs into unity.

The Commons listened to this in deep silence. Reports of the king's rough handling of the dissenters at the Hampton Court Conference had spread through the realm with the speed of light and had affected the elections. Reform-minded men had flocked to the polls and sent their counterparts from the country to join the already influential Reform minority in London to the session. In the past many men had not bothered to attend Commons; on this occasion, extra seats had to be ordered. There was a feeling in the air of a gathering crisis—to which James appeared oblivious.

A man who believed himself to be God's representative on earth was unlikely to leave any matter unresolved. James went on to call himself the Prince of Peace and to discuss a peace with Spain as though it were already accomplished. The Commons, whose members were in sympathy with the Dutch rebels, the Huguenots of France, and the Calvinists of Geneva waited in vain to hear a kind word for these. They heard, instead, that their king had "no desire" to prosecute Papists, though he had reservations about priests who placed the pope of Rome above James I of England.

They heard, in fact, far more than they wanted to hear of the king's attitudes, opinions, and plans and far less than they had hoped about the long-pent complaints of England. James finally came to a halt and departed, hugely pleased with himself and leaning—as ever—on the arm of a handsome young man. Members of Commons were left astonished. Within weeks they were locked in struggle with the Crown.


The first argument came over a disputed election. The king had decided the Court of Chancery could resolve such disputes. Chancery had ruled that Sir Francis Goodwin, elected by small landowners in Buckinghamshire over a Privy Councillor—Sir John Fortescue, who obtained the votes of the gentry—could not be seated. A second election was held, and Fortescue, unopposed, won.

Commons decided this proceeding could not stand. It summoned Goodwin to take his seat. Matters immediately grew complex. The House of Lords wanted to know what Commons had done and was told it had no constitutional right to ask. Then the king suddenly sent an order that Commons should discuss the issue with Lords. Commons, surprised, prepared an explanation to James, explaining the laws of England. It was surprised, in its turn, to learn the king's philosophy of law.

The new king of England believed that "all matters of privilege came from him," and therefore "could not be turned against him." Precedents did not matter, for they came from "the reigns of minors, tyrants, women —and foolish kings." Commons was to confer with the judges of Chancery; it was clear James meant by this that his judges should prevail.

Commons, however, was well stocked with lawyers. These drew together a bristling document justifying their procedure, citing innumerable rights regarding its membership, and sent it to the king. His response was thunderous. He declared he was "distracted in his judgment" by their arguments and commanded, as "an absolute King," that they confer with the judges of Chancery in his presence and that of his Privy Council.

That response was read aloud in the House of Commons. The members were stunned and sat in silence. Sir Henry Yelverton, ambitious for high office, took the king's part. "The Prince's command is like a thunderbolt. His command on our allegiance is like the roaring of a lion. His command brooks no contradiction," he said.[4]

By then Cecil moved behind the scenes to calm the situation. Although no longer a member of Commons, he had a useful instrument in Sir Francis Bacon, who had been among the throng knighted by the new monarch. Bacon passed the word, both conversationally and in veiled public speeches, that the Privy Council had prevailed upon the sovereign to show mercy to lesser mortals.

A conference was held, that was marked by great civility on all sides. Commons announced it would make some minor changes in its rules, so this particular dispute would not recur. The king beamed. The Devil had created contention, but God had turned it to good and enabled James to prove his bounty and grace. There were deep bows and flowery words, But when it was all over, the House of Commons had not only won its right to decide the qualifications of its own members, but had looked deeply into the new king. Its members were not impressed by the sight.

That argument, however, was only one. Straw men of huge proportions were rising on all sides. A convocation under the iron directives and harsh intentions of Richard Bancroft had drawn together a host of new canons —church laws. The new structure for the Church of England eliminated much that was obsolete, but added over forty special rules against Puritan dissenters. Penalty for noncomformity to any of these was suspension, the loss of position for the clerics, or excommunication.

Commons, however, held many men who had accepted the theories of Knox, Calvin, and Buchanan. Like Lord Burghley under Elizabeth, they had no liking for the High Commission, its mandatory oath that forced men to testify against themselves, its conformity, or its power. The Beale books claiming the Magna Carta forbid such practices had sunk deep and taken root. The whole issue of canon law, in fact, was anathema to the lawyers of Commons. They preferred the common laws of England, the national— as opposed to the ecclesiastical—legal structure.

While Bancroft and his fellow bishops drew their new regulations, Commons proposed its version of Knox's *Book of Discipline* to the Church. That suggestion fell on unsympathetic ears, and Commons then petitioned the king.

The king, however, was growing angry. He had learned that debates in the House of Commons were far different than in a Scots Parliament that met with the king's list of demands in hand for a few muted days, voted obediently, and then went home. Instead Sir William Maurice repeatedly rose to propose that King James be called an emperor and sat down to general laughter.

Commons brought up the matter of purveyances, in which the court commandeered and consumed the substances of regions through which it traveled. There was also an ancient system of wards, in which nobles collected revenues from districts they once protected that had long out-grown the need. The system of wards was handed down from William the Conqueror and Commons wanted it abolished. The Crown responded that if it lost purveyances, it would need money to make up for the loss. Commons in turn sent the king a series of laws, long since ratified, making many such abuses already illegal. The lawyers would not compensate the Crown for abandoning abuses it should not continue. The system of wards, which covered both estates, minors, females, and counties, was far more complex and needed further study by all parties.

Then Commons told the king that he could not change the religious laws of the nation without its approval. It also argued the matter of common citizenship between Scots and Englishmen at great length, and speeches were made about the poverty-stricken Scots that created great indignation among James's personal entourage. It was feared Scots merchants would flood England, evade taxes, and create disorder. The question of the differ-ent laws of the realm brought up the issue of who would draw new laws for both kingdoms. How would such men be chosen, and by whom?

The longer the matter was examined, the more obvious it became that James's idea that the two kingdoms could be made one "in a month or less" was a fantasy, an impossibility. The proposed change of name of the realm was delayed; commissioners were appointed to study all the complexities of the king's proposals.

Meanwhile, James sought to both force and direct the activities of the Commons. He could not seem to understand that members were free to express their opinions; he sent rejoinders and admonitions and made speeches at them in response. By June 1604 the City of London was beginning to reflect satires, tavern limericks, and stories about the strange new king of England. Commons itself decided the sovereign—the Great Instructor—needed some lessons to study. A lengthy document entitled *An Apology*—a word that then meant "explanation"—was prepared. This document traced the liberties and rights of Englishmen back to antiquity in a style Buchanan had introduced years before, using much the same sort of reasoning as his *History of Scotland*. The rights of Englishmen, in this theory, were as old as the monarchy, were as firm as the right of every man to hold his property, and could not be taken by any power. Commons left no area untouched. It repeated its claim that no man could order religious beliefs, not even a king. It openly questioned why the new king needed more money in peace than his predecessor needed during a time of rebellion in Ireland and when the war with Spain raged fiercely. It mentioned the king's vast estates and the licenses he distributed to his favorites and concluded on a note that headed directly against a theme he often raised. "The voice of the *people,*" said Commons, "is said to be as the voice of God."[5]

Cecil and his associates came running to stifle that document and to keep the Commons from making a formal presentation to the king. Such a confrontation would make an argument between Commons and the Crown that could tear the country apart; it had to be diverted. Commons was assured the king would read and consider the matters brought to his attention; the king was persuaded to take no public notice of the protest. Nevertheless, James decided to suspend the session. He appeared before Commons on July 7, 1604, in a mood much different from the one in which he had launched its deliberations.

He began his comments on their activities with a certain amount of civility, but was soon carried away by irritation. To general astonishment, the king of England began to scold the members of Commons—whose collective wealth could have purchased all his court—as though they were deficient schoolchildren. "I will not thank you where I think no thanks due," he said in part. He then caught himself and mentioned that their members contained many persons of ability, but before long he was haranguing. He compared them to the rude Parliament of Scotland, subservient, impotent, and unrepresentative, and gave Scotland greater credit. There, he said, proving his memory was fallible or else trusting that the English were uninformed, "I ruled upon men not of the best temper, and was heard not

only as a King, but as a counselor. Contrary, here nothing but curiosity
from morning to evening, to find fault with my propositions. There all
things warranted that came from me. Here all things suspected."

He was bitter about the Reformers among them. "I did not think they
had been so great," he said, "in your House." Then he came very close to
losing his temper altogether. "You have done many things rashly," he said,
"I say not you meant disloyally . . . I only wish you had kept better form.
I like form as well as matter. It shows respect. . . ."[6]

James had flaunted his learning so long that he had come to believe
he had a monopoly; the discovery that other men were also learned filled
him with indignation.


While taverns rocked with laughter at the king's discomfiture, Ben
Jonson mounted a play—immediately successful—called *Eastward Ho*. The
title came from the Thames water taxis, whose oarsmen would shout "Eastward Ho" or "Westward Ho" for passengers going one way or the other
at numerous river points. The dialogue was filled with topical references,
including descriptions of the fabulous wealth of Virginia, where even chamber pots were made of gold—and where Scots were few. Sir Petronel Flash,
regarding a half-drowned man washed ashore at Cuckold's Landing,
affected a thick burr and said, "I ken the mon well. He's one o' my 30 pound
knights." This transparent burlesque of the king and the host he had honored earned Jonson an arrest, but sent his popularity soaring.

The City was, in fact, feverish. The plague had killed 30,000—almost
a fifth of its population. The survivors wanted to experience all possible joys;
the great international problems of the Elizabethan period had vanished
with the decline of Spanish menace. People were bored by high drama and
great goals and turned toward pleasures of every sort.

The return of the court restored patronage and sent a waterfall of
business trickling from the staid establishments of the north side down to
the theaters, taverns, whorehouses, and gambling dens of the south. Rents
soared; property values doubled, tripled, and quadrupled. Office space was
so scarce that men did business among the tombstones of St. Paul's and even
inside the cathedral itself.

Whitehall was the scene of the largest, most lavish, and most continu-
ous party of all. The great candelabras blazed all night. Masques, feasts,
dancing, and gaming continued to all hours. The numbers of courtiers,
women, office seekers, attendants, and hangers-on increased astronomi-
cally. Forty-eight Gentlemen of the Bedchamber crowded two hundred
gentlemen "extraordinary." Ushers, grooms, clerks, pages, messengers, and
servants surrounded a court of 1,500 persons. Men lay in wait for James

everywhere, burning for favors, for preferment, for privilege. His every appearance was in the midst of a crowd. The king seemed unable to maintain any order, regularity, or decorum over this elegant mob; the high court of the Tudors dissolved into disorder and confusion.

In view of this dishevelment, it was all the more remarkable that on July 16, 1604, with the king's approval, only a week after Parliament was prorogued, Bancroft issued the new 104 canons of the Church of England. They were of unprecedented rigor and gave all clergymen who refused to accept their every dot, comma, and phrase until November 30, 1604, to conform or lose their posts.

King James's pursuit of peace produced a series of surprises beginning in mid-1604. He had launched his effort in the beginning of his reign by a dramatic step, intended to prove his goodwill and to end the war with Spain. It consisted of ending the "Letters of Marque"—governmental permits— for English privateers to sail against the ships of Spain.[7]

Spain, as well as most of Europe, was amazed. By a stroke of the pen the new king of England halted the use of England's most famous and effective weapon against Madrid at a time when Spain was visibly weakening. At the same time, he diminished his own crown revenues though his expenses were soaring.

His action had other unexpected results. It snuffed England's glory on the seas and eliminated a flourishing wartime industry. It also converted that industry from a respectable, privately financed effort on the nation's behalf into a peacetime series of criminal ventures. The privateers, stripped of legal status, were converted into pirates. In a very short time, they threatened English vessels as well as French, Spanish, Dutch, and all others. Not bound by any rules of war, they committed atrocities. A new criminal marine menace emerged that increased dangers to all commerce.

Oblivious to these results, the king then turned his wisdom toward the terms of a treaty with Spain. It was clear from the start of the peace negotiations that the king of England held no high opinion of the great dreams that had convulsed all western Europe for more than a generation. One such dream had obsessed Philip II, who mobilized his country to restore the old order of Christendom. In the course of this great effort, the Spanish faith was altered into an instrument of Spanish expansion.

Philip II had struggled against a different vision based on the theories of Calvin, as expanded by Knox. That vision had soared far beyond Luther's desire to be free of the Vatican controls and to restore a simplified Christian faith. Where Luther had worked with the nobility to suppress social revolution, the followers of Knox had sought to combine such a revolution with their faith and to destroy the supremacy not only of the Vatican, but also of sovereigns. Buchanan and others had popularized these ideas and carried them into the world so intertwined that they provided catalysts for change in all areas.

These theories had converted the Huguenots of France, inspired the rebels of the Netherlands, altered Scotland, and penetrated deep into the intellectual life of England. As the prize pupil of Buchanan, James VI had been the hope of the Reform in England. His muted encouragement of the Vatican while he sought the throne of England was largely unknown and dismissed by the more worldly as a sign of naïveté.

The Reform expected that, as king of England, James would press the war against Spain to a notable victory. In the course of this effort, he would ally himself with the Dutch rebels. Some hoped for an actual merger between the two countries, which would place England on the Continent again as part of a new nation that would extend from Scotland to the Netherlands. Henry IV feared that possibility. At the same time, Henry IV hoped for an alliance against Spain. The Huguenots and the more ardent English Reformers expected that if James moved positively, the influence of the Reform would spread across all northern Europe, swing uncertain German states, and create a power that would press hard against Rome and Madrid.

Instead, the new king arrived from the North, surrounded by the high pro-Vatican Scots nobles of the party of his mother, Mary Stuart. He was surrounded by more Catholics in Whitehall. He listened to Lord Henry Howard, long a secret Catholic, who was now among the most influential at court and who had been raised to earl of Northampton. Howard openly expressed the view that the Dutch had rebelled against their lawful sovereign and even asked his Convocation of Bishops if a Christian king could assist rebels against a Christian monarch.

The rebels of the Netherlands learned this with dismay and sent a special agent to James to plead their case. He was refused the king's presence. Rumors cascaded through England's court and were carried in diplomatic bags to the confusion of Europe. Henry IV now regretted that he had made so many jokes about James, that he had once laughingly suggested he might send one of his bastards to repeat the performance of William the Conqueror, or that he had called the Scots Solomon "the son of David."

The king himself was serenely indifferent to the worries he created. His position was that he sought peace with everyone. His instructions to Cecil and other negotiators was to work toward that end. Cecil did his work well; the three "cautionary" towns of Brill, Flushing, and Rammekins remained in English hands. No change was made in the permission given Henry IV to recruit English volunteers to help the Dutch, and his expense in such efforts was applied against money he owed England. But trade with Spain and England was to be renewed; Madrid promised not to turn the Inquisition against English seamen. In return, James allowed his policy of leniency toward Catholics in his realm to speak eloquently of his own toleration.

By the time the treaty was concluded in August 1604, relations between James I and Spain appeared better than since the days of Mary Tudor. Queen Anne was thrilled to learn and to share with the king the information that the Spanish wanted to marry their infanta to England's Prince Henry.

When the treaty was signed in August 1604, the king was in rare good humor. A great banquet was held, and the Spanish were lavish in their admiration of the ornate, gleaming silver service that appeared. James was gracious enough to give it to them on the spot.

Sir Dudley Carleton watched that gesture with disgust. "We cannot say this King hath been behindhand in liberality," he wrote, "for at this one instance he hath given away more plate than did Elizabeth in her whole realm."[8]

Sir Dudley understated the case. James Stuart had given away far more than silver; he had abandoned the great Calvinist dream that had driven and sustained the men who had crowned him in infancy so many years before.

**27** King James wanted to eclipse the glory of Elizabeth's England by a greater glory of his own. Despite the fact that the English Parliament had delayed in moving toward a union with Scotland, James abruptly announced himself king of Great Britain by his own proclamation.

The Privy Council muttered against this self-conducted baptism. Members said it was "provocative . . . a mere shadow without the substance." Others whispered that Francis Bacon had encouraged the monarch. As usual, James was offended at the murmurs and declared that Great Britain was the name that "God had given the island."[1]

Another of God's preferences, apparently, was that men should stop smoking, a fashion introduced by Sir Walter Raleigh. That former hero was still smoldering, like a quiescent volcano, in the Tower, but London alone enjoyed 7,000 tobacco shops. In these, customers puffed on long-stemmed pipes provided by the proprietors. In such cloudy establishments men passed the pipe and indulged in gossip—some of which was highly disrespectful to the Crown.

A *Counterblast Against Tobacco,* authored by His Majesty himself, suddenly appeared. Smoking was described as ". . . loathsome to the eye, hateful to the nose, harmful to the brain, dangerous to the lungs, and in the black stinking fumes thereof, nearest resembling the horrible Stygian smoke of that pit that is bottomless."[2]

Cecil was alarmed and came running. To his surprise, he learned the king wanted to halt all commerce in tobacco. None was to be allowed into England; its cultivation in Virginia and other colonies was to be halted. The tobacco shops were to close, and the people would abandon—of course— a habit of which their king disapproved.

The secretary explained how important the commodity had become to England's commerce. He mentioned the taxes and the livelihoods involved, the loss of revenue to the nation, and the nearly unanimous medical opinion at the time that tobacco was a powerful curative for many illnesses. In the course of this, he touched, naturally enough, on the great loss of revenue such an embargo and such an edict would have upon the Crown itself. James graciously allowed himself to be persuaded—but the *Counterblast* remained in circulation among the other great writings—*Dæmonologie, Basilikon Doron,* and poems—for which the king was already famous.

The king was annoyed by other English habits as well. The bishops had begun their purge of the dissident clergymen who refused to accept the new canons of the Church. Some of these drew up a petition and presented it to James when he was hunting at Royston in November 1604. Nothing could more infuriate the monarch: hunting was sacred, uninterruptible, and not to be stained by petitioners.

"I have daily more and more cause to hate and abhor all that sect," he wrote Cecil. On the heels of that petition another arrived, this time signed by gentlemen, lay sympathizers with the Reform. The king was aroused enough to attend a meeting of his council, where he "most bitterly inveighed against the Puritans, saying that revolt in the Low Countries, which had lasted ever since he was born and whereof he never expected to see an end, began first by a petition for the matter of religion, and so did all the troubles in Scotland; that his mother and he from their cradles had been haunted with a Puritan devil which he feared would not leave him to his grave; and that he would hazard his Crown but he would suppress these malicious spirits."[3]

Petitions seemed to James equivalent to rebellion; he was indignant that such instruments appeared against him—and could not accept the fact that they were legal in England. That denial was a serious matter. Many dissenting ministers had petitioned the Courts of Common Law and been sympathetically heard by judges who themselves resented the great authority of the High Commission. One result was that the Courts of Common Law had issued many "prohibitions" against High Commission rulings. Another was that petitions rained upon these courts from ministers faced with the loss of their livelihoods.

Bancroft, who was acting as head of the bishops at this period, asked the Star Chamber—the legal tribunal of the Privy Council—whether the High Commission could banish nonconforming ministers, administer its mandatory oath in examinations—and whether petitions were legal.

The Star Chamber, now composed of the king's men or men—like Cecil—whose beliefs were less firm than his father's—declared the High Commission held its authority from the king, and all three of its rights were upheld. That meant that the Reform was not only to be repressed, but stifled so its cries could not be heard.

The king received these verdicts with huge satisfaction; he was verified in his idea that he was the source of all law—and that those who disagreed were against the law. Yet as the numbers of ministers ejected from their churches began to increase, divisions broadened in the Church of England. Clergymen who had been able to reconcile their differences were now parted by them, and congregations became disturbed.

The king's leniency toward Catholics had led to their emergence into outdoor services, at some of which thousands attended for the first time in years. James had been asked to apply the laws against these, but had turned a blind eye. It was his belief that he could reconcile the differences between the Church of England and the Vatican, much as he himself represented a union of Scotland and England. James had begun to believe he was a divine instrument sent to bring peace and harmony to all mankind.

He was so caught by this vision that he sent one of his Scots favorites, Sir James Lindsay, to Rome to talk to the pope. Lindsay was so profuse in his descriptions of James's respect for the pontiff and his desire to see peace and goodwill reign that the Vatican was sent into transports of joy.

The pope excitedly appointed a committee of twelve cardinals to gather arguments and prepare the way for a great conversion. He ordered Masses to be held and petitioned heaven to assist these efforts. Rumors swept through Rome and then over all Europe that the king of England would soon astonish the world.

Meanwhile, James had made Richard Bancroft the new archbishop of Canterbury. That was tantamount to bringing the ghost of Whitgift back from the grave in more vigorous form. The appointment made it clear the suppression of Reformers in the Church of England would continue.

That suppression contrasted with James's leniency toward England's Catholics, who were now openly defying the laws against public demonstrations of their faith, and gave credence to the rumor that now swept both England and Europe regarding James's imminent conversion.

The king was among the last to learn of this expectation. He received it in stages, in a series of shocks. The first came in the form of a message from Madrid. Before Prince Henry could contract to marry the Spanish infanta, the Spaniards demanded that the heir to England's throne be sent to Madrid, "to be educated in the True Faith." James recoiled at that.

He had not recovered from the collapse of that negotiation before he learned that Lindsay had convinced the pope that James could be converted. The king was both astonished and outraged. He could not recall precisely what he had told Lindsay; he had said so many things. But he had not expected to be converted by the pope. If the truth were known, he had expected to convert the pope.

The realm entered its Christmas festivities at year's end with both the people and their monarch greatly upset. The English were confused and suspicious; Cecil was disturbed and concerned—the king was irritated at a world that refused to conform to his ideas.

After he had recovered from the holy days and their delights, James discussed the now seething religious situation with his Privy Council. As usual, he spoke against the Reform bitterly. But for the first time he showed that he was aware matters had grown awry. Following Cecil's advice, presented in many obsequious forms, he issued orders that the laws against Catholics be applied.

The results were breathtaking. Within weeks over 5,000 Vatican followers found themselves hauled into prisons and before the Courts of Common Law for failing to attend services of the Church of England. The leniency was over—not so much on the part of the king—but on the part of the governmental officialdom, which was securely in the hands of the Reform.

The Catholics were taken aback. They had watched, first with suspicion and finally with trust, the enlarged leniency that James had created. They had heard the rumors of his conversion with tearful thanksgivings and heartfelt prayers. It seemed to many the king had tricked them. Lured out of concealment by false hopes, they were abruptly confronted with arrest, fines, loss of property, or prison. The blackmail and system of bribes that had flourished beneath the surface at their expense increased to onerous new levels.

The realm, in other words, was growing as disordered as the court. The king's expenses were huge, and Cecil used desperate expedients to keep James's luxurious ship, with its ravenous and teeming passengers, afloat. He began the quiet sale of crown lands to raise cash. The secretary, however, had other worries of which money was only a symptom.

Large numbers of ministers were being cast out of the Church of England. Each of these ministers represented a congregation and had a following among the people, and many regions were affected. They turned toward members of Parliament—the same Parliament that had already reminded James it held authority on grounds more substantial than his approval.

That Parliament, besieged with petitions, armed with new grievances, was displeased with James's new foreign policy in which a promiscuous pursuit of peace with all and influence with none dominated the king's thoughts. It was due to meet in February 1605. The secretary suggested to the king that the session be delayed. James agreed. He turned his attention back to his hunting and to efforts to subjugate, through newly appointed bishops, the Kirk of Scotland. Cecil, relieved, turned toward some mysterious activities that had attracted his attention.

On the surface, life in England appeared much the same. The king enjoyed his hunt and traveled from one great house to another in a continual round that consumed the countryside, burdened his hosts, and added to his own expenses. At Royston a favorite hound named Jowler vanished, and the King was vexed. Soon Jowler appeared with a note tied to his collar.

"Good Mr. Jowler. We pray you speak to the King (for he hears you every day, and so doth not us) that it will please his Majesty to go back to London, for else the country will be undone; all our provision is spent already and we are not able to entertain him any longer."[4]

The king laughed and forgot the matter. Government business reached him by messenger and was examined late at night before the King fell asleep. His companions had to double as secretaries, but since they also had to accompany him on the hunt, they were left little time to work. "We are all become wild men wandering in a forest from morning to evening," said the earl of Dunbar, one of his Scots favorites.

Cecil, who had been elevated to earl of Salisbury for the triumphant Spanish treaty that ended a war without victory, sent streams of carefully composed reports, suggestions, and reminders, each heavily wrapped in lavish compliments.

While the king enjoyed his pleasures, his little secretary toiled late into the night. Cecil was a widower with two children. Some considered him a mere drudge—but that was an underestimation. The younger son of the great Burghley was fond of gambling and had indulged in some famous love affairs.[5]

Under James, however, Cecil's time for private pleasure vanished. He was burdened with all the worries of the realm. At the same time, he was uncomfortably aware that his position was resented; he himself, hated. His presence and diligence kept Francis Bacon from rising, held the schemes of the intriguing earl of Southampton in check, and even provided an unwelcome, though unstated, discipline upon the king.

When Cecil first discovered the Gunpowder Plot remains one of the many secrets of history. All that appears clear in retrospect is that it came to his attention at a time when James was confronted by an angry Parliament and a divided realm and when Cecil badly needed a means to restore the credit, as well as the situation, of the king.


The plot began with Robert Catesby and Thomas Percy, two relatively poor gentlemen related to illustrious families, and broadened to include Thomas Winter and John Wright. The gentlemen believed they needed someone who knew about explosives, who was able to keep a secret, who was sympathetic to their cause, and whose courage was established. He proved to be Guy Fawkes. Which of the group first conceived of the idea of blowing up Parliament, with the king, the ministers, the lords, and their retainers, remains uncertain.[6]

But it is known the conspirators could not keep a secret. They informed the Jesuits through the confidential channels of the confessional. The provincial of the order in England, Father Garnett—one of the most closely watched men in the realm—sent the news to the Vatican and asked for advice. In response, he was told to lay low, to play dumb.

The conspirators rented a house next to Parliament and began tunneling. For gentlemen of that age and time, the effort was a ghastly one for which they were totally unsuited. Weeks passed. They worked with inadequate tools and flagging strength against walls nine feet thick. Naturally, they made little headway at penetration, but their imaginations flourished. Candles flickered and every outside noise made them tremble; they imagined they heard unearthly sounds in the air about them as timbers creaked and the wind rustled. To their horror, water began to seep around their feet; their project appeared doomed by maddening physical details.

Their fears increased when they heard loud noises from the other side of the wall. Exploring these noises, they discovered they had been scratching at the wall at a point directly opposite some cellars under the House of Lords. The cellar nearest the conspirators was sublet from Mr. Whynniard—a minor court official—by Mrs. Bright, who sold coal.

Thomas Percy, identifying himself as an agent of his relative the earl of Northumberland—a great peer, but one under constant surveillance by the Crown—bought all Mrs. Bright's coal and also rented the cellar itself from her. Not an eyebrow was raised. The transaction was concluded with extraordinary dispatch. No questions were asked.

Certainly, the conspirators did not ask any questions. Somehow they got rid of the coal. They then mysteriously obtained and placed 36 barrels of gunpowder in the cellar. Where they obtained this large, lethal cargo seems, neither then nor later, to have become an issue. Then they placed large iron bars over the barrels, about 1,000 billets of wood over the bars, and 500 faggots over the billets—for concealment.

By that time other details of the plot had greatly expanded. At least thirteen men were informed of all its details, including Francis Tresham. The conspirators engaged in disputes over the fact that blowing up the court and Parliament would carry away a number of Catholics as well. Mysterious warnings were sent to persons whom one or another of the principals wanted to spare.

In addition the plotters had spent months on the developments they hoped to direct after their great blow. These contingency plans included kidnapping either the king's younger son, Prince Charles, and/or the Princess Elizabeth to place one or the other on the throne.

The matter of escape had not been overlooked. Horses were obtained and placed at strategic places along the line of flight; houses of refuge arranged. Tresham, however, believed that hints and mysterious warnings were not enough: his brother-in-law, Lord Monteagle, should be specifically spared. He was outvoted, since the plotters were afraid such an exception might reveal their entire plan.

Finally, the conspirators were ready—though barely in time. Parliament was due to open November 5, 1605, and that date was almost upon them. They decided to disarm suspicion by leaving the door of the cellar wide open, as though nothing within deserved concealment. Guy Fawkes —who looked as little like a merchant as a griffin—was chosen to stand guard. He strode slowly back and forth across the entrance with measured steps befitting the veteran of a thousand sentry posts, his fierce moustache bristling, his sword at an angle, his hat pulled low.

Meanwhile, Tresham sent a cryptic letter to his brother-in-law, Lord Monteagle. The peer received it while at dinner with friends. He read it with alarm and at once sent it to the earl of Salisbury, Robert Cecil himself.

Cecil read the letter and shook his head, saying that it baffled him— but that he knew of a greater intelligence who would, no doubt, be able to penetrate its strange meaning. He had the letter sent by messenger to the king.

James took the letter, sat down, and read. It said, in part:

> . . . Out of the love I bear to some of your friends, I have a care of your preservation, therefore I would advise you, as you tender your life, to devise some excuse, to shift off your attendance at this Parliament. For God and men have contrived to punish the wickedness of this time. . . . For though there is no appearance of any stir, yet I say they shall receive a terrible blow this Parliament, and yet they shall not see who hurts them .[7]

James started out of his chair, his eyes rolling, shouting "Treason!" and tore around the room. As he limped through his suite, he stopped suddenly. "Gunpowder," he muttered and sat down to read the letter again.[8]

They had tried to murder his father with gunpowder.

The king, aflame with excitement, but speaking with far more deliberation than usual, told Cecil his interpretation; and the little minister staggered as though stricken by His Majesty's powers of penetration.

Moving together in an enterprise of great importance, they called in the earl of Suffolk, the lord chamberlain, into whose care the houses of Parliament and other crown properties were entrusted.

Suffolk himself, leaving most of his attendants outside in the street, descended to the cellar. His eyes surveyed the great soaring mound of wood and faggots, enough to fuel an army, and asked the awesome guardian its purpose.

"Firewood," muttered Fawkes, and added the name of the earl of Northumberland.

Suffolk grunted and departed.

At midnight Sir Thomas Knevet and a group of strong deputies crept, in their stocking feet, down the stairs, entered the room with a rush, and grappled with Fawkes, who fought desperately. In his pockets they found matches; under the faggots, the powder and train. From then on, matters became spectacular.


The news of Parliament's deliverance and the escape of the king coursed through the City while bells tolled, bonfires were lit, and messengers ran in all directions. A guard was placed around the residence of the Spanish ambassador, and in the Tower the king's men bent eagerly over Guy Fawkes as he was racked.[9]

The veteran proved brave, and his confession was slow in coming. The government, meanwhile, issued circulars with the names of the principal conspirators—except for Tresham—listed. The king appeared before Parliament on November 9, 1605, and told the gathering how blessed it was in his escape. He took full credit, which Cecil repeatedly verified, for having saved all their lives by the shrewdness with which he had penetrated the letter to Lord Monteagle. He spoke at great length at having been spared, but added that had he not been saved, he would have preferred to die in such honorable company, rather than in "an alehouse, or a stew, or some such filthy place."[10] The king had a curious mind.

The nation was told, as were the Scots some years earlier, that it owed thanks to God for its deliverance; November 5th was declared a day of thanksgiving forever.

Meanwhile, Cecil's dragnet spread across the realm. The conspirators fled in various directions, but were quickly caught, killed, or captured—and the government prepared its case. Parliament, prorogued to reflect upon the mysterious ways of the Almighty and puny men alike, was to meet again in January after the holidays—and after the government had investigated and tried the plot.

The king, for his brave speeches, "is in terror," wrote the Venetian ambassador. "He does not appear nor does he take his meals in public."[11]

He huddled with his favorite Scots, remained in his apartments, and was often depressed. There was good reason. James had thought he had left peril of his life behind in Scotland; he was alarmed to discover that paradise held serpents.

It was the activity of the government under Cecil, however, that appeared most interesting. Fawkes and his associates were tried, after being exposed to the usual denunciations. The case against them was based largely on confessions extracted by torture. Oddly enough, many circumstantial matters of genuine interest, such as their source of illegal gunpowder and the like, were allowed to remain unexamined.

At the same time, investigations went forward to discover the extent of the Vatican involvement in the plot. On December 5, 1605, Sir Edward Coke, diligent on behalf of the Crown, intent upon examining the contents of Tresham's rooms, came upon a Vatican argument for "Equivocation." It dealt with the eternal problem of whether an honest man could lie in a just cause. The Vatican thought there were occasions when the truth could be legitimately denied.

The discovery came hard upon the heels of one conspirator's admission that he had revealed the plot to a priest during confession. That sent the hounds coursing after the larger game that interested Cecil and the Reform-minded members of the government.

While these grim investigations went forward, the court turned, during the Christmas and New Year's festivities, toward a social event it considered highly important: the marriage of the young earl of Essex and Lady Frances Howard.

The groom was only fourteen years old and somewhat immature even for his age. The bride was a year younger but her figure was already full and inviting. Their union brought together the heir of Elizabeth's famous favorite and the Howard family, which—under the cultivation of Lord Henry Howard, the earl of Northampton—was now ascending toward great power. James took a great interest in the event, believing that it strengthened his own supports. Ben Jonson,[12] then at the height of his powers, wrote the main masque, which was designed by Inigo Jones.

The ladies wore white velvet, with headdresses of heron feathers; the gentlemen were dressed in crimson satin; the bride danced with the twelve-year-old Prince Henry, among others. The bridegroom, who could not dance, watched from the sidelines.

Shortly after these festivities, the young earl was sent abroad to Europe to continue his studies under a traveling tutor and to mature. His bride, now the countess of Essex and a married woman, made her home with her great-uncle, the earl. In a very short time she became one of the reigning beauties of the court.

By January 21, 1606, when Parliament finally met, the government had finished its work with Fawkes & Company. It was cheated out of Tresham by tuberculosis, but his head was cut off his cadaver and publicly displayed as a traitor anyway. On the thirty-first of the month, Robert Winter, Grant, and Bates were executed in St. Paul's Churchyard. The next day Fawkes, Rokewood, and Keys were executed at Westminster before immense crowds, with excruciating cruelties.

Father Garnett, the head of the English Jesuits and an important object of the governmental dragnet, was arrested at Hindlip, where he and another priest named Oldcorne had hidden in a tiny closet for days in a watched house. Conveyed in a carriage to London at Cecil's special order, the defendants were questioned by the Privy Council.

James had forbidden torture for Garnett, but it was used on his servant, Owen. The torture was more effective than the experts intended: they nailed Owens' thumbs to a beam above his head for initial questioning. The first session elicited nothing in particular. But when they came to him for his second, Owens was dead. It was agreed that terror, in his case, had worked too well.

The trial of Father Garnett was mounted in March 1606 with the full trappings of a great occasion of state. The commissioners included five earls including Salisbury (Cecil), the lord chief justice, and other high dignitaries, with Sir Edward Coke heading the prosecution. King James, who was absorbed by the spectacle, sat behind a specially constructed lattice. The proceedings were dramatic and political.

Coke spoke about the vast, international conspiracies of the Jesuits and dwelt on previous plots. His voice rose with indignation as he reached the latest perfidy of the order, as exemplified by Garnett. "A false traitor against the most mighty and renowned King . . . whose virtues are rather with amazed silence to be wondered at, than able by any speech to be expressed." [13]

Behind his lattice the king heard oratory that exceeded any in his experience. It was the contention of the government that a plot against everything decent in England had been exposed. When Coke ended, the earl of Northampton picked up the theme and spoke interminably. He later issued an even longer pamphlet about the Gunpowder Plot and its implications, which joined dozens of others that appeared.

The king, with some assistance from his bishops, devised a new oath for Catholics as a result of his narrow escape. It embodied his theory that the pope could not be supreme over the king of England. He believed loyal Catholics could take such an oath; pamphlets poured from Rome denying that was possible and attempted to explain why the impossibility did not imply disloyalty.

The air was suddenly heavy with controversy between James and Rome, where before the Gunpowder Plot it had been warm and hopeful. The trial of Father Garnett ended, and the Jesuit went to his death on May 3, 1606, while the entire Vatican army of propagandists prepared their multitudes for news of a fresh martyr.

Shortly after Father Garnett's execution, all Europe was papered with tracts describing a miracle. One of the straws used on the scaffold, said the Vatican writers, was picked up by a spectator as a memento and was found to have, on its husk, a perfect image of the face of the new saint.

In England, however, other Catholics found the events surrounding the Gunpowder Plot to be less felicitous. The earl of Northumberland, whose only involvement was to have had a relative among the conspirators, was fined £30,000 and clapped into the Tower for a time. Lord Mordaunt, whose absence on the day of the planned explosion had been noted in Parliament, was fined £4,000 for the coincidence.

On a larger scale, however, the effects of the Gunpowder Plot upon the realm were awesome. The people of England, who had been muttering darkly against the king the previous autumn, were imbued with new patriotic sentiments. Parliament was so overtaken with relief that it voted new "supply"—money—to the monarch with unwonted alacrity, and the session was closed until fall. Even the king's course was altered, and his tendency to draw closer to Rome was deflected into channels of dispute.

Only a philosopher could have appreciated the many ironies involved or realized how adroitly Cecil had exploited the spontaneous activities of dangerous though amateurish plotters to realize opposite ends. At the moment, all that was clear was that the emergence of the Gunpowder Plot was oddly fortuitous, and its results constituted another of fortune's unexpected and inexplicable gifts to James Stuart.

# 28

"One day a great feast was held, and after dinner the representation of Solomon his Temple, and the coming of the Queen of Sheba was made before their Majesties. The lady who did play the Queen's part did carry precious gifts . . . but forgetting the steps arising to the canopy overset her caskets into his Danish Majesty's lap and fell at his feet, though I rather think it was in his face. Much was the hurry and confusion; cloths and napkins were at hand to make it clean. His Majesty then got up and would dance with the Queen of Sheba, but he fell down and humbled himself before her and was carried to an inner chamber and laid on a bed of state, which was not a little defiled with the presents of the Queen which had been bestowed on his garments, such as wine, cream, jelly, beverage, cakes, spices and other good matters. The entertainment went forward . . . now did appear Faith, Hope and Charity. Hope did assay to speak but wine had rendered her endeavors feeble . . . Faith left the Court in a staggering condition . . . Peace laid upon the pates of those who did oppose her coming."[1]

The occasion was only one of many held in celebration of the arrival of King Christian IV of Denmark, Queen Anne's brother. Christian was addicted to drink and found himself among congenial company. The court was merry, in its own fashion, during the summer of 1606.

Christian departed, and James went back to his eternal "progress" from one abode to another: from the environs of London to Oxford, from Oxford to Hampton Court, from Hampton Court back to Royston and from there to Huntington and then to Hinchinbrook and then to Ware. Each move required long trains of carts, carriages, and horsemen; each was marked by the abandonment of a vast amount of litter and debris from a fouled nest toward one newly cleaned.

The size and apparent importance of the court was somewhat deceptive. In reality, James had recreated the pattern of his rule in Scotland years earlier. A man of firm character and clear vision was tending to the realm, to the myriad but essential details of government, to the selection of persons for high office, to the collection of revenues, and to the expenses of the Crown.

In effect, Cecil—the earl of Salisbury—was the uncrowned and largely unseen ruler of England. All important appointments fell under his eyes, and he was careful to see that these did not flow from the court. One of these was the elevation of Sir Edward Coke, who had done such yeoman work for the Crown, to the position of chief justice of the Court of Common Pleas. Another was to hold Sir Francis Bacon at bay. The great polymath had issued another of his eloquent books—this time *On the Advancement of Learning*—but, like the king himself, his soaring words were belied by crawly behavior. Cecil neither trusted nor liked Bacon.

A more important matter was the Crown expense. Inflation elevated the price of all commodities and services, but the king's expense outstripped even this factor. James had an unfortunate and lifelong habit of lavishing costly pensions and gifts on men he liked. His numerous abodes with their individual servants, stables, animals, keepers, grounds, and furnishings—all kept in readiness for his arrival—cost a great deal of money. Queen Anne was extravagant. Young Prince Henry had his own court, and though he kept within his budget, it was an added expense. The debt of the Crown in 1606 was over £500,000—and Parliament's generosity in voting £250,000 was insufficient to cover it. Cecil raised some money for James by a forced loan at no interest—a procedure that had obvious limitations. More money was raised at 10 percent interest—another obviously risky proceeding. The earl of Dorset, Chancellor of the Exchequer, was understandably worried.

King James turned his attention toward the condition of religion in Scotland. He had harbored resentments about the ministers of the Kirk, though with poor grace, for many years. Now, convinced he had laid the basis for improvement at the Hampton Court Conference in England, he sent for eight of the leaders of the Kirk. The command was issued to James Melville himself, who had once called the king "God's silly vassal"; Melville's uncle Andrew; and six others.

Ostensibly, the king wanted to engage the clergy of Scotland in the same sort of discussion he held with the English bishops and dissident ministers at Hampton Court. But events in Scotland, set into motion at James's orders, belied such peaceful purposes.

Shortly after arriving in England in 1603, James had forbidden the General Assembly of the Church of Scotland to meet at all. In 1605 a handful dared to defy that order. James sent a favorite—the earl of Dunbar —north to punish those responsible. Sixteen of the Scots ministers were tried for treason. The trials were underway when Melville and his companions arrived, in response to James's commands, in England in September 1606.

The king met them as though seated on a mighty throne—as indeed he was. He was surrounded by his own newly created Scots bishops, his favorite Scots nobles, and members of the Scots Privy Council—many of whom were Catholic. He wanted to know their opinions on his supremacy and on the illegal General Assembly. Melville, who had to speak on his knees, defended his faith, the Kirk, and the assembly. He called the King's Advocate—the prosecutor—"the accuser of the Brethren." James caught at the phrase.

"What?" he cried. "Methinks he makes him the anti-Christ! By God, it is the Devil's name in Revelation! He has made the Devil of him!"[2] He swept out; the phrase had provided an excuse for which he had only waited.

Pending the king's decisions, Melville and the others were ordered to attend Church of England services. The English bishops, with rare malice, saw to it that they were confronted with music and elaborate rituals at the feast of St. Michael. James Melville, Andrew's nephew, was questioned regarding the supremacy issue—and asked whether it should go to the pope, the king, or the presbytery. He was firm in favor of the presbytery, and was told that was treason, according to the laws of England. "Not by ours," he replied.

He was mistaken; it was James's intention to have "one faith and one King." Out of those who had attended the forbidden assembly, sixteen lost their parishes and positions. Six were banished from the realm for life; eight others sent to remote exile in their own land. When the six who were to leave forever "went down to their boat at Leith in October 1606 . . . the people who crowded to see them go . . . heard them singing the Twenty-Third Psalm" as the ship vanished into the night.[3]

A month later, the leader of the Scots dissidents—Andrew Melville—was subjected to humiliations and hauled before the English Privy Council. There the archbishop of Canterbury, Bancroft, ordered him to kneel. He refused. Attendants were called to force him to his knees, but when they let go, he rose again. When Bancroft came close to a charge of treason in his statements regarding the Church of Scotland, Melville lost his temper. Turning on Bancroft, he seized the ornate lawn sleeves of the English prelate and shook them, shouting they were "Romish rags—and part of the Mark of the Beast."[4]

The Privy Councilors were astonished and half rose from their seats; Bancroft tried to pull himself free and the attendants came running. Melville had to be wrestled out of the chamber; his voice could be heard shouting in the corridors as he was led away. It was not long before he was in the Tower. Shortly afterward the king's bishops assumed the control of the Scots Kirk. James's victory seemed complete.

While James dug a pit for the Kirk of Scotland, the English Parliament reconvened in mid-November 1606. The king appeared, launched into another long criticism of those who had written the Petition of Grievances in the last session, and castigated the members at length because Scotland and England were not yet united. He swept away and left a great many men burning in anger behind him.

Members arose to say the Scots would descend from the north like locusts. The speeches grew so violent that Cecil persuaded the king to recess the gathering until the following February. The king was willing; he had begun to believe that the entire institution of a Parliament was a threat, as indeed it was, to his prerogatives.

In February 1607, when the debate resumed, his irritation increased. Sir Christopher Pigott rose to denounce all the Scots as "beggars, robbers and traitors." He reminded his countrymen that all the kings of Scotland had, in the past, been murdered by their subjects—an only slight exaggeration. He compared the status of a Scotsman to an Englishman as resembling that between a criminal and a judge. James was informed immediately and wanted Pigott tried for treason. Cecil was forced to shuffle matters and the outspoken member was persuaded, through various expedients, off the center of the stage.

Sir Nicholas Fuller, a lawyer who had turned, through defending dissident ministers, into a fervent Puritan of a sort now beginning to arise, took up the argument. He compared the Scots to starving cattle, avid to feed upon the rich lands of England. He accused them of crowding into English schools and elbowing aside English students. He also put his finger on a fallacy in James's argument that since the king was a Scot, all Scots could become English. Suppose, he wanted to know, some future sovereign came from Spain? Could England then expect all Spaniards to claim citizenship in England?

James, drawn toward these debates by an incurable belief that his own persuasions were better than any other man's, appeared and orated again —to no avail. Parliament was going into the subject hair by hair and would not be hurried. The matter dragged.

To take the king's mind off this vexation and also to maintain his ascendancy, Cecil offered James the magnificent palace of Theobalds. The king was delighted; it was the mansion he admired above all. He gave Cecil a royal palace at Hartfield and properties spread over twelve counties in exchange.

Both men were pleased with the transaction, and on May 27, 1607, Cecil entertained the king at Theobalds for the last time. The occasion was marked by another masque created by Jonson. It was more dignified than those the court usually watched, but then, so was Cecil.

The diminutive secretary then turned toward the construction of a final great mansion for himself. Building and improving properties was one of his delights. He was interested in every aspect of architecture and art, as well as real property and its values. From 1607 onward the earl of Salisbury was engrossed, in those odd moments when the state did not engage him, with architects, bricklayers, artisans, and craftsmen of all sorts. He planned the most magnificent home of his age; it was a project that apparently took him out of himself and his cares.

These increased at almost the same moment he traded Theobalds to the king. The House of Commons brought up the matter of the High Commission. Established by Elizabeth, it had been running roughshod for a long time, but James had revived its energies when it had appeared to have outlasted its purpose.

The issue spilled from Commons to the Court of Common Pleas, where Sir Edward Coke sat as chief justice. Coke was the most learned lawyer and perhaps the most formidable personality in England. Tall, reasonably good-looking, gifted with eloquence, he worshipped the Common—or national—law of the realm. Once the matter of the High Commission reached him, he dominated his associate judges into considering its powers. Coke's attitude was very clear: he did not believe the courts of any church, under whatever name, should have greater powers than the common courts of the realm. He ruled, in fact, that only Parliament could approve the commission's orders.[5]

Shortly after that ominous ruling, Coke came into conflict with the High Commission over the case of Sir Nicholas Fuller—a lawyer who had come to believe, and who loudly proclaimed, that the High Commission was misusing powers to which it was not entitled. Fuller cited Beale, the Magna Carta, the powers of Parliament, the inherent right of men not to be forced to testify against themselves, and other reasons that he distributed in Commons, in common law courts, in defending clients, in obtaining prohibitions against the commission, and everywhere else. The commission arrested him for "schism and erroneous opinions." Fuller appealed to the Court of Common Law—to Coke.

The chief justice decided to tread lightly. After mulling the matter with eleven other judges, he finally let the commission have its way because it was entitled to sentence heretics. But he let the issue of its other powers remain unconfirmed.[6] The king was not appeased. His nostrils warned him of danger in the air. He told Cecil that "if ecclesiastical dignity . . . be turned into contempt . . . the kings thereof shall not prosper in their government."

As a child of the Scots revolution, he knew what could happen when subjects overruled men the king had placed in authority. To him it was very clear. No bishops; no king.


The king's attention was diverted at a tourney. One of the horses fell and its rider was injured. The king drew near and recognized a former page from his court in Scotland, Robin Ker. Ker had grown into young manhood. The king looked at bright blue eyes, wavy auburn hair, a perfect complexion, and a flashing smile that appeared despite a broken leg. James asked a few questions and was answered in Scots as broad as his own. He was enchanted and ordered the young man carried to the royal apartments.

A number of persons ran to tell Philip Herbert, later the earl of Montgomery, that the king had found a new interest. Herbert shrugged; his was a position easily obtained but not altogether pleasant to keep. Meanwhile, the king gave orders that nobody but himself and the physicians were to visit the injured object of his attention.

"He is a Scot lad," he said, "who hath much need of better language."[7] He visited the invalid's room often, in an eerie and distorted repetition of how his own mother had once visited Lord Darnley.

By the time the young invalid was able to get about again, the court was amused to learn the king had acquired a new Gentleman of the Bedchamber. "The Prince leaneth on his arm, pinches his cheek, smooths his ruffled garments, and when he looketh . . . directeth his discourse to divers others. This young man doth much direct all art and device; he hath changed his tailors and tiremen many times, and all to please our Prince, who laugheth at the long grown fashion of our courtiers and wisheth for change every day."[8]

Among other changes the young Scot experienced was one of name: Robin Ker became Robert Carr—a switch that convinced many Englishmen he came of no particular background. That was not true; he was a younger son of the laird.[9]

Carr's ascendancy came with a rush, however, for which the English were not prepared. They knew the king's leaning toward handsome young men and were not naïve about its meaning. But James had kept his tendencies under at least quasi-control for many years and had not succumbed completely to his inclinations since the days of Esmé Stuart. Since then he had married and fathered three living children and had played the role of family man with some success. Suddenly, at the age of forty-one, he relapsed completely; openly succumbed to homosexuality and fell in love with a nineteen-year-old youth of no great intelligence.

News of the king's infatuation reached Cecil at once. The secretary—never without resources—searched among his papers for some counter pawn and emerged, with admirable speed, with Thomas Overbury.

Overbury was an honor graduate from Queen's College, Oxford, and had studied for law at Middle Temple. He came from a landed and respectable family in Gloucester, where his father was a judge. When and how he became one of Cecil's agents was the secretary's secret.

In 1601 at the age of twenty, Overbury appeared in Edinburgh, ostensibly to make friends at James's court on the eve of his succession to the throne of England. At that time, Overbury made many acquaintances, was kind to the young twelve-year-old page Robin Ker, and apparently kept that friendship alive in later years. Later Overbury was sent to France and the Low Countries by Cecil for purposes that remain hidden. He appeared at the English court soon after Robert Carr was raised by the king.

Carr was delighted. His old friend was just the man to assist him. James was teaching Carr the intricacies of Latin and wanted to make a learned man of him. Overbury was already learned; he became the favorite's secretary and private mentor. Cecil relaxed.

In April 1608 the earl of Dorset—Shakespeare's model of the fatuous Polonius—rose shakily to his feet in the course of a trial being held before the Privy Council and confronted a prisoner. The earl fumbled inside his robes for some papers, glared at the accused, shouted, "Here is this that will strike you dead," staggered back, and fell dead himself.

That was how Cecil inherited, in addition to his other tasks, the post of lord treasurer of England.

Around England the international situation, unhinged by James's hasty peace with Spain, slowly settled into new forms. The Dutch had fought Spain to a stalemate. But before a treaty could be signed, the French and the English had to approve the details, since they had been involved both strategically and financially in the long struggle.

James was interested only in peace, but Cecil bargained for England. The Dutch proposed a three-nation alliance against Spain; a sort of truncated new Protestant League. The king of England was not interested in that. In fact, his High Commission was forcing a steady trickle of Calvinists, now identified in England as Puritans, out of the country. These refugees joined the stream of English Catholics who fled numerous disabilities placed upon them.

Such emigration is only an indicator of domestic discontent; it does not represent its actual extent. Many persons might want to leave an unhappy country, but cannot for reasons of poverty, lack of courage, family ties, or a tangle of similar causes. The fact was, however, that people fled James's England. The land that had once harbored refugees from Europe was now sending Europe its own.

These developments did not concern the king. He was more interested in some Vatican arguments issued in the name of Cardinal Bellarmine, a great Vatican scholar and polemicist against the oath that James was forcing upon English Catholics. Nothing touched the king of England more quickly than intellectual debate: he seemed to confuse words with reality and argument with action.

Commandeering the services of some clerics whose names were not acknowledged, James issued a thunderous tract, *An Apology in Reply to Bellarmine,* in early 1608. The king's entourage marveled at the ease with which he created this effort and he was immensely proud himself: several editions were printed for distribution around Europe.

Another important James project was the matter of an estate for his new favorite, Sir Robert Carr. That young man had introduced his new secretary to the sovereign. In short order, the smiling secretary became Sir Thomas Overbury. The two made a formidable combination; Overbury was able to screen innumerable matters of business that Carr could bring to the attention of the king. The partners were soon thriving, but James liked to be more than generous.

Cecil, tireless and apparently omniscient, learned of the king's latest minor worry from Overbury and had his experts undergo a search. They returned with the information that Sir Walter Raleigh's only remaining estate—the manor of Sherborne—by a technicality, could be regained by the Crown. The king was pleased and ordered that proceedings be started.

Cecil was, in all truth, infinitely resourceful. As lord treasurer of the realm in addition to being its spymaster, secretary, and secret ruler, he had the responsibility of saving James, in spite of himself, from bankruptcy. The debt of the Crown had soared to nearly £600,000. The secretary increased the sale of Crown lands and realized over £400,000 by that step.

Next he turned toward the matter of taxes. A favorable court ruling enabled him to levy duties on all goods flowing into England—but he was too shrewd to do that by fiat. Instead he held a series of conferences with the business community and lowered some duties while raising others. By that means he increased the Crown revenues by over £100,000 a year.

Cecil was working against time and attempting to maintain the Crown until 1610. In that year the "supply" voted by Parliament would be exhausted and the subject could be raised again. Cecil decided to form a great contract, by which Commons would have many of its grievances recognized and reformed, and the king would receive enough to live in proper style.

These labors took their toll. Cecil had worked incredibly for many long years, beginning when he was very young. Now his hair turned prematurely, and the small, thin figure seemed careworn. Yet he plunged into his own affairs as though planning to live forever; his great new mansion began to take expensive and elaborate form.

In October 1608 the courts ruled the Crown could take Sherborne away from Raleigh. The news sent a wave of indignation through the land; the imprisoned hero had outlasted his period of disgrace and had been steadily climbing back to popularity. Many prominent persons visited him in his comfortable Tower apartment; his work on the *History of the World* had drawn the attention of scholars and intellectuals. Prince Henry—a manly, athletic youth attracting general admiration—was said to have said, "Only my father could keep such a bird in a cage."[10]

Lady Raleigh, it was said, appeared at court and threw herself at the king's feet to beg for the estate, but James muttered, "I maun have it; I maun have it for Carr," and turned away.[11]

The king had need of comfort that season. Cardinal Ballarmine, joined by the redoubtable Father Parson, answered his *Apology* with a brilliant salvo that made the king's effort appear juvenile. James was appalled. He had never before been addressed in such elegantly learned invective. His resentment was made keener by the fact that the Vatican reprinted a groveling letter he had written years before and sent to the Vatican by Sir John Elphinstone.

The letter stung fiercely. It was picked up with delight by the Catholics of England and struck the Crown defenders dumb. No possible answer seemed available, but James turned savagely on Elphinstone, who had been proudly living under his new title of Lord Balmerino. He had been tricked, said the king. His ambassador had added words he had not dictated nor read. Pressure was applied, and Balmerino had to go to his knees before the world and admit he was a slave by testifying the king's charge was true.

Balmerino was then sent to the Privy Council where Cecil and others went through a sad charade of questioning, while the Scotsman repeated his degradation. James was jubilant; he genuinely believed he had fooled the world. He called his favorite clergymen around him, held secretaries in long labors, assigned research tasks to teams, and threw himself into the struggle to reply to critics that now seemed to flower from every churchbush in Catholic Europe. His ego was like jelly—easily penetrated, but self-healing.

A word war with the Vatican was only one sector of James's intellectual concerns, however. Another was the matter of the High Commission. His bishops—more than any other group—represented his realm to James. And despite the fact that Chief Justice Coke and the other judges of the Courts of Common Law knew His Majesty was behind his High Commission, the same Courts of Common Law judges kept issuing "prohibitions" against the High Commission's rulings, fines, imprisonments, and even procedures.

The king called for conferences, events he considered supreme actions, at which all issues would be resolved. The Privy Councillors attended; the bishops spoke eloquently. The judges of the Court of Common Law appeared impressed and convinced—but their prohibitions continued.

In February 1609 Chief Justice Coke and some others were called to Whitehall to rehash the issues. The scene was impressive. King James was there with jewels gleaming from his hat and sparkling on his clothes; the Privy Council was seated in stern dignity. The icily competent archbishop of Canterbury, Bancroft, and his lesser bishops were all assembled.

The archbishop spoke about the king and his powers. All judges, being only representatives of the king, said he, could be overruled in their judgments since their judgments were only extensions of his. Coke disagreed. The king, he said, could not intervene in a court. He then quoted the Magna Carta, which—he said—gave the Courts of Common Law the right to provide justice "from the highest to the lowest."

The king reacted like a man on a hot stove. The judges were like Papists, he shouted, who quoted Scriptures to suit their own purposes. If he chose, he could sit on the bench himself; he had reason and therefore he could judge. Coke demurred. The king could reason, but he did not know the law; the king "ought not to be below any man, but under God and the law."

At that James flew into a genuine rage. He shook his fist at Coke and some thought he would strike him. The chief justice threw himself on the floor and begged to be pardoned if his zeal had carried him too far.[12]

James had reason to be angry. The issue he thought buried forever, banished from Scotland in the dark of night, immured in the Tower with Andrew Melville, burned in the books of Buchanan, had arisen inside the very precincts of his power in England. His mother, Mary Stuart, had argued the position he now adopted, that the sovereign was above the law. But it was clear England would not accept that reasoning from him anymore than it had from his mother.

Yet he was in no remote realm where armed men could be summoned to stop the argument. England and the world were far more civilized than they had been in Mary Stuart's time or in Elizabeth Tudor's heyday. The anger, the raised fist, the shouts of treason dithered into apologies and explanations and polite interventions. The chief justice of England left, all humility; the bishops congratulated the king on his perceptions; the Privy Councillors added their praises; the conference ended.

Yet nothing had ended. The High Commission continued to haul men before it, and the Courts of Common Law continued to issue prohibitions against its proceedings, penalties, and procedures. The printing presses continued to roll, and the ranks of those who called themselves Puritans were joined by utterly nonreligious men who simply detested the idea of an ecclesiastical High Commission ruling over their minds.

In Europe the Dutch won nine United Provinces from the grasp of Spain. A twelve year's truce was signed, guaranteed by Henry IV of France and the Emperor Rudolf II of Germany. Cecil managed, finally, to insert a guarantee from England, but the Dutch were no longer friends with the king of England. They gave refuge to the Separatists pursued by the High Commission; some of them arrived and formed a colony at Delft. They numbered thousands, but James was indifferent.

The king thought in large terms, sweeping measures, vast projects. He had wanted, a few years earlier, to apply his ecclesiastical wisdom to the Irish and had been disappointed to discover legal impediments prevented him from forcing religious change upon them. The earls of Tyrone and Tyrconnel, powers in Ulster, finally fled and sought help from Spain. That help was not forthcoming. England, at least for the moment, was master of Ulster as well as the rest of the island.

It was suggested that territories be divided among the Irish and the English who had fought in the area. James decided the English and Scots should have these lands, and the Irish could be contented with what remained. This colonial attitude, which sowed the seeds of hatred and division for centuries to come, was among James's many accomplishments.

Meanwhile, he enjoyed his court, and Carr. His new favorite was perfect for him in every way—including a capacity for bisexuality. James liked men who liked women; he was not jealous of their heterosexual affairs. On the contrary, he enjoyed hearing details; they seemed to help convince him of women's inferiority.

Carr's eye had fallen, naturally enough, upon the beauteous countess of Essex. Unfortunately, she was the mistress of Prince Henry. Few men would have ventured into competition with the heir to the throne, but Carr's opinion of himself had risen with his position.

The prince was disgusted to learn that the beautiful young countess was receptive to the favorite. An athletic, serious young man, he had gradually realized his father's nature with inner loathing. Their relations were amiable enough on the surface, but James did not much care for this masculine offspring who was not overfond of books, who was reserved, who studied the use of weapons and the arts of war. They were poles apart; the distance between them was greater even than most sovereigns maintained toward their "rising suns."

A courtier, unaware that the countess had shifted her favors, seeking to gain favor with Prince Henry, handed him a glove Lady Frances had dropped. He thought the prince might want to return it personally. "Why should I be bothered about a glove stretched by another?" the prince asked sharply.

As usual, there was more to the moves and shifts at court than the eye could follow. The countess of Essex—"little Fanny Howard"—lived with her great-uncle, the earl of Northampton. The earl wanted the controls of state, the controls handled so long and so firmly by Cecil. Where Cecil had placed Overbury beside Carr, the earl had put forward his own pawn: his great-niece, the countess. She smiled, Carr moved forward, and all the Howards watched closely.

While these intensely personal maneuvers were underway at court, Cecil was concerned with foreign matters. The secretary watched the creation of a Protestant Union of German princes under King Christian IV of Denmark and Frederick IV, the elector of the Palatinate. In response, a Catholic League formed under Maximilian, the duke of Bavaria.

To King James these maneuvers seemed of less importance than his endless pamphlets against the Vatican. He sent a stream of agents over Europe to suppress replies to his own diatribes. The king, when he chose to move on foreign affairs, moved clumsily. Early in 1609 he demanded the Dutch stop fishing in English waters. That step, hastily taken, did not help his relations with a growing commercial competitor.

Then in March 1609 the duke of Cleves died, leaving no heir and many claimants. That situation threatened to set the German Protestant Union against the Catholic League. Henry IV was very active inside this issue. James was urged to join the Protestant side, but he wanted only peace, blessed peace. Cecil, nevertheless, was pulled into the situation because England's assistance was needed to assist the Reform claimants.

At the same time, Henry IV of France was amazingly active on a number of related issues. Henry was involved in the discussions of German territory, the discussions regarding fishing rights—and renewed his discussions of the large debt France owed England. The mention of possible money brought James to attention, and Cecil was ordered to negotiate.

Again, all was not as it seemed. The king of France was also dealing with Venice. He talked in muffled tones to the Dutch. He was in touch with the Protestant Union in Germany.

Henry IV was, in fact, creating a web against Spain and doing it without a sound. He had studied James with some bafflement for a number of years. The combination of benevolent words and almost total passivity regarding the interests of England had, for a long time, seemed too unreal to be credited. Finally, however, the king of France realized that James was interested only in money for his comforts and was against war because it required more energy and courage than he possessed. It would be necessary, therefore, to trap the king of England, to place him in a position where events would govern his actions—rather than attempt to gain his active alliance. Henry IV was busy, in 1609, arranging such events.

King James was happy with Carr. The favorite accepted his rise gracefully; he and his secretary, Sir Thomas Overbury, were prospering beyond their dreams and their world seemed very bright.

It was a period when offering costly bribes to officials was taken for granted; Carr and Overbury were besieged. Yet Carr was careful not to inflate his own importance beyond the king's patience. He developed the habit of telling the king about every present and every suitor. James's trust increased as Carr's prosperity grew large.

Sir Thomas Overbury's role was as behind-the-scenes adviser, general factotum and secretary, confidant and friend. When Carr pursued the beauteous young countess of Essex, it was Overbury who wrote clever little notes that were folded into hearts and sent quietly through the corridors; Overbury who composed the witty yet ardent poems then considered essential in courtship.

Yet the Howards did not like Sir Thomas. They were too well aware that what Overbury knew, Cecil knew, and they whispered against the favorite's secretary. The earl of Northampton, whose cringing before the king contrasted with his lofty attitude toward upstarts, newcomers to the nobility, and ordinary people, called Overbury "the Scab."

The young countess, busy in bringing Carr close, was also disdainful of Overbury, but was willing to bide her time—until her young husband suddenly returned from his long sojourn abroad. His return was watched with glee by many malicious eyes; the eighteen-year-old countess was aghast. She had almost forgotten about him.

The earl was tall, serious, polished after tasting the pleasures of travel, and obviously mature at nineteen. It was common knowledge that he had been too young to consummate his marriage when it took place in late 1605; many malicious observers wondered whether he had heard that substitutes had happily appeared. It was soon clear the earl did not know—or chose not to know. He was anxious to claim his bride. The countess screamed. "To be carried by him into the country would," she cried, "be an insufferable torment."[13]

She turned toward Carr, but he was away from court, hunting at one of innumerable sylvan hideouts with the king. Her great-uncle, the earl of Northampton, took some curious measures. He introduced her to a Mrs. Anne Turner, a familiar figure on certain court levels. Mrs. Turner was a widow and the mistress of Sir Arthur Mainwaring, who was at Prince Henry's court. She was a dressmaker and a clever one—for she worked with Inigo Jones in designing costumes for his masques. She was also inventive: she had compounded, or said she had, a new yellow starch that lifted and made stiff the fashionable ruffs of the day. These creations became a fad; yellow became a reigning color.

Northampton's purpose in putting his great-niece together with Mrs. Turner was mysterious. The widow was pretty, "of fair visage for outward behavior, but . . . little less than a flat bawd." She was a procuress, a secret Catholic, and a spy for Northampton and worked closely with many figures on the edge of London's shuddery underworld. One was Dr. Simon Forman, an astrologist, a clairvoyant, a mixer of elixirs and, sometimes, poisons. Forman and Mrs. Turner were very close and often combined their talents on behalf of wealthy court clients.

Perhaps it was a coincidence that the young earl of Essex fell suddenly and dangerously ill before he could carry his young countess off to his country estate in Staffordshire.


Sir Edward Coke examined the words of the Act of Supremacy that had established the High Commission. It gave the church court the right to try cases of heresies, schisms and . . . enormities. Coke's attention fastened on the word *enormities*. He decided an offense had to be enormous before the commission's jurisdiction applied.[14] That pulled a linchpin out of the entire structure of the commission and made it possible to define almost any offense as relatively minor—and therefore beneath the commission's powers. Enormities, after all, are not common.

A stream of prohibitions broke loose. Coke himself, obsessed, authored a stream of arguments against the commission, using not only the Magna Carta but bones of precedents exhumed from the deepest of legal cemeteries; other judges of the Courts of Common Law followed suit and lawyers did the same. The Puritans rained pamphlets; the result was that a genuine body of literature that ranged from the heights of scholarship to the depths of propaganda inundated the realm.

One such book, composed from the king's viewpoint, sponsored by the archbishop of Canterbury, was a law dictionary called *The Interpreter*. It stated that James was an absolute king—and therefore above the law. It circulated among the king's supporters and created great indignation elsewhere.

Cecil, however, was intent upon money. He had reduced James's debts, created a budget, and narrowed the king's needs. He appeared before Commons and spoke in very conciliatory terms, pleading that "they not wreck the Ship of State at the entrance of the harbor." Trained in Elizabeth's school, Cecil put the needs of the king first—and the grievances of Commons second. That was unfortunate, but the response to his Great Contract was initially very favorable. The Commons wanted to examine its details, but its clarity and order appealed to the business instincts of many members.

On March 21, 1610, the king appeared before Parliament. He had many things to say. He told them again that kings were gods and could do as they pleased. Fortunately, he was a good king and would obey the laws he made. He deplored the rise of prohibitions against the High Commission and called for restraint. That led him, by association, to the subject of economizing. Restraints should be a general practice. He continued in this vein for some time, in the sort of soliloquizing schoolteachers allow themselves before their captives, and departed—leaving behind a general feeling of disgust.

In that mood, Commons turned toward its multiple grievances against the Crown. Because they were stated in specifics, later observers seem to believe that was all the members were concerned about. The facts were far more serious. The activities of the High Commission and attempts to force all Englishmen into an iron ecclesiastical mold along distastefully Catholic lines had created simmering resentments. Commons gave some indication of its temper when it discussed *The Interpreter*—the legal dictionary written by a Cambridge University professor. Declaring its identification of the monarchy with total power beyond the law to be contrary to the Magna Carta and the rights of Englishmen, the House had the book burned by the common hangman and banned from the realm.

The right of the king to tax imports, known as "impositions"—a word that acquired, from this argument, a new meaning—was also dragged out, stamped upon, discussed, and denied. The king reappeared in May 1610 to say the courts had approved this right and angrily declared other kings collected taxes without worrying about Parliaments. He warned Commons not to meddle with his prerogatives. That started a new fire; the members turned toward a definition of prerogatives. Cecil groaned inwardly, but his hopes were still high. Discreet soundings convinced him the Parliament believed it was merely laying the groundwork for a genuine understanding. If its grievances were relieved, the king could have his money.

In Europe, King Henry IV of France signed a treaty with the Protestant Union and prepared to intervene in German affairs. The disputed dominions of the dead duke of Cleves were between the Netherlands, the Rhine, and Germany. Henry IV massed 30,000 men to march against Julier, another 14,000 to combine with the duke of Savoy against Milan, and a third 25,000 near the Pyrenees to invade Spain.

The French king was going to separate the Hapsburgs and complete the reduction of Spain that James I had left uncompleted. He had the support of the Dutch, the Danes, and the Protestant princes of Germany and was confident that England would either join his effort or lose every ally and all standing in the world.

Before leaving Paris, the king of France had his second wife, Marie de Médicis, daughter of the grand duke of Tuscany, declared regent, and named a council to advise her. Before taking that step, he also had Marie crowned at the abbey church of St. Denis on May 13, 1610. Due to join his northern army on May 19, Henry passed through the streets of Paris on the afternoon of May 14, 1610, to pay a visit to the duke of Sully, who was indisposed. In the Rue de la Ferronière some carts blocked his passage. The king's carriage was briefly halted, and a man named François Ravaillac— a fanatic Catholic—jumped up on the wheel of the royal coach and struck at the king. "I am wounded," Henry cried, and the assassin struck again. The second blow penetrated his heart, and Henry IV, with all his plans and hopes, died immediately.

While all Catholic Europe rejoiced at the demolition of the leader of its enemies, King James decided the time was appropriate to have Prince Henry named Prince of Wales.

Cecil was attempting to persuade Parliament to accept the Great Contract and to believe the sovereign would stay within a generous budget when all London broke out in a rash of fetes, celebrations, masques, banquets, dances, plays, gifts, and speeches.

Taking brisk advantage of the season and the presence of so many from court, Ben Jonson staged *The Alchemist.* He had a wonderful time abusing scholarly quacks of all sorts. In one scene Sir Epicure Mammon gloated to the audience over his discovery of how to make gold out of all base metals.

"This night," he said rubbing his hands, "I'll change all that is metal in my home to gold, and early in the morning will I send to all the plumbers and the pewterers, and buy their tin and lead up, and to Lothbury for all the copper. I'll purchase Devonshire and Cornwall and make them into perfect Indies. I mean to have a list of wives and concubines equal with Solomon, who had the stone elixir alike with me. I will make me a back, with the elixir, that shall be as tough as Hercules, to encounter fifty a night."

It was, from all accounts, a time of merriment. England had grown fond of Prince Henry, whose interests promised a vigorous future for the realm; few begrudged him honors.

Parliament, however, was not diverted from its complaints against the prince's father, King James. The festivities had hardly died away when, in July 1610, a delegation presented him a list of grievances, laboriously scrawled by clerks on a single immense scroll. James unrolled it with a sentiment that approached awe; his irrepressible wit broke through the solemnity of the moment. The complaint was so long, said his Majesty, that he might use it as a tapestry.

Later he sent Commons a series of replies, almost item by item, regarding its desires. He gave way on many minor matters, but held fast on the Church. Yet it was the Church and the High Commission, which James used to hammer the Church into conformity, that was the issue that loomed above all others. Commons recessed for the summer with both parties beginning to have second thoughts.

The king had grown into the habit of giving his courtiers drafts upon the Treasury for money. During the summer of 1610 one such draft reached Cecil. It was for £10,000. The secretary-treasurer had begun to suspect the king did not realize the size of such a sum. To make sure, he had the gold coins brought to the palace and stacked, in an immense, glittering array upon a table. Then he escorted the king to the room. James was transfixed, astonished. He wanted to know whose money it was, and Cecil explained it was his, but he had given it away. James spread himself across it with both arms, shouting he was being deceived, and "scrabbled out two or three hundred coins," saying that was enough; he would keep the rest.[15]

Cecil departed softly, but he did not smile. He had penetrated a mind that was, beneath a veneer of learning forced upon it, childlike and immature. The king, later, was similarly displeased. It seemed to him he had not been treated with sufficient respect; he feared the story would go the rounds and he would appear ridiculous.

The young earl of Essex recovered from his illness and carried his countess off to Chartley, in Staffordshire. She went unwillingly, and later

he said he received "not so kind a glance as she would throw to a dog." Once
they were inside the huge country manor, the beauty established herself as
impregnable. She refused to see her husband except at meals, surrounded
herself with servants, never emerged from her apartment except at night.
The earl stormed and shouted, pleaded, sought to break through her barricades in vain.

She wrote letters back to London, including many to Mrs. Turner and
to Simon Forman, the physician. They were as candid as the confessional:
". . . he hath not lain with me," she wrote, "and I would not suffer him to
use me. My father and mother are angry but I had rather die a thousand
deaths over, for besides the suffering I shall lose his [Carr's] love if I lie with
him. . . ."[16]

She asked Forman for "philters" to reduce her husband's "lusty"
spirit. Unfortunately, the physician himself suddenly died. His wife—a pale,
depressed, mouselike creature—carefully went through all the forbidden
books and objects, letters and mementos, the instruments of magic and the
sexual illustrations and statuettes, the love elixirs and the aphrodisiacs, the
locked boxes and the concealed records and put them carefully away.


Queen Anne—Danish Anna—was walking in the palace gardens with
her ladies when two men appeared. They were Sir Robert Carr and Sir
Thomas Overbury, deep in conversation.

"There goes the king's keeper," the queen said bitterly, "and the keeper
of the king's keeper."

Her voice carried, and Overbury looked toward them and laughed
derisively. He was very sure of himself.

Cecil himself was not so sure. During the summer the king's speeches
and attitudes were discussed with supporters, friends, and neighbors by the
members of Commons; they returned to a renewed session in October 1610
less inclined to help the king. Nevertheless, the Great Contract terms had
been drawn and Commons expected it to go through. It was the king himself
who decided against it.

He had been listening to his courtiers, including Sir Robert Carr, who
expressed great indignation that so great a monarch could be hindered by
so many small men. Sir Edward Coke and others had raised a new issue that
struck the king very hard: proclamations. James enjoyed making proclamations; he was now told he could not make any laws in that manner—and
that henceforth his proclamations could only remind the realm of existing
law.

Parliament gathered in October 1610 and listened while a letter from
the king was read aloud. It gave way a little, but not very far. Members rose

to call for greater concessions. In response, James informed Commons it must give him all the money he needed to pay his debts at once and increased the amount formerly asked.

Angry debate arose, and the festering subject of the king's Scots favorites emerged into the open. The words were so angry that rumors reached the court that Commons wanted to send all Scotsmen home. Carr, alarmed, carried this news to the king. James wrote Cecil an angry diatribe, blaming the secretary for everything, calling his attention to the fact he had been patient for seven long years. The results were "more disgraces, censures and ignominies than any Prince did endure." Then he grew bitter. He had "followeth your Lordship's advice in having patience, hoping for better issue. . . . [but] He cannot have assinine patience. . . ."[17] Only a House of Hell, James wrote angrily, would treat him the way Commons had.

Cecil read these reproaches and watched the king lose his temper with great disappointment. He thought he had come very close to closing the gap. In reality, a gulf yawned that money could not span. The king and his bishops were caught in a dream of a past that had never existed, but which they insisted upon creating. The Crown and Commons were talking past one another; the people were disturbed and divided, extremists were increasing in numbers, and a malaise spread through the land. Bancroft, the archbishop of Canterbury, died almost unnoticed under the lowering clouds.

Cecil called in architects and began to plan an elaborate tomb, a monument to himself for his descendants. His health was bad, but not bad enough for such a step. Perhaps he had premonitions.

In January 1611 the king abruptly dissolved Parliament. He wanted to send a number of the members of Commons to the Tower and was barely dissuaded. Elizabeth had done it; why should not he? It was difficult to explain that Elizabeth had been loved, and he was not.

He blamed Cecil for all his troubles. The court, which hated the secretary, agreed with one voice. Sir Robert Carr, reigning gloriously as the king's lover, led the pack. Sir Thomas Overbury showed signs he would also like to switch, but Overbury had no patron to whom to switch. The name Scab clung to him; the earl of Northampton hoped to become the next secret ruler of the realm—and he had no plans for the favorite's favorite.

In February 1611, in an act of total defiance, James distributed £34,000 among six Scots courtiers. A month later, he made Carr an English peer with the title of Viscount Rochester. That placed a Scot in the English House of Lords. The king, however, was not finished. He gave Rochester the royal grant of the castle in that city. He made him keeper of Westminster. He placed him on the Privy Council. He also made him a Knight of the Garter—an honor Elizabeth and all England kept rare and that he himself did not receive for many long years as king of Scotland and heir to his predecessor.

The king also appointed George Abbott, formerly the bishop of London, new archbishop of Canterbury. His selection was a surprise; Abbott was weak and inexperienced. James, however, treasured such defects; he believed he could provide all the counsel the archbishop needed.

It was obvious that a shift in power was underway, directed from the court. Cecil, however, was a hard man to displace. He answered the king's reproaches with dignity, but managed to overcome them and pursued the high state business for which time, training, and natural talent had equipped him.

The death of Henry IV dramatically changed the international situation. His widow was now dowager queen and regent of France and ruled in the name of the nine-year-old King Louis XIII. Ardently Catholic, long disappointed because her husband had not approved a marriage between their children and the children of Philip III of Spain, she proceeded to sit cautiously while Henry's carefully constructed plans slowly dissolved.

James belatedly realized how close these plans had come to drawing him into a major war, the one situation he abhorred above all others. Yet the Protestant League could not be left without a strong anchor. Cecil began to push James into that sort of arrangement. As part of the strands by which he sought to move the king, he opened marriage negotiations between the youthful Frederick V of the Palatinate and Princess Elizabeth, who was blooming into healthy womanhood.

The secretary, however, struggled against many factors. He had been a great power for a long time, perhaps too long. He was remote from the ordinary life of the realm and associated with the past, with the years of Elizabeth. It was known he had been an enemy of Raleigh, and that hero's long confinement, which turned him into a martyr, was laid at Cecil's door. He had been a rival of the folk hero, the Essex whom Elizabeth had doted over. He was no longer liked by the king—if indeed, he had ever been liked.

The secretary had not lost his remarkable ability to emerge with new ideas, however. The failure of the Great Contract had left the Crown in desperate financial straits while the king indulged in renewed orgies of generosity. Cecil, aware of the great lure hereditary titles held for his countrymen, suggested that baronets—little barons—be created.

James was pleased; he held all titles except his own very lightly. A survey was made of the eligible and conditions drawn. The price would be a little over £1,000—payable in three installments. Cecil thought of everything. By that means, some money was raised to stave off the inevitable day of reckoning for the Crown. But it did little to stop the decline of Cecil's influence.

The power of Viscount Rochester began to soar, as did the influence of the earl of Northampton. Men began to drift out of Cecil's orbit. Rochester, once notably respectful, grew notably disrespectful. In December 1611 the secretary became very ill. He recovered, but fell ill again in February 1612.

The doctors examined him and diagnosed a tumor; one suggested a trip to take the waters at Bath. He made the effort, though the trip took five days in a springless carriage. He prayed aloud most of the way; a retinue of servants followed and he talked to Sir Walter Cope and Michael Hicks, his traveling companions, about sin. After a day or two, it was clear the waters would not help. He started home, but collapsed on the way. Recovering slightly, he moved again and fell again. In that fashion he reached Marlborough, where he died holding his chaplain's hand. He was 47.

**29** The news of Cecil's death left the king unconcerned. Most, however, openly rejoiced. An avalanche of denunciations poured forth in amazing volume from almost every quarter. The earl of Northampton, who had squirmed beneath Cecil's cool and measuring eyes for years, was gleeful. He spoke of "the death of the little man for which so many rejoice and so few do much as seem to be sorry."[1] His sneer was echoed, though more elegantly, by Sir Francis Bacon, who wrote an essay *On Deformity*.

In the taverns, where the sins of the mighty land like droppings from above, a limerick went the rounds:

Here lies, thrown for the worms to eat,
Little bossive Robin that was so great.
Not Robin Goodfellow or Robin Hood
But Robin the encloser of Hatfield Wood.
Who seemed as sent from Ugly Fate
To spoil the Prince and rot the State,
Owning a mind of dismal ends
As trap for foes and tricks for friends,
But now in Hatfield lies the Fox
Who stank while he lived
And died of the Pox.[2]

Amazingly, the loss of his right arm was hailed as good fortune for the king. The general opinion was that James—learned and devout—had been misled by the secretary. It was an opinion he himself held, just as he had held a low opinion of the Regent Morton, who had subdued Scotland; the Secretary Maitland, who had put that realm in order; and all the other men who had worked for him through the years. The king decided he would endure no more such unworthy servants, but would rule his realm himself —with Robert Carr, the Viscount Rochester.

Meanwhile, the new authorized version of the Bible in English slid slowly, soundlessly, but deep into the intellectual life of the country. Presented to James the year before, the final result of almost eight years of labor by 46 of the foremost classicists and scholars of the land under Sir Henry Savile, the new translation was a stunning achievement. The splendor and sonority of its language, produced when English was bursting with energy, recreated the vividness of the original Greek better than any religious literary effort before—or since.

Until its appearance, the English had used the Tyndale Bible and later the Coverdale Bible; the Vatican had issued its own mandatory version in the Vulgate. The King James version, as it was termed with unconscious irony, quickly replaced all others in the English Reform world. The huge team of scholars who labored over it included men of both Reform and Anglo-Catholic inclinations; the results were balanced and learned and achieved the status of revealed truth among millions with astonishing speed. The Church of England promoted its use, as a matter of mandatory course, to the pulpit. First hundreds and then thousands of households began to save toward its purchase. In a very short period, at a time when cynicism, corruption, and decay had permeated all levels of government and political life, when the theater was both bawdy and revolutionary, when illegal pamphlets and books poured out of the underground to dispute both Church and Crown, the new Bible traveled through subtle avenues to alter England. Its effects upon the sovereign who gained undying fame by having his name attached to it were far removed from his expectations.

The king, in fact, considered himself the great authority in the realm in matters of religious belief. His attention had been drawn to the writings of Vortsius, a theologian at Leiden. The mighty king of England decided that Vortsius's theories were wrong and put pressure on the Dutch to ruin the professor. While this argument was underway, the King learned that heretics persisted under his own rule. One such sinner was a man named Wightman, convicted by Bishop Neile of holding forbidden opinions; another was named Bartholomew Legate. James ordered Legate brought before him. The king continued to believe—despite mountainous evidence to the contrary—that his personal powers of persuasion were too formidable for ordinary men to resist. He questioned Legate, who denied the divinity of Jesus. The king had him removed and then turned toward the question of punishment.

Elizabeth had burned heretics; why should not James? The king had neither qualms nor doubts; he was determined that he would enjoy the same prerogatives as his predecessor. His advisers counseled that legal opinion

would be wise. James agreed, providing the outcome was according to his
own view, and suggested that Sir Edward Coke be kept out of the matter.
Sir Francis Bacon, Coke's rival, assured James there would be no problem.
A mock trial was held in the Consistory Court, which obtained a ruling
from the High Commission. Working speedily, the king's men rushed Legate to Smithfield, where he was burned at the stake on March 18, 1612.
A few days later Wightman was also done to death.

These executions were greeted with silence. King James waited, but
heard no praise. The English had too often denounced the autos-da-fé of
Spain to be easy over their king's cruelty. Even James, insensitive to the
opinions of other men though he was, never repeated the performance. He
stopped with the distinction of being the last monarch of England who had
men burned alive for failing to agree with his arguments.


Fortunately, other matters intervened to attract the attention of both
king and country. The negotiations to marry the Princess Elizabeth to the
youthful elector of the Palatinate, Frederick V, were concluded. During the
summer of 1612, James himself, acting through Rochester, who had become
his intermediary with the world, dickered to marry Prince Henry to various
brides.

The young prince attracted considerable attention, and his popularity
aroused his father's jealousy. On one occasion when Henry was at court,
the king saw so many persons crowded around his son he could not bear
it and said aloud, "Will he bury me alive?"[3]

The prince, however, was anxious to avoid difficulties with his father.
A little over average height, he was described by his tutor as "strong and
well made . . . with somewhat broad shoulders and a small waist, of an
amiable majestic countenance, with hair of auburn colour, long-faced and
broad forehead, a piercing grave eye, a most gracious smile, a terrible frown,
courteous, loving and affable."[4] He was a notable athlete and spent long
hours training in armor; he often visited the shipyards and studied military
and naval matters. There was little doubt the prince loathed his father's
homosexual coterie, but he was careful not to make that a public or even
a personal issue.

Nevertheless, all England sensed that a realm under the direction of
Prince Henry would be far different from one under James. The country was
beginning to learn that its fabled position on the seas under Elizabeth had
vanished under James. Dutch shipping was everywhere, and everywhere
crowding the English, if not off the seascape, at least into darker corners.
Holland had three times the number of English ships; the fabled English
navy was sitting, rotting, at anchor.

It was Prince Henry who made the future shine. A slogan appeared, author unknown: The Hope of Protestantism. Limericks—the voice of the people—put lyrics to music.

Henry the Eighth pulled down abbeys and cells,
Henry the Ninth shall pull down Bishops and bells.[5]

His father, with his stubborn belief that all beliefs but his could be reconciled, maneuvered to marry him to a Catholic princess. By the end of summer 1612, his eye was on one of the daughters of the pro-Spanish Marie de Médicis of France.

Before that negotiation was concluded, the elector of the Palatinate arrived in person in England in October 1612. He was sixteen, the same age as Princess Elizabeth. Pleasant and open, with brown curly hair, he fitted the princess as though born to do so; the sight of the two young people together charmed the realm.

Princess Elizabeth was "attractive and endearing." Educated at the home of Lord Harington, she had been at court since 1608 and managed to remain decent and unaffected, happy and outgoing ever since. She and her elder brother—surprising products of such a father—were very close.

The new alliance was very popular, though its author was forgotten. The Palatinate was a small but wealthy Protestant area in Germany; the elector was not a king, but was certainly a sovereign. James, as usual, offered lavish festivities and entertainments to the future bridegroom, and the court turned merry, until a shadow fell.

Prince Henry complained of headaches and was bled by the physicians. They fed him various medicines to alleviate an increasing illness: boiled Sene and rhubarb. They were encouraged when this brought on "a great store of putrified choler."[6]

The prince resisted these attentions and struggled out of bed to play tennis. For several weeks he tried to conduct his usual regimen, but was pale and finally had to go back to bed. The doctors then tried powdered unicorn horn in julep. No record remains of where they obtained this curious prescription. The prince then complained that his head still hurt, so the physicians shaved his hair and applied the still-warm bodies of freshly killed pigeons and roosters. His condition grew worse.

On November 1, 1612, however, he improved and visitors were allowed. The king arrived; so did Queen Anne and Princess Elizabeth, accompanied by the elector. They smiled and spoke cheerfully, and the prince replied in kind. His younger brother, Prince Charles, twelve years old, came and stared quietly. They departed, one by one, and the doctors moved around the bed.

During the next few days news trickled from the sickroom that the prince was sinking. His sister, Princess Elizabeth, came several times to see him, but was turned away. The king, meanwhile, fled to Theobalds; Queen Anne immured herself in Denmark House. The doctors had warned of contagion; the prince had typhus. Princess Elizabeth made several more efforts to get into the sickroom by disguising herself. The apologies of the physicians were profuse, but she was turned away.

Instead George Abbott, the archbishop of Canterbury appeared— awesome in his robes. The archbishop's voice rose and lowered as he dirged prayers and exhorted the dying boy to remain firm in his faith. Prince Henry's last words were, "Where is my dear sister?"

The embalmed body lay in its coffin a month awaiting burial, in a chamber draped in black velvet, while all England mourned. One night a naked young lunatic appeared and claimed to be Prince Henry's ghost. He was held briefly in the porter's lodge and then sent to a madhouse.

Yet Prince Henry's ghost did, in a sense, hover over England for a long time. There was still an heir—the younger son, Charles. He was a stick of a boy, bookish and withdrawn. Prince Henry had teased him a lot; and Charles, six years younger, would weep and hide in a corner. But the hope of Protestantism was dead, and a wave of foreboding and gloom swept over the land.


King James did not believe in long periods of mourning. He ordered feasts and festivities in honor of the elector and signed the marriage articles on behalf of his daughter soon after Prince Henry's death. The union was surrounded by elaborate protocols. The contract had to be followed by an official betrothal. That was announced on November 27, 1612.

These steps did something to alleviate the distress created by Prince Henry's death. Dark rumors of poison, however, circulated through the realm. Suspicion was cast upon the earl of Northampton, a man whose secret Catholicism was considered dangerous and whose scheming, haughty personality made him obnoxious to many. The earl was aroused at these charges and had some persons hauled to court and punished for them.

The marriage between Princess Elizabeth and the elector was performed in February 1613, on St. Valentine's Day. The next morning, according to Chamberlain, a chronicler of the times, "the King went to visit these young turtles" and wanted to know the details of their wedding night.

Great, costly, and clumsy celebrations were mounted. The throng at court during some masques was so dense that ladies were forbidden to wear farthingales; there was not enough room. The newlyweds sailed away April 25, 1613, living symbols of the Reform cause in England and visible signs that King James I was, at last, serious about leading the Protestant alliance. That alliance had suffered a great loss by the death of Henry IV and the neutralizing of France by his widow, Marie de Médicis.

Nevertheless, the Protestant Union in Germany was active and held many territories; the Catholic League was able to maintain only a balance. Holland, Denmark, and other powers were staunch for the Reform. If England was bold, it could weld another combination that could replace Henry's plans.

Cecil had left the king, therefore, in a promising position internationally, provided he had the force to exploit it. Many of the king's advisers were against such an effort. The earl of Northampton was their leader; he was firmly pro-Vatican. The Spanish, watching the situation, had many reasons to worry. Rumors had swept England during the autumn of 1612, in the wake of Prince Henry's death, of poison, plots, and invasion. These alarms had caused special patrols to be raised among the leaders of the country gentry; lawyers rose to urge the courts to apply the laws against Catholics with more severity and regularity.

Madrid watched all this very closely. It had "pensioners" in high places. One was Queen Anne; another was the countess of Suffolk; another was the earl of Northampton; another was Sir Francis Bacon; these names were followed by a long list.[7]

Spain's situation, however, lent itself to exaggerations. The power that held the Indies and the Americas; straddled Iberia; ruled Belgium, Milan, Naples, Sicily, the western Mediterranean islands; and dominated commerce with Asia and Africa was still monstrous in sweep, immense in influence and importance. But Spain was decaying at the core. The court was extravagant and pleasure-mad while its revenues of bullion from America were declining. Bureaucracy was expanding; the navy was a shadow of its former glory; monasteries and convents had become warehouses of indolence; taxes oppressed the productive. Spanish literature began to reflect a deep-seated pessimism.

Madrid did not lack intelligent men, however. Spain was suffering, but still loomed beyond any other single power. Its leaders decided to play for time, to play one of its allies against another, and to maneuver. To deflect England from replacing the France of Henry IV as leader of a coalition against Madrid was crucial. After a quiet search, the duke of Lerma selected Don Diego de Sarmiento, one of Spain's most experienced and impressive diplomats, to go to London.

The ambassador and his entourage arrived in May 1613 on two galleons that sailed into Portsmouth harbor. En route to anchorage, the Spanish captain exchanged courtesies with the flagship of the English Channel fleet, which was in the port. Later the Spaniard was told it was the custom for foreign vessels to keep their flags lowered in English ports, as long as the English navy was present. He told the ambassador, who promptly forbade him to strike his colors.

The English threatened to sink the Spanish ships unless their customs were obeyed, and Don Diego sent a note to King James. He explained the situation and said he intended, if the galleons were sunk, to sink with them. The king sent word back to his naval forces to drop their demand. The king's decision ended the display of English pride. It recognized that spirit in the Spaniards, however, and established Don Diego, before anyone met him at court, as the formidable agent of a greater power.

Sarmiento arrived at a time when King James had taken the control of the government into his own hands and was determined to rule the realm his own way. That way had opened wide with the death of Cecil, and even wider with the passing of Prince Henry.

The courtiers, who had been barricaded from the government by Cecil and whose influence had been shaded by the brightening prospects of Prince Henry, surged forward like men finally allowed inside a treasure house. The earl of Northampton, leader of the Howard family, clutched at power at last. A relative, Thomas Howard, was lord admiral; his son-in-law, Lord Knollys, held important posts; the earl of Suffolk—another Howard—was lord chamberlain; Sir Arthur Lake, Cecil's assistant, joined them. The earl was very pleased; he relayed the king's wishes to the Privy Council and wrote letters—much as Cecil had done, to the king's various hunting centers. The council was not so pleased; it found itself dealing with details and blocked from the larger issues of the realm.

Northampton found it difficult to deal by correspondence; he lacked Cecil's unerring tact and facility for mingling the comical with the serious. He cringed; he blamed all mishaps on Cecil's legacies, but it was soon clear that more was needed. The old earl's problem was that Robert Carr, now the earl of Rochester, was not on his side. Rochester—and Rochester's man, Sir Thomas Overbury—was against him. There was no doubt that it was Overbury's influence that was dominant.

The earl of Northampton, however, was a key figure in the pro-Vatican party of England. That party was now moving close to ascendancy over the king. The Reform, which had its strength in Commons, had no equal avenue to the Crown, since Parliament was dissolved, and the king had no apparent intention of ever calling new elections. Yet Reform leaders like the

Lord Chancellor Ellesmere and such ironly anti-Catholic figures as the archbishop of Canterbury could at least rely upon Overbury's influence to keep Northampton and his associates from growing too strong.

Northampton's next move was interesting. He summoned his great-niece, the countess of Essex, back to court. Her arrival was something of an event, for she had a sensational story to tell. Her husband, said the countess, had never consummated their marriage, though she had spent three terrible years in his company. She wanted a divorce.

Overbury was appalled. He was quick enough to realize that the countess of Essex wanted to change husbands. If she succeeded, his own influence would be lost as Carr vanished into the folds of the Howard family. All sorts of repercussions would result; the pro-Spanish, pro-Vatican party would rise again—and he himself would tumble down to oblivion.

Events, however, turned very quickly. Sir Thomas Overbury was bright and intelligent, but he was only an individual of modest rank pitted against a great family. He argued with Carr, called the countess a strumpet, and threatened to reveal that he himself had authored the letters and poems Carr had palmed off as his own. The viscount laughed; he could not take that seriously.

Overbury had very few instruments at hand beyond his wits and his pen. He wrote a poem called *The Wife*. It was a hymn to chastity, was widely circulated through the court, and aroused attention. He wrote another titled *Character: A Mistress Made Wife*, whose target was obvious. The countess was furious and suggested to Sir David Wood, a truculent sort who had a grudge against Overbury, that he challenge Sir Thomas and run him through. She added it would be worth £1,000.

"I am loath to go to Tyburn for any lady's pleasure," Wood told her.

The countess had reason to be concerned. She and Rochester were meeting secretly at the residence of Mrs. Turner—the little dressmaker who often rented rooms to persons from court for such purposes—and Overbury knew about the meetings.

One night a servant, lingering late in the Privy Gallery, overheard the favorite and his secretary in a memorable argument. The hour was late, and Rochester was returning to his apartment when he was suddenly accosted by Overbury.

"What do you here at this time of night?" asked the viscount.

"Will you never leave the company of that base woman?" asked Overbury fiercely. "Seeing that you so neglect my advice, I desire that tomorrow morning we part, and that you will let me have that portion that you know is due me. Then I will leave you free to yourself, to stand on your own legs."

"My legs are strong enough to bear me," said Rochester and pushed past.[8]

The argument did not end their association, however. Overbury was truly indispensable to Rochester. But the earl of Northampton was pleased to learn the friends had neared the parting of the way. Through complex channels he saw to it that the king also learned. While that took effect, the earl counseled the favorite regarding his secretary. "Unless you curb his greatness and abate his pride," he said, "he will in time be your equal in power. . . ."[9]

It was cleverly done. The king sent word through the archbishop of Canterbury that Overbury should prepare himself for an overseas assignment. Sir Thomas was appalled. He was being banished, and he knew he would not return. He appealed to Rochester, who apparently told him to refuse the appointment. The favorite would handle matters with the king.

Overbury sent his refusal to the king, but was shortly afterward called in to the Privy Council and offered the post of ambassador to Russia—a land then, as now, considered distant, barbaric, and mysterious. Overbury repeated his objections and, to his consternation, was immediately taken into custody and carried off to the Tower for high contempt.

He entered on April 21, 1613, still bewildered, still staring, and was told he was to have no visitors. The speed of his fall took his breath away. Staring at the turnkey as the massive iron door was locked, he saw a broad, knowing grin spread across the man's face. For the first time, Overbury felt a cold chill of fear.


With Northampton's Scab out of the way, matters moved swiftly. A conference was held at Whitehall, in which Northampton and the earl of Suffolk appeared to discuss the complaint of their beautiful young relative, and the earl of Southampton and Lord Knollys (related to the Howards by marriage) appeared for the earl of Essex. Incredibly, the divorce had become a matter of state.

The position of Essex was that he was willing to be rid of the lady—but he would not accept the charge of being unable to be a husband. By orders of the king, as filtered through his army of sycophants, that issue was beside the point. The countess could not be disputed. The men fell into a wrangle; it was a time when men could quibble forever. They emerged, at length, with an agreement that the countess's word would be accepted and that the earl would also have his way: a truly monstrous *non sequitur* that James himself had reached.

The king was in his element. No man enjoyed bedroom details as much, and no other could have emerged with his explanation for what appeared incredible. Witchcraft was at the bottom of it, said the king. Leaning back, glass in hand, he recalled tangled tales of strange spells and dark mysteries from Scotland, and courtiers scurried to read, on command, his *Dæmonologie.* The earl of Essex was perfectly normal; he had simply been bewitched.

The court was fascinated. The Essex divorce was the best play of the season and drew everyone's attention. The issue spread from court to country and lent itself to every sort of wonder and speculation. A commission was created, headed by the archbishop of Canterbury; Bishops Neile, Andrewes, and King; two members of the Privy Council; and four lawyers.

The proceedings were wrapped in the elegant garments of the law, but their essence was prurient. The countess of Essex had to appear before another special committee composed of four elderly peeresses and two midwives for an examination. Whether she actually endured this test was —then and now—uncertain. All that was recorded was that a heavily veiled figure arrived and was examined by the midwives. The veiled female was dressed, however, in the countess's clothes; and none ventured, apparently, to ask for the veils to be removed. Examined, the mystery female was pronounced *virgo intacta.* The news sent a wave of laughter through the land and inspired endless speculations about the identify of the mystery maid.

Everybody settled down to enjoy the next stage of the drama, and their expectations were fulfilled when it was learned that George Abbott, the archbishop of Canterbury, who had earned his honors by bowing to every royal thought, simply could not accept the latest reasoning of the king.

Don Diego de Sarmiento was a brilliant conversationalist—which meant not only that he could tell wonderfully funny stories and also turn serious—but that he could listen so astutely, so sincerely, that he could respond to the nuances and turns of another man's speech without losing the threads of his own thought.

He charmed King James into the only true friendship—clear of homosexual implications—that the monarch ever developed with another man. Sarmiento liked to hunt, liked to pun, and could speak Latin very well. He was versed in the stately courtesies of the great masculine court of Madrid, the most powerful, polished, and learned in the western world at that time. As an emissary from that greater court, he reflected its magnificence in state appearances, as well as in the ability to enter into the hunter's world that James loved so much.

"While hunting with the King," wrote the Venetian ambassador, "he vies with him in putting his hands in the blood of bucks and stags, doing cheerfully everything that his Majesty does and in this way," he ended darkly, "he has gained his favor." [10]

Actually Sarmiento had many ways. The Venetian ambassador noticed one way, Arthur Wilson noticed another. "The King took delight to talk to him," wrote Wilson, "for he was full of conceits and would speak false Latin on purpose in his merry fits to please the King. . . ." He would pretend, at such moments, that he could do no better, telling the King he spoke Latin "like a gentleman, while the King spoke it like a scholar." [11]

Yet the ambassador could grow tall on occasion. He recognized important issues at once. Shortly after his arrival, one such issue arose over a Spanish lady, Donna Luisa de Carvajal, who lived at the embassy, employed many English servants, and engaged in various Catholic activities. After Sarmiento's arrival, she left the embassy and assumed residence in Spital-fields. The archbishop of Canterbury, whose agents had been watching Donna Luisa, had her taken into custody and placed her in custody in his own palace. The ambassador, learning of this discreet house arrest, immediately sent his wife to keep Donna Luisa company while he demanded her release from the council. At the same time, he sent a letter with the same request to the king, ignoring that it was late at night.

James dictated a reply, saying the lady had broken the laws of England and drawing attention to the fate of any who so violated the religious rules of Spain inside Spanish territory. However, being merciful, reasonable, and amiable—James was never loath to admire his own attributes—the king would release the lady if she left the realm.

Sarmiento's answer was quicker than thought. If Donna Luisa were expelled, who had done no wrong—then Don Diego de Sarmiento de Acuña would leave with her. That night Donna Luisa was freed without conditions by the king.


The death of Cecil the year before had opened gates for men he had held back. One of these was Sir Francis Bacon. Bacon had prospered; he was one of the great figures of the era, but he had not prospered as much, or risen as high, as he wanted to rise. A couple of years over fifty, author of renowned books that had attracted international attention, he was far too learned—and too immodest about his learning—to please James. Nevertheless, Bacon persisted. He composed papers of advice; he made suggestions, and he always had a plan. Some of them worked sometimes; some, never; some were never tried; others were tried in part.

In 1613, knowing the king considered Sir Edward Coke "perverse" in his persistent rulings against the High Commission as chief justice of the Court of Common Law, Bacon suggested a different job for Coke—chief justice of the King's Bench—a position informally known as chief justice of England. In such a post, Coke would defend the king's peace in criminal cases. It was a high honor, but a deceptive one, because it was less profitable.

Coke would be placed where he could apply the law against criminals, be reduced in terms of compensation—and a more pliant man could replace him in Common Law. A stairstep was thus opened up that would leave the position of attorney general open for Sir Francis Bacon. It was complicated, smooth—and James liked it.

In the summer of 1613 the earl of Northampton placed Sir Gervase Helwys into a badly needed post as lieutenant of the guard of the Tower. At the same time, Richard Weston was named Overbury's keeper.

Weston was an old acquaintance of Mrs. Turner; he had once been her husband's assistant. Unfortunately, his career had encountered some rough spots; he had once been jailed himself, for coining sixpences.

Mrs. Turner and the countess of Essex, who was waiting for the commission headed by the archbishop of Canterbury to rule on her divorce, had now time to handle the matter of Sir Thomas Overbury, whom the countess called "that scum of men; that devil incarnate."

The two women then contacted, probably through Mrs. Turner's incredibly varied acquaintance, James Franklin, a Yorkshireman who had a slight reputation in medicine. Franklin began to prepare prescriptions for Overbury, for the prisoner was able to send out for food, through Weston. Later Franklin declared he had supplied aquafortis (nitric acid), arsenic—black to mix in pepper and white to be mixed in salt—ground glass, cantharides, corrosive sublimate, and various other toxic poisons.

The prisoner, meanwhile, sent a stream of letters to Rochester. Their tone began indignantly, but as the weeks and months passed, grew polite, then questioning, and finally pleading. Rochester sent back soothing replies, at inconsistent intervals. He was attempting to straighten matters; he was working for Overbury's release, but powerful forces were against him.

Meanwhile, the commission was tied into knots by the reluctance of the archbishop of Canterbury to accept the witchcraft theory of the king. Bishop Andrewes, a great favorite of the king, had similar qualms. The king spoke to both at great lengths and swung Andrewes. But the archbishop of Canterbury composed a lengthy letter, filled with quotations from many irrelevant sources. Beneath the verbiage it was clear the bishop did not believe any witches were at work in England, but could not discover a way to say it.

By September, the commission was tied and could reach no verdict. The information, coming on top of the archbishop's objections, cast a shadow over Lady Essex and the entire situation.

The condition of Sir Thomas Overbury was, by then, grave. He wrote:

> This morning, I find a great heat continue in all my body; and the same desire of drink and loathing of meat [solid food] and my water is strangely high. . . . The same sewering [diarrhea] and vomiting. Yesterday about 8 o'clock . . . I fainted.[13]

His elderly parents came from the country to see him, but were turned away. Lady Essex, meanwhile, had grown impatient. Franklin's prescriptions were taking too long, though Weston had carried them, mixed into his food, to the prisoner. Investigating further, the countess discovered that Overbury was occasionally visited by one of the king's physician's, Dr. Mayerne, and in Mayerne's absence, by a French apothecary named Lobell.

She and Mrs. Turner managed to reach the apothecary's assistant—a young boy named William Reeves. Reeves was admitted into Overbury's cell the night of September 14, 1613. He gave Sir Thomas an enema of sublimate of mercury, one of the most painful of caustic poisons.

Overbury gasped and writhed on the floor. Reeves hid his face in hands, unable to bear the sight. Weston shoved him out and locked the door. He did not have to tell him to keep his mouth shut.

In the afternoon of the following day, Overbury's body was wrapped in a winding sheet, dumped into a coffin, and buried in quicklime.

The earl of Northampton wrote Robert Carr, the Viscount Rochester:

> Sweet Lord, Overbury being viewed, there was found in his arm an issue, and on his belly twelve kernals . . . as big as sixpence; one issue on his back with a tawny plaster on it; this was strange and ugly. He stank intolerably . . . he was cast into the coffin with a loose sheet over him. God is gracious in cutting off ill instruments.[14]

That night the countess of Essex appeared at a court function. She was dazzling in green velvet lined with gold-patterned white satin, wearing one of Anne Turner's yellow, starched ruffs, but with the line of her dress cut very low to show her magnificent breasts. She had red jewels around her neck, yellow feathers in her hair, and looked radiant.

Ten days later, after the king had added two more members to the panel, the commission handed down a ruling that declared the Essex marriage invalid—by a majority of two.

The wedding of the favorite and the reigning court beauty was the high point of the Christmas festivities. The bride wore white and entered the ceremony with her hair loose and flowing—the signs of virginity. But shortly before she left her apartment with her bridesmaids, she handed a messenger £20 for young William Reeves and some other sums of money for Franklin and his associates and gave instructions that Reeves should be sent out of the country. Then she gathered her train, turned with a flashing smile, and left to get married.

The king was short of money, as always, but he sold Crown lands worth £10,000 in order to buy jewels for the bride. He raised Carr to earl of Somerset. He made a graceful joke about it, saying he was only doing it to keep Frances Howard a countess.

By 1614, only three years after Cecil thought he had reduced the king's debts to manageable proportions, the Crown owed Gargantuan sums ranging somewhere between £600,000 and £750,000. Crown servants were unpaid; every department was in arrears; the forts, harbors, navy, armories, and supplies of the government insufficient and decayed; and several enormous loans were due. The new earl of Somerset, the greatest power in the realm next to His Majesty, discussed this situation in council. Sarmiento, who apparently had a chance to see him in action at this high gathering, thought he handled himself well. "He showeth much temper and modesty, without seeming to press and sway anything. But afterward the King resolveth all business with him alone. . . ." [15]

With the Crown confronting a fiscal crisis, the new earl of Somerset announced at council that he would personally lend the King £20,000; the offer was made to prime the pump and persuade other men to put up their fortunes. They were not so certain as Somerset, however, of receiving theirs back from the king's hands or through the king's prerogatives. There seemed no other course than to call for elections and appeal to a new Parliament.

James was reluctant. He considered Parliaments troublesome instruments, if not inherently seditious. His mood was not a happy one. His health was beginning to falter, pains invaded his right foot, and he sometimes had trouble walking. Yet he needed money.

Sir Henry Neville advised the king's friends to make a special effort to have men elected to Commons who would work for the Crown. That effort was called an "undertaking" and was soon discovered. The realm was outraged, and the king's supporters were given the ironic name of "undertakers." The results boomeranged on the manipulators, and more extreme Reformers arrived in Commons than ever before. Each was burning with zeal.

Sir Francis Bacon, a genius of the abstract, had also advised the king.

It was his opinion ordinary men should not be allowed voice or vote in matters of state. He suggested that James seek to persuade the Commons to forget about new laws and address itself only to the matter of Crown finances.

When James appeared before the gathering he followed, somewhat vaguely, Bacon's advice. He spoke against the Papists, which had always been a popular position and was fatherly about the fact that his daughter had delivered a son in the Palatinate. He wanted the child named in the succession to the throne rather than his mother, a woman. Finally he added that the Crown needed money. Shortly afterward, assured by his entourage his first effort had been successful, the king appeared again for another long and irritating speech. He had learned Commons was considering new bills. Perhaps it would be best if each were brought to him, and discussions were held. In that way, harmony would reign supreme. He wanted, he said, a Parliament of love.[16]

The results were predictable. Commons was not going to discuss anything with the king until the questions upon which the last Parliament was dissolved were settled. Impositions had to go. The king's men protested in vain; Bacon—as an attorney general—was barely allowed to sit, and it was decided that in the future no attorney general could sit at all. Some of the King's spokesmen mistakenly called attention to the powers of kings in France and Spain. They were shouted down; the comparison was with tyrants.

Wentworth, a Puritan lawyer, recalled how the king of France had died under an assassin's knife "like a calf before a butcher." Other speakers, surprisingly outspoken, rose to echo his thought. At last word came from the House of Lords for a conference; the proceedings in Commons had created indignation in the upper chamber. Bishop Neile, who had voted for Lady Essex's divorce, denounced Commons. Members rose to propose punishments against bishops.

At that point, a member rose to abuse the courtiers around the king, and another began to orate against the Scots. The proceedings in Commons suddenly deteriorated into wrangles, side issues, irrelevancies. While these strange eruptions were underway, the earl of Northampton, whose political ideas belonged to the previous century, whispered to the king that Parliaments were useless. The proper course, he said, was to dissolve this rebellious group, negotiate a marriage between Prince Charles and the Spanish infanta, receive an enormous, a glittering dowry with which to pay off all debts, relax the laws against Catholics, and rule as an absolute king.

That advice was congenial to the king. The disjointed proceedings in Parliament enhanced its timeliness. It did not occur to James, nor apparently, to many others, that the attempt to stack the elections in favor of the

Crown had inspired the pro-Vatican faction to do the same. The result, for the first time in English history, was an assembly divided into pressure groups whose intentions were to overcome, rather than reflect, the opinions of their countrymen.

The earl of Northampton, for instance, was known to be the sponsor of some of the more outspoken members. The earl's recommendation that James should turn toward Spain and the Vatican was not only cunningly timed as an alternative toward a frighteningly unruly Parliament, but delivered at the same time that word came from Madrid regarding a possible marriage. A huge dowry was hinted, sufficient to pay all the king's debts and expenses for years to come. James responded like a man seeing a vision —and sent for Sarmiento.

The ambassador arrived as impassive as ever, but even his well-trained control almost slipped when the king of England asked him whether Spain would support a dissolution of the English Parliament. James's meaning was clear enough: he would never convene another Commons. Sarmiento grew vague and talked about Madrid's desire to see an orderly rule in all countries. That was enough for James; he had enlisted the ambassador. He dissolved Parliament.

The court mocked the Addled Parliament that had met a little over two months and whose Commons had not succeeded in obtaining royal approval of even a single measure. Yet the proceedings had been deeply significant. Commons, once the support of Tudor kings, had been converted into a Crown target. King James's theories had prevailed for the moment, but at the expense of badly needed support. In effect, the Addled Parliament reflected a growing division between the Commons and the Crown.

The king proceeded to deepen that gap. He ordered that the papers and notes prepared by the members of Commons who had met in conference with the House of Lords be seized and burned before the Privy Council. Four outspoken members—Wentworth, Hoskins, Neville, and Chute— were sent to the Tower.[17] Their incarceration was not notably long, but the meaning of the king was emphasized.

Later, James discussed Parliament with Sarmiento. He complained of insolence and hoped the Spaniard would send a true report, "not as it is told by the gossips in the streets." That exchange seemed puzzling, but the king was adroit in his own way. Sarmiento went back to his embassy and for the first time wrote seriously about a marriage between the infanta and Prince Charles. He wrapped the suggestion inside another. If he could persuade James into open toleration of Catholicism, then perhaps the Vatican faith could so undermine the Reform in England that an effective alliance could be achieved—marriage or no. It began to look as though the cornerstone of the Protestant coalition could be removed.

The earl of Northampton had a tumor in his thigh that forced him to bed during the closing days of the Parliament. It festered and gangrene began to appear. Surgeons entered the situation and performed clumsily. The gangrene spread. Worms were at work on the earl before he died a week after Parliament. He left behind no friends, no mourners, but a record of evil and dark behavior that seeped even from his grave.

The earl of Somerset became lord chamberlain, the king's first minister. The earl of Suffolk, whose countess was on the payroll of Spain, became lord treasurer. That post was papered with debts and had virtually no funds. The king was operating now on forced credit; his suppliers could not be attached for their own debts as long as they worked with the Crown—but working with the Crown extended their own debts—for the king did not pay.

The pro-Spanish faction was in control of the king and the government for the first time since the days of Mary Tudor. Many nobles and bishops were deeply alarmed. The Catholics in the population were hopeful, but the Reform had grown to a majority—and was displeased.

Carr, now grown rich, launched a benevolence for the king. It resembled a vast national charity drive, which the favorite sparked by a grand contribution. Pliant bishops came forward with gifts of costly plate. Officials toured the countryside and the towns, asking for pledges from various regions. The pressure started at the top and traveled downward; all men were asked to volunteer their offerings. Some protested the king should ask Parliament for money. Others refused altogether, saying they could not be forced into voluntary action. The campaign soon became embarrassing; it was clear the realm had little love and less money for James. Force replaced persuasion and the effort grew naked: the Crown was extorting money in illegal ways.

The king, meanwhile, returned to his eternal trundles through the countryside. His peregrinations had grown endless, though his health was beginning to fail. He hunted from a carriage; his wild rides had ended. He traveled, as always, with a huge entourage that was followed, at a little distance, by another far more ragged assembly of drabs, scullions, gypsies, pickpockets, and other strange types that camped around the court for its crumbs. But the king was lonely. Carr was married and his wife was more congenial than James; the favorite was busy with state affairs. He developed a tendency to grow impatient and to avoid embraces.

That situation was noted with keen interest by Reformers. They had been outmaneuvered by the Howards, who now seemed in total control, but the Reformers had learned a lesson. If the way to the king was through a young man, then they would find one. The search involved many men secretly ashamed of their task. Some indication of how low James Stuart had carried proud England was provided by the fact that the searchers included even the august archbishop of Canterbury.

During the summer of 1614, the king traveled to the estate of the earl of Suffolk and then to Bletsoe, Kirby, and Apethorpe. At Apethorpe in August an extraordinary young man appeared before him: one of the perverted parade of possible candidates for his affections. He was twenty-two and the second son of a widow. Tall, gracefully muscular, he had an oddly small head and an almost pretty face.

His name was George Villiers. He had been outfitted and coached by Sir John Graham, one of the Gentlemen of the Privy Chamber. How Graham found him is unknown, but young Villiers was ambitious enough —and unscrupulous enough—to break an engagement with the daughter of Sir Roger Aston in order to enter the contest for the king. It is known, however, that the young man had his mother's anxious support. She wanted her son to succeed.

James stared; the young man bowed low. When he rose, it was clear he would stay at court. Within two months the favorite, Somerset, was aware of him and intervened to prevent his being a Gentleman of the Bedchamber, but Villiers became a cupbearer.

In that position he was among those who waited upon the king at dinner. James's dinners are fondly reviewed by certain scholars, for they were marked by the presence of clergymen and much windy discussion on theological issues, interspersed with scatology. In reality, they were peculiar. Military men were excluded. The king, being easily scared, had rules forbidding the wearing of swords; and any sort of physical confrontation was, of course, forbidden.

Villiers knew this, of course; he had learned a lot, very quickly, about James and his court. Yet, when one of his fellows jostled him while serving table, Villiers turned around and gave him "a box on the ears." The penalty for striking anyone in the king's presence was to lose a hand; the gathering was appalled. But the king laughed. He had always had a liking for certain exaggerations of masculinity, providing they were in his service. Villiers remained unpunished; the stricken man was banished.

During the turn of the year 1614, several obscure changes took place. One was the publication of a book by Sir Thomas Overbury, entitled *Char-*

*acters: A Mistress Made Wife.* The reappearance of this posthumous volume composed in hatred against her by a man long dead had a terrible effect upon the countess of Somerset and her husband. It was as though the grave suddenly yawned and a hand appeared.

Another event was the sly movement of Sir Thomas Lake, once an assistant to Cecil and now, as one of the two secretaries of state, an assistant to Somerset. Lake was never known to author a project or make a memorable suggestion. He was cautious and colorless, and he gravitated toward power. Sometime during the holiday season, he became known as the most important member of a coterie rapidly collecting around the cupbearer, George Villiers.

The combination sent Somerset into great excitement. His temper, once famous for being placid, began to sputter. He rushed to the king with complaints that base whispers and false allegations were being raised against him and invaded the king's bedchamber at odd hours—peering, like a jealous husband, for signs of alien occupancy. His new condition made him less attractive to the king, who began to recall his royal prerogatives.

Early in 1615 James wrote one of his inimitable letters. He scoffed at Somerset's complaints about whispers, libels, calumnies. "I never knew . . . any such Court faction as you describe," he said coldly. "Never any man, directly or indirectly, let fall to me anything . . . to lessen your credit with me."

As the letter proceeded, however, it turned into angry charges. The king had a pent-up case against Somerset that broke into the open. ". . . a piece of ground cannot be fertile," James wrote, "if by its own natural rankness, or evil manuring, it become fertile with weeds . . . a strange phrenzy took you, so powdered and mixed with strange streams of unquietness, passion, fury, and insolent pride, and . . . a settled kind of obstinacy, as chokes and obscures those excellent and good parts that God hath bestowed upon you."

Once released, the torrent turned into flood. The earl had refused to sleep in the royal bedchamber. The king warned Somerset that ". . . you might lead me by the heart, but not by the nose." He ended by demanding that Somerset change his ways.[18]


The earl of Somerset was not, however, alone in the world. He was surrounded by Howards and their multitude of connections. They were numerous and powerful, and they mounted as many whispers in favor of the earl as their opponents did against him. The king had expressed his anger and then relapsed into indolence; the realm had to be managed by someone and he had no alternative men in mind.

When the king visited Cambridge University in March 1615, he was accompanied by a large group. Someone noticed that all the ladies present were connected, in one or another way, with the Howard family. The visit was a huge success; an obscene comedy titled *Ignoramus* that assaulted common law advocates sent James into delighted paroxysms of laughter.

James needed his sense of humor regarding the common law and its lawyers, for Sir Edward Coke, though transferred to the King's Bench, was again issuing prohibitions against the High Commission and its proceedings, again citing the common law on an immense variety of cases.

One of these attracted widespread attention and involved an elderly rector named Edmund Peacham.[19] Peacham had complained against his bishop in the Consistory Court and was deprived of his orders by the High Commission for his temerity. The High Commission also searched his rooms, and papers containing bitter remarks about the Church and Crown were discovered in a locked desk drawer. A new, far more serious charge, based on the find, was lodged against him: treason.

That charge was laid before the Privy Council, which had Peacham conveyed to the Tower.

The old man, Bacon wrote, was questioned "before torture, in torture, between torture and after torture" but would not admit to any treason. His questioners, as is customary in such cases, insisted he was a member of a group or a conspiracy; they were aware his opinions reflected a considerable measure of popular sentiment. It was a period when—because of the benevolence and the pro-Spanish policy—there was a great deal of hard feeling toward the king. James, aware and fearful, now traveled with a large number of running footmen around his carriage to keep possible assassins, à la Henry IV's Ravaillac, at a safe distance.

Since Peacham would not confess to treason, his interrogators thought they needed the decision of the King's Bench before he could be put to death, which was James's desire. That brought the king and Bacon & Company up against Sir Edward Coke again. James sought to isolate the chief justice by having his associates brought before him to tell him their verdict, one by one, in advance. The King had odd ideas.

Coke was called in last, but refused to answer—saying he needed time to study the case. When it came before him, he ruled Peacham innocent, since his writing, being secret and private, had not "disabled the King's title."

In this disordered and argumentative climate, the king turned toward a matter highly important to him, if not to the realm: the promotion of George Villiers. He had developed a routine for these undertakings, with which Queen Anne was disgustedly familiar. He liked to have the queen suggest that he bestow some honor or another on his young men. That, believed the king, prevented her later reproaches. The archbishop of Canterbury, one of the powerful men who now clustered around Villiers, pleaded his case with her.

That was unusual, but Canterbury had learned, through his many agents, that the favorite, Somerset, had been dealing with Sarmiento, the Spanish ambassador. Somerset was attempting to attach himself to the king's foreign plans to bolster his own situation. It was essential to the Reformers to elevate a favorite who could be differently directed.

Queen Anne warned the archbishop he was "simply making a future scourge," but Abbott persisted. His persuasions were conveyed through the corridors; Somerset and his friends appeared outside the king's bedchamber and waited with the archbishop while the queen entered. She emerged with the news that Villiers would be knighted, made a Gentleman of the Bedchamber, and given a pension of £1,000 a year.

The bedchamber, by then, had taken on a very peculiar character. The king himself slept in a round bed about which three other beds were arranged to serve as a sort of barricade. His lifelong fears and restlessness had grown remarkably; he drank almost constantly.

The growing indolence of the English Crown pleased Madrid. France was neutralized because its dowager queen was pro-Spanish. If England could be kept out of Europe, the Spaniards could move in Germany to upset, divide, and scatter the League of Protestant States.

The Huguenots of France began to organize against the dowager; the realm teetered on the brink of a new civil war. The Dutch moved with great energy on the seas, competing with England to England's loss. This might have been overcome if James could make up his mind, but the king of England had a serious marriage negotiation underway for Prince Charles with France. By July 1615, he told Sarmiento he thought it might be possible to discuss similar possibilities with Spain.

That turn marked a peak in the power of the Howards and the earl of Somerset, who played some part in it and seemed higher and stronger than ever. He asked the king for the wardenship of the Cinque Ports—a lucrative post vacant since the death of the earl of Northampton. That was a mistake based on a mistake. James Stuart considered himself a great expert in all international matters and deeply resented others attempting to share his accomplishments. The wardenship of the Cinque Ports was suddenly given to Lord Zouche—who had not even applied for the honor.

Even the earl could read this omen, but others began to pile rapidly.

One summer day in 1615 Sir Humphrey May appeared in Somerset's office in Whitehall to warn that Sir George Villiers would soon appear to offer his services. Somerset said fiercely he did not want Villier's services, and Sir Humphrey replied, in a careful, neutral voice, "It is the King's wish that you should."

A little later Villiers entered and made his bow. Somerset rose and said, in a choked voice, "I will have none of your services and you shall have none of my favour. I will, if I can, break your neck, Of that be confidant."[20]

Brave words, but ugly whispers were circulating. The posthumous book by Sir Thomas Overbury had restored his name and memory at court. Seated behind his ornate desk, listening at council or—even worse—talking with his countess, the earl of Somerset could not shake the lengthening shadow of the man who had once been his best friend. That memory brought others, and Somerset decided, as had other falling English favorites before him, to make himself safe before events grew worse. He directed Sir Robert Cotton to draw a pardon to "cover the greatest possible number of offenses" and brought it to the king.

James was pleased. It was clear Somerset was now ready to accept the fact that their affair was ended; he assured the earl the formality would be handled with dispatch. To prove it, the king attended a meeting of the Privy Council in July 1615—a rare condescension. In the king's presence Somerset declared he only asked for such a document because his enemies had grown so numerous. James spoke along the same lines and closed by saying, "Seal it at once, for such is my pleasure."[21] Without the seal it was worthless.

Ellesmere, the lord chancellor, demurred. He said such a sweeping pardon would allow the earl, if he chose, to decamp with the crown jewels and escape prosecution. Somerset intervened to say the document was based on one given to Cardinal Wolsey. The king rose—he detested arguments—and repeated, "I have ordered you to pass the pardon," and swept from the room. Outside he was besieged with protests, to which he listened uncertainly. That night, anxious to get back to the country, he fled amid his running footmen. Somerset remained, sickened by the realization the pardon had not been sealed and haunted by wonder. What was known?

Sir Ralph Winwood, who was in charge of the investigation, knew a great deal. He had the confession of William Reeves, the apothecary's apprentice who had administered the fatal enema to Overbury, in hand. Later during the summer of 1615 he obtained a series of statements from Sir Gervase Helwys, the lieutenant of the Tower. By September 1615 enough evidence was in hand to tell James.

Sir Edward Coke, chief justice of the King's Bench, retired every night at exactly nine o'clock and rose at three. At one in the morning a messenger knocked, loudly officious, on his door. It was opened by Coke's son.

"I come from the King and must immediately speak to your father," said the messenger.

"If you come from ten Kings you shall not," said young Coke, "for I know my father's disposition to be such that if he is disturbed in his sleep he shall not be fit for any business. But if you will do as we do—you shall be welcome. About two hours hence my father will arise, and you may then do as you please."[22]

The messenger waited. At precisely 3 A.M. the monster arose and rang his bedside bell. The man entered and handed him the king's letter.


James had no choice: the issue was murder, the evidence already collected was ominous, and the relationship between Somerset and Overbury had been notorious. The earl was at Royston with the king when word of all this reached them, and his protests were tearful.

His defense, apparently developed during premonitory months, was that a political faction was attempting to destroy him. He named Sir Edward Coke as the architect, and Lord Chancellor Ellesmere as the intellectual leader of the effort. Going to his knees, he reminded James of how Ellesmere had aided in the trial of Mary Stuart, but James pushed him toward the door. He would have to convince the Privy Council; matters were out of the king's hands. Somerset rushed to London.

He appeared before the council, and their frozen faces warned of his peril. Back in his City residence, the earl sent agents to seize all Mrs. Turner's papers—but men had been there well in advance; the move was another self-betrayal. He scrabbled through letters to Northampton that concerned Overbury, scratched out passages, changed dates—and finally burned some of them. He was engaged in this task when word came, on October 17, 1615, for the earl and countess of Somerset to remain in their apartments. They were under house arrest.


Richard Weston, Sir Thomas Overbury's keeper, was the first to go on trial. He looked at the bench, dense with personages. Sir Edward Coke presided; Sir Francis Bacon sat beside him.

Somerset had sent lawyers to counsel Weston. They had told him that a man who did not enter a plea could not be found guilty. If he was never found guilty, his estate could not be seized by the Crown, and his family would avoid destitution. No plea, no trial. No trial, no punishment. It all sounded very simple—but the lawyers were against Sir Edward Coke.

Coke listened to the prisoner's decision not to plea and then responded. His voice was soft at first but gradually grew louder, until it sounded like Nemesis.

The prisoner, Coke said, could be persuaded to plea, "and to have weights laid upon him—no more than he was able to bear—which little by little were to be increased. He could then be exposed in an Open Place, near to the Prison. In the Open Air, being naked. And, lastly, he was to be preserved with the coarsest Bread that could be got, and water out of the next sink or puddle to the place of execution. And on that day he had water he should have no bread, and that day he had bread he should have no water. In this torment he was to linger as long as Nature could linger out, so that oftentimes men lived that extremity eight or nine days."[23]

Weston pleaded guilty. He endured long questioning, gave his statement, and was carried away to be hanged.


Mrs. Turner's trial started November 7, 1615. Sensational disclosures emerged. Sir Edward Coke produced a parchment bound with tanned strips of human skin and unfurled it, revealing cabalistic formulas written in human blood and containing crosses and sacred names placed in unspeakable combinations. As he did so, the scaffolding that supported a large number of onlookers suddenly gave a loud, unearthly creak, creating panic.[24]

Mrs. Turner's notorious position as procuress for persons at court provided many of the spectators with private reasons for concern. She had not only designed dresses for masques, but had rented rooms for assignations, sold powders and charms, medicines and aphrodisiacs. Her paraphernalia included wax figures of male and female genitalia, copulations, and perversions. Her papers were cryptic and hinted at many dark matters; she had an extensive collection of books on witchcraft, black magic, and Devil worship. Sir Edward Coke thundered at her to reveal all her secrets, and many persons trembled with her.

The king, an absorbed observer who had given the investigators a running series of suggestions and who was himself attempting to persuade a confession from Somerset, grew upset at the chief justice. Coke began to ask Mrs. Turner about Prince Henry. Had she known the prince or anyone near him?

That series of inquiries raised a larger specter than Sir Thomas Overbury's. The mystery of the healthy Henry's abrupt death coiled in the mind of all England. The disclosures of Overbury's murder had already thrilled the country with horror at the unsavory nature of the king's favorite and persons in the court; Coke touched a sensitive nerve.

Sir Francis Bacon, the king's man, intervened to turn the trial back toward the murder at hand. That brought matters to a somewhat abrupt close. The little dressmaker ascended the scaffold as the year 1615 came to its end. To her horror, and to the vast amusement of a large crowd, the executioner appeared with yellow-starched ruffs on his sleeve and a larger yellow-starched ruff around his neck. Her fashion died with her.

Sir Gervase Helwys, the Tower lieutenant, was next. He had known efforts were made to poison the prisoner under his care, and he had allowed these efforts to proceed. He was found guilty and condemned to death. Franklin, the expert mixer of evil potions, followed. By then Sir Edward Coke was hinting again about Prince Henry and succeeded in dragging Sir Robert Cotton into the situation. Cotton had been an intermediary between Somerset and the Spanish ambassador and had no knowledge of Overbury's murder, but Coke was after traitors as well as murderers and bayed down a track that alarmed the Crown.

Helwys and Franklin went to the gallows, and the countess of Essex was delivered of a daughter. She asked upon entering the Tower not to be placed in the cell that Overbury had once occupied. The earl was already inside.

The Somersets could only be tried by their peers. Therefore their case was out of the hands of Coke and in the hands of Attorney General Sir Francis Bacon. The jury would consist of the House of Lords—both secular and ecclesiastical. The countess appeared May 24, 1616. Bacon rose to speak. The murder of Overbury had darkened the Crown immeasurably. All England shuddered at the activities of the countess of Somerset and Mrs. Turner and the earl and all their sinister instruments. The king and his relationships were the subjects of shame; the introduction of Prince Henry's name into the issue by Coke, the partial revelations of highly placed persons in the pay of Spain, shook the realm.

Sir Francis Bacon made a great effort to turn this around. It was the king and his desire to see justice done—no matter whom it touched—that had bared the scandal, said the attorney general. In a rationalization James's apologists have used ever since, Sir Francis insisted that it was the king's keen and searching mind that had penetrated all mysteries and commanded all punishments. James was unafraid of revelations, said the attorney general, and placed all men equal under the law.

Having defended the king, Sir Francis then summarized the case against the countess, coupling it with the king's great and well-known capacity for mercy. The countess was asked for her defense and she replied, in a low, hushed voice, "I can much aggravate but nothing extenuate my fault. I desire mercy and that the Lords will intercede for me with the King."[25]

"The lady is so touched with remorse," said Sir Francis, "that grief surprises her from expressing of herself."

Ellesmere pronounced the sentence of death, and the countess was led away, but the moment had already lost interest. All eyes were fixed upon the trial of the earl, scheduled for the following day.

England had waited for that day many months. Pamphlets, letters, limericks, lampoons, satires, anonymous books had already appeared:

I.C.U.R. [I see you are]
Good monsieur Carr
About to fall.[26]

The king had offered Somerset a pardon if he would confess, but the earl had refused. Instead he stood, hour after hour, with the earl of Essex —the man he had replaced and demeaned—posed conspicuously opposite him. The king waited; the realm waited. They had a common curiosity. Would the favorite, when his turn came to defend himself, reveal all he knew?

It was said the court had placed strong men with capes near the earl, ready to muffle his words if he dared venture beyond the scope of the questions put to him or his own explanations of the Overbury murder. To the wonder of many, the earl did not—but it was really no wonder. His chances of living depended on the king's mercy—which would vanish at a single word.

Somerset argued with considerable spirit until the windows darkened, arousing reluctant respect. He was found guilty and taken away; the king was told it was all over. He plunged into his carriage and left the City at once.

Later, after negotiations back and forth, they were released from the Tower and sent under custody to a comfortable country manor. The countess's death sentence was lifted, but the earl's was only reprieved. They lost much of their wealth, but enough remained for comfort. There was only one twist. They could not leave their residence for any greater distance than three miles—and they had to live together.

The result was that the earl and countess of Somerset lived many long years in mutual loathing. It was said they never spoke to each other at all. James had taken a lover's revenge.

# 30

In early 1616, King James I decided to dispense with navigators and steer the ship of state himself. Unfortunately, he worked at the task only intermittently. That created difficulties, but they were minor compared to the fact that he chose a destination that was not marked on any chart. It was a port no monarch then or now has ever reached, but which remains one of great visionary goals of mankind: peace.

James had selected *Beati Pacifici* as his motto: Blessed Are the Peacemakers. Unfortunately, western Europe was maneuvering toward war. The great argument between the Vatican and the Reform created a vast gulf in art, literature, political thought, and future plans between Mediterranean and northern Europe. Germany, a mosaic whose many principalities were only theoretically ruled by an elected emperor with no central authority, reflected these differences and was like a group of tinder boxes ready to break into flames at a scratch.

Spain was aware that northern Europe hoped to sever the Hapsburg rulers of Iberia from their pro-Vatican relatives in Austria. Madrid maneuvered skillfully to conceal its weaknesses and to keep its enemies divided. The effort succeeded brilliantly in France, where the plans of Henry IV had been ended not only by the assassin's knife, but by a diplomatic success with his widow, the Dowager Queen-Regent Marie de Médicis. A double marriage between the French and Spanish royal houses not only pulled Catholic France toward Spain, but led to unrest among the French Huguenots. France was, as a result, no longer a menace to Spain.

At the same time, Madrid read its dispatches from Ambassador Sarmiento in England with close attention. Spanish fears flared when James I married his daughter, Princess Elizabeth, to the elector of the Palatinate, a prince who was titular leader of the Protestant League of Germany. If that step were to be followed by an alliance between England and Holland, Spain would be in jeopardy. The Dutch and English together could sweep Spain off the seas. That would mean Spanish silver and gold from Mexico and Peru would halt, Spain's commercial trade with Africa and Asia would be severed, and its empire would crash.

At first, Sarmiento attracted James's attention by telling him the king of Spain—with all his many kingdoms and vast problems—longed to confer with a monarch of recognized intellectual attainments, a figure who regarded the world through unselfish eyes. Gradually, the Spanish ambassador extended these sentiments into a discussion about a possible alliance between the two great powers. This, in turn, led to discussions of a marriage between Prince Charles and the infanta. Such a marriage would bring James a dowry of anywhere between £600,000 and £1 million. That was more than enough to settle all James's money problems and at the same time enhance his role as peacemaker of the world.

At first, the discussions seemed nebulous. When Sarmiento wrote Madrid, he was given a series of demands that James would have to meet: the children of the union would have to be Catholic; the pope's permission was necessary—and so on. For a time that seemed to chill the subject; the trial of the Somersets diverted attention.

During the winter of 1615–1616 the king listened to Reformers who wanted to displace the Howards and their pro-Spanish policy. For a time he encouraged their hopes. But he needed money. When he asked their thoughts regarding money, the only answer that Sir Ralph Winwood and the archbishop of Canterbury could suggest was a new Parliament. James was against that; Parliaments were anathema.

He turned toward Sarmiento and asked about the latest news from Madrid. The Spaniard declared the prospects for a marriage linking the two countries appeared excellent, except for the deplorable fact that James was already discussing the same marriage possibilities with the French.

The king then turned back to his administration and cleared his decks, so to speak, for his great journey toward the port of peace. He began by appointing, to the disappointment of the Reform, the Catholic earl of Worcester to the high post of lord chamberlain. At the same time, he gave his new favorite, Sir George Villiers, the lucrative post of Master of the Horse. The Reformers, scrambling to keep matters in balance, pushed forward the name of Sir Walter Raleigh.

The move was almost instinctive. All Reform England now looked back upon the reign of Elizabeth as a golden age. It was a time when English mariners attracted the attention of the world, when the English sailed the seas without fear, and when England was the hope and refuge of Protestantism.

Raleigh was that glory in the flesh. His exploits were famous and his writings had burnished his name. In his comfortable apartment in the Tower he had somehow kept that fame alive and had entertained high personages and conjured dreams. Lord Ellesmere, now in his late seventies, well recalled the days of glory. The archbishop of Canterbury was concerned over the king's moves toward Spain; these men and others began to press for Raleigh's release. They thought of the hero as a symbol of the policy they wanted to recreate. Their hope was that the realm would rise to push the king toward that policy.

In 1596, Raleigh had published a book called *Discovery of Guiana*. It was based on a trip he had made to that region, where he had discovered friendly Indians. It was an immensely popular book and was translated into many languages, and it brought a vision before men's eyes that in time became a cliché. Raleigh was famous for his travels, but he was a man whose imagination was, literally, boundless. Raleigh's most famous tale was told to him by the Indians. They spoke of a great, hidden kingdom far up from the delta of the Orinoco, along the shores of a lake called Parima, where rose a city made of gold. This secret realm, richer even than that of the Incas, was known among the Indians as El Dorado.

For years Raleigh wanted to go back to that region; he grew fanatically convinced he had turned back on the very rim of the gold fields that supplied El Dorado. That, at least, was the story that floated from the Tower over England and Europe. Behind the scenes, Raleigh put together still another story for Winwood, Ellesmere, and others.

Sir Walter would outfit an expedition, as of old, and sail toward Guiana. There was a treasure fleet that belonged to Spain which sailed off the coast of Mexico. It contained enough gold to save King James. If Raleigh came back, as in the days of Elizabeth, with that gleaming cargo, who would expect anything but the past returned, the days of glory alive again? The vision was shining enough to carry to Villiers. His intercession gained Raleigh a provisional release and permission to begin outfitting an expedition.[1]

The hero was no longer the flashing figure that had, however briefly, charmed Elizabeth. He walked out of the Tower for the first time in thirteen years, on March 19, 1616. In his middle sixties, he looked around at the world from which he had been held so long with the sparkling eyes of a boy.

At the same time, James told the Privy Council that preliminary conversations were underway with Spain regarding a possible marriage between Prince Charles and the infanta. The council, deeply divided, with no clear policy of its own, was in no condition to say much. Its composition had grown misshapen. The archbishop of Canterbury was against Rome, and bishop Andrewes considered Geneva the font of all difficulties. One secretary of state, Sir Ralph Winwood, wanted to go to war against Spain, and the other, Sir Thomas Lake, was for peace at any price. Sir Francis Bacon thought only of serving the king, and the earl of Arundel represented the old nobility.[2] The king, in command, sat back and orated about religious unity; the Peacemaker believed an alliance with Spain was the cornerstone of such an enterprise. Raleigh was not the only dreamer in the realm.

A month later, in April, 1616, the king sprang another surprise. He sold the three "cautionary towns" of Flushing, Brill, and Rammekins back to the Dutch for £215,000. His reasons were persuasive for those fortunate enough to hear them. The sites were expensive to maintain and could become the cause of contention if Spain and the Netherlands should not renew their truce, but resume fighting. England might be dragged into an unwelcome war. Beyond all that, there was James's desperate need for money.

That need was so great that the king next turned toward selling the peerage itself. Cecil had invented the somewhat ridiculous title of baronet, which made knighthood hereditary. James had less imagination or could not be bothered conceiving a new class. He proposed to make real barons out of any men who could produce £10,000 for the honor. Two appeared at once: Sir John Roper and Sir John Holles. One was made Lord Teynham; and the other, Lord Houghton.

Then James turned around and gave half the £20,000 he had realized from the sale to Lord Hay. Lord Hay, a Scot whom the king had known all his life, was to go to Paris and present some impossible conditions to the dowager queen to impel her to break off marriage negotiations regarding Prince Charles. James wanted these ended, but he did not want the onus for taking the step.

Hay, who had delayed the trip on grounds that he could not afford the expense, arrived in Paris at the head of a huge entourage. The magnificence of their costumes and the show they made astonished the largest city in Europe. Legends were told about it. The Parisians claimed the English shod their horses with silver shoes. Hay was pleased; so was his master. Both were men of impoverished backgrounds; both believed in great displays. Hay returned with the French negotiations ended, though he was not able to convince the Frenchmen that England was unhappy over the outcome. The great show had dazzled, but had not deceived.

That left, as far as King James was concerned, only one problem area remaining: the courts of England. James believed that judges, like bishops, should be obedient to the sovereign. His great opponent in that belief was Sir Edward Coke.[3]

Sir Edward had ruled against the High Commission in his former post and continued to rule against it when he became chief justice of the King's

Bench. He ruled, in 1616, against the mandatory oath of the High Commission on the grounds that it put men in peril of penal laws. The bishops argued fiercely, but the matter was swallowed in an even greater argument that rose between Coke and the Court of Chancery. Chancery was headed by Lord Ellesmere, who ruled favorably on a matter in which James was interested. Coke declared Chancery did not have such authority and ruled the other way.

That brought James raging to the scene. He summoned twelve judges before him on June 9, 1616. His attitude was that they were ignorant men and their opposition to his desires was insupportable. On their knees they begged his pardon, and as he questioned each in succession, each man humbly admitted his error and reversed his judgment. Only Sir Edward Coke resisted, saying he would have to consider the matter.

The king called Coke a sophist and dismissed him. He was pleased with himself and pleased with Sir Francis Bacon, who had argued exhaustively on his behalf.

James was so pleased that he appeared in the Star Chamber on June 20, 1616, to explain how the courts of England and its judges should conduct themselves.

His argument was that God had appointed the king, and "the mystery of the King's power is not lawful to be disputed. . . . The absolute perogative of the Crown is not subject for the tongue of a lawyer, nor is it lawful to be disputed. It is atheism," he continued, "and blasphemy to dispute what God can do; good Christians content themselves with his Will . . . so it is presumption and high contempt in a subject to dispute what a King can do, or say that Kings cannot do this or that, but rest in that which is the King's will revealed in this law."[4]

After this oration, James departed, amid his usual cluster of courtiers, who assured him he spoke with the tongue of an angel.

A week later, on June 26, 1616, Sir Edward Coke was called before the Privy Council and charged for not having listened to Bacon's arguments and for not giving way before the king. On the thirtieth, Coke was called back to hear James's judgment on him, a reversal of position for the most famous judge in England. His punishments were shrewdly mixed. He was deprived of his seat on the Privy Council and was told to remain off the bench and to go home and "employ his leisure" in looking over his reports and to correct all "extravagant and exorbitant opinions" he found in them.

On the surface, the king had scored an impressive victory. He had humiliated Coke and forced eleven of the highest judges in the land to their knees. The king turned toward his pleasures with great private satisfaction; Sir Francis Bacon saw his own chances for advancement open wide.

Beneath the surface, however, the king had created a new problem, one that had not existed before. England was proud of its justice and teeming with lawyers. The Reform propaganda had based its resistance to the High Commission on common law rights. The subjugation of Sir Edward Coke was accepted, by the most serious elements in the realm, as the abandonment of the rights of England. Sir Edward became a martyr, symbol of the common law—and his name began to shine.

When Sir George Villiers was first made a knight and Gentleman of the Bedchamber through the intercession of the archbishop of Canterbury, he was pleasingly grateful. He went to the archbishop and thanked him and asked his advice. The older man beamed and grew sententious.

Later, when Villiers became Master of the Horse and King James began his arguments with Sir Edward Coke, Villiers went to Sir Francis Bacon and asked his advice. Bacon, as charmed as the archbishop, wrote many pages of sage aphorisms. In the end, they all added up to "obey the Crown." Sir Francis did not, of course, put that worship in ignoble terms: he used a premise that greedy intellectuals have often since used in similar circumstances. "Power to do good," said Sir Francis, "is the highest aspiration of mankind."[5]

What Villiers thought of Bacon's effort remains unknown. All that remains is the picture of a young man to whom everyone seemed attracted. Bishop Godfrey Goodman, watching carefully, wrote, "Sir George Villiers had kept much company with the gentlemen waiters, who sometimes after supper did leap and exercise their bodies. But [he] of all others was most active; he had a very lovely complexion; he was the handsomest bodied man of England; his limbs were so well compacted, and his conversation so pleasing, and of so sweet a disposition. And truly his intellectuals were very great; he had a sound judgment and was of a quick apprehension. . . ."[6]

These qualities helped him rise very quickly, but he had others of which the good Bishop Goodman did not write. The king was growing older and his vices had grown stronger. He kissed Sir Henry Rich, who had a remarkably smooth and handsome face, full on the lips before the court. Sir Henry turned away with an expression of disgust and spat on the floor. That disgust and that gesture offended James, and Sir Henry had to leave the court.

Villiers, in contrast, welcomed the king's overtures. Selected like earlier favorites for his looks, he made no pretense—for no pretense was possible with James in his maturity: ". . . the love the King showed was as amorously conveyed as if he mistaken their sex and thought them ladies," wrote Francis Osborne, "which I have seen Somerset and [Villiers] labour to resemble, in the effeminateness of their dressings, though in whoreson lookes and wanton gestures, they exceeded any part of womankind my conversation did ever cope withall. Nor was his love, or what else posterity will please to call it . . . carried on with a discretion sufficient to cover a lesse scandalous behavior; for the kings kissing them after so lascivious a mode in publick, and upon the theatre, as it were, of the world, prompted many to imagine some things done in the tyring-house [bedroom] that exceed my expressions . . ."[7]

Villiers played his role with an apparent gusto that was astonishing. He managed to be playful and eloquent at the same time, and before the king knew him a year, he found his company indispensable. James was in his fiftieth year, and his health had grown erratic. He had arthritic attacks in cold, damp weather, accompanied by swelling feet. "The pains are acute," the physician, Malverne, wrote, "raging by night, now worse, now milder." The attacks were miraculously soothed when Villiers appeared. He could calm the king, flatter him into a good humor, and make him laugh.

That was more than his physicians could accomplish. James obeyed no rules and followed no regimen excepting his own immediate desires. He gorged himself on whatever dish appealed at the moment and was fondest of fresh fruits, because they were easy on his remaining teeth. Liquor began to affect him; his drinking increased as his capacity decreased.

Yet in summer 1616 the king of England was a happy man. He had Villiers, the perfect favorite, at his side and was supreme in the realm. His handling of the judges had seemed, to both the king and his coterie, marvelous. Prospects for continued peace appeared good, and the court was somehow—by bribes and extortions and subterfuges of various sorts—able to maintain its careless luxury. James was persuaded, by the Bishop Montagu among others, to have his many writings—or the many writings in his name —collected into a huge folio titled *The Work of the Most High and Mighty Prince James.* It was dedicated to the only superior that the king now recognized: Jesus Christ.

Later in the summer of 1616 the king made Villiers Viscount Buckingham "with the greatest alacrity and princely cheerfulness." The king delighted in these ceremonies and rejoiced in the smiles of his favorite and happily returned the toasts that the courtiers raised in both their honors. He seemed entirely unaware of—or at least indifferent to—what Osborne described as the results. "His favorites . . . or minions," said the observer, "were like burning glasses . . . interposed between him and the subject, multiplying in the heat of oppressions in the general opinion, though in his own he thought they screened him from reflexions upon the crowne. . . ."[8]

Villiers not only rose; he carried his family with him. It was a period when a family operated much as a corporation would behave in later centuries. Any advancement in position or influence was immediately announced through the familial telegraphs of letters and conversations. The new Viscount Buckingham had already introduced his mother, Lady Compton, to the king, and she pushed forward two more sons—Sir John Villiers and Sir Christopher Villiers. Sir John was described as "a weakling in mind and body," and Sir Christopher as "dull and unattractive."

Nevertheless, Villiers wanted all his family to rise. The court learned that Buckingham had a flair in using his influence. He was the closest man to the king in every sense, his companion and the sharer of his confidences, his secretary and his shield against the world. James had never been without men to play one or another of these roles, but Buckingham was the only one in his life who would play them all at once.

His ascendancy was amazing. Early in 1616 young Charles, still known in England as the duke of York, extravagantly admired a ring Villiers was wearing, begged to be allowed to wear it, and then lost it. James rebuked the heir to the throne and reduced him to tears. Later in the year, Charles playfully—and he was rarely playful—turned a water fountain on Buckingham. On that occasion, James boxed his son's ears.

In November 1616, however, Charles was made the Prince of Wales. He was sixteen. A slender, solemn, and not very bright boy, he grew up at a court where drunkenness and profligacy were common. An undertone of sexuality of all sorts permeated the palace; Charles remained aloof. It was not that he was virtuous so much as he was dim.


Sir Edward Coke reluctantly sent the king a report, in which he discovered several minor—very minor—errors in his own previous judgments. That gesture was deemed insufficient. On October 10, 1616, Sir Edward virtually withdrew the opinions that had so angered the king, but was now caught by Buckingham, the favorite.

The wife of Sir Edward Coke had so many grievances against him she refused to use his name and was known instead as Lady Hatton—the name of her first husband. Nevertheless, the Cokes had a beautiful daughter—Frances Coke—to whom a considerable inheritance was due. Sir John Villers, elder brother of the favorite, fixed upon the heiress as the woman he wanted to marry.

Lady Compton, Villier's grasping mother, sought to arrange the union and was asked if, in the event it occurred, Sir Edward would retain his post as chief justice. Word came back from the favorite that could be arranged —provided Coke also contributed a large sum of money. At that point,

Coke resisted, saying the king's favor was "too dear."

In November, 1616, word came that the famous jurist was dismissed.


In January 1617 Villiers was made earl of Buckingham, a Knight of the Garter and a member of the Privy Council. The king had already made him wealthy and given him estates equal to his new rank; the favorite used his influence to increase these already astonishing gifts.

Around him other men were moved upward as well. Sir Francis Bacon had crawled since the days of Elizabeth with his eyes fixed upon high office. As attorney general he had been outstanding in his efforts on behalf of the king; he watched the illness of the eighty-year-old Lord Ellsemere, the lord chancellor, with careful patience.

Meanwhile, he discussed his expedition with Sir Walter Raleigh. The hero had put all his money into the venture, as well as all he could persuade others to invest. His flagship was named, appropriately, *Destiny*. *Destiny* would be followed by thirteen other vessels. While it was built and Raleigh's little fleet was being prepared, it attracted considerable attention. Even Bacon was drawn by curiosity. In the course of remarks, Raleigh mentioned the treasure fleet of Mexico as though accidentally.

"But that would be piracy," said Bacon, recoiling in horror. He shared many attributes with his king.

Raleigh smiled. "Did you ever hear of men who are pirates for millions?" he asked easily. "They who aim at small things are pirates."[9]

Raleigh had, however, many admirers. In Europe the Huguenots of France discussed the possibility of outfitting some ships to join him against Spain; the treasure could finance a rebellion. The duke of Savoy, at war with Spain, was interested in the venture. Venice, the Dutch, some of the Protestants of Germany and Scandia all wished him well. These wishes, however, were not accompanied by money—and Lord Ellesmere, the lord chancellor, Raleigh's greatest patron in England, was eighty years old and sick.


By March 1617 Raleigh's prospects darkened. The duke of Savoy had decided to end his war against Spain. Sarmiento, the Spanish ambassador, after several months of delays, was able to assure James that prospects for a marriage between Prince Charles and the infanta looked promising. At the same time, he raised serious objections to Raleigh's trip—not for the first time.

James was so elated at the news that a Spanish marriage was now really possible that he made a public announcement of the fact. Madrid, in turn, was so pleased that James made their growing détente known to the world that it raised Sarmiento to Count Gondomar. Sir John Digby was sent back to Madrid as ambassador with terms—James wanted at least £500,000—to launch negotiations.

This development sent shudders through the Reform areas of northern Europe and much of England—but James's court and council were now heavily loaded with pro-Vatican individuals. Its balance was further tipped when Lord Ellesmere, an ardent Reformer, died. Sir Francis Bacon succeeded as head of Chancery. Since he was not a peer, his title was lord keeper.

Other steps of the ladder opened in sequence. Sir Henry Yelverton, who was solicitor general, was slated to become attorney general. Yelverton, however, discovered the favorite in his path. Buckingham was now so strong that he believed no man should advance without paying him tribute. Sir Henry, ordinarily compliant, grew indignant and refused, and his appointment was delayed. It was not until a great many parties were drawn into the matter that Buckingham gave way and the new earl made his reasons clear. It was not money; he had moved beyond that need— "but if so important an office was disposed of without his influence being seen in the matters, men would fancy he had lost his credit with the King."[10]

Buckingham's power spread through the court and the government. His mother, Lady Compton, was tireless; his brothers, cousins, and hangers-on were insatiable. The favorite was capricious; he would assist men and then turn on them suddenly and ruin them. Nevertheless, there was a stream of applicants, candidates, hopefuls, and ambitious men who flowed toward him. Sir Edward Coke, having spent an entire winter in lonely boredom, decided to meet Buckingham's price. If Sir John Villiers wanted to marry one of his daughters and if he had to add money to honey, he would do so.

That arrangement was relayed to Buckingham just as he and the king, at the head of a huge caravan, began a trip to Scotland.

James had, some time earlier, approved of Five Articles for the Kirk. James had learned, however, that the articles were ignored. The Scots worshiped as they had during the days of Andrew Melville. Having settled all the affairs of England, James decided only his own irresistible presence could resolve the lingering resistance of Scotland.

Over £100,000 was extorted from the merchants of London for the king's journey. Raising that sum had been difficult and James blamed his lord treasurer, the earl of Suffolk. For the moment he deferred that subject, however, until he had reduced his countrymen.

James, the product of the Reform, hated it from the bottom of his heart. In England the Church had knelt before him as God's representative; he determined the Scots would do the same. To prepare them to adopt the Church of England liturgy, he had an organ sent ahead, which landed at Leith. Soon after its arrival, English sculptors arrived carrying effigies of patriarchs and saints. These objects, to be installed at Holyrood, inspired riots. The Scots bishops were so alarmed they wrote to London, asking the king to defer his plans or to at least remove the objects that caused so much trouble. James was annoyed.

He crossed the border on May 13, 1617, and entered Edinburgh on the sixteenth. He enjoyed the progress north immensely, and the Scots made costly preparations to welcome him. These included pageants and floats, speeches, purses of gold, and crowds, to which he had grown accustomed. He attended services at Holyrood and listened to a trained choir and the peals of the organ in the chapel with great satisfaction. They had not been heard in that site since the days of his mother, Mary Stuart. Then he ordered all the Scots Privy Councillors, the bishops, and his other creatures to show, by their obedience, how services were conducted in England.

Speaking before a session of the Scots Parliament, he told the members they represented "a barbarous people." He advised them to adopt more of the English customs than simply smoking tobacco or wearing fine clothes. He then proceeded to tell the nobility of Scotland that it should relinquish its ancient feudal rights, as their counterparts had in England. They listened to this stonily, but the king persisted. His only accomplishment was to force a grudging competence from them to support the clergy.

After that, the king turned toward the clergy, the real objects of his mission. His argument was that "whatever His Majesty should determine . . . for the Church, should have the force of law." That raised a storm, and James retracted somewhat. But, as ever, he returned to the substance of the move almost at once. He would not rule on doctrine, he said, but on forms. Ministers rose to protest; several were forced into exile as a result.

In July 1617 James held a meeting at St. Andrews with the bishops and hectored them at length. Between these sessions, which tired him quickly, he drank, hunted, and toured. He visited Stirling and Glasgow, Hamilton, Dumfries, and other sites. Matters in Scotland had settled in his long absence; the country was not overly prosperous but had grown relatively peaceful and calm. The appointment of bishops had not changed the forms of worship; most men saw little difference in the ecclesiastical moves James had made. His trip, however, changed all that—for he was intent upon changing the forms and the Reform.

James was accompanied in this effort, and on his trip, by a man whose name was already creating discord in England: Laud, the dean of Gloucester. Laud was against Puritanism in all its forms, and it never seemed to occur to him that intolerance is not made admirable because its targets are unpopular. He forced conformity and had created great unrest in Gloucester and other English towns by his refusal to allow even slight deviations from the letters of James's rules.[11]

The High Commission had begun to flag under the opposition of the common law judges and lawyers, but Laud revived its efforts—and extended them into the congregations. As usual, when zealotry appears, it created resistance. Demonstrations broke out in England at the time James traveled north to prove his rise in the world to his countrymen; Laud was, in part, responsible.

In Scotland James called a General Assembly. It included nobles as well as James's bishops; Knox had long before established a combination of nobles and ministers. Bishop Spottiswoode, humble before the king, urged obedience to his great authority and wisdom. No seats were provided for ministers; they huddled in the back, while the nobles and bishops sat in dignity. A letter from James was read aloud, warning that resistance was useless, since the new articles and other measures were ordered by royal authority. Those who questioned that authority were questioning the power that God gave a Christian king.

Enough bishops and nobles voted in favor of acceptance to carry the matter. Demonstrations erupted in Edinburgh; ministers were summoned for recalcitrance; a High Commission was established to enforce conformity.

James turned southward immensely pleased with himself. He had created machinery to make Scotland like England and to forward his old dream of uniting the two realms. The Reform he hated was now beneath the power of the sovereign. He believed he had, at last, laid to rest the ghosts of John Knox and George Buchanan and all the other men who had told him in his youth that subjects could rightfully depose their sovereigns, as they had deposed his mother, Mary Stuart.

In reality, he had revived the rusted machinery of revolution by moving against the Kirk in Scotland and the Reform in England. In Mary Stuart's time the Reform had been directed against the Vatican and traditional Catholicism. James Stuart, stressing his divine right, provided a new target: the bishops and the king of both realms.


The world did not rest while James summered in Scotland. Sir Walter Raleigh sailed from Plymouth at the head of fourteen ships while Gondomar, the Spanish ambassador, watched with displeasure. His protests forced James to obtain a letter from Raleigh, vowing not to fight against Spaniards anywhere. In addition, the Spaniard received a secret map of Raleigh's travel plans.

In France assassins ended the life of the Italian favorite of the dowager queen and a Huguenot faction persuaded the young Louis XIII to assume the reins of government.

In England Sir Edward Coke told the favorite's mother, Lady Compton, of his change of heart. Buckingham, traveling with James, kept many messengers busy and wrote back his pleasure. Bacon, however, was displeased. The last man on earth who should be allowed to rise, in his opinion, was Sir Edward Coke.

The new lord keeper had, in fact, grown very grand. He had taken office in great state, attended by a hundred men. The absence of the king and his favorite left Bacon to receive foreign ambassadors, and he had the sensations, however, fleeting, of holding ultimate power. The Chancery Court, which he now headed, began to move at a more rapid pace; his reports to the king were somewhat smug. Yet he did not forget his political manners; he was careful to send Buckingham a stream of flattering letters.

It was the Coke-Villiers marriage that led Bacon astray. Sir Edward Coke was now anxious to give his daughter to the favorite's brother. He was also of the opinion his wife, Lady Hatton, could pay the extra sums involved. Lady Hatton did not agree; neither did her daughter. Both fled from Hatton House and an impasse developed.

Bacon, hearing of the deadlock, wrote a letter to Buckingham. The letter offered advice—a practice to which Bacon was addicted; he advised mankind. He urged Buckingham to keep his brother away from a family as unsettled as the Cokes and also warned against restoring his old rival to any official post.

Unfortunately, Buckingham's mother, Lady Compton, acting under her son's direction, appeared before the council, asking for a warrant so that Sir Edward Coke could regain custody of his daughter. Bacon, sitting as lord chancellor, brusquely refused the request. That earned him the undying hatred of one of the most vitriolic and obnoxious women in the realm. She turned to another judge, Sir Ralph Winwood, who granted the warrant at once.

Then, armed with the warrant and a number of armed men, Buckingham's mother and Sir Edward Coke traveled to the estate of a cousin of Lady Hatton. They rapped on the door but it remained closed. The former chief justice of England then seized a heavy log, broke the door down, and dragged his protesting daughter to his coach.

The following day a distraught Lady Hatton rushed to the Privy

Council to protest. Bacon, as the mighty lord chancellor, declared the lady in the right. He suggested various severe punishments for Coke. To his surprise, a fellow judge produced a letter from King James approving the marriage between the Coke heiress and Sir John Villiers. Bacon was overruled, though an order went out for Coke. He appeared and thundered about the rights of a father. Sir Henry Yelverton soothed him. In the end the Cokes left together, hand in hand.

Bacon, however, persisted. He wrote James a long letter, repeating his objections and characterizing Coke. Toward its close he added that he would not change his mind for Buckingham—but only for the king. In response, he received a long tirade from the king and a much shorter but terrible letter from the favorite that ended. "I'm sorry, for I was your friend." The lord chancellor was in trouble.

Sir Edward Coke, however, traveled north to greet the returning king and favorite and was well received. Sir Henry Yelverton made the same effort and managed to ingratiate himself. Buckingham raged to him about Bacon. With a touch of malice, Yelverton wrote the lord chancellor the details of the favorite's tirade, saying in part, that Buckingham had said "the Lord Keeper was showing the same ingratitude to him as he had formerly shown Essex and Somerset." That was a deadly stroke; it could bring to the surface a widespread but deep-rooted disgust of Sir Francis Bacon that could seriously injure him.

Sir Francis wasted no time in hurrying to meet his masters, but neither would receive him. Instead, he was told the earl of Buckingham would talk to him later in London.

By September the royal party was home in Whitehall, and the lord chancellor, officially attired in the hope of a royal audience, appeared. He was directed to Buckingham's apartment and led to a room "with scrapers and lackeys, where he had to sit on a wooden chest with his Purse and Seal."

He waited a long time. Two days, in fact. At the end of this penance the great intellectual, almost sixty years old, was told the terms upon which the favorite would see him. He agreed to them. The door then swung open, and Sir Francis Bacon entered to kneel humbly and kiss the feet of the twenty-five-year-old earl of Buckingham—the king's Steenie. Then he was pardoned.[12]

Sir Edward Coke was restored to his place as Privy Councillor in late September 1617. King James himself appeared and could not help but notice how eyes continued to turn toward the restored member. "I, James," he said, "am neither a god nor an angel, but a man like any other. Therefore I act like a man and confess to loving those near to me more than any other men. You may be sure that I love the Earl of Buckingham more than anyone else, and more than you who are here assembled. I wish to speak in my own behalf and not to have it thought to be a defect, for Jesus Christ did the same, and therefore I cannot be blamed. Christ had his John, and I have my George."[13]

The following day Frances Coke married Sir John Villiers at Hampton Court. The king was present to give his blessing and to give them orders not to rise from their beds the following morning until after he had visited them. But Sir Edward Coke was not made chief justice again. He had the honor of being a member of the Privy Council, but was given no other office. A great bitterness began to rise within him, as he watched the attentions of Buckingham and his mother, Lady Compton, and the king himself, turn toward Lady Hatton—his wife.

The Villiers family wanted the Hatton money. They attended a party she gave, and the king knighted four of the guests who were present that evening. He kissed Lady Hatton repeatedly as he departed. She found herself the belle of the season—but when the Villiers learned she would hold her own money, favor departed as abruptly as it had arisen.

Nevertheless, the Coke lesson was not lost on the realm. The figure of the earl of Buckingham was merging into that of the king.

The end of December 1617 found Sir Walter Raleigh ill with fever in a ship lying off Guiana. He had only ten vessels left of the fourteen with which he started; storms and illness had taken the rest. Only five of his ten vessels could enter the Orinoco; the others drew too much water to pass over the shoals. He sent them up the river with 250 fighters and 150 seamen without him; he was too weak to travel. They included his nephew, George Raleigh, and his son, Wat—Walter. Keymis, the trusted assistant who had been up that river with him in the 1590s, was in charge overall. Raleigh saw them leave with a great mixture of emotions and prayed for their success with a fervor that would have surprised the people who considered him an atheist.

Sir Ralph Winwood, Raleigh's supporter, died. That left one vacancy of the two offices of secretary of state. For a short time James and Buckingham thought they could manage it themselves, but they soon grew tired of such details. Their choice was Sir Nicholas Naunton, an obscure and obedient man, who paid for the honor by making the favorite's younger brother,

Sir Christopher, heir to lands worth £500 a year. The interests of the favorite had become synonymous with those of the Crown.

"My Lords," said the King on New Year's Day, 1618, "I drink to you all, and I know that you are all welcome to my George, and he that doth not pledge with all his heart, I would the Devil had him."[14]

He made Buckingham a marquis that day, the first he had ever made in England. He raised some other men, as was customary. Sir Francis Bacon, having kissed the right feet and handled suits in Chancery with notable dispatch, became a peer at last: a baron. He chose the title Lord Verulam.

With the exception of the king's debts, which had risen to nearly £750,000, matters appeared well in hand. There was an obvious need for economies, and both the king and Buckingham talked grandly of putting the government in order. But neither were men of detail. James liked to talk and to drink and to hunt. Buckingham himself was not a man of letters. His was a verbal ability, though he was shrewd and could cross-examine astutely. He and James finally abandoned their efforts to manage everything, in a sort of boredom—but not until they agreed upon Sir Lionel Cranfield. Cranfield was a successful businessman brought into governmental matters by the long-dead earl of Northampton of the dark plots and devious ways. Since then Cranfield had proven ingenious in various projects; he became a sort of floating expert for the Crown.

In Madrid whole committees, commissions, and flocks of theologians worked on the problems attendant upon a marriage between a Spanish princess and the English Prince of Wales. Sarmiento—or Count Gondomar as he had become—struggled to reconcile two worlds that had drifted far apart. The Vatican had struggled against the Reform so long that its own faith—especially in Spain—had grown into something almost new. The Church of England, which prided itself on being an ancient form of Catholicism, had become a hybrid all its own. The ideas of James and the Spanish cardinals required more than translators; they were almost comically apart. Nevertheless, Gondomar kept sparks of hope flickering, and the size of the Spanish dowry impelled James to make a continuing series of concessions.

By early 1618, however, these concessions were not as important to Madrid as either James or Gondomar believed. Matters were growing tense in Europe, especially in Germany. The Emperor Matthias had no heir. The Hapsburgs of Vienna and Madrid decided to support Ferdinand II, the king of Bohemia. The Reform knew Ferdinand and did not like the idea. As king of Bohemia, he had ordered his mainly Reform subjects to adopt the Vatican faith or be deported. Reform services were suppressed.

In May 1618 a rebellion against Ferdinand began in Bohemia and opened with a dramatic scene. Three of the king's councillors were thrown out of the windows of the council chamber in Prague. Defenestration, as it is known, was a favored Czech method. A provisional government was declared, and the Reform began a new revolution.


The news was slow in reaching England, where the king and Buckingham were finally moving against the Howards. They had offended in a peculiar way. Having succeeded once with Somerset and been succeeded in that triumph by the introduction of a new young man named Villiers, the Howards had set a new beauty contest in motion. One of their more spectacular entrants was a younger son of Sir William Monson. They made great efforts with him, dressing him elaborately and "washing his face every day with posset curd."[15] They did not rest with one effort, however. The court was gradually inundated with effeminate young men, some of whom apparently penetrated the king's bedchambers and who subsequently believed themselves to be the coming favorite.

The king and Buckingham both became aware these hopefuls were making the court ridiculous; Buckingham was furious. The great Howard family, which still held many important governmental posts, found itself under attack.

The instrument of that attack was Sir Lionel Cranfield, who headed a series of investigations. One, exploring the state of the navy under the earl of Nottingham—a Howard—discovered that nearly half the forty-three ships of the fleet were unseaworthy. Corruption had penetrated every crevice of naval activities; the situation was so bad that independent observers declared a new navy could be constructed from scratch for less money.[16] Nottingham was doomed by these discoveries; Buckingham was appointed to a special board that would, henceforth, supervise this service.

Another Howard—the earl of Suffolk—was lord high treasurer. It was learned that the earl's obnoxious wife, who had long collected a pension from Spain, also extracted bribes from everyone with whom her husband conducted business. James, furious, ordered the countess to leave court and even London itself. After a brief absence, the countess returned. The king flew into a passion and said he would have her removed from the city "in a cart, like a common whore."


Sir Walter Raleigh's men traveled up the Orinoco and reached the region Keymis recalled as holding the gold mines of El Dorado. It had, however, been many years since he and his captain had been to that area, and in the meantime a Spanish town called San Tomé had been created. It was, however, located near a mine. The story of the battle that took place between the English and Spanish at that site varies according to the writers, but there is no doubt about the deaths, the firing of the town, and the breaking of Raleigh's pledges of peace. Young Raleigh was killed. The English survivors crawled back down the great river. When Keymis reported the catastrophe, Sir Walter's words were so bitter that Keymis committed suicide.

It took some months for the expedition to straggle back across the Atlantic; news of its failure arrived with its first two vessels in May 1618. Gondomar appeared before the English Privy Council to demand satisfaction; he claimed James had promised to send Raleigh to Spain for punishment. That information created an uproar; both the king and Gondomar, the Catholic and Reform issues, were flaming subjects. Gondomar insisted, however, that such an agreement had been made and Buckingham spoke in its favor.

News of these discussions created widespread indignation. A member of the Spanish embassy had the misfortune, at this time, of running over a child in his carriage. All London erupted in a riot. Thousands descended upon the embassy to throw rocks and were barely restrained. The king apologized and issued orders the city should not only do the same, but punish those responsible. Gondomar, as always, took a high tone and said he did not know how his master would react to such activities.

On July 15, 1618, the Spaniard departed. All the Catholic priests in English prisons were released as a sort of departing honor, and over a hundred trailed the ambassador's coach to embark upon his ship with him. Gondomar had every reason to be pleased; he had made himself a virtual minister of a foreign state while serving his own with complete loyalty. His recall was by no means a sign of disfavor; the rebellion in Bohemia was like a burning torch near a haystack. His masters in Madrid wanted to know what England would do, what it could do, and what Spain's approach toward James should be in the next stage of developments.


James agreed, before his Privy Council, to send Raleigh to Spain for punishment; and the news had created widespread indignation when the adventurer himself, with the tattered remnants of his expedition, arrived at Plymouth in June 1618. He started for London, but was soon joined by his cousin Sir Lewis Stukely. Stukely was a vice admiral and took the hero into custody, but their progress toward London was slow. Raleigh feigned illness and several times came close to escape. In these efforts, his connections with the French were revealed. Meanwhile, he composed a defense—an *Apology*.

The *Apology* was an argument that the Guiana Territory was open to all, that Spain had no right to claim all the Americas as its own. The king, however, clung to the letter of the agreement. There was never, in all James's life, a reason to fight—not even, in his own life, self-defense. He appointed a commission consisting of Bacon, the archbishop of Canterbury, Sir Edward Coke, and several others to judge the matter.

Meanwhile, Raleigh was subjected, in grim custody in the Tower, to a variety of efforts to confess that he deliberately misled the king. Raleigh was tangled in the innumerable stories he had told; he was an incurable fabulist. He added to these in confinement. He presented quite a problem. James was afraid to have him tried in open court, lest demonstrations on his behalf—and against Spain—occur. The wrangle continued into the autumn.

The Raleigh issue was only one of many. The earl of Suffolk, whom the countess had so effectively undermined by her criminalities and her indiscretions, was hauled before the Star Chamber on charges of corruption. Under examination, these dwindled to accepting gifts and bribes, and Bacon —now Lord Verulam—was sarcastic. New Year's gifts, he said, were accepted by all—but New Year did not extend to all year. These proceedings droned along at the same time as the Raleigh brouhaha.

Had Raleigh returned a year before, or a year later, his fate might have been different. But he returned at the time that the Reformers in Bohemia launched their rebellion. Acting on the advice of Gondomar, back in Madrid, the Spaniards suggested that King James I of England—*Beati Pacifici* —act as peacemaker.

The suggestion came after James had already received a letter from the Bohemian Reform rebels, asking his assistance. Spain, however, had pointed toward what James considered the right sort of assistance. He grasped at the chance to shine—and to improve the world. He composed a reply to Madrid, saying he had heard the side of the rebels; would the Spaniards now enlighten him of the other side?

That response was received with enormous glee in the Spanish capital; Gondomar sent his private confessor to acquaint Sanchez, the new ambassador from Spain to London, on how to talk to James. The Protestant world, alarmed, began to pour men toward James to divert him from Spain, to suggest brides other than the infanta for Prince Charles.

In October 1618, under these lowering skies, Sir Walter Raleigh appeared before the king's commission to hear, from Bacon, that he would be executed "for abusing the confidence of the King . . . and injuring subjects of Spain." That reason, however, could not safely be made public. Instead, the lawyers found, as lawyers always seem to find, a technicality. Raleigh was still under a sentence of death for complicity in the Cobham plot of

1603. It was decided to execute that sentence; another would be redundant.

On the evening of October 28, 1618, Lady Raleigh, who had a small velvet bag set aside for his head, visited her husband and told him she had obtained permission to dispose of his body. He smiled and said, "Bess, thou mayst dispose of that dead . . . which thou hadst not always the disposing of . . . alive."

Lady Raleigh left at midnight, and Raleigh prepared himself for his last public appearance. He was composed enough to write some last verses on the flyleaf of his Bible. Then he slept.

The following morning was chilly. On the way to the scaffold, Raleigh saw a bald-headed man and handed him his cap, saying "You have more need of it than I." On the stage before a large crowd, he mounted a last defense. Finished, he turned to the executioner and asked to see the axe. Running his finger along the edge, he said, "Sharp medicine—but a sound cure for all diseases." The crowd hummed its approval; Raleigh was behaving like a hero. Lying down, he heard someone shout that he ought to face his head toward the east, and he lifted his head to make a last retort. "What matter," he said, "how the head lie, so the heart be right?"

A little later, in the midst of his last prayers, he gave the signal and the gleaming blade flashed down once, then twice—and his head was held aloft. His last verse left the realm with words by which to remember him:

> Even such is Time that takes on trust
> Our youth, our joys, and all we have,
> And pays us back with age and dust;
> Who in the dark and silent grave,
> When we have wandered all our ways,
> Shuts up the story of our days.
> But from this earth, this grave, this dust,
> The Lord shall raise me up, I trust.[17]

Prince Charles was in his eighteenth year when he quarreled during a tennis game with Buckingham. The King was upset and insisted they must become friends. That was part of his eternal attitude; but Buckingham, looking at the silent young man, had even deeper thoughts. The King was 52 and showed his age. He limped noticeably when he walked; his lifelong pacing had largely stopped. He sat in a chair most of the time; he even traveled in a chair. He loved his horses but was content to have them exhibited; his riding days were over. It was time, and perhaps more than time, that farsighted men began to regard the heir.

In 1618, therefore, the favorite arranged an elaborate feast. He called it the Feast of Friends. It was the sort of playlet of which the king was fond, and he made much of the occasion. Prince Charles was the honored guest before whom people rose and to whom they addressed flowery speeches; his name and Buckingham's were coupled. The prince's elder brother, Henry, could not have been so pressured, but Henry was dead. Charles had been a timid boy with thin legs so weak the physicians had, at one time, recommended iron braces. He had outgrown that, but he remained a somewhat sticklike figure who seldom spoke. He was almost abject in his anxiety to please his father and his father's friend.

Seated between them, with James planting kisses on first one and then the other, the prince smiled uncertainly. He was apparently unable to face, even in his imagination, the facts of homosexuality. It was disloyal to think about such a subject and impossible to conceive of his own father engaged in the postures and practices it entailed. He had, therefore, long ago stopped not only his ears but his mind as well. He looked at Buckingham's tall, athletic form, the deep blue eyes that could shine so warmly, the perfect complexion—and his mind glided past the odd, small hands and the curiously bisexual features—to accept a great and important court statesman.

Buckingham's hand was on his shoulder, and the favorite pleaded for the prince's friendship. Charles took it and, with that acceptance, accepted his father and all his rationalizations: his relationship with Steenie and his duty to cling to them both. In that acceptance he never wavered.

Queen Anne had watched favorites rise and fall. She and her husband, King James, had not lived together since they inherited the crown of England. Her great hope had been Prince Henry. After his death her interest in political matters had waned, though she was in favor of the Spanish marriage of Prince Charles for a time. By the end of 1618 she suffered from dropsy, and her life—an innocent one filled with games, parties, her ladies, and dogs—began to diminish. The new relationship that flowered between her only remaining son and Buckingham may have depressed her, for Anne of Denmark began to speak very bitterly about the king. He was puzzled; he could not account for it. Her health declined subtly; her appearances became less frequent, and her parties stopped. By early 1619 she was bedridden and not improving.

In February the king went to Newmarket to enjoy the races. While there, he fell ill, and Queen Anne, alone except for servants, physicians, and clergymen, sank toward her end. Prince Charles was summoned toward the end of the month, but his mother had nothing to say to him. She told him to return the next day and told the bishops the same. Someone urged she make a will, and she said, "Tomorrow will do." It was not until after midnight and during the first hours of March 2, 1619, that she realized she was dying.

The news of her death reached James at Newmarket and depressed him —but not on Anne's account; it was the grim reminder of passing time that he felt most. Such thoughts sent him into melancholia, a condition increased by heavy drinking. He left Newmarket for Royston suffering from arthritis and the stone. By the middle of March he was seriously ill. His physicians hardly knew which of his problems to handle or in what order. He had ". . . pains in the joints and nephritis with thick sand, continued fever, bilious diarrehea . . . bitter humours boiling from his mouth so as to cause ulcers on his lips and chin, fainting, sighing, dread, incredible sadness, intermittent pulse."[18] He finally voided three stones, suffered fits of vomiting, and began to recover.

In the middle of the siege, he thought he was dying and called Prince Charles. James recommended Buckingham to him; that pact was their bond. He also muttered about the Spanish marriage and the miracles it would bring. But by the end of March 1619 he began to recover; by April he was carried to Theobalds in a chair. There, enjoying the sensation of renewed life, he had deers run past him and as soon afterward as possible was back following the hunt. Told that fresh deer blood was good, he began to stand in the opened cadavers of freshly killed carcasses. He was soon gorging on fresh fruit and resumed drinking heavily.

Queen Anne presented a problem in death; the expenses of her funeral were difficult to raise. Her body was eviscerated on March 6, 1619, and the entrails buried in the Henry VII Chapel at Westminister. On the ninth of the month the cadaver was carried to Denmark House, where her ladies took turns in sitting with it and its catafalque. Their dreary vigil continued as days and weeks passed into months.

Finally, on May 13, 1619, money having been somehow produced, Queen Anne received an elaborate funeral. The king, basking in the joy of his own recovery and the congratulations of the realm—for a change of monarchs was always an anxious and troublesome matter—did not mourn long or deeply. Some dignitaries from Lorraine arrived two weeks late for the queen's funeral and were astonished to discover the entire court had forgotten her passing. King James, determined to cheer London with his presence, appeared on June 1, 1619, in "a pale blue satin suit with silver lace and a blue and white feather, more like a wooer than a mourner."[19]

Great changes took place in Europe while James was voiding his kidney stones. In Germany the death of Emperor Matthias meant the princes of the German States had to elect a successor. Both the Hapsburgs and their Reform opponents maneuvered for position, but it was clear neither side would accept a leader from the other.

In Holland a national split yawned between the Calvinists and a spreading group known as Arminians. Their differences were both theological and political. After turbulent scenes and bitter arguments, the Calvinists resorted to force. The ruler of Holland, an Arminian, was overthrown. His place was taken by Maurice of Orange, a fervent Calvinist. That development did not bode well for a continuance of the truce between Holland and Spain, which was due to expire in 1621.

Reflections of these divisions appeared all over the landscape of England. The Church of England was dominated by Arminian and early Lutheran ideas. These included a sort of muted Catholicism complete with surplices and incense, images of saints and details of liturgy and worship —and the theory of obedience to the prince. The names of these movements varied from place to place, but their similarities to one another were as remarkable as their differences. Men the Dutch called Calvinists were known as Huguenots in France, Puritans in England, and Presbyterians in Scotland. Men called Arminians in Holland were similar to Lutherans in Germany and the favorite bishops of James I in the Church of England.

Their differences with one another extended as far as their mutual differences with the Vatican and were reflected in their tastes in art and music and their styles in clothes and even in speech. Short-haired men in sober suits contrasted with long-haired men in velvet and ribbons. The divide between the careless courtiers who gathered around Mary Stuart and their stern opponents in the Congregation in Scotland had spread through England and across northern Europe.

All these divisions came to a boil in Bohemia, where Calvinist rebels against the Vatican faith had declared a provisional government and were in possession of most of the realm. Calvinists everywhere thought Bohemia could become the lever to destroy the pro-Vatican power of the Hapsburgs in Germany and plotted a coalition against Austria. Their leader in this effort was Christian of Anhalt, but the man Christian proposed to carry the banner was young Frederick V, elector of the Palatinate and son-in-law of King James of England.

Frederick sent Baron Dohna to James to ask for his help, but the king wanted no part of rebels. The suggestion of Spain that James be a peacemaker was far more congenial. Using money he could not afford, he sent his extravagant old friend Lord Hay, now Viscount Doncaster, to the incredibly complex scene. Doncaster, who believed displays of wealth were somehow synonymous with intelligence, traveled across Europe with an entourage of 150 richly dressed courtiers. He arrived at Heidelberg to find Frederick absent and learned Silesia and Moravia had decided to join the Bohemian rebels. An army, similarly inspired, was moving against Austria. Meanwhile, 10,000 troops, quietly assembled in the Catholic Netherlands, were moving quietly from one Catholic territory to another toward the scene. When Frederick returned and received James's ambassador, he learned Doncaster had no messages; he was merely gathering information. He had "come as a white sheet of paper, to receive impressions . . ."

Frederick was upset. He was in the path of armies. He wanted James to assist him; England was a member of the Protestant Union. While that word was sent to London, the earl of Doncaster—still trailed by 150 companions, rushed to Dresden, passed through Munich, and eventually found Ferdinand at Salzburg, on his way to be elected emperor. He was told there that German princes could solve their own problems; King James was not needed as a mediator.

Doncaster then trundled to Frankfurt, saying he would talk to the Bohemians. At Frankfurt he found a Spanish ambassador, Oñate, who told him the time for conversation was over. Meanwhile, word came from the Bohemians that if England had no intention of assisting, its delegation was not wanted.

The unhappy peacemaker had, by that time, attracted sardonic laughter; the earl of Doncaster had been placed by his master in an impossible situation.

His master, however, would never believe that. King James saw himself as the peacemaker of Europe and that vision was unshakable. The Dutch sent agents to urge him to come down from that mountain and offered—if he would abandon the Spanish marriage project—a daughter of Maurice instead. They dangled a dowry large enough to pay all his debts. The Reform leaders in England mounted similar inducements. A new Parliament would be summoned and would vote him £800,000 in subsidies.

But James was adamant. It was not money that moved him; he was no longer interested in money. His subjects would provide, somehow, for his needs. He wanted to occupy a lofty position in the minds of men and to direct the destinies of the world. He and Spain together would resolve the arguments and divisions of Europe.

While James held to his dream, Ferdinand was elected emperor. At almost the same moment in August 1619, the Bohemians announced Ferdinand was not their choice as king—and offered the crown to Frederick V, James's son-in-law.

Baron Dohna returned to England to renew his pleas for support. Tactfully, he said that Frederick needed James's advice. The king of England, however, turned toward Spanish agents to discover their opinions, kept Dohna dangling—and before he could compose a response—learned that Frederick had decided to accept a crown. Frederick, he said, had decided to take his own counsel. Very well; let him handle his own troubles.

That attitude contrasted with a great enthusiasm for the leader of the Protestant League, however, and the king had to soften his remarks in public. He would have to study the laws of Bohemia, he said, to see if his son-in-law's election was legal.

James was, in fact, indignant. He sent instructions to Doncaster, who was still floating unhappily and expensively across Europe, to revisit all the capitals and to explain that the king of England had no hand in the follies of his son-in-law and that England's offer to mediate was sincere—and still open. The king of England wanted to assure all intriguers of his sincerity. The response was more than disdainful: it emboldened Spain to make more specific plans to intervene.

While an international storm gathered, the favorite, Buckingham, completed the demolition of Howard family influence in the government. The earl of Suffolk and his countess were briefly imprisoned and fined; their fall dragged down Sir Thomas Lake as well. The last highly placed Howard, Lord Wallingford, though blameless of any misconduct, was forced to resign mastership of the Court of Wards. It was a clean sweep that left Buckingham supreme.

The favorite grew stronger as the king grew weaker. His severe illness had left him shaken; his addictions now fastened upon him. Tillières, the French ambassador, wrote young Louis XIII about James I.

"It seems to me," he said, "that the intelligence of this King has diminished. Not that he cannot act firmly and well at times, and particularly when the peace of the kingdom is involved. But such efforts are not as continual as they once were. His mind uses its powers only for a short time, but in the long run he is cowardly. His timidity increases day by day as old age carries him into apprehensions, and vices diminish his intelligence."[20]

A series of subtle shifts were underway, in other words, between the king and Buckingham. The favorite had grown indispensible; the king wrote Steenie little notes embarrassing in their revelations, addressed to his "sweet wife," "Sweet heart," "Sweet Steenie gossip." The younger man wrote back to his "Dear Dad, and "Your dogge, Steenie." It was a marriage.

The marriage could withstand any shock and took no heed of the outside world. The archbishop of Canterbury, now old, wrote pleading that the king aid the Bohemian rebels for religion's sake—but the letter was brushed aside. News that Frederick and his English wife, Elizabeth, had been crowned amid wild scenes of jubilation in Prague in November 1619 filled the King with indignation. The thought that subjects could depose one monarch and choose another filled him with anger; he decided that Frederick was a usurper—unworthy of assistance.

His opinion was mirrored in the Vatican. The Jesuits called Frederick a Winter King and said he would not last a season. The ruler who was considered entitled to Bohemia, Ferdinand, then huddled with Maximilian of Bavaria. Maximilian was a Catholic, but neither man considered religion superior to power. A complex arrangement was made, in which Maximilian received large promises for his intervention. At the same time, Madrid, despite its financial problems, drew into the negotiation. The Catholic League, dormant for years, revived as though by magic. The winter passed amid the clanking sounds of backstage machinery. When these noises were reported to James, he grew angry. "What do you know?" he shouted. "You are ignorant. I know quite well what I am about. All these troubles will settle themselves . . ."[21]

The year 1620 opened with ministers thundering from the pulpits of England about the threat to the Reform on the Continent. The king, well aware the clergy played the role of journalists to the people and could— by artful selection—convince them in almost any direction, gave orders that no prayers could be mounted for Frederick as king of Bohemia. It was a title to which he had no legitimate claim. At the same time, word was passed from the court to the bishops to restrain orations on the whole issue.

"A strange father," said William of Orange when this was reported to him. "He will neither fight for his children or pray for them."

Strange indeed. James had, a year earlier, issued a little book entitled *Meditations on the Lord's Prayer*. It did little to add any majesty to the subject. In 1620 he turned toward the sections in the Gospel of St. Matthew that described the mock coronation of Jesus and drew comparisons with his own difficulties.

Intense pressures were being exerted. The Dutch subsidized Frederick in Bohemia. They sent an ambassador to James to urge that he share their efforts—and warned that plans were underway to invade the Palatinate. That was serious, for Heidelberg was a key location to the control of Germany. Dutch troops moved toward the Rhine; General Spinola gathered a force for Spain.

In Madrid the arguments swayed both ways. Philip III was afraid of going to hell and his priests warned him he would if he did not move. The issue, therefore, was in the hands of the king of England. If England moved, Spain would not. In the English court men beseeched Buckingham to move James, and the favorite did his best—to no avail. The best that could be done was to allow volunteers to be raised for the coming struggle.

In this tense confrontation, Count Gondomar arrived from Spain on March 5, 1620, at Dover. He was conducted in state to the bishop of Ely's mansion in Hatton Garden, where a Catholic chapel had been prepared— at the king's order—for his convenience. He arrived when England was seething with anti-Vatican and anti-Spanish sentiment. The execution of Raleigh, troubles in the Indies, subversion in Germany, threats to Holland, plots at home—in all directions the subterranean intrigues of Spain seemed at the root of all trouble. Yet Gondomar smiled.

Just before he saw James, the Spanish ambassador talked to Sir John Digby, who warned him the court teemed with his enemies. In response, Gondomar said his master had behaved admirably; it was the king of England who had broken his promises. Digby left and entered the rooms where James was waiting, reappeared, and beckoned.

"I hear from Buckingham," said James, "that you squeezed his sore finger hard enough to hurt him. I remember hearing that Montagu . . . once did the same to Burghley, when he had the gout."[22] He could not be squeezed, he went on to say. Then he began to complain. He had done everything in his power not to offend, but everyone was complaining. Four years ago he had one anti-Spanish Sir Ralph Winwood; now he had three hundred Winwoods in his court.

"I give you my word as a gentleman, as a Christian and as an honest man," he said, taking Gondomar's hand, "that I have no wish to marry my son to anyone except your master's daughter, and I desire no alliance but that of Spain." He took off his hat and wiped his forehead with a handkerchief; liquor makes a man sweaty.

Gondomar replied that he was sorry. But he could not forget the king had power and could remedy matters.

"All that is needed is that we two should talk these matters over together," James said. Then he put the question that was burning in all minds. "Do you think the Emperor intends to attack the Palatinate?"

"What would you do," Gondomar asked, "if anyone had taken London from you?"

"Well," James answered weakly, "I hope God will arrange everything for the best."

Gondomar bowed deeply and did not smile; he did not dare. In a few words, he had learned James would remain neutral.

Buckingham had other matters in mind. He had discovered Lady Catherine Manners, heiress of the earl of Rutland, richest peer in England. The favorite was a curious man, genuinely bisexual—which is rare at any time. His heterosexual activities at court were not impeded by his relations with the king, who doted upon salacious details. At the same time, these activities did much to confuse observers and to maintain the facade of normality that Buckingham could so deftly assume when it suited his purposes.

Rutland was a Catholic and against the marriage, but his daughter was in love. Despite the meddling of the favorite's mother, who now enjoyed the title of countess of Buckingham, Lady Catherine was anxious for the union. She even converted from Catholicism. The marriage was very quiet, with only the king and the earl present as witnesses. Yet it had consequences.

Gondomar's return had impelled James to relax laws against Catholics as a means of forwarding the Spanish marriage of Prince Charles. Buckingham, who had been sympathetic to the Reform war party, began to cool. He now had a beautiful and amiable wife, whose sympathies—despite her professed conversion—remained Catholic. Frederick of Bohemia and the Palatinate, engrossed in worries, had not sent fulsome congratulations to the favorite. At the same time, a dispute had arisen between Dutch and English ships in the East Indies; as lord high admiral, the favorite considered that a personal insult.

The combination of factors of a secretly Catholic wife, fancied insults from the Reformers of Europe, a need to remain close to the king—and the king's fondness for Gondomar—drew Buckingham closer to the Spanish ambassador. He even, at one point, suggested an alliance between England and Spain against Holland. That proposal was very attractive to James and to Prince Charles, who was the only other man drawn into the conversation.

Gondomar, however, relayed the discussions to Madrid, and they flowed from there to Brussels, where they were assessed as nonsense. The reputation of the king of England, already abysmal, sank even lower.

It was during this summer that a handful out of the thousands of Separatists, who fled from the England of Elizabeth, Whitgift, James, and Bancroft to Holland, decided to part from their fellows. The world pressed them in even a Calvinist country; their young people were being attracted along worldly paths. They were able to borrow from the Virginia Company and enlisted the help of Sandys, who asked James to issue them a permit to sail to the English colony in the New World.

James granted an easy assent, but was mildly curious. "What profit might arise from those parts?" he asked.

"Fishing," someone said.

"So God hae my soul," said the King, laughing. "T'was the Apostle's calling."[23]

After exasperating delays, the Puritans, as they were called, sailed past Land's End on September 6, 1620. Their small boat, the *Mayflower*, vanished over the horizon at the same time news reached England that the Spanish general, Spinola, had attacked the Palatinate.

On September 24, 1620, the Spanish ambassador appeared before James at Hampton Court. His arrival was greeted indignantly by the king. He had been "cheated into the belief" that Spinola was only interested in the recovery of Bohemia; he had been treated with gross disrespect. He had been kept in the dark.

Gondomar was at his loftiest. No promise had ever been given that the Palatinate would not be invaded; as an ambassador he was given no such news to tell the king of England. The king, however, shrieked that he could not be prevented from defending his children and ended in a flood of angry tears. Gondomar was ushered away while the king sat weeping.

For several weeks the king blustered, and the need to call a Parliament was clear. The Spaniards, however, had timed their move precisely. While the cumbersome machinery of the English court spun uselessly, Spinola's armies ran through Bohemia. Frederick, in his early twenties, had no qualities of leadership or experience with which to rally a defense. He had wasted his time in conversations, banquets, and dreams. On October 29, 1620, his polyglot army of Hungarians, Czechs, and adventurers collapsed in combat outside the walls of Prague. The Winter King, who had actually lasted a year, more or less, went into flight. The Czech nobles and revolutionaries were taken, hanged, imprisoned, or dispersed; a new German aristocracy appeared to take their places.

The news reached London in late November and cast a pall of gloom over the court. Prince Charles locked himself into his apartment for days. James muttered to everyone around that he knew this would happen. There were other developments, however, that he did not know about. In Madrid the king had agreed to marry the infanta to the son of the German Emperor Ferdinand. This arrangement, deeply secret, was to be kept from the king of England. Instead, Gondomar was provided with a letter from Madrid, saying the marriage between the same infanta and Prince Charles now looked more promising than ever. Armed with this treacherous document, the ambassador added another line. If James's son-in-law, Frederick, would abandon his claim to Bohemia, the Palatinate might remain in his hands. That promise, issued while military operations against the Palatinate were barely beginning, was one at which James clutched.

Restored to high graces, Gondomar then scuttled an effort of the French, who proposed a marriage between Prince Charles and their Princess Henrietta Maria, by telling James that Naunton, the secretary of state, had said James would marry his son to the highest bidder. The king flared and dismissed Naunton. The French ambassador was awed. Gondomar, he wrote his master, "is not only an ambassador but one of the first councillors of state of this kingdom, being day and night at the palace of Whitehall, where the most secret councils are confided to him and where they listen to his advice and follow them. . . ."[24]

The dismissal of a high official on the complaint of a foreign ambassador created astonishment and indignation among the English. Even the archbishop of Canterbury, whose presence was distasteful to Gondomar, was kept from council. Thomas Scot, a Norwich minister, produced a clever pamphlet, purportedly a verbatim transcript, describing Madrid's glee at the execution of Raleigh and the clear path toward world domination opened by the policies of the English king. In response, James issued a proclamation forbidding the English to discuss "causes of state."

The year 1621 opened with the distribution of new honors on the eve of a new Parliament—the third of James's reign. Bacon, glittering at the summit and ensconced in York House as lord chancellor of the realm, was raised another notch in the peerage to Viscount St. Albans. He gave a huge banquet to celebrate the event, and his longtime admirer and favored artist, Ben Jonson, delivered verses composed in his honor:

> With a title more to his degree
> England's High Chancellor, the destined heir,
> In his soft cradle, to his father's chair,
> Whose even threads the Fates spin round and full,
> Out of their choicest and their warmest wool.[25]

Parliament opened toward the end of January 1621. Its composition was greatly altered from the one James had addressed seventeen years earlier. Commons held more Puritans; they had grown into a majority. The House of Lords had expanded through James's practice of handing peerages to favorites and selling them to others. Almost half the secular lords were recent creations.

The great issue surrounding the Crown and Commons was James's foreign policy—but he had warned all England that such matters were within his prerogative alone and could not be discussed. Thomas Scot, the author of *Vox Populi,* had been forced to flee the country. Dr. Everard, another minister, had been put in prison for inveighing against Spanish cruelties in their colonies. When Gondomar passed through Fenchurch Street in his chair an apprentice had shouted, "There goes the devil in his dungcart."[26]

The king's injunctions, however, placed a lid on Parliament before it could protest. He appeared and spoke for an hour. After his usual description of Commons as an advisory group to the Crown assembled at his pleasure, he dwelled on his need for money, praised Buckingham, the lord admiral—and promised he would defend the Palatinate. He was carried out in a chair; he had grown feeble and had trouble walking.

Commons, however, was cheered by his promises about the Palatinate. The Privy Council had recommended an army of 30,000 and an expenditure of nearly £1 million; James was afraid to mention such a sum and reduced it to £500,000. The figure, however, chilled wartime ardor; the English were more in favor of a sea war against Spain. Their experience in sending armies to Europe had many failures on record. Nevertheless, Commons voted the king £160,000 for his expenditures, as a sort of evidence of goodwill and hope.

Forced to avoid a deep discussion of foreign matters, Commons turned toward burning grievances banked since the time of Elizabeth, which James had not only allowed to smolder, but had fueled. These involved Crown monopolies that had passed from hand to hand though court patronage, largely controlled by Buckingham and his followers. Commons was led in this attack by the most formidable legal advocate in the realm: Sir Edward Coke.

Buckingham and his brothers had forced Coke into an unwanted marriage for his daughter and extorted money from him, holding out the lure of a restoration to his high position as chief justice. Those hopes had ended in a seat on an impotent and often-ignored Privy Council—and nothing more. The great lawyer burned with resentment and led Commons down a path where the figure of the magnificent Marquis of Buckingham was clearly visible.

Commons wanted monopolies ended. They restricted trade; they were unfair; they were obtained—as everyone knew—by bribes, collusion, and court favor. The king and Buckingham alike were alarmed at the tone of the onslaught; the favorite was particularly upset because three of his relatives were principal targets—Sir Giles Mompesson, Sir Edward Villiers, and Sir Christopher Villiers. Other names arose as well, and one offender was thrown into the Tower by Commons at Coke's suggestion.

Sir Edward Coke, however, was not to be placated by the punishment of instruments; he was after greater game. Rummaging through his vast mental warehouse of precedents, laws, and the rights of Commons, he had unearthed a rusty but formidable weapon that had lain unused since 1485: impeachment of Crown ministers by Parliament.

A secret poll of Commons found a majority anxious to test the power of this nearly-forgotten right and, more surprisingly, a majority of Lords. On closer examination, however, that sentiment in the upper chamber was not unreasonable. The holders of proud old titles felt demeaned by the presence of so many upstarts among them; Buckingham—the most powerful of them all—was especially loathed.

Coke brought powerful arguments to bear. It was not the instruments who abused monopolies alone who should be examined and punished, but those who placed those instruments into position. His fingers pointed to the great judges who had ruled obnoxious practices legal. Eyes turned and regarded Chief Justice Mandeville and the great lord chancellor himself—Bacon.

James was startled and had himself carried into the House of Lords, where he summoned Commons before him. He began, as usual, on a high tone. Upon what did they base their claims to omnipotence? Their precedents were culled from "times of confusion and anarchy." His tone diminished, however, and toward the end he turned plaintive. For the first time in many years, a glimpse of the helpless young king of Scotland appeared in his conclusion.

"Before Parliament met," he said, "My subjects, whenever they had any favor to ask, used to come either to me or to Buckingham. But now, as if we both ceased to exist, they go to Parliament. All this is most disrespectful. I will . . . tell you a fablé. In the days when animals could speak, there was a cow burdened with too heavy a tail. Before the end of winter came, she had it cut off. When the summer came, and flies began to annoy her, she would gladly have had her tail back again. I and Buckingham are like the cow's tail, and when the session is over, you will be glad to have us back again to defend you from abuses."[27]

Commons listened and went into conference with the House of Lords. Mandeville and Bacon were called and protested against the procedure. Coke looked at the Lords and asked if their House supported the protest, and a deep silence ensued. The issue was, therefore, grave. Impeachment proceedings were underway in all but name; if the Commons discovered grounds, the king's ministers were no longer under his protection.

Bacon pointed out the peril. "Those that will strike at your Chancellor," he said, "it is much to be feared—will strike at your crown."[28] His words were lost in Buckingham's fears. The favorite ran to the dean of Westminster, a shrewd but kindly prelate, for advice. He was told to swim with the tide or drown. Both James and Buckingham switched with comical speed. The king declared he could not defend wrongdoing. That had been his attitude when Somerset was threatened and had served him well.

On March 13, 1621, Buckingham himself appeared in the Lords and denounced his brothers and the system of monopolies, declared he was unfamiliar with Parliaments, but was learning—and was anxious to learn. His surrender was enough; Commons passed a bill against monopolies, convinced the King would approve it; and the question of impeachment faded, for the moment, from the forefront of attention. It was, however, an ominous indication that the suppressed theories of Buchanan, which stressed the ancient rights of subjects against their sovereigns and lords, were rising from the earth of England.


In Holland young Frederick, ousted from Bohemia, beset in the Palatinate, rode into the Hague in April 1621. His wife, the daughter of James, had been warned not to come to England; her father feared becoming entangled. The king of England, however, had a last chance to intervene to improve the situation. The Spanish-Dutch truce was due to end in the autumn; Madrid was anxious to finish its efforts in Germany in order to meet the threat of that war. If England sent the troops that Commons approved and if James moved to range himself beside Holland, young Frederick's rule in the Palatinate could still be saved.

Instead, the king sent Sir John Digby on another peace mission. The effort was not hopeless. The costs of intervention in Germany had been expensive to Spain, and its limited objectives realized. Bohemia was now restored to the Vatican faith; the Vienna Hapsburgs, strengthened; the Protestant Union, in disarray. The Spanish told Digby that Frederick of the Palatinate could keep his original birthright if England did not help Holland against Spain.

Unfortunately, Digby received these assurances on March 31, 1621—the day the king of Spain, Philip III, died. On his deathbed he called his heir and the infanta and said, "Maria, I am sorry that I must die before I married you, but your brother will take care of you." Turning to the future Philip IV, he said, "Prince, do not forsake her till you have made her an Empress."[29]

That deathbed injunction, awesome to the Spanish mind, was a closely held secret in the Spanish court. Even Gondomar was not told; he was busy keeping the king of England convinced that the infanta would marry the Prince of Wales.

The lord chancellor of England, Viscount St. Albans and Lord Verulam, had no time to relax as the dread question of impeachment faded away. Instead Sir Lionel Cranfield, the best financial mind in government, rose in Commons to complain against Bacon's Bills of Conformity. In effect, these were immunities conferred by debtors in the Court of Chancery. Sir Edward Coke pretended surprise. He could not believe such orders could issue from any court. An inquiry was demanded, and the instigators of the new, special hunt to corner Bacon were pleased.

Within days persons appeared and testified that Bacon had accepted bribes. Speeches were mounted, and it was decided the evidence presented should be sent to the House of Lords. Bacon took to his bed, where Buckingham visited him and found him "very sick and heavy."

The chancellor could not have been improved by the favorite's visit, for King James—told about Bacon's new troubles—said "he was sorry a man whom he hath preferred should be guilty of such great crimes."[30]

The king then suggested that he appoint a special commission of six lords and a dozen members of Commons to try the lord chancellor. It was a move straight out of Elizabeth's book; James planned to stack the commission in Bacon's favor. He did not understand that Sir Edward Coke could penetrate any veil and was not to be cheated out of the destruction of Bacon. "Let us see," said Sir Edward, "that this gracious message taketh not away our Parliamentary proceeding."

Reminded of their powers, the lords selected to sit in judgment as a body. Meanwhile, the first complaint was seconded. A third appeared, and a fourth, and a fifth. The lords examined the witnesses and some odd behavior emerged. Bacon had taken money from litigants and then ruled against them. Yet even as the inquiry proceeded, it seemed, for a time, that the lord chancellor might escape. Buckingham was working for him, and James was under great pressure to dissolve Parliament.

This altered Bacon's mood from concern to confidence. He asked that a real trial be held, in which the charges be brought into the open. Unfortunately, the charges kept mounting. By the twentieth of April, 1621, only three months after the glittering banquet where Ben Jonson had read his adoring verse, someone brought Bacon a copy of the evidence, and the lord chancellor's resistance collapsed. All the bribe-givers had not been disappointed.

Bacon wrote James a letter that revealed his personal standards. "He that hath taken bribes is apt to give bribes," he said. "I will go farther, and present your Majesty with a bribe. For, if your Majesty give me peace and leisure, and God give me life, I will present you with a good history of England, and a better digest of your laws."[31]

He also sent the lords a long, learned letter saying he was about to resign and protesting the purity of his motives. Word was returned that it was not enough; he would have to admit his wrongdoing. Messengers were sent to Bacon in bed and returned saying, "The Lord Chancellor will make no defense . . . meaneth to acknowledge corruption, and to make a particular confession, and after that a humble submission." Five days later he sent explanations—but not denials—for the long list of thirty-seven charges placed against him.

The lords were unwilling to take any chances with him and some went to his bedside to verify his signature. "My Lords," he said huskily from the bed, "it is my act, my hand, my heart. I beseech your Lordships to be merciful unto a broken reed."[32]

The reed, however, was not broken; it was slender enough to bend in any direction. Some peers arrived to take away the great seal, and one wished matters had been better for the man in the bed. "The worse the better," Bacon sighed dramatically.

After he was found guilty, a debate broke out. The upshot was that Bacon could keep the title of Viscount St. Albans, but could never again hold public office. A long list of fines and imprisonment at the king's pleasure was added for the record, but everyone knew James would repeal those—if Bacon would beg. Nobody doubted either reaction.

Parliament was far from finished, however. Sir Henry Yelverton, former attorney general and king's man par excellence, was brought from the Tower—where he was confined at the king's pleasure—to the House of Lords.[33] His testimony was needed in the exhaustive investigation underway into the abuse of gold and silver thread patents.

Accused of complicity with the missing Mompesson—Buckingham's favorite—Yelverton said he had acted well for the king; that was the cause of his troubles. Chief Justice Mandeville, who had himself walked over hot coals in Parliament, protested Yelverton slandered the Crown.

Summoned again, Yelverton refused to retract. He had been threatened, he said, "with the ill-will of the all-powerful favorite, who stood ever at his Majesty's hand, ready to hew him down." Turning to Buckingham, Yelverton said fiercely, "I dare say if my Lord of Buckingham had but read the articles exhibited in this place against Hugh Spencer, and had known the danger of placing and displacing officers about a king, he would not have pursued me with such bitterness."[34]

The sudden reminder of homosexuality, similar to that between Edward II and his favorites, shocked the House. Cries were raised to stop the speaker; nobody wanted to confront the specter that so suddenly appeared. Yelverton was choked off, convicted of slander, and hustled off the scene.

Buckingham, incredibly, said the reaction showed that he himself was "Parliament proof."

Nevertheless a nerve had been exposed that James could not endure. On May 28, 1621, James sent a sudden order for Parliament to recess until the following February. Commons and Lords alike rose in surprise, and a real concern about the international drift of England came boiling to the surface. "The country is in a dangerous state," Sandys said, "our religion is rooted out of Bohemia and Germany. It shall soon be rooted out of France."[35]

Others spoke in similar vein, and a *Declaration* was drafted, saying the entire realm would support the king if he moved in the Palatinate in the event his peace making efforts failed.

The king, however, was displeased. His subjects had dared to discuss the destiny of the realm and to meddle in concerns of their prince. As soon as Parliament recessed, Sandys, Seldon, and the earl of Southampton were arrested. James denied the arrests had any connection with the statements these men had made in Parliament or outside it; the denials were transparently false. The conciliatory mood of the country, as expressed in the Commons pledge of national support for intervention in the Palatinate, dissipated at once.

The general discontent was not lifted when Buckingham, attempting to prove he was a moderating influence, emerged from Theobalds on July 16, 1621, and made a tour of those imprisoned. Yelverton, Sandys, Southampton, Seldon, and others were all released while the favorite beamed. Far from gaining him popularity, the gesture was accepted as a demonstration of power.

Through the summer and early autumn of 1621, the Dutch prepared to renew their struggle against Spain, suspended for twelve years by a truce. The hopes of the Hague had been that England might join in this effort, but James had placed his entire confidence in Gondomar and Madrid. A series of incidents involving Dutch and English merchant ships, engaged in fierce competition in the East Indies, had exacerbated relations between the two countries.

These arguments excited Buckingham, who took himself seriously as lord high admiral. He urged a war with Holland. He was seconded by Sir Lionel Cranfield, a businessman whose mind was bounded by immediate profits. Buckingham and Cranfield were a difficult combination to oppose. When joined by the Spanish ambassador, Gondomar, they were almost irresistible—at least for James.

The king's conviction that Gondomar was his personal friend and a man of towering ideals was verified, or seemed to be verified, when the new pope, Gregory XV, appointed a committee of cardinals to study a dispensation regarding the marriage of Prince Charles and the infanta. The subtle diplomats of Madrid had managed to persuade the Vatican into innocent complicity in their great deception of the king of England.

James's trance was broken, briefly, when Sir John Digby returned from Europe toward the end of October 1621. He carried dreadful news regarding both Frederick and the fortunes of the Reform. Maximilian of Bavaria had invaded the Upper Palatinate. Spanish troops were already in the Lower Palatinate. Frederick was under a ban by the emperor; and his mercenary, Count Mansfield, was nearly out of control. The situation was grim for the young elector, the Hapsburgs were strengthening their control, the German states were tilting toward the Vatican, and the Protestant Union was in near-collapse.

A sudden flurry of decisions issued from the English court. Money was sent to Frederick; he was urged to abandon his pretensions to Bohemia. James issued a call for Parliament to reconvene November 20, 1621. The hopes of the Reform soared again; certainly the king would have to appeal for funds and support and clarify his foreign policy for the realm. James, however, sent a secret message to Gondomar, telling him to ignore whatever was said in Parliament and to be sure that the king of England would not approve of any steps that might displease the king of Spain. No ambassador, before or since, has ever enjoyed such an eerie influence over a foreign government.

Parliament was opened, in the name of King James, by John Williams, dean of Westminster, favorite of Buckingham, and now keeper of the great seal. The king, it was said, was indisposed. As usual, during these indispositions he was off in one of his progresses, accompanied by various Villiers ladies and their children. He had grown fond of such company because he had learned that by so encircling himself he could be sure the favorite would be at hand, day and night.

Williams's speech sounded, to the Commons, more like "a divine than a statesman or orator." He urged the Parliament to "avoid all long harangues, malicious and cunning diversions"—and to postpone all business, except funds for the Palatinate, until the next meeting in February. Digby rose and described the terrible situation of Frederick. Cranfield—now lord treasurer—urged Commons to vote large sums. Digby, a professional diplomat, also insisted the king of Spain was attempting to restore peace in the

Palatinate. Since Spanish troops were part of that tangled problem, this attempt to square the circle of events with James's ideas created incredulity.

The fact was that most members had already decided that Frederick was a foolish monarch who had not the wit to cut his losses when that was practical. The members wanted a war against Spain at sea and a return to the foreign policy of Elizabeth and to the domestic policy of Burghley years before. One member after another rose to take issue with the king's opinion that a royal marriage would end the deep-seated controversies of Europe. The debate began politely, with such orators as Phelips pointing to the great wheel of Madrid which propelled the smaller wheels of Catholic German princes into motion. Then Sir Edward Coke arose.

Coke had brought Bacon down and driven Mandeville out as chief justice. He had aroused Buckingham's enmity, but was protected by Commons.

Coke began with a long dissertation on the quarrel between the Vatican and Elizabeth, reviewed the machinations of Jesuits and the Armada, and then proceeded to place all the evils of the western world on the doorstep of the Vatican. The sheep scab came from Spain. Syphilis came from Naples, a Spanish possession. The Spanish ambassador headquartered in London maintained open house for Spanish and pro-Vatican conspirators. As he talked, his recollections of past dangers, difficulties, and disasters merged into the present and extended to the future; Commons' anti-Spanish sentiments rose with his voice.

John Pym—a man whose name would ring in revolutionary annals— picked up the theme the following day. He charged that the Papists would press first for toleration, then for equality, then for superiority, and then for the extirpation of all contrary beliefs. He urged strict administration of anti-Catholic laws and a special oath of belief in the Reform for all around the king and a special commission to discover and punish those who did not attend Church of England services. These speeches and proposals sounded as though the days of Elizabeth had returned.

By December 1621 the discussions ended in a petition to the king to rally the Protestant states and to make war on Spain. Since no marriage could be arranged under such conditions, that decision was implied.

Agents rushed a copy of this inflammatory document to Gondomar before the official version reached James himself. The king was at Newmarket, and the Spanish ambassador sent him an amazing letter. He said that he would have immediately left England if he did not already know that King James would punish the insolence of Commons. "It would have been my duty to do so [leave]," he said, "as you would have ceased to be a king here, and I have no army with which to punish these people myself."[36]

"God give me patience," James cried. His impatience, however, was not directed against Gondomar, but against Commons. He sent a fierce letter—James could be fierce on paper—saying some "had debated and argued in public on matters far beyond their reach and capacity," tending to "high dishonour and trenching upon his prerogative royal." Members were warned not to meddle with "mysteries of state." There was to be no discussion of the prince's Spanish marriage, nor anything said against the honor of the king of Spain. He warned the members he considered himself "free and able to punish any man's misdemeanors in Parliament"—and would not be sparing.[37]

That raging letter was read aloud on December 4, 1621. The Commons grew very sober. Issues were being raised that struck at the very existence of Parliament. As usual, when matters grew serious, men grew very quiet. A careful response was drafted, saying the issues of religion and marriage had been discussed as part of the Palatinate problem, to which the king himself had drawn their attention. Then, at the very end, the Commons said the king's letter "doth seem to abridge us of the ancient liberty of parliament for freedom of speech, jurisdiction and just censure . . . and other proceedings . . . the same being our undoubted right and inheritance from our ancestors, without which we cannot debate or clearly discern of things in question before us. . . ."[38] They asked that James clarify his position.

A delegation was appointed to carry this response to the king. It found him at Newmarket in good spirits. "Bring stools for the ambassadors," he called when the members appeared. That sign that he considered their claims to amount to sovereignty was followed by a rambling discourse, filled with the usual oaths and digressions, along the same lines. They left with another giant letter the king had dictated between drinks. It repeated the points he had already made, blamed Frederick's ambitions for the troubles in Germany, and defended the king of Spain. Meanwhile, their claim to rights and inheritances were wrong; their "privileges were derived from the grace and permission of his ancestors and himself." James would never lack words.

Unfortunately, his words were carrying them beyond the issues of the moment into deeper waters. The question of the Palatinate receded. Even the matter of the prince's Spanish marriage appeared no longer burning; it was not that immediate. As far as voting money for the Crown was concerned, some members observed they were being placed in the position of merchants forced to pay for unknown and unstated goods. The king's advisers were alarmed. Williams, that worldly prelate, urged moderation upon the king. James then sent another letter saying he had no intention of withdrawing the "privileges" of Parliament.

During the Christmas holidays all parties huddled in some perplexity. The proceedings of Parliament had been once again muddled by James. It was impossible to debate any question without angering a king who did not believe other men should talk. While Commons regarded the latest impasse, another letter came from James, instructing them either to vote funds his ministers had said were indispensable or he would be able to wait until the next session. In any event, he ordered a Christmas recess.

In gathering gloom the members assembled and drew together a petition. This time they spelled their rights in detail and said they had freedom to discuss and debate and to immunities from punishment for using their rights. They repeated the historical basis for their position. It was decided not to go through the motions of presenting this to the king. The statement was entered into the *Journals.* After that clear move, the members left for their Christmas vacation on December 19, 1621.

The king received the news with anger, and Gondomar said he doubted if the king of Spain could negotiate with any monarch whose control over his own subjects was so tenuous. Buckingham added similar words. On December 27, 1621, to prove his strength, James ordered Sir Edward Coke to the Tower. Other arrests followed. On December 30, 1621, the king arrived in Whitehall and sent for the *Journals* of Parliament. With his Privy Council and judges watching, he tore the pages containing Parliament's protestation out with his own hands. Prince Charles, watching his regal father, was shown how to behave.

The next question was whether Parliament should be dissolved. It seemed highly academic, but the king pretended to seek the advice of his Privy Council. The councillors assembled and sat in dim silence, until Lord Pembroke said, "The King has declared his will; it is therefore our business not to dispute but to vote."

"If you wish to contradict the King," Buckingham said, "you are at liberty to do so. . . . If I could find any reasons I would do so myself, even though the King is present."[39] He flashed his brilliant eyes toward James, who smiled adoringly in return.

As soon as the dissolution of Parliament was voted upon by the king and his flaccid council, the marquis of Buckingham hurried to tell Gondomar. The Spanish ambassador wrote, in stern pride, to Madrid. "This King," he said in part, "will never summon another Parliament as long as he lives, or at least not another composed as this one was. *It is the best thing that has happened in the interests of Spain and the Catholic religion since Luther . . . a hundred years ago.*"[40]

The Spaniard turned the event around so his masters could regard the various facets. James would not be able to help his son-in-law Frederick in Germany. As for England, wrote Gondomar, "This wretched people are desperately offended against him, but they are without union among themselves, and have neither leaders nor strong places to lean against. Besides, they are rich, and live comfortably . . . it is not likely there will be any disturbance.''

The notice of dissolution appeared on January 6, 1622. The king managed to get on a horse that day and rode in the park at Theobalds. Unfortunately, he chose a stubborn animal that rushed toward the New River and then abruptly stopped. James was thrown over and landed head first in the icy waters ''so only his boots could be seen.'' Sir Richard Young jumped in and pulled him out; ''there came much water from his mouth and body.''[41] He rode home, went into a warm bed, and was none the worse for the experience.

The accident was minor and of little consequence, yet it seemed symbolic. The dissolution of Parliament left James with only the support of Spain, and no man knew when it would reveal its true intentions.

# 31

"I will govern," said King James, "according to the common weal—and not according to the common will."

The king proceeded to declare he would send 8,000 foot soldiers and 1,600 horses to the aid of his son-in-law, Frederick—and would raise the money without Parliament. New taxes were levied on wines and imports. A new benevolence was declared: a forced loan to the Crown. It was resisted; dark mutterings were heard. A lawyer's servant was racked for predicting rebellion; another was executed.

Rumors swept the realm that the king would convert and a manuscript was passed from hand to hand titled *Tom Tell Truth,* in which James was described as a defender of the Vatican faith. The writer traced the influence of Gondomar to the growth of Spanish control of the West Indies and the loss of protection to European Protestants—while the king indulged in depravities with his favorites.

The Reform, long muted, began to emerge more and more openly. A young minister at Oxford University named Knight raised his voice in arguments that sounded like echoes of John Knox. Taking the story of Ahab and his persecution of Elijah, he said it was "lawful for subjects when harrassed on the score of religion, to take arms against their Prince in their own defense." Taken into custody, he said he had quoted the opinions of Pareus, a professor at Heidelberg.

The king reacted like a man confronted with a scorpion. Libraries and bookstores were ransacked, and Pareus's *Commentaries* were burned at Oxford, Cambridge, and London. The universities proved their hatred of free intellects by forcing undergraduates to swear against Pareus's ideas. Life under the Scholar King was dangerous for other scholars.

In the midst of these scenes the count of Gondomar sailed, in April 1622, for home. Few men can play a role for years without finally believing it, and Gondomar was no exception. He had spent his own fortune to maintain a high state in England and was sailing to a land that had behaved the same way, on a high scale, before the entire world. Madrid was living on the verge of bankruptcy and had long since succumbed to opulent displays. Its currency was debased; its empire was creaking; and it was living by tricks, ruses, strategems, and wits.

Those wits had encouraged the pro-Vatican faction in France by marriage. They gained when young King Louis XIII appointed Cardinal Richelieu his first minister, and Richelieu suppressed Huguenots. The same clever intelligences had tilted the balance in the German states. Frederick was fighting for his territories in the Palatinate, and his prospects grew darker every month.

Yet the war with Holland strained Spain. Gondomar was going home to a land dense with monasteries, teeming with beggars, dominated by priests, where the young King Philip IV was led by his adviser, Zuñiga. The diplomat had followed orders brilliantly, but he and his fellow Spaniards had led Europe into a quagmire where men had lost sight of their goals.

Toward the end of his English stay, however, the count's mind returned to old hopes. An alliance between wealthy England and needy Spain would salvage a collapsing situation. James might not actually convert, as the Vatican so often dreamed, but the children of a Spanish marriage could certainly turn the balance in England in years to come. The count thought of the disdain of Madrid with dismay, but regarded Prince Charles—that marvel of austere obedience—with more hope.

Moved by impulse, he called the prince to one side. "Perhaps," he said, "it may be necessary for you, yourself, my Lord, to come to Madrid. There, once your virtues are seen and understood, I am sure this matter can become successful."[1]

Charles nodded, eyes shining with sincerity. He promised that if Gondomar called, he would respond.

The spring and summer of 1622 witnessed the bloody decline of Frederick's grasp in the Palatinate. James sent man after man to the scene in vain attempts to mediate; they were treated with scant courtesy. The king of England was no longer the laughing stock of Europe; he was now simply ignored. In Spain the English ambassador, Sir John Digby, discovered Madrid in a mood of high exaltation.

The Englishman, however, was granted an audience with the infanta, who thanked the Prince of Wales for his regard—and his hopes. The Spaniards assured Digby their hopes were as high as his master's—but word had not yet emerged from the Vatican. As news arrived that Frederick's retreat was now centered around Heidelberg, his capital, the Spaniards were soothing. Gondomar arrived, and Digby was told the issue of the Palatinate and the Spanish marriage were to be considered together by the Council of State in Madrid.

Lulled by these assurances, the king played happily with his favorite's baby while all England watched, with mounting bitterness, the steady collapse of Protestant territories in Europe. The great Calvinist dream receded while the Vatican's influence continued to spread.


One result was a spectacular increase in Puritanism in England. The policies of Elizabeth now appeared, in retrospect, clear and lucid. The intricacies of that female Tudor were unknown or forgotten in the soft glow of retrospect; all that was visible was the hideous corruption of the English court and the manner in which its unmanliness had eroded the pride, prestige, and posture of the realm.

The king seemed utterly oblivious to this mood. In August 1622 writs were issued releasing English Catholics imprisoned for their religion. James said his intent was to prove tolerance at home, while he pleaded for tolerance for Reformers abroad. That explanation was not accepted; it was widely believed the king was acting under Spanish pressure.

Such suspicions were well founded. The king sent assurances to Madrid through Buckingham, who wrote Gondomar a stream of letters. Regarding the treatment of Catholics in England, the favorite said, "they are in all points as your heart could wish . . . it shall not be lawful hereafter for them to rail against the Pope or the doctrine of the Church of Rome . . . but alas, now that we have put the ball at your feet . . . from other parts of the world the effects appear contrary."

Buckingham then went on to tell the count that word had been received from the Vatican that the sovereign of England must accept complete conversion of Crown and realm. The situation in the Palatinate remained grim and efforts to mediate had failed. He ended by a plain appeal: ". . . hasten the happy conclusion of this match. The Prince is now two and twenty years of age. . . . Your friends here are all discomfited with this long delay. . . . As for the pact of your true friend and servant Buckingham, I have become odious already, and counted a betrayer of both king and country."

Finally, the most powerful peer in England wrote the Spanish diplomat, "I will end to you, my sweet friend, as I do in my prayers to God— Only in thee is my trust, and—Haste, haste, post haste!"[2]

Not long afterward Heidelberg fell.


The marquis of Buckingham purchased the mansion of New Hall, in Sussex, from the earl. In celebration of his occupancy, he ordered a great party to which his now numerous attendants and relatives, supporters and sycophants were invited. The king himself could be counted among the latter. Steenie could override James at will, but the old man's clutch remained as feverishly doting as ever.

The favorite also had a constant admirer in the thin, dignified figure of Prince Charles. The prince was his father's son in many ways. His tongue was too large and tended to get in the way of his speech when he was excited. He dressed, however, with singular care. He had no apparent interest in women, and it was rumored he was impotent. That rumor was started, apparently, by women of the court who had tried their lures on the prince and found him completely oblivious. The same lack of interest, approaching blindness, was noted by the numerous homosexuals of the court. Prince Charles was unaware of such undercurrents.

Like his father, he was a passionate hunter and a reckless rider, but showed little courage in other areas. Long cowed by his voluble parent, he seldom responded to argument, was cautious in his opinions, and tended to straddle every issue when forced to speak. "He was born," said Gardiner, "to be the idol of schoolmasters."[3]

The heir to the crown of England was a strange, odd, inhibited figure who clung to the shadow of Buckingham as though the favorite were his elder brother. In return, Buckingham protected him, spoke for him, and treated him to his confidences—or at least some of them. Together at the great party that celebrated the favorite's latest palace, the odd triangle that ruled England smiled happily. A great many new honors were distributed among their following and some serious men given credit for arduous labors.

At first, news of the debacle in the Palatinate brought arguments inside England for war. Buckingham, who now suggested avenues to James rather than listened to the king, watched while the Privy Council decided to call upon the king of Spain for the help he had so often promised. Madrid was to demand that the emperor of Germany return Heidelberg to Frederick, as well as refrain from taking the last territories held by the elector. Then a peace settlement was to be reached, which Spain, England, and the emperor would arrange.

If the emperor refused, Spain was to send an army to enforce such an arrangement or to allow passage for an English army to do so, through Flanders. If no answer was received in ten days, the Spanish marriage was to be cancelled.

The king watched this passively; he had grown strangely weak, like a man sinking into his dotage. Matters of state had passed into Buckingham's control. The favorite dared not openly oppose the strong tides mounted against Madrid inside England. But Buckingham was still convinced, apparently, that all the realm was wrong and James's policy was right. He composed a secret message to Gondomar that, as lord admiral of the English navy, he planned to "take his friend with him in secret, to bring back that beautiful angel." Both messages—one official and one secret— were entrusted to Endymion Porter. When Porter left the council chamber, bystanders who waited outside greeted him with shouts. "Bring us war! Bring us war!"[4]

Some changes had taken place in the Spanish capital by the time Porter arrived in November 1622. The secretive minister, Zuñiga, had died, and his nephew, Olivares, was supreme. The secret letter to Gondomar created satisfaction, and the Englishman was told the Prince of Wales would be welcome. The king, however, was off hunting and could not be approached.

Olivares heard Porter ask about Spanish intentions in the Palatinate and gave a brusque reply. It was absurd, he said, to expect the king of Spain to go to war against his uncle, the Catholic League, and the Hapsburgs of Austria. Turning away, he concluded, "As for marriage, I know not what it means."[5]

That comment agonized Gondomar. He was fervent for the union, which he had virtually created. His arguments were that the Vatican was unrealistic; a junta was created in Madrid to draw up more reasonable terms. Meanwhile, a great behind-the-scenes dispute began to boil in the Spanish royal family. The confessor to the infanta said to her, "What a comfortable bedfellow you will have. He who lies by your side and who will be the father of your children is certain to go to hell."[6] The princess, who was only 17, had hysterics.

Porter returned to England in early January 1623. The Council of State in Madrid had shown the English a huge mass of documents regarding the Spanish marriage. Many of the articles had been relaxed; a dowry of £500,000 was included and the demands regarding the Palatinate had been rendered vague.

The Spaniards—like James, Buckingham, and the English Catholics— were operating under several delusions. Olivares thought a settlement could be reached in the Palatinate if the elector's children were raised in the Vatican faith. They could inherit, in other words, what Frederick would lose by his folly. Count Gondomar, on the other hand, thought the Prince of Wales could be converted to Catholicism if he came to Madrid. That would end the Vatican objections. The count did not know that Philip IV had no intention of breaking the deathbed vow he had given his father regarding his sister. The Spanish king forced Olivares to send a secret message to the Vatican, telling them the negotiations were not serious and virtually pleading that the Holy See forbid the union.

Meanwhile, King James remained deceived. When Porter arrived from Madrid in early 1623 carrying the Spanish terms, he read them eagerly. Spain offered £500,000 in dowry, asked for tolerance for English Catholics, and offered assurances that the troubles in the Palatinate would be amicably resolved. The king was jubilant; he and his son signed the articles immediately. James's euphoric humor was not even diminished by news that Maximilian of Bavaria had been named elector of the Palatinate.

Instead, while Englishmen spoke bitterly in the privacy of their homes, Lord Admiral Buckingham made preparations to travel to Spain with a fleet of ten ships to escort the infanta to her new home. Yet, astonishingly, this was not enough for Buckingham. Lounging in conversation with the stiff and silent Prince of Wales, the marquis began to speculate about the infanta, a poor girl, destined from birth for the bed of a stranger, never to be wooed for herself alone. As he talked, an idea occurred to him, and his eyes began to sparkle. Charles should go to Spain incognito to woo the infanta himself.

The more he turned that thought around, the more it glittered. A deed of knight-errantry badly needed in a jaded world. Charles never crossed Buckingham; that would have been inconceivable. The marquis put his hand on the prince's shoulder. Why wait long months for a fleet to be readied? They would ride through France and astound the world together. Spain would see what men England held; the infanta would be wooed as should all beautiful women.

They rushed to the king, who was miserable with his arthritis and his gout, and told him the plan. He could not resist Buckingham; he gave way at once.


The following day James realized what had been said and agreed and was horrified. Buckingham appeared to discuss arrangements, and the king began to babble about the dangers of such a trip. If any harm fell upon the prince, he said, he would be blamed. The whole project was mischief. Folly. It was heartbreaking that such a proposal should be pressed upon him; he burst into tears—which now flowed often and easily.

Prince Charles, his tongue thick, reminded the king he had promised. Buckingham, more formidable, said curtly that if the king was going to break promises as soon as he made them, he could never be trusted, could never be believed by anyone. No doubt, he continued, James had broken the vow of secrecy already, and some knave had brought up these objections. Who was he?

The king defended himself feebly; he had kept the secret. Next, he was forced to admit he would keep his word. Who would accompany the Prince of Wales and the marquis of Buckingham? Names were suggested, and they settled upon Francis Cottington, Charles's secretary, and Endymion Porter. Cottington was sent for, and as he entered the room, Buckingham whispered to the prince that he would oppose the project.

"Cottington," said James, his voice shaking, "here is Baby Charles and Steenie, who have a great mind to go by post into Spain to fetch home the Infanta, and will have but two in their company. They have chosen you for one. What think you of going?"

Cottington's breath left him, and he froze. Then, recovering, with a sidelong look at Steenie, he said he did not think well of such a trip. "With Prince Charles in their hands," he added, "the Spaniards would simply increase their demands."

James threw himself on his bed and wept. "I told you all the time," he wailed. "I am undone. It will break my heart if you follow your resolution." He buried his face and kicked his heels.

Steenie turned on Cottington, eyes blazing, and said all the king had wanted to know was the condition of the roads.

"Nay, by God, Steenie," said the king from the bed, "you are much to blame to use him so. He answered me directly to my question and yet you know he says no more than I told you before he was called in."[7]

---

On the evening of February 18, 1623, Jack and Tom Smith, wearing false beards and with one groom, hailed a boatman to carry them across the Thames. The man thought it strange they ordered him not to land outside the regular place at Gravesend, but instead told him to let them off farther up the bank.

As they left, one of the bearded men, muffled to the eyebrows, handed the boatman a purse. He opened it as they mounted their horses and disappeared into the dark, then stared after them with surprise and suspicion. He had been given a purse filled with gold.

Informed that two men, possible duelists off to break the law, had crossed the Thames under suspicious circumstances, the Gravesend authorities sent a man to overtake them for questioning, but the Smith horses were too fast.

A king's carriage, carrying Boiscot, master of ceremonies, and Sir Henry Mainwaring, lieutenant of Dover Castle, was proceeding in the early morning along Dover Road when they saw three horsemen approaching. While they waited for the horsemen to reach them, the trio abandoned the road and galloped across an open field.

Mainwaring put his head out the coach window and ordered his escort to go after them and hold them for questioning in Canterbury. But when he arrived in the town, he found men bowing and flustered. Tom Smith had taken off his beard and revealed himself to be the marquis of Buckingham, George Villiers himself. His companion was the Prince of Wales.

They were seasick crossing the Channel in a vessel that Cottington and Porter had obtained, but their passage was otherwise uneventful. In France the party, now numbering five, rode from Boulogne to Montreuil. Two days later, on February 23, 1623, they were in Paris. Strolling about, they saw the king and Marie de Médicis; that night they managed to watch the rehearsal of a masque in which the Princess Henrietta Maria was to participate. The Prince of Wales did not mention her in his letter to the king, but word of their identities had seeped through the gardens, and the princess was thrilled. She was only 14.


Their departure and the mode they chose created consternation in England. The Privy Councillors appeared before James to ask if the rumors were true, and he put his best face upon matters. His son, he said, was following the example of Lord Darnley, his grandfather. The king reminded his listeners that he himself had gone to Denmark, at great risk, it now appeared, to claim his own bride.


On the evening of March 27, 1623, the new earl of Bristol was told a Mr. Smith was at his door in Madrid and would not leave. Bristol, who had been warned, opened the door himself and bowed low as the marquis of Buckingham, traveled-stained and saddlesore, limped painfully into the embassy. The Prince of Wales, who looked unusually cheerful and fit, followed quietly.

One of Gondomar's spies, watching the building, flew to the count with the news. He was delighted. It was obvious to him the prince would not have dreamed of coming to Madrid, so secretly and with no crowd of attendants, if he did not plan to be converted.

The count went to the royal palace and rushed upon Olivares, who was at dinner. "What brings you here so late?" Olivares asked. "One would think you had got the King of England in Madrid."

"If I have not got the King, at least I have got the Prince," Gondomar said triumphantly.[8]

Olivares was speechless. The news put him into a dreadful position, and it took all his abilities to congratulate Gondomar. As soon as the count left, the Spanish favorite went to the king, who was in bed, and told him the news. The response of the king was not favorable to the Prince of Wales. Olivares felt almost physically pained.

The marquis of Buckingham and his impulsive gesture created an immense international mess. In the Vatican grave cardinals gathered to discuss the situation; the Reformers of Europe were appalled and ministers thundered. Orders were issued from the palace to celebrate the safe arrival of the adventurers in Spain, and the king's men went about setting off firecrackers and starting bonfires. Observers noted, however, that the fires died for lack of attendance, and the crowds remained indoors.

Neither the prince nor Buckingham, in Madrid, were accustomed to life without crowds of servants, attendants, and hangers-on. They sent to England for money, for clothes, for servants; Charles was to request horses and even tilting equipment. Their reaction to Spanish efforts toward conversion were not what Gondomar had expected or Olivares had hoped.

Prince Charles and Buckingham were summoned to a conference on religion. Four friars appeared while Olivares leaned forward hopefully. One asked about the prince's doubts regarding his faith and was informed no such doubts existed. Olivares suggested the English heir be enlightened, and efforts were made. Charles, after listening, asked that the Bible passages quoted be repeated in French. They were, and he said the interpretation was strained. Buckingham then wanted to know what was happening. Charles told him, and the marquis jumped up from his chair, pulled off his hat as an expression of contempt, threw it on the floor, and jumped up and down on it. That ended that particular session.

King James, however, was hopeful in his now lonely state. "I sent you," he wrote, "your robes of the order, which ye must not forget to wear on St. George's Day . . . it will be a goodly sight for the Spaniards to see my two boys in them. . . ." A ship was dispatched bearing servants, clothes, money, jewels, and all the other necessities the knights-errant might need for their inconspicuous pursuit of the infanta.

Two of the prince's chaplains appeared with this cargo, bearing candlesticks, tapers, wafers for Communion, basins, flagons, an alter, fonts, palls, linen coverings, and all the other articles and symbols for a Church of England chapel, which was to be created in the embassy. The ministers were told not to abuse the Vatican or the Spaniards in their sermons and carried huge armloads of the immense works of the Mightie Prince James I of England, in Latin and English, as well as prayer books and other articles to edify the most Catholic country in the world.[9]

This move by James, which he considered only fair, since the infanta was going to hold Vatican services in England, almost ruptured the entire charade. Olivares had the Prince of Wales moved inside the royal palace to apartments commensurate with his rank and announced that heretics would be barred, as well as heretical services—if necessary by force.

The Vatican, drawn against its will but fascinated by the possibilities inherent in the situation, finally issued its demands upon England. They were sweeping. The infanta was to have a chapel in England; all Catholics were to be free to their beliefs and relieved of any oaths to the English king; all children of the marriage were to be raised in the Vatican faith from the age of twelve. The demand was a virtual ultimatum that the English king dismiss the laws of his realm at the order of the Vatican.

By May 1623 Olivares and Buckingham had exchanged hard words and were no longer speaking. The Prince of Wales, however, had not been trained to argue. He said he and his father would set aside the laws of England and sign the articles. The consent of Parliament, he agreed, might take a little time—but he was sure it could be obtained.

While Charles was bending and Buckingham boasting, the Spanish lodged their English attendants on the opposite end of town in quarters too cramped for comfort. In a few weeks it was clear so many English were not wanted in Madrid, and the prince sent most of them home. From week to week new conditions were conceived regarding the marriage. First the Vatican said it would hear of no change. Then the Spanish Council announced the infanta would have to remain in Spain for a full year after the ceremony to see if England would follow all its agreements. Olivares himself appeared, smiling, to carry that news and Buckingham became abusive. The Spanish favorite looked at his English counterpart and murmured that his presence did not assist matters.

Nevertheless, matters moved toward a marriage, though the people of Spain were indifferent and the people of England loathed the idea. The king of Spain announced that all English galley slaves were released, an act of goodwill that succeeded in scraping an old sore. Other pleasant gestures were made; festivities mounted. Lope de Vega wrote a play in honor of the prince, and Valázquez painted a memorable portrait showing the young man standing stiffly, somewhat like a statue in fancy clothes.

A meeting between the prince and the infanta was arranged by the court. The protocol of Spain had grown Byzantine and formal; every step and move for such an appearance was charted in advance. The prince was handed a script; the infanta had another. The princess performed as she was instructed; but Charles, the least spontaneous young man on earth, pretended to be overcome with her beauty and inflamed with passion, cast his script aside, and began to protest his burning love. The infanta recoiled in horror, wide-eyed. Attendants rushed forward to hasten the Prince of Wales out of the room while the Spaniards rolled their eyes, gestured, and broke into angry comments.

The king of England, meanwhile, had a chapel prepared for the infanta. He went to survey the work and noticed the people standing around were gloomy and silent. He tried a jest: "We are preparing a Temple to the Devil," he said—and when he saw his attempt at exaggeration was taken seriously, fled.

The king had not heard from Steenie or Baby Charles, as he called them, for over a month and was very worried, when Cottington returned. Now a baronet and Sir Francis Cottington, the prince's secretary told James in detail how serious the situation had grown; how difficult the Spaniards were making matters—and how far-reaching the demands of the Vatican had become. The king was shaken:

> My sweet boys, your letter by Cottington hath stricken me dead. I fear it shall very much shorten my days, and I am the more perplexed that I know not how to satisfy the people's expectations here, neither know I what to say to our Council . . . come speedily away, if ye can get leave, and give over all treaty. And this I speak without respect of any security they can offer you, except ye never look to see your old dad again, whom I fear ye shall never see, if you see him not before winter. Alas! I now repent me sore that I ever suffered you to go away. I care for match, nor nothing, so that I may once have you in my arms again. God grant it! God grant it! God grant it! Amen, amen, amen.[10]

The following day he listened to Cottington again and said he would sign anything. He seemed to believe the prince and Buckingham were held in captivity, as he himself had been held so often in Scotland. The great sophisticated world of western Europe had never really penetrated James; he had behaved as king of England as though he was still the poverty-stricken sovereign of a poor and backward nation, who had to plead, crawl, and beg for peace and protection from stronger realms.

Frantic, he sent word to Charles to sign and to marry and to come home. It was clear where his fears rested; his instructions ended with his hope that none would seek to bar the prince's passage from Spain.

While these secret negotiations were underway, the king tried to pretend all was well and went hunting. "He is stupefied," said one observer. James himself, forgetting his role of all-confident sovereign, turned to a servant one day and asked, "Do you think I will ever see the Prince again?" and burst into tears.[11]

The prince, meanwhile, acted like a lovesick youth in his first effort. He craned out the window to see the shadow of the princess pass before the curtains of her rooms. He wrote poems and had them sent to her, though she knew no English and he no Spanish. Receiving James's permission to sign the articles, he told Olivares, and that imperturbable eminence said he was pleased; it meant a delay of only four more months. Perhaps the marriage could be held in September; the infanta could leave the following March.

Charles then asked for that in writing. The following day he told the king of Spain he agreed to all, and the Spaniards planted illuminations throughout Madrid as a sign of success. Still they waited, for it was the king of England whose words would settle the matter—not his son's.

In Whitehall the king went through motions. He convinced his council to agree for the sake of the return of the prince. James used gold plate, but all the guests at the banquet, except the incurably foppish earl of Carlisle, appeared dressed in black. After the banquet, the king signed the marriage contract with secret clauses nobody in the realm knew about—but which were suspected.

Weeks passed while the documents traveled to Spain, but matters there were also strained. The Spanish had grown to hate Buckingham, who had demanded women, who drank too much, who insulted numerous nobles, and who made himself generally obnoxious. Even the English ambassador, Bristol, stopped speaking to the favorite, whom James—in an attempt to make equal in rank to Olivares—had elevated to a duke.

When word came that James had signed all the articles, Olivares was almost at his wits' end. New clauses were added as afterthoughts. One was a demand that the future king of England listen to the persuasions of Catholic priests at any time they wanted to make them. Others were equally insulting. Charles nodded and said he agreed. "Is it possible?" asked Olivares. "I would as soon have expected my death."[12]

While Charles was giving way, however, he had Buckingham write a letter to James, asking the king to call him home. The prince was subtly changing. Olivares, who studied him deeply, decided he was both weak and obstinate. He did not really believe the infanta could be trusted to him; he promised too easily and too much.

Nevertheless, further delay seemed impossible; even Olivares ran out of excuses. Prince Charles solemnly signed proxies and took an oath on August 28, 1623. He took his leave of the queen of Spain and the infanta and assured them all the Catholics of England would be under his protection.

On September 2, 1623, Charles said goodbye to King Philip IV and their conversation was cordial. Buckingham, however, had aroused deep contempt and anger. The Spaniards, usually coldly correct in disdain, were surprisingly vocal in their feelings. At the moment of parting, the English duke exchanged angry words with Olivares.

Charles, however, was a correct young man, a type not unfamiliar in Spain. He left in a royal coach, attended by a large escort. Cardinal Zapata sat in the coach with him and asked if he wished the carriage to be open. A hint of Charles's feeling appeared abruptly. "I should not dare to give my assent," he said, "without sending first to Madrid to consult the Junta of Theologians."

Nevertheless, he continued to play his role. In Segovia he wrote a letter to the king of Spain, repeating his promises. It was sent to Madrid, and the strange young man then wrote another letter to Bristol, the English ambassador, saying that the marriage by proxy should not take place until guarantees that the infanta would not enter a convent were received. Once such guarantees were sent, the prince would issue the necessary permission. The second letter, however, was not to be given to the ambassador until after the pope had sent his approval of the latest arrangement. The prince, in other words, would throw some last minute delays of his own—from a safe distance.

On September 12, 1623, Charles and Buckingham reached Santander and English ships. Behind them the infanta set about preparations for marriage. On October fifth, the prince and the duke arrived at Portsmouth. They rode at once to York House, arriving a little after daybreak. News of their coming—without the infanta—spread as fast as the rising sunlight. Bells began to peal in London, and crowds surged into the streets. The adventurers were met by the Privy Council, but were in a hurry to get to the king. They were furnished a coach and traveled past roaring crowds cheering the Prince of Wales; it was assumed he had broken free of Spanish enchantments and come home to his people.

London had not seen such scenes of joy since the headiest days of Elizabeth. Tables were brought out into the streets, and rich men placed food before the poor. A cartload of felons on the way to death were pardoned because they crossed the path of the prince. Over a hundred bonfires were counted between St. Paul's and London Bridge.

Charles's first words to his father were, "I am ready to conquer Spain, if you will allow me to do it." The prince and Buckingham were closeted with the king for hours. When they emerged, James radiated joy.

His happiness did not last long. The duke of Buckingham and Prince
Charles had returned from their sojourn in Spain like two brothers—and
like two brothers, they combined against the king. Where James had hoped
to resolve the problems of the Palatinate in concert with Madrid, Buckingham and Prince Charles were now breathing war with Spain itself. James
was deeply shaken; his entire foreign policy was in jeopardy, and his favorite
had joined with his heir to dominate him.

While the king, virtually crippled now by arthritis and gout, struggled
to put his foreign policy back together, the Prince of Wales and the duke
of Buckingham appeared in London and held a secret meeting with a dozen
Privy Councillors who had been participating in the Spanish negotiations.
The councillors, sworn to secrecy, listened to a long, highly colored account
of their adventures in Spain from Buckingham.

Every so often the duke would turn to the prince for verification, and
Charles would nod solemnly. It was, said one observer later, almost as
though together they were one man, with Buckingham being the voice.
Buckingham would relate insults, slights, lies. "Is that not so, My Lord?
Did they not so?" "Aye," the prince would say. "Aye." And again, "Aye."[13]

Meanwhile, James wrote Madrid, outlining his solution of the Palatinate problems and asking for the infanta's dowry in cash. Bristol was
instructed to return in twenty days if these terms were not met. The English
ambassador also received orders from Prince Charles to delay the proxy
marriage until further notice. Both father and son could be peremptory—
at a distance.

Meanwhile, the pope's approval of the marriage contract was received
in Madrid. Other news, more serious in nature, created consternation in
Olivares and Philip IV. Buckingham's denunciations and the complicity of
Prince Charles spelled the ruin of Spanish hopes just as much as they did
the hopes of James. War with England was an event no man in Madrid
wanted to see.

Nevertheless, when Bristol appeared to delay the wedding until a
satisfactory treaty had been reached over the Palatinate, the Spaniards were
firm. The Hapsburgs of Spain would not fight the Hapsburgs of Vienna over
Frederick V. If the marriage arrangements hinged on such a new clause,
which involved many more princes of Europe, then there would be no
marriage.

In England the Privy Councillors sat in wonder. They had been forced
to agree to arrangements with Spain that were now being broken. Buckingham and the Prince of Wales were as urgent in their new direction as they
had been in their old.

King James, meanwhile, was told that Spain would surrender its territories in the Palatinate in the autumn. He was cheered, but Buckingham was angered. The twelve Privy Councillors presumably conversant with the Spanish negotiations slowly realized they had been kept in the dark. They voted to inquire into past arrangements and secret clauses, and Buckingham abused them. He rushed from the council chamber with Prince Charles toward Royston. Once there, they pressured James into signing a letter forbidding such an inquiry. Then Buckingham stood guard over the king while the prince rushed back to say he would never marry the infanta.

The direction of the realm was being taken from the hands of James and into the hands of his son and his favorite. The king was pressured into calling for a new Parliament. He had not wanted to do that, but he could not argue long or hold out very long. The session was due to open February 12, 1624, but was delayed by the death of the duke of Lennox. James was losing his old friends and supporters; familiar faces were vanishing.

Finally, the king was carried in to Lords. His eyes had sunken, and his face showed the signs of years of dissipation. His confidant tone and the jokes, the careless curses, and the references to his divinity were gone. He spoke of his hopes for peace and for the first time said he sought their advice. He had hoped much of Spain, but now knew better. The whole story, he said, would be told to them by the secretaries—and by the Prince of Wales and the duke of Buckingham. "Never King gave more trust," he ended. "Ye may freely advise me, seeing of my princely fidelity you are invited thereto."

"I pray you," he said, "judge me charitably, as you will have me judge you. . . ."[14] The ghostly echo of Biblical words and phrases always rang in James's rhetoric.

He was carried out of sight in his chair like Father Time giving way, in an artist's cartoons, to the vigorous figure of the duke of Buckingham. That eminence gave orders the Parliament would assemble in the great Hall of the palace, instead of in the Painted Chamber. There they would hear the man who was now, in all but name, the king of England.


Buckingham made a considerable oration against Spain. Later, Commons met in official business. Buckingham's report was read; the Spanish marriage was denounced. The king's requests for money were passed over; but measures to repair the fleet, assist the Dutch, defend Ireland, and strengthen national defenses were passed.

To general surprise the king was not pleased. He wanted funds for fighting in the Palatinate. But he had not himself spoken against Spain and reminded Commons he had not approved Buckingham's report. Prince Charles was so angry that he refused to speak to his father, but Buckingham came boldly in to storm at the king.

The king temporized. He had always dreaded the thought of war; he pleaded that England needed allies. Buckingham snatched at that thought and expanded upon it. France could help—and the French royal family had a princess to marry. Henry Rich, Viscount Kensington, was sent to Paris to revive the idea of a marriage between the Princess Henrietta and Prince Charles. Buckingham knew the Reformers of England would see little difference between an alliance with the pro-Vatican rulers of France, oppressors of the Huguenots, and Madrid. But he also knew that a joint campaign conducted by combined French-English forces to restore his lost Palatinate to the Elector Frederick would be so popular that it would drown other consideration.

The French were very receptive. Cardinal Richelieu was not anxious to see Spain's domination of the continent continue. The queen believed her daughter could advance the Vatican faith in England. The young king, Louis XIII, was—as usual—indifferent.

Negotiations proceeded rapidly. Both countries agreed on the selection of Count Mansfeld as their joint field commander. Mansfeld arrived in London and immediately charmed James, whose pleasure at handsome and virile men had grown compulsive. The count was known as a fighter for the deposed Elector Frederick in London and was therefore popular. Few knew that his behavior as a general had been calamitous. Arrangements were made to give Mansfeld £20,000 a month and 13,000 men. France agreed to match the money and the men. It was hoped that France would recover some lost territory and that James's son-in-law and daughter would regain their domain—the gods of war permitting.

These developments so alarmed the Spaniards that their diplomats in London took an unprecedented step. Their circumstances were difficult; they were under constant watch and were barred from seeing the king alone. They decided, therefore, to present James with the true picture of the duke of Buckingham, culled from his behavior in Madrid and the Spanish observations of his activities both in Europe and in England.

The results were interesting. They charged that the duke had brought whores into his apartments in Madrid and that he had deliberately created situations that broke the Spanish marriage. They charged he was plotting to marry his son to the king's granddaughter in Europe so that his heirs could be part of the royal family. They charged he would break the French alliance as he had the Spanish. They also castigated the English Parliament as an unruly and rebellious gathering and declared the king of England was being misrepresented to his subjects by the duke, who was ruling by deceit.

James demurred. He could not believe all that, but he had allowed the Spaniards an audience. They told him that Buckingham had promised he —James—would be deposed if he did not declare war against Spain.

James, agitated, took a coach to Windsor, stopping at St. James on the way. Prince Charles came out, with Buckingham beside him. The king was crying and repeated what he had been told. Buckingham was furious, and after reading the details of the charges, fastened his suspicions on Cranfield, the earl of Middlesex. Middlesex was a businessman to whom a war spelled financial chaos. He could not understand such activities; he had secretly intrigued against Buckingham's policy. He had also been talking to the king.

Charges arose against the lord treasurer out of the air overnight. They were laid before the House of Lords on April 15, 1624—prepared by Coke and Sandys. The weapon of impeachment, only threatened before, was now polished and ready. It fell upon Middlesex on May 13, 1624. He was sent to the Tower, banned from office, and heavily fined.

Buckingham gloated and preened himself. He believed he had achieved an outstanding victory. The king turned on him sharply. "You are a fool," he said. "You are making a rod by which you will be scourged yourself."

To Prince Charles, who was standing silently nearby as usual, James added another word. "You will live to have your bellyful of impeachments," he said prophetically.[15]

Having used impeachment, Commons next turned to the matter of patents, and passed a bill placing these under the Common Law Courts. It was then prorogued until November. King James alone in the realm realized the significance of the shift that Buckingham and Prince Charles had accomplished by turning against him. The Crown's prerogatives had been reduced, and those of Parliament made immensely stronger. There had never been anything wrong with James's intelligence; it was his character that was deficient.

The King was barely able to follow events after Parliament vanished, temporarily, from the landscape. Negotiations were underway with France regarding a marriage—and the terms soon involved the Catholic issues. The king decided they could not be met. A letter was drafted to France to that effect. The French ambassador in England, Effiat, hurried to Buckingham, who was taking the cure at Wellingborough.

The duke immediately accompanied the Frenchman back toward court. On their way, they met a French courier. Buckingham asked for the dispatches, broke open the seals, read them, stuffed them in his pocket, and continued until he reached the king. The startled James was conveyed into a private room. When they emerged, a greatly altered dispatch was sent to France.

It reached Richelieu, who drafted an article restating Catholic de-

mands. Matters went back and forth, and James was pressed by the duke
to give way, item by item and article by article. Prince Charles was now
beside the favorite; they combined against the sinking king. By November
1624 the terms were signed that pleased the cardinal.

The same series of concessions to Catholics that had created such a gulf
so often before began again. On December 24, 1624, the courts were forbidden to apply laws against the Vatican followers and Catholics in prison were
released.

The king, meanwhile, was in serious bad health. He dictated a personal
letter to Buckingham; his hands being too crippled to hold a pen:

> If I cannot content myself without sending you this billet, praying
> God that I may have a joyful and comfortable meeting with you, and
> that we may make at this Christenmass a new marriage—ever to be
> kept thereafter. For, God so love me, as I desired only to live in this
> world for your sake . . . I had rather live banished in any part of the
> world with you, than live a sorrowful widow-life without you. And so
> God bless you, my sweet child and wife, and grant ye may ever be a
> comfort to your dear dad and husband.[16]

It was a love letter, written by a man 59 years old, to a middle-aged
bully who had once been his smooth-cheeked lover.

Preparations mounted to send troops to Europe under Count Mansfeld. The count was a robber on a great scale, unaccustomed to paying much
attention to matters of supply or payment to his troops. These gathered at
Dover in considerable misery, consisting of conscripts seized almost at
random from among the poor and the helpless. Unpaid, with no orders, they
wandered about the shipping region foraging for themselves.

The original plan had been to land in Calais to involve the French in
the great enterprise to regain the Palatinate. The French were not ready for
that and attempted to persuade the Dutch to receive the troops instead. The
Dutch, however, knew Mansfeld and his methods—which were as hard on
allies as on enemies. Mansfeld, however, declared he would carry his men
across to Flushing. He finally departed with his destination uncertain, on
January 31, 1625. He found Calais closed against him and proceeded to
Flushing, where the vessels carrying the men cast anchor.

Poorly clad against freezing weather, the men huddled on the ships for
several days. They were then transferred to boats to carry them to Gertruidenberg, near Breda. Three regiments arrived. The other three were
caught in snows and cold winds. They arrived hungry, having been unfed

for several days. Gertruidenberg had no food for them and forty or fifty died every day. Mansfeld, from a warm distance, sent £2,000 for provisions.

Word was sent back to England asking for assistance, and word was received from England—in one of King James's last messages to his subjects —that they should proceed to the Palatinate. Meanwhile, wretched men died. By March 1625 only 3,000 were still alive out of the original 12,000. When Christian of Brunswick at last arrived on the scene, only a few hundred wasted men were able to greet him.

English naval preparations were better organized and in better hands. Twelve ships of war and a hundred transports were made ready. The duke of Buckingham organized for war as well as the marriage of Prince Charles. The duke was now all-powerful. His instruments sat on the Privy Council, and his relatives or creatures held all offices.

The king, fading, huddled in his stained, padded clothes. He was as remote from the life of England as he had once been remote from the life of Scotland. Yet he still had moments. He was at Theobalds on March 1, 1625, watching deer, when news reached him that the duke of Hamilton had died. He was greatly affected. "I shall never see London more," he said. Then he fell ill with what was vaguely known as the "ague."

"An ague in spring is physic for a King," his servants said, but he was not consoled.

On the seventeenth of March, 1625, he felt better. Buckingham's mother, fussing about him, insisted he drink a posset prepared by a doctor she liked, and James suffered a frightening relapse. His physicians said they would not attend him any further unless the countess and her doctor stayed out of the case. The countess, greatly upset, went to the king on her knees and begged for help against "these charges."

"What charges?" asked James, puzzled.

Weeping, the countess said she and her physician were being accused of poisoning the king.

"What?" said James faintly. "Poison?" and fainted.

But he recovered and seemed to be mending when the countess and her physician returned with another posset. James drank it and promptly had another relapse.

On the twenty-fourth of March James was sinking; his ailments had grown so numerous he kept their pangs at bay only with copious quantities of beer. The royal physician advised abstinence. He sent, finally, for Lancelot Andrewes, a saintly cleric, but Andrewes himself was ill. Meanwhile, news came that several aged but good old Scots nobles whom he had always liked had died.

Finally, Lord Keeper John Williams, competent and cool, arrived to tell James he was dying.

James, given Communion, asked that Prince Charles be summoned; Buckingham could already be heard in the hall.

By the time the prince arrived, the fiancé of a new French Catholic princess, his father had been deprived of a chance to make a deathbed statement by a stroke that left him unable to speak. Even worse, the stroke had unhinged his jaw so that it hung laxly on his chest in a ghastly simulacrum of death. Phlegm choked him; servants kept running in and out with fresh towels.

Then God—a satirist whose scale is beyond all mortals—sent an attack of dysentery. On Sunday, March 27, 1625, just before noon, James was carried away in an outgoing tide of his own shit.

No fool was ever so fertile in the invention of fallacies or left behind so many enduring errors to plague the human race. His theory that peace can be purchased by cowardice helped move Europe into the Thirty Years' War in his own day—and many more since.

Hailed as a scholar, he sought to kill the thoughts of other men. Yet as he died in his filthy bed, the words of Buchanan were coursing through England's political underground, and the theories of Knox were creating a new church.

James inherited a realm proud in the world, filled with riches, clear in purpose, and strong in its sense of destiny. He left it racked with dissension, economically gutted, sown thick with the seeds of revolution, sinking into incoherent wars.

None of his descendants escaped the results of his follies. Prince Charles's Catholic marriage entangled all the Stuarts into eternal religious troubles with their English and Scots subjects. His attempt to continue the theories of Elizabeth and his mother, Mary Stuart, that sovereigns are above the law and created by divine sanction, led his son, Charles I, to the executioner's block and Louis XVI to the guillotine.

Even the passage of centuries has not completely destroyed or extirpated the amazing virulence of James Stuart's arguments. Intellectuals still echo his desire "to govern according to the common weal and not according to the common will." Governments still exist that believe, as did James and the Vatican of his day, that men can be held in mental prisons. And these arguments are still opposed by those who believe in Knox's living God and by those who agree with Buchanan that men cannot be governed without their own consent—though the names of these men and their associates, and the great tectonic revolution they launched, are barely recalled.

# NOTES

1.  George Buchanan's father was a Highlander named Thomas Buchanan, who spoke Gaelic; his mother—Agnes Heriot—spoke Scots and was from the Lowlands. The boy himself was born in 1506 near the village of Killearn in Stirlingshire and is thought to have attended grammar school in Glasgow. He had an early facility for language and was obviously gifted; an uncle—James Heriot—sent him to the University of Paris when Buchanan was about fourteen years old in 1520.

    The transition was startling: Scotland was a sparsely settled country whose largest city capital, Edinburgh, had a population of only 15,000 whereas Paris held 200,000. The great congeries known as the University of Paris was, in itself, immense and populated by a polyglot collection of students from all parts of Europe. Their ages ranged the scale from lads like Buchanan to men of thirty-five; many continued to wear the clothes of their lands of origin—and a number were in greasy rags. Most lived on the Left Bank of the Seine; bands of them prowled the streets of the city at night—and murders were not unknown among them. Living conditions were horrendous; the tenements on the bank and the rooms in such colleges as the Scots maintained at the university were icy in winter, sweltering in summer. Students in Buchanan's circumstances slept on the floor atop a mound of smelly rushes; in the classrooms only the teacher had a stool—the students sat on the floor. Years later Buchanan described the scene: "Some," he wrote of the students, "are sound asleep and others are thinking of everything else but the book they are reading. One is absent, but has bribed his neighbor to answer to his name when the roll is called. Another has lost his stockings, and another cannot keep his eyes off a big hole in his shoe. One pretends to be ill, and another is writing a letter to his parents. And so the rod is never idle, sobs never cease, and cheeks are never dry from tears." Lessons and books alike were in Latin—for which Buchanan, luckily, had a facility that was to later make him famous. But in his first two years he was often hungry, often ill, and, he said later, always unhappy.

In 1523 Buchanan's uncle died, and he returned to Scotland. He arrived when the air was thick with war clouds; the Scots regent, the duke of Albany, drafted an army in the name of the boy king, James V, to invade England. Buchanan, swept in the tide; attired in a leather, iron-plated jacket; wearing a steel cap; given a sword, buckler, knife, and shield, marched with the rest. The expedition was a disaster and during its return, in icy November, was caught in a snowstorm in which many froze to death. Buchanan, a slender seventeen, barely made it home to suffer the rest of the winter in bed.

A year later, Buchanan returned to the University of Paris, with food and lodging assured by a post as bursar of the Scots College. These fundaments were barely enough to keep him alive, but the university was seething in the battle between the medieval Scholastics and the followers of the New Learning—the northern equivalent of the Renaissance. The struggle had various names; some called it Scholastic and Classic. Buchanan was a Classicist—a term that attracted a number of definitions. Great debates between the orators of the two sides took place. Buchanan contributed epigrams and verse. In 1526 he graduated as Master of Arts and received a plum in the form of a regency at Ste. Barbe—the most famous college in the university.

By that time Buchanan had become a friend of Budé and created a sensation by discarding the antique Latin grammar used at his college and by translating to Latin the English grammar of Linacre. That thrust him forward at a time when Francis I of France was encouraging new scholars, when Erasmus was softening the impact of Luther's arguments, and when the Crown was optimistic. Levels of scholarship, in fact, soared high. Chairs of Greek and Hebrew were established; studies of mathematics and geography were transformed; a great printing house was established that was often visited by the queen of Navarre. The Royal College was looked upon as a New Learning headquarters and aroused the bitter opposition of the theological faculty head, Nicholas Beda. Beda's example fired a Spanish student, older than his fellows, limping from a wound in the wars, named Ignatius Loyola.

The split was deep and dangerous. Beda believed the study of Greek would reawaken the lures of paganism; and the study of Hebrew, the tenets of Judaism. Together they would usher doctrines into society that would first weaken, then loosen, and finally sever the tapestry of Christianity. Buchanan's achievement in changing an established Latin grammar was, to Beda, a part of this perilous new course. The issue of the Royal College, therefore, introduced from the top, created disruption.

Buchanan was part of the scene, but France was not his native land, and he had no hope of rising with the new stars of the Royal College. Instead he left after three years with an established reputation to become tutor to the young earl of Cassillis. Back in Scotland, he appeared at the court of the young King James V, who was himself just coming into his powers. James was well aware that Scotland was backward and plagued with a corrupt crowd of priests and monks; he especially loathed the Franciscans. Discovering that Buchanan was a gifted poet with a biting wit, the king of the Scots encouraged him to write a lampoon about the Franciscans. The results were scurrilous and hilarious; the poem went the rounds of the country and created a scandal. Buchanan, despite the protection of the king, had to flee.

His flight led through London in 1539, but danger there was also great. Henry VIII was sending men to their deaths for heresy according to his own shifting definitions of these deviations. Buchanan proceeded to Paris and there discovered that James Cardinal Beaton, serving as ambassador from Scotland, was diligent in searching out impious scholars. Francis I, as was the habit of kings, now repented his encouragement of the New Learning and had turned against its exponents. Buchanan was lucky to get out of the place and even luckier to land a post in Bordeaux, where a good friend—André de Gouvêa—headed a college. A chair of Latin was created for Buchanan, and he settled for the quiet life.

At Bordeaux, Buchanan wrote a play in Latin verse called *Baptistes*. He later claimed the effort was inspired by events in England under Henry VIII, and he had that cruel king, Anne Boleyn, and Sir Thomas More in mind. In any event, the play was, on the surface, about John the Baptist and Herod. It was cast in the antique mold with a chorus and was staged at the Bordeaux College several times. Montaigne, a pupil of Buchanan, later recalled playing one of the parts. It took no great powers of analysis to see that the author was talking about tyranny—and it passed, in arduously hand-copied manuscripts, from hand to hand throughout Europe—and made Buchanan famous. It was to circulate, in fact, for over a hundred years. It was translated into English by John Milton during revolutionary times in England—and was, in fact, one of the inspirational works of that event. It was translated into French and Dutch—and it helped get Buchanan into trouble with the Inquisition.

He landed in that vise circuitously as a result of accompanying Gouvêa to Portugal, in response to an invitation from King John III, who was anxious to rejuvenate the University of Coimbra. Gouvêa died in 1547, and the Inquisition used the event as a sign to move against the avant-garde professors of the university.

While they held Buchanan, the Inquisitors traced his background and activities. After six months, the evidence was collected, and Buchanan, together with two Portuguese professors, was ordered tried. He was accused of being "badly disposed" toward the Faith and belonging to the "sect of Luther." Proofs were collected that he had made jokes at Church practices and eaten meat during Lent, had consorted with Jews and even shared their Passover Feast. These were not grave accusations: unlike most men whose lives were searched by these subtle investigators, no offenses against morals had been uncovered—and no incidents of which Buchanan was ashamed. Nevertheless, his situation was scary: he was in the hands of men from a country different from his own, infused with the passions of Mediterranean Christianity, who could take fire and consume him if he responded improperly.

The records of his trial were obtained many years later and show that he answered both well and honestly. He had wavered, but never joined the Lutherans; he had indeed written against Franciscans, but not in malice so much as in fun—and he added he had not associated with Jews in Scotland because there were no Jews in that country. His inquisitors listened and sent him back to his confinement in the monastery of St. Bento during the pleasure of their general. He busied himself while waiting for their conclusions by translating the Psalms into Latin verse. In time these also became popular and famous, and their serene rhythms give no hint that the author was suspended in dread.

His sentence, when it was finally delivered, was relatively mild. He was released, after seven months, but forbidden to leave Lisbon. He broke that regulation as soon as possible and took passage on a Cretan ship to England on the last day of February 1552. From there, he somehow managed to get back to France.

Like Knox, Buchanan had been involuntarily drawn into the

vortex of the Reform. Unlike Knox, he did not take fire, but the experience of the Inquisition turned him against the Vatican forever. While Knox was busy in England, Buchanan lived quietly as a teacher —sometimes for a college and sometimes in the household of the Marshal de Brissac—kept quiet, and watched events. They were grim. Francis I died, and his successor, Henry II, embarked upon a campaign of terror against heretics. He created a *chambre ardente* for the purpose, and the cells of the Conciergerie, which included some below the surface of the Seine, were dense with prisoners; the Grand Châtelet, with cells too small for the captives to stand up or lie fully down, were similarly filled. Buchanan watched; studied the literature that streamed from Geneva—and, like many of his contemporaries, felt that not all the beauty of the Vatican liturgy nor the treasures of its art could overcome his growing aversion to the cruelty of its campaigns.

In 1561, when Lord James Stewart and the Scots Council decided to invite Mary Stuart to the throne of Scotland, Buchanan returned home. He found himself hailed by his countrymen, who were immensely proud that the greatest poet and best-known Latinist of all Europe was one of their own. When the beautiful, young, nineteen-year-old queen established her little court at Holyrood, Buchanan became one of its stars. He helped the young queen select books from abroad, works by Erasmus, Rabelais, Ariosto, Ronsard, Horace, and other writers, old and new; composed a new dedication of his own famous translations of the Psalms to her. They often read together after dinner surrounded by Gobelin tapestries, their steps made soft by Persian rugs. Their conversation was in French, a language they each loved. She was nineteen, had been a queen of France, and was at her charming peak. He was fifty-five and had lived the hard, pinched life of a teacher-scholar. For the first time, he enjoyed the comfort, prestige, and beauties of life at the top. In those winters— and winters were cold in Scotland in the 1560s, even colder than usual —with the fireplace blazing cozily while icy winds howled outside, it was no wonder that Buchanan, for the first time, fell a little bit in love.

2. Henry Stewart, Lord Darnley, was born December 7, 1545. A memorable painting, which hangs in Windsor Castle, shows him at the age of seventeen. He is standing with his six-year-old younger brother; behind them stretches a great but strangely empty room with two high, narrow windows visible in the distance. Both the boys are dressed in black; Darnley's ruff is high and close. He is wearing a dress sword, and one gloved hand is visible; the other—bare—is resting on his little brother's shoulder. Something about the arrangement—all

black, white, and gray—conveys a haunting sense of frozen child-hood, of isolation amid great vacant spaces.

Their lineage was high indeed and spanned both England and Scotland. Their father, the earl of Lennox, was generally considered a weak man, but revealed great ambition in all his efforts. He moved into the circle of the English royal family when he married Lady Margaret Douglas—a formidable, proud, imperious woman whose mother had been Lady Margaret Tudor, elder sister of King Henry VIII.

The marriage moved Lennox into assisting Henry's effort to subjugate Scotland; his reward was a promise to be made governor of that realm during a planned occupation. Henry's effort failed, and Lennox fled south, but was rewarded with great estates. His countess made herself memorable by openly scorning both Anne Boleyn and her daughter, Elizabeth. The countess of Lennox, née Douglas, harbored a lifelong resentment over the fact that Henry VIII had excluded his elder sister and all her descendants from the English throne because of their Vatican faith.

When Mary Tudor sat on the throne of England, the countess of Lennox, her first cousin, had shared that Vatican faith with the sovereign and took precedence over the Princess Elizabeth. She was rumoured to have urged Elizabeth's death. Even Elizabeth's accession to the throne did not cow the countess; she continued to call her "that fool bastard."

To the countess of Lennox, therefore, Mary Stuart was not only a relative, but the rightful heir to the throne of England. If her own eldest son, Lord Darnley, who was the nearest prince of the blood in England, could marry the Queen of Scots, then Elizabeth's hold on her throne could be threatened.

Darnley was raised toward this objective. After Mary Stuart's husband, the French boy King Francis II, died in December 1560, an intense maneuvering began around her possible return to Scotland, and the countess sent the seventeen-year-old Darnley to that country. There the tall, handsome young noble held long conversations with the Guise family. News of this was reported in London, and Elizabeth was sufficiently annoyed to have the countess brought before her in court. The countess protested that a marriage between the Queen of Scots and her son Darnley was suitable—and then added their union would assure an orderly succession if Elizabeth died without children. Elizabeth, however, recalled that the pope had annulled the marriage of the countess's parents. Then, after questioning her cousin's legitimacy, she had her put under house arrest to cool off.

After this, it was amazing that the Virgin allowed Darnley to go to Scotland. Some observers wondered whether it was not a trap, but Elizabeth was less calculating and more emotional than such an analysis deserves. She had no fears, once she attained the throne—neither the earl of Lennox nor his heir, Lord Darnley, aroused any in her.

Sir James Melville, sent to England by Mary Stuart to discuss the negotiations between the Queen of Scots and the Queen of England regarding Lord Robert Dudley, found the Virgin in excellent humor. She was elevating Dudley to be earl of Leicester, and Melville was invited to watch. As her favorite knelt before her, Elizabeth could not resist putting her hand down and tickling him. Then, having made her feelings clear to the world, she turned to the Scotsman and asked how he liked the new earl. Melville, never at a loss, congratulated the Englishman in having "a Princess who could see and reward good service."

"Yet," said the Queen of England, "you like better yon long lad," and pointed toward Lord Darnley, who as the highest noble in England, carried the sword of honor for the occasion. Melville protested that Darnley was beardless and therefore lady-faced. He was so convincing that his deprecations have been used ever since as a valid analysis, though Sir James had no such opinion. According to his *Memoirs,* he had already been contacted by the countess of Lennox and the earl and was secretly trying to obtain permission for Darnley to go to Scotland. The young prince—for such he was known in England—was very tall, as were so many of the Stewarts, including his mother and Mary Stuart, Queen of the Scots. Darnley was somewhere between one and three inches over six feet, and Melville described him later as not only of "high stature, long and small, even and straight but . . . well instructed in all honest and comely exercises." He was an excellent rider and a graceful dancer and gifted enough to write remarkably good verse. He was also fond of music and pleasant conversation—and far too large physically to be taken lightly as a presence. Melville, however, dismissed him so easily to Elizabeth that she herself followed suit—and allowed him to go to Scotland, as she had earlier allowed his father.

Darnley danced with all the ladies of the court of Scotland without showing any signs of special favoritism, played tennis with David Rizzio—an Italian who had grown important as the queen's secretary —and charmed everyone he met. He was so outstanding that the queen's infatuation seemed too well-placed not to be sincere. Perhaps, for a time, it was.

3.   Robert Dudley was born about 1533, the third son of Sir John Dudley.

The Dudleys were a family of intriguers and adventurers who became prominent in the reign of the first Tudor king of England, Henry VII. At that time, Edmund Dudley had married Elizabeth Grey, daughter of Viscount Lisle, a connection that placed his descendants into kinship with several ancient noble English families. Edmund's activities created notoriety and widespread enmity, and he was beheaded, and the family was stripped of its possessions and their names attainted when Henry VIII succeeded. Sir John Dudley, however, so successfully served Henry VIII that he became Viscount Lisle and then earl of Warwick; he held a series of impressive posts and elevated the family even higher than before.

Raised in the court, Robert Dudley was the same age as Elizabeth and one of the companions for her brother, Edward VI. At the age of seventeen, he was discovered in an affair with the youthful Amy Robsart, daughter of Sir John Robsart. They were married June 5, 1550, at a glittering court ceremony the day after one of his elder brothers, Lord Ambrose Dudley, was married to Lady Anne Seymour. The union of Robert Dudley and Amy Robsart was described by Cecil as a *nuptiae carnales.*

Robert Dudley's father undermined Somerset, the lord protector, managed to unseat him and have him beheaded, rose to rule England under the name of the boy king, and made himself duke of Northumberland. When Edward VI died at the age of fifteen, Northumberland attempted to set aside the succession and place Lady Jane Grey on the throne. That cost him his dukedom and his head; all the Dudleys were clapped into prison and sentenced to death, but Mary Tudor soon remitted the sentences. While Robert Dudley was in the Tower, however, and the new Queen Mary was still uncertain of her seat, Princess Elizabeth arrived in the same fortress as a prisoner on Easter Sunday, 1554. Robert Dudley, her same age and lifelong confidant, sold some land to obtain money to bribe her keepers to treat her well. Released after Mary Tudor's marriage to Philip II of Spain, Robert Dudley retired to his wife's estate in Norfolk. He reappeared at court in 1557, served well in France on behalf of Philip II and Mary Tudor, was restored to favor, and was among the first to rush to Hatfield to greet Elizabeth on her accession.

It was soon clear to all that the new queen was in love with him. By 1559 their relationship was so notorious the Spanish ambassador, de Quarda, wrote Madrid that Lord Robert Dudley had ordered his wife, Amy Robsart Dudley, to be poisoned so he could marry the English queen. Tall, dark, athletic, versed in Latin and Italian, a notable politician with all the charm that talent implies, he was given lucrative monopolies and rapidly made himself a power in the realm. He hated Cecil above all rivals and plotted incessantly to replace him as the first minister on the Privy Council. His relations with Elizabeth have been subjected to immense speculations then and since. Because the depths of her love were unquestionable, there will always remain a speculation that his affections were based upon her station.

In 1560, Dudley succeeded in putting Cecil into disgrace and was ensconced in an apartment next to the queen's. His wife lived alone at Cumnor Hall, three miles from Oxford. She was rumored to be seriously ill. A general belief existed that either her death or a divorce would soon be arranged and that Dudley would marry Elizabeth. On Sunday, September 8, 1560, when Amy Robsart's broken-necked body was found at the foot of a staircase at her home, a great wave of suspicion arose that she had been murdered. Dudley, informed at Windsor, sent a cousin to investigate. The event had occurred when Lady Dudley was alone and the servants away; an inquiry returned an official verdict of accidental death. The scandal, however, could not be quelled, and Elizabeth restored Cecil, after telling him she had finally made up her mind not to marry Robert Dudley.

4. Syphilis appeared in Europe toward the end of the fifteenth century and was at first believed to have originated in the army of Charles VIII during its attack upon Naples in 1495. So many of his polyglot troops were affected that the attack was halted, and the disbanded soldiers spread the disease as they returned to homes throughout Europe. It was called the Neapolitan disease, the French and Polish disease. Each nation blamed its worst enemy nation as the source of origination. The French termed it the Spanish disease and said it came from the New World. Medical Historian F. F. Carwright, however, in *Disease and History* (New York: Crowell, 1972) identifies it bacteriologically with the African disease of yaws and believes it was carried to the New World by African slaves and from thence to Europe—a theory that does not negate the Naples legend.

By the middle 1500s it was called the French pox in England, the *grosse vérole* in France, *bubas* in Spain. The name *syphilis* was coined by Girolamo Frascatoro in Verona in a poem in 1530. The illness hit every level and was spread, apparently, by any sort of contact including kissing, handshakes, through contaminated glasses, and so forth. Erasmus commented on it; a third of Paris was once held infected; both parents of Catherine de Médicis died of it within a few weeks of her birth. Henry VIII had syphilis that may have caused his remarkable character and personality deterioration; Ivan the Terrible had it; Mary Tudor shows signs of having inherited it, as did James I. Treatment was with mercury administered both orally and in "vapor" baths. It was centuries before the stages of the illness were recognized as connected; its multiple disguises remain often unrecognized even today.

5.   Mary M. Luke, *Gloriana: The Years of Elizabeth I* (New York: Coward-McCann & Geoghegan, 1973), p. 228.

6.   Stefan Zweig, *Mary Queen of Scotland and the Isles* (New York: Viking, 1935), p. 65.

7.   James Stewart was born 1531, the natural son of James V of Scotland and Lady Margaret Erskine Douglas. Lord James Stewart was almost king of Scotland; his royal father sought a papal dispensation so that he could marry Lady Margaret. The pope refused to allow the lady to divorce her husband, Douglas of Lochleven. James V then married Mary of Guise, who became the mother of Mary Stuart.

There is no record, either then or later, that Lord James Stewart ever sought to become king or resented his half sister's inheritance. He was popular, sensible, and influential from an early age. His father settled the income of the Priory of Saint Andrews upon him at the age of seven, and Lord James graduated from the University of Saint Andrews in 1545. He traveled to France in 1548 and fought against the English briefly, Scotland then being at war with that country.

The king of France settled estates upon Lord James and a number of other highly placed Scots nobles as part of a long-range plan to unite Scotland and France. Returning from that sign of favor from France to Scotland in 1552, however, Lord James Stewart held a secret meeting in London with the famous Scots revolutionary, John Knox.

The two men presented a study in contrasts. Lord James was only 21; Knox was 38 and looked much older. His sufferings as a galley slave of France had marked him physically, and his survival from that ordeal had given his conviction of divine mission an iron cast. Famous in England as well as Scotland, he was rising high in the country that gave him sanctuary; at the time he met with Lord James, the fiery Knox had made himself so notable in the Protestant England of Edward VI that the duke of Northumberland planned to make him bishop of Rochester. Lord James Stewart, on the other hand, was a member of the Scots royal family, held a high income from a Vatican trust in Saint Andrews, had just returned from receiving favors from Europe's "Most Christian" monarch, Henry II, and was held to be a loyal Catholic.

Vatican propagandists thundered about their secret meeting in St. Paul's Cathedral in London for years after it was discovered and believed that the course of the Scots revolution was plotted between these two unlikely partners. They were handicapped in proving this theory so far as the conversation between the two men was concerned, however, since no record was made, and neither ever revealed what passed between them. But there is no doubt the Vatican observers were accurate in claiming that Lord James Stewart's swing away from the Vatican could be dated from that event, and there is also no doubt that in the long view of later events, it was the assistance of Lord James Stewart and his influence among the high nobility of Scotland that brought the revolutionaries together with key members of the ruling group of the realm to achieve eventual success.

A year later, in 1553, the situation was altered dramatically. Edward VI died, the duke of Northumberland failed to seat Lady Jane Grey, and Mary Tudor—fanatically pro-Vatican—was Queen of England. By year's end, John Knox was in flight, and persecution of English Reformers was in full course.

In Scotland the Queen Mother moved adroitly. In order to become regent and displace the earl of Arran, whom the French king had made French duke of Châtelherault, she forbade persecution of the Scots Reformers. With their assistance, she became regent of Scotland in 1554. She then began a policy of swinging the realm into the orbit of France. That policy was popular with pro-Vatican Scots nobles, but was unpopular with the Reform elements and a growing number of nobles who had been converted to the new faith. Lord James Stewart was among these.

Lord James Stewart was among those who invited John Knox to Scotland in 1555. Knox arrived in the autumn and set the country on fire. He held house meetings, traveled from Edinburgh to Montrose, to Midlothian, where he was met by Lord Erskine, who was later earl of Mar; the lord of Lorne, heir to the earl of Argyll—and Lord James Stewart. These careful leaders sent the revolutionary from one great house to another. Church authorities issued a summons in May 1556 for Knox to appear, but Mary of Guise was persuaded to intervene and to quash the proceedings. That emboldened Knox and the Reformers; the firebrand appeared in Edinburgh and converted the capital. Knox left Scotland for Geneva soon afterward, but he left behind a handbook for revolution, instructions on how to organize—and Lord James Stewart among his followers.

By autumn 1556 the Scots nobility was torn between lures offered by the king of France—who wanted his heir, the dauphin, to marry Mary Stuart—and the maneuvers of Mary of Guise to start a new war with England. Knox was first asked to return and by year's end asked to wait. While he waited, the regent gathered a force to invade England, but the Scots nobility rebelled against the project.

Their rebellion took a form new in revolutions. A common band was drawn, or covenant. The term came straight from Knox's lexicon, in which Biblical terms were updated into contemporary moves. The signers included the earl of Morton, Erskine of Dun, and the lord of Lorne, and they pledged to defend Christ and His Congregation against Satan and Anti-Christ. Lord James Stewart did not sign this first band of the Lords of the Congregation. He thought the timing was premature; a rising against Mary of Guise would bring French intervention.

In December 1557 Mary of Guise and the Scots Parliament appointed nine commissioners to go to France to negotiate a marriage contract between Mary Stuart and the dauphin. Lord James was among these. They sailed in February 1558. In France in April 1558 the duke of Guise and his brother, the cardinal of Lorraine, persuaded Mary Stuart to sign her Scots inheritance over to France if she died without children or to hold that realm until the costs of her upbringing and education had been repaid. She also signed a document making the first two irrevocable. She then married the dauphin on April 24, 1558.

In France four of the nine Scots commissioners died mysteriously, and Lord James Stewart himself almost died; he had a bad stomach forever after. Poison in the court of Catherine de Médicis was generally—and creditably—suspected as the cause of this decimation.

The survivors returned to Scotland in October 1558, having agreed that Mary Stuart's husband, the dauphin, should have the crown matrimonial—that is, during the life of the Queen of Scots. Their return was at a time of rising disturbances; the Vatican prelates in Scotland had burned to death an elderly parish priest converted to the Reform for the crime of teaching his new faith to children. Riots erupted in Edinburgh; Reform demands were presented to Mary of Guise.

In November 1558 Elizabeth succeeded to the throne of England, and the Scots Parliament met and ratified the marriage of Mary Stuart to the French dauphin. The regent, Mary of Guise, had no more need to placate the Reform elements and during the spring of 1559 made plans to restore the Vatican supremacy in the realm. Four Reform ministers were summoned to appear in May 1559 on charges of heresy. Reform nobles urged Mary of Guise not to press the issue and meanwhile sent word to Knox to return to Scotland. He arrived 2 May 1559. He discovered the regent had issued a number of pro-

Vatican edicts of unexpected severity. At the same time, Elizabeth in England had grown irritated because the dauphin on his accession as King Francis II and his Queen Mary Stuart in France had added the arms of England to their new arms of combined France and Scotland.

In May 1559 Knox's speeches inspired crowds to invade and pillage various Catholic churches in Scotland, the regent marshaled French troops, and various Reform nobles gathered forces of their own. Lord James Stewart appeared, in this critical juncture, as a conciliator between the various forces. He first negotiated a temporary settlement between the regent and the Reform, whose terms were a success for the Reform. Then he switched sides, saying the regent was not sincere and was merely stalling till she could receive more troops from France. She charged in response that Lord James Stewart was aiming at the crown.

Lord James convinced the watchful English otherwise by inviting the earl of Arran—a convinced Reformer and heir to the duke of Châtelherault, leader of the Hamiltons and next in line of legitimate succession after Mary Stuart—to come back to Scotland from France. The fact was Lord James Stewart was that rare exception during a time of revolution and strife: an honest man. As such—and as virtually the only such man—his positions influenced everyone. England began to send the Reformers of Scotland money. In October 1559 the Reform leaders formally deposed Mary of Guise and established a committee consisting of Châtelherault, the earl of Arran, and Lord James Stewart to govern the realm.

The move combined, as was inevitable, religious and political policies. William Maitland of Lethington, secretary of state under Mary of Guise, switched sides. Maitland wanted a union between England and Scotland. His crossing over closed the situation; from that time forward, Lord James Stewart would consider the victory of the Reform at home and an alliance with England abroad as the two irreplaceable elements in all his activities.

Mary of Guise was not without supporters and strength, however. The third earl of Bothwell on the border was on her side; French troops were in possession of Leith; reinforcements from France could be expected. Elizabeth hated rebels and was against intervention, but Cecil played upon her annoyance with Mary Stuart and the irritation over English quarterings on the escutcheon of the French king so adroitly that she finally permitted the duke of Norfolk to gather an army.

The decision to intervene was timely; Lord James had been declared an outlaw by the regent and was hard pressed by the French forces. John Knox, in his later history of these events, said Lord James and the earl of Arran fought for twenty-one days without taking their clothes off. It was, on the basis of both his and other reports, a bitter winter.

The year 1560, however, dawned on the sight of an English fleet in the Firth of Forth. An English army meanwhile was approaching from the south. A French relief fleet was wrecked by a storm en route. In February 1560 Lord James Stewart signed an agreement with England at Berwick. It was a pact against France. It repeated the legitimate status of Mary Stuart as Queen of Scots and her husband as King Matrimonial. But it bound Scotland to fight alongside England in the event of war with France.

For the first time a religious rebellion had gained an ally in a great power, though from Elizabeth's viewpoint the issue was to protect England against French occupation of Scotland. The Treaty of Berwick broke the centuries-long Auld Alliance between Scotland and France and broke Henry II's dream of making Scotland a French province. It also declared that Mary Stuart had no claim on the throne of England, though it verified her title as Queen of Scots. The last two clauses were to be resisted by that queen for her entire life; she would never sign that treaty.

After the treaty was signed, there was a struggle to defeat Mary of Guise that attracted international attention on almost every level. The papacy watched anxiously to see whether its hold on a sovereign nation would be broken for the first time. The French watched in agony as the efforts of years began to crumble, virtually as soon as they were grasped. London was anxious to end an ancient threat. Madrid held aloof; its leaders were religiously concerned, but politically pleased.

By April 1560 the English had 11,000 troops in Scotland. Lord James Stewart and Maitland negotiated during a siege of the regent at Edinburgh Castle. Beset, the remarkable woman fell finally ill—fulfilling another of the many eerie prophecies of John Knox—and died on June 10, 1560. By July 1560 the French were driven from Scotland, and the Congregation was triumphant over the Vatican.

In August 1560 the Scots Parliament established the new faith in the land and outlawed Catholicism. A *Book of Discipline* along Calvinistic lines was created. Long discussions were held regarding the Scots crown. It was proposed that Elizabeth marry the earl of Arran and unite the two realms. That was a sacrifice the Virgin did not want to make. Cecil urged that she do so, but Elizabeth would not hear of such a proposition.

As usual, she took months to reach such a clear decision and did not announce it until December 1560—at which time Scotland learned that the youthful King Francis II of France had died of an abscessed ear that had spread to his brain. That meant the French threat was gone, in a dynastic sense.

In early 1561 Lord James Stewart went to France to talk to his half sister, Mary Stuart. His purpose was to probe her mind and assess her intentions and abilities. He also served as an intermediary between his half sister and the Congregation. He wanted her to come home. He assured the Congregation she would not seek to overthrow its victories—and he assured her she could attend Mass of her own in her own palace. She listened and assessed him in her turn. Mary Stuart's eye was on the throne of England—a throne to which all Europe or virtually all Europe considered her the legitimate heir. Lord James Stewart, with his clear eyes and calm face, erect bearing and lucid speech, appeared unaware of such calculations. To a woman familiar with the licentious and amoral court of France, such a figure seemed almost comic; a *naif* in the great world. Lord James, however, was a convert of John Knox. He looked upon his young half sister as a child playing at sophistication in a world whose deeper meanings are too terrible to be taken lightly.

8.  John Knox was born near Haddington in 1514. Little is known of his antecedents beyond the fact that his mother's name was Sinclair and that he often used that name during his underground periods. He attended Haddington Grammar School and graduated from the University of Saint Andrews, where one of his teachers was John Major, the famous Scots Scholastic. In 1536 Knox received the degree of Bachelor of Divinity and was ordained a priest at twenty-two by special dispensation.

Knox practiced as a country lawyer for several years, since posts as a priest were overcrowded; there is no record he ever served a Vatican church or parish. At the age of thirty—short, broad-shouldered and swarthy—he became tutor to the sons of Sir Hugh Douglas, laird of Longniddry. At this post the tides of the Reform revolution began to reach him, though his readings of Augustine and Jerome had already aroused his religious bent. In 1545 Knox was swept by emotion on hearing George Wishart, who toured the region during a period when Arran, regent of Scotland, was briefly receptive to the proposition of Henry VIII to marry the infant Mary Stuart to Prince Edward of England.

Wishart, also a graduate of Saint Andrews, was tall, slender, bearded, and eloquent. He introduced the practice of singing by con-

gregations and denounced the liturgy of the papacy as theatrical
trickery, the custom of praying to saints—and all the evils and injus-
tices of society. Knox followed Wishart when he left Longniddry,
became one of his bodyguards, and carried a two-handed sword—a
violation of his priest's status.

On January 12, 1546, Wishart sent Knox back to Longniddry.
Later that evening Wishart was captured by the border earl of Bothwell and turned over to Vatican authorities. James Cardinal Beaton
had Wishart condemned for heresy at the Castle of Saint Andrews and
executed at the stake, thus creating great indignation and a martyr for
the Reform.

On May 29, 1546, sixteen young men led by William Kirkcaldy
of Grange killed a sentry, penetrated the castle, stabbed Cardinal
Beaton to death, urinated on his cadaver, and hung it naked on the
battlements. The coup placed the key fort in the hands of the Reform,
enraged the regent, Arran, and the Queen Mother Mary of Guise, and
pleased Henry VIII of England.

A stream of Reform sympathizers poured toward the castle,
Knox among them. For months the keep was the scene of demonstrations, speeches, and lectures. Knox joined these and exhibited remarkable abilities as an orator; it was predicted he would end as had
Wishart. In July 1547 the castle was besieged by Arran's troops
ashore and a French fleet from the sea. The French landed with
cannon, overcame resistance, and carried 120 of the defenders off in
war galleys—Knox among them. As a slave, he was given a loose
brown robe, canvas breeches, and a red cap and chained to an oar.
The experience was to prove his turning point.

His fame spread among the prisoners; despite a near-fatal illness,
he survived to be exchanged in March 1549. Accepted by the English
government, he was given a post in Berwick, a teeming border town
only a day's ride from Longniddry. There his oratory attracted
streams from across the border and much attention throughout England. The duke of Northumberland heard him and carried him back
to London, where Knox attracted international attention by the vigor
and acuity of his theological debates. Geneva was attracted; Northumberland decided to make him bishop of Rochester.

In October 1552 Knox held a secret London meeting with Lord
James Stewart and established important connections with the Reform nobles of Scotland. In December 1552 Cecil sent him to the
Chelsea home of the duke of Northumberland, where the Duke was
surprised to have his offer of a bishopric refused.

Knox was forced to flee England after the death of Edward VI and the accession of Mary Tudor and became one of the famous group of Reform religious leaders named, somewhat foolishly, as the "Marians" by historians. In Geneva the Scot became well acquainted with Calvin, who rated him an equal, proved a formidable propagandist and theologian, and played a shaping part in the doctrines of the Church of England in exile.

In 1555 he was invited to Scotland to assist the Reform. He launched Bible readings by lairds, established discussion groups, created a movement that spread through all classes and pioneered revolutionary methods since grown familiar to the world. He began to develop theories that extended religious dispute into the political sphere and questioned the ancient Christian doctrine of obedience to evil princes as "scourges of God." He also married Marjory Bowes, daughter of an ardent English follower, Mrs. Elizabeth Bowes.

In 1558, after years of difficulties created, at least in part, by three women sovereigns (Mary of Guise in Scotland, Mary Tudor in England, and Catherine de Médicis in France), Knox issued his famous *Blast of the Trumpet Against a Monstrous Regiment* [rule] *of Women*. As a political document, it sank deep; it contained many citations from misogynists ancient and modern against women, but also argued that insurrection "against the foolish consent of an ignorant multitude" was ethical—provided such a rebellion was inspired by Knox's version of Christianity. The effort created a sensation and has convinced later generations Knox hated women and at the time was accepted as political propaganda. Virtually every monarch regarded its thrust as anarchistic; Elizabeth in England, new to her throne, took it as a personal insult.

Returned to Scotland in May 1559, Knox found his stream of advice, pamphlets, and letters had created the Lords of the Congregation among the nobility and the Congregation among the people; both combined to threaten the Regent Mary of Guise, and the Vatican faith in the realm. His speeches inspired crowds to sack churches of their statues and ornaments, altars and paintings during the summer of that year and to oust the papacy and the French by autumn.

Knox was the intellectual author of a *Confession for Scotland* in the wake of that victory and also of a *Book of Discipline* designed to establish a new church organization in the land. Because the Scots nobles wanted to retain their Vatican titles and incomes, the *Book of Discipline* was rejected—a great blow to Knox. The restoration of Mary Stuart was another defeat; Knox predicted the young queen would divide the realm and seek to reintroduce Catholicism as the official religion. He was accurate in this prediction as well as many others. Nevertheless, he succeeded in establishing his version of Calvinistic doctrines in the land, created the Kirk, and laid the foundations of what would later be known as the Presbyterian Church.

Alone among his contemporaries, Knox could see eternal principles and long-range results. His theories inspired George Buchanan later and were to enter into the stream of world history. Although maligned during his lifetime and still fiercely hated outside the realm he transformed from a barbaric to a civilized land, there is little doubt that this incredible leader, who sank beneath notice as a slave, spurned the highest offers of the world, and was called a magician in his own life, did more to alter the course of history and all our lives than any of his contemporaries. No saint, but certainly no more a sinner than other men, he remains one of the great, though greatly misunderstood, personalities of the ages.

9.   Jasper Ridley, *John Knox* (Oxford: Oxford University Press, 1968), p. 393.

10.   David Rizzio was from Piedmont. He arrived in Scotland in the train of the ambassador from Savoy, M. de Moret, in 1561. Queen Mary Stuart was in need of a basso to complete a quartet in the palace; Rizzio proved able and available. The circumstance appeared curious; the Queen of Scots was engaged in a voluminous, secret correspondence with various pro-Vatican capitals and personages in Europe, and Rizzio—a foreigner of unknown antecedents (excepting to the Savoyard ambassador and the queen)—was soon moved into the post of personal secretary. Maitland, laird of Lethington, who was secretary of state, was not pleased to discover the queen's new man—a short, swarthy and apparently ugly figure—was engaged with her in mysterious matters.

That mingled irritation and suspicion were shared by other high nobles, for Rizzio, according to the *Memoirs* of Sir James Melville, seemed always to be whispering to the queen—even in public—and even during occasions of state. His influence grew rapidly, however, and Melville says ". . . those who had great actions of law . . . addressed themselves to him . . . whereby in short time he became rich."

Rizzio did not hide his influence. He blossomed in fine clothes and created great resentment. Melville thought it wise to warn the queen her foreign secretary, whom she said handled "her French matters," was growing embarrassing. Indignantly, Mary replied she could "dispense her favours to such as she pleased."

By the time Darnley appeared on the scene, Rizzio had grown very strong; it was rumored he aimed at becoming chancellor of the realm—and that he wanted to become a peer of Scotland. The Scots burned with resentment. Yet Darnley made friends with Rizzio, and the Italian, who had a brother at court, seemed securely placed in 1565. Inevitably, rumors collected that he was intimate with the queen —but these remained below the surface—at first.

11.  James Hepburn was born in 1535. His family held the titles of Hailes and Bothwell. Several of his forbears distinguished themselves by befriending widows of the kings of Scotland. The first Lord Hailes was close to Queen Joan, widow of James I; the second Lord Hailes was close to Mary of Guelderland. His father, the third earl, sought to marry Mary of Guise and divorced his wife when young James was only nine toward that end.

The boy was then raised by his great-uncle Patrick, bishop of Aberdeen, a notorious womanizer. John Knox describes the bishop— whose title was honorary but whose income was not—as "a true servant of the King of love." An anecdote by Knox underscores the bishop's proclivities. "After supper," wrote Knox, "he asked of his gentlemen that should truly declare how many sundry women every one of them had had and how many were men's wives." The answers varied, but the bishop's number topped them all—nor was his bragging empty. He legitimatized his children, says Gore-Browne, "in batches . . . by different mothers. The only difficulty . . . was to think of names."

The atmosphere in the bishop's palace at Spynie, near Elgin, therefore, helped shape James Hepburn. Later he was sent to the University of Paris, where he was an apt scholar, learned to speak beautiful French, proved to have some talent in writing, and developed a lifelong love of reading. He inherited the earldom of Bothwell and hereditary offices as sheriff of Berwick, Haddington, and Edinburgh; the bailie of Lauderdale; the post of lord high admiral of Scotland; and the castles of Hailes and Crichton, in 1557—the same year the Lords of the Congregation signed their covenant. True to his family tradition, he remained faithful to the regent, Mary of Guise.

At the age of twenty-four, Bothwell formed a famous liaison with the fabled Janet Beaton, widow of Sir Walter Scott of Buccleigh, who had already enjoyed three legal husbands and a string of lovers, had borne seven children, and was considered a female magician because of her remarkably enduring beauty and youthful appearance. She was 43 when Bothwell appeared at her side.

During the civil war, Bothwell fought ably on the side of the regent, Mary of Guise, and seriously interfered with the Lords of the Congregation and the English by capturing a messenger from Elizabeth carrying 3,000 crowns. In London, Cecil took note of the earl's proclivity for effective field action and decided that, since Bothwell could not be wooed from the French, he should be taken. The civil war came to an end, however, with the death of the Regent Mary of Guise. Bothwell prudently fled the realm.

His journey abroad took him to Germany and Denmark, where he met Anna Throndsen, daughter of a retired Danish admiral. Anna was dark and had a dowry of 40,000 silver dollars, and Bothwell vowed marriage; intimacy followed. The Earl's resolve faded, however, when the 40,000 pieces of silver proved exaggerated; but when he left Denmark for France to pay his respects to Mary Stuart, the Danish beauty followed. Bothwell kept her hidden in Flanders while he appeared at the French court; his appearance of substance was due to the sale of her jewels. Bothwell met Mary Stuart in France when she was eighteen and queen of France. At the time of the death of her youthful husband in Flanders, he was among the Catholic nobles sent by Mary Stuart back to Scotland to prepare for her return.

In 1561 after Mary Stuart returned to Scotland, Bothwell was large at her court and a member of her Privy Council. In Edinburgh, Bothwell made peace with John Knox, who had hopes for his conversion—and struck up a conspicuously close relationship with the earl of Arran, heir to the duke of Châtelherault and a disappointed man. Arran had been mentioned as a suitable marriage partner for Elizabeth in lieu of Mary Stuart's return, but Elizabeth rejected that proposal. He was next mentioned as a suitable husband for Mary Stuart, but the Queen of the Scots was not interested. Bothwell, according to Arran, suggested that they kidnap the Scots queen and force her into a union. The proposition was bold enough to unhinge Arran, whose mental balance was precarious; he had an embarrassing public breakdown and accused the earl. His story was confusing and not generally believed, though in view of Bothwell's later behavior may well have been true. Arran was invalided and Bothwell placed in light custody at Edinburgh Castle pending an inquiry; he soon escaped with the connivance of Mary Stuart.

As he fled to France, his ship was sent into Berwick by a storm. He was immediately arrested by the English, who had neither forgotten nor forgiven the matter of Elizabeth's 3,000 crowns. Sir Thomas Randolph wrote Cecil about the man the English now held. "As mortal an enemy to our nation as any man alive," he said. "Despiteful above measure, false and untrue as a devil." Cecil had Bothwell placed in Tynemouth Castle. Anna Throndsen, bereft in Edinburgh, left for Norway. In due course, Bothwell, in captivity, received a single Portuguese piece—as a token (Gore-Browne). The English then transferred Bothwell to the Tower, where he remained for over a year. He was not released until the marriage negotiations between Elizabeth and Mary Stuart, in which the English queen believed she could force Lord Robert Dudley upon the Queen of Scots. Once released at Mary Stuart's request, Bothwell continued to France where—at Mary Stuart's suggestion—he was given command of the king's Scots Archers, bodyguards. Once Darnley appeared in Scotland and the earl of Moray rose in opposition, Mary Stuart sent for Bothwell to come home. He was the only man she knew who could not be overawed; she considered him loyal and helpful in times of emergency.

Bothwell reappeared in Edinburgh; Jane Beaton came from the border to serve behind the scenes as his procuress. The earl brought his personal man of all work, French Paris, who was—he said later —terrified of him. He was not the only one; Bothwell had matured into an oddly disturbing presence.

12. Antonia Fraser, *Mary, Queen of Scots* (London: Weidenfeld and Nicolson, 1969), p. 305.
13. Zweig, *Mary Queen of Scotland and the Isles* (op. cit.), p. 122.
14. Caroline Bingham, *The Making of a King: The Early Years of James IV and I* (London: Collins, 1968), pp 26–27; Zweig, *Mary Queen of Scotland and the Isles* (op. cit.), pp. 136–137. Bingham cites and Zweig draws upon the *Memoirs* of Lord Herries.
15. Ibid.
16. Ibid.

*Notes to Chapter 2* (pages 26–36)

1. James Anthony Froude, *History of England from the Fall of Wolsey to the Death of Elizabeth,* 12 Vols. (London: Longman, Green, Longman, Roberts & Green, 1863–1872), Vol. 8, p. 304.
2. Mary M. Luke, *Gloriana: The Years of Elizabeth I* (op. cit.), p. 250.
3. Froude, *History of England* (op. cit.), Vol. 8, pp. 307–309.
4. Ibid., p. 343.
5. Meredith H. Davison, *The Casket Letters* (London: Vision Press, 1965), Appendix A, "The Maladies of Mary Queen of Scots and Her Husbands," pp. 311–312.
6. Froude, *History of England* (op. cit.), Vol. 8, p. 358.
7. Ibid., p. 354.
8. Maurice Lee, Jr., *James Stewart, Earl of Moray* (New York: Columbia University Press, 1953), pp. 182–184; Froude, *History of England* (op. cit.), Vol. 8, p. 357.

9.  Luke, *Gloriana* (op. cit.), p. 250.
10. Sir James Melville, *Memoirs of His Own Life* (London: Chapman & Dodd, 1922), pp. 84–85.
11. Davison, *The Casket Letters* (op. cit.), Appendix A, pp. 313–315.
12. Froude, *History of England* (op. cit.), Vol. 8, p. 363.
13. Davison, *The Casket Letters* (op. cit.), p. 120.
14. Froude, *History of England* (op. cit.), Vol. 8, p. 379.

*Notes to Chapter 3* (pages 37–48)

1.  Legends accumulated around the exact nature of the king's death. Sir James Melville, a contemporary, said in his *Memoirs* that "the King was taken forth, and brought down to a stable, where a napkin was stuffed in his mouth, and he therewith suffocated." Others said men from the Douglas clan were in the garden into which the king fled, and that women of the neighborhood later said they heard the young man pleading for his life. Hay of Tallo and Hepburn of Bolton, two of Bothwell's men, declared on their scaffolds that they had lit the charge of dynamite, fled into the garden where Bothwell and some companions were standing, and fled, leaving these grim figures waiting for the blast. Tradition, a witness more reliable than historians like to believe, credits Archibald Douglas with the actual deed and says he used a towel soaked in vinegar. All the versions and all the known facts, however, agree on one central point: it was cold murder.
2.  Mary M. Luke, *Gloriana: The Years of Elizabeth I* (op. cit.), pp. 270–271.
3.  Stefan Zweig, *Mary Queen of Scotland and the Isles* (op. cit.), p. 205.
4.  James Anthony Froude, *History of England* (op. cit.), Vol. 9., p. 50.
5.  A hagbut was an early version of a harquebus, a gun operated by a trigger and matchlock. It was the most advanced hand weapon of the time and greatly feared.
6.  Frank Arthur Mumby, *The Fall of Mary Stuart: A Narrative in Contemporary Letters* (Boston: Houghton Mifflin, 1922), p. 226.
7.  Froude, *History of England* (op. cit.), Vol. 9., p. 55.
8.  Sir James Melville, *Memoirs of His Own Life* (op. cit.), p. 88.
9.  Ibid.
10. Ibid.
11. Antonia Fraser, *Mary Queen of Scots* (op. cit.), p. 374.
12. Froude, *History of England* (op. cit.), Vol. 9, p. 93.
13. Luke, *Gloriana: The Years of Elizabeth I* (op. cit.), p. 288.

*Notes to Chapter 4* (pages 49–53)

1. Jasper Ridley, *John Knox* (op. cit.), pp. 465–469.
2. "You may assure these Lords that we do detest and abhor the murder committed upon our cousin and King; but the head cannot be subject to the foot, and we cannot recognize in them any right to call their Sovereign to account," wrote Elizabeth to Throckmorton in Scotland. She went on to threaten revenge; there is no doubt she was far more deeply shocked at the idea of a Sovereign being held accountable to the law than she was at any of the events in the northern kingdom.

   For further insight into the Virgin's attitudes, see Froude, *History of England* (op. cit.), Vol. 9, pp. 129–130, as well as Luke's *Gloriana, The Years of Elizabeth I* (op. cit.), pp. 290–295.
3. William Cecil, Elizabeth's fabled adviser, was born in 1520 into a family of Welsh descent that had identified its interests with those of the Tudors—and England. His grandfather, David, had campaigned with Henry VII in his successful effort to become king; his father, Richard, was a successful businessman favored by Henry VIII. William himself was a court page, graduated from St. John's College, Cambridge, and studied law at the Inns of Court. He made an early and apparently impulsive marriage; it was his last impulsive act. His first wife died leaving him one son; he remarried—choosing Mildred Cooke, daughter of Sir Anthony Cooke, governor to the youthful Prince Edward. His bride was phenomenally learned and could converse in both Greek and Latin. William soon came to the favorable attention of Henry VIII; the young man became part of a rising Reform element of "new men."

   He served as a court-martials judge in Henry VIII's Scots campaign and learned something of armies, generals, campaigns, and Scotland in the process. He rose to become personal secretary to Somerset, the lord protector under the boy King Edward VI. When Somerset was overthrown, Cecil was briefly imprisoned in the Tower, but was released and made the extraordinary switch to Northumberland, Somerset's rival and successor. When Northumberland sought to set aside the Princess Mary in the line of succession in favor of Lady Jane Grey, Cecil demurred. Finally forced to sign in agreement, he managed to make his reluctance clear. That saved his life when Northumberland failed and Mary Tudor inherited the crown.

   To the open disgust of such convinced Reformers as John Knox, Cecil attended Mass under Bloody Mary as faithfully as he had rejected the Vatican faith under Edward VI and the Protectors. Cecil, however, was convinced—as were all the political theorists of his time

—that no state could endure that was divided by two religions. Nevertheless, his inner inclinations were toward the Reform; his family fortunes were based in large measure on confiscated Catholic properties. During Mary's five years and five months of rule, his contributions to the crown were only intermittent; he devoted himself to business and building his great houses in Burghley and London. He increased his wealth, but lived austerely in a personal sense, though certainly with all the pomp and attendants appropriate to his high status. He also kept in subtle contact with Princess Elizabeth and, when she succeeded to the throne, was her most trusted adviser and first minister.

Slight, pale, reticent, dignified, he was the living symbol of sophistication; no man ever knew the world better than William Cecil. He understood the workings of the law, of finance, of political maneuver, and of power. If he had been irreligious, he would have been the most dangerous man in England; fortunately for Elizabeth and her subjects, Cecil's faith extended beyond sects. He regarded order as the first principle of civilization, and no lure could shake that conviction. He managed to steer Elizabeth along Reform lines, lines that bounded their mutual inheritances, and did so with an adroitness and a disarming approach that was, in the long run, inescapable. Historians have always had trouble in assessing William Cecil; von Ranke doubted he was truly great "because he was not original"—but he was original. He led Elizabeth and England out of the insane excesses and brutal whims of Henry VIII when, in addition to multiple disorders, syphilis affected the great king's judgment, into a realm whose established religion retained the traditions of Christianity without the excesses of the Vatican and the mass appeal of the Reform without the fanaticism of revolutionaries. No pattern is more difficult to sustain than moderation to men of large vision; it requires an iron self-control and an ability to deal patiently with the less endowed. William Cecil himself had no doubt about his most effective tactic. "I have gained more," he said, "by . . . forbearing than I ever did by my wit." That took a very great man indeed.

4.     Reported by the English ambassador, Sir H. Norris, to Cecil; cited by Froude, *History of England* (op. cit.), Vol. 9, pp. 133–134.

5.     Ibid., Vol. 9, p. 139.

6.     David Harris Willson, *King James VI and I* (New York: Oxford University Press, 1956), p. 19.

*Notes to Chapter 5* (pages 54–60)

1.  Frank Arthur Mumby, *The Fall of Mary Stuart* (op. cit.), p. 291.
2.  Maurice Lee, *James Stewart, Earl of Moray* (op. cit.), pp. 208–209.
3.  Sir James Melville, *Memoirs of His Own Life* (op. cit.), p. 97. "It [the conversation] cut the threads of love and credit betwixt the Queen and him forever," Melville added.
4.  Robert Gore-Browne, *Lord Bothwell and Mary Queen of Scots, A Study of the Life, Character and Times of James Hepburn 4th Earl of Bothwell* (Garden City, N.Y.: Doubleday, Doran & Company, 1937), pp. 395–408.
5.  James Anthony Froude, *History of England* (op. cit.), Vol. 9, pp. 203–204.
6.  Jasper Ridley, *John Knox* (op. cit.), pp. 476–479.
7.  Mary Stuart had gutted the Treasury. Moray, having placated the Kirk by presiding over many concessions to its clergy, was also confronted with the need to raise a force to restore order. He was under heavy financial strain at a time when civil war loomed in the realm. To raise funds, he pawned the royal plate. He proved human enough, however, to give some of Mary Stuart's jewels to his own wife. He has been greatly criticized for this by historians.
8.  Froude, *History of England* (op. cit.), Vol. 9, pp. 213–220.
9.  Ibid., pp. 220–221.
10. Ibid.
11. Ibid., p. 223.

*Notes to Chapter 6* (pages 61–73)

1.  Maurice Lee, *James Stewart, Earl of Moray* (op. cit.), p. 22.
2.  James Anthony Froude, *History of England* (op. cit.), Vol. 9, pp. 237–239.
3.  Ibid., pp. 393–394.
4.  Jasper Ridley, *John Knox* (op. cit.), p. 483.
5.  Froude, *History of England* (op. cit.), Vol. 10, p. 118.
6.  Ibid., Vol. 9, p. 521.
7.  Ibid., Vol. 10, p. 34.
8.  Lee, *James Stewart, Earl of Moray* (op. cit.), pp. 273–275.
9.  Ridley, *John Knox* (op. cit.), pp. 488–489.
10. Adam and Charles Black, *Black's Picturesque Tourist of Scotland* (Edinburgh: R. & R. Clark, 1875), p. 192.
11. Froude, *History of England* (op. cit.), Vol. 10, p. 103. Elizabeth had,

at last, realized that Mary Stuart was a dangerous woman. It was at
about that time that the Virgin composed her famous sonnet about
her cousin:

Those dazzled eyes with pride, which great ambition blinds,
Shall be unsealed by worthy wights, whose foresight falsehood binds
The Daughter of Debate, that eke discord doth sow,
Shall reap no gain where former rule hath taught still peace to grow.

12. Robert Chambers, *The Life of King James the First,* 2 Vols. (Edin-
    burgh: Constable & Co., 1830), Vol. 1, pp. 44–45. "All is well if the
    babe is well," said Lennox as he was carried into the castle. He died
    the following day after giving young James and others pious advice.
13. Mary M. Luke, *Gloriana: The Years of Elizabeth I* (op. cit.), p. 367.
14. The first edition appeared in 1571 and was printed in London by John
    Day, and a copy was soon placed in the hands of Mary Stuart,
    immured in her comfortable prison at Sheffield. She wrote Fénelon,
    the French ambassador to England, immediately. Saying the book
    bore neither a printer's name or place of origin, she wanted the king
    of France to express outrage to Queen Elizabeth and to demand its
    suppression. When Fénelon gave Elizabeth that message, the English
    queen replied the book had issued from Scotland, where she had no
    influence.
15. Ridley, *John Knox* (op. cit.), p. 503.
16. Ibid., p. 517.
17. Froude, *History of England* (op. cit.), Vol. 10, p. 475. John Knox's
    reputation has been greatly darkened by many generations of anti-
    Christian historians who take a peculiar relish in accusing Christian
    leaders of violating their faith by showing signs of human error. That
    sort of interpretation betrays both theological ignorance and political
    prejudice. John Knox, for example, was one of the greatest of all
    fighters against tyranny. The Vatican of his day had fallen into its
    lowest position and was more a temporal power than a religious one.
    To suppress the Reform and to maintain its revenues and privileges,
    it used the rack, the faggot, and the Inquisition; attempted universal
    censorship and thought control; and allied itself with retrograde lead-
    ership. Knox identified this position as inherently evil, despite re-
    deeming qualities. To fight against such a tyrannical institution was
    hardly a sign of intolerance; to use any but the most exciting weapons
    of rhetoric and exhortation would have been insufficient for the task.
    The true measure of John Knox, as for all men, must be found in the
    examination not so much of what he said, but what he did. In his own

life he was surrounded by men and women who found him a kindly and forgiving pastor and leader. When his great revolution triumphed in Scotland, he did not set up a new reign of terror, nor were men purged for their beliefs. The burnings and stranglings that had marked James Cardinal Beaton were not imitated. Instead a system of universal education was launched, and one of the most backward and savage realms in all western Europe launched its impressive contributions toward world culture. An age that has watched incredible political butcheries with notable lack of indignation has little reason to scorn the founder of the Presbyterian Church.

18.  Suicide is suspected; accounts are vague. It seems likely, however, that his death disappointed his captors, who wanted to hang him.

19.  Ridley, *John Knox* (op. cit.), p. 519.

*Notes to Chapter 7* (pages 77–88)

1.  James Anthony Froude, *History of England* (op. cit.), Vol. 11, pp. 11, 76.

2.  Elizabeth was short, fine-boned, and thin. She suffered from migraines. Medical authorities also believe she suffered from amenorrhea (absence of menstruation), that this condition convinced her she was sterile, and therefore that marriage would not produce the heir for which England longed. She was also subject to melancholia. In 1562 she had smallpox. She was afflicted for years with a running ulcer above one ankle. That ulcer was aggravated by the standard treatment at the time, which, instead of advising rest for the afflicted limb, advised activity. The ulcer condition, commonly associated with varicose veins, had also afflicted her father, Henry VIII.

     See Sir A. MacNulty, *Henry VIII: A Difficult Patient* (London: Christopher Johnson, n.d.); also Luke, *Gloriana: The Years of Elizabeth I* (op. cit.), Chapter 18, fn. 29 and pp. 171–172, 185–187, 301, 303, 309, 378–379, 637–638, 689–691.

     For an estimate of Elizabeth's stature, see Melville, *Memoirs of His Own Life* (op. cit.), p. 55.

3.  Froude, *History of England* (op. cit.), Vol. 11, p. 70.

4.  Ibid., pp. 73–74.

5.  Caroline Bingham, *The Making of a King* (op. cit.), p. 83.

6.  Ibid., p. 82.

7.  The ancient isolation of England was broken in equally large part, however, by the Reform movement. Refugees from the Low Countries had driven "tens of thousands" across the Channel with their "arts and industries" and established the English in the textile trades.

The end of the ancient English alliance with Spain had inspired a great increase in the English maritime industries, though most vessels of the period were still small. The combination of privateering, trade, exploration, and discovery created a great intellectual ferment as tales of new lands and people, customs and laws appeared; the English knowledge of the significance of the Spanish Inquisition was deepened by the agonizing experiences of English seamen caught in those dreadful toils; England became a great and wealthy international center where information, commerce, international travel, and observations carried men in the reign of Elizabeth far beyond the ideas and limitations of their forbears. The same sequence affected France, Spain, Portugal, and other countries of Western Europe.

8.  Bingham, *The Making of a King* (op. cit.), p. 84.

9.  Ibid., pp. 99–100.

10. *Baptistes* was a revolutionary play; Buchanan himself told the Portuguese Inquisition the model was Henry VIII and that he had Anne Boleyn in mind for Salome and Sir Thomas More for John the Baptist. The king was, of course, Herod. Almost a century after it was written (in Latin), John Milton translated it into English, with Charles I in mind as Herod, and it appeared in London amid a flood of revolutionary pamphlets and literature in the 1640s.

11. George Buchanan, *Glasgow Quatercentenary Studies* (Edinburgh: James Maclehose and Sons, Publishers to the University, 1907), p. 447.

12. Ibid.

13. David Harris Willson, *King James VI and I* (op. cit.), p. 20.

14. Robert Gore-Browne, *Lord Bothwell and Mary Queen of Scots* (op. cit.), Chapter 35. Bothwell, after leaving Bergen, Norway, was shipped to Copenhagen. There he was imprisoned in comfortable circumstances for a time, and on January 8, 1568, dictated an explanation of his relationship with Mary Stuart. The document, self-serving but interesting, ran to 6,000 words. Later, after discovering nobody would ransom him and unwilling to release him for fear of creating political troubles, the Danes placed him in a dungeon at Dragsholm.

15. Bingham, *The Making of a King* (op. cit.), p. 103.

16. Froude, *History of England* (op. cit.), Vol. 11, pp. 116–117.

17. Adam and Charles Black, *Black's Picturesque Tourist of Scotland* (op. cit.), p. 193. The heads were removed in 1777, after their weight threatened the ceiling.

18. Froude, *History of England* (op. cit.), Vol. 11, p. 118. He quotes Sir Thomas Randolph, the English observer, as saying "all the devils in Hell were stirring."

19.   Willson, *King James VI and I* (op. cit.), p. 30.
20.   Ibid.
21.   Bingham, *The Making of a King* (op. cit.), p. 116.

*Notes to Chapter 8* (pages 89–93)

1.   Froude, *History of England* (op. cit.), Vol. 11, pp. 121–122.
2.   This masterpiece has been strangely neglected by modern historians, but manuscript copies of it created a sensation exceeded only by the printed version. As soon as it appeared, the scholars of the Reform poured congratulations. The first Edinburgh edition was followed by one from Leiden or Antwerp; Lord Burghley was among the avid readers of the work. At least four editions were exhausted in the first two years of publication, and Andrew Melville forced his students at Saint Andrews to read *De Jure* more assiduously than even Calvin's *Institutes* (according to Bishop Spottiswoode).

Counterblasts appeared almost at once and mounted into a fusillade through succeeding years. Official (later) condemnations did not extirpate the work, but spurred many to read a volume so dangerous as to cause such an outcry. It played an important role in the English Revolution against Charles I and even in 1660 provoked the Privy Council into new efforts to suppress English editions. Oxford University condemned it numerous times through several generations, the latest being in 1680. Hobbes, Milton, and virtually all the English Reformers and revolutionaries still heralded for their views and contributions to political history pored over this seminal effort of George Buchanan, whose name has been forgotten while theirs still radiates. Much of later Whig literature in England is based upon *De Jure;* its influence on European thought was less direct, though contributory. Jean Bodin *(De La République)* was a far more important political writer in Europe. The French Huguenots also contributed to a great torrent of thought, which Buchanan's work joined at many points. In his own time, Buchanan expressed arguments in favor of tyrannicide more extreme than any government then or now would find acceptable. Yet, despite the fact that other thinkers were more lucid and that some of his theories anticipated Rousseau, there remains little doubt that Buchanan brought the attitudes and the lyric ability of the Humanist school of Latinists into a blend with the revolutionary doctrines of the Reform more effectively than any other writer of his century—or any for a century afterward. It was, in other words, a political tract of tremendous brilliance that lit fires in every landscape of northern Europe. It surrounded the fall of Mary Stuart and the efforts of the Scots Reformers with an immediate and thrilling argument delivered with poetic force that carried the personalities and issues onto the world stage. Its ideas and theories were absorbed into the stream of western Europe so deeply that they cease to carry the impact of novelty or the illusion of exclusivity; Buchanan's success was so great that his imitators overwhelmed his memory.

3. Caroline Bingham, *The Making of a King: The Early Years of James VI and I* (op. cit.), p. 90.

4. John Calvin, elected by secret ballot by the citizens of Geneva over an opposition party called the Libertines, directed an effort to create a model community and operated an international center against the Vatican. The major part of Calvin's efforts were directed toward the creation of a Reformed Church in France. Hundreds of French refugees poured into Geneva and were later joined by others from various states of Germany, England, Scotland, et al. Special schools and colleges were created and a great conglomeration of printing houses established; Geneva became the revolutionary center for new doctrines. Its leaders pioneered approaches in terms of missionaries, pamphlets and propaganda, training in secret organizations in unfriendly areas, and networks of underground travel and assistance that have since grown familiar to the world in the hands of imitators whose purposes constitute a great perversion of the principles of the originators.

Interestingly enough the hiding places behind chimneys and in cellars of the stone farmhouses in the valleys of Dauphine Alps used by Calvin's ministers en route from Geneva to France are still held secret and were last used by the Resistance to Hitler during World War II. The fact that this underground railroad is still held useful and necessary for future possibilities provides striking evidence that tyranny is as virulent a danger today as ever at any time in the past.

The Calvinists came from the elite bourgeoisie of France and represented the better educated elements. Their education was improved at Geneva itself by lectures, studies, discussions, and examinations that soared beyond standards ever before known in a group sense. Graduates traveled under assumed names with false papers and were harbored by secret congregations. The religious nature of their activities was intertwined with politics, since religion and politics were then facets of a single overarching theory regarding the proper nature of society; the role of the individual and the sovereign; the nature and significance of law, custom, behavior, and morality.

Within ten years these efforts created a counterforce to the Vatican in France and resulted in religious civil war; books from Geneva constituted the largest printing center in all Europe; a publishing, ink, paper, translation, and distribution center was established; in time Geneva also became a center of munitions manufacture.

There is little doubt, however, that the instrument of the printing press (first used by the Jews who had been expelled from Spain to print Orthodox works) was the most important weapon of Calvinism. It produced the inconspicuous and silent arguments that men could read in privacy and that prepared their minds and hearts for the physical appearance of Calvinist pastors, ministers, agents, and sympathizers.

There are many remaining mysteries regarding Geneva in the time of Calvin and Beza. Its efforts were so distilled, so effective and so impressive that underlying questions arise. The question of funding is only one such mystery, for although the printers and other galaxy of subsidiaries that ring the ecclesiastical leaders of Geneva are known to have been entrepreneurial in nature, the source of their capitalization is unknown. There is also the mystery of how the leaders of a single relatively small anti-Establishment city ringed by the Catholic powers of France, Savoy, Lorraine, and the Spanish Netherlands could so quickly establish so many connections in farflung European financial circles. It is known that Geneva itself was protected by the Republic of Berne, which—with suspicious providentiality—embarked upon an aggressive campaign that resulted in the conquest of all the surrounding territory between Geneva and the mountain ranges that ring it on three sides.

In an intellectual sense, however, the growth of Calvinism appears less mysterious. But despite its great influence in Holland, France, and other regions, its theories did not result in a frozen doctrine. John Knox was able to extend them in Scotland—but Knox was, after all, Calvin's equal. Beza, who succeeded Calvin, considered Knox one of the greatest of all men—and Knox's doctrines were not, though they coincided in great measure, entirely identical with Calvin's.

See Fernand Braudel, *The Mediterranean and the Mediterranean World in the Age of Philip II*, 2 Vols. (New York: Harper & Row, 1973), Vol. 2, p. 760; Robert M. Kingdon, *Geneva and the Coming of the Wars of Religion in France, 1555–1563* (Geneva: Libraire E. Droz, 1956).

5.   Froude, *History of England* (op. cit.), Vol. 11, p. 125.
6.   Ibid., Vol. 11, p. 154.

*Notes to Chapter 9* (pages 97–105)

1.   James Anthony Froude, *History of England* (op. cit.), Vol. 11, pp. 272–273.

2.	David Harris Willson, *King James VI and I* (op. cit.), pp. 36–37.
3.	Caroline Bingham, *The Making of a King* (op. cit.), p. 138.
4.	Willson, *King James VI and I* (op. cit.), p. 34.
5.	Froude, *The History of England* (op. cit.), Vol. 11, p. 328.
6.	Ibid., p. 327.
7.	Sir James Melville, *Memoirs of His Own Life* (op. cit.), p. 141.
8.	Ibid.
9.	Froude, *History of England* (op. cit.), Vol. 11, p. 297.
10.	Willson, *King James VI and I* (op. cit.), p. 35.
11.	It was nicknamed The Maiden because it had never been used; Morton—who had it copied from a machine he had once seen in Italy—was its first victim. His severed body, covered only by a beggar's blue gown, lay untended all afternoon on the scaffold, since his former supporters did not dare reveal themselves by coming forward to take it away; eventually the porters took it to the place where criminals were interred. Chambers, *The Life of King James the First* (op. cit.), Vol. 1, pp. 75–76.
12.	Bingham, *The Making of a King* (op. cit.), p. 142.
13.	Mary M. Luke, *Gloriana: The Years of Elizabeth I* (op. cit.), p. 469.

*Notes to Chapter 10* (pages 106–115)

1.	Mary M. Luke, *Gloriana: The Years of Elizabeth I* (op. cit.), pp. 462–464.
2.	David Harris Willson, *King James VI and I* (op. cit.), p. 36.
3.	Harold J. Grimm, *The Reformation Era 1500–1650* (New York: Macmillan, 1954), p. 452.
4.	Froude, *History of England* (op. cit.), Vol. 11, pp. 463–464.
5.	Ibid., p. 469.
6.	Willson, *King James VI and I* (op. cit.), p. 41.
7.	Froude, *History of England* (op. cit.), Vol. 11, pp. 480–490.
8.	Scottish National Portrait Gallery.
9.	Froude, *History of England* (op. cit.), Vol. 11, pp. 492–493.
10.	Ibid.
11.	Robert Chambers, *The Life of King James the First* (op. cit.), Vol. 1, pp. 79–80.

*Notes to Chapter 11* (pages 116–120)

1.	Froude, *History of England* (op. cit.), Vol. 11, p. 502.
2.	Willson, *King James VI and I* (op. cit.), p. 44.
3.	Froude, *History of England* (op. cit.), Vol. 11, p. 503.
4.	Ibid., p. 504.

5.  Willson, *King James VI and I* (op. cit.), p. 44.
6.  Bingham, *The Making of a King* (op. cit.), pp. 175–176.
7.  P. Hume Brown, *George Buchanan and His Times* (Edinburgh: Oliphant, Anderson & Ferrier, 1906), pp. 80–82.
8.  Bingham, *The Making of a King* (op. cit.), p. 176.

*Notes to Chapter 12* (pages 121–130)

1.  Actually he said more than that and certainly more than was necessary. He told Bowes "that his mother being defeated, and desperate in her intended plots and purposes, and seeing how matters were likely to proceed between Her Majesty and him, was now affecting to desire an amicable arrangement . . . but was only casting a bone to stick between their teeth. He wished his mother would give over her plots . . . she was a determined Papist and French to the heart—" and more. Froude, *History of England* (op. cit.), Vol. 11, pp. 547–548.
2.  Froude, *History of England* (op. cit.), Vol. 11, p. 534.
3.  Ibid., p. 552.
4.  Caroline Bingham, *The Making of a King* (op. cit.), p. 184.
5.  Froude, *History of England* (op. cit.), Vol. 11, p. 588.
6.  Francis Walsingham came from a well-known family in Kent that had been among those who prospered in the despoliation of the Vatican holdings in England. An ardent Reformer, Francis Walsingham was born about 1530 and was a student at Cambridge when Mary Tudor inherited the English throne. He fled during the persecution years of Bloody Mary and spent considerable time in France, Germany, and, presumably, Geneva. Returned under Elizabeth, he became a member of Parliament and an agent for Cecil.
    Dark and silent, he impressed Elizabeth as somehow alien; she called him Sir Moor. He was dedicated, intelligent, and indifferent to public credit—a combination that made him an excellent spymaster. The network he inherited and eventually operated on behalf of the Crown was that established by a system of bribery by Thomas Cromwell under Henry VIII; in Walsingham's hands it relied more upon ideological loyalties in the intermingled religious political cold and hot war of his day. Compared to the Italian states, steeped in plots, intrigues, and conspiracies; compared to Spain and its hordes of mercenaries; or the Vatican with its hundreds of thousands of priests of many varieties, Walsingham's network, says Garrett Mattingly, the noted Renaissance historian, "dwindles on inspection" in terms of size to a network hardly larger than that maintained by a first-rate ambassador. Yet it was efficient and sufficient.
    Walsingham so detested his mission to Scotland that it made him

ill, and he paused to restore himself at frequent intervals along the way. He made the trip in a carriage and was escorted by 140 gentlemen on horseback; there was to be no doubt about his high position and the honor he was bestowing upon James VI, or the prince of Scotland, as James was officially known in England.

7.   Froude, *History of England* (op. cit.), Vol. 11, p. 592.
8.   Ibid., p. 599.
9.   Charles Williams, *James I* (New York: Roy Publishers, n.d.), p. 57.
10.  Conyers Read, *Mr. Secretary Walsingham and the Policy of Queen Elizabeth,* 3 Vols., Repr. (Boston, Harvard University Press, 1967), Vol. 11, p. 221.
11.  Froude, *History of England* (op. cit.), Vol. 11, p. 614.
12.  The English-speaking world appears to have accepted the erroneous idea that the period was the Age of Elizabeth. In reality it was the Age of Philip, at least as far as western Europe was concerned.
13.  The calculation was made by Don Bernardino de Mendoza, the Spanish Ambassador cited by Froude, *History of England* (op. cit.), Vol. 11, p. 616.
14.  Don Bernardino was almost glad to leave, though indignant at the disgrace. "The insolence of these people," he wrote, "so exasperates me that I live only to be revenged on them . . . I will walk barefoot over Europe to compass it." His hatred was reciprocated by the English Reformers.
15.  Leonard W. Levy, *Origins of the Fifth Amendment* (New York: Oxford University Press, 1968), pp. 109–135.

*Notes to Chapter 13* (pages 131–138)

1.   Maurice Lee, Jr., *John Maitland of Thirlestane and the Foundation of the Stewart Despotism in Scotland* (Princeton, N.J.: Princeton University Press, 1959), pp. 53–56.
2.   Fontenay's coded letters were read, some years later, after being decoded, by Walsingham's secretary and are quoted in every description of James Stuart. See Froude, *History of England* (op. cit.), Vol. 11, pp. 663–664. David Harris Willson, *King James VI and I* (op. cit.); Robert Ashton, ed., *James I by His Contemporaries, An Account of His Career and Character* (London: Hutchinson & Co., 1969), pp. 1–3.
3.   Froude, *History of England* (op. cit.), Vol. 11, pp. 669–670.
4.   Ibid., Vol. 12, p. 42.
5.   Ibid., pp. 41–42.
6.   Ibid., p. 43.
7.   Ibid., pp. 17–18.

*Notes to Chapter 14* (pages 139–144)

1.  Levy, *Origins of the Fifth Amendment* (op. cit.), pp. 136–138.
2.  Ibid., p. 147.
3.  Ibid.

*Notes to Chapter 15* (pages 145–148)

1.  The adventurer, who had swaggered as earl of Arran, lost that title as the result of this Raid of Stirling. The Hamiltons, back on the scene, had their properties and position restored. The erstwhile earl then dropped back to being simply Captain James Stewart. He watched events from a safe distance and in 1587, when it appeared that Secretary John Maitland was in difficulties, sent a letter to James charging his onetime associate with various crimes. That brought him back to attention, and he had to flee into a remote area—Bewley, in Rosshire —where his wife owned a small property. In 1596, after Maitland's death, the captain pleaded with James to be allowed back at court, but the memories of his days of glory were still too green, even after so many years. Nevertheless, he had hopes and managed to create a small coterie and to stay at a stronghold in Ayrshire. In that location he received warning that James Douglas of Torthowald lived nearby. Douglas—a nephew of the earl of Morton, whom Stewart had helped have executed—had promised to avenge that deed. Stewart boasted he was not afraid. Hearing that, the Douglas sought him out and caught up with him at the Pass of Catslack, between Clydesdale and Ayrshire. Stewart was dragged from his horse and killed; his head was cut off, fastened to the head of a spear, and planted on the walls of Torthowald Castle. The cadaver was left in a ditch and eaten by dogs and swine. A yardstick of how Stewart had been regarded was provided by the fact that his murder was ignored by all authorities. See Robert Chambers, *The Life of King James the First* (op. cit.), pp. 102–104.
2.  Froude, *History of England* (op. cit.), Vol. 12, p. 131.
3.  Ibid., Vol. 12, p. 158.

*Notes to Chapter 16* (pages 149–167)

1.  Maurice Lee, Jr., *John Maitland of Thirlestane* (op. cit.), pp. 75–76.
2.  Willson, *King James VI and I* (op. cit.), p. 71.
3.  Froude, *History of England* (op. cit.), Vol. 12, pp. 247–248.
4.  Ibid., p. 250.
5.  Willson, *King James VI and I* (op. cit.), p. 72.

6.   Mary M. Luke, *Gloriana: The Years of Elizabeth I* (op. cit.), p. 495.
7.   Ibid., p. 501.
8.   The Privy Council appointed a committee to sift through this vast trove; members included Shrewsbury, Knollys, Burghley, Cobham, and Walsingham. Letters were found from innumerable members of the nobility who had sought to ensure themselves against a change in regime—and many, now aware they were under suspicion, went to extraordinary efforts to clear themselves by mounting vehement opposition to the Queen of Scots. See Froude, *History of England* (op. cit.), Vol. 12, pp. 255–256.
9.   Froude, *History of England* (op. cit.), Vol. 12, p. 277.
10.  Lee, *John Maitland of Thirlestane* (op. cit.), p. 100.
11.  The white headdress and veil were French mourning colors Mary Stuart had assumed, long years before, after the death of her first husband, the boy King Francis II. Her habit of resuming these colors on later occasions (she had several portraits painted in them) seems a simple matter of presenting herself at her most appealing. Certainly, she was not in mourning for Bothwell, whom she pretended to have forgotten.
12.  Stefan Zweig, *Mary Queen of Scotland and the Isles* (op. cit.), p. 326.
13.  Ibid.
14.  Froude, *History of England* (op. cit.), Vol. 12, p. 315.
15.  Ibid., p. 327.
16.  Luke, *Gloriana: The Years of Elizabeth I* (op. cit.), p. 531.
17.  Ibid., p. 544.

*Notes to Chapter 17* (pages 171–176)

1.   Maurice Lee, Jr., *John Maitland of Thirlestane* (op. cit.), p. 105.
2.   Walsingham sent a memorandum to Maitland in which he outlined the reasons why Scotland should remain a strong ally of England. His argument was that the northern realm could not defeat England without outside help—and that such help would not fight to place James Stuart in possession of the fruits of victory. On the other hand, with Mary Stuart out of the way, the path of a peaceful succession was opened—and would remain open so long as the two kingdoms were allied. See Lee, *John Maitland of Thirlestane* (op. cit.), pp. 107–109.
3.   A very complex movement was mounted against Gray, in which he was simultaneously charged with trafficking with the agents of the Vatican and accepting a bribe from the English to connive at the execution of Mary Stuart. It culminated in Gray's

banishment from the realm, and he was forced to surrender properties in favor of the earl of Huntly. His period in the sun had been brief; he left behind an ineradicable impression of unscrupulous amorality. See Lee, *John Maitland of Thirlestane* (op. cit.), pp. 113–114.

4. Drake's foray not only delayed the Armada, but dealt it a deadly blow whose effectiveness would only emerge later. See Garrett Mattingly, *The Armada* (Boston: Houghton Mifflin, 1959), pp. 93–120.

*Notes to Chapter 18* (pages 177–184)

1. Maurice Lee, Jr., *John Maitland of Thirlestane* (op. cit.), pp. 117–118.
2. Levy, *Origins of the Fifth Amendment* (op. cit.), pp. 191–192. The Separatists were the forerunners of the Puritans.
3. Similar charges against military men are currently popular again.
4. The Clink, from which the name comes, was a prison in Southwark, England.
5. Levy, *Origins of the Fifth Amendment* (op. cit.), pp. 152–155.
6. Garrett Mattingly, *The Armada* (op. cit.), pp. 175–186.

*Notes for Chapter 19* (pages 185–191)

1. Charles Williams, *James I* (op. cit.), p. 90.
2. Garrett Mattingly, *The Armada* (op. cit.), pp. 205–206.
3. James and Maitland pressed these demands upon Sir William Ashby, and the Englishman, whose orders were vague, promptly agreed. In return, James issued the pronouncement of support that England wanted to hear.
4. Mattingly, *The Armada* (op. cit.), pp. 216–217.
5. Mary M. Luke, *Gloriana: The Years of Elizabeth I* (op. cit.), p. 565.
6. William Camden, *History of Princess Elizabeth,* repr. (New York: AMS Press, 1970).
7. James Anthony Froude, *History of England* (London: Longman, Green, 1872), p. 499 (synopsized).
8. Mattingly, *The Armada* (op. cit.), pp. 323–324.
9. Ibid.

*Notes to Chapter 20* (pages 192–197)

1. The major part of the losses of the Armada were due to storms around Scotland and Ireland—and disease. The legend that the Irish butchered those unfortunate enough to be cast upon their shores are, in the

main, untrue. They were butchered—but by the orders of the English lord deputy, Sir William Fitzwilliam, and by soldiers under his command. Several hundred Spaniards were harbored in Scotland—where no English troops were quartered. According to Mattingly, "the Armada still had sixty-eight fighting ships on July 30th. On September 3rd, Medina Sidonia could still count forty-four. These obeyed his orders and followed his course . . ." All reached Spain, including the ten Indian Guard galleons, eight Andalusians, seven out of ten Portuguese, six Biscayan. These survivors were, however, racked with disease, lack of rations—and injuries. Philip II, to his eternal credit, said "the Armada . . . might have suffered a worse fate." He issued no reproach, sympathized with the agonized duke of Medina Sedonia, and began to plan a new effort. But the portraits of the mighty king of Spain, which until then showed a man wearing the smooth, self-contained, and sure face of success, forever after showed him white-faced, drawn, worn; his eyelids lowered; and his expression remote, like a man who has suffered an irredeemable loss.

2.   Garrett Mattingly, *The Armada* (op. cit.), p. 384.
3.   Ralph Roeder, *Catherine de' Medici and the Lost Revolution* (New York: Garden City Publishing Co., 1939), p. 603.
4.   Maurice Lee, Jr., *John Maitland of Thirlestane* (op. cit.), p. 177.
5.   David Harris Willson, *James VI and I* (op. cit.), p. 99.
6.   Ibid., p. 177.
7.   Lee, *John Maitland of Thirlestane* (op. cit.), p. 182.
8.   Helen Georgia Stafford, *James VI of Scotland and the Throne of England* (New York: D. Appleton Century, 1940), p. 49.
9.   Lee, *John Maitland of Thirlestane* (op. cit.), pp. 184–185.
10.  Ibid., p. 186.
11.  Ralph Roeder, *Catherine de' Medici and the Lost Revolution* (op. cit.), p. 610.
12.  Thomas B. Macaulay, *Burleigh and His Times,* Essays, Vols. III (Twentieth Century Edition, n.d.), p. 104.
13.  Mary M. Luke, *Gloriana: The Years of Elizabeth I* (op. cit.), p. 606.

*Notes to Chapter 21* (pages 198–203)

1.   Charles Williams, *James I* (op. cit.), p. 179.
2.   Thomas B. Macaulay, *Burleigh and His Times,* Essays, Vol. III (Twentieth Century Edition, n.d.), p. 104.
3.   Robert Chambers, *The Life of King James the First* (op. cit.), pp. 140–142. (Spelling modernized.)

4.    Maurice Lee, Jr., *John Maitland of Thirlestane* (op. cit.), fn. on p. 206.
5.    Ibid., p. 215.

## Notes to Chapter 22 (pages 204–208)

1.    To avoid creditors. Elizabeth's rejection of Walsingham, puzzling to many, had a simple explanation: the Virgin never forgave him for his entrapment of Mary Stuart.
2.    Leonard W. Levy, *Origins of the Fifth Amendment* (op. cit.), pp. 150–151.
3.    Helen Georgia Stafford, *James VI of Scotland and the Throne of England* (op. cit.), p. 58.
4.    David Harris Willson, *King James VI and I* (op. cit.), p. 100.
5.    Ibid., p. 109. The immediate cause for Elizabeth's letter, however, was to persuade him to seal the border and to end the refuge that the Scots Reformers offered to English Protestants fleeing from the High Commission.

## Notes to Chapter 23 (pages 209–232)

1.    H. R. Trevor-Roper, *The Crisis of the Seventeenth Century: Religion, the Reformation and Social Change* (New York: Harper & Row, 1968), Chapter Three, "The European Witch Craze," pp. 105–115.
2.    Henry Charles Lea, *Torture* (Philadelphia: University of Pennsylvania Press, 1973), p. 146.
3.    William Roughead, *The Rebel Earl* (Edinburgh: W. Green & Son, 1926), pp. 17–29.
4.    Ibid., p. 10.
5.    David Mathew, *James I* (London: Eyre & Spottiswoode, 1967), p. 75.
6.    Roughead, *The Rebel Earl* (op. cit.), p. 10.
7.    David Harris Willson, *King James VI and I* (op. cit.), p. 106.
8.    Ibid., pp. 106–108.
9.    Helen Georgia Stafford, *James VI of Scotland and the Throne of England* (op. cit.), p. 68.
10.   Maurice Lee, Jr., *John Maitland of Thirlestane* (op. cit.), pp. 243–244.
11.   Ibid., p. 246.
12.   Leonard W. Levy, *Origins of the Fifth Amendment* (op. cit.), pp. 188–195.
13.   Stafford, *James VI of Scotland and the Throne of England* (op. cit.), Chapter III, pp. 78–123, "The Spanish Blanks."
14.   Willson, *King James VI and I* (op. cit.), pp. 111–112.
15.   Roughead, *The Rebel Earl* (op. cit.), pp. 42–43.

16.  Stafford, *James VI of Scotland and the Throne of England* (op. cit.),
     pp. 100–101. The Virgin wanted the Catholic earls of Scotland pun-
     ished, not forgiven.

17.  Robert Chambers, *The Life of King James the First* (op. cit.),
     pp. 205–206.

18.  Lee, *John Maitland of Thirlestane* (op. cit.), pp. 270–271.

19.  Stafford, *James VI of Scotland and the Throne of England* (op. cit.),
     p. 108.

20.  Lee, *John Maitland of Thirlestane* (op. cit.), p. 272.

*Notes to Chapter 24* (pages 233–260)

1.  Maurice Lee, Jr., *John Maitland of Thirlestane* (op. cit.), pp. 284–288.

2.  Ibid., p. 289.

3.  Ibid., Appendix II, p. 302.

4.  Francis Bacon was born in 1561 at York House when his father, Sir
    Nicholas Bacon, was lord keeper of the great seal. Sir Nicholas was
    a friend and ally of William Cecil, whom he resembled; the two men
    married sisters. Francis was the younger son. He distinguished him-
    self in his studies at an early age, spent three years at Cambridge, and
    was in France serving as an assistant to the English ambassador when
    his father unexpectedly died. Returned to England, he studied for the
    law at Gray's Inn. He sought help from the Cecils, but Sir William
    did not care for him; he was elected to Parliament at the age of 23
    and irritated Elizabeth by defending the Reform element. The error
    was the last of that sort he ever made; he was never again to speak
    for any proposition not favored by the Crown.

    Bacon obtained, after a long interval, a series of minor legal posts
    for the government; as Robert Cecil began to show signs of brilliance,
    he found his way blocked by a contemporary and very capable rival.
    That led Bacon into some maneuvers against the Cecils. They were
    abortive until the rise of the earl of Essex, whom Francis served as
    adviser. By that time Francis Bacon's proclivities had emerged, to the
    disgust of his mother. "I pity your brother," she wrote regarding
    Francis to his elder brother, Anthony, "because of his debts. But so
    long as he pitieth not himself but keepeth that bloody Percy . . . yea
    as a coach companion and bed companion . . . a proud, profane, costly
    fellow whose being about him I verily fear that God mislike . . . surely
    I am utterly discouraged." Nor was Percy the only one. Old Lady
    Bacon went on to tick off the entourage: ". . . that Jones never loved
    your brother indeed, save for his own credit, living upon your brother
    and thankless though bragging . . . It is most certain that till Enny,

a filthy, wasteful knave and his Welshmen one after another . . . did so lead him in a train he was a towardly young gentleman, and a son of much hope . . . I will not have his cormorant seducers and instruments of Satan to him committing foul sin by his countenance, to the displeasing of God"—and so on.

Essex went to great efforts to have Francis Bacon made attorney general, but the Virgin did not like Bacon, whose brilliance was not of the sort she appreciated. He was, said Arthur Wilson, a contemporary, "more a man in some things and less than a woman in others." When he grew prosperous—which he did, far more than most—he kept about him "prodigal and expensive youths . . . his indulgence to them, and familiarity with them, opened a gap to infamous *Reports,* which left an unsavoury Tincture on him; for where such leeches are there must be putrid blood to fill them." Some sense of that underlay Aubrey's famous description, concluding that Francis Bacon's eyes were "delicate, lively, hazel Eies—like the Eies of a Viper."

5.  Robert Ashton, ed., *James I by His Contemporaries* (op. cit.), pp. 174–175, from James Melville's Diary.
6.  Edith Sitwell, *The Queens and the Hive* (Boston: Little, Brown & Co., 1962), p. 413, citing *Purgatory Proved by Miracles.*
7.  David Harris Willson, *King James VI and I* (op. cit.), pp. 123–124.
8.  Ibid., p. 125.
9.  Helen Georgia Stafford, *James VI of Scotland and the Throne of England* (op. cit.), pp. 182–183.
10. Mary M. Luke, *Gloriana: The Years of Elizabeth I* (op. cit.), p. 624.
11. Edith Sitwell, *The Queens and the Hive* (op. cit.), p. 419.
12. Luke, *Gloriana: The Years of Elizabeth I* (op. cit.), p. 639.
13. Lytton Strachey, *Elizabeth and Essex,* (New York: Harcourt, Brace, 1928), pp. 168–169.
14. Ibid., p. 174.
15. Luke, *Gloriana: The Years of Elizabeth I* (op. cit.), p. 646.
16. Ibid., p. 651.
17. Sitwell, *The Queens and the Hive* (op. cit.), p. 457.
18. The official version of all this was printed in Edinburgh in 1600 on the fifth of August and was called *Gowries Conspiracy: A Discourse of the Unnatural and Vyle Conspiracie Attempted against the Kings Majesties.* Unofficial though equally confusing versions have been appearing at intervals ever since. See Chambers, *The Life of King James the First* (op. cit.), pp. 242–269; Andrew Lang, *James VI and the Gowrie Mystery* (New York: Longmans, Green & Co., 1902); Ross Williamson, *Historical Whodunits* (New York: Macmillan, 1965). All these various accounts and their bulky companions

agree on the underlying incredibility of King James's version of the event.

19. Willson, *King James VI and I* (op. cit.), p. 128.
20. Luke, *Gloriana: The Years of Elizabeth I* (op. cit.), pp. 669–672.
21. Ibid., pp. 682–683.
22. Her remarks lingered long in history as her Golden Speech.
23. Luke, *Gloriana: The Years of Elizabeth I* (op. cit.), p. 684.
24. Sitwell, *The Queens and the Hive* (op. cit.), p. 475.
25. Ibid.
26. Ibid., p. 689.
27. Luke, *Gloriana: The Years of Elizabeth I* (op. cit.), pp. 690–691.

*Notes to Chapter 25* (pages 263–280)

1. Aston had formerly been James's barber.
2. Robert Chambers, *The Life of King James the First,* 2 Vols. (op. cit.), Vol. 2, p. 74.
3. David Harris Willson, *King James VI and I* (op. cit.), p. 148.
4. Ibid., p. 188.
5. David Cecil, *The Cecils of Hatfield House* (Boston: Houghton Mifflin, 1973), p. 129.
6. Samuel Rawson Gardiner, *History of England,* 10 Vols. (London: Longmans, Green & Co., 1893), Vol. 1, p. 100.
7. Willson, *King James VI and I* (op. cit.), p. 165.
8. Gardiner, *History of England* (op. cit.), Vol. 1, p. 121.
9. Edward Coke was born at Mileham, in Norfolk, in 1552. A graduate of Cambridge, he was admitted to the bar in 1578, came to the attention of the Cecils and, under their patronage, rose rapidly. The case against Essex was his first great test. The case against Raleigh, another Cecil project, was his second. Coke made the most of his opportunity, as he was to make the most of every situation in his life.
10. David Mathew, *James I* (op. cit.), p. 138.
11. Ibid., p. 124.
12. Ibid., p. 125.
13. Willson, *James VI and I* (op. cit.), p. 204.
14. Gardiner, *History of England* (op. cit.), Vol. 1, pp. 153–154.
15. Willson, *James VI and I* (op. cit.), pp. 205–206.
16. Ibid., p. 207.
17. Gardiner, *History of England* (op. cit.), Vol. 1, p. 157.
18. Ibid.
19. Willson, *King James VI and I* (op. cit.), p. 208.

20. Ibid.

21. Gardiner, *History of England* (op. cit.), Vol. 1, p. 159.

*Notes to Chapter 26* (pages 281–289)

1. David Harris Willson, *James VI and I* (op. cit.), pp. 250–251.
2. Ibid.
3. Ibid.
4. Samuel Rawson Gardiner, *History of England* (op. cit.), Vol. 1, p. 169.
5. Ibid., p. 185.
6. Ibid., p. 191.
7. Maurice Lee, Jr., *James I and Henry IV* (Urbana, Ill.: University of Illinois Press, 1970), p. 17.
8. J. P. Kenyon, *The Stuarts* (London: B. T. Batsford, Ltd., 1958), p. 48.

*Notes to Chapter 27* (pages 290–300)

1. David Harris Willson, *King James VI and I* (op. cit.), p. 252.
2. Robert Chambers, *The Life of King James the First* (op. cit.), Vol. 2, p. 93.
3. Willson, *King James VI and I* (op. cit.), p. 209.
4. Chambers, *The Life of King James the First* (op. cit.), Vol. 2, p. 85.
5. Scandal linked his name with Lady Suffolk, Lady Derby, and Lady Walsingham, among others.
6. The project, one of the most celebrated in English history, remains the inspiration for one of its great holidays. It has been examined and reconstructed in books, plays, and essays in exhaustive detail. Yet the most interesting facet—the use to which Cecil bent the plot—is conspicuously absent from the dramas about it so often mounted.
7. Samuel Rawson Gardiner, *History of England* (op. cit.), Vol. 1, p. 248.
8. Chambers, *The Life of King James the First* (op. cit.), pp. 109–110.
9. Mute evidence of the severe effects of the torture are provided by Fawkes's signature before the pains, when his strokes are bold and sure—and afterward, when they are shaky and indecipherable.
10. Willson, *King James VI and I* (op. cit.), p. 226.
11. Ibid., p. 227.
12. Ben Jonson enjoyed a long vogue at court and was a great admirer of Sir Francis Bacon.
13. David Mathew, *James I* (op. cit.), p. 154.

*Notes to Chapter 28* (pages 301–321)

1.  Robert Ashton, ed., *James I by His Contemporaries* (op. cit.), pp. 242–244.
2.  Samuel Rawson Gardiner, *History of England* (op. cit.), Vol. 1., pp. 305–316.
3.  Ibid.
4.  David Harris Willson, *James VI and I* (op. cit.), p. 318.
5.  Leonard W. Levy, *Origins of the Fifth Amendment* (op. cit.), p. 231.
6.  Ibid., p. 239.
7.  Lucy Aikins, *Memoirs of the Court of King James the First,* 2 Vols. (London: Longman, Hurst, Rees, Orme and Brown, 1822), p. 329.
8.  G. P. V. Akrigg, *Jacobean Pageant, or The Court of King James I* (Cambridge, Mass.: Harvard University Press, 1963), p. 178.
9.  Gardiner, *History of England* (op. cit.), Vol. 2, p. 42.
10. Willson, *King James VI and I* (op. cit.), p. 280.
11. Gardiner, *History of England* (op. cit.), Vol. 2, p. 46.
12. Levy, *Origins of the Fifth Amendment* (op. cit.), pp. 243–244.
13. Miriam deFord, *The Overbury Affair* (Philadelphia; Chilton, 1960), p. 20.
14. Levy, *Origins of the Fifth Amendment* (op. cit.), pp. 244–245.
15. G. P. V. Akrigg, *Jacobean Pageant* (op. cit.), p. 91.
16. Miriam deFord, *The Overbury Affair* (op. cit.), pp. 22–23.
17. Willson, *King James VI and I* (op. cit.), p. 266

*Notes to Chapter 29* (pages 322–347)

1.  David Harris Willson, *King James VI and I* (op. cit.), p. 269.
2.  David Cecil, *The Cecils of Hatfield House* (op. cit.), p. 280.
3.  Willson, *King James VI and I* (op. cit.), p. 281.
4.  Ibid.
5.  John Heneage Jesse, *Memoirs of the Court of England,* 6 Vols. (Boston: Francis P. Nicolls & Co., n.d.), Vol. 1., p. 178.
6.  G. P. V. Akrigg, *Jacobean Pageant* (op. cit.), pp. 134–135.
7.  Even Robert Cecil's name was later discovered on the list of the English who accepted regular payments from Madrid—and performed services for that realm. Historians have not discovered any important pro-Spanish decisions on Cecil's part, but have found his reports to that realm in the files.
8.  Akrigg, *Jacobean Pageant* (op. cit.), p. 182.
9.  Miriam deFord, *The Overbury Affair* (op. cit.), p. 29.
10. Willson, *King James VI and I* (op. cit.), p. 363.
11. Ibid.

12. Gardiner, *History of England* (op. cit.), Vol. 2, pp. 221–223.
13. deFord, *The Overbury Affair* (op. cit.), p. 35.
14. Akrigg, *Jacobean Pageant* (op. cit.), p. 203.
15. Willson, *King James VI and I* (op. cit.), p. 343.
16. Ibid., pp. 345–346.
17. Gardiner, *History of England* (op. cit.), Vol. 2, pp. 247–249.
18. Willson, *King James VI and I* (op. cit.), pp. 350–351.
19. Leonard W. Levy, *Origins of the Fifth Amendment* (op. cit.), pp. 251–253.
20. Akrigg, *Jacobean Pageant* (op. cit.), pp. 188–189.
21. Willson, *King James VI and I* (op. cit.), p. 352.
22. Akrigg, *Jacobean Pageant* (op. cit.), p. 193.
23. Ibid., p. 195.
24. Gardiner, *History of England* (op. cit.), Vol. 2, pp. 342–343.
25. deFord, *The Overbury Affair* (op. cit.), p. 88.
26. Akrigg, *Jacobean Pageant* (op. cit.), p. 200.

*Notes to Chapter 30* (pages 348–388)

1. Raleigh's friends had to add a bribe to their persuasions to gain the favorite's intercession.
2. Samuel Rawson Gardiner, *History of England* (op. cit.), Vol. 3, p. 72.
3. David Harris Willson, *King James VI and I* (op. cit.), pp. 380–382.
4. Gardiner, *History of England* (op. cit.), Vol. 3, p. 22.
5. The aphorism has since become a favorite of power-hungry intellectuals. "There was something in the bent of his genius," says Historian Gardiner of Bacon, "which led him to pay exaggerated reverence to all who were possessed of power."
6. Robert Ashton, ed., *James I by His Contemporaries* (op. cit.), p. 122.
7. Ibid., p. 114.
8. Ibid., pp. 113–114.
9. Gardiner, *History of England* (op. cit.), Vol. 3, p. 48.
10. Ibid., p. 80.
11. Ibid., pp. 241–247.
12. Ibid., pp. 96–97. Gardiner gives the polite version of this episode. The impolite version, accepted by Macaulay among others, and quoted here, is based on the version of Sir Anthony Weldom, who played a revolutionary role in the times of Charles I.
13. Ibid., p. 98.
14. Willson, *King James VI and I* (op. cit.), p. 395.
15. George Macaulay Trevelyan, *England Under the Stuarts* (London: Methuen & Co., 1924), p. 114.
16. Gardiner, *History of England* (op. cit.), Vol. 3, pp. 203–205.

17.  Ibid., pp. 149–152.
18.  Willson, *King James VI and I* (op. cit.), p. 404.
19.  G. P. V. Akrigg, *Jacobean Pageant* (op. cit.), p. 270.
20.  Willson, *King James VI and I* (op. cit.), p. 412.
21.  Ibid., p. 413.
22.  Gardiner, *History of England* (op. cit.), Vol. 3, pp. 337–338.
23.  Ibid., Vol. 4, p. 156.
24.  Willson, *King James VI and I* (op. cit.), p. 416.
25.  Gardiner, *History of England* (op. cit.), Vol. 3, p. 393.
26.  Ibid., Vol. 4, pp. 118–119.
27.  Ibid., p. 49.
28.  Lord Macaulay, *The Works of Lord Macaulay*, Essay on Lord Bacon (Twentieth Century Edition, n.d.), Vol. 4, p. 82.
29.  Gardiner, *The History of England* (op. cit.), Vol. 4, pp. 189–190.
30.  Ibid., p. 68.
31.  Ibid., p. 92.
32.  Macaulay, *Works*, Essay on Lord Bacon (op. cit.), Vol. 4, p. 84.
33.  Yelverton had fallen afoul of Buckingham.
34.  Gardiner, *History of England* (op. cit.), Vol. 4, p. 112.
35.  Ibid., p. 127.
36.  Willson, *King James VI and I* (op. cit.), pp. 421–422.
37.  Gardiner, *History of England* (op. cit.), Vol. 4, pp. 249–250.
38.  Ibid., p. 252.
39.  Ibid., p. 265.
40.  Ibid., p. 266.
41.  Willson, *King James VI and I* (op. cit.), p. 424.

*Notes to Chapter 31* (pages 389–408)

1.   Samuel Rawson Gardiner, *History of England* (op. cit.), Vol. 4, p. 369.
2.   Ibid., pp. 356–357.
3.   Gardiner, whose history of the reigns of James I and Charles I is considered by most professional historians to be the best.
4.   G. P. V. Akrigg, *Jacobean Pageant* (op. cit.), p. 342.
5.   Gardiner, *History of England* (op. cit.), Vol. 4, p. 384.
6.   Ibid., pp. 387–388.
7.   Akrigg, *Jacobean Pageant* (op. cit.), pp. 345–346.
8.   Gardiner, *History of England* (op. cit.), Vol. 5, pp. 10–11.
9.   Ibid., pp. 35–36.
10.  David Harris Willson, *King James VI and I* (op. cit.), pp. 437–438.
11.  Gardiner, *History of England* (op. cit.), Vol. 5, p. 59.

12. Akrigg, *Jacobean Pageant* (op. cit.), p. 357.
13. Ibid., p. 381.
14. Gardiner, *History of England* (op. cit.), Vol. 5, p. 183.
15. Ibid., p. 231.
16. J. P. Kenyon, *The Stuarts* (op. cit.), p. 71.

# ACKNOWLEDGMENTS

The publisher and the author acknowledge with appreciation the permissions granted by the following copyright holders and others for excerpts used in this book:

Akrigg, G.P.V., *Jacobean Pageant, or the Court of James I,* Harvard University Press, 1963, and Hamish Hamilton, London.

Ashton, Robert, ed., *James I by His Contemporaries, An Account of His Career and Character,* Hutchinson Publishing Group Ltd., 1969.

Bingham, Caroline, *The Making of a King: The Early Years of James VI and I,* Collins, 1968.

Cecil, David, *The Cecils of Hatfield House,* Houghton Mifflin Company, 1973.

Selections from Maurice Lee, Jr., *John Maitland of Thirlestane and the Foundation of the Stewart Despotism in Scotland* (copyright © 1959 by Princeton University Press), pp. 56–289. Reprinted by permission of Princeton University Press.

Luke, Mary M., *Gloriana: The Years of Elizabeth I,* Coward, McCann and Geoghegan, 1973.

Mattingly, Garrett, *The Armada,* Houghton Mifflin Company, 1959.

Willson, David Harris, *King James VI and I,* used with permission of the Estate of David Harris Willson and Jonathan Cape Ltd.

# SELECTED BIBLIOGRAPHY

Aikins, Lucy. *Memoirs of the Court of King James the First.* London: Longman, Hurst, Orme and Brown, 1822.

Akrigg, G. P. V. *Jacobean Pageant, or the Court of James I.* Cambridge, Mass.: Harvard University Press, 1963.

Anthony, Katherine. *Queen Elizabeth.* New York: The Literary Guild, 1929.

Ashley, Maurice. *England in the Seventeenth Century.* Baltimore: Penguin Books, Inc., 1967.

Ashton, Robert, ed. *James I by His Contemporaries, An Account of His Career and Character.* London: Hutchinson & Co., Ltd., 1969.

Aylmer, G. E. *A Short History of Seventeenth Century England 1603–1689.* New York: New American Library, 1963.

Bax, Clifford. *The Silver Casket, Being the Love Letters and Love Poems, Attributed to Mary Stuart, Queen of Scots* (now modernized or translated). London: Home & Van Thal, Ltd., 1946.

Belloc, Hilaire. *How the Reformation Happened.* New York: Robert M. McBride & Co., 1928.

Bingham, Caroline. *The Making of a King: The Early Years of James VI and I.* London: Collins, 1968.

Black, Adam and Charles. *Black's Picturesque Tourist of Scotland.* Edinburgh: R. & R. Clark, 1875.

Braudel, Fernand. *The Mediterranean and the Mediterranean World in the Age of Philip II,* Vol. I. Translated by Sian Reynolds. New York: Harper & Row, 1972.

———.*The Mediterranean and the Mediterranean World in the Age of*

*Philip II,* Vol. II. Translated by Sian Reynolds. New York: Harper & Row, 1973.

Bridenbaugh, Carl. *Vexed and Troubled Englishmen 1590–1642.* New York: Oxford University Press, 1968.

Brown, P. Hume. *George Buchanan and His Times.* Edinburgh: Oliphant, Anderson & Ferrier, 1906.

Bruce, John, ed. *Letters of Queen Elizabeth and King James VI of Scotland.* Camden Society, 1849. Repr. New York: AMS Press, 1968.

Camden, Carroll. *The Elizabethan Woman.* New York: Elsevier Press, 1952.

Campbell, Douglas. *The Puritan in Holland, England and America.* New York: Harper, 1893.

Cartwright, Frederick D., and Bidiss, Michael D. *Disease and History.* New York: Crowell, 1972.

Cecil, David. *The Cecils of Hatfield House—An English Ruling Family.* Boston: Houghton Mifflin, 1973.

Chambers, Robert. *The Life of King James the First.* 2 Vols. Edinburgh: Constable & Co., 1830.

Clark, Sir George. *The Wealth of England from 1496 to 1760.* London and New York: Oxford University Press, 1954.

_____. *The Seventeenth Century.* New York: Oxford University Press, 1961.

Cole, Rufus. *Human History—The Seventeenth Century and the Stuart Family.* Human History. 2 Vols. Freeport, N.Y.: Bond Wheelwright, 1959.

Cook, E. Thornton. *The Royal Line of France.* Freeport, N.Y.: Books for Libraries Press, 1967.

Cunningham, J. V. *The Renaissance in England.* New York: Harcourt, Brace & World, 1966.

Davison, Meredith H. *The Casket Letters, A Solution to the Mystery of Mary Queen of Scots and the Murder of Lord Darnley.* London: Vision Press, 1965.

Dawson, Christopher. *The Movement of World Revolution.* New York: Sheed & Ward, 1959.

deFord, Miriam Allen. *The Overbury Affair.* Philadelphia: Chilton, 1960.

Disraeli, Isaac. *The Literary Character and an Inquiry into the Character of James I.* Edited by Benjamin Disraeli. London: Routledge, Warner and Routledge, 1859.

Donaldson, Gordon. *The First Trial of Mary, Queen of Scots.* New York: Stein and Day, 1969.

Elliott, J. H. *The Old World and the New 1492–1650.* London: Cambridge University Press, 1970.

Foxe, John. *Foxe's Book of Martyrs.* Edited by Marie Gentert King. Old Tappan, N.J.: Revell, 1968.

Fraser, Antonia, *Mary, Queen of Scots.* London: Weidenfeld and Nicolson, 1969.

Fraser, George MacDonald. *The Steel Bonnets.* New York: Knopf, 1972.

Froude, James Anthony. *History of England from the Fall of Wolsey to the Death of Elizabeth.* 12 Vols. London: Longman, Green, Longman, Roberts & Green, 1863–1872.

_____. *Historical and Other Sketches.* New York: Funk & Wagnalls, 1883.

Gardiner, Samuel Rawson. *History of England from the Accession of James I to the Outbreak of Civil War.* 10 Vols. London: Longmans, Green & Co., 1891.

_____. *The First Two Stuarts and the Puritan Revolution 1603–1660.* New York: Crowell, 1970.

Garrett, George. *Death of the Fox* [Raleigh]. Garden City, N.Y.: Doubleday, 1971.

Gelder, H. A. Enno Van. *The Two Reformations in the 16th Century—A Study of the Religious Consequences of Renaissance and Humanism.* The Hague: Martinus Nijhoff, 1964.

Gibb, M. A. *Buckingham.* London: J. Cape, 1939.

Gibbs, Philip. *The Reckless Duke.* New York: Harper, 1931.

Glasgow Quatercentenary Studies. *George Buchanan.* Glasgow: University Press, 1906.

Gooch, G. P. *English Democratic Ideas in the Seventeenth Century.* New York: Harper & Brothers, 1959.

Gore-Browne, Robert. *Lord Bothwell and Mary Queen of Scots, A Study of the Life, Character and Times of James Hepburn 4th Earl of Bothwell.* Garden City, N. Y.: Doubleday, Doran & Company, 1937.

Graham, Fred W. *The Constructive Revolutionary John Calvin and His Socio-Economic Impact.* Richmond, Va.: John Knox Press, 1971.

Green, John Richard. *A Short History of the English People.* 3 Vols. New York: Colonial Press, 1899.

Green, V. H. H. *Renaissance and Reformation.* London: Edward Arnold Publishers, Ltd., 1967.

Grimm, Harold J. *The Reformation Era 1500–1650.* New York: Macmillan, 1965.

Haller, William. *The Rise of Puritanism Or, The Way to the New Jerusalem as Set Forth in Pulpit and Press from Thomas Cartwright to John Lilburne and John Milton, 1570–1643.* New York: Harper & Row, 1957.

Hardy, B. C. *Arbella Stuart, a Biography.* London: Constable, 1913.

Harrison, George B. *A Jacobean Journal.* London: G. Routledge & Sons, 1946.

Hill, Christopher. *Society and Puritanism in Pre-Revolutionary England.* New York: Schocken Books, 1967.

_____. *Reformation to Industrial Revolution—The Making of Modern English Society,* Vol. I: 1530–1780. New York: Random House, 1967.

Hill, John E. C. *The Century of Revolution 1603–1714.* Edinburgh: T. Nelson, 1962.

Hughes, Philip. *The Church in Crisis—A History of the Twenty Great Councils.* London: Burns & Oates, 1961.

_____. *A Popular History of the Reformation.* Garden City, N.Y.: Hanover House, 1957.

Hume, David. *History of Great Britain, the Reigns of James I and Charles I.* Harmondsworth, U.K.: Penguin, 1970.

Inderwick, F. A. *Sidelights on the Stuarts.* London: S. Low, Marston, Searle & Irvington, 1888.

Innes, Donald A. *Leading Figures in English History; the Tudor and Stewart Period.* Freeport, N.Y.: Books for Libraries, 1967.

Ives, E. W., ed. *The English Revolution 1600–1660.* New York: Harper & Row, 1968.

James I. *The Essayes of a Prentice in the Divine Art of Poesie; A Counterblast Against Tobacco.* Westminster: A Constable, 1895.

_____. *The Political Works.* New York: Russell & Russell, 1965.

Jesse, John Heaneage. *Memoirs of the Court of England during the Reign of the Stuarts including the Protestorate,* 6 vols. Boston: Francis A. Niccolis & Co., n.d.

Johnston, Arthur, ed. *Francis Bacon.* New York: Schocken, 1965.

Kendrick, T. D. *British Antiquity.* London: Methuen & Co., 1950.

Kenyon, J. P. *The Stuarts.* London: B. T. Batsford, Ltd., 1958.

Kingdon, Robert M. *Geneva and the Coming of the Wars of Religion in France 1555–1563.* Geneva: Libraire E. Droz, 1956.

Knappen, M. M. *Tudor Puritanism—A Chapter in the History of Idealism.* Chicago: University of Chicago Press, 1970.

Lang, Andrew. *James VI and the Gowrie Mystery.* New York: Longmans, Green & Co., 1902.

Lea, Henry Charles. *Torture.* Philadelphia: University of Pennsylvania Press, 1973.

Lee, Jr., Maurice. *James Stewart, Earl of Moray—A Political Study of the Reformation in Scotland.* New York: Columbia University Press, 1953.

_____. *John Maitland of Thirlestane and the Foundation of the Stewart Despotism in Scotland.* Princeton, N.J.: Princeton University Press, 1959.

———. *James I and Henry IV.* Urbana, Ill.: University of Illinois Press, 1970.

Levy, Leonard W. *Origins of the Fifth Amendment.* New York: Oxford University Press, 1968.

Linklater, Eric. *The Royal House.* New York: Doubleday, 1970.

Luke, Mary M. *A Crown for Elizabeth.* New York: Coward-McCann, 1970.

———. *Gloriana: The Years of Elizabeth I.* New York: Coward-McCann & Geoghegan, 1973.

Lyon, Hastings, and Block, Herman. *Edward Coke, Oracle of the Law.* Boston: Houghton Mifflin, 1929.

MacDonald, Hugh. *Portraits in Prose—a Collection of Characters.* Freeport, N.Y.: Books for Libraries Press, 1969.

McElwee, Wm. Lloyd. *The Wisest Fool in Christendom.* New York: Harcourt, Brace, 1958.

Mackenzie, Agnes Mure. *The Scotland of Queen Mary and the Religious Wars 1513–1638.* Edinburgh: Oliver & Boyd, 1957.

Mackie, J. D. *John Knox.* London: The Historical Association, 1968.

Mackie, R. L. *A Short History of Scotland.* New York: Praeger, 1963.

Mackinnon, James. *Calvin and the Reformation.* New York: Russell & Russell, 1962.

Mathew, David. *James I.* London: Eyre & Spottiswoode, 1967.

Mattingly, Garrett. *The Armada.* Boston: Houghton Mifflin, 1959.

———. *Renaissance Diplomacy.* Boston: Houghton Mifflin, 1955.

Melville, Sir James. *Memoirs of His Own Life.* London: Chapman & Dodd, Abbey Classics Edition, 1922.

Neale, J. E. *The Age of Catherine de' Medici.* London: Bradford and Dickens, 1959.

New, John F. H. *Anglican and Puritan: the Basis of their Opposition.* Stanford, Calif.: Stanford University Press, 1964.

Nichols, J. B. *Progresses, Processions and Magnificent Festivities of King James I.* London: J.B. Nichols 1828.

Nogueras, Henri. *The Massacre of Saint Bartholomew.* Translated by Engel. London: George Allen & Unwin, Ltd., 1959.

Parry, J. H. *The Age of Reconnaissance.* New York: New American Library, 1964.

Rait, Robert S., ed. *Lvsvs Regius; Being Poems and Other Pieces by King James I of Great Britain.* Westminster: A. Constable, 1901.

Ranke, Leopold von. *A History of England Principally in the Seventeenth Century,* Vol. I. Oxford: Clarendon Press, 1875.

Ridley, Jasper. *John Knox.* Oxford: Oxford University Press, 1968.

Roche, Owen J. A. *The Days of the Upright—The Story of the Huguenots.* New York: Clarkson N. Potter, Inc., 1965.

Roeder, Ralph. *Catherine de' Medici and the Lost Revolution.* New York: Garden City Publishing Co., 1939.

Roughead, William. *The Rebel Earl and Other Studies.* Edinburgh: W. Green & Son, Ltd., 1926.

Schmidt, Albert-Marie. *John Calvin and the Calvinistic Tradition.* London: Longmans, 1960.

Sitwell, Edith. *The Queens and the Hive.* Boston: Little Brown & Co., 1962.

Smith, Preserved. *The Age of the Reformation.* New York: Henry Holt and Company, 1920.

Snow, Vernon F. *Essex the Rebel.* Lincoln, Nebr.: University of Nebraska Press, 1970.

Stafford, Helen Georgia. *James VI of Scotland and the Throne of England.* New York: D. Appleton-Century, 1940.

Strachey, Lytton. *Elizabeth and Essex.* New York: Harcourt, Brace, 1928.

Thomson, E. McC. *The Chamberlain Letters; a Collection of the Letters of John Chamberlain Concerning Life in England from 1597–1626.* New York: Putnam, 1965.

Trevelyan, G. M. *History of England.* 3 Vols. New York: Doubleday, 1953.

Trevor-Roper, H. R. *The European Witch-Craze of the Sixteenth and Seventeenth Centuries and Other Essays.* New York: Harper & Row, 1969.

————. *George Buchanan and the Ancient Scottish Constitution.* The English Historical Review, Supplement 3. London: Longmans, 1966.

Watt, Hugh. *Reformation and Revolution.* Edited by Duncan Shaw. Edinburgh: Saint Andrew Press, 1967.

Wedgewood, C. V. *The Thirty Years War.* London: Jonathan Cape, Ltd., 1938.

White, R. J. *A Short History of England.* Cambridge: Cambridge University Press, 1972.

Williamson, Hugh Ross. *Historical Whodunits.* New York: Macmillan, 1965.

Willson, David Harris. *King James VI and I.* New York: Oxford University Press, 1956.

Winwood, Sir Ralph. *Memorials of Affairs of State in the Reigns of Queen Elizabeth and King James I.* New York, AMS Press, 1972.

Zweig, Stefan. *Mary Queen of Scotland and the Isles.* New York: Viking, 1935.

# INDEX